Using Human Rights Law in English Courts

MURRAY HUNT

B.A., B.C.L., (OXON) LL.M. (HARVARD)
Barrister

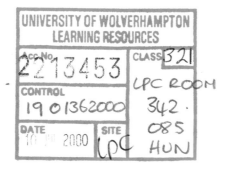

· HART ·
PUBLISHING

OXFORD
1998

This book is dedicated to my parents,
Jean and Bob Hunt

Hart Publishing
Oxford
UK

Distributed in the United States by
Northwestern University Press
625 Colfax
Evanston
Illinois 60208-4210 USA

Distributed in Australia and New Zealand by
Federation Press Pty Ltd.
PO Box 45,
Annandale, NSW 2038,
Australia

© Murray Hunt 1997 and 1998

Hardback published 1997; reprinted 1997
Paperback first published 1998

Hart Publishing is a specialist legal publisher based in Oxford, England.
To order further copies of this book or to request a list of other
publications please write to:

Hart Publishing, 19 Whitehouse Road, Oxford, OX1 4PA
Telephone: +44 (0)1865 434459 or Fax: (0)1865 794482 or 434459
e-mail: hartpub@janep.demon.co.uk

ISBN 1–901362–00–0 (hbk)
ISBN 1–901362–72–8 (pbk)

Typeset in 10pt Sabon
by SetAll, Abingdon
Printed in Great Britain on acid-free paper
by Biddles Ltd., Guildford and Kings Lynn

Alexander Maxwell Law Scholarship Trust

Maurice W. Maxwell whose family founded Sweet & Maxwell, the law publishers, by his Will established a charitable trust to be known as the Alexander Maxwell Law Scholarship Trust in memory of his great great grandfather. The Trust is committed to promoting legal research and writing at various levels by providing financial assistance to authors whether they be experienced legal practitioners, those in the early years of practice or at postgraduate level.

The author of this book received financial assistance from the Trust to enable him to complete the work.

The Trust calls for applications for awards from time to time. Anyone interested in its work should write to The Clerk to the Trustees, Alexander Maxwell Law Scholarship Trust, c/o Sweet & Maxwell, 100 Avenue Road, Swiss Cottage, London NW3 3PF.

Foreword

Over sixteen years ago I wrote an article analysing the different ways in which English judges might have regard to the European Convention on Human Rights ("the Convention") despite its unincorporated status. Whilst outlining the case law as it was then and examining the possibilities, I expressed caution as to the practical impact that the convention was likely to have on the outcome of cases. That prediction proved correct in the years following, but, in this important book, Murray Hunt demonstrates how judicial recourse to binding international human rights standards has developed more recently. He has produced a remarkable analysis of the differing judicial techniques and trends. I am very pleased to have been asked to write this foreword and to have the opportunity of recommending this book most warmly. It is an excellent work by a very able member of the Bar. The themes Murray Hunt examines are both topical and of long term relevance.

The book is topical, particularly on the issue of incorporation of the Convention. Towards the end of 1996 a Labour Party Consultation document was published on how this should be done. At the heart of the incorporation question is the balance between the respective roles of Parliament and the courts in giving domestic effect to the Convention.

Those still opposing incorporation stress the importance of maintaining intact the prerogatives of Parliament and of not placing the courts in a position of having to decide whether to give effect to the general provisions of the Convention over specific statutory provisions. There is the fear that, if judges can give effect to the Convention, Parliamentary democracy, which is the cornerstone of our constitutional tradition, will suffer.

I do not share this fear. If Parliament decides that judges should give effect to the Convention in cases before them, their authority to do so will be securely rooted in constitutional tradition. As this book shows, problem cases today arise mostly when no specific legislative provision has been made for individual rights in a particular unanticipated context. Currently, our courts have to strain in such cases to give effect to fundamental rights enshrined in the Convention. In many cases, as Murray Hunt indicates, sometimes through the common law and sometimes through EC law, effect can be given to the Convention. Often, however, these techniques do not avail. The results are patchy. The domestic effectiveness of the Convention remains unpredictable.

The United Kingdom, however, has committed to secure to everyone in its jurisdiction the rights protected in the Convention. The European Court of Human Rights has pointed out that:

"By substituting the words 'shall secure' for the words 'undertake to secure" in the text of Article 1, the drafters of the Convention also intended to make it clear that the rights and freedoms . . . would be directly secured to anyone within the jurisdiction of the Contracting States. That intention finds a particularly faithful reflection in those instances where the Convention has been incorporated into domestic law" (*Ireland v United Kingdom* (1978) 2 EHRR 25 at 103, paragraph 239).

The domestic legal status of the Convention would be enhanced by Parliamentary incorporation. We are the only State Party to the Convention, in which the Convention or an equivalent national bill of rights can still not be applied routinely by domestic courts when relevant. Incorporation is long overdue.

Incorporation is also desirable from the international perspective of the Convention system. Since 1980, particularly since 1989, many countries of Central and Eastern Europe have become parties to the Convention. This happy development, however, has meant that the pressure on the Convention system has intensified, both in terms of volume of cases and the gravity of issues. Increasingly, the European Court of Human Rights has to confront cases involving allegations of grave violations of minority rights where local remedies appear non-existent and/or ineffectual. It is wrong that the Court's capacity to give attention to such vital cases is reduced because the volume of United Kingdom Strasbourg cases is much higher than it would be were our courts clearly empowered to give effect to the Convention domestically.

Finally, I remain of the view, expressed 16 years ago, that greater use of the Convention by our courts should sensibly be coupled with greater attention to fundamental rights by Parliament. It is welcome to see the role of Parliament feature prominently in the Labour Party's consultative paper on incorporation.

I urge those still fearful of incorporation to study this book. The picture that emerges of judicial decision-making is sensible and re-assuring. Incorporation of the Convention would occur against the context of the prevailing judicial ethos, which has at its core respect for Parliamentary democracy.

This book is published at a very opportune time. Its analysis will not be superceded if and when the Convention is incorporated. Courts are still likely to have to determine the scope of the presumption of Convention compliance when confronted with an apparently inconsistent statutory provision. Murray Hunt provides the best analysis of this issue yet published. Further, even if the convention is incorporated, other important international instruments seem likely to remain unincorporated and thus subject to the judicial techniques and constraints examined in this book.

This book deserves to be widely read. Murray Hunt is to be congratulated for writing it. In introducing the first edition, I look forward before too long to a second edition in which, I hope, Murray Hunt will have the task of examining how our courts have handled incorporation of the Convention, based, I would expect, on his first hand experience of appearing as counsel in many of the leading cases.

Peter Duffy
Essex Court Chambers
London, December 1996

Preface to the Paperback Edition

Since this book was first published, the Labour Government elected on 1 May 1997 has introduced into Parliament its Human Rights Bill, the aim of which, according to the accompanying White Paper, is "to make more directly accessible the rights which the British people already enjoy under the European Convention on Human Rights" (*Rights Brought Home: The Human Rights Bill*, CM 3782, 24 October 1997, para. 1.19). The appearance of this paperback edition provides an opportunity to explain briefly the significance of this development for the book's general thesis that there already exists a legal basis for according special status to human rights law in English courts.

The principal means proposed by the Bill for making Convention rights more directly accessible are the enactment of, first, a requirement that legislation be read and given effect in a way which is compatible with the Convention so far as it is possible to do so, and, second, an obligation on public authorities to act in a way which is compatible with the Convention on pain of being found to have acted unlawfully if they do not. The effect of such legislation, if enacted in the form in which it is proposed, will be to accelerate, in relation to the European Convention on Human Rights, the legal recognition by courts of precisely the "interpretive obligation" for which this book argues. The book's attempt to demonstrate the scope that already exists for protecting fundamental rights through an "interpretive" approach thereby becomes more immediately relevant to legal practice. At last the courts generally, rather than a few judges, will feel compelled to discover in the context of the ECHR the interpretive flexibility and ingenuity which they have developed in their accommodation of European Community law. The availability of a declaration of incompatibility, where it is impossible to interpret legislation so as to achieve compatibility with the Convention, should help to develop an imaginative interpretive approach, as courts are likely to be reluctant to grant such declarations, just as for many years they were reluctant to find domestic legislation to be incompatible with Community law.

In addition, the enactment of such a specific interpretive obligation by Parliament, in relation to one of the international human rights treaties to which the UK is a party, makes it more important than ever that the full legal basis for judicial recognition of the fundamental nature of human rights law is properly understood, for at least two reasons. First, if the Convention is to take root in English legal and political culture, to become "more subtly and powerfully woven into our law" as the White Paper envisages, courts must do more than treat the Human Rights Act as merely another piece of legislation, to be interpreted and applied like any other statute, armed with the canons of interpretation derived from a traditional premise of parliamentary sovereignty. They must recognise that, like the European Communities Act 1972, it enjoys a special status by virtue of its subject-matter. Second, the special treatment accorded to the European Convention on Human Rights must not be allowed to prejudice the evolving domestic status of other human rights treaties to which the UK is a party but which remain unincorporated. The enactment of the Human Rights Act by Parliament does not mean to say that the status of such other instruments in domestic law is in any way diminished.

There is currently reason to be optimistic on both scores. In relation to the first concern, both the White Paper and the Human Rights Bill are replete with at least implicit acknowledgments by the Government that this is legislation of a special kind. The Bill, for example, expressly establishes obligations on judges in relation to the interpretation of future as well as past legislation, and introduces the novel device of a judicial declaration of incompatibility between legislation and the Convention. It sees the Convention itself as a "living instrument", subject to "dynamic and evolving interpretation" in the light of present day conditions and changing social attitudes (para. 2.5). And it clearly envisages a significant change in the judicial role, requiring courts to balance for themselves the protection of individuals' fundamental rights against the demands of the general interest of the community (paras 2.5–2.6). The contrast between the bold and innovative tone of this 1997 White Paper on the Convention and the constitutional conservatism of the 1967 White Paper which considered accession to the European Community (*Legal and Constitutional Implications of United Kingdom Membership of the European Communities* (Cmnd. 3301) (considered in chapter 2)), could hardly be greater.

As for the concern about the future domestic status of international human rights law other than the Convention and its case-law, it is not without significance that the draft legislation itself does not presuppose that before the Act is passed Convention rights are of no effect. As is clear from the draft legislation's long title, "An Act to give further effect to rights and freedoms guaranteed under the European Convention on Human Rights", the legislation's premise is not that the Convention needs "incorporating" in order to give *any* effect to its rights and freedoms, rather it is that the legislation is required in order to make them *more* effective than they currently are in English law. If the long title remains in that form, Parliament will have signified its acknowledgment that the days of dualistic purity are no more, a fact potentially of some significance for the status of other international human rights instruments not yet made part of domestic law.

A timely reminder of the steadily evolving common law judicial obligation in relation to such other instruments was recently given by Lord

Browne-Wilkinson in the House of Lords in *R v Home Secretary, ex p. Venables and Thompson* [1997] 3 WLR 23 at 49F-50B. In considering the lawfulness of applying to a child detained under the Children and Young Persons Act 1933 a tariff based on a policy adopted for adult mandatory life prisoners, Lord Browne-Wilkinson had regard to relevant provisions of the UN Convention on the Rights of the Child, which had been brought to the court's attention by the third party intervention of JUSTICE. In saying that his conclusion has been reinforced by the provisions of that Convention, Lord Browne-Wilkinson said that, although it was not incorporated into English law,

> it is legitimate in considering the nature of detention during HM pleasure . . . to assume that Parliament has not maintained on the statute book a power capable of being exercised in a manner inconsistent with the treaty obligations of this country.

In so saying, Lord Browne-Wilkinson was not merely taking a significant step in the evolution of a common law presumption of interpretation that statutory powers cannot be exercised in a way which is inconsistent with international treaty obligations, he was also delivering a timely reminder that such common law presumptions of interpretation apply to international obligations such as the UN Convention on the Rights of the Child, notwithstanding their unincorporated status.

But while at present there may be some cause for optimism, it will only become apparent over the longer term whether the ECHR can truly be said to have taken root in English law, and to have done so without prejudice to the domestic status of other unincorporated human rights instruments. It is hoped that this book, as well as demonstrating the possibilities inherent in an "interpretive" approach to the protection of fundamental rights, will help to articulate the common law basis onto which the legislation about the Convention will be grafted, and out of which a steadily strengthening interpretive obligation in relation to other instruments may continue to be fashioned by the courts.

MURRAY HUNT

Oxford
November 1997

Preface and Acknowledgements

This book is an attempt to take up the challenge identified by Lord Scarman more than twenty years ago when, in his 1974 Hamlyn Lectures, he heralded the arrival of a "new dimension" to English law. The new dimension consisted mainly of the international human rights movement and the European Community of which Britain had recently become a member, and the challenge was how England's common law system could accommodate these new and important influences. Lord Scarman's well-known conclusion was that, for the English legal system to respond successfully to this challenge, it would be necessary for Parliament to engraft a new, constitutional dimension onto the common law by enacting and entrenching a Bill of Rights.

In this book I attempt to show that, whether human rights law is incorporated or unincorporated, its practical effectiveness depends ultimately on the proper articulation of a common law basis for according it a special, or "constitutional", status. By placing the contemporary debate about the domestic status of human rights law in the context of wider constitutional themes, the book attempts to demonstrate that much of that debate is conducted on a false premise derived from a theory of parliamentary sovereignty that, in practice, has already passed into history. There already exists very considerable scope for using unincorporated international human rights instruments, such as the European Convention on Human Rights, in English courts, but even if those instruments, or any of them, were to become legislatively incoporated, the difference it makes in practice will be minimal unless the common law basis for the special status of such law is properly articulated. Not only does the common law have the resources to achieve what Lord Scarman feared could only come about through legislative constitutional change; a proper understanding of its role as constitutional bedrock is a necessary prerequisite to such change having much practical effect.

The book is therefore, in effect, an extended argument for the articulation of a legal basis to underpin the special status accorded to human rights law in English courts. As matters stand, with all the key international human rights instruments unincorporated, the book argues for a common law interpretive obligation on domestic courts, whereby they recognise that they must strive to construe domestic law in such a way as to give effect to the human rights norms contained in those international treaties to which the UK has committed itself. As the book goes to press, however, it is looking more likely than at any other time in British history that the UK will soon have a domestic Bill of Rights. Both of the principal opposition parties favour incorporation of the European Convention on Human Rights into English law, and the

Labour Party has published a consultation paper on incorporation. This book's central thesis is unaffected by whether or not incorporation takes place. It argues for the recognition of a particular legal basis for the courts' human rights jurisdiction and advocates a general approach to human rights adjudication, both of which apply equally whether or not Parliament has legislated to make the ECHR "part of" English law. As the Canadian experience with its 1960 Bill of Rights demonstrates, even a legislatively approved Bill of Rights which purports to be entrenched against future legislative repeal will not provide effective protection if the courts called on to apply its provisions remain wedded to an out-dated, essentially sovereigntist constitutional framework.

The book has been written with both practitioners and academic lawyers in mind. I hope that practitioners will be interested in the possibilities which exist for making more effective use of human rights law domestically, and that academics and law students will find the approach sufficiently theoretical to be of interest. Although the book is based substantially on an analysis of primary legal materials, it attempts to engage, no doubt rather clumsily, with some larger themes. It does so in the conviction that these more abstract ideas can only acquire some practical significance if some attempt is made to bridge the divide between theory and practice.

The scheme of the book, in broad outline, is as follows. Chapter 1 charts the changing domestic status of international legal norms, against the contemporary background of growing globalisation, increasing international interdependence and the declining importance of the nation-state as an organising concept. It provides the theoretical framework for the transcendence of the crude monist/dualist dichotomy argued for in the rest of the book. Chapters 2 and 3 examine the impact of EC membership on traditional sovereignty theory and seek to demonstrate the important modification of fundamental premises which has taken place in practice. It is argued that the constitutional imagination unleashed by the need to accommodate the supremacy of Community law, as well as both its direct and indirect effect, has great potential if deployed in the judicial protection of human rights.

Chapters 4 and 5 trace the domestic career of international human rights law, and in particular the European Convention on Human Rights, through three phases. In Phase I, in the 1970s, the courts assumed that they were under an obligation to interpret domestic law in such a way as to achieve conformity with the UK's Convention obligations. Phase II was a period of curious bifurcation, as the courts reasserted sovereignty and dualism to keep the Convention out of administrative law, at the same time as referring to it relatively freely in the course of interpreting and developing the common law. In Phase III, which dates from about the beginning of the 1990s, the clear emergence of a common law human rights jurisdiction has made the insulation of administrative law from the influence of the Convention unsustainable, and Chapter 6 chronicles the many and various ways in which the Convention has increasingly featured in administrative law in recent years.

Chapter 7 explores the still largely untapped potential for using human rights law more directly in domestic courts when the case is in the field of Community law. Chapter 8 concludes the study by assessing the extent to which English courts have now accepted a full interpretive obligation to construe domestic law consistently with international human rights law, and asks whether recognising such an obligation and using such law makes much difference to the outcome of cases. It sounds some alarms about emerging trends, such as the marginalisation of Convention case-law and the enthusiastic embrace of the "margin of appreciation", before concluding that the true obstacle to the effective use of human rights law will remain so long as English courts remain resistant to overtly recognising the concept of proportionality.

Appendix I contains a chronological table of cases, reported and unreported, in which English courts have made some reference to the European Convention on Human Rights, the Universal Declaration of Human Rights and the International Covenant on Civil and Political Rights. Other international human rights instruments, such as I.L.O. Conventions and the U.N. Convention on the Rights of the Child have occasionally, though rarely, been referred to by English courts, but these have not been included in the table in order to reflect the focus of the analysis in the text. That analysis has concentrated on the instruments enshrining the more traditional rights and freedoms for the simple reason that, so far, these have generated more case law. However, the arguments the book makes apply equally to those other instruments, which it is to be hoped will benefit from the enhanced domestic status now enjoyed by instruments such as the ECHR.

In bringing the book to publication, I have incurred debts of gratitude too numerous to detail in full, and would like to thank generally all those who have helped in so many different ways. Particular thanks are due to Christine Gray for her comments on chapter 1, Rabinder Singh and Mike Taggart for their comments on substantial parts of the manuscript, and Gráinne de Búrca who read and commented on the draft in its entirety. Their comments and suggestions were invaluable.

Thanks for research assistance are due to Izumi Parkin for the fine job she did checking footnotes under pressure of time, and to David Waterston and David Watson for their excellent work in helping to compile the table at Appendix I. The Alexander Maxwell Law Scholarship Trust provided the generous financial assistance which paid for that research and also enabled me to take time away from practice.

I would like to thank my colleagues at 4/5 Gray's Inn Square, including the clerks and staff, whose forbearance has made possible my absence from chambers whilst completing this project. In particular I would like to thank Michael Beloff for his unerring support and encouragement at every stage; Alan Moses, who (at least during his days at the Bar) was prepared to take serously the views advanced in this book; Richard McManus, who wasn't, but has never tired of arguing enthusiastically about them; and above all Rabinder Singh, Helen Mountfield and David Wolfe, whose professional commitment to public interest lawyering I admire and whose personal friendship I greatly value.

I would like to acknowledge also help of a more general kind from David Dyzenhaus, Peter Duffy, Ronald St. John Macdonald, Karen Reid and Stephen Phillips, all of whom have contributed to the knowledge and experience on which the book is based.

I am grateful to Richard Hart and Jane Parker for being prepared to risk an unknown author to launch Hart Publishing. I have been fortunate to benefit from their considerable experience and expertise as publishers, as well as from their unfailingly patient and understanding manner. Their professionalism and hard work has brought the book to publication with exceptional speed. I wish Hart Publishing the success it undoubtedly deserves.

Finally, special thanks are due to Gráinne de Búrca, who in various ways played a large part in the formulation of the book's ideas and arguments.

The book takes account of the law as it stands at the beginning of 1997.

MURRAY HUNT

Oxford
December 1996

Contents

Table of Cases

Other jurisdictions

European Court of Human Rights

European Court of Justice

Table of Statutes

Table of Statutory Instruments

Table of EC Instruments

Table of International Instruments

1

The Changing Domestic Status of International Legal Norms

1. INTRODUCTION

In the course of the last twenty-five to thirty years, a great variety of factors has combined to undermine both the explanatory and the justificatory power of the traditional account of the United Kingdom's constitutional arrangements.[1] Those years have witnessed a number of developments of great constitutional significance, including a dramatic increase in the powers of the regulatory state, the declining effectiveness of traditional mechanisms of governmental accountability and, more recently, the shrinking of the "public" domain as a result of privatisation, deregulation and the contractualisation of government. Each of these has, in different ways, contributed to a growing awareness of an ever-widening chasm between what constitutional actors do in practice and the roles which traditional theory purports both to describe and to justify.

Arguably, however, no single factor has been more significant in exposing this gap between theory and practice than the international dimension which, during the same short period, domestic constitutional practice has been forced to accommodate. Not only has the UK been an active participant in the formulation of the considerable number of international human rights treaties adopted over this period, and ratified most of them, but, in two instances in particular, it has gone a significant step further. First, it has accepted the right of individual petition to the European Commission of Human Rights in Strasbourg and recognised as compulsory the jurisdiction of the European Court of Human Rights[2] under the European Convention on Human Rights ("the ECHR").[3] Second, and probably even more importantly from a constitutional point of view, it has become a member of the European Community.

In 1974, when these last two events of constitutional significance were still relatively recent, Sir Leslie Scarman, with characteristic foresight, delivered his Hamlyn Lectures in which he heralded the arrival of a "new dimension" to

---

[1] Precisely what is meant by the "traditional account" is explained below.

[2] *Declarations recognising the competence of the European Commission of Human Rights to receive individual petitions and recognising as compulsory the jurisdiction of the European Court of Human Rights*, Cmnd. 2894.

[3] *The European Convention for the Protection of Human Rights and Fundamental Freedoms*, Cmnd. 8969.

English law.[4] The new dimension consisted largely, though not exclusively, of the challenge from the human rights movement and the "Common Market", as it was still then known. Lord Scarman believed that the common law system had the principles and flexibility necessary to meet the challenges, but he predicted that, if it was to do so successfully, it would need to engraft a new, constitutional dimension onto the common law by legislatively entrenching a bill of rights.[5] Today, more than two decades on, the type of legislatively introduced constitutional reform hoped for by Lord Scarman has not been forthcoming, but fundamental constitutional change has nevertheless taken place, as English courts have been forced to accommodate momentous developments in the legal system of the European Community, as well as the increasing normative force of the European Convention on Human Rights and other international human rights instruments.[6]

The aim of this book is to draw together these profound influences on the domestic constitution and, by studying in detail the judicial response to them, to demonstrate the inability of the traditional account to provide a satisfactory foundation for the domestic status of international human rights law. By placing the contemporary debate about the status of such norms in the context of wider constitutional themes, and in particular the internationalisation and Europeanisation of constitutional practice, it seeks to demonstrate that much of that debate is conducted on a problematic premise derived from a theory of parliamentary sovereignty that, in practice, has already passed into history. Until it is overtly acknowledged that the theoretical framework has shifted, it will be argued, the place of international human rights norms in domestic law will remain vulnerable to the resurrection of theoretical anachronisms. This theoretical adjustment, it will be suggested, is of significance for much more than the domestic status of international human rights. In particular, it has implications for the courts' conception of the nature of their function in public law in modern conditions. Even a statutorily incorporated ECHR, or other legislatively approved domestic bill of rights, purporting to be entrenched against future repeal, will fail to provide effective protection so long as the courts called on to apply its provisions remain wedded to an unthinkingly sovereigntist constitutional framework.

What has been referred to above as the "traditional account" of the UK's constitutional arrangements, and will be referred to variously throughout as

---

[4] Sir Leslie Scarman, *English Law—The New Dimension*, Hamlyn Lectures, 26th Series (London: Stevens, 1974).

[5] Ibid. at 15 and Part VII.

[6] In particular the International Covenant on Civil and Political Rights ("the ICCPR"), which, like the ECHR, has its own mechanism for adjudicating on alleged breaches of its provisions. As will be seen throughout this book, however, the influence of the ICCPR on English law has been remarkably slight, due in part, no doubt, to the UK's failure to ratify the Optional Protocol granting the individual right of petition to the Human Rights Committee: see F. Klug, K. Starmer and S. Weir, "The British Way of Doing Things: The United Kingdom and the International Covenant on Civil and Political Rights, 1976–94" [1995] PL 504. A list of the other international human rights treaties to which reference has been made by English courts can be found at Appendix I.

the classical, received or orthodox account, is the familiar Diceyan version, which is too well known to bear recounting in detail here.[7] Suffice it to say for present purposes that, for Dicey, the British constitution rested on twin foundations: the absolute and continuing legal sovereignty of Parliament and a judicial commitment to a rule of law ideal which, subject only to Parliament's sovereign will, guaranteed the protection of an individual's private rights of property and analogous freedoms from state interference. Each of these foundations has been challenged by international and, in particular, European influences with which they are in fundamental tension. The traditional civil and political rights protected by the Diceyan rule of law have begun to look dated, as the substantive values protected in both the international human rights instruments and the positive law of the European Community have gone far beyond the narrow catalogue of property and analogous civil rights traditionally protected by the English common law. Today, international instruments and Community law embrace a much wider lexicon of aspirations, including so-called second and third generation rights which are more often "positive" in the sense that they require state action for their protection or realisation.[8] However, it is the modern inadequacy of Dicey's other foundation, the sovereignty of Parliament, that provides this book's principal focus, for it is that particular aspect of the Diceyan account which has proved the main theoretical stumbling block to the successful constitutional accommodation of the international dimension generally, and of international human rights in particular.

The inadequacy of the very concept of "sovereignty" in making sense of reality in today's interdependent world is now a well documented phenomenon.[9] In a series of recent essays, for example, MacCormick has persuasively argued that sovereignty has undergone a metamorphosis, which requires a more subtle understanding of its meaning and *locus*.[10] As MacCormick points out, "sovereignty" is a property conventionally ascribed to states, or to their governing authorities, and "sovereign power", whether legal or political, is ultimate power, power which admits of no superior power or higher authority.[11] The concepts of the sovereign law-maker within the

---

[7] A.V. Dicey, *An Introduction to the Study of the Law of the Constitution*, 10th edn. with introduction by E.C.S. Wade (London: Macmillan, 1959).

[8] This is not to say that more classical civil and political rights do not sometimes require positive state action for their protection; it is merely to say that the "freedom from state interference" paradigm of Dicey's classical liberalism cannot accommodate the social, economic, cultural and environmental rights now widely recognised as being "fundamental".

[9] For an interesting view of the phenomenon from the perspective of the "new political thinking" in the Soviet Union, shortly before that nation-state's disintegration into many smaller nation-states, see V.S. Vereshchetin and R. A. Mullerson, "International Law in an Interdependent World" (1990) 28 *Columbia Journal of Transnational Law* 291.

[10] N. MacCormick, "Beyond the Sovereign State" (1993) 56 MLR 1; "Sovereignty, Democracy and Subsidiarity", ch. 7 in R. Bellamy, V. Bufacchi and D. Castiglione (eds.), *Democracy and Constitutional Culture in the Union of Europe* (London: Lothian Foundation Press, 1995); "The Maastricht–Urteil: Sovereignty Now" (1995) 1 ELJ 259.

[11] Bellamy et al., *Democracy and Constitutional Culture* (above n. 10) at 98.

domestic legal system and the sovereign nation-state as the basic unit of the international legal system have both been increasingly transcended by legal and political developments, with inevitable consequences for the particular conception of law which those concepts have traditionally underpinned.

Take first the developments on the international plane which have combined to undermine the concept of the sovereign nation-state.[12] The post-War period has seen a paradigm shift, away from the traditional position whereby only sovereign states could be the proper subjects of international law, towards the general recognition of individual citizens as the bearers of international rights and obligations.[13] There have emerged entirely novel international, transnational and supranational legal orders, supplanting the traditional framework in which sovereign states formerly conducted their affairs with one another, and conferring rights on citizens enforceable against their states through international or supranational mechanisms.[14] Not only has there been a notable proliferation of multilateral agreements between states, regulating an ever-increasing range of activities which were previously the exclusive preserve of the sovereign nation-state, but the nature of such agreements has changed, away from the traditional paradigm of treaties concerning the relationship of one state to another, towards a new model of treaties concerned with the relationship of states with their own citizens.[15] Above all, the rapid progress towards European integration that has been made since the Treaty of Rome, especially in the last decade since the signing of the Single European Act, together with the maturation of the European Convention system for the protection of human rights, have increasingly restricted the national sovereignty of European nation states.

In short, although "globalisation" and "interdependence" may seem fashionable epithets, they reflect the undeniable present reality that, in today's world of political and economic transnationalism, nation states can no longer consider themselves masters of their own destiny. The modern state no longer finds itself a free actor in the international sphere, nor even unconstrained domestically. Instead, its freedom of action is limited by a vast array of inter-

---

[12] For an interesting and concise account of the developments which have conspired to undermine the concept of the sovereign nation-state as the traditional unit of politics, and thus helped to precipitate a crisis for the orthodox account of British constitutionalism, see J. Morison and S. Livingstone, *Reshaping Public Power: Northern Ireland and the British Constitutional Crisis* (London: Sweet and Maxwell, 1995), at 13–17, 54–62, and ch. 6.

[13] See eg. C. Chinkin, *Third Parties in International Law* (Oxford: Clarendon Press, 1993); R. Higgins, *Problems and Process: International Law and How We Use it* (Oxford: Clarendon Press, 1994), ch. 3 esp. 48–55.

[14] For the argument that the paradigm shift within international law has overturned not only the concept of state sovereignty, but the equally state-centred concept of citizenship, and that both concepts are fundamentally at odds with the paradigm of constitutionalism and human rights, see L. Ferrajoli, "Beyond sovereignty and citizenship: a global constitutionalism" in R. Bellamy (ed.), *Constitutionalism, Democracy and Sovereignty: American and European Perspectives* (Aldershot: Avebury, 1996), ch. 10.

[15] See eg. V. Leary, *International Labour Conventions and National Law* (Dordrecht: Martinus Nijhoff, 1981) at 1.

national legal commitments which operate as very real constraints on the policy choices open to a national government. As McCrudden and Chambers observe,[16]

"a strong current has been carrying Britain in the direction of an increasing acceptance of supra-national, and for the most part European, laws and institutions which may in practice limit domestic freedom of action and circumscribe national sovereignty."

The fact that since November 1993 citizens of the UK are also citizens of Europe is perhaps the most potent symbol of this transition from the old international order of sovereign nation states to the relatively untested new world of overlapping domestic and international legal orders.[17] It is developments such as these which have led some writers to go so far as to talk of the demise of sovereignty in its classical sense and the dwindling of the nation state.[18]

The accommodation, at the national level, of these developments in the international sphere has inevitably placed enormous strain on a traditional constitutional account which presupposes the existence of a single sovereign law-maker within a sovereign nation-state.[19] It would have been surprising indeed had the metamorphosis of national sovereignty on the international plane not begun to influence the traditional presupposition of parliamentary sovereignty on the domestic plane.[20] It is not simply that the domestic Parliament's freedom to legislate as it chooses is now circumscribed by international obligations, some of which are enforceable through international mechanisms created for that very purpose. The rather less direct, but equally significant, effect of these developments is that international law in the emerging new paradigm is dependent on the domestic legal order of the nation-states to give practical effect to its norms. So the developments outlined above do not amount to the progressive subordination of national legal systems to a superior international order, but rather herald the arrival of a new interdependence of national and international legal orders, in which each presupposes the independent validity of the other. This "mutuality of recognition", as MacCormick has described it, necessitates the use of a quite

---

[16] C. McCrudden and G. Chambers (eds.), *Individual Rights and the Law in Britain* (Oxford: Clarendon Press, 1994), at 4.

[17] Article 8 of the EC Treaty, as amended by the Treaty on European Union 1992. The significance of European citizenship for the domestic status of international human rights norms is considered in more detail in ch. 7 below.

[18] See eg. MacCormick, in Bellamy et al. (eds.), *Democracy and Constitutional Culture* (above n. 10) at 95 and 104; M. Newman, *Democracy, Sovereignty and the European Union* (London: Hurst, 1996) at 4–15. For the contrary thesis, that the rhetoric of European integration has played a crucial role in preserving the nation-state as an organisational concept, see A. Milward, *The European Rescue of the Nation-State* (London: Routledge, 1992), reviewed approvingly by I. Ward, "The European Constitution and the Nation State" (1996) 16 OJLS 161.

[19] More detailed consideration of the variants of the traditional account, such as the so-called "continuing" and "self embracing" schools of sovereignty theorists, is postponed until ch. 2.

[20] MacCormick refers to these two senses of state sovereignty as "internal" and "external" sovereignty in Bellamy et al. (eds.), *Democracy and Constitutional Culture* (above n. 10) at 99.

different vocabulary from that in which legal discourse about the domestic status of international norms has traditionally been conducted. In place of language reflecting the traditional notion of a nation-state "internalising" norms from an "external" source, the language of "interpenetration" and "interdependence" better reflect the partially overlapping and interacting nature of today's national and international legal orders.[21]

The many and varied responses of English courts to this challenge are considered in detail in chapters 2 to 7 below. It will be seen that whilst in practice English courts have gone some considerable way towards accommodating the new international dimension to the UK constitution, at least in the context of European Community law and occasionally, though more sporadically, in the context of international human rights law, they have largely contrived to do so by maintaining at the theoretical level the fiction that such accommodation requires little, if any, modification of their sovereigntist premise, on the preservation of which the legitimacy of the judicial function is perceived to depend. As a result, even in the face of all these challenges from Europe and beyond, the sovereigntist account has proved remarkably durable even as it has become increasingly untenable.

One of the aims of this book is to suggest, as just one aspect of the much broader re-conceptualisation of constitutional thinking now widely called for,[22] a more appropriate judicial response to the challenge presented by these momentous changes, yet a response which, it will be argued, remains consistent with the judiciary's legitimate constitutional role in a representative democracy. The purpose of this introductory chapter is briefly to demonstrate, against this contemporary background of increasing international interdependence and the declining significance of the sovereign nation state, the way in which the domestic status of international legal norms is already changing in the UK. This book is not the place to consider at length the well-rehearsed debate in international law scholarship about the relationship between international law and domestic law.[23] Indeed, one of the claims which will be made is that the old opposition between monism and dualism which has dominated that debate has to a large extent been left behind by modern developments. However, it is necessary briefly to explain the historical and theoretical relationship between the orthodox account of the British constitution and the

---

[21] See eg. H.J. Steiner and P. Alston, *International Human Rights in Context: Law, Politics, Morals—Text and Materials* (Oxford: Clarendon Press, 1996), ch. 11.

[22] See eg. Morison and Livingstone, *Reshaping Public Power* (above n. 12); MacCormick, in Bellamy et al. (eds.), *Democracy and Constitutional Culture* (above n. 10); Ferrajoli in Bellamy (ed.), *Constitutionalism, Democracy and Sovereignty* (above n. 14).

[23] For a detailed account, readers are referred to the extensive international law literature, eg. I. Brownlie, *Principles of Public International Law*, 4th edn. (Oxford: Clarendon Press, 1990), ch. II; R. Jennings and A. Watts (eds.), *Oppenheim's International Law*, 9th edn., Vol. I (Harlow: Longman, 1992) at 52–86, esp. 52–63, 81–6; A.D. McNair, *The Law of Treaties* (Oxford: Clarendon Press, 1961, repr. 1986), chs. IV and XIX; F.A. Mann, *Foreign Affairs in English Courts* (Oxford: Clarendon Press, 1986), 97–112 and *Studies in International Law* (Oxford: Clarendon Press, 1973), ch. VIII; F.G. Jacobs and S. Roberts (eds.), *The Effect of Treaties in Domestic Law*

traditional view of the status of international law in domestic courts. It will be seen that the question of the status of international legal norms in the domestic legal system cannot be dissociated from deeper questions of what counts as "law", or what norms are legally relevant, in a particular legal system. These are questions which English courts have been conspicuously reluctant to consider overtly, despite the magnitude of the constitutional changes wrought largely by their own practical responses to these international pressures.

2. THE RELATIONSHIP BETWEEN PARLIAMENTARY SOVEREIGNTY AND DUALISM

Like so much else in the UK's constitutional firmament, the status of international law in the domestic legal system continues to bear the unmistakeable mark of Dicey's influence. The possibility that international law constituted a limitation on the otherwise absolute authority of Parliament was one of the heresies which Dicey sought to refute in the course of his well-known attempt to prove the existence of Parliamentary sovereignty as a legal "fact".[24] He insisted that an Act of Parliament was never invalid merely because it was opposed to the doctrines of international law and that there was simply no legal basis for the theory that judges may overrule an Act of Parliament on the ground that it went beyond the internationally permissible limits of Parliamentary authority. It was, in Dicey's view, a simple fact of legal practice that a modern judge would never listen to a barrister who presented such an argument.[25] On this view, if domestic legislation clearly conflicts with a treaty obligation which has not been statutorily incorporated into domestic law, the courts are constitutionally bound to give effect to the domestic provision, even though this involves a breach of the state's obligations in international law. Courts cannot hold the statutory provision void, disapply it, ignore it or otherwise render it of no effect on the ground that it contravenes a treaty to which the UK is a signatory or otherwise breaches general principles of international law.

For Dicey, this much followed inexorably from the absolute and continuing nature of Parliamentary sovereignty. The same premise, however, also has implications for less drastic uses of international legal norms. It not only

(London: Sweet and Maxwell, 1987), esp. Introduction (F. Jacobs) and ch. 12 (R. Higgins on the U.K.); R. Higgins, *Problems and Process* (above n. 13), ch. 12 ("The Role of National Courts in the International Legal Process"); "The Relationship Between International and Regional Human Rights Norms and Domestic Law" (1992) 18 CLB 1268.

[24] Dicey, *Introduction* (above n. 7) at 62–63. The heretical example cited by Dicey, at 62 n.2, was *Ex parte Blain* (1879–80) 12 Ch. D. 522 at 531, where Cotton LJ suggested, *obiter*, that "there might be a question" about the duty of the court where an Act had "clearly gone beyond the power of the English legislature."

[25] Ibid. at 63.

prevents such norms from being judicially recognised as superior to a domestic statute, but it precludes unincorporated international treaties from being of *any* legal relevance in domestic courts.[26] Individual citizens cannot seek to rely on an international treaty as a source of rights enforceable in domestic courts unless that treaty has undergone incorporation into domestic law so as to make a claim on the basis of it "justiciable" by domestic courts.[27]

A number of rationales have been suggested for the traditional requirement that treaties be legislatively incorporated before they are capable of having domestic legal effect.[28] One justification which has traditionally been offered is that treaties are "non-justiciable" because their performance, as well as their making, is within the executive's prerogative power of the conduct of foreign relations.[29] As Loveland rightly observes, however, this rationale for the requirement of incorporation is a relic of the days of unreviewable prerogative power, yet it continues to be heard notwithstanding that since the House of Lords decision in the *GCHQ* case the exercise of prerogative powers is no longer unreviewable.[30] In any event, even if the power to conclude a treaty remains an unreviewable exercise of prerogative power after *GCHQ*, that alone cannot be a good reason why its terms are non-justiciable, particularly where the treaty is of such a nature that it is clearly meant to confer rights on individuals. As Loveland points out, that is to conflate two issues which are quite distinct: on the one hand, the power to make treaties, and, on the other, that treaty's subsequent effect in domestic law.

Despite its persistence, the prerogative powers rationale is today only a secondary justification for the requirement that treaties be legislatively incorporated before they are capable of having legal effect. The principal rationale is undoubtedly the doctrine of the separation of powers underpinning Dicey's

---

[26] See A.W. Bradley and K.D. Ewing, *Constitutional and Administrative Law*, 11th edn. (London: Longman, 1993), at 73–4, 326–7, 331–5 for the traditional account of the relationship between legislative supremacy and the domestic status of treaties.

[27] See eg. *J.H. Rayner (Mincing Lane) Ltd.* v. *Department of Trade and Industry* [1990] 2 AC 418 at 476F–477A, (Lord Templeman), 483C (Lord Griffiths) and 499E–501B (Lord Oliver) for a recent reiteration of many of these propositions. The case is considered in more detail, nn. 87–97.

[28] In federal jurisdictions, of course, there is a separate rationale not present in a unitary state, namely the preservation of the constitutional division of legislative competence. On this, see eg. K. Wiltshire, "The Federal Dimension" in P. Alston and M. Chiam (eds.), *Treaty-Making and Australia: Globalisation versus Sovereignty?* (Annandale, NSW: Federation Press, 1995), at 74.

[29] The justification is criticised by I.D. Loveland, *Constitutional Law: A Critical Introduction* (London: Butterworths, 1996) at 590–1. The examples cited by Loveland are *Rustomjee* v. *R* (1876–77) 2 QBD 69 at 74 and *Blackburn* v *AG* [1971] 1 WLR 1037, in both of which treaties were held to be non-justiciable in domestic courts because the executive's prerogative power to enter into treaties was not amenable to judicial review. See also De Smith, Woolf and Jowell, *Judicial Review of Administrative Action*, 5th edn., (London: Sweet and Maxwell, 1995), ch. 28 at 991–5.

[30] *Council of Civil Service Unions* v. *Minister for the Civil Service* [1985] AC 374. Lord Oliver in *Rayner* [1990] 2 AC 418 at 499F–500B, for example, relied on *Rustomjee* and *Blackburn* in explaining that an unincorporated treaty was outside the purview of the court "because it is made in the conduct of foreign relations, which are a prerogative of the crown."

theory of the absolute and exclusive legal sovereignty of Parliament. International treaties are entered into by the executive government pursuant to its prerogative power to conduct foreign affairs, but, according to the terms of the constitutional settlement of 1688, the executive lacks the constitutional authority unilaterally to alter the domestic law of the country. Subordinating the executive to Parliament's legislative supremacy was, after all, what the great constitutional upheavals of the seventeenth century were all about. Courts therefore must not treat an international treaty entered into by the executive as a source of enforceable legal rights and obligations until Parliament has blessed it with legitimacy and truly "legal" pedigree by incorporating it into domestic law by statute. For the courts to recognise such treaties as law without Parliament's legitimation would undermine the principle which Craig has distilled from Dicey, the "legislative monopoly" of Parliament,[31] by conferring *de facto* legislative authority on the executive.

There is no shortage of examples of English judges deducing these various dualist conclusions from the premise of parliamentary sovereignty. Shortly before Dicey wrote his famous lectures, for example, it had been held in *The Parlement Belge* that the Crown could not rely in the courts on an immunity conferred by a convention between the Crown and Belgium, which, had it been applicable, would have had the effect of extinguishing, without the authority of Parliament, the subject's right to recover compensation for damage to property.[32] That, it was said, would be a use of the treaty-making prerogative of the Crown "without precedent, and in principle contrary to the laws of the constitution."[33] The same rule was exported to the Empire by the Privy Council, as is shown by a classic formulation of the orthodox position in the judgment of Lord Atkin, giving the decision of the Privy Council in *AG for Canada* v. *AG for Ontario*.[34] The case concerned a dispute between the federal government of Canada and the provinces over the validity of federal labour legislation passed in performance of treaty obligations. Lord Atkin referred to the "well-established rule that the making of a treaty is an executive act, while the performance of its obligations, if they entail alteration of the existing domestic law, requires legislative action."[35] An executive incurring a treaty obligation which involves alteration of domestic law was said to take the risk of getting Parliament to pass the necessary legislation, because Parliament remained absolutely free to choose whether or not to fulfil the treaty obligations imposed upon the state by its executive.

---

[31] P.P. Craig, *Administrative Law*, 3rd edn. (London: Sweet and Maxwell, 1994), ch. 1; *Public Law and Democracy in the United Kingdom and the United States of America* (Oxford: Clarendon Press, 1990), ch. 2.

[32] (1879) 4 PD 129.

[33] Ibid. at 154, per Sir Robert Phillimore.

[34] [1937] AC 326 at 347–8.

[35] Ibid, at 347.

"The nature of the obligations does not affect the complete authority of the Legislature to make them law if it so chooses."[36]

That courts were drawn to such a pure dualist position was not surprising in view of their rather unsophisticated premise of Parliament's absolute and exclusive sovereignty. Indeed, in a case dating from the period earlier this century during which the dualist position was being most forcefully articulated, its logic was pursued relentlessly to what now seems the astonishing conclusion that recourse to the relevant international obligation was not even permissible as an aid to the construction of legislation introduced in order to implement the obligation. In *Ellerman Lines* v. *Murray*, the House of Lords took the view that if the statutory language was unambiguous, it was not proper to resort to the convention being implemented in order to give the statutory words a meaning other than their "natural meaning", even though the Convention itself was contained in a schedule to the Act.[37]

Both the historical and the theoretical connections between parliamentary sovereignty and the UK's dualist inheritance are therefore clear. It is the democratic and separation of powers concerns expressed in the doctrine of parliamentary sovereignty which primarily explain the rule that an international treaty is without domestic legal effect until it has been "transformed" into domestic law by legislation.[38] Such a stance is generally contrasted in the literature with "monism". This takes a variety of forms but for present purposes can be taken to refer broadly to the view that international law is not only automatically a part of but is also supreme over domestic law. Some versions of the monist theory of the relation between national and international law manifest a clear association with liberal constitutional theories of the protection of individual rights. Hersch Lauterpacht, for example, consistently argued that the individual is the subject of international law, which takes precedence over domestic law even in the sphere of nation-states' legal competence.[39]

Such an association between dualism and sovereignty theory on the one hand and monism and rights theory on the other is of course an oversimpli-

---

[36] [1937] AC 326 at 348. For more recent statements of the same position see *Inland Revenue Commissioners* v. *Collco Dealings Ltd.* [1962] AC 1 at 18–19, where Viscount Simonds described an argument that the plain words of a statute should be disregarded, and words implied in order to observe the comity of nations and the established rules of international law, as "an extravagance to which this House will not, I hope, give ear"; *Cheney* v. *Conn* [1968] 1 WLR 242 at 246G–247E; and many of the cases discussed in chs. 4 and 5 below in the specific context of the domestic status of international human rights law.

[37] [1931] AC 126. See eg. Lord Tomlin at 147. The correctness of *Ellerman Lines* has since been doubted: see Lord Wilberforce in *James Buchanan* v. *Babco* [1978] AC 141 at 153D.

[38] The translation of international treaties into domestic law which dualism requires is usually described as "transformation", and can be either general or special. The former is where a constitutional provision makes all treaties part of domestic law automatically on ratification; the latter where, in the absence of such a constitutional provision, the treaty only becomes part of domestic law on the passage of specific implementing legislation. In the UK, of course, the dualist requirement of transformation of international treaty obligations takes the latter form.

[39] See eg. H. Lauterpacht, *International Law and Human Rights* (London: Stevens, 1950).

fication; as will be seen below, in reality the supposedly antithetical positions of monism and dualism are two extremes on a spectrum of possible approaches to the domestic status of international law. In the meantime, however, the contrast helps to make the point that the effect of Dicey's influence on generations of both practising and academic lawyers has been to perpetuate, at the theoretical level, an ostensibly "dualist" approach to the question of the relationship between domestic law and international treaties and to bequeath, at the practical level, a legal culture of resistance to the use of international law before domestic courts.[40]

3. CUSTOMARY INTERNATIONAL LAW AND THE COMMON LAW

It might be thought that the premise of parliamentary sovereignty on which the English dualist tradition rests ought to dictate, as a matter of logic, that all international law is wholly irrelevant in the national legal system unless it has been specially transformed into domestic law by statute. In practice, however, the rigour of pure dualism has always been mitigated to some extent by the fact that English courts have purported to take a more monistic approach to international norms which qualify as customary international law. Such norms are automatically recognised by the courts as part of the common law, without the need for any specific legislative act of transformation. This approach to the status of customary international law is a remnant of Blackstone's boldly pronounced view that

"the law of nations . . . is here adopted in its full extent by the common law, and is held to be part of the law of the land."[41]

While this is no longer true as far as treaties are concerned, as was seen in the previous section, Blackstone's view appears to have survived the rise of parliamentary sovereignty as far as customary international law is concerned. In *Chung Chi Cheung* v. *The King*, for example, Lord Atkin said:[42]

"The courts acknowledge the existence of a body of rules which nations accept amongst themselves. On any judicial issue they seek to ascertain what the relevant rule is, and, having found it, they will treat it as incorporated into the domestic law, so far as it is not inconsistent with rules enacted by statutes or finally declared by their tribunals."

---

[40] R. Higgins, "The Role of National Courts in the International Legal Process", ch. 12 in *Problems and Process* (above n. 13), at 206 and 218.

[41] Blackstone's *Commentaries on the Laws of England*, vol. iv, ch. 5. Lord Mansfield in *Triquet* v. *Bath* (1764) 3 Burr. 1478, 97 ER 936 at 938, was of the same view, adding that "the law of nations was to be collected from the practice of different nations and the authority of writers."

[42] [1939] AC 160 at 168. See also *West Rand Central Gold Mining Co.* v. *R* [1905] 2 KB 391. As will be seen below, the limitation that the customary international law rule must not conflict with a common law precedent has now arguably been relaxed.

The label generally used to describe this judicial practice of automatic recognition of customary law is "incorporation".[43]

It is true to say that the survival of the more monistic approach to customary international law has not always been beyond controversy. There has been much debate over whether the authorities support the doctrine of incorporation or impose a requirement of transformation before customary international law will be judicially recognised as part of domestic law. There are certainly decisions which appear to proceed on the assumption that customary law is only part of domestic law in so far as it has been adopted in some way, such as by legislation, governmental assent or established usage. In *Mortensen* v. *Peters*, for example, a Scottish court was at pains to point out that it was "not a tribunal sitting to decide whether an Act of the Legislature is *ultra vires* as in contravention of generally acknowledged principles of international law", reiterating the supremacy of an Act of Parliament and the duty of the court to give effect to its terms.[44] International law, so far as a domestic court was concerned, was said to be the body of doctrine regarding the international rights and duties of states which had been adopted and made part of domestic law.[45]

It is also true that even where the doctrine has been recognised it has generally been subject to strict conditions and qualifications which have minimised the extent of its apparent derogation from dualism.[46] Thus a norm of customary international law would only be recognised as automatically a part of the common law if it could be proved to exist. The criteria for the recognition of customary international law are vague and uncertain, requiring a court to have regard to evidence of state practice and to the received international opinion of jurists to establish its existence or content. And even if such problems of proof could be surmounted it would only be recognised to the extent that it was not in conflict with a domestic statutory provision or, at least until relatively recently, a common law precedent.

Nevertheless, the weight of authority and opinion seems to favour the view that rules of customary international law are automatically part of the common law, albeit that they are overridden by inconsistent statutes. The extent to which the approach of English courts to customary international law can be said to be monistic may be heavily qualified, but, even within these con-

---

[43] Although the term "incorporation" is frequently heard in the context of the debate over whether international instruments such as the ECHR or the ICCPR should be made part of English law, the translation of treaty obligations into domestic law is referred to in the literature as "transformation", which is to be distinguished from the incorporation of customary law. The language of "adoption" will be avoided altogether in the interests of clarity, since it is used variously in the literature, sometimes to mean incorporation of customary law and sometimes to mean transformation of treaties.

[44] (1905–06) F (JC) 93 at 100, per Lord Justice-General Dunedin.

[45] See also *R* v. *Keyn* (1876) 2 Ex D 63.

[46] See Brownlie, *Principles*, (above n. 23) at 44–7, for consideration of this debate, concluding that on balance the authorities support the doctrine of incorporation. See also Jennings and Watts (eds.), *Oppenheim's International Law* (above n. 23) at 56–60.

straints, the doctrine of automatic incorporation of customary international law is clearly a means whereby some domestic effect can be given to international law, notwithstanding its untransformed status.

How is such automatic incorporation of customary norms of international law to be explained, given the dualist stance described above in relation to international treaties? The answer, it is suggested, lies in a proper appreciation of the rationale behind the requirement that treaty law be specially transformed. It has already been seen that the principal explanation for that requirement is that Parliament's legislative monopoly would be undermined if treaties entered into by the executive automatically became law enforceable in domestic courts. The recognition of customary international law, by contrast, is no more subversive of Parliament's legislative monopoly than the very existence of the common law itself. International law of this kind is seen by the courts, not as executive legislation, but as the international equivalent of the domestic common law, the product of universal practice rooted in morality recognised on an international scale. Moreover, to the extent that it conflicts irreconcilably with laws emanating from Parliament, customary international law, like the common law itself, must give way, and its automatic recognition by courts can therefore be reconciled with the theory of ultimate parliamentary sovereignty.

4. THE INTERNATIONAL TREATY PRESUMPTION

The account so far given of the status of international norms in domestic courts suggests a predominantly dualist position, subject only to the qualification that customary international law is judicially recognised as being automatically part of the common law. Although that qualification is, on the face of it, limited, in that customary international law is only automatically a part of domestic law in so far as it is not inconsistent with statute, its significance should not be underestimated. That significance becomes apparent on closer consideration of the nature of the relationship between parliamentary sovereignty and the common law.

According to the traditional, most expansive account of parliamentary sovereignty, the interpretation of statutes is a straightforward matter of discovering and applying Parliament's historical intention when enacting the relevant legislation. In reality, of course, Parliament's "intention" is seldom discoverable by any linguistic or factual inquiry, but is constructed by the courts against a background set of assumptions rooted in the common law.[47]

---

[47] Dicey himself relied on the mediating role of the judges in the exercise of their interpretive function in his attempt to reconcile his otherwise contradictory foundational principles of the sovereignty of Parliament and the rule of law: *Introduction* at 413–414. In Dike's view, parliamentary sovereignty is challenged "every time a court construes or interprets an Act of Parliament": C. Dike, "The Case Against Parliamentary Sovereignty" [1976] PL 283 at 291.

In carrying out their inevitably interpretive function, courts in practice achieve a degree of entrenchment for common law values by deploying presumptions of statutory interpretation of varying strengths.[48] One of the best known examples is the presumption that, in the absence of clear language to the contrary, Parliament did not intend to impose retrospective criminal liability.

Since, as was seen in the previous section, the values recognised by the common law include some of those protected in international law, it would be surprising if unincorporated international law were treated as wholly irrelevant by the courts whenever Parliament had legislated in the same field. In practice, the apparent purity of the dualist position has often been compromised by the courts when interpreting statutes, and, as with the more familiar domestic qualifications of pure sovereignty theory in favour of common law values, the main vehicle for this compromise has been a presumption of statutory interpretation, based on Parliament's presumed intention when enacting the statute in question. Notwithstanding the frequently uncompromising judicial statements of the dualist position, including the refusal even to have regard to the relevant international obligation when construing implementing legislation, a rule of construction gradually emerged, to the effect that where legislation is passed to implement an international treaty, it is to be presumed that Parliament intended to fulfil its international obligations.

In *Salomon*, for example, there arose a question of construction of a statute which was clearly based on an international convention but which neither included that convention as a schedule nor made any express reference to it.[49] Diplock LJ began impeccably, reciting the received dualist wisdom that an international treaty is irrelevant to any issue in domestic courts so long as no legislative steps have been taken to fulfil the obligations thus incurred. Even when implementing legislation has been enacted, he held, if its terms are clear and unambiguous they must be given effect by the courts whether or not they fulfil the treaty obligations, because Parliament's sovereign power extends to breaking treaties, for which the only remedy lies elsewhere than in domestic courts.[50] This much is standard dualist dogma, but Diplock LJ went on to add an important qualification. Any ambiguity in the terms of the implementing legislation, he said, triggered a presumption that Parliament does not intend to act in breach of international law, including specific treaty obligations, and the treaty itself therefore became relevant to the exercise in construction. In choosing between the possible meanings of the ambiguous legislation, the

---

[48] For accounts of such statutory interpretation in terms of Dworkin's theory of law and adjudication, see D. Dyzenhaus, *Hard Cases in Wicked Legal Systems: South African Law in the Perspective of Legal Philosophy* (Oxford: Oxford University Press, 1991) and T.R.S. Allan, *Law, Liberty, and Justice: The Legal Foundations of British Constitutionalism* (Oxford: Clarendon Press, 1993), esp. chs. 4 and 6.

[49] *Salomon* v. *Commissioners of Customs and Excise* [1967] 2 QB 116. The statute and treaty were the Customs and Excise Act 1952 and the Convention on Valuation of Goods for Customs Purposes 1950 respectively.

[50] Ibid. at 143B–F.

presumption required the court to prefer the meaning which was consonant with the treaty obligations.[51] In addition, it was said to be no obstacle to such use being made of a treaty to resolve statutory ambiguities or obscurities that the statute itself made no mention of the convention which it was its purpose to implement. It was sufficient if that intention was apparent from extrinsic evidence such as a comparison between the subject matter of the statute and the treaty.[52]

After *Salomon*, then, it was clear that resort to a convention as an aid to interpretation of a statute was permissible on two conditions being satisfied: first, that the terms of the legislation were not clear but were "ambiguous", in the sense of being reasonably capable of more than one meaning; and, second, that there was cogent extrinsic evidence that the enactment was intended to fulfil obligations under a particular convention. The case was soon being cited as authority for the legitimacy of judicial resort to unincorporated conventions, notwithstanding the dualist stance to which the courts were theoretically committed. In *Post Office* v. *Estuary Radio*, for example, the *Salomon* presumption was applied to the construction of an Order in Council,[53] and in *Corocraft Ltd.* v. *Pan American Airways Inc.*, *Salomon* was again cited as authority for construing legislation so as to be in conformity with international law rather than in conflict with it.[54] This marked a significant progression beyond the earlier cases, in particular *Ellerman Lines* v. *Murray*, in which resort to the international treaty had been held to be impermissible even as an aid to the interpretation of implementing legislation.

Thus, while in theory a dualist stance towards international law would seem to be required by judicial acceptance of Parliament's legislative monopoly which flows from the most expansive theory of the sovereignty of Parliament, in practice the bright lines of dualism are blurred in two ways. First, by the judicial recognition that customary international law is already part of the common law without the need for any overt act of transformation by statute; and, second, by the common law presumption of statutory interpretation that Parliament intends to legislate consistently with the country's international obligations, at least when enacting implementing legislation. In this way, judges have contrived to give practical effect to a hybrid of the monist and dualist approaches when interpreting domestic law, whilst at the same time maintaining at the theoretical level a commitment to a dualist

---

[51] Ibid. at 143F–144A. Compare Lord Denning MR at 141F, who preferred to express himself in terms of a general obligation, rather than a presumption of interpretation: "we ought always to interpret our statutes so as to be in conformity with international law." Russell LJ, at 152C–D, agreed with the views of the other two on reference to a treaty in aid of construction of a statute "plainly intended to carry out its terms", but thought that the views expressed may be strictly speaking *obiter* because in his view the question of construction could be resolved by wholly conventional techniques of statutory interpretation.

[52] Ibid. at 144A–145B.

[53] [1968] 2 QB 740 at 757C, per Diplock LJ.

[54] [1969] 1 QB 616 at 653B–C, per Lord Denning MR.

stance towards international treaties underpinned by the sovereignty of Parliament, which could be invoked to preclude reference to such international law as and when convenient.

These qualifications of dualistic purity mean that in practice the stance of English courts towards international legal norms is much more of a compromise between monism and dualism than is commonly supposed.[55] Moreover, each of these qualifications of the pure dualist position has been expanded in significant ways in recent years, in a development which, it will be argued, reveals both to be particular manifestations of a more general interpretive principle that English courts ought to interpret and apply domestic law consistently with the UK's international obligations. First, there has been an important shift in the courts' approach to the question of the domestic status of customary international law, towards a greater receptiveness. Second, in a judicial development which is clearly not unrelated to the first, there has been a gradual relaxation of the conditions for the application of the treaty presumption, resulting in a considerable enhancement of its strength and a correspondingly greater degree of domestic protection for the values contained in international treaties. The inevitable effect of the combination of these trends has been to render domestic law more permeable by international standards.

5. A GREATER RECEPTIVENESS TO CUSTOMARY INTERNATIONAL LAW

It will be recalled that, as classically formulated by Lord Atkin in *Chung Chi Cheung*, rules of customary international law are automatically part of the common law to the extent that they are not inconsistent with either statute or precedent.[56] In *Trendtex*, however, an approach which is more receptive to customary international law appears to have been adopted.[57] In that case, Lord Denning MR invoked the judicial practice of consistently giving effect to changes in international law "without the aid of any Act of Parliament" as justification for his view that "the rules of international law, as existing from time to time, do form part of our English law."[58] International law was said to know no rule of *stare decisis*, which meant that if a domestic court was satisfied that a relevant rule of international law had changed, the court could give effect to that change in English law, notwithstanding the existence of domestic precedents to the contrary. Applying this approach in the case itself, a majority of the Court of Appeal held that the defendant bank could not claim sovereign immunity, despite precedents to the contrary, because in inter-

---

[55] See eg. Pescatore's description of the UK as "radically dualist" in Jacobs and Roberts (eds.), *The Effect of Treaties in Domestic Law* (above n. 23) at 191.

[56] [1939] AC 160 at 168.

[57] *Trendtex v. Central Bank of Nigeria* [1977] QB 529.

[58] Ibid. at 553B–554H.

national law the scope of that immunity had been reduced to cover only executive and not commercial acts of government.[59]

Debate has long raged over the extent to which *Trendtex* heralds a new departure in the approach of English courts to the domestic status of customary international law. The debate has focused on whether the *ratio* of the majority's decision is that changes in customary international law are automatically a part of the common law such that they override all inconsistent precedents, or only those which were based on the rule of customary international law which is now obsolete. Duffy has argued for a "modified narrow view" of the decision in *Trendtex*, whereby the *rationes* of precedents based on obsolete international law are interpreted as being that the points in question are governed by international law.[60] Such a reading is acknowledged to be a reformulation of the ratio of earlier cases, but to have the advantage of allowing contemporary changes in international law to be judicially recognised consistently with the doctrine of precedent.

Whichever view of the scope of *Trendtex* is preferred, it is clear that the decision represents a greater willingness on the part of courts to treat customary international law as part of the common law. The decision could therefore be said to represent the adoption of a more receptive, or, if it makes sense at all to turn the bivalent language of the monist/dualist debate into a matter of degree, a more "incorporationist" approach than the traditional formulation of the so-called doctrine of incorporation. Subsequent cases have confirmed the *Trendtex* approach, referring, for example, to the "duty of English courts so far as possible to keep in step with the settled practice of other nations."[61] Such a development clearly has important implications for the domestic status of international human rights instruments such as the ECHR and the ICCPR, insofar as they, or any part of them, are capable of constituting customary international law, particularly as the meaning of their provisions is constantly evolving in the course of their interpretation by the bodies established to enforce their provisions.

6. STRENGTHENING THE TREATY PRESUMPTION

It was seen above that, notwithstanding a professed commitment to a theoretical premise of dualism, English courts had in practice developed a presumption of statutory interpretation, to the effect that where Parliament has enacted domestic legislation to give effect to an international convention, it was presumed to have intended to fulfil the country's international obligations

---

[59] Shaw LJ agreed with Lord Denning MR, ibid. at 578G–579F; Stephenson LJ dissented on this point, at 571D–572B.

[60] P.J. Duffy, "English Law and the European Convention on Human Rights" (1980) 29 ICLQ 585 at 600–1.

[61] *Standard Chartered Bank* v. *International Tin Council* [1987] 1 WLR 641 at 648.

under that convention. According to the formulation of that presumption by Diplock LJ in *Salomon*, international obligations could be looked at by courts as an aid to the construction of implementing legislation where there was both ambiguity in the statutory language and cogent extrinsic evidence that the statute was intended to give effect to a particular convention.[62]

However, in the subsequent case of *Garland*, Lord Diplock formulated the presumption slightly differently.[63] He said,

> ". . . it is a principle of construction of United Kingdom statutes, now too well established to call for citation of authority, that the words of a statute passed after the Treaty has been signed and dealing with the subject matter of the international obligation of the United Kingdom, are to be construed, if they are reasonably capable of bearing such a meaning, as intended to carry out the obligation, and not to be inconsistent with it".[64]

This represented an expansion in the scope of the treaty presumption in two important ways. First, the requirement of ambiguity in the statutory language as a precondition to using the treaty as an aid to construction appears to have been dispensed with. It is certainly not mentioned expressly, and, as will be demonstrated below, the requirement that the words must be "reasonably capable of bearing such a meaning" is quite different from a precondition of ambiguity. Second, the range of legislation to which the presumption applied appears to have been extended beyond implementing legislation to any legislation "dealing with the subject matter of the international obligation." Each of these developments broadening the scope of the treaty presumption has significant implications for the domestic status of international treaties, including international human rights instruments, and in particular for their relevance to the interpretation of domestic statutes.

(a) Dropping the Ambiguity Requirement

Consider first the apparent dropping of the ambiguity requirement. This aspect of Lord Diplock's evolving formulation of the presumption between *Salomon* and *Garland* can in fact be traced all the way back to *Salomon* itself, which contains at least two clear precursors of the subsequent development. First, in the course of argument in that case, though not in the judgment,

---

[62] *Salomon* v. *Commissioners of Customs and Excise* [1967] 2 QB 116 at 143F–144A.

[63] *Garland* v. *British Rail Engineering Ltd*. [1983] 2 AC 751. The case is considered at length in ch. 2 below.

[64] Ibid. at 771A–B. As will be seen in ch. 2, although *Garland* concerned Art.119 of the EC Treaty which was directly applicable anyway by virtue of s.2 of the European Communities Act 1972, Lord Diplock's formulation of the treaty presumption was not confined to the EC context but was intended as an authoritative statement of the general position on the legal relevance of international obligations. Where the international obligation was one made directly applicable by s.2, the ordinary common law presumption applied *a fortiori*.

Diplock LJ had said "[w]hen the Crown has entered into a treaty the courts will so far as possible construe a domestic Act in conformity with the treaty, so that the Crown in its judicial capacity does not sleep while in another capacity it watches."[65] This strongly suggests that Diplock LJ considered it to be the *duty* of courts (as an emanation of the Crown) to construe domestic legislation, if they could, so as to be in conformity with the UK's international obligations, quite independently of any specific parliamentary intention that the legislation ought to be so construed.

Second, as was noted above, Diplock LJ in *Salomon* had dutifully recited the dualist platitudes that it was the duty of the court first to construe the legislation in isolation, and, if that construction yielded a clear and unambiguous meaning, to give effect to it, even if that involved a breach of the country's international obligations.[66] The terms of the treaty only became relevant to the judicial interpretive task once the court had *first* decided that there was an ambiguity or lack of clarity in the statutory language. The dualist credentials of this abstract formulation could not be faulted. However, when it came to applying this approach to the particular case, Diplock LJ showed some reluctance towards keeping the international convention out of sight while first construing the statute on its own. Significantly, he admitted that, had he not read the construction put on the statutory words by the judge below, he might have been misled into thinking that the words were too clear and unambiguous to necessitate any reference to the convention, and that since his own construction differed from that of the judge below, it would be "hubristic" to assert that the words were capable of only one meaning and to refuse to look to the convention as an aid to their construction. This shows that he was alive to the very real danger inherent in a preliminary ambiguity requirement, namely that words considered on their own, in isolation from any wider context, often do not appear to be ambiguous (in the sense of capable of more than one meaning).[67] Nevertheless, he felt constrained to "observe the rules" and deal first with the construction of the words used in the statute before turning to the convention.[68]

A similar unease with the artificiality of first construing the domestic law in isolation from the international treaty was again in evidence in Diplock LJ's judgment in *Post Office* v. *Estuary Radio*, in which, "[w]hile recognising that the Order in Council is the document which we have to construe", he found

---

[65] [1967] 2 QB 116 at 132D–E.

[66] Ibid. at 143D–F. Diplock LJ even went so far as to cite in support the ultra–dualist authority of *Ellerman Lines* v. *Murray* [1931] AC 126, which was subsequently disapproved by Lord Wilberforce in *Babco* [1978] AC 141 at 153D.

[67] Whether there is any difference between words being "ambiguous", "unclear" and "reasonably capable of more than one meaning" is considered in section 9 below.

[68] [1967] 2 QB 116 at 145B–D. For an extreme example of the dualist insistence on construing the domestic statute first, in isolation even from directly effective European Community law, see the decision of the Court of Appeal majority in *Macarthys* v. *Smith* [1979] 3 All ER 325, considered in ch. 2 below.

it convenient to look first at the relevant convention before doing so.[69] In *The Eschersheim*, Lord Diplock appeared to stray even further from the theoretical purity of his abstract statement in *Salomon*, by making no mention whatsoever of any preliminary requirement of ambiguity.[70] There he simply said that, as the relevant Act was passed to enable the government to give effect to the obligations in international law which it would assume on ratifying the convention to which it was a signatory, the rule of statutory construction laid down in *Salomon* and *Post Office* v. *Estuary Radio* was applicable. This meant that if there was any difference between the language of the statutory provision and that of the corresponding provision of the convention, the statutory language should be construed in the same sense as that of the convention, if the words of the statute were reasonably capable of bearing that meaning.[71]

Orthodox theory could no doubt be stretched to accommodate this greater judicial willingness to refer to international conventions as an interpretive guide to the meaning of domestic legislation without first deciding that the statute, construed on its own, is ambiguous. It could say, for example, that the development amounts to an acceptance by the courts that the very existence of the international obligation is capable of being a source of ambiguity, in the sense that, when considered alongside the statute, it may reveal an alternative meaning which the statutory words are capable of bearing but which would not have suggested itself had the statutory words been considered by themselves. By characterising the development in this way, ambiguity is at least nominally retained as the valve by which to regulate recourse to international instruments as aids to interpretation.

A preferable way of viewing the development, it will be argued, is as the abandonment of the precondition of ambiguity and the transformation of the international treaty presumption from a presumption triggered by ambiguity to a general presumption rebuttable only by clear language to the contrary.[72] The development is better characterised in this way because it recognises that what has taken place is essentially a "constitutionalisation" of the subject-matter of the presumption. Discarding the ambiguity precondition, it will be argued, is a necessary step in recognising the nature of the treaty presumption as a particular manifestation of a broader judicial *obligation* to construe domestic law so as to be in conformity with international law, rather than a

---

[69] [1968] 2 QB 740 at 755B. At 757C, however, he reverted to dualist orthodoxy when, citing *Salomon*, he referred in the abstract to there being "a presumption that the Crown did not intend to break an international treaty ... and if there is any ambiguity in the Order in Council it should be resolved so as to accord with the provisions of the Convention in so far as that is a plausible meaning of the express words of the Order."

[70] [1976] 1 WLR 430.

[71] Ibid. at 436C. The statute and convention were the Administration of Justice Act 1956 and the International Convention Relating to the Arrest of Seagoing Ships (1952) respectively.

[72] A distinction drawn by J. Bell & G. Engle (eds.), *Statutory Interpretation*, 3rd edn. (London: Butterworths, 1995), at 166, to distinguish presumptions operating "at a higher level" as expressions of fundamental constitutional principle. The argument that the ambiguity precondition has been abandoned is developed in section 9 below.

mere permission to have regard to the unincorporated international law as a supposed aid to uncovering Parliament's historical intention at the time it enacted the legislation.

(b) Extending the Presumption to Non-Implementing Legislation

Even such a total repudiation of the ambiguity requirement as a precondition of legitimate reference to an unincorporated treaty, however, would not necessarily be inconsistent with a sovereigntist view of the judicial function, in which the courts consider it to be their constitutional role to discover and give effect to some historically extant legislative intention. So long as the other of Lord Diplock's conditions in *Salomon*, that there be cogent evidence that the legislation was intended to implement a particular convention, were maintained, the courts could continue to justify their reference to the international convention in terms of fulfilling the legislative intention to give effect to the treaty.[73] The significance of Lord Diplock's formulation of the presumption in *Garland*, however, is that not only has it dropped the preliminary requirement of ambiguity, but it has also dispensed with the requirement that the legislation which falls to be construed must be shown, by some extrinsic evidence, to be implementing legislation.

The origins of this evolution in the scope of the presumption can again be traced to *Salomon* itself, which was, for its time, a liberalising decision in this respect. Diplock LJ rejected an argument that the terms of the convention could not be consulted to resolve ambiguities in a statute unless the statute itself contained some express reference to the international convention which it was the statute's purpose to implement. Such an express reference was held to be unnecessary if it was apparent from a comparison of the subject-matter of the statutory provision and the convention that the former was enacted to carry out the government's obligations under the latter. By the time of *Garland*, Lord Diplock clearly felt able to carry this evolution even further by making explicit that courts are entitled to have regard to international treaties to help construe statutes, which neither expressly nor impliedly, implemented those obligations, but which merely concerned the same subject matter.

(c) The Reasons Behind the Gradual Strengthening of the Presumption

This relaxation of the conditions for the application of the international treaty presumption marks a significant stage in its evolution to the status of a presumption of general application, rather than one triggered by ambiguity. That

---

[73] Brownlie, *Principles* (above n. 23) at 49, sees the requirement of evidence that the statute was intended to implement obligations under the relevant convention as the only necessary principle.

evolution of the presumption has come about gradually; Lord Diplock's more liberal approach to its application was by no means without precedent.[74] A decade before *Salomon*, in *Smith* v. *East Elloe Rural District Council*, for example, the great common lawyer Lord Reid, giving examples of the many cases in which general words in a statute are read down by courts so as not to conflict with fundamental principles, said that such general words would be given a limited meaning "so as not to conflict with international law".[75] Similarly, that rather less consistent common lawyer, Lord Denning MR, in *Salomon* itself formulated the presumption in more general terms than Diplock LJ in the same case, saying "we ought *always* to interpret our statutes so as to be in conformity with international law",[76] and in *Corocraft* he described it as being the "duty" of English courts to construe legislation so as to be in conformity with international law and not in conflict with it.[77] Scarman LJ in *Pan American World Airways Inc.* v. *Department of Trade* also thought it proper for a court to have regard to an international convention when choosing between competing constructions of English law.[78]

Indeed, in formulating the treaty presumption in this way, Lords Diplock, Reid, Denning and Scarman were doing nothing more dramatic than returning to the general presumption of conformity with international obligations acknowledged to exist even by Dicey himself. For although, as has been seen, he set out in unequivocal terms the doctrine of the supremacy of Parliament over international law, he also recognised the existence of a presumption of statutory interpretation whereby judges would presume a legislative intent not to contravene international obligations. Faced with dicta in some cases which appeared to suggest that international law might be the source of limits on Parliament's own *vires*, and that courts might refuse to enforce statutes going beyond those proper limits, Dicey explained them away as amounting to nothing more than a presumption of intended conformity with international obligations:

---

[74] Nor does *Garland* stand alone in its relaxation of the *Salomon* conditions for resorting to unincorporated international instruments. See the cases cited by Brownlie, *Principles* (above n. 23) at 49 n.3 for examples of judicial reference to treaties in the absence of ambiguity; and see *Ahmad* v. *ILEA* [1978] QB 36 and *Williams* v. *Home Office* (No. 2) [1981] 1 All ER 1211 for examples of the presumption being applied to non-implementing legislation.

[75] [1956] AC 736 at 765.

[76] [1967] 2 QB 116 at 141F (emphasis added).

[77] [1969] 1 QB 616 at 653B-C.

[78] [1976] 1 Lloyd's Rep. 257, at 261 col.2–262 col.1. See also the various cases in the mid-1970s, considered in ch. 4 below, in which the courts applied a strong version of the treaty presumption in relation to the ECHR. For evidence of governmental acceptance of a general treaty presumption see eg. G. Howe, "The European Communities Act 1972" (1973) 43 International Affairs 1 at 9, referring to "the rule of interpretation which requires [the courts] to construe our domestic law, if possible, in a way that is in line with our international obligations", and the parliamentary debates on the European Communities Bill, as recounted by Forman, "The European Communities Act 1972: The Government's Position on the Meaning and Effect of its Constitutional Provisions" (1973) 10 CMLRev 39 at 52 and 53, considered in ch. 2 below.

". . . the judges, when attempting to ascertain what is the meaning to be affixed to an Act of Parliament, will presume that Parliament did not intend to violate . . . the principles of international law, and will therefore, whenever possible, give such an interpretation to a statutory enactment as may be consistent with the doctrines . . . of international morality."[79]

The absence from that statement of any reference to a precondition of ambiguity, or restriction of the presumption's applicability to implementing legislation, is particularly striking, emanating as it does from the author to whom responsibility is usually attributed for the prevailing legal culture of resistance to the domestic reception of international norms. Ironically, the conditions which in the intervening years came to be attached to Dicey's presumption were the consequence of the ascendancy enjoyed by the doctrine of parliamentary sovereignty which he articulated so forcefully.

The modern strengthening of the treaty presumption can be explained by a combination of influences on both the international and domestic plane. On the international plane, as has already been noted in section 1 above, the significance of national sovereignty has been steadily eroded in an ever more interdependent international community. Domestic judges have not been wholly blind to the implications of these developments for the doctrine of parliamentary sovereignty and other constitutional certainties formerly taken for granted. In particular, as will be seen in chapters 2 and 3, English judges have been forced to push out the frontiers of their interpretive function in order to accommodate the supremacy and direct effect of European Community law and the indirect effect of such law as is non-directly effective.

Meanwhile, on the domestic plane, the traditional rationales on which dualism theoretically rested have also been seriously weakened. Since 1924, treaties have been ratified in accordance with the so-called Ponsonby Rule, whereby the Crown does not proceed with ratification until the text of the treaty it is proposed to ratify has been laid before Parliament for 21 days. During that time there is an opportunity, in theory at least, to challenge the terms of the treaty. While this falls far short of legislative scrutiny, it goes some way towards diminishing the "executive legislation" rationale for the incorporation requirement. Courts have often relied on the fact that statutory instruments (executive law-making with Parliament's prior authorisation) lie before Parliament before their adoption, as an indication of their democratic pedigree and a reason why judges should be slow to strike down their provisions on judicial review, and there seems no reason in principle why courts should not equally take notice of the opportunity for Parliament to object to the ratification of treaties.

More importantly, perhaps, a number of features of the contemporary political landscape have helped to undermine the idea of parliamentary sovereignty by weakening the democratic imperative which in theory

---

[79] Dicey, *Introduction* (above n. 7) at 62–3.

underpinned it. These now go far beyond the mere fact that, as Cunningham succinctly puts it, the traditional rationale for the incorporation requirement "ignores the realities of executive influence in the legislature in the modern British constitution."[80] Today, ruthless party discipline, an unfair electoral system, a fragmented and largely ineffective opposition, and the declining respect for and authority of the people's representatives are all well documented shortcomings of this country's present constitutional arrangements.[81] Though well beyond the scope of this book, these and other deficiencies in the democratic machinery must be acknowledged for the part they have undoubtedly played in weakening the constitutional objections to courts having regard to international law which Parliament has not yet incorporated. When Parliament and the executive are no longer thought to be in any meaningful sense separate entities, or representative of the citizenry, the rationales for dualism, based on democratic and separation of powers concerns, are seriously undermined. Moreover, the common law renaissance in administrative law which these failings of the political system have called forth, as judges have felt compelled to fill the obvious gaps in governmental accountability, has helped to engender a climate in which judicial revision of the status of international law in the domestic legal system seems much less controversial than during sovereignty's heyday.

One further influence which helps explain the modern strengthening of the treaty presumption is the advent of a more internationalist outlook amongst the senior judiciary. Signs of a new receptiveness to the experience and learning of other jurisdictions has led Lord Bingham to talk of "a new dawn of internationalism" replacing the mood of introversion which prevailed among the English legal community during the first half of this century.[82] Elsewhere, the same judge, reflecting on the impact of international conventions on municipal law, has expressed the hope that, in the field of interpretation, the judges "are all internationalists now."[83] The new internationalism has in part been forced upon the judges by the UK's accession to the European Community and its acceptance of the jurisdiction of the European Court of Human Rights, but in part it is undoubtedly the product of the emergence of an international judicial community, pooling their experience and cross-fertilising ideas at international conferences. At a time of great upheaval in

---

[80] A.J. Cunningham, "The European Convention on Human Rights, Customary International Law and the Constitution" (1994) 43 ICLQ 537 at 552.

[81] The high level of interest in constitutional reform from political commentators of both left and right is itself evidence of the malaise: see eg. W. Hutton, *The State We're In* (London: Jonathan Cape, 1995); A. Marr, *Ruling Britannia: The Failure and Future of British Democracy* (London: Michael Joseph, 1995); P. Johnson, *Wake Up Britain!* (London: Weidenfeld and Nicholson, 1994); S. Jenkins, *Accountable to None: The Tory Nationalization of Britain* (London: Hamish Hamilton, 1995); F. Mount, *The British Constitution Now* (London: Heinemann, 1992).

[82] T.H. Bingham, "There is a World Elsewhere: The Changing Perspectives of English Law" (1992) 41 ICLQ 513 at 515, 519 and 526–8.

[83] B. Markesinis (ed.), *The Gradual Convergence: Foreign Ideas, Foreign Influences and English Law on the Eve of the 21st Century* (Oxford: Clarendon Press, 1994) at 166.

the world's political ordering, comparative constitutionalism has enjoyed a revival, and the globe-trotting judge[84] has been a full participant in the international exchange of ideas. The experience has led some to dream of the emergence of an international common law, including an international common law of human rights.[85]

In short, what has come about as a result of these many and varied influences is a gradual evolution of the international treaty presumption, reflecting shifts in judicial conceptions of the relative normativity of law emanating from different sources, and resulting in a greater permeability of domestic law by international norms.

7. THE ATAVISTIC DUALISM OF ENGLISH COURTS

It would be misleading to suggest, however, that there is any inexorable trend towards greater judicial receptiveness to international legal norms. It is not surprising that, despite the significant developments charted in the two preceding sections, English courts have continued to display the atavism which invariably attends beguilingly clear-cut legal concepts such as sovereignty and dualism. This atavism manifests itself in two ways. First, by continuing to insist that the international treaty presumption is subject to a precondition of ambiguity, the courts have reserved to themselves a discretion as to whether or not to refer to unincorporated international norms. Any presumption of statutory interpretation, being couched in the fictitious language of discovering Parliament's historical intention, keeps a court's sovereigntist options open in the sense that it can always resort to what it asserts to be "Parliament's clear intention." The treaty presumption therefore preserves the opportunity for courts to avoid having to consider unincorporated international law at all by finding that domestic law is clear or unambiguous. The second way in which the courts' atavistic dualism manifests itself is by overstating the scope of the doctrine of the non-justiciability of international treaties. In *Blackburn* v. *Attorney General*, for example, in the context of a challenge to the Government's proposed signature of the Treaty of Rome, thereby acceding to the European Communities, Lord Denning MR said "[i]t is elementary that these courts take no notice of treaties as such . . . until they are embodied in laws enacted by Parliament, and then only to the extent that Parliament tells us."[86]

---

[84] The phrase is Taggart's, "Legitimate Expectation and Treaties in the High Court of Australia" (1996) 112 LQR 50 at 54.

[85] Lord Cooke, "The Dream of an International Common Law", in C. Saunders (ed.), *Courts of Final Jurisdiction: the Mason Court in Australia* (Sydney: Federation Press, 1996), at 138.

[86] [1971] 1 WLR 1037 at 1039G–H. See, to the same effect, the comments of Lord Denning MR and Phillimore LJ in *McWhirter* v. *Attorney General* [1972] CMLR 882 at 886 and 887, a similar challenge brought after the Treaty of Accession was signed but before its implementation by Act of Parliament. Contrast Lord Denning's views in the early cases concerning the domestic status of the ECHR considered in ch. 4 below.

The same tendency to exaggerate the extent of the non-justiciability of unincorporated international treaties was also very much in evidence in the course of the *International Tin Council* litigation.[87] The case raised the question of the justiciability of the Sixth International Tin Agreement, which had not been incorporated into English law, in the context of an action to recover the Tin Council's debts from its constituent members. In the House of Lords, Lord Oliver took a very restrictive view of the competence of domestic courts to take cognisance of and to construe treaty obligations entered into by the UK. He regarded it as axiomatic that domestic courts could not have the competence to adjudicate upon or enforce rights arising out of international agreements entered into by sovereign states, because of two fundamental principles of constitutional law. First, such agreements were concluded by the Crown in the exercise of the royal prerogative, the exercise of which could not be challenged in domestic law. Second, the royal prerogative did not extend to altering the law or conferring rights on individuals or depriving individuals of rights which they enjoy in domestic law without legislation. For Lord Oliver, the axiom that a treaty is not self-executing meant that

> "[q]uite simply, a treaty is not a part of English law unless and until it has been incorporated into the law by legislation. So far as individuals are concerned, it is *res inter alios acta* from which they cannot derive rights and by which they cannot be deprived of rights or subjected to obligations; and it is outside the purview of the court not only because it is made in the conduct of foreign relations, which are a prerogative of the Crown, but also because, as a source of rights and obligations, it is irrelevant."[88]

Although Lord Oliver hastened to make clear that these propositions of constitutional principle did not mean that domestic courts must never look at or construe a treaty, he kept within narrow confines his definition of when a court could do so: where a treaty was directly incorporated into domestic law by Act of Parliament; where a statute was enacted to give effect to the UK's obligations under a treaty; where parties to a contract had incorporated into it the terms of a treaty; or where domestic legislation, though not incorporating the treaty, nevertheless required resort to be had to its terms for the purpose of construing the legislation. However, Lord Oliver was careful to point out that domestic courts could only legitimately make reference to unincorporated treaties in such situations for "evidential" purposes. The conclusion of an international treaty, which states were parties to it and what its terms were, were all questions of fact as far as the domestic court was concerned, and the question of its legal effect in international law was said to be not justiciable by municipal courts.

---

[87] *J.H. Rayner (Mincing Lane) Ltd.* v. *Department of Trade and Industry* [1990] 2 AC 418 at 476F–477A, 483C, 499E–501B.
[88] Ibid. at 500C–D.

Lord Templeman took a similarly restrictive view of the status of international treaties in domestic law.[89] In his view, the constitutional division of functions was quite clear: the Government may negotiate, conclude, construe, observe, breach, repudiate or terminate a treaty; Parliament may alter the laws of the UK; and the courts must enforce those laws. Judges had no power to grant specific performance of a treaty or to award damages against a sovereign state for breach of a treaty or to invent laws or misconstrue legislation in order to enforce a treaty. Except to the extent that a treaty became incorporated into the laws of the UK by statute, the courts of the UK had no power to enforce treaty rights and obligations at the behest of a sovereign government or at the behest of a private individual. The position was quite simply that treaty rights and obligations are not enforceable in the courts of the UK unless incorporated into law by statute.[90]

By contrast, in the Court of Appeal in the same case, Kerr LJ had shown a rare judicial awareness of the English tendency to revert to dualistic purity, and warned against carrying the doctrine of the non-justiciability of unincorporated treaties too far.[91] The danger as he perceived it was that reliance on the doctrine of non-justiciability could all too easily involve an approach which tended to preclude all reference to the terms of a treaty and to inhibit the court in its duty to decide justiciable issues. In Kerr LJ's view, a court must always bear in mind that whether or not a matter connected with an unincorporated treaty was justiciable depended not on whether the arguments or evidence required reference to the contents of such a treaty, but on the nature of the issue under consideration. To guard against the danger of the doctrine of non-justiciability being extended beyond its proper scope, he reminded courts that it only rested on two general principles.

The first such principle was that, since unincorporated treaties have no legislative effect, they do not form part of the law of this country, and no private rights or obligations can therefore be derived from them. The second was that, although treaties are agreements intended to be binding on the parties to them, they are not contracts which our courts can enforce, and therefore any issue between the parties to an unincorporated treaty is a non-justiciable issue in our courts. That, however, was as far as the doctrine of non-justiciability of unincorporated treaties went.[92] In particular, Kerr LJ was anxious to make clear that

---

[89] Ibid. at 476F–477A.

[90] Ibid. at 483C. Contrast Lord Templeman's position in R v. *Secretary of State for the Home Department, ex p. Brind* [1991] 1 AC 696, discussed in ch. 4 below, in which he was the only member of the House of Lords not to take this point as the ground for dismissing an argument based on the European Convention on Human Rights.

[91] [1989] Ch. 72 at 163D–167B.

[92] Ibid. at 163F–164E. Kerr LJ. criticised the trial judge, Staughton J., for taking too expansive a view of when a claim is "founded on a treaty" and therefore non-justiciable. See [1987] BCLC 667 at 687e–689d, 701f–703f.

"[i]t does not preclude the decision of justiciable issues which arise against the back-ground of an unincorporated treaty in a way which renders it necessary or convenient to refer to, and consider, the contents of the treaty. Indeed, any contest as to whether or not an issue connected with an unincorporated treaty is justiciable will usually require some reference to the treaty. Apart from this, a court must be free to inform itself fully of the contents of a treaty whenever these are relevant to the decision of any issue which is not in itself a non-justiciable issue."[93]

Kerr LJ also rejected the suggestion, which is commonly heard in cases involving unincorporated treaties, that when a court looks at an unincorporated treaty, it is then precluded from applying any process of interpretation to its provisions. He rightly pointed out that reading a treaty involves seeking to understand it, which may necessarily involve some interpretation of its terms.[94]

The contrast of approaches could hardly be starker.[95] The approach of Lords Templeman and Oliver in the House of Lords exemplifies the tendency, inherent in the sovereigntist approach, to treat unincorporated treaties as being beyond the competence of a domestic court to consider, and to believe the fallacy that such a conclusion is compelled by fundamental constitutional principles.[96] Kerr LJ's approach, on the other hand, acknowledges that the unincorporated status of international law is not an obstacle to its legal relevance before a domestic court and that an unincorporated treaty may be relevant to an issue which is otherwise justiciable. As Kerr LJ pertinently observed in the course of his judgment,

"it appears excessively insular, and perhaps in these times almost absurd, to prohibit reference to the underlying international instruments as an aid to the intended effect" of domestic legislation.[97]

8. THE SPECIAL STATUS OF INTERNATIONAL HUMAN RIGHTS NORMS

So far, this chapter has concerned itself with the changing domestic status of international norms generally, regardless of their content. In fact, as will be seen in the following chapters, domestic law has become particularly permeable by international human rights norms, suggesting that they may enjoy a

---

[93] [1989] Ch. 72 at 164B–D. See also Ralph Gibson LJ., in *Rayner* (above n. 87) at 240A–B, who pointed out that the rule did not prohibit reference to unincorporated treaties in all circumstances and for any purposes, and that the question was what was meant by "relying on the provisions of a treaty".

[94] Ibid. at 164G–H.

[95] See R. Higgins, *Problems and Process* (above n. 23) at 207, who contrasts their Lordships' treatment of the issue as a short question of construction of the plain words of a statutory instrument with Kerr LJ's obvious interest in the international law dimension.

[96] See also *British Airways* v. *Laker Airways* [1984] QB 142 at 192D, *per* Sir John Donaldson MR.

[97] [1989] Ch. 72 at 165C-D. The more restrictive approach of the House of Lords was, however, followed by the House of Lords in *Arab Monetary Fund* v. *Hashim (No. 3)* [1991] 2 AC 114.

special status, by virtue of their subject-matter. Indeed, there is a steadily growing body of opinion amongst commentators and theoreticians that many of the norms contained in the international human rights treaties such as the ECHR and the ICCPR, and in the jurisprudence of the bodies charged with their interpretation, enjoy a special status and therefore are either automatically part of domestic law, by virtue of their customary status, or at least coincide with the content of customary domestic law (ie. common law). If this is so, the treaty presumption can be expected to be of even greater strength where the subject-matter of the international treaty is human rights.

(a) International Human Rights Treaties as Customary International Law

So far in this chapter, a distinction has been drawn between treaties on the one hand and customary international law on the other. To the extent that treaties are capable of evidencing, or evolving into, customary international law, however, that distinction breaks down.[98] In a series of articles in the second half of the 1970s, Drzemczewski drew attention to the "interpenetrative development" of customary human rights law and the English common law, and argued for the recognition by English courts of the existence of an international common law, comprising international human rights instruments, including the European Convention.[99] The argument was essentially that instruments such as the Convention are the expression of customary international human rights law and as such form part of the common law via the doctrine of incorporation, without any need for legislation.[100] Adopting the wide interpretation of the *Trendtex* decision, as meaning that domestic courts are bound to apply customary international law as it changes, even where that involves departing from common law precedents to the contrary, Drzemczewski argued that the substantive provisions of the Convention, as interpreted by the Court of Human Rights, were already an integral part of domestic law which domestic courts were therefore under a duty to enforce.

---

[98] Article 38(1)(b) of the Statute of the International Court of Justice implicitly recognises that treaties can constitute customary international law when they constitute "evidence of a general practice accepted as law". As Higgins points out, *Problems and Process* (above n. 23) at 19, in practice the clause is interpreted as if it read "*evidenced by* a general practice accepted as law". On the role of treaties in the development of customary human rights norms, see generally T. Meron, *Human Rights and Humanitarian Norms as Customary Law* (Oxford: Clarendon Press, 1989). On the "overlap" between treaty and custom see Higgins, op. cit at 28–32.

[99] A. Drzemczewski, "The Applicability of Customary International Human Rights Law in the English Legal System" (1975) 8 HRJ 71; "European Human Rights Law in the United Kingdom: Some Observations" (1976) 9 HRJ 123, at 125–6; "The Implementation of the United Kingdom's Obligations under the European Convention on Human Rights: Recent Developments" (1979) 12 HRJ 95, at 98–101; "British Courts and the European Human Rights Convention: An Unsatisfactory Situation" (1979, October) Topical Law 38, at 40–41, 52.

[100] See Meron, (above n. 98) at 114–17 for consideration of British cases recognising human rights as customary law.

In the case of the ECHR, Drzemczewski's argument about the domestic applicability of international human rights instruments was reinforced by the Convention's *sui generis* nature. He pointed out that although the Convention is an international agreement which takes the form of a treaty, in substance it has given rise to a new type of law which defies classification as either international or domestic law.[101] Rather than being a simple contract between states based on traditional international law concepts such as reciprocity, sovereignty or nationality, it is, says Drzemczewski,

> "a treaty of a normative character which is developing an evolving notion of 'Convention law' which interpenetrates and transcends both the international and domestic legal structures."[102]

The uniqueness of the Convention resides, of course, in its system of institutions for ensuring the protection of the rights it guarantees. The existence of a right of individual petition to the supranational machinery, accepted by the UK in 1966, further enhances the transnational status of the Convention,[103] and justifies talk of the Convention establishing a "new legal order" transcending the former relationship between domestic and international law.[104] The subject-matter of its guarantees, being classical civil liberties and human rights of the kind usually found in national constitutions, further contributes to its unusual character as a sort of supranational constitution.

Drzemczewski's thesis of the direct applicability of the Convention has been criticised. Duffy, for example, responded that English courts were unlikely to accept the argument that the Convention was part of the common law, and argued that, even if they did, it would be of very little practical consequence because the Convention would still only be a part of domestic law to the extent that it did not conflict with contrary statutes and precedents.[105] Duffy's criticism focused on the likelihood that English courts would take a conservative approach to the domestic effect of customary international law, in the sense that even if they recognised the Convention to be part of the common law they would still accord priority to domestic law in the event of conflict. As will be seen in chapters 4 to 6 below, that prediction has been borne out by experience, at least until the rapid developments of the last few years.

---

[101] A. Drzemczewski, *European Human Rights Convention in Domestic Law: A Comparative Study* (Oxford: Clarendon Press, 1983), at 22–34.

[102] Ibid. at 33.

[103] Article 25 of the ECHR. Although the ICCPR also has its own enforcement mechanism, it will be recalled that the UK has so far refused to accept the right of individual petition to the UN Human Rights Committee under the Optional Protocol.

[104] See eg. A.H. Robertson and J.G. Merrills, *Human Rights in Europe: A Study of the European Convention on Human Rights*, 3rd edn. (Manchester: Manchester University Press, 1993). The *sui generis* nature of the Convention arguably renders irrelevant the 19th century cases such as *Cook* v. *Sprigg* [1899] AC 572 and *Rustomjee* v. *The Queen* (1876) 2 QBD 69 relied on by the House of Lords in *Rayner* [1990] 2 AC 418 at 499F–500B as being authoritative on the question of the domestic status of unincorporated treaties.

[105] "English Law and the European Convention on Human Rights" (above n. 60) at 599–605. Duffy's criticism is based on his "modified narrow view" of the *Trendtex* decision.

Drzemczewski's thesis faces an even greater hurdle in terms of orthodox theory, however, in the shape of Parliament's repeated refusal to incorporate the European Convention into domestic law. A number of Bills have been introduced proposing incorporation of the Convention and so far all have failed to secure a Parliamentary majority.[106] Although the extent to which such legislative silence or omission can legitimately be taken as an indication of parliamentary "intention" is naturally a matter of some controversy, it is clear that English judges feel constrained by the failure of repeated attempts to incorporate the Convention by legislation. Judicial restraint in recognising the Convention as part of English law has also been due in part to an acute awareness of the discrepancy between the adjudicative and interpretive techniques which the application of the Convention's provisions requires, and the traditional English approach to adjudication based on the model of the private law-suit and sovereignty-based techniques of statutory interpretation.

(b) The Historical Relationship between the ECHR and the Common Law

Notwithstanding these obstacles, considerable support can be marshalled for Drzemczewski's thesis that the Convention, or at least part of it, already has domestic legal status by virtue of being customary international law. Consideration of the historical relationship between the common law tradition and the contents of the European Convention, for example, reveals the extent to which many of the provisions of the Convention have their origins in an attempt to articulate some of the most fundamental values of the English common law. In recent years, important historical work has been done, much of it using archive material which has become available under the 30 year rule, which has revealed the full extent of the UK's involvement in the drafting of the Convention and the clear influence of the UK's representatives on the content of its substantive protections.

Lord Lester, for example, has shown that British lawyers played an important role in the drafting of the text of the Convention, and that in doing so they drew upon sources of English law which had long ago attained customary status: the writ of *habeas corpus*, Magna Carta, the Petition of Right, the English Bill of Rights, the Scottish Claim of Right and the Act of Settlement, for example.[107] More recently, Marston has traced the genesis of the

---

[106] See most recently Lord Lester's Human Rights Bill 1995, HL Deb Vol. 560 cols. 1136–74 (25 January 1995); HL Deb Vol. 561 cols. 762–84 (15 February 1995); HL Deb Vol. 562 cols. 1692–702 (29 March 1995); HL Deb Vol. 563 cols. 1271–85 (1 May 1995). See Lester, "The Mouse that Roared: The Human Rights Bill 1995" [1995] PL 198.

[107] A. Lester, "Fundamental Rights: The UK Isolated?" [1984] PL 46 at 49–55 and "Taking Human Rights Seriously", the 1993 Paul Sieghart Memorial Lecture. See also his speech in the House of Lords during the second reading of his Human Rights Bill, above n. 106 at col. 1136. The close historical relationship between the contents of the common law and those of the Convention has also been acknowledged by Lord Browne–Wilkinson, "The Infiltration of a Bill

Convention even further back, and demonstrated the role played by the UK in the wider human rights background from which the Convention emerged in the aftermath of the Second World War.[108] In 1947, the UK Government published a "Draft of an International Bill of Rights" which the Foreign Office had prepared to submit to the UN's Commission on Human Rights, set up to formulate an international bill of human rights in fulfilment of the UN Charter's aim of achieving international co-operation in promoting and encouraging respect for human rights and fundamental freedoms.[109] The contents of the draft bill provide an interesting insight into what rights and freedoms the government of the day considered to be recognised as fundamental by the English common law. The listed freedoms included life, liberty, religion, expression, assembly and association, and freedom from slavery. The comments on the substance of the text included a reference to "the firm foundation which these principles have in the deepest convictions of Parliament and the people."[110]

The UK Government's draft bill was to influence the contents of the European Convention. Indeed, as Marston's detailed analysis of the official papers at the time of the Convention's adoption has shown, the UK exerted an important influence on the substantive provisions of the Convention. Following the establishment of the Council of Europe in 1949, steps were taken towards drafting a human rights convention pursuant to the Council's aim, contained in its founding Statute, of achieving greater unity through "the maintenance and further realisation of human rights and fundamental freedoms." When the Committee of Experts met in March 1950 to formulate a draft Convention, the UK Government circulated a draft of 15 articles containing definitions of and limitations on specific human rights taken from the UN's Universal Declaration.[111] The Committee put forward the UK proposal as one of two alternative draft conventions. The Conference of Experts, established by the Committee of Ministers, put forward a draft Convention based on the UK's proposal as far as the definition of the rights to be contained in the Convention were concerned. According to a memorandum dated 25th July 1950, uncovered by Marston, the Cabinet was told that the present draft of the Convention

"contains a definition of the rights and limitations thereto which follows almost word for word the actual texts proposed by the UK representatives . . . and which

of Rights" [1992] PL 397 at 404: "[i]t was those very freedoms enjoyed by us over the centuries which were principal sources of the ECHR itself."

   108 G. Marston, "The United Kingdom's Part in the Preparation of the European Convention on Human Rights, 1950" (1993) ICLQ 796.
   109 The idea that the UK should submit a draft text of such an international bill of rights was conceived in the Foreign Office, "[i]n view of the extremely good record of this country in the matter of human rights": see Marston, op. cit. at 797.
   110 Ibid. at 798.
   111 *Collected Edition of the Travaux Préparatoires of the European Convention on Human Rights*, Vol. IV, at 14–16.

is thought to be consistent with our existing law in all but a small number of comparatively trivial cases."[112]

In respect of those cases it was envisaged that it may be necessary on accession to take advantage of the right to make reservations.

Although elements within the Labour Government of the day objected to the Convention because of its contents (for example, both the Chancellor of the Exchequer, Sir Stafford Cripps, and the Lord Chancellor, Lord Jowitt, saw the Convention as being inconsistent with the policy of a planned economy), the principal objection was not to the content of the Convention but to the proposed individual right of petition and the jurisdiction of the European Commission and Court of Human Rights. Apart from the concerns of the Colonial Secretary, that acceptance of the individual right of petition would destabilise the colonies, the main concern was that to permit an appeal to a supranational court would compromise parliamentary sovereignty. These concerns were accommodated by the amendment of the draft Convention to make the right of individual petition and therefore the jurisdiction of the Convention institutions optional. Following these amendments, the UK signed the Convention on 4th November 1950 and was the first country to ratify it on 8th March 1951.

In the event, no amending legislation was adopted to implement the Convention, nor were any reservations entered to cover any provisions of UK law which might arguably not conform to the Convention. Although, as Marston suggests, this was probably a consequence of the Attlee Government's desire to create the impression that the Convention was merely a statement of general principles, rather than an internationally binding legal instrument,[113] it also serves to reinforce the view that at the time there was thought to be little or no discrepancy between the substance of the Convention and English law, and therefore that the Convention was merely a restatement of principles already enshrined in the common law.

In addition to the historical evidence of the relationship between the common law and the Convention marshalled by Lester and Marston, further indirect support for Drzemczewski's thesis is to be found in the large number of cases, beginning in the late 1970s, in which it has been asserted by courts that the Convention is merely declaratory of rights or principles which are already part of the common law.[114] In many such cases, although the court has not expressly recognised the Convention as customary international law, nor always been explicit about developing the common law so as to be in conformity with the Convention, there seems little doubt that the way in which

---

[112] Marston, (above n. 108) at 811.

[113] Ibid. at 826.

[114] Indeed, as will be seen, this has been one of the main ways in which domestic courts have made reference to the Convention. As Clapham notes, *Human Rights in the Private Sphere* (Oxford: Clarendon Press, 1993) at 24, "the Convention has been used mostly to buttress the principles already contained in the common law".

the common law has been articulated, in terms of fundamental rights or principles, has been influenced by the Convention. That indirect influence, it is suggested, is an example of the interpenetration and transcendence of Convention and domestic law described by Drzemczewski, and for which the recognition of the Convention as customary international law was intended by him to be the vehicle.

(c) Theoretical Support for the Special Status of Human Rights Norms

Drzemczewski's thesis, that the rights in the Convention, or some of them, are automatically part of the common law by virtue of their status as customary international law, also finds support at the theoretical level from other writers. Higgins, for example, is of the view that some of the rights contained in the Convention and other international treaties are not the product of the international agreement in which they happen to be articulated, but ante-date those instruments and as such are part of the common law by virtue of being rules of general international law.[115] Some would go even further and argue that, not only is recognition of the Convention as customary international law, and therefore as part of domestic law, not prohibited by the rule requiring legislative incorporation of international treaties, but is positively required by the rationale which underpins that rule. The traditional rationale for that rule, it will be recalled, is the protection of the public against unaccountable executive law-making to the disadvantage of the people.[116] Where the obligation entered into by the executive is to the benefit of the public and imposes a burden on the executive itself, as do human rights instruments such as the ECHR, it is arguable that the same rationale *requires* the courts to recognise that the executive is bound by those obligations.[117]

Brudner makes a similar if more theoretical argument, also derived from the rationale behind the existing rules governing the domestic enforceability of international law. He offers a theory according to which the domestic enforcement of human rights covenants such as the Convention is consistent with legislative supremacy.[118] He argues that if international treaty obligations are enforceable by a domestic court, it is either by virtue of having become part of municipal law or by virtue of some theory which distinguishes those treaty obligations whose domestic enforcement would compromise legislative

---

[115] R. Higgins, "The Relationship between International and Regional Human Rights Norms and Domestic Law" (1992) 18 CLB 1268 at 1272. As Meron notes, (above n. 98) at 115, "[s]uccessful invocation of customary human rights norms requires that a liberal approach be adopted to treaties as a source of customary law."

[116] The facts of *The Parlament Belge* (above n. 32) illustrate the danger well.

[117] See E. Lauterpacht, "International Law and Her Majesty's Judges", F.A. Mann Memorial Lecture 1993 (unpublished).

[118] A. Brudner, "The Domestic Enforcement of International Covenants on Human Rights: A Theoretical Framework" (1985) 35 UTLJ 219.

supremacy from those whose enforcement would be consistent with that principle. Brudner's argument could be said to amount to the application on the international plane of the common lawyer's faith in reason. Customary international law is automatically a part of domestic law because it is an expression, not of executive will, but of a common human reason, the same reason that is historically embedded in the domestic common law. The rationale for the requirement of special transformation is to ensure the subordination of the executive to the democratic will, and it therefore has no application to international instruments which are not the product of such executive discretion but the purpose of which is to advance a transcendent common good of the human community. It follows that international human rights treaties are of such a kind as to be no more in need of transformation than rules of international custom and, although they happen to be articulated in treaties, their applicability in domestic courts without such transformation is no more inconsistent with the democratic will than the automatic incorporation of such customary rules.[119]

Whatever the precise theoretical basis preferred, it is clear that there is now a very substantial body of academic opinion which regards international human rights norms as being qualitatively different from other international legal standards when it comes to deciding their domestic status notwithstanding their non-incorporation in national law.[120] Whether or not human rights treaties, and the body of jurisprudence which has grown up around them, are correctly regarded as constituting customary international law, there can be little doubt that the views considered above have helped to establish a climate of opinion in which judicial resistance to giving some domestic effect to international human rights standards is increasingly difficult to sustain.

(d) The Bangalore Principles

International recognition of this worldwide phenomenon was achieved in 1988 in the shape of what have become known as the Bangalore Principles. An international judicial colloquium on the domestic application of international human rights norms held in Bangalore, India, produced a summary of the discussions which had taken place at the colloquium in the concluding statement of the Convenor, former Chief Justice Bhagwati of India.[121] The principles

---

[119] For a rival argument from a positivist perspective that the ECHR is already part of English law, and that dualism does not apply to treaties concerning human rights, which are of a special kind, see D. Beyleveld, "The Concept of a Human Right and Incorporation of the European Convention on Human Rights" [1995] PL 577.

[120] Clapham, for example, *Human Rights in the Private Sphere* (above n. 114) at 14, n.2, considers it unnecessary to explain the effect of international law generally in the internal legal order of the UK, because the ECHR has "a rather special role."

[121] The participants included judges from ten countries. Britain's representative was Anthony Lester QC.

can be found in full in Appendix II, but their substance should be briefly considered since they represent an important staging post in the gradual evolution of the judicial approach to international human rights norms in common law countries.

The Convenor's summary began, significantly, by asserting the universality of fundamental human rights and freedoms, and noting that they find expression in constitutions and legal systems throughout the world as well as in the international human rights instruments. Those instruments, and the body of jurisprudence which had emerged interpreting particular rights and freedoms, were recognised as providing "important guidance" to national courts in cases concerning such rights and freedoms. The fact that unincorporated international conventions are not directly enforceable in most common law countries was expressly acknowledged, but there was an enthusiastic welcome for the growing tendency of national courts to have regard to those international norms for the purpose of deciding cases where domestic law, whether constitutional, statute or common law, was uncertain or incomplete. Such a practice was said to be within the proper nature of the judicial process and compatible with well-established judicial functions. The colloquium participants called for international human rights norms to be still more widely recognised and applied by national courts, whilst recognising that there are limits to the legitimacy of that process. They acknowledged, for example, that national courts must take full account of local laws, traditions, circumstances and needs when using international norms to remove uncertainty from national law, and that where national law is clear and inconsistent with the international obligations of the state concerned, in common law countries the national court is obliged to give effect to national law.

In 1988 the Bangalore Principles constituted a timely recognition of the development then taking place throughout the common law world, whereby national courts were beginning to refer to ratified but unincorporated human rights treaties as a source of guidance in constitutional and statutory interpretation and in their development of the common law. In a far-sighted contribution to the colloquium, the President of the New South Wales Court of Appeal, Justice Kirby, urged judges to "struggle for release from a too narrow and provincial conception of its role and duties", and to adapt the judicial method to applying the developing norms of international law concerning human rights.[122] Rejecting the discredited notion of the judicial function as the value-free application of neutral principles, yet remaining sensitive to the limits of the judiciary's legitimate role because of its relative lack of democratic accountability, Kirby recommends that judges use the inevitable space for value choice, which flows from the interpretive nature of their function, to seek to ensure compliance with international obligations where appropriate. In his view, it is the duty of judges to apprise themselves of the gradual

---

[122] M.D. Kirby, "The Role of the Judge in Advancing Human Rights by Reference to International Human Rights Norms" (1988) 62 Austr. LJ 514 at 529.

evolution of international human rights law and to use it as a source of guidance in deciding the meaning of domestic law. Only if judges and advocates deliberately adopt such an "internationalist" approach to their function, taking international human rights law as the starting point in statutory construction and common law development, will domestic law be appropriately located in the international setting which now exists.

As will be seen in later chapters, at the time of the formulation of the Bangalore Principles, the UK was on the threshold of an important transition as far as the domestic status of international human rights norms was concerned, and the Principles are a useful measure of the worldwide progress towards acceptance of the legitimate use which could be made of such norms by national judges.[123] Since 1988, as Kirby has pointed out in subsequent contributions, something of a sea change has come about in the approach of English courts, as well as in Australia and New Zealand.[124] Throughout the common law world, it seems, there has been a marked increase in judicial willingness to refer to relevant human rights principles in reaching conclusions about the meaning of national law, be it constitutional, statutory or common law.[125] That trend amounts to a modification of the common law's earlier principle of maintaining a strict separation between domestic law and unincorporated international law, in recognition of the importance of the content of the international laws on human rights. The development is bound to attract criticism from those who continue to see force in the traditional rationales underpinning the dualist inheritance, but, as Kirby has argued, it seems a particularly apt judicial response to the modern reality of globalisation and increasing interdependence, and has the potential to bring about a gradual harmonisation between internationally accepted principles and municipal law.

9. THE AMBIGUITY FALLACY

A notable feature of the Bangalore Principles is their apparent incorporation of the ambiguity/uncertainty requirement as a precondition of reference to international human rights instruments. Domestic courts are said to be entitled to have regard to international obligations "for the purpose of removing ambiguity or uncertainty from national law", but where national law is clear

---

[123] As will become apparent in chs. 4 to 6 below, Kirby, ibid. at 515, rather over-estimated the extent to which the approach he advocates was already well-established in England.

[124] Kirby, "The Role of International Standards in Australian Courts" in Alston & Chiam (eds.), *Treaty-Making and Australia: Globalisation versus Sovereignty?* (above n. 28), 81 at 83; "The Australian Use of International Human Rights Norms: From Bangalore to Balliol—A View from the Antipodes" (1993) 16 UNSWLJ 363.

[125] In England it would seem that the continuation of that trend owes nothing to the influence of the Bangalore Principles. According to a LEXIS search, no English judge has yet referred to them.

and inconsistent with international obligations the national court must give effect to it. This acknowledgment of the limits of the development is clearly a concession to the continued sovereignty of national law-making institutions, but it appears to go further by erecting ambiguity or uncertainty in domestic law into a precondition of any reference to unincorporated international law.[126]

Although in England, in the human rights context, the ambiguity precondition appears to be supported by high authority,[127] it will be argued throughout this book that such a precondition is misconceived. In the absence of theoretical clarity about the precise status of international law in domestic law, the courts have transformed the simple notion that unambiguous domestic law overrides inconsistent international law into a precondition of ambiguity which must first be established before the international instrument even becomes relevant.[128] But that conclusion does not follow from the recognition of Parliament's ability to legislate inconsistently with unincorporated international law. It is one thing to say that, in the event of irreconcilable conflict, domestic law prevails over international law. It is, however, quite another thing to say, as English courts consistently say, that it is only *permissible* for a court even to have regard to unincorporated international law where there is some prior and independent ambiguity or uncertainty in domestic law. The persistence of the ambiguity requirement is not so much a logical consequence dictated by any theoretical premise, as a symptom of a sovereignty-inspired legal culture which instinctively views norms contained in unincorporated treaties as being necessarily external to the interpretive task of judges.

For courts to repudiate the ambiguity requirement, it is not necessary to go as far as Loveland suggests, and invite the House of Lords to reverse the common law rule so that in future courts presume that a treaty whose terms are justiciable and intended to bestow rights and obligations on individuals is "part of" domestic law until Parliament expressly says otherwise.[129] It merely requires courts to reconsider the cases concerning the international treaty presumption, and in particular those decisions of Lord Diplock (especially *Garland*) which are so often cited as if they were authority for the ambiguity requirement. Those authorities, it has been argued, can conscientiously be read as supporting the view that English courts are under an obligation at common law to interpret domestic law (both common law and statute) in

---

[126] Although note that in para. 4 of the Principles reference is made to having regard to international norms where domestic law is "uncertain *or incomplete*" (emphasis added). For consideration of the significance of the distinction between ambiguity/uncertainty and incompleteness, see the discussion of Scarman LJ's judgment in *R v. Secretary of State for the Home Department, ex p. Phansopkar* [1976] QB 606 in ch. 4 below.

[127] *R v. Secretary of State for the Home Department, ex p. Brind* [1991] 1 AC 696. See also *Oppenheim's International Law* (above n. 23) at 62 n. 35.

[128] In fact, as will be seen in chs. 4 to 6, English courts have so far failed to adopt a consistent approach to whether ambiguity is a precondition of reference to international human rights law.

[129] Loveland, *Constitutional Law* (above n. 29) at 592.

such a way as to make it consistent with the UK's international obligations.[130] In short, English courts have been asking the wrong question. Instead of asking "is the domestic law ambiguous?", they should have been asking "can the domestic law be read in a way which avoids a conflict with international law?". To answer that question properly, it will always be necessary for the domestic court to have regard to the terms of those obligations, without first having to undertake the wholly artificial exercise of construing domestic law in isolation to determine whether it is "ambiguous".

Even if this argument in relation to international law generally is thought to be too radical a departure from present practice, it will also be argued, less ambitiously, that ambiguity has no role to play in the case of international human rights norms. For if the views expressed by the various authors considered above are correct, and the rights and values in international human rights law such as the ECHR are in effect already part of English law by virtue of being customary international law, it follows that "ambiguity" cannot be a precondition of consideration of those international norms.[131] Those norms are an ever-present part of the common law context in which every act of judicial interpretation takes place, and, as such, not only can but *must* always be considered as part of the interpretive exercise, as a matter of judicial obligation.

Would the dropping of the ambiguity precondition which is recommended here be likely to make any difference in practice? Provided English courts can also overcome their undoubted cultural resistance to considering and interpreting international law material, it is suggested that in practice it could make a very real difference to the level of compliance with international obligations achieved by domestic courts through interpretation. When the starting point of the domestic court is that the international treaty is only relevant when there is ambiguity in the statutory language considered on its own, it is almost inevitable that the court will pay no regard to the international obligation when first deciding the meaning of the domestic provision. The court therefore will not have the benefit of the argument that there are two possible meanings of the provision, one consistent and the other inconsistent with the international obligation, because that obligation has to be kept out of sight while the court reaches its decision about the "plain meaning" of the statute, as if it exists in an international vacuum. As well as making it more likely that the meaning of the domestic provision will appear to be clear on its face,[132]

---

[130] As Brudner observes, (above n. 118) at 232, the adoption of such a strong presumption of statutory interpretation, that when Parliament legislated it did so intending not to violate its international obligations, could be seen as the domestic adoption of the customary international norm requiring state parties to conform their domestic laws to their external obligations.

[131] Higgins, "The Relationship Between International and Regional Human Rights Norms and Domestic Law" (1992) 18 CLB 1268 at 1273–4.

[132] Recall Diplock LJ's candid admission in *Salomon* [1967] 2 QB 116 at 145B–D, considered in section 6(a) above.

this gives less conscientious courts a supposedly respectable justification for refusing to consider the international obligation on the ground that it is irrelevant, an opportunity which experience suggests is all too frequently seized upon by busy judges anxious to get through their list.

If, on the other hand, the court's starting point is a generally applicable presumption that the statute is to be read consistently with international obligations, it must consider whether Parliament has expressed itself with sufficient clarity to preclude a construction which is consistent with the relevant international obligation. On the latter approach, the international obligation forms part of the very context in which the court decides on what the possible meanings of the relevant provision are, rather than being artificially kept out of sight until the court has decided whether there is an ambiguity which the instrument could help to resolve. The easy option for a domestic court, of ruling the international obligation irrelevant because the language of the domestic provision is supposedly "clear", is therefore pre-empted, since the very existence of the obligation is a factor in the interpretive inquiry into statutory meaning.

If the requirement of ambiguity is dropped as a precondition of reference to international law, does it have any role left to play? The answer must surely be that it does not. The preservation of sovereignty in the ultimate sense described above does not require its retention. On the contrary, there is then only room for a concept of "non-ambiguity". As was explained above, even if the presumption is generalised to the extent advocated here, so that the relevant international norms, while not founding a domestic cause of action, can only be excluded from the interpretive context by an express statutory provision to that effect, the theoretical possibility remains of the presumption being displaced if, after having considered the domestic law in the light of the international norm, it is impossible to give it a meaning which achieves consistency. So instead of asking if there is ambiguity which can be resolved with the "assistance" of international law, on this approach the court should ask, having automatically considered the international law alongside the national law, whether the domestic law is unambiguously (in the sense of irreconcilably) in conflict with the international norm.

This emphasis on the "unambiguous" rather than the "ambiguous" is more than mere semantics. It will make a practical difference to the likelihood of a court making a conscientious attempt to interpret domestic norms so as to reflect the content of international norms. Preserving *any* role for ambiguity risks it being applied by courts as a preliminary requirement, a gateway to the consideration of international law, which undermines the generality of the presumption.[133] The presumption of conformity must be general, in the sense that its applicability must never depend on a prior finding of ambiguity in

---

[133] Even Higgins, one of the strongest advocates of the recognition of a general presumption, appears to waver on the role of ambiguity: see eg. *Problems and Process* (above n. 23), at 6–7; (1992) 18 CLB (above n. 23) 1268 at 1274.

domestic law. Only then can it meaningfully be said to impose an interpretive *obligation* on the court, that is, a *duty* to arrive at an interpretation, if the limits of language permit, which is in conformity with international norms.[134]

Recognising the ambiguity requirement for the fallacy that it has become would therefore clear the way for the recognition of a full interpretive obligation on domestic judges to interpret domestic law in such a way as to be consistent with international law, or at the very least with international human rights law. If courts were to bring to that interpretive function the dexterity to which, it will be seen in chapters 2 and 3, they have grown accustomed in their role as Community law judges, greater domestic effect would be secured for international legal norms, yet Parliament would remain supreme in the ultimate sense that, in the event of irreconcilable conflict, domestic law prevails over international law. Not only is this a course which it is open to courts to take on the present state of the authorities, but it would be an entirely appropriate judicial response to the global developments outlined in the introduction to this chapter.

10. CONCLUSION: BEYOND THE MONIST/DUALIST DICHOTOMY

Although the trend has been uneven, the developments charted in this chapter (the greater receptiveness to customary international law, the gradual strengthening of the treaty presumption and the growing recognition of the special status of international human rights norms) together represent discernible progress towards an ever more explicit transcendence of the monist/dualist dichotomy, particularly in relation to the international law of human rights. The effect of those developments is to blur the bright line which dualism seeks to draw between incorporated and unincorporated international law.

At the very least they reveal what the theoretical antithesis of monism and dualism only serves to conceal, which is that the domestic status of international legal norms is in reality a matter of degree. The language of "incorporation" presupposes a dualist position derived from an uncompromising premise of the sovereignty of Parliament. The question of the domestic status of international law in that binary framework is an "in/out" question: has the international norm been made "part of" domestic law or not? The concepts and the language lack the sophistication to capture the more nuanced reality that there are many different ways in which international law may be of relevance to an issue before a domestic court. A norm of international treaty law may not be "part of" domestic law in the sense that it gives rise to a right or

---

[134] For a possible example of such an irreconcilable conflict, unable to be resolved by interpretation, see *R v. Saunders* [1996] 1 Cr App R 463, in which Parliament had expressly authorised in s. 434(5) Companies Act 1985 that answers given by a person to questions put by DTI inspectors in the exercise of their investigative powers may be used in evidence against him.

obligation which is directly enforceable in domestic courts and on which individuals may therefore found their case, but, insofar as judicial recourse to it is permitted by the treaty presumption, to assist in the interpretation of domestic statute law, or its customary or near-customary status provides guidance in the development of domestic common law, it is clearly of legal relevance.

The courts' increasing willingness to forsake dualistic certainties therefore lends support to Brownlie's observation that the theoretical constructs of monism and dualism have tended to obscure the realities of the status of international law in the domestic legal system.[135] That is a sentiment now widely shared.[136] Judicial practice seems better accommodated within more pragmatic theories to which, as Brownlie points out, more and more jurists are turning as an alternative to the monist/dualist dichotomy.[137] As this book hopes to demonstrate, to reject both dualism and monism does not entail the abandonment of the quest for a tenable theoretical position between these two extremes which can both explain and justify the legal relevance which is in practice accorded to unincorporated international human rights law in domestic courts.

One final observation requires to be made, concerning the implications of this transcendence for the language in which debates about the status of international law have traditionally been conducted. If this chapter's thesis about the changing domestic status of international norms is accepted, an entirely different vocabulary is required in order to be able meaningfully to discuss the question of the domestic status of international law. That vocabulary will have to reflect the fact that the underlying concepts are better described in shades of grey than in black and white, and that legal systems no longer occupy separate spheres but now overlap and interact.

O'Neill, discussing the internal legal effects of membership of the European Union on the English and Scottish legal systems, has used the label "reception" to describe the concept of evolutionary legal change by which the standards, tests, values and general approaches of one legal system influence and penetrate another.[138] Reception, unlike the all or nothing concept of incorporation, is itself a matter of degree. He distinguishes, for example, between

---

[135] Brownlie, *Principles* (above n. 23) at 56.

[136] See eg. Bernhardt in R. St. J. MacDonald, F. Matscher and H. Petzold (eds.), *The European System for the Protection of Human Rights* (London: Martinus Nijhoff, 1993), who refers to monism and dualism as the two "dogmatic alternatives" in the debate about the relation between national and international law; Frowein in Jacobs & Roberts (eds.), *The Effect of Treaties in Domestic Law* (above n. 23) at 63, who considers the monist–dualist debate to be passé; and Jacobs, ibid. at xxiv, who regards the antithesis as an oversimplification which must be viewed with caution.

[137] Brownlie, (above n. 23) at 34–5. Such theories are referred to in the literature as "theories of co-ordination". Brownlie's own preference is for such theories, due to their greater explanatory power: ibid. at 57.

[138] A. O'Neill, *Decisions of the European Court of Justice and their Constitutional Implications* (London: Butterworths, 1994), at 2.

partial reception, which involves the borrowing of discrete legal concepts or doctrines by one legal system from another, and "substantial partial reception", which may in turn evolve into full reception, which occurs when the receiving legal system effectively subordinates itself entirely to the donor system, the norms of which it acknowledges to be internally superior. As well as being a matter of degree, reception can take place in different modes: direct reception occurs where one system's standards and concepts are imposed on another, whereas indirect reception is more akin to osmosis of legal ideas and concepts. By leaving behind the black and white language of incorporation, this more nuanced vocabulary of reception more aptly describes the reality of judicial compromise of the pure dualist position which this chapter has sought to demonstrate. It will be used throughout this book as shorthand for the various ways in which English law has assimilated legal norms emanating from sources other than the UK Parliament.[139]

[139] The language of "reception" may, however, fail to acknowledge the mutuality of the evolutionary dynamic; English law, for example, has in various ways contributed to the development of both Community law and the law of the Convention. See eg. D. Wyatt, "European Community Law and Public Law in the United Kingdom" in Markesinis (ed.), *The Gradual Convergence* (above n. 83) at 188; R. Higgins, "The Role of National Courts in the International Legal Process" in *Problems and Process* (above n. 23), ch. 12.

2

The Implications of European Community Membership for Sovereignty Theory

1. INTRODUCTION

The purpose of this and the following chapter is to demonstrate the effect which the UK's membership of the European Community has had on the traditional theory of parliamentary sovereignty.[1] In particular, these chapters seek to challenge the frequently heard claim of constitutional traditionalists, that the judicial response to Community membership has wrought no fundamental changes on the UK constitution, because the courts are merely doing what the sovereign Parliament "authorised" them to do in the European Communities Act 1972. The aim is to show that, in order fully to accommodate all the constitutional implications of Community membership, courts have in practice modified the premise of parliamentary sovereignty in significant respects. In so doing, it will be argued, they have transcended the sterile old debate about whether a sovereign Parliament can bind its successors, and demonstrated that the true nature of the sovereignty of Parliament cannot be derived from any *a priori* theory, but lies, like the common law itself, in the keeping of the courts.

There are essentially two justifications for what might appear at first sight to be a lengthy digression from this book's principal concern, the domestic status of international human rights law. The first is that the story of the gradual reception of Community law into UK law demonstrates that, contrary to what is commonly supposed, the constitutional doctrine of the sovereignty of Parliament, properly understood, presents no fundamental theoretical objection to judicial recognition of the interpretive obligation for which this book argues, that is, an obligation to construe domestic law so as to conform with international human rights norms. The second justification is that, as will be seen in more detail in chapter 7, the UK's membership of the European

---

[1] References to "traditional" sovereignty theory include both the theory of "continuing" and "self-embracing" sovereignty. The latter is widely referred to in the literature as the "new" view of sovereignty, after R.F.V. Heuston, "Sovereignty" in *Essays in Constitutional Law*, 2nd edn. (London: Stevens, 1964) at 6, but, in the light of more recent developments, must now take its place as a mere variant of what, from today's perspective, can properly be described as the traditional view that Parliament is sovereign.

Community has necessitated the participation of its courts in the gradual emergence of, not only a common law of Europe, but a common European constitution. That gradual process of European constitutionalisation, it will be argued later, is an important source of legitimation for an obligation on English courts to interpret domestic law in conformity with internationally recognised human rights standards. It is therefore of the utmost importance for this book's central thesis that the theoretical basis on which UK courts participate in that wider European project be understood, for only then can the way begin to be cleared through the common misconceptions which currently prevent proper regard being paid to international human rights law by domestic courts.

No version of sovereignty theory, it will be argued, can provide that understanding. The evolution which has taken place in the status enjoyed by Community law in English courts in the period since accession, that is, the gradual judicial recognition of the direct effect and supremacy of Community law, and the more recent judicial acceptance of an obligation to interpret domestic law consistently with non-directly effective Community law, cannot be explained in sovereignty theory's limited terms. According to such theory, either every step the courts have taken since accession was authorised in advance by Parliament's expression of its sovereign will in the European Communities Act 1972,[2] or there has been a "legal revolution", or change of grundnorm, a discontinuity in the sovereign to which the courts regard themselves as owing allegiance.[3] The former is fanciful, and by reference to legislative history can be shown to be false even on its own terms. The latter simply fails to capture the gradual, piecemeal way in which the evolution (rather than the revolution) has been brought about. The explanation for that evolution must be found in a more sophisticated theory of constitutional change which acknowledges the ultimate common law foundation of the sovereignty doctrine,[4] and can accommodate its modification by courts over time.[5] The process by which constitutional change comes about can only be

[2] As will be seen below, this is the explanation of the self-embracing sovereigntists. See eg. G. Winterton, "The British Grundnorm: Parliamentary Supremacy Re-examined" (1976) 92 LQR 591, at 613–17; Irvine, "Judges and Decision-Makers: The Theory and Practice of *Wednesbury* Review" [1996] PL 59 at 75: "the constitutional developments which have accompanied British membership of the European Union, startling as they may seem, have all been sanctioned by Parliament itself."

[3] This is the explanation of the continuing sovereigntists. See eg. H.W.R. Wade, "The Basis of Legal Sovereignty" [1955] CLJ 172 at 189; "Sovereignty and the European Communities" (1972) 88 LQR 1; "What has Happened to the Sovereignty of Parliament?" (1991) 107 LQR 1. Wade's contributions, spanning four decades, show no discontinuity in the theory to which he owes allegiance.

[4] See Dixon, "The Common Law as an Ultimate Constitutional Foundation" (1957) 31 ALJ 240; A.W. Bradley, "The Sovereignty of Parliament—in Perpetuity?" in J. Jowell & D. Oliver (eds.), *The Changing Constitution*, 3rd edn. (Oxford: Clarendon Press, 1994) ch. 4 at 85–9.

[5] For an example of such an approach, articulated prophetically before the UK had formally beome a member, see S.A. de Smith, "The Constitution and the Common Market: A Tentative Appraisal" (1971) 34 MLR 597, at 612–14. See also, to similar effect, Lloyd, *The Idea of Law* (Harmondsworth: Penguin, 1964) at 191–2.

properly understood by stepping outside of the circular debates about whether or not a sovereign Parliament can bind its successors.

To make good this claim, it will be necessary to trace in some detail in this and the following chapter the successive steps by which European Community law has attained the status it enjoys today in our courts, asking at every stage what justifies the latest advance. To arrive at a convincing account of the precise role played by the European Communities Act 1972, it is necessary to return briefly to pre-accession days to consider the way in which the constitutional implications of membership were then perceived by constitutional actors, and how it was proposed to reconcile membership with the UK's constitutional tradition.

2. THE CONSTITUTIONAL IMPLICATIONS OF ACCESSION TO THE EUROPEAN COMMUNITY

The UK's unusual constitutional arrangements inevitably meant that becoming a member of the European Communities would cause internal constitutional difficulties. In particular, its historical adherence to the doctrine of parliamentary sovereignty and its ostensibly dualist approach to the domestic status of international law were likely to present, or at least be perceived to present, a very real obstacle to devising means of complying with certain minimum requirements of membership, such as the domestic application of self-executing provisions of Community law. These constitutional difficulties of accession caused by the UK's peculiar constitutional tradition were further compounded by important developments in the nature of the Community legal order brought about by the European Court of Justice. The UK had missed the opportunity in the 1950s to influence the drafting of the Treaties establishing the Communities, and by the time the UK Government had woken up to the fact that "Europe is now faced with the opportunity of a great move forward in political unity and . . . we can—indeed we must—play our full part in it",[6] as an applicant for accession it had no choice but to take the Communities as it found them.

In its early case-law, the Court was at pains to establish that what the Treaties had constituted was unique and quite unlike any other system of international law. It stressed that the Treaties establishing the Communities had brought into being a "new legal order" for the benefit of which the States had limited their sovereign rights, albeit within limited fields, by transferring sovereignty, and the subjects of which included the nationals of Member States.[7] This conception of the Communities as a new legal order without

---

[6] In its 1967 White Paper, *Membership of the European Communities* (Cmnd. 3269) (hereinafter, "*Membership*"), being Prime Minister Wilson's statement to the House of Commons on 2nd May 1967.

[7] Case 26/62, *N.V. Algemene Transporten Expeditie Onderneming van Gend en Loos* v. *Nederlandse Administratie der Belastingen* [1963] ECR 1.

precedent in international law was a creation of the Court, motivated probably by a practical concern that national courts in more dualist countries might
otherwise regard the Treaties as having no greater status than any other international law, and justified in legal terms largely by reference to the spirit and
objectives of the Treaties.[8] The vehicles for the realisation of this judicial
conception were the two concepts of direct effect and the supremacy of
Community law.[9]

The concept of direct effect, whereby certain provisions of Community law
can be relied on by individuals before national courts without further implementation,[10] was derived from the novel character of the Community by the
Court of Justice in *Van Gend En Loos*.[11] The Court stressed that it was an
important feature of the new legal order that it conferred rights on individual
citizens which became part of their legal heritage and which national courts
were bound to protect. In the case itself, Article 12 of the EC Treaty was held
to have direct effect and could therefore be invoked directly by individuals
before their national courts. Such decentralised enforcement of Community
law by individual citizens was justified by the practical need to secure the
effectiveness of Community law throughout the Member States.

The concept of supremacy, whereby directly effective Community law takes
precedence over inconsistent national law, was equally a creation of the Court
in its early decisions. Like the doctrine of direct effect, the supremacy of
Community law is nowhere mentioned in the Treaties, but in *Costa* v. *ENEL*
the European Court of Justice held that it followed from the very nature of
the new legal order that national courts are bound to give primacy to
Community law over any inconsistent national law, including subsequent legislation.[12] Although this notion of the supremacy of Community law is conceptually distinct from the notion of direct effect, the two are inextricably
linked. Direct effect alone would not achieve the uniform application and
effectiveness of Community law if Member States were at liberty to adopt
inconsistent national measures which prevailed over Community measures.
Community law had to be supreme over national law, as well as directly effective, if the Community was to achieve its ambitious goals.

---

[8] For a challenge to the claim of Community law to be *sui generis*, in contrast to traditional
public international law, see D. Wyatt, "New Legal Order, or Old?" (1982) 7 ELRev 147.

[9] For accounts of direct effect and supremacy from a Community law perspective, see Craig
and de Búrca, *EC Law: Text, Cases and Materials* (Oxford: Clarendon Press, 1995), chs. 4 and 6
respectively; Weatherill and Beaumont, *EC Law: The Essential Guide to the Legal Workings of the
European Community* 2nd edn., (London: Penguin Books, 1995), chs. 11 and 12; Hartley, *The
Foundations of European Community Law*, 3rd edn., (Oxford: Clarendon Press, 1994), ch. 7.

[10] The concept of "direct applicability" was present in the Treaty in a limited form, Article
189 EC providing that regulations are to be "directly applicable" in all Member States. However,
the Treaties make no provision for the direct effect of other Community measures, including even
their own Articles.

[11] [1963] ECR 1.

[12] Case 6/64, *Flaminio Costa v. ENEL* [1964] ECR 585.

It is against this background of the early constitutional evolution of the Communities that the UK's accession must be seen. By the late 1960s, membership of the Communities required acceptance of the twin constitutional principles of direct effect and supremacy. Indeed, the Commission's *Opinion on Accession* was careful to emphasise that the requirements that certain Treaty provisions and acts of Community institutions were directly applicable, and that Community law takes precedence over any national rules conflicting with it, were essential features of the new legal order established by the Treaties.[13] Accession was said by the Commission to entail recognition of the binding force of those principles.

Such recognition was not a straightforward matter in the UK, however, due to the continued spell cast over all constitutional actors by the doctrine of Parliamentary sovereignty. In chapter 1, the relationship between the doctrine of parliamentary sovereignty and the UK's tradition of dualism was explained, but a more detailed explanation of the variants of the doctrine was deliberately postponed until the present chapter. Sovereignty theorists can be divided into two camps, labelled by Hart the "continuing" and the "self-embracing" school.[14] Continuing sovereigntists, led by Wade, argue that Parliament's sovereign will must always be obeyed by the courts, save in one case: Parliament cannot detract from its own continuing sovereignty by purporting to bind its successor Parliaments.[15] It follows that for continuing sovereignty theorists, the doctrine of implied repeal is an inherent part of sovereignty theory: it merely expresses the logical consequence that courts must give effect to Parliament's most recently expressed intention, even where an earlier Parliament has purported to restrict the later Parliament's freedom of action in some way. In support of their view, they rely on well-known decisions such as *Ellen Street Estates*, in which it was held that the legislature cannot bind itself as to the form of subsequent legislation, nor enact that in a subsequent statute dealing with the same subject matter there can be no implied repeal.[16] Self-embracing sovereigntists, on the other hand, argue that Parliament's sovereignty extends to binding its successors as to the manner and form in which legislation can be passed.[17] It follows that on this view of sovereignty, limitations as to manner and form are not impliedly repealed by later inconsistent legislation, or legislation passed ignoring those limitations.

The two schools of thought agree on one important fundamental, however: subject to a disagreement about binding successors, Parliament is the sovereign lawmaker. The disagreement is over the nature and extent of that sover-

---

[13] *Opinion of EC Commission on Application for Membership received from UK, Ireland, Denmark and Norway*, 29 September 1967 (COM (67) 750), at 80–1.

[14] H.L.A. Hart, *The Concept of Law* (Oxford: Clarendon Press, 1961) at 146.

[15] See in particular Wade, "The Basis of Legal Sovereignty" [1955] CLJ 172.

[16] *Ellen Street Estates Ltd. v. Minister of Health* [1934] 1 KB 590 at 597, per Maugham LJ. *Vauxhall Estates Ltd. v. Liverpool Corporation* [1932] 1 KB 733, to similar effect, is also cited in support.

[17] See Heuston (above n. 1), ch. 1.

eignty. The common premise means that the two views have much in common. For example, both subscribe to the dualist requirement, that treaties be incorporated into domestic law by legislation before they are cognisable by domestic courts, since this is a manifestation of Parliament's sovereignty in the sense of the exclusivity of its law-making power vis-à-vis the executive. Continuing and self-embracing sovereigntists would therefore be agreed that the Treaty establishing the Community would have to be incorporated into domestic law by Act of Parliament. Similarly, providing for the direct internal application of existing regulations and other directly applicable provisions, and for their supremacy over existing domestic law, was not a problem for either version of sovereignty theory. That much could be done by the incorporating legislation entirely consistently with traditional understandings of the sovereignty of Parliament.

But the nature of the commitments which accession would involve also engaged other aspects of the doctrine on which the two camps disagreed. The difficulty arose for continuing sovereigntists in providing for the direct applicability of future directly effective Community legislation and for the supremacy of any Community law, existing or future, which was inconsistent with future British legislation. For continuing theorists, these engaged also the supposedly illimitable and indivisible nature of Parliament's sovereignty, which prevented it not only from imposing limits on itself by binding successor Parliaments, but also from transferring even part of its sovereign law-making power to any other body. The problem, then, was that for the requirements of direct effect and supremacy to be satisfied, the statute by which the provisions of Community law were given effect, or any Community law thus incorporated, could not be vulnerable to implied repeal by a later inconsistent statute, nor could the courts be powerless to hold the later inconsistent national law invalid. Yet both of these were apparently precluded for all time by the principles derived from continuing sovereignty theory that no Parliament can bind its successors, and no court can hold an Act of Parliament invalid. Any proposal that the UK become a member of the Communities would therefore have to find a satisfactory way of reconciling the requirements of Community membership with these manifestations of that particular version of the doctrine of Parliamentary sovereignty.[18]

It was self-evident that acceptance of the requirements of Community membership was inconsistent with, at the very least, the continuing view of the sovereignty of Parliament. But since membership required member states to make whatever constitutional changes were necessary to facilitate acceptance of Community obligations, the question was not so much how to accommodate Community law within the national legal system, as how to accommodate the national legal system to Community law.

---

[18] For an early consideration of the constitutional difficulties involved in accession, see P.B. Keenan, "Some Legal Consequences of Britain's Entry into the European Common Market" [1962] PL 327 at 331–3.

The first detailed insight into how the problem was perceived by the UK Government is to be found in the 1967 White Paper, *Legal and Constitutional Implications of United Kingdom Membership of the European Communities*.[19] The White Paper was an attempt by the Government to assess the implications of membership for the country's laws and legal systems and for the legislative functions of Parliament.[20] The document was remarkable for its constitutional conservatism and its seemingly deliberate attempt to minimise the legal and constitutional implications of membership. The overall tone was distinctly defensive, suggesting that it was drawn up neither to inform the debate nor to inspire any enthusiasm for membership, but rather to meet the possible objections of critics, and to reassure them that membership would not involve any great departure from Britain's traditional modes of governance.[21] Surprisingly, no mention was made of *Costa v ENEL*, or the important development it represented, and the principle established in *Van Gend En Loos*, that private individuals may be able to rely directly on provisions of Community law, was only obliquely referred to in a passage aiming to reassure that there was no reason to think that the impact of Community law would weaken or destroy any of the basic rights and liberties enjoyed under the law of the UK.[22]

As Mitchell rightly observed, the recurring theme of the *Implications* White Paper was one of "no change". It sought at every turn to play down the constitutional significance of membership and to smooth over the possible constitutional difficulties which membership might raise. Thus, for example, the concept of treaty provisions which are intended to take effect directly as law in each Member State was said to be "by no means unknown to the law of the UK", but the examples given were provisions in various conventions relating to carriage by air or sea and to the regulation of fisheries, and embodied in domestic law by legislation passed for that purpose.[23]

---

[19] Cmnd. 3301 (hereinafter "*Implications*"). For commentary see J.D.B. Mitchell, "What do you want to be inscrutable for, Marcia?" (1967–8) 5 CMLRev 112; N. March Hunnings, "Constitutional Implications of Joining the Common Market" (1968–9) 6 CMLRev 50; A. Martin, "The Accession of the United Kingdom to the European Communities: Jurisdictional Problems" (1968–9) 6 CMLRev 7.

[20] Ibid, at para. 1.

[21] As Mitchell observed at the time, op. cit. (1967–8) 5 CMLRev 112 at 113, there is a marked contrast between the timorous and conservative tone of the *Implications* White Paper and the enthusiastic, forward-looking tone of the earlier 1967 *Membership* White Paper. As subsequent experience has shown, Government pronouncements on Europe have never managed to escape from this tension between, on the one hand, the rhetoric of being at the heart of an exciting and dynamic development in the building of a new political entity, and, on the other, the downplaying of the impact that this development will have on the traditional British way of conducting the nation's political affairs.

[22] Mitchell has since claimed that there is good evidence to suggest that the White Paper was written some years before, at a time when the true constitutional nature of the Communities had not yet become apparent: J.D.B. Mitchell, "The Sovereignty of Parliament and Community Law: The Stumbling Block That Isn't There" (1979) International Affairs 33, at 45.

[23] *Implications*, at para. 3.

In the midst of the many assertions that the various requirements of membership created "no new problem" or involved no constitutional innovation,[24] one novel feature of the Community Treaties was admitted: the bestowal of powers on the Community institutions to issue subordinate instruments which may have direct internal effect in the Member States.[25] The legislation necessary to give effect to Community law in the UK would therefore have to cover not only directly effective provisions in force at the time of accession, but those coming into force subsequently as a result of instruments issued by the Community institutions.

Such acceptance in advance of future directly effective Community provisions as part of the law of the UK was admitted by the White Paper to be without precedent.[26] But even this admitted constitutional innovation was rendered reassuringly unthreatening by its conceptualisation in the familiar, sovereignty-friendly terms of a delegation of legislative power to the Community institutions: "these instruments, like ordinary delegated legislation, would derive their force under the law of the United Kingdom from the original enactment passed by Parliament."[27] The reasons why delegation of legislative power as the vehicle for giving direct effect to future Community instruments is inadequate, as far as Community law's requirements are concerned, will be returned to below. It is sufficient for present purposes to note that the *Implications* White Paper avoided confronting the constitutional difficulty, preferring to use the familiar model of legislative delegation. It was not surprising, then, that no mention was made anywhere in the White Paper of the even more problematic fact, made clear by the decision in *Van Gend En Loos*, that direct effect is itself a dynamic concept, in the sense that the criteria by which Community measures are judged to be directly effective are themselves subject to development by the European Court of Justice.[28]

Similarly evaded by the White Paper was the question of how directly effective Community law could be accorded precedence over national law consistently with the doctrines that Parliament cannot bind its successors and courts cannot question the validity of any Act of Parliament. The White Paper accepted the need for giving Community law precedence over domestic law, but failed to address how this could be done.[29] It was merely said to follow from the fact that Community law takes precedence that the UK legislation giving effect to Community law "would have to do so in such a way as to

---

[24] See, eg., ibid at paras. 21, 22, 23 and 27.

[25] Ibid, at para. 4.

[26] Ibid, at para. 22.

[27] Ibid.. Making Community regulations "a form of delegated legislation" was also the method anticipated by Keenan, (above n. 18) at 332.

[28] Indeed, the White Paper did not dwell at all on the fact that a Member State's constitutional obligations flowing from membership of the Community could not be determined once and for all at the time of accession, but were subject to constant development by the European Court of Justice as a result of its dynamic approach to interpreting the Treaties.

[29] Ibid., at para. 23. Consistently with the White Paper's defensive tone, no mention is made of the emotive term "supremacy".

override existing national law so far as inconsistent with it". It was envisaged that this would be done expressly, rather than by implication, and that Parliament could enact consequential amendments or repeals from time to time. As for the future, "within the fields occupied by Community law Parliament would have to refrain from passing fresh legislation inconsistent with that law."[30] There was conspicuously no mention of any role for the courts in invalidating such inconsistent legislation. Rather, the White Paper seemed to envisage the supremacy of Community law as being guaranteed by nothing more than Parliamentary self-restraint. That this was the White Paper's understanding seems to be confirmed by the protestation that such self-restraint involved no constitutional innovation, because it already had to be exercised in the light of other international treaty obligations such as those under the UN Charter or the European Convention on Human Rights. No distinction was seen between the nature of the restraint under those treaties and the nature of the restraint imposed by the requirement that directly effective Community law be given precedence over domestic law.

The unspoken reason for the White Paper's evasiveness on the supremacy question was its clear acceptance of continuing sovereignty theory as its premise. As Mitchell observed, the Lord Chancellor in the House of Lords debate on the White Paper revealed more explicitly the assumption on which the UK Government was proceeding, when he said, "There is in theory no constitutional means available for us to make it certain that no future Parliament would enact legislation in conflict with Community law."[31] In other words, there was no alternative but to rely on legislative self-restraint as the guarantor of the primacy of Community law, because parliamentary sovereignty meant that Parliament could not bind its successors, and any later national legislation would impliedly repeal the directly effective Community law, or the statute by virtue of which that law had effect, to the extent to which they were inconsistent.[32]

3. THE EUROPEAN COMMUNITIES ACT 1972

The legislative attempt to reconcile what, according to continuing sovereignty theory, were the irreconcilable demands of the two legal orders, is to be found

[30] *Implications* White Paper, at para. 23.

[31] (Above n. 19) 112 at 118. Mitchell's view, even in 1967, was that it was highly doubtful that the doctrine of parliamentary sovereignty existed at all in the form in which it was generally expressed, and that there was no real constitutional obstacle to Parliament both transferring legislative sovereignty and limiting its successors to passing legislation which was consistent with Community law. In his view, ibid. at 120, "the stumbling block was merely that the draftsmen of the White Paper had timorously accepted too readily a traditional view, which largely lacks foundation."

[32] Keenan, (above n. 18) 327 at 333, similarly could see "no suitable way of avoiding this difficulty", citing *Ellen Street Estates* as the reason why even an interpretation statute providing that the statute giving effect to Community law could only be expressly repealed "would appear to have no effect."

in sections 2 and 3 of the European Communities Act 1972 ("the ECA 1972"). In those sections, Parliament provided its answer to how the supremacy and direct effect of Community law could be constitutionally achieved. This part of this chapter subjects those provisions, and their legislative history, to detailed consideration with a view to assessing the extent to which Parliament in 1972 was prepared to contemplate modification of the UK's own constitutional fundamentals in order to facilitate Community membership. It will be seen that the legislative approach to the problem of how to avoid conflicts between the two distinct legal orders is considerably more sophisticated than the analysis in the *Implications* White Paper. What emerges from a simple linguistic analysis of the provisions themselves, and of the parliamentary debates that preceded their adoption,[33] is that, far from accommodating the supremacy and direct effect of Community law within what was commonly supposed to be an immutable constitutional tradition of continuing Parliamentary sovereignty, the ECA presaged, at least in some respects, a significant evolution away from such traditional constitutional understandings. As will be seen in the next chapter and the remainder of this, that evolution was some time in coming about, but its implications for sovereignty theory, and the ECA's role in the modification of that theory, provide instructive analogies for the similar evolution which has already begun in the domestic status of international human rights norms.

(a) Direct Effect

Parliament's solution to the problem of how to give direct effect to Community law is contained in s.2(1), the essence of which provides:

> "All such rights . . . from time to time created or arising by or under the Treaties . . . as in accordance with the Treaties are without further enactment to be given legal effect . . . in the United Kingdom shall be recognised . . . in law, and be enforced . . . accordingly; and the expression 'enforceable Community right' and similar expressions shall be read as referring to one to which this subsection applies."[34]

This sub-section makes the sole constitutional innovation which the *Implications* White Paper admitted would be necessary. By the inclusion of

---

[33] See J. Forman, "The European Communities Act 1972: The Government's Position on the Meaning and Effects of its Constitutional Provisions" (1973) 10 CMLRev 39 for detailed consideration of the House of Commons debates on the European Communities Bill. In what follows, consideration is given to the parliamentary debates, partly in order to show that the explanation of the self-embracing sovereigntists is wrong on its own terms, and partly because, since *Pepper* v. *Hart* [1993] AC 593, reference to legislative history is permitted as an "aid" to statutory interpretation.

[34] The sub-section in full is considerably more complicated, referring, comprehensively, to powers, liabilities, obligations, restrictions, remedies and procedures which are to be recognised and available in law, and be enforced, allowed and followed accordingly.

the words "from time to time" and "without further enactment", it purports to give the force of law in the UK not only to directly effective Community law already in force at the date of accession, but also to such law coming into existence in the future without any further measure of implementation being necessary. In the course of the Act's passage, Enoch Powell argued that the words "without further enactment" went further than was necessary to give effect to the concept of direct applicability in Article 189 of the EC Treaty, which, he argued, did not exclude re-enactment by the national legislature.[35] Other amendments were also proposed which would have interposed Parliament between the making of a Community measure and its taking effect in the UK, but the Government insisted that the concept of direct applicability required nothing less than that directly effective Community law apply domestically in its own right, without Parliament's legislative intervention.[36] As had been pointed out in 1967, such prospective conferral of legal status as that achieved by s.2(1) ECA was without precedent in UK law.[37]

In fact the sub-section is arguably even more innovative in its attempt to deal with a further problem which the *Implications* White Paper had not even mentioned. As *Van Gend En Loos* had made clear, the idea of direct effect is itself a fluid concept, subject to evolution and refinement as the case-law of the European Court of Justice develops. By the inclusion of the words "in accordance with the Treaties", s.2(1) implicitly acknowledges that what is needed in order for a measure to be directly effective, and whether a particular provision is directly effective, are matters of Community law, on which the European Court of Justice has the final say. Therefore Parliament in this sub-section was not only authorising in advance the reception into English law of provisions yet unmade, it was also purporting to authorise in advance any changes by the ECJ in the criteria for such reception.[38] Such blank-cheque legitimation of future law not only from an external source but of uncertain definition was truly without precedent.

What exactly then is the juridical nature of s.2(1) ECA 1972? According to conventional sovereignty theory, there were really only two ways in which to make directly effective Community law part of UK law. The first was to treat directly effective Community law as any other international law, requiring incorporation by statutory transformation. The second was by the "delegation of legislative power" model which was crudely envisaged by the *Implications* White Paper.[39] On this latter view, directly effective Community

---

[35] Powell, HC Deb., Vol. 835, cols. 1366–70, (April 25 1972).

[36] Rippon, HC Deb., Vol. 835, col. 1358 (April 25 1972); Howe, HC Deb., Vol. 835, col. 1580 (April 26 1972); Howe, HC Deb., Vol. 840, cols. 1873–4 (July 13 1972). See Forman, (above n. 33) at 44–5.

[37] *Implications* (1967), para. 22.

[38] A momentous change of this type was brought about by the ECJ within a year of the UK's accession, and in the first Art. 177 reference made by a UK court, when it held in *Van Duyn* v. *Home Office* Case 41/74 [1974] ECR 1337, [1975] Ch. 358 that measures in Directives could be directly effective.

[39] Op cit. at para. 23.

law would, in the national legal system, take the form of delegated legislation passed by Community institutions pursuant to legislative power granted them by the Westminster Parliament.[40]

Several writers have maintained that s.2(1) involves no constitutional innovation because the effect it gives to Community law is explicable on the basis of either incorporation or delegation. Collins, for example, claims that the way in which Community law has been given effect in the UK is "wholly orthodox and wholly consistent with the previous practice on the transformation of international obligations into the municipal sphere."[41] Clarke and Sufrin appear at different times to embrace both explanations, talking first of s.2 being "foreshadowed" by the passage in the *Implications* White Paper analogising directly effective Community law with delegated legislation,[42] and then explaining s.2(1) as giving legal effect to directly effective Community law in the UK "without any further incorporation procedure", which is said to be the expression of "a familiar technique ... in a new context".[43]

In fact, even on sovereignty theory's own terms, s.2(1) ECA cannot be explained away as effecting either incorporation or delegation. Incorporation might explain perfectly well how Community law already in existence at the time of enactment became directly applicable, but it cannot account for future directly effective Community law becoming automatically part of domestic law without any further act of incorporation. Quite apart from the purely semantic objection, that "prospective incorporation" seems something of an oxymoron, one need only recall from chapter 1 the traditional rationale for the requirement of incorporation to see that, on sovereignty's own terms, incorporation will not do. Statutory incorporation of international law is demanded by sovereignty theory primarily in order to preserve Parliament's legislative monopoly as against the executive, by ensuring that Parliament has the opportunity to scrutinise and, if necessary, reject obligations entered into by the executive. The sub-section subverts that rationale by providing for the prospective automatic acceptance into English law of Community measures in the preparation of which the executive, but not Parliament, will have participated. As for delegation as an explanation of how future Community law becomes directly effective, the breadth of the novel prospective device

[40] The nature of the premise is revealed by a comparison with Wade's view that legislation passed under the Parliament Acts 1911 and 1949 is "a species of delegated legislation": H.W.R. Wade, "The Basis of Legal Sovereignty" [1955] CLJ 172 at 193.

[41] L. Collins, *European Community Law in the United Kingdom* 4th edn., (London: Butterworths, 1990), at 23.

[42] D.N. Clarke & B.E. Sufrin, "Constitutional Conundrums: The Impact of the United Kingdom's Membership of the Communities on Constitutional Theory" in M.P. Furmston, R. Kerridge, & B.E. Sufrin (eds.), *The Effect on English Domestic Law of Membership of the European Communities and of Ratification of the European Convention on Human Rights* (The Hague: Martinus Nijhoff, 1983), 32 at 42.

[43] Ibid, at 46, where the authors, rejecting Lord Denning's famous metaphor of the "incoming tide", characterise s.2(1) as a conduit (a "Channel Tunnel") by which new directly effective Community law is "transported" into UK law.

employed in s.2(1) seems quite incompatible with the notion that directly effective Community law is merely delegated legislation. The section's recognition of the concept of an "enforceable Community right" defined in "accordance with the Treaties", for example, is suggestive more of a transfer of sovereign legislative power than of an authorisation to make laws as a delegate.[44]

The inescapable fact is that, even when read through the prism of traditional sovereignty theory, the language of s.2(1) reads neither like an ordinary incorporation of international law, nor like a conventional delegation of legislative power. Rather it reads like a legislative recognition of the *sui generis* nature of the Treaties establishing the Communities and of the novel concept of the direct effect of instruments made in pursuance of them. But this rather begs the question of what exactly it is that s.2(1) does. Mitchell takes the rather extreme view that s.2(1), indeed the entire ECA, although politically necessary, was not legally necessary.[45] In his view, it merely derives legal consequences rather than creates them. If by this he meant to suggest that even without the passage of the ECA English courts would have started unilaterally giving direct effect to Community law, his view would have to be rejected. The Act clearly did something. It appears to be almost universally accepted that directly effective Community law has the force of law in the UK by virtue of s.2(1). Yet how has it acquired that force if the sub-section effects neither an incorporation nor a delegation?

One possible explanation of the juridical nature of s.2(1) ECA is that, rather than a delegation or incorporation section, it is a jurisdiction section, bestowing on UK courts a Community law jurisdiction. UK courts, left to their own devices, were unlikely simply to have arrogated this jurisdiction to themselves, at least not at this early stage of the UK's membership, and legislation was therefore necessary in order to confer on courts a new capacity as Community law courts.[46] Indeed, this explanation of the nature of the sub-section draws some support from statements by the Government during the parliamentary debates. Solicitor-General Geoffrey Howe, for example, emphasised that the effect of the sub-section was that directly effective Community law applied "as law" in the UK and not "as part of the law of the UK".[47] The point of

---

[44] De Smith, (above n. 5) at 610 points out the inappropriateness of the delegation solution, observing that directly applicable Community law would be "a very extraordinary kind of delegated legislation."

[45] Mitchell, at above n. 22 at 40. See also "What Happened to the Constitution on 1st January 1973?" (1980) 11 Cambrian Law Review 69 at 76–6..

[46] Perhaps a useful analogy is the Judicature Acts 1873–5, and in particular the bestowal of an equitable jurisdiction on the common law courts, to be administered alongside (but not fused with) the common law jurisdiction.

[47] See also the similar distinction drawn by J.P. Warner, "The Relationship Between European Community Law and the National Laws of Member States" (1977) 93 LQR 349 at 351, between Community law becoming "part of English law", which it has not, and it becoming "part of the law of England", in the sense of part of the law applicable in England, which it has. See also Forman, (above n. 33) at 55, who considers that the ECA should be regarded as a mere "stepping-stone" to enable Community law to be interpreted in accordance with the basic concept of uniform applicability in all member states.

the distinction was that a UK court applies Community law as law, existing alongside but separate from UK statute and common law. Section 2(1) ECA, in other words, respected the independent nature of the Community legal order by scrupulously keeping the national legal order separate from it whilst still contriving to facilitate the application of Community law by UK courts. Such an explanation of the nature and role of the sub-section, as facilitating the exercise by English courts of a distinct Community law jurisdiction, is entirely consistent with the evolutionary theory of gradually changing judicial obligation preferred by this book, both in relation to Community law and in relation to international human rights law. That theory accounts for subsequent developments in the domestic status of Community law not exclusively in terms of the statute by which the courts first acquired their jurisdiction, but in terms of changing judicial attitudes to the nature of that jurisdiction in the light of broader political developments. However its precise juridical nature is characterised, the irresistible conclusion is that, as a statutory provision, section 2(1), like the new international legal order it recognises, is itself *sui generis*, and irreconcilable with a theory of exclusive and indivisible Parliamentary sovereignty.

Arguably, just such a novel provision was required in order for the UK to comply with the requirement of membership that direct effect must be given in domestic law to appropriate Community law provisions. The achievement of s.2(1) is that it secures the direct effect of Community law without losing its character as Community law.[48] The nature of Community law, as part of a distinct and autonomous legal order, is preserved. This is something which neither incorporation nor delegation could achieve. When international law is incorporated, it is transformed into domestic law. Section 2(1) does not effect any such orthodox conversion of international obligations into domestic law. It requires courts to give direct effect to Community law without transformation, and so treats Community law quite differently from other international law. The Government was aware that the independent nature of the Community legal order made transformation inappropriate. Solicitor-General Howe, for example, argued that to make Community law expressly the law of the UK, in the same way as the rest of the law of the UK is made, was founded on a complete misunderstanding of the nature of Community law.[49]

Similarly, the delegation "solution" would fail to preserve the specific character of Community law, by treating directly effective Community law as a subordinate instrument of the national legal system. It is also difficult to see how the delegation explanation could co-exist with recognition of Community law's supremacy. Community law which ranked as ordinary delegated legislation could hardly be supreme over other UK law of the same rank as its "parent" statute. Both incorporation and delegation, being creatures derived

---

[48] See J.D.B. Mitchell, S.A. Kuipers & B. Gall, "Constitutional Aspects of the Treaty and Legislation Relating to British Membership" (1972) 9 CMLRev 134, at 137.
[49] HC Deb., Vol. 839, col. 263 (June 20 1972). See Forman, (above n. 33) at 41.

from sovereignty theory, would submerge Community law into national law and so destroy the constitutional theory of the Community as a new and distinct legal order to which the Member States had effected a transfer of their sovereign powers.[50] Section 2(1) avoids that result, but does so in a way that cannot be reconciled with any conventional understanding of parliamentary sovereignty.

This preservation of Community law's special character by s.2(1) is further reinforced by s.3, which provides, so far as relevant:

> "(1) For the purposes of all legal proceedings any question as to the meaning or effect of any of the Treaties, or as to the validity, meaning or effect of any Community instrument, shall be treated as a question of law (and, if not referred to the European Court, be for determination as such in accordance with the principles laid down by and any relevant decision of the European Court or any court attached thereto).

> (2) Judicial notice shall be taken of the Treaties, of the Official Journal of the Communities and of any decision of, or expression of opinion by, the European Court or any court attached thereto on any such question as aforesaid; . . ."

These provisions again neatly demonstrate the *sui generis* status of Community law in national courts.[51] Unlike questions of foreign law, which are treated as questions of fact to be proved by expert evidence, questions of Community law are to be treated as questions of law by national courts. But whereas the interpretation of incorporated international law is a matter for national judges, since it is their task to interpret national law, questions of Community law are to be determined in accordance with the case-law of the European Court of Justice, of which judicial notice must be taken, along with the Treaties and the Official Journal. Although not expressly incorporated by this section, the procedure under Article 177 EC, whereby a national court can make a preliminary reference to the ECJ, is also clearly presupposed by both sub-sections (in the words "if not referred to the European Court" in s.3(1) and the reference to "any . . . expression of opinion by the European Court" in s.3(2)). Taken together, ss.2(1) and 3 ECA 1972 amount to an ingenious but wholly novel means of implanting directly effective Community law into the national legal system in a way which does not sacrifice Community law's special nature as an integral part of a separate legal order.

---

[50] See Mitchell, (above n. 19) at 117. The importance of conceiving of the Community as a distinct legal system, to which there had been a transfer of jurisdiction by the Member States' legal systems, was articulated by Advocate General Lagrange in *Costa* v. *ENEL* [1964] ECR 585 at 602–3.

[51] According to Forman, (above n. 33) at 53, "it was recognised by the Government that Community law constitutes a single system of law . . . separate from but taking effect alongside the national systems."

(b) Supremacy

It is arguable that ss. 2(1) and 3 of the ECA 1972, read together, not only succeed in ensuring that direct effect is given to appropriate provisions of Community law, but also settle the question of the relationship of such directly effective Community law to national law.[52] According to this view, by providing in s.3(1) that any question as to the "effect" of the Treaties or of any Community legislation must be determined in accordance with the principles of the ECJ's case-law, Parliament was requiring national courts to follow the Court-made principle of supremacy of Community law over inconsistent national law, which was already by this time an established principle in the case-law of the Court. It is as if the principle of supremacy is itself given direct effect in national law by s.3(1). This certainly appears to be what Geoffrey Rippon M.P., Chancellor of the Duchy of Lancaster, had in mind when introducing the European Communities Bill in the House of Commons:[53]

> "By accepting the directly applicable law in clause 2(1) and accepting the jurisprudence of the European Court in clause 3(1) the Bill provides the necessary precedence. In relation to statute law, this means that the directly applicable provisions ought to prevail over future Acts of Parliament in so far as they might be inconsistent with them."

Yet despite this ministerial view that the combination of ss.2(1) and 3(1) fulfilled the UK's obligation to ensure the supremacy of Community law by "provid[ing] the necessary precedence", the Act contains a separate provision in s.2(4) which is clearly intended to address the question of supremacy. The relevant part of s.2(4) provides:

> " . . . any enactment passed or to be passed . . . shall be construed and have effect subject to the foregoing provisions of this section."[54]

Included amongst the "foregoing provisions" of s.2 are the provisions of s.2(1) giving the force of law in the UK to directly effective Community law. The explicit reference to enactments "to be passed" makes clear that Parliament was attempting to deal in this section with the relationship of future legislation to directly effective Community law. Since it appears on the face of it that Parliament has attempted by this part of s.2(4) to subordinate all Acts of Parliament, present and future, to directly effective Community law, it is again relevant to inquire into the precise juridical nature of this provision.

---

[52] See eg. T.C. Hartley, *The Foundations of European Community Law*, 3rd edn. (Oxford: Clarendon Press, 1994), at 262.

[53] H.C. Deb., Vol. 831, col. 278, (Feb. 15 1972).

[54] As various commentators have observed, eg. Bradley, (above n. 4) at 37, there is a striking similarity between this provision and s.2 of the Canadian Bill of Rights 1960, which provides: "Every law of Canada shall . . . be so construed and applied as not to abrogate any of the rights or freedoms herein recognised and declared."

Confining the inquiry to begin with to the statutory language alone, there appears to be a range of possible answers lying on a spectrum, delimited at one extreme by the view that s.2(4) is a mere interpretation section and at the other by the view that it is a substantive entrenchment device.[55] This orientation of the possible meanings on a spectrum is significant, because it reflects the fact that the concepts of interpretation and entrenchment, far from being analytically distinct as is commonly supposed, are matters of degree. At some point on the spectrum one begins to merge into the other.

The view of s.2(4) as an interpretation section sees it as laying down a rule of construction to guide the courts in their task of statutory interpretation. On this view it functions in the same way as either a common law presumption or an Interpretation Act provision, that is, dictating a particular outcome unless a contrary intention appears in the legislation. In the case of s.2(4), the outcome dictated by the rule of construction is a reading of legislation which is consistent with Community law, unless Parliament has indicated an intention at variance with such a meaning. Such an expressly enacted presumption of interpretation had been suggested by some writers as a means of giving effect to the supremacy of Community law even before the European Communities Bill had appeared.[56] As a pure matter of statutory language, the strongest textual support for this view of the nature of s.2(4) is the presence in the sub-section of the words "shall be construed". The lack of any express provision as to what remedy a court should give in a case of inconsistency may also implicitly support the view that the sub-section was only intended to lay down a rule of construction rather than confer on the courts a power to set aside or disapply a statute for inconsistency with Community law. Indeed, far from containing a power to invalidate a statute, the inclusion of the words "have effect subject to" could be taken to suggest that it was envisaged that an inconsistent Act should have some effect.

At the opposite end of the spectrum, the view of s.2(4) as a substantive entrenchment device sees it as imposing a limitation of substance on the power of Parliament to legislate inconsistently with directly effective Community law. On this view, UK law which is inconsistent with Community law is invalid and the courts must have the power to declare such law invalid. This does not cause any particular difficulties for sovereignty theory where the inconsistent statutory provision was passed before accession, or even after accession but before the relevant Community measure. In such cases, the relevant domestic provision can be said to have been impliedly repealed, either by the ECA in the former case or by the Community measure which is given effect through the ECA in the latter case. But the case of post-accession legislation which is inconsistent with a prior Community provision does create difficulties for sovereignty theory. In such a case, supremacy can only be

---

[55] J. Jaconelli, "Constitutional Review and Section 2(4) of the European Communities Act 1972" (1979) 28 ICLQ 65.

[56] See eg. de Smith (above n. 5) at 612; Martin, (above n. 19) at 22.

afforded to the Community measure by nullifying or not applying the offending provisions of the domestic statute. This view of the nature of the sub-section, which implies that a transfer of legislative power has taken place, is most strongly supported by the inclusion of the words "shall . . . have effect subject to" in addition to "shall be construed . . . subject to" directly effective Community law. This strongly suggests that what was envisaged was more than a mere rule of construction.

Jaconelli suggests that a third possibility exists, as a *via media* between the two extremes of s.2(4) as an interpretation section and s.2(4) as a substantive entrenchment device.[57] This is the view that s.2(4) renders Acts of Parliament which are inconsistent with directly effective Community law "inoperative" in the circumstances of the particular case, as opposed to "null", "void", "invalid" or "repealed". It is said that this is, at least formally, reconcilable with sovereignty theory, because it does not involve the court in any invalidation of Acts of Parliament. However, it would appear to be just one of a number of possible points on the spectrum between the two extremes already outlined, and therefore no attempt is made here to present it as a distinct interpretation. In terms of where on that spectrum it lies, however, it would appear to be very close to the entrenchment end.[58]

In view of such uncertainty as to the meaning of s. 2(4) ECA from the actual terms used, the conventional inquiry would turn to the drafting and legislative history of the sub-section to discover whether it was indeed the intention of the drafters of the legislation, and Parliament's understanding in enacting it, that directly effective Community law should take precedence over later inconsistent national legislation. Although, since *Pepper v Hart*, it is now permissible to have recourse to Hansard to discover the parliamentary "intention" behind the provision in s. 2(4), no court which has since been confronted with an apparent conflict between a domestic statute and Community law has yet taken advantage of this new opportunity. The reason may well be that, as might be expected in the case of such a politically controversial piece of legislation, for which the Government was by no means assured of a majority, the various statements made on this point during the passage of the European Communities Bill are ambiguous and often contradictory.

Some ministers were quite clear that s. 2(4) contained a rule of construction, requiring courts to construe subsequent Acts which appeared to be inconsistent with directly effective Community law in such a way as to achieve consistency rather than conflict, but ultimately giving precedence to the English statute in the event of irreconcilable conflict.[59] On the other hand, as was seen above, Geoffrey Rippon MP spelt out in quite unequivocal terms in

[57] Jaconelli, (above n. 55) at 66.

[58] See Mitchell, at (above n. 22) for the view that the supremacy of Community law does not require a court to pronounce provisions invalid in any event; it is sufficient to declare them to be inoperative in so far as they are inconsistent with directly effective Community law.

[59] See eg. Lord Colville, HL Deb. Vol. 333, col.s 1026–7, (8 August 1972).

the Second Reading Debate that the provisions of the Bill meant that directly applicable Community law "ought to prevail over future Acts of Parliament in so far as they might be inconsistent with them", suggesting that in his view directly effective Community law was substantively entrenched against future repeal.[60] But in almost the same breath he claimed that this only involved any constitutional innovation "to the extent clearly set out in the 1967 [*Implications*] White Paper" and sought to reassure the House that "[o]f course nothing in this Bill abridges the ultimate sovereignty of Parliament."[61] He went on to quote with approval the statement of Lord Gardiner, the Lord Chancellor, to the House of Lords in 1967:

> "The United Kingdom legislation would be an exercise of Parliamentary sovereignty and Community law existing and future would derive its force as law in this country from it. The Community law so applied would override our national law so far as it was inconsistent with it. Under the British constitutional doctrine of Parliamentary sovereignty no Parliament can preclude its successors from changing the law."[62]

This apparent championing of entrenchment at the same time as defending the continuing sovereignty of Parliament by the minister promoting the Bill shows the difficulty in using parliamentary material to elucidate the meaning of the relevant provisions of the ECA. Not only do Government ministers contradict each other, sometimes they contradict themselves.[63]

Solicitor-General Howe's account of the nature of s. 2(4) was rather more coherent.[64] He distinguished between the different situations in which a conflict between a statute and Community law might arise: inadvertent conflict, deliberate conflict and repeal of the ECA. He reassured Parliament that its *ultimate* sovereignty would remain intact, in that it would retain its ultimate power to repeal the Act. Where an inadvertent conflict arose, Howe suggested that the courts would try to interpret the statute so as to give effect to Community law; significantly, he considered this to be merely an application of the courts' traditional approach to interpreting legislation in accordance with Treaty obligations. It was in the intermediate case of deliberate conflict, whilst remaining a member, that Howe was least able to provide a clear answer. He thought that the courts would give effect to a statute which made absolutely clear its intention not to comply with a particular Community obligation, for example by including the phrase "notwithstanding s. 2 of the ECA 1972", but he qualified his answer with the words "as the

---

[60] HC Deb., Vol. 831, col. 278, (15 February 1972).

[61] Ibid; as noted by F.A. Trindade, "Parliamentary Sovereignty and the Primacy of European Community Law" (1972) 35 MLR 375.

[62] HL Deb., Vol. 282, col. 1202, (8 May 1967).

[63] Ministers also resisted an Opposition amendment to the effect that nothing in the Act should be taken to affect Parliamentary supremacy, arguing that such an amendment was unnecessary because Parliamentary sovereignty was not threatened.

[64] See Forman, (above n. 33) at 52.

matter now stands." This suggests that Howe subscribed to the view that the sovereignty of Parliament was something which could change over time, depending on the attitude of the judges to Acts of Parliament, and that the nature of s. 2(4) ECA was that of a guide to the courts in the carrying out of their common law interpretive functions.

Even if it were absolutely clear, whether from the statutory language or the legislative history, that Parliament by s.2(4) did intend to depart from traditional understandings of the continuing sovereignty of Parliament by purporting to bind its successors, that would not alone be determinative of the question whether there has been an actual modification of sovereignty theory. The sovereignty of Parliament is a relational concept which describes the relationship between Parliament and the courts. An attempt by one Parliament to bind its successors is not enough on its own to disprove the theory that Parliament is sovereign in the continuing sense.[65] The proof of "the filling to the s.2(4) sandwich"[66] is in the interpretation. The proper question to ask is not whether traditional understandings of sovereignty can be maintained in the light of the provisions of the ECA 1972, but whether they can survive the judicial interpretation of those provisions in the years since their adoption.

4. DIRECT EFFECT BY INCORPORATION

The early case-law in which the ECA fell to be interpreted reveals considerable judicial uncertainty as to the precise juridical nature of ss. 2(1) and (4), and it was some time before any consistency in judicial approach began to emerge. The earliest examples of UK courts considering Community law occurred in the context of competition law, no doubt because by this time Articles 85 and 86 of the Treaty of Rome had already been held by the ECJ to be directly effective. Following the entry into force of the ECA 1972 on 1st January 1973, defendants to existing infringement actions in the Chancery Division sought to amend their defences so as to rely on those Treaty provisions. Although none of these cases directly raised the question of what an English court was now to do in the event of a conflict between Community law and national law, they contain important clues as to what the courts perceived to be the effect of the ECA.

In the first case in which the Court of Appeal had to consider the Treaty, *Application des Gaz SA* v. *Falks Veritas Ltd.*,[67] the view that s.2(1) ECA had effected an "incorporation" of directly effective Community law seemed to be

---

[65] There have been other, much discussed examples of attempts to bind successor Parliaments. See eg. Northern Ireland Constitution Act 1973, s.1, providing that Northern Ireland shall not cease to be part of the UK without the consent of the majority of the people of Northern Ireland voting in a border poll.

[66] As Clarke & Sufrin call the middle clause of s.2(4) ECA 1972, (above n. 42) at 49 and 62.

[67] [1974] 1 Ch. 381.

the most popular with the Court. The plaintiffs in an action for infringement of copyright appealed against the granting of an application by the defendants to amend their defence so as to allege infringements of Articles 85 and 86 of the Treaty, arguing, *inter alia*, that questions under the Treaty should be dealt with in separate proceedings altogether. In the course of dismissing the plaintiffs' appeal, Lord Denning MR made observations on the status of the Treaty which revealed his view as to the effect of the ECA. The Treaty, he said, had been "given legal effect in the UK" by the ECA and was therefore "part of our law. It is equal in force to any statute. It must be applied by our courts."[68]

Although Lord Denning concluded that "Articles 85 and 86 are part of our law" without expressly mentioning s.2(1) ECA, it seems reasonable to infer from his comments that at this stage his view of the effect of the Act was that it had incorporated the Treaty, apparently in its entirety, into English law, where its status was equivalent to that of a statute. This was certainly the view of Stamp L.J. (with whom Roskill L.J. agreed), who, unlike Lord Denning, did expressly mention s.2(1) ECA. In his view, the juridical nature of that provision was that it effected an incorporation or transformation of the Treaty provisions which were to be treated by a UK court "as if . . . contained in an enactment of the Parliament of the UK."[69] A defence based on the provisions of the Treaty of Rome was therefore "a defence in English law".

Incorporation therefore rapidly found judicial favour as the best explanation of how directly effective Community law had come to have the force of law in the UK by virtue of the ECA, but the limitations of this explanation were already apparent in Lord Denning's assertion that Community law was "equal in force to any statute". Although doubtless uttered to counter the proposition that Community law was of any lesser status, the notion of equality with national statutes cannot accommodate the principle of the supremacy of Community law when the two are in conflict, and therefore highlights the limits to the "incorporation" explanation of what was achieved by s.2 of the ECA 1972.

5. COMPETING SUPREMACIES

A settled judicial view on the question of the supremacy of Community law was much slower to emerge. The early judicial responses to the problem of what to do in the face of a conflict between a statute and Community law cover virtually the entire range of possibilities, from the reassertion of the

---

[68] [1974] Ch. 381, at 393B–C. Lord Denning expressed similar views in *H.P. Bulmer Ltd.* v. *J. Bollinger SA* [1974] Ch. 401 at 418E–419C, immediately after his famous metaphor that "the Treaty is like an incoming tide. It flows into the estuaries and up the rivers. It cannot be held back."

[69] [1974] 1 Ch. 381 at 399E.

absolute duty to follow the latest expression of the will of the sovereign Parliament at one extreme, to the apparent acceptance that Community law must always take precedence at the other, with various compromise positions between the two. As was characteristic of this particular period in English legal history, the Master of the Rolls somehow contrived to occupy, at different times, every conceivable point on this spectrum.

Lord Denning it was, for example, who was responsible for the most unreconstructed denial of the supremacy of Community law in the face of a later inconsistent Act of Parliament. In his view in *Gaz* and *Bulmer* of the equality of status of Community law and statute, and in his omission to mention s.2(4) ECA in either of those cases, Lord Denning had either overlooked the principle of the supremacy of Community law or was choosing not to address it until a conflict arose. When that opportunity presented itself, in *Felixstowe Dock & Railway Co.* v. *British Transport Docks Board*, he adopted an extreme position denying supremacy, or indeed any effect at all, to Community law once an English statute had been passed.[70] The plaintiff Company, which had entered into an agreement with the Docks Board whereby the Board agreed to take over the Company subject to the passage of a private Act of Parliament giving the Board the necessary statutory authorisation, sought a declaration that the agreement was void on the ground, *inter alia*, that it was contrary to Article 86 EEC because the attempt to take over the port of Felixstowe was an abuse by the Board of a dominant position. Lord Denning, having observed that "Article 86 is now part of English law",[71] found there to be no abuse of any dominant position, but went on to add:

> "It seems to me that once the Bill is passed by Parliament and becomes a Statute, that will dispose of all this discussion about the Treaty. These Courts will then have to abide by the Statute without regard to the Treaty at all."

This flagrant denial of the primacy of Community law amounted to a regression even from his former questionable position according the Treaties equal status with domestic legislation.

Yet Lord Denning it was again at the opposite extreme, appearing to accept the full implications of the supremacy of Community law in *Shields* v. *E. Coomes (Holdings) Ltd.*, in which the Court of Appeal dismissed an employer's appeal against an equal pay award to a female counterhand at a betting shop, under the provisions of the Sex Discrimination Act 1975 and the Equal Pay Act 1970 ("the EPA 1970").[72] The Court rejected the employer's argument that the male employee was paid a higher hourly rate because of the "deterrent" and "protective" functions he served in the shop, which was in an

---

[70] [1976] 2 Lloyd's Law Reports 656 . Scarman LJ's judgment in the same case is considered below.

[71] Ibid, at 662 col. 2.

[72] [1978] 1 WLR 1408. The amended Equal Pay Act 1970 came into force in December 1975, so both statutes post-dated the ECA 1972.

area in which trouble was likely to occur. It held that there were no differences of practical importance between their work and that there was no material difference other than sex because the male counterhand had been employed purely because he was a male and not because he was trained in security duties.

Having heard argument from the Equal Opportunities Commission on the law of the European Communities on equal pay and discrimination, in particular Article 119 of the Treaty and the Equal Pay Directive,[73] Lord Denning made several general observations about the relationship between Community law and national law. He described the principle of the supremacy of Community law as one of the two principles of great importance established by the ECJ and by which, according to s.3(1) ECA, the UK courts must abide. The principle was said to arise

> "whenever there is a conflict or inconsistency between the law contained in an article of the Treaty and the law contained in the internal law of one of the member states, whether passed before or after joining the Community. It says that in any such event the law of the Community shall prevail over that of the internal law of the member state."[74]

Lord Denning envisaged supremacy being given to Art. 119 over an Act of Parliament in the event that Parliament were to pass a statute inconsistent with that directly effective article of the Treaty. For example if the EPA had given the right of equal pay only to unmarried women, Lord Denning thought that a married woman could bring an action in the High Court to enforce her right to equal pay under Art. 119.

In this case, then, Lord Denning appeared to take the view that UK courts are bound by s.3(1) ECA to give effect to the principle of supremacy of Community law, which may include giving precedence to Community law over a later inconsistent statute. Defenders of sovereignty theory have said that these comments were strictly speaking *obiter*, since on the facts of the case there was no conflict between national law and Community law.[75] But they do not appear to have been *obiter* for Lord Denning, who, towards the end of his judgment, claimed that it was only "by giving supremacy to Community law" that he had resolved his difficulties in overcoming the industrial tribunal's finding that the differences between the work done were of practical importance.[76] Although this part of Lord Denning's judgment is not

---

[73] Art. 119 had been held to be directly effective by the ECJ in Case 43/75 *Defrenne* v. *SABENA* [1976] ECR 455; [1976] ICR 547. The Equal Pay Directive (Council Directive 75/117/EEC) was not directly effective.

[74] [1978] 1 WLR 1408 at 1415A–B.

[75] See eg. O. Hood Phillips, "Has the 'Incoming Tide' Reached the Palace of Westminster?" (1979) 95 LQR 167 at 170.

[76] [1978] 1 WLR 1408 at 1419G. Even if not *obiter*, Lord Denning's is clearly a minority view, as the other two members of the Court of Appeal reached the same result without mentioning the supremacy of Community law. Orr LJ, ibid. at 1423, thought that the argument on Community law had been heard for the purpose of helping to construe the English statutes, and

very clear, the suggestion is that, had it not been for the existence of the provisions of Community law, he would not have found the work to be "like
work" within the meaning of s.1(4) of the Equal Pay Act. It is also true that
Lord Denning's example of a statute "inconsistent" with Art. 119 is a case of
under-implementation rather than contradiction. But elsewhere in his judgment Lord Denning makes perfectly clear that he envisages primacy being
given to Community law to resolve "inconsistency" as well as mere ambiguity or omission.[77] It is true that the case concerned the interpretation of legislation designed to implement Community law. It is also true that Lord
Denning's comments cannot be taken as going so far as to say that national
courts should give primacy to Community law even if the national statute
expressly shows that Parliament intended to contradict Community law on
that matter. Nevertheless, Lord Denning's comments in *Shields* go a long way
towards accepting the full implications of the supremacy of Community law.

Whereas Lord Denning's dictum in *Felixstowe* appears to be an isolated
example of outright judicial rejection of the supremacy of Community law,
he was not alone in his apparent view in *Shields* that UK courts were now
under a duty to accord supremacy to Community law even over a later inconsistent Act of Parliament. In what appears to be the earliest reported case concerning Community law following the passage of the ECA, *Aero Zipp
Fasteners* v. *YKK Fasteners (UK) Ltd.*, Graham J. also appeared to take a view
of the effect of the ECA verging on entrenchment.[78] In an action for infringement of a patent, he refused the plaintiffs' application to strike out an amendment to the defence which relied on Articles 85 and 86. In doing so, he
considered the effect of the ECA 1972. It had been passed, he said, to implement the UK's obligations under the Treaty of Accession, and "enacted that
relevant Common Market law should be applied in this country, and should,
where there is a conflict, override English law."[79] The choice of language
suggests that Graham J. was in no doubt about the effect of the Act.
"Override" is not even a word used by the drafter of the ECA, and leaves no
room for equivocation about what a court is to do in the event of a conflict
arising.

---

held that the applicant did not need any such assistance; Bridge LJ, ibid. at 1424–5, acknowledged
that Art. 119, being of direct effect, had to be "applied as part of our law under the provisions
of s. 2 ECA", and that the non-directly effective Directives could help resolve some ambiguity in
implementing legislation, but held the meaning of the English statutes to be perfectly clear, so
there was no need to have any resort to Community law.

[77] Eg. ibid, at 1419G.

[78] [1973] CMLR 819.

[79] Ibid, at 820. Graham J.'s dictum is cited approvingly by Advocate General Warner, (above
n. 47), at 364, as an example of an English judge properly recognising that the ECA gives effect
to the primacy of Community law over national law in national courts. Contrast the traditionalists' rearguard action, exemplified by Hood Phillips, (above n. 75), at 170, arguing that Graham
J's dictum is not in point because the case did not concern a conflict between Community law
and a later statute, and that the word "override" used by Graham J. is "ambiguous."

Two further examples can be given of early decisions appearing to lend support to the entrenchment view. It appears from the report of *Re an Absence in Ireland* that the case is an early example of Community law prevailing over a later UK statute.[80] In allowing an appeal by a claimant for invalidity benefit, on the ground that he was not disqualified from receiving such benefit during his absence from Great Britain, the National Insurance Commissioner appears boldly to have held that the provisions of a 1971 Community regulation overrode the inconsistent statutory ground of disqualification in the Social Security Act 1975.[81] Although there is no mention in the report of the ECA 1972, so we are left to infer his justification, the language of "override" leaves little doubt as to precisely what the Commissioner considered himself to be doing.[82]

Finally, it is arguable that an even earlier acceptance of the supremacy of Community law can be found in the judgment of Scarman LJ. in the case in which Lord Denning had been at his most antediluvian, *Felixstowe*.[83] He considered the Company to be arguing that the agreement with the Board was designed to facilitate the abuse of a dominant position at a later stage, which was tantamount to saying that the Bill, if it became an Act, would itself establish an abuse of a dominant position by the Board. Scarman LJ. considered this argument on its merits, rejecting it only because there was "no evidence at all" that the Act would bring about such an abuse, and the case therefore "does not . . . give rise to the problem of a conflict between the Treaty of Rome and a subsequent Act of Parliament."[84] This rejection of the implicit challenge to the forthcoming Act on its merits is in stark contrast to Lord Denning's approach, since it clearly presupposes that the court has jurisdiction to consider such a claim. It was only because there was no evidence that the Act would make an abuse of a dominant position inevitable that no question of a conflict between Community law and a later national law arose. Although Scarman LJ. did not expressly disagree with Lord Denning, nor overtly accept the principle of supremacy, it seems implicit in his consideration of the merits of the Company's claim that, if such evidence had existed, he would have been prepared to accord primacy to Article 86 over the later inconsistent statute.[85] Otherwise it is hard to imagine why it was necessary to consider at all whether there was any evidence that the Act would itself make inevitable an abuse of a dominant position contrary to the Treaty.

---

[80] [1977] 1 CMLR 5.

[81] The relevant provisions were Council Regulation 1408/71, Articles 38 and 39, and Social Security Act 1975, s. 82(5)(a).

[82] Again the unequivocal language did not deter Hood Phillips, (above n. 75), at 169–70, from characterising the case as an example of the application of a mere presumption of interpretation that the statute was not intended to conflict with Community law.

[83] [1976] 2 Lloyd's Law Reports 656.

[84] Ibid, at 664 col.1.

[85] The matter is left to inference. The ECA 1972 was not cited by any of the judges in *Felixstowe*.

None of these cases, however, are sufficiently clear to be capable of providing unqualified support for the proposition that UK courts must now accord precedence to Community law over a later inconsistent statute. None, except perhaps *Re an Absence in Ireland*, in which the issue was not satisfactorily discussed, had involved a direct conflict between Community law and a provision of national law. No judge had yet expressly considered the effect of s.2(4) ECA, the very provision in the Act intended to deal with the question of supremacy. Even Lord Denning in *Shields*, whose judgment amounted to probably the clearest acceptance so far of the principle of supremacy, had relied on s.3(1) ECA as the source of UK courts' obligation, and had not even mentioned s.2(4). It was not until the decision of the majority of the Court of Appeal in *Macarthys v Smith* that a UK court unequivocally declared that the effect of s.2(4) ECA was to require courts to give precedence to directly effective Community law in the event of a conflict with domestic law, even where the domestic provision had been enacted subsequently to the Community provision.[86]

Macarthys was another equal pay case raising even more directly than *Shields* the constitutionally problematic question of the proper relationship between directly effective Community law and subsequent national legislation on the same subject. The female applicant was employed as a stockroom manageress and was paid £10 a week less than the previous male stockroom manager, who had left his job with the employers four and a half months before she was appointed. In equal pay proceedings before an industrial tribunal she claimed that she was employed on like work as the previous employee and was therefore entitled to equal pay under the Equal Pay Act 1970, as amended by the Sex Discrimination Act 1975 ("the SDA 1975").[87] The tribunal allowed her claim and the employers' appeal to the EAT was dismissed.[88] On the employers' appeal to the Court of Appeal, the question was whether the domestic provision, which provided for the comparison of contractual terms "where the woman is employed on like work with a man in the same employment",[89] only permitted comparison to be made with the work of a man in contemporaneous employment and, if so, whether Community law required any different result.

The majority of the Court of Appeal, Lawton and Cumming-Bruce L.JJ., adopted an approach which, for the first time, made it impossible to avoid the difficult questions of what a court was to do when faced with a conflict between directly effective Community law and a subsequent statute, and what the effect of s.2(4) ECA was in such circumstances. Notwithstanding anything

---

[86] [1979] 3 All ER 325.

[87] This was not in fact her original claim. Her case had begun by comparing her work with that done by the office manager, but during its presentation her male predecessor in the post was substituted as the comparator, thus raising the point so perfectly designed to test the position of the UK courts on supremacy. See [1978] 1 WLR 849 at 850G (EAT).

[88] [1978] 1 WLR 849. The decision of the EAT is considered further below n. 143.

[89] EPA 1970, s. 1(2)(a)(i).

in the ECA, these two judges took the stringently dualist view that the correct approach was first to ask what was the meaning of the English statute.[90] That was to be discovered by applying the ordinary English rules of statutory construction, which included the rule that words in a statute have their ordinary and natural meaning unless such a meaning is manifestly inconsistent with the context or gives rise to such absurdity or injustice that Parliament cannot have intended it. Adopting this ultra-traditional approach to statutory interpretation, the meaning of the relevant part of the EPA 1970 was said to be clear and unambiguous.[91] Its grammatical construction and use of the present tense were said to be consistent only with a comparison between a woman and a man in the same employment at the same time. Since the plain meaning of the provision was clear from the words themselves, which gave rise to no ambiguity, it was held not to be permissible to go outside the Act, for example by looking at the Treaty as an aid to construction, in order to read the words in a sense other than that of their "ordinary" meaning.[92] Reference to the provisions of Art. 119 EEC to help discover the meaning of the provision was, on this view, an illegitimate exercise. The terms of the Treaty, or any interpretation of it by the ECJ, could not affect the meaning of the English statute.

The majority judges therefore treated directly effective Community law as if it were any other unincorporated international law for the purposes of construing national legislation, rigidly applying traditional canons of construction complete with an ambiguity precondition before recourse to such law was even permissible as an interpretive aid.[93] However, the majority recognised that it was not free to ignore Art. 119 and simply apply what it considered to be the Act's plain meaning, because Art. 119 gave rise to individual rights which the courts must protect.[94] That obligation was said to arise both from the decisions of the ECJ, making clear that Art. 119 has direct effect, and from s.2 ECA. Since they were unclear as to the meaning of Art. 119, they held that it was necessary to make a reference to the ECJ to discover whether that Article applies to such a case.

There can be no doubt that these two judges fully understood the implications of their making a reference in these circumstances. As Lord Denning pointed out in his dissenting judgment, if it transpired that there was a conflict between Community law and the statute as they had interpreted it, they would have to give priority to Art. 119 over the statute.[95] Indeed, it was

---

[90]   [1979] 3 All ER 325 at 332b (Lawton L.J.) and 334h (Cumming-Bruce L.J.).

[91]   Ibid. at 332c–h (Lawton L.J.) and 334j-335a (Cumming-Bruce L.J.).

[92]   See eg. Lawton L.J., ibid. at 332h–j and Cumming-Bruce L.J. at 335j.

[93]   When the case returned to the Court of Appeal from the ECJ, Cumming-Bruce L.J. reiterated that it was not appropriate to look to the Treaty as an aid to construction unless there was ambiguity in the English statute: [1981] 1 QB 180 at 201G–202A. For criticism of the judicial insistence on statutory ambiguity as a precondition of reference to international law, see ch. 1.

[94]   Lawton L.J., [1979] 3 All ER 325 at 333h–334a.

[95]   Ibid, at 331e. Lord Denning's dissent is considered in the following section.

expressly envisaged by Cumming-Bruce LJ. that if the ECJ were to hold that the terms of the Treaty were inconsistent with the provisions of the EPA, "European law will prevail over that municipal legislation."[96] Lawton LJ. was slightly more circumspect, saying only that the case could be "of constitutional importance" if the ECJ's opinion on the reference conflicted with the clear terms of the statute,[97] but the tenor of his judgment is the same and certainly supports Lord Denning's understanding of it. For the first time, then, more than six years after the passage of the ECA 1972, a UK court had explicitly held that it was under a duty to give priority to Community law where it was in actual conflict with a later domestic statute. This appeared to amount to an explicit judicial endorsement of the entrenchment view of s.2(4) ECA, and therefore, by necessary implication, to be a rejection of the theory of continuing sovereignty.

Yet significantly, though unsurprisingly, the majority did not consider their conclusion to involve any compromise of Parliamentary sovereignty. For them, the reconciliation with sovereignty theory was straightforward. Far from subverting the sovereignty of Parliament, they believed that they were in fact applying it, because Parliament, "by its own act in the exercise of its sovereign powers", has enacted that European Community law is to be given direct effect (s.2(1)) and accorded supremacy (s.2(4)).[98] It followed that the Court was merely implementing the will of Parliament expressed in the 1972 Act, in the absence of any indication in the subsequent Act that Parliament had changed its mind. As Lawton LJ. put it:

"Parliament's recognition of European Community law and of the jurisdiction of the ECJ by one enactment can be withdrawn by another. There is nothing in the EPA 1970, as amended by the SDA 1975, to indicate that Parliament intended to amend the ECA 1972 or to limit its application."[99]

The Court of Appeal majority in *Macarthys* therefore relied on the sovereignty of Parliament as its justification for limiting the sovereignty of Parliament. For, whatever the lip-service paid to sovereignty, the result of the majority's approach is that s.2(4) ECA has achieved a degree of entrenchment of directly effective Community law, in the sense that it will take precedence over later inconsistent national law unless Parliament has made very clear in the subsequent statute its intention to limit or amend the ECA 1972. Simply to legislate in direct contradiction of Community law is not, on this approach, a sufficient indication of such intention. This cannot be squared with the theory of Parliament's continuing sovereignty, which, it will be recalled from the discussion earlier in this chapter, necessarily entails the so-called doctrine of implied repeal. On the majority's view in *Macarthys*, Parliament remains

---

[96] Ibid, at 335j–336a.
[97] Ibid, at 332a.
[98] Lawton L.J., ibid. at 334e–f.
[99] Ibid, at 334f–g.

sovereign, not in the "continuing" sense in which orthodox constitutional theory had for so long believed, but in the less expansive sense that it was free to legislate inconsistently with directly effective Community law provided it made its intention to do so sufficiently explicit. For all practical purposes the supremacy of Community law over national law was therefore acknowledged, and the supposed obstacle of continuing sovereignty shown to be illusory.

6. THE EMERGENCE OF A "CONSTRUCTION APPROACH" TO THE SUPREMACY OF COMMUNITY LAW

(a) Lord Denning's Construction Approach

The statutory entrenchment approach of the Court of Appeal majority in *Macarthys*, however, did not settle the question of the domestic supremacy of Community law once and for all. Ironically, in the very same case in which a UK court had at last confronted the question of what to do in a case of irreconcilable conflict, and spoken with a clear voice, albeit a majority one, on the effect of s. 2(4) ECA, there emerged a competing view in the form of the dissenting judgment of the Master of the Rolls. This time Lord Denning managed to occupy a compromise position mid-way between his two extremes in *Felixstowe* and *Shields*. Although formulated in a dissenting judgment, Lord Denning's latest approach requires careful consideration, because it was around this alternative approach to the supremacy of Community law that a judicial consensus was eventually to emerge during the 1980s.

Whereas the majority asked first what was the ordinary and natural meaning of the English provision, construed in isolation from Community law, Lord Denning reversed the order in which national law and Community law were to be considered, looking first to the principle of equal pay for equal work in Art. 119 of the Treaty. For Lord Denning this seemed to follow from the fact that that provision "takes priority even over our own statute".[100] It was true that if domestic legislation contravenes such a directly applicable principle, or is inconsistent with it or fails properly to implement it, the Treaty provided for enforcement measures to be taken against the UK by Community institutions, but Lord Denning's understanding of the effect of the ECA 1972 was that domestic courts need not wait until that procedure has been gone through.

> "Under s.2(1) and (4) ECA 1972 the principles laid down in the Treaty are 'without further enactment' to be be given legal effect in the UK; and have priority over 'any enactment passed or to be passed' by our Parliament. So we are entitled and I think bound to look at Art. 119 of the EEC Treaty because it is directly applicable here; and also any directive which is directly applicable here."[101]

---

[100] [1981] 1 QB 180 at 328b.
[101] Ibid, at 329a.

The correct approach, therefore, was for courts to look first to see what directly effective Community law requires in relation to equal pay for men and women, and only then to look at domestic legislation on the point, "giving it, of course, full faith and credit, assuming that it does fully comply with the obligations under the Treaty." In construing the domestic statute, courts were said to be entitled to look to the Treaty as an aid to its construction, and, if necessary, "as an overriding force", and if, by some legislative oversight, the statute was deficient or inconsistent with Community law, it was the courts' "bounden duty" to give priority to Community law.[102] This approach was based on the statutory presumption that Parliament, whenever it passes legislation, intends to fulfil its obligations under the Treaty. Proceeding on that assumption, the question for Lord Denning in this case was whether Parliament, in enacting the EPA and SDA, had fulfilled those obligations.

Looking first at what the relevant Community law required, Lord Denning thought that Art. 119 was reasonably clear on the point at issue. In his view, it clearly applied to cases where the woman is employed on like work in such close succession to a man that it is just and reasonable to make a comparison between them.[103] He then turned to the EPA to see if that principle in the Treaty had been successfully carried forward into domestic legislation. Reading the relevant provision in the EPA as it stood, he admitted that on its face it appeared to contemplate only cases where the woman was employed at the same time as a man. The use of the present tense and of the phrase "in the same employment" carried that connotation. But that literal interpretation did not exhaust the possible meanings the words could bear. Lord Denning was prepared to take a broad purposive approach to their construction. The EPA and the SDA 1975 were intended as a single code intended to eliminate discrimination against women, and should therefore be construed as a harmonious whole. To achieve that harmony it was necessary to read the statutory provision, not as if it included the words "at the same time", but as applying to cases where a woman is employed at the same job doing the same work 'in succession' to a man.[104]

By considering the Treaty and the domestic statutes together in this way, it was possible to construe them so as to avoid a conflict between Art. 119 and the provision in the EPA, and this exercise in construction therefore had the advantageous result that the UK was in conformity with its obligations under the Treaty. On Lord Denning's approach, "both under the Treaty and under the statutes"[105] a woman should receive equal pay for equal work when employed at the same job in succession to, as well as at the same time as, a man. Because he thought the meaning of Art. 119 was clear, and that it was

[102] Ibid. at 329b–c.
[103] Ibid. at 330b.
[104] Ibid. at 330h.
[105] Ibid. at 331c.

possible to construe the UK's implementing legislation so as to give effect to that meaning, he would have dismissed the employer's appeal without making a reference to the ECJ, but he agreed to make such a reference in view of the uncertainty of the other two members of the Court of Appeal.[106]

Lord Denning's approach to according supremacy to directly effective Community law was therefore in stark contrast to that of the majority. They accepted unreservedly that European law prevails over national legislation in the event that an inconsistency arose, but they were not prepared even to have regard to the relevant Community law when construing the domestic provision if the meaning of the statute was "clear". Lord Denning, on the other hand, was prepared to construe domestic law in the light of directly effective Community law in order to prevent such inconsistency from arising in the first place.[107] There was, nevertheless, one significant point on which Lord Denning and the majority were agreed, and that concerned the reconciliation with parliamentary sovereignty. Just as Lawton L.J. had been careful to point out that nothing in the majority's judgment in any way detracted from Parliament's sovereignty, so Lord Denning was equally careful to point out that nothing in his quite different approach was incompatible with that constitutional fundamental:

> "If the time should come when our Parliament deliberately passes an Act with the intention of repudiating the Treaty or any provision in it or intentionally of acting inconsistently with it and says so in express terms then I should have thought that it would be the duty of our courts to follow the statute of our Parliament. I do not however envisage any such situation. . . . Unless there is such an intentional and express repudiation of the Treaty, it is our duty to give priority to the Treaty."[108]

Parliament's sovereignty therefore remained intact in the ultimate sense that it could still legislate inconsistently with Community law, provided it made express its intention so to do.

Unlike his apparent embrace of the Community law principle of supremacy in *Shields*, which had caused alarm amongst traditionalists, Lord Denning's "construction" approach in *Macarthys* was hailed by adherents to the theory of continuing sovereignty as the right approach to the problem of how to recognise the supremacy of Community law consistently with basic constitutional commitments. It found favour with commentators such as Hood Phillips, for example, whose view of s.2(4) ECA was that it laid down "a rule of construction for giving effect to UK statutes",[109] requiring UK courts to

---

[106] See text following n. 94 above. Surprisingly, this was the first reference to be made to the ECJ by the Court of Appeal: see Lawton LJ, ibid. at 331j.

[107] Lord Denning's views on what a court was to do if a conflict was unavoidable are considered below, text following n. 111.

[108] Ibid, at 329d–e. However, the question was left a little more open by Lord Denning's repetition of his own dictum in *Blackburn* v. *Attorney-General* [1971] 1 WLR 1037 at 1040, that if Parliament should expressly legislate inconsistently with Community law, "we will consider that event when it happens."

[109] "High Tide in the Strand? Post-1972 Acts and Community Law" (1980) 96 LQR 31.

strive to reconcile an Act with Community law if reasonably possible. Starting from the continuing sovereignty premise that "the ECA could not bind Parliament in the future", Hood Phillips criticised the majority of the Court of Appeal in *Macarthys* for having unnecessarily created "a constitutional issue", by backing themselves into a corner from which there was no way out if the ECJ ruled that the relevant provision of Community law had a meaning which was inconsistent with their interpretation of the UK statute. Lord Denning's approach, by contrast, avoided such a constitutional issue arising in the first place by looking to the relevant Community law first and then reading the domestic statute so as to achieve consistency if at all possible. Such a construction approach was said to respect "the basic principle of the constitution", and gave effect to Parliament's uncontravened wish, expressed in s.2(4) ECA, that future Acts shall be construed and have effect subject to Community law.[110]

However, by focusing on that part of Lord Denning's dissent in which he sought to construe the domestic statute so as to avoid a conflict with Community law, the defenders of continuing sovereignty were too selective in what they saw. As Allan has made clear, Lord Denning's approach was not confined to statutory "construction" in the narrow sense permitted by their theory.[111] At various points in his judgment he made quite clear that, where conflict cannot be avoided by construing the language of domestic law in the light of Community law, the latter is to be given precedence. This much is clear from his comments to the effect that the principle of equal pay in the EEC Treaty "takes priority even over our own statute";[112] that the court is entitled to look to the Treaty "not only as an aid [to construction] but as an overriding force";[113] and that "it is our bounden duty to give priority to Community law" in the event of inadvertent conflict.[114]

Lord Denning clearly was not saying that, if a statute is incapable of being construed so as to be in conformity with directly effective Community law, it must take precedence over that Community law. In such a case, where, even on Lord Denning's more flexible approach to statutory interpretation, the language of the domestic provision simply cannot be made to bear a meaning necessary to achieve consistency, Lord Denning undoubtedly agreed with the majority that the courts must still give priority to Community law over the irreconcilably inconsistent national law. The only virtue of his approach for continuing sovereigntists such as Hood Phillips, therefore, was that his more flexible approach to construction made such overt conflicts much less likely to occur.

[110] Ibid. at 32.
[111] T.R.S. Allan, "Parliamentary Sovereignty: Lord Denning's Dexterous Revolution" (1983) 3 OJLS 22.
[112] [1979] 3 All ER 325 at 328b.
[113] Ibid, at 329b–c.
[114] Ibid.

Indeed, this much was made explicit when the case came back to the Court of Appeal from the ECJ after the ruling on the preliminary reference.[115] The ECJ had held that the principle in Art. 119, that men and women should receive equal pay for equal work, was not confined to situations in which men and women were contemporaneously doing equal work for the same employer, but applied to a case where a woman was paid less than a man who was previously employed doing like work for the same employer. Lord Denning said:[116]

> "It is important now to declare—and it must be made plain—that the provisions of Art. 119 of the EEC Treaty take priority over anything in our English statute on equal pay which is inconsistent with Art. 119."

This was no sudden change of heart on Lord Denning's part. As was shown above, his preparedness to find that in a case of conflict the Community law provision overrode the statute, and must be given priority, was already manifest in his earlier dissent. Having agreed to make the reference, Lord Denning now joined the majority in treating the case as one of irreconcilable conflict between Community law and a later English statute, and thus was revealed the full extent of the overlap between his approach and the reasoning of the majority, which the sovereigntists had found constitutionally unacceptable.

For Lord Denning, as for the majority, Community law must prevail over the domestic provision if the latter cannot be construed so as to achieve conformity. In Allan's words, "the two approaches run into one another".[117] Hood Phillips and the defenders of continuing sovereignty had overlooked the fact that Lord Denning's "construction" approach was based on the statutory presumption, not only that Parliament intended not to legislate inconsistently with Community law, but that it intended in cases of actual unavoidable conflict that the inconsistent domestic legislation should not be applied by the courts. A presumption of such strength is more than the theory of continuing sovereignty can accommodate within its notion of "construction", because it necessarily abandons the notion of implied repeal and requires express wording to be used if the courts are to be expected to give effect to an inconsistent statute over directly effective Community law. Since this inevitably means that Parliament in 1972 succeeded, at least to this extent, in binding its successors, it is more than continuing sovereigntists can countenance.

(b) Lord Diplock's Construction Approach

It was probably a belated recognition of this fact that led Hood Phillips to desert Lord Denning and welcome as "the correct approach" the alternative

---

[115] [1981] QB 180.
[116] Ibid. at 200E–F.
[117] *Law, Liberty and Justice* (Oxford: Clarendon Press, 1993), at 276.

and, on the face of it, more sovereignty-friendly construction approach adopted by the House of Lords in *Garland*.[118] The question at issue in that case was whether the employer's discriminatory provision of concessionary travel facilities as a retirement benefit was within the scope of s.6(4) SDA 1975, which excepted "provision in relation to . . . retirement" from the Act's prohibition of discrimination on grounds of sex. The industrial tribunal had dismissed the claim on the ground that the employer's scheme was a provision in relation to retirement and therefore within the scope of the exception in s.6(4) SDA. The EAT allowed the employee's appeal, holding that the words of the exception created by s.6(4) ought not to be construed so widely as to include "a privilege that has existed during employment" and is allowed by the employer to continue after retirement. The Court of Appeal, however, allowed the employer's appeal, holding that "provision in relation to . . . retirement" in s.6(4) was a wide expression and included any provision *about* retirement.

In none of these proceedings had the court's attention been drawn to the relevant Community law, Art. 119 EEC and two Council Directives, the Equal Pay Directive and the Equal Treatment Directive.[119] The claim had been dealt with by all three courts on the footing that it turned upon the true construction of s.6(4) SDA 1975, but without any consideration being given to the fact that equal pay without discrimination on grounds of sex is required by Art. 119, or that the application of that article had been the subject of two directives, or that as a result of the ECJ's decision in *Defrenne* v. *Sabena*, Art. 119 gave rise to directly effective rights.

The House of Lords insisted that these matters of Community law were relevant to the proper construction of the domestic statute, and referred to the ECJ the questions, first, whether the discrimination was contrary to Art. 119 EEC or the two Directives, and, second, if so, whether that article or either of the directives was directly applicable so as to confer enforceable Community rights upon individuals. Following the ECJ's answers in the affirmative, the House of Lords allowed the employee's appeal, holding that, in the light of those answers, the correct construction of s.6(4) was that adopted by the EAT, since that was the only construction consistent with Art. 119. The justification given by Lord Diplock for taking this approach to construing the statute has already been encountered in chapter 1, but in the present context it is necessary to quote it at even greater length:

". . . even if the obligation to observe the provisions of Art. 119 were an obligation assumed by the UK under an ordinary international treaty or convention and there were no question of the treaty obligation being directly applicable as part of the law to be applied by the courts in this country without need for any further enactment,

[118] *Garland v. British Rail Engineering Ltd.* [1983] 2 AC 751 (ECJ & HL); O. Hood Phillips, "A Garland for the Lords: Parliament and Community Law Again" (1982) 98 LQR 524.
[119] As pointed out by Lord Diplock, ibid. at 770F. The Directives were, respectively, Council Directive 75/117/EEC, and Council Directive 76/207/EEC.

it is a principle of construction of UK statutes, now too well established to call for citation of authority, that the words of a statute passed after the Treaty has been signed and dealing with the subject matter of the international obligation of the UK, are to be construed, if they are reasonably capable of bearing such a meaning, as intended to carry out the obligation, and not to be inconsistent with it. A fortiori is this the case where the Treaty obligation arises under one of the Community treaties to which s.2 ECA applies."[120]

In this important passage, Lord Diplock made clear the basis on which his construction approach rested. It was the ordinary common law presumption of statutory interpretation concerning treaty obligations, which applies with particular force where the treaty obligation is given domestic effect by s.2 ECA.

Although *Macarthys* was not cited by name, Lord Diplock seems to have had it in mind when he said that, had the attention of the Court of Appeal been drawn to Art. 119 and *Defrenne*, he had no doubt that they would have construed s.6(4) SDA so as not to make it inconsistent with Art. 119, consistently with statements made by Lord Denning "in previous cases".[121] Certainly, Lord Diplock's approach seems implicitly to reject the approach of the majority in that case in favour of the approach in the dissenting opinion of Lord Denning. Unlike Lawton and Cumming-Bruce LJJ., who maintained a strictly dualist dichotomy between the exercise of construing the UK statute and that of ascertaining what Community law requires, Lord Diplock's approach was to refer the questions of interpretation and direct applicability of Community law to the ECJ *before* attempting to construe the Act himself.[122] He expressly said that the whole point of making the reference was to provide the court with material to aid it in the construction of the domestic statute.[123] Moreover, this insistence on making a reference was in the face of the employee's extreme reluctance to raise a question of Community law at this stage if the result was that there would have to be a reference to the ECJ.[124] She asked the House of Lords to treat the case as an ordinary case of construction of an English Act, by hearing argument on the proper construction of s.6(4) SDA, arguing that it was a novel proposition to say that the House of Lords, before it answers a question of construction of an English Act, must send it to the ECJ for its views. The House of Lords' rejection of that argument, and insistence on making a reference despite the opposition of both parties, strongly suggests that in the view of the House of Lords a UK court must now, of its own motion, ascertain the UK's Community law obligations *before* embarking on the exercise of construction of the domestic statute.

---

[120] [1983] 2 AC 751 at 771A–C.

[121] Ibid. at 771F.

[122] See Lord Diplock's unease at the artificiality of the dualist approach of first construing domestic law in isolation in *Salomon* [1967] 2 QB 116 at 145B–D and *Post Office* v. *Estuary Radio* [1968] 2 QB 740 at 755B, considered in ch. 1.

[123] Ibid. at 772B.

[124] Ibid. at 753F–754D, 754G–H.

(c) The Two Versions Compared

Which of the construction approaches is to be preferred, Lord Diplock's or Lord Denning's? The latter's approach in *Macarthys* was welcomed by Allan as a "dexterous revolution".[125] This was not only because his judgment exposes the fallacy of the continuing sovereigntists' view that one Parliament cannot curtail the unlimited sovereignty of its successors. That would not be sufficient to distinguish Lord Denning from the self-embracing sovereigntists who had always questioned that aspect of the sovereignty doctrine, at least insofar as it purported to prohibit restrictions on the manner and form in which future legislation is passed. For Allan, the approach taken by Lord Denning has the much greater significance that it exposes the fallacy of the supposedly fundamental rule underlying *both* views of parliamentary sovereignty.[126] Both views shared the positivist assumption that at the foundation of the legal system lay a fundamental rule or ultimate principle, and the puzzle to be solved was what was the true nature of that rule: was Parliament's undoubted sovereignty continuing or self-embracing? In Allan's view, Lord Denning has short-circuited that debate by revealing that what is supposedly a fundamental rule is in fact indeterminate, because the sovereignty of Parliament is ultimately a matter of judicial interpretation.

Allan's crucial insight in his comment on *Macarthys* is that non-application, or even disapplication, of an Act of Parliament, is all of a piece with statutory interpretation; they are merely points along an interpretive spectrum. Since Parliament's "intention", if it can meaningfully exist at all, can never be historically discoverable, any recourse to such intention as a justification for the meaning given by courts to a statutory provision is necessarily a constructive intention, and in the construction of that intention the courts invoke common law principles of interpretation.[127] Such common law principles themselves secure a degree of entrenchment; how much depends on the strength accorded to them by the courts in the interpretive exercise. When a principle acquires such force that clear legislative language is required in order to defeat it, a degree of entrenchment has occurred. But there is nothing essentially different about this compared to *any* exercise in statutory interpretation. In Allan's words, "it is one and the same judicial process."[128]

Allan applauds Lord Denning in *Macarthys* for breaking out of the circularity in which the sovereignty theorists are ensnared, and in the process exemplifying this interpretive approach. Lord Denning certainly embraced a more expansive conception of statutory construction than was usual in

---

[125] Above n. 111.
[126] Ibid. at 29.
[127] See also C. Dike, "The Case Against Parliamentary Sovereignty" [1976] PL 283.
[128] Above n. 111 at 31. For a similar treatment of the supposed distinction between the "application" and "interpretation" of statutes, see *Law, Liberty and Justice* (above n. 117) at 266–7.

English law, a conception within which there was room for the non-application of inadvertently conflicting legislation. Lord Diplock in *Garland*, by comparison, appeared to have a more limited view of the legitimate limits of interpretation. He deliberately left open the question of whether directly effective Community law could ever be impliedly revoked, or whether only an express statement of Parliament's intention to legislate inconsistently with Community law would suffice to achieve that result. Again the importance of his words merits their citation in full:

> "The instant appeal does not present an appropriate occasion to consider whether, having regard to the express direction as to the construction of enactments "to be passed" which is contained in s.2(4), anything short of an express positive statement in an Act of Parliament passed after January 1 1973, that a particular provision is intended to be made in breach of an obligation assumed by the UK under a Community treaty, would justify an English court in construing that provision in a manner inconsistent with a Community treaty obligation of the UK, however wide a departure from the *prima facie* meaning of the language of the provision might be needed in order to achieve consistency."[129]

The question was said not to arise in *Garland* because the language of s.6(4) SDA was reasonably capable of bearing the meaning which was consistent with Art. 119. The words of the sub-section could bear the narrow meaning adopted by the EAT "without any undue straining of the ordinary meaning of the language used."[130]

Obviously no firm conclusion can be drawn from a dictum expressly leaving the question open. However, it does not seem unreasonable to infer from Lord Diplock's comments that he was not prepared to go as far as Lord Denning in *Macarthys*, who had held that only an express positive statement of Parliament's intention to legislate inconsistently with directly effective Community law would suffice to have that effect. The very way in which Lord Diplock stated the question he declined to answer, in terms of the extent of departure from the *prima facie* meaning of the statutory language which may be necessary to achieve consistency, together with his references to the notions of language being "unduly strained" and "reasonably capable" of bearing a meaning, suggest that, for him, achieving consistency with Community law may sometimes require a greater straining of statutory language than is within the bounds of legitimate judicial interpretation. Therefore, although he left the question open, it seemed implicit in his judgment that, unlike Lord Denning, he considered there to be a linguistic limit to achieving consistency through construction. That limit is reached when the statutory language cannot be made to bear the meaning necessary to reconcile it with Community law. In such a case, Parliament's intention to legislate inconsistently with Community law must be inferred and the directly effective Community law is impliedly repealed.

[129] [1983] 2 AC 751 at 771C–D.
[130] Ibid. at 771E.

Lord Denning's approach in *Macarthys* therefore achieved a greater degree of entrenchment for Community law than Lord Diplock's weaker construction approach in *Garland*. The difference, however, is one of degree rather than kind. Both are forms of entrenchment. Both focus on the interpretive role of judges in a way which is capable of transcending the inevitable conundrums which attend the traditional acceptance of the sovereignty of Parliament as the premise from which all else flows. The essential difference resides only in the degree to which each judge is prepared to recognise an evolution of judicial obligation away from the uncomplicated fealty traditionally owed to the UK Parliament.

Lord Diplock was prepared to interpret statutes flexibly and creatively in the light of Community law, so as to avoid inconsistencies wherever possible, but was not prepared to go beyond what he considered to be the legitimate bounds of interpretation. Although apparently closer to traditional ideas of sovereignty than Lord Denning, even this approach amounts to a significant modification. Implied repeal is theoretically preserved, but is likely to be a rare event as the court will strive to find an interpretation which avoids inconsistency arising. Lord Denning, on the other hand, was not only prepared to go further than Lord Diplock in attempting to arrive at an interpretation of a domestic statute which avoided conflict, but was prepared to give precedence to Community law in cases of irreconcilable conflict. Parliament was still sovereign, not only in the ultimate sense that it could repeal the ECA, but also, it would seem, in the slightly less ultimate sense that Parliament could still, in any given statute, express its intention to legislate inconsistently with Community law. For Lord Diplock, by comparison, Parliament did not need to express its intention so explicitly: it was enough if the language of the statute could not be given a meaning which was consistent with the relevant Community law without going beyond what for him were the more tightly drawn bounds of legitimate interpretation.

Although in this respect the difference between the two construction approaches was more one of degree than of kind, there was one important difference between the two, concerning their view of the foundation of the courts' jurisdiction in relation to Community law. The tendency amongst most commentators has been to treat the House of Lords decision in *Garland* as being based on s.2(4) ECA and as establishing that the sub-section is to be read as laying down a principle of construction to be used in cases of potential conflict between domestic legislation and Community law.[131] Hood Phillips, for example, claims that the House "founded their jurisdiction specifically on s.2(4) of the European Communities Act".[132] Not only is this

---

[131] See eg. Bradley & Ewing, *Constitutional and Administrative Law*, 11th edn. (London: Longman, 1993), at 147.

[132] Above n. 118 at 526. Hood Phillips criticised the Times Law Report of the case for having "missed this point" and for emphasising instead "an irrelevant reference . . . to a judge-made presumption of statutory interpretation in relation to treaties generally." As will be seen below, the Times law reporter had it right.

incorrect, because Lord Diplock only expressly mentioned s.2(4) in the *obiter dictum* considered above, but such an interpretation of the case fails to capture an important element of the reasoning. Lord Diplock considered the court's jurisdiction to be founded, not on s.2(4) ECA, but on a principle of construction of general application, namely the international treaties presumption, which was said to apply with even more force where the relevant international obligation was directly effective, as certain provisions of Community law are recognised to be by s.2(1) ECA. While it is true that Lord Diplock went on to refer, in the passage cited above, to s.2(4) as containing "an express direction" as to the construction of future enactments,[133] it is quite plain that he did not consider this section to be the basis of his jurisdiction to construe domestic law in the light of Community law. That jurisdiction was ultimately derived from the general common law principles of construction according to which meaning is to be given to statutory language in the light of relevant international obligations. The role of s.2 ECA was merely to make into an *a fortiori* case the construction of statutes in which Parliament had legislated in the same field as Community law.

This is to be contrasted with the approach of Lord Denning in *Macarthys*, which was more explicitly based on s.2(4) ECA and made no use of the general principle of statutory interpretation concerning treaty obligations. For Lord Denning, the duty of the court to give priority to Community law in cases of inadvertent conflict was "the result of s.2(1) and (4) of the ECA 1972".[134] When applying the ECJ's decision, he stressed that it was not a matter of Community law supplanting UK law. Rather, Community law was part of UK law by virtue of the ECA and was given priority by the ECA itself. It was therefore simply a familiar case of conflict between two parts of UK law and of a court having to decide which one takes priority.[135]

All this suggests that it is Lord Diplock rather than Lord Denning who is the ingenious exponent of the interpretive approach favoured by Allan. By explicitly and exclusively basing his approach on s. 2(4) ECA 1972, Lord Denning could be said to go little, if any, further than the self-embracing sovereigntists.[136] His reliance on a "statutory presumption" is premised on the notion of the courts as statutory delegates, authorised by nothing more than legislation (the ECA) to rank law from different sources in a particular way,

---

[133] (Above n. 118) 524 at 771C.

[134] [1979] 3 All ER 325 at 329c.

[135] [1981] QB 180 at 200E–F and 201B–C.

[136] As Allan points out, though, (above n. 111) at 26, the ECA does not itself expressly impose any manner and form requirement on future legislation, but the result of Lord Denning's interpretation is that in future Parliament must use express words to make clear its wish to legislate inconsistently with Community law. He could therefore be said to have gone further than a self-embracing sovereigntist would be prepared to go. See also Craig, "Sovereignty of the United Kingdom Parliament after *Factortame*" (1991) 11 YEL 221 at 251–2, who points out that to accept the supremacy of Community law is really to accept restrictions on the *area of power* of the UK Parliament, rather than on the mere manner and form in which legislation is passed, and is therefore as unacceptable to self-embracing theorists as it is to continuing theorists.

unless that instruction itself is expressly countermanded. Ultimately, as will be seen in chapter 3 below, this conception of what the courts are doing when they accord supremacy to directly effective Community law cannot account for the courts' changing attitude to the sovereignty of Parliament.

Lord Diplock's approach, on the other hand, being more rooted in the common law, in that it made use of the general common law principle of statutory interpretation concerning treaty obligations, is both more sophisticated and potentially more far-reaching in its implications. It is more sophisticated because it does not ultimately depend on the notion of courts as mere implementers of parliamentary will, but is more deeply rooted in a consistent philosophy of the nature of what judges do when they interpret statutes. And it is potentially more far-reaching because it is based on a common law presumption of general application rather than a particular statutory provision in the ECA, and is therefore not only unconstrained by the terms of the ECA, but is capable of application outside the context of Community law, for example in relation to human rights law. This crucial difference between the two approaches was only concealed by the fact that Lord Diplock was not prepared to go as far as Lord Denning at this particular stage in expanding the scope of legitimate interpretation. That greater reluctance was not surprising in view of Lord Diplock's starting point, articulated in anticipation of the UK joining the Community, which seemed close to an acceptance of the theory of continuing sovereignty, complete with its doctrine of implied repeal.[137] Nevertheless, the fact that in *Garland* he expressly left open the question whether only express words could rebut the presumptive principle of construction distinguishes him from the continuing sovereigntists, for it suggests that he considered the principle to be capable of judicial change and development over time.

(d) The Common Law Origins of the Construction Approach

This view, that there is an important difference between the foundation of the two versions of the construction approach, is supported by consideration of the origins of that approach. Responsibility for the emergence of the construction approach is usually attributed to Lord Denning in his dissenting judgment in *Macarthys*. In fact, when its origins are traced a little further back, it is found that when it first emerged, far from having a statutory foundation in the ECA, it was a common law response to a perceived lack of a such a foundation.

For some time following the entry into force of the ECA 1972, there prevailed in the industrial tribunals and the EAT a misapprehension as to the

---

[137] See his Lord Upjohn Lecture, "The Common Market and the Common Law" (1972) 6 Law Teacher 3, at 8. He spoke to the same effect in the House of Lords debate on the European Communities Bill, HL Deb, Vol. 333, col. 1029, (8 August 1972).

proper forum for the assertion of directly effective rights under Community law. This was the result of a decision of the EAT in *Amies v. Inner London Education Authority*, in which a female art teacher claimed that her employers had discriminated against her on grounds of sex, contrary to Article 119 EEC, by appointing a male art teacher to the post of department head.[138] The employee was forced to rely directly on Article 119 because the events of which she complained had taken place on a date before the Sex Discrimination Act 1975 had come into force. The appeal tribunal, dismissing the claim, held that even if Article 119 created such an enforceable general right not to be discriminated against on grounds of sex, neither the industrial tribunal nor the EAT had jurisdiction to rule on whether there had been an infringement of an "enforceable Community right" before the SDA came into force. As statutory tribunals, their jurisdiction was said to be limited to that which had been expressly conferred on them, and an individual who sought to rely directly on a Treaty Article should seek a declaration from the High Court, the successor to the inherent jurisdiction of the courts of common law and equity.

The error was soon corrected by Lord Denning in *Shields*, who held that Community law applies not only in the High Court but also in the industrial tribunal and in the EAT.[139] Nevertheless, it was under the influence of this jurisdictional misapprehension that the construction approach first saw the light of day. In *Snoxell v. Vauxhall Motors Ltd.*,[140] female machine part inspectors claimed equality of pay with male inspectors who had been "redcircled", that is, placed in a protected pay category. Phillips J., giving the decision of the EAT, accepted the view of Bristow J. in *Amies* that a claimant before an industrial tribunal could not seek to enforce directly an "enforceable Community right" such as that under Art. 119.[141] However, since the decision of the ECJ in *Defrenne v. Sabena*, Art. 119 had to be directly applied in the courts of member states. The correct approach for industrial tribunals and the EAT was said to be to give effect to the *Defrenne* case by construing and applying the EPA in conformity with Art. 119. By so construing and applying the domestic statute subject to, and so as to give effect to, the principle in Art. 119, it would be unnecessary for a claimant to make a separate claim in the High Court relying directly on the Treaty article.[142] But the Act was capable of a broad construction, and only by giving it such a construction was it possible to honour the obligation, resulting from *Defrenne*, to apply Art. 119 directly in the courts of member states. Adopting this approach

---

[138] [1977] ICR 308.

[139] [1978] 1 WLR 1408 at 1415D–F.

[140] [1978] QB 11.

[141] Ibid, at 26E–F.

[142] Ibid, at 27B–C. It is not suggested why the EAT considered statutory tribunals to be under any obligation to give effect to *Defrenne*. This can only have been by virtue of s.2(1) or 3(1) ECA, but the EAT did not consider these provisions to confer jurisdiction on them with regard to directly enforcing directly effective Community rights. The reason for the distinction is not clear.

of construing the EPA in the light of Art. 119, the EAT went on to hold that the relevant statutory provision had to be interpreted in such a way as to ensure that the principle of Art. 119 was observed in practice. So although the EAT did not consider s.2(1) or 3(1) of the ECA to confer jurisdiction on statutory tribunals to enforce directly effective Community rights, it did consider statutory tribunals to be under an obligation to give effect to *Defrenne*. The explanation for this, in the absence of statutory authority, can only have been the acceptance of a principle of construction similar to that articulated by Lord Diplock in *Garland*.

The same approach was in evidence in *Macarthys* itself in the EAT, where, it will be recalled, the question of statutory construction which arose was whether a claimant under the EPA 1970 can compare the work done by her with that done by an employee in the same employment but whose employment ceased before she took up her employment.[143] Phillips J. admitted that there was "not much doubt" about the "ordinary meaning of the language used"[144] and that the employers therefore had in their favour the literal words of some parts of the Act. But there was no doubt that strange results followed from that literal construction; for example, a woman would have no claim under the EPA in a situation where she replaced a male employee the day after his departure but was paid half as much as he had been. The question therefore, as Phillips J. saw it, was whether the tribunal was obliged to construe the Act according to the ordinary meaning of the language, however strange the results might be, or whether it would be justified in the circumstances of the case in construing the Act so as permit comparison with a previous employee.

The EAT concluded that it was permissible to construe the Act so as to allow a comparison of the situation of a woman with that of a former employee. A number of justifications were offered for why such an approach was permissible, but the most significant was that based on the direct effect of Article 119. The EAT, deriving some assistance from the approach taken by the EAT in *Snoxell* v. *Vauxhall*,[145] said that what has to be given effect to is the principle of Art. 119 that men and women should receive equal pay for equal work. An Act which permitted the strange results which followed from the literal construction "would not be a successful application of the principle."[146] However, the EAT acknowledged the limitations of its approach to construction, accepting that "what we cannot do is to construe [the Act] in such a way as in effect to introduce a new scheme for which it does not provide." It recognised the danger that its liberal construction might be seen as the judicial introduction of a new scheme based on the comparison of posts or jobs rather than of individuals, but that danger could be avoided.

---

[143] [1978] 1 WLR 849, at 851C.
[144] Ibid, at 851H.
[145] [1978] QB 11.
[146] At 853C.

So the construction approach was first conceived by a statutory tribunal which did not consider itself entitled to give direct effect to directly effective but non-implemented Community rights, and therefore considered that the only way to honour the international obligation to give effect to such rights was to interpret national law in the light of them. The significance of the adoption of this construction approach by the statutory tribunals, so long as they laboured under the *Amies* jurisdictional misapprehension, should not be under-estimated. The tribunals believed that they required express statutory authority in order to give direct effect to Community rights. They lacked that authority, yet they clearly considered that they were under an obligation to secure that result by construction if possible. The only possible justification for their taking such an approach was that they recognised a strong presumption that Parliament intends to legislate consistently with its treaty obligations. Moreover, that presumption was not triggered by ambiguity. In *Snoxell*, Phillips J. admitted that there was not "any particular ambiguity or obscurity in the EPA 1970." The meaning of the relevant provision, s.1(3), was said to be "clear enough." Similarly in *Macarthys* the EAT found there to be not much doubt about the ordinary meaning of the language used. These tribunals did not consider that statutory authority was necessary to justify adopting an approach to statutory interpretation which aimed to achieve consistency with the UK's international obligations.

7. CONCLUSION

This chapter has explored the main constitutional implications of Community membership for the UK, namely how, if at all, sovereignty theory can accommodate the requirements that Community law be given direct effect and accorded supremacy over national law. It was seen that the Government's response to the challenge this posed to traditional constitutional theory, in its *Implications* White Paper, was a model of constitutional conservatism, as it did its utmost to avoid political controversy by treating Community law as if it were any other source of international law which could be incorporated into domestic law by ordinary statute and as easily removed. If the White Paper were to be believed, membership of the Community was entirely compatible with the continuing theory of the sovereignty of Parliament.

The legislative response, in the European Communities Act 1972, was more imaginative, and seemed more clearly to contemplate the possibility of a gradual evolution in the doctrine of parliamentary sovereignty consequent on membership of the Community. Some of the Government's ministers were clearly prepared to countenance at the very least a version of self-embracing sovereignty as the minimum constitutional modification necessary so long as the UK remained a member of the Community. However, it would be impossible to say that this was in any meaningful sense the "intention" of the 1972

Parliament when enacting the relevant provisions of the ECA, as the most cursory glance at the parliamentary debates reveals. As Wade has observed, commenting on the parliamentary reaction to subsequent Community law developments, "in 1972 the root problem of sovereignty was never quite cleanly disposed of."[147] Members of Parliament who were concerned that the Act foreshadowed the end of Parliament's sovereignty were bought off with ministerial assurances that Parliament remained sovereign, that it was theoretically incapable of binding its successors; in short, that the doctrine of continuing sovereignty was alive and well.

Despite the innovative form of the legislation, the judicial response was, at least during the early years following accession, as constitutionally unimaginative as the White Paper. The sovereignty-derived concept of incorporation was preferred as the explanation for how directly effective Community law had come to have the force of law in the UK, by virtue of s. 2 of the ECA 1972 and, as de Smith had correctly predicted, judicial recognition of Parliament having subordinated itself to a superior law-maker was not at all readily forthcoming.[148] From the late 1970s, however, a growing number of individual judges were prepared to abandon the theory of continuing sovereignty and hold that inadvertently inconsistent domestic law had to give way to Community law, relying on s. 2(4) ECA as mandating such a consequence. But no sooner had the self-embracing theorists appeared to gain the ascendancy, than the construction approach emerged as an alternative means of according supremacy to Community law, through a more flexible approach to the interpretation of domestic statutes. The advantage of the construction approach was that, ostensibly at least, it was more consistent with traditional notions of the judicial function, in that, by making inconsistency unlikely, it avoided the necessity for courts to set aside or disapply an Act of Parliament in the event that it was found to be inconsistent with Community law. Rather, it enabled courts to rescue such Acts by giving them, if possible, a creative interpretation which eliminated the conflict.

Of the two versions of the construction approach on offer, Lord Denning's was, on the face of it, the least consistent with the traditional theory of continuing sovereignty, since it extended, in cases of irreconcilable conflict, to the disapplication of the later inconsistent statute. Lord Diplock, by comparison, was not prepared to accept quite the same degree of interpretive flexibility, and probably would still have accorded precedence to a domestic statute where it could not be interpreted consistently with Community law without distorting its meaning. Paradoxically, however, it is Lord Diplock's approach which provides a foundation for the constitutional accommodation of Community law which has the potential to transcend the old debate about Parliament binding its successors. While Lord Denning relied exclusively on

---

[147] H.W.R. Wade, "What has Happened to the Sovereignty of Parliament?" (1991) 107 LQR 1 at 3.

[148] Above n. 5 at 613.

the ECA as the justification for according priority to Community law, and so appeared to locate himself firmly within the sovereignty tradition, Lord Diplock treated the statute as merely confirming a pre-existing common law principle of construction.[149] Like Solicitor-General Howe in his contributions to the debate on the European Communities Bill,[150] and de Smith in his appraisal of the constitutional impact of Community membership,[151] Lord Diplock regarded the sovereignty of Parliament as having a common law foundation, and therefore as being capable of evolution over time. As will be seen in chapter 3, it is only through such a theory of evolutionary constitutional change, rather than any cruder version of sovereignty theory, that the subsequent developments in the domestic status of Community law can be plausibly explained.

---

[149] In fact the best account of the constitutional evolution taking place probably lies somewhere between the two approaches, because the statute no doubt played some role in the evolution of the judicial view of the strength of the treaty obligation. As Bradley observes, (above n. 4) at 107, fundamental changes in the relationship between courts and Parliament are "unlikely to come about except when Parliament itself gives a definite lead by means of legislation, which the courts accept as being effective to achieve its stated purposes." To acknowledge the role played by statute in this way does not mean to say, however, that European Community law owes its effect and supremacy exclusively to the ECA 1972.

[150] Above n. 64.

[151] Above n. 5 at 612–14.

3

The Inadequacy of Traditional
Sovereignty Theory Exposed

1. INTRODUCTION

In chapter 2, the challenges posed to traditional sovereignty theory by the
UK's membership of the European Community were explained, and the early
judicial responses to those challenges described. It was seen that, for many
years after accession, courts tended to downplay the constitutional impact of
Community law by asserting that it could be easily accommodated within the
UK's constitutional tradition, and in particular with little, if any, modification
of the central plank of that tradition, the sovereignty of the UK Parliament.
The purpose of the present chapter is to demonstrate how, as the European
Communities Act 1972 has receded into history and the ECJ has made new
demands of national courts, so the inadequacy of traditional sovereignty
theory to account for the domestic status now accorded to Community law
has been exposed.

Although the important constitutional developments traced in this chapter
have taken place in the context of European Community law, they are of
much wider significance for this book's principal concern, the more general
question of the domestic status of international human rights norms. The
eventual unequivocal acceptance by English courts of the supremacy of
Community law over statute in a case of irreconcilable conflict, for example,
has falsified the traditional view that no court could ever hold legislation to
be invalid. More significantly, as far as international human rights law is concerned, the experience of UK courts in giving effect to the interpretive obligation stipulated by the European Court of Justice in relation to non-directly
effective Community law has demonstrated the possibility of a mid-way position between making unincorporated law directly effective and giving it some
indirect effect by interpreting domestic law in the light of it. It has shown that
English courts can, both in fact and theory, accommodate the notion of a
strong interpretive obligation to construe domestic law consistently with unincorporated law from an external source, at the same time as preserving a commitment, albeit attenuated, to the *ultimate* sovereignty of the domestic
Parliament.

The Community law concept of indirect effect through such an interpretive
obligation, it will be argued, has great potential if deployed judicially in the

protection of human rights. As this chapter seeks to demonstrate, for English courts to recognise such an obligation would be at least as legitimate as giving indirect effect to non-directly effective Community law, once it is openly acknowledged that the justification for so doing is no longer to be found, if ever it was, in the European Communities Act 1972, nor in any version of sovereignty theory, but has its basis in the gradual judicial acceptance of the growing normativity of Community law as the political and legal integration of Europe proceeds.

2. THE LIMITS OF A SOVEREIGNTY-BASED CONSTRUCTION APPROACH

The attraction of the so-called "construction approach" was that it offered a means of according supremacy to directly effective Community law which appeared to be reconcilable with Parliamentary sovereignty. If a statute could be interpreted consistently with the relevant directly effective Community law provision, it avoided the necessity for courts to set aside national legislation and, if only superficially, preserved the courts' loyalty to expressions of parliamentary intent. A more flexible and creative approach to the interpretation of statutes seemed a modest modification of the traditional constitutional function of the courts compared to a re-assertion of the power to strike down legislation, a power to which they had not laid claim since the days of Coke. The reconciliation with sovereignty was all the greater where the basis for the construction approach was said to be the "rule of construction" contained in s. 2(4) ECA 1972. On this version of the construction approach, the recognition of the supremacy of Community law was achieved by means of an approach to statutory construction based ultimately on the assumption of parliamentary sovereignty, rather than by any acceptance by courts of a more "constitutional" role when deciding on the meaning of statutory language.

The price of such an accommodation with sovereignty, however, was continuing uncertainty as to what a UK court was to do when the limits of statutory interpretation within such a sovereignty framework were reached, as inevitably they would be. The limits of a construction approach reconcilable with sovereignty were reached when a conflict arose between directly effective Community law and a statutory provision which was incapable of resolution by sovereignty-derived construction, because the statutory words could not possibly bear the meaning necessary to achieve consistency. In such circumstances, the only way to respect the supremacy of Community law was to give no effect to the English statute, or even, if necessary, "disapply" it, neither of which can be reconciled with the theory of continuing sovereignty. While Lord Denning had shown that he was prepared to go that far in *Macarthys*, subject to an express assertion of Parliament's will to the contrary, Lord Diplock's ostensibly more cautious version of the construction approach in *Garland* seemed to suggest that in such a case of irreconcilable conflict courts would give effect to the latest expression of Parliament's will, and treat the later statute as having impliedly repealed the earlier inconsistent Community law, contrary to the Community law doctrine of supremacy.[1]

Surprisingly, it was several years after *Macarthys* and *Garland* before English courts were confronted with a situation which made it impossible to finesse the question of the supremacy of Community law by treating it as a mere matter of statutory "construction" which could be fitted within a traditional sovereignty framework. When, finally, such a case presented itself in the well known *Factortame* litigation, English courts, eventually, did not shrink from accepting that the earlier inconsistent Community law takes priority, thereby unequivocally abandoning in this context the doctrine of implied repeal derived from the traditional notion of continuing sovereignty.[2] Unfortunately, as will be seen, the courts missed the opportunity to ground this important constitutional development in the common law foundation suggested by Lord Diplock in *Garland*, preferring instead to minimise the modification of Parliamentary sovereignty by claiming, like Lord Denning in *Macarthys*, that it was Parliament itself that required such acceptance of supremacy, in the ECA 1972. By so doing, they ensured that English courts remain, for the time being at least, locked in the logical conundrums of sovereignty theory, even while recognising the supremacy of Community law over a later Act of Parliament.

The supremacy question arose in a much more focused way in *Factortame* than in the earlier cases concerning the equality legislation. In both *Macarthys* and *Garland* the question was essentially whether the domestic statute had defined the circumstances in which an individual has a remedy against another private party sufficiently widely to give full effect to the directly effective Community law right in Art. 119. In *Factortame*, by comparison, the allegation was that the impugned legislation directly deprived the applicants of their enforceable Community rights. Part II of the Merchant Shipping Act 1988, and the regulations made thereunder,[3] introduced a new regime for the registration of British fishing vessels in an attempt to protect the British fishing quota, under the EC common fisheries policy, from the practice of "quota-hopping". Under the previous regime, governed by the Merchant Shipping Act 1894, it was possible for a ship to be registered as British, even though its ownership was vested in people or companies abroad. The 1988 Act

---

[1] As was argued in the last chapter, Lord Diplock's clear awareness of the possibility of judicial obligation changing over time showed that he was not a continuing sovereigntist. Rather, his implicit acceptance in *Garland* that Community law could still be impliedly repealed by an irreconcilably inconsistent statute reflected a judgment that by 1980 the conditions for a further evolution in judicial obligation did not yet exist. For the continuing sovereigntist, by contrast, Parliament is sovereign for all time, or until some legal "revolution" brings about a discontinuity in the sovereign to which judicial allegiance is owed.

[2] *R v. Secretary of State for Transport, ex p. Factortame* [1990] 2 AC 85 and *R v. Secretary of State for Transport, ex p. Factortame (No. 2)* [1991] 1 AC 603.

[3] Merchant Shipping (Registration of Fishing Vessels) Regulations 1988 (SI 1988 No. 1926).

established new criteria for registration as a British vessel. In future, only vessels owned by British citizens domiciled and resident in the UK or by companies 75% of whose shareholders and directors were British citizens domiciled and resident in the UK, could be registered as British.

The owners of fishing vessels previously registered as British under the old regime, but effectively disqualified from registration under the new criteria, applied for judicial review of the legality of both the Act and the regulations on the ground that they contravened Community law by depriving them of their directly effective rights under the EC Treaty.[4] The applicants' substantive claim therefore raised directly the question of what an English court would do when confronted with an irreconcilable conflict between directly effective Community law and a subsequent national statute incapable of being rescued by the construction approach. This unavoidable challenge to traditional sovereignty theory was even more focused due to one other important feature of the case. Because they stood to suffer considerable financial loss in the meantime, the applicant companies also sought interim relief, in the form of an interim injunction to restrain the Secretary of State from enforcing the provisions of the statute and regulations, and an order "disapplying" those provisions in so far as they affected the applicants. Here, then, was a case bound to test the degree of UK courts' acceptance of the supremacy of Community law.

One of the most remarkable features of the *Factortame* litigation is the contrast between, on the one hand, the readiness of all the courts who considered the case to recognise that directly effective Community law must prevail over inconsistent subsequent legislation and, on the other, the extreme reluctance of all save the Divisional Court to accept, as the logical implication of such recognition, that courts must be prepared to grant interim relief by disapplying an Act of Parliament. The fact that the supremacy of Community law over subsequent inconsistent statutes was taken for granted throughout the progress of the case through the courts was probably due to the apparent concession on behalf of the Secretary of State in the Divisional Court that, if the ECJ gave a ruling favourable to the applicants as to the extent of their directly effective Community law rights, the English courts would have to give those rights priority over any provisions of the 1988 Act which might be inconsistent with them. It is clear that the Divisional Court was proceeding on this basis when it decided to make an Art. 177 reference to the ECJ, requesting a preliminary ruling on the substantive questions of the extent of the Community rights claimed by the applicants and the compatibility of the 1988 Act with those rights.[5] The Court of Appeal was in no doubt that this was

---

[4] The Treaty rights relied on were the right to establish themselves in business anywhere in the Community (Arts. 52 and 58), the right to participate in the capital of the applicant companies (Art. 221) and the right to freedom from discrimination on grounds of nationality (Art. 7).

[5] Neill LJ, [1989] 2 CMLR 353 at 373–4.

the law.[6] Similarly, Lord Bridge in the House of Lords observed that it was "common ground" that, in so far as the applicants succeeded in establishing their rights in the ECJ, those rights would prevail over the restrictions imposed by the Act and the Divisional Court would be obliged to make appropriate declarations to give effect to those rights.[7] There was, in other words, unequivocal recognition that directly effective Community law prevails over subsequent national legislation.

All this might be thought to be uncontroversial in light of the position already taken by the Court of Appeal in *Macarthys*. There, it will be recalled, although Lord Denning had originally preferred to accord supremacy to the relevant Community provision by means of his construction approach, when the case came back from the ECJ he joined the majority in making clear that, in cases of irreconcilable conflict between the domestic statute and Community law, the courts are bound to accord priority to the directly effective Community law.[8] In this respect, it might be thought, *Factortame* does little more than make clear that Lord Denning's more far-reaching approach in *Macarthys* is to be preferred to Lord Diplock's more limited approach in *Garland*. However, what does, on the face of it, appear to be new about *Factortame* is the step which the Divisional Court was fearless, and the House of Lords eventually compelled, to take: granting interim relief to restrain an Act of Parliament from taking effect.

The Divisional Court held that it had jurisdiction to grant such interim relief, and ordered that the Act be disapplied and the Secretary of State be restrained from enforcing it in respect of any of the applicants. The Court of Appeal, however, allowed the Secretary of State's appeal against the order for interim relief on the ground that, under the British constitution, a court had no jurisdiction to grant such an interim order disapplying a statute. Bingham LJ described it as a "constitutional enormity" to require the Secretary of State to act contrary to the clearly expressed will of Parliament when the unlawfulness of that expression has yet to be established.[9] The House of Lords also held that English courts had no jurisdiction, as a matter of English law, to grant interim relief in terms that effectively set aside an English statute before the ECJ had ruled that the statute infringed Community law. They claimed to be prevented from doing so by two rules of national law. First, there was said to be a presumption of validity, which meant that an Act of Parliament was to be assumed to be compatible with Community law unless and until it

---

[6] Bingham LJ, [1989] 2 CMLR 353 at 403–4.

[7] [1990] 2 AC 85 at 140C–D.

[8] Nevertheless in the light of the narrower approach subsequently taken by Lord Diplock in *Garland*, and the UK Government's usual determination not to surrender an inch of sovereignty without a fight, it does seem surprising that the Crown was prepared to concede the impossibility of implied repeal.

[9] [1989] 2 CMLR 353 at 407. See to similar effect Lord Donaldson MR at 397 ("any attempt to interfere with primary legislation would be wholly unconstitutional") and Mann LJ at 408 ("this court is obliged to defer to the Sovereignty of the Queen in Parliament").

was established to be incompatible. Second, the courts were said to lack jurisdiction to grant an interim injunction against the Crown in judicial review
proceedings.[10] Nevertheless, the House of Lords was prepared to accept that
Community law, as opposed to national law, might empower or require the
courts to grant interim relief to protect putative Community rights and
referred this question to the ECJ. The ECJ's ruling on the reference was that
if, in a case concerning Community law, the sole obstacle which precluded a
national court from granting interim relief is a rule of national law, it must
set aside that rule.[11] The House of Lords, now accepting that it had jurisdiction to grant such interim relief, albeit under Community law rather than
national law, held that this was an appropriate case in which to exercise that
discretion and granted the interim relief sought.[12]

Why was the House of Lords initially so reluctant to grant the interim relief
sought, given their apparent acceptance of the supremacy of directly effective
Community law over later inconsistent legislation? Surely, as Lord Bridge
himself eventually acknowledged in *Factortame No. 2*, the granting of interim
relief by national courts was "no more than a logical recognition of that
supremacy"?[13] The explanation for why this logic was not apparent to Lord
Bridge the first time around is to be found in the fundamental premise from
which he derives his view of Community law's supremacy. For Lord Bridge
in *Factortame*, as for Lord Denning in *Macarthys*, Community law derives its
force from the ECA 1972, and owes its supremacy solely to Parliament's own
intention expressed in s. 2(4) ECA. As he made clear in *Factortame No. 1*, in
his view, directly effective Community law rights prevail over a subsequent
inconsistent Act of Parliament because the effect of that sub-section is to write
into each Act of Parliament passed after the 1972 Act an implied provision
that the Act shall take effect subject to directly effective Community law. So
in this case s. 2(4)

". . . has precisely the same effect as if a section were incorporated in Pt. II of the
1988 Act which in terms enacted that the provisions with respect to registration of
British fishing vessels were to be without prejudice to the Community rights of
nationals of any Member State of the EEC."[14]

Ultimately then, even Lord Bridge's approach to giving supremacy to
Community law in *Factortame* comes down to a construction approach, and
has its foundation in the sovereignty of Parliament.

---

[10] On these aspects of the House of Lords decision, see N.J. Hanna, "Community Rights All
at Sea" (1990) 106 LQR 2.

[11] Case C-213/89, [1991] 1 AC 603.

[12] *R v. Secretary of State for Transport, ex p. Factortame Ltd. (No. 2)*, ibid.

[13] Ibid. at 659C.

[14] [1990] 2 AC 85 at 140C. Compare the technical drafting suggestions made by sovereigntists
at the time of accession, to insert into every subsequent Act of Parliament some formula stating
that it conforms with Community law. See eg. H. W. R. Wade "Sovereignty and the European
Communities" (1972) 88 LQR 1 at 4.

Given his sovereignty premise, it is hardly surprising that Lord Bridge did not initially see the logic that leads from the recognition of Community law's supremacy to the granting of interim relief disapplying an Act of Parliament. The sovereignty premise pulls in precisely the opposite direction, as was evident in Lord Bridge's reasoning when refusing to grant the interim relief in *Factortame No. 1*. Although the presumption of validity and the unavailability of injunctive relief against the Crown were the ostensible reasons for refusing to grant interim relief, it was clear that underlying the reluctance of Lord Bridge to disapply the statute was a strong sense that to do so was constitutionally inappropriate in the light of the sovereignty of Parliament which the courts still professed to respect. He was concerned, for example, that Parliament's will in the 1988 Act would have been subverted in the event that interim relief was granted and the applicants failed in the ECJ to make out their claim that they had been deprived of enforceable Community rights.[15] The effect of making such an order might be to confer on the applicants rights "directly contrary to Parliament's sovereign will" and by the same token to deprive British fishing vessels "as defined by Parliament" of their share of the UK quota.

Even when the case came back from the ECJ, with the logic of the required approach now revealed, the House of Lords persisted in its strictly dualist approach to the effect and supremacy of Community law. Not only did it clearly proceed on the basis that the jurisdiction of English courts to grant interim relief against the Crown existed only as a matter of Community law not national law, but Lord Bridge reiterated his view that the source of the courts' duty to accord supremacy to Community law was the ECA 1972.[16] This time he went further than explaining the mechanism by which sections 2(1) and 2(4) ECA achieved that result, and sought to justify his interpretation of the effect of those provisions by reference to Parliament's state of knowledge when it enacted them. Parliament was said to have been well aware in 1972 that Community law took priority over the national law of member states and, therefore, whatever limitation of its sovereignty Parliament had accepted when it passed the ECA was entirely voluntary. According to Lord Bridge, under the terms of that Act it had always been clear that it was the duty of a UK court to override any rule of national law found to be in conflict with any directly enforceable rule of Community law.[17] There was therefore nothing novel in according supremacy to Community law, nor in granting interim relief to protect putative Community law rights.

These observations by Lord Bridge were made in response to public comments which had suggested that the Court of Justice's ruling was "a novel and dangerous invasion by a Community institution of the sovereignty of the UK

---

[15] [1990] 2 AC 85 at 143.

[16] [1991] 1 AC 603 at 659A–B.

[17] This was a somewhat surprising assertion in view of the debate which had raged over the effect of s. 2 ECA 1972 since its enactment: see ch. 2 above.

Parliament."[18] The constitutionally unprecedented step of a judicial order dis-applying an Act of Parliament had captured the public and political imagination in a way which the Court of Appeal's less dramatic non-application of legislation in *Macarthys v Smith* over a decade earlier had failed to do. The Attorney General was asked to make a statement to the House of Commons on the "juridical implications" of the ruling of the ECJ.[19] Such was the level of public criticism that Lord Bridge felt compelled to answer what he considered to be the "misconception" on which such comments were based. The great irony in his response was that, in his attempt to rebut the misconception, he exemplified the very judicial attitude which helps sustain it. There can be little wonder that public misconceptions arise when courts not only continue to profess the sovereignty of Parliament whilst demonstrably limiting it, but justify those limitations by invoking the sovereignty of Parliament itself.

Did Lord Bridge have any alternative way of justifying the House of Lords decision in *Factortame No. 2*, or are English judges forever condemned to these logical conundrums by the doctrine of parliamentary sovereignty? Wade has sought to explain the development in *Factortame* in terms of the continuing theory of sovereignty: what has happened is a "constitutional and legal revolution", a redefinition of the sovereign by removing the old unqualified sovereignty of Parliament, whose Acts are now second-tier legislation, subject to a higher law.[20] In other words, there has been a shift in the rule of recognition, brought about by an essentially political choice on the part of the judges. However, as Craig points out, Lord Bridge's reasoning in *Factortame No. 2* does not fit well with the traditional theory of continuing sovereignty.[21] That reasoning is said to be more an example of the self-embracing view, according to which the 1972 Parliament bound its successors. Such an explanation, Craig explains, is more attractive to the judiciary, since it attributes responsibility for the shift to Parliament rather than the courts, and so avoids the courts being seen to make what, according to the continuing theory, is a "political choice", at the boundary of the legal system.

There is, however, an alternative way of seeing the *Factortame* decision, which relies on neither version of traditional sovereignty theory. The decision can be seen as a demonstration of the evolutionary process by which law from a source other than Parliament is received into the domestic legal system, by the gradual judicial strengthening of the common law principle of construction as the relevant international obligations assume greater normative significance. This evolutionary theory of constitutional change is certainly of much greater explanatory power than the theory of continuing sovereignty.

---

[18] [1991] 1 AC 603 at 658G–H.

[19] HC Deb., Vol. 175, WA141–3 (26 June 1990).

[20] H.W.R. Wade, "What Has Happened to the Sovereignty of Parliament?" (1991) 107 LQR 1 at 2.

[21] Craig, "Sovereignty of the United Kingdom Parliament after *Factortame*" (1991) 11 YEL 221 at 252.

The lack of descriptive power of that theory is self-evident in Wade's own criticism of the House of Lords for not making more explicit the nature of the fundamental change which in his view their decision in *Factortame* brings about. He complains that not a word was said about the "constitutional revolution" being silently brought about, and of "how smoothly the courts may discard fundamental doctrine without appearing to notice."[22] These criticisms only serve to expose the lack of descriptive power of the theory of continuing sovereignty today. The reason nothing was said about constitutional revolutions or discarding fundamental doctrine in *Factortame* is that the development was the culmination of a much more gradual evolution than Wade's theory can accommodate.

On this view, Lord Bridge's approach in *Factortame No. 2* can be seen as being rooted in the common law, much as Lord Diplock's had been in *Garland*. Although Lord Diplock had not in 1981 felt able to recognise anything stronger than a common law presumption rebuttable by evidence of contrary intention, there is nothing inherent in his common law approach to confine the courts to such a weak presumption. Indeed, it is arguable that by 1990, when *Factortame* was decided, European political and legal integration had accelerated sufficiently to warrant a court taking the view that what the common law now recognised as being required by the supremacy of Community law was considerably stronger than it had been for Lord Diplock ten years earlier.[23]

3. NON-DIRECTLY EFFECTIVE EC LAW AND THE INTERPRETIVE OBLIGATION

So far this book's consideration of the constitutional implications of Community membership has confined itself to the constitutional accommodation in the UK of the Community law principles of the direct effect and supremacy of those Community measures which are directly effective. It has been seen that, by and large, courts have sought to minimise the impact of that accommodation on the doctrine of Parliamentary sovereignty, by maintaining that Community law derives both its direct effect and its supremacy from the ECA 1972, an explanation which increasingly strains credibility. How UK courts would deal with the effect of provisions of Community law which were not directly effective, however, was quite another matter. Whether such non-directly effective provisions were within the scope of s. 2(1) ECA 1972, and could therefore derive some domestic legal status from that

---

[22] Above n. 20, at 4.

[23] For evidence of further stages being reached, since *Factortame*, in the domestic evolution of the obligation to give supremacy to Community law, see *R* v. *Secretary of State for Employment, ex p. Equal Opportunities Commission* [1995] 1 AC 1 and *R* v. *Secretary of State for Employment, ex p. Seymour-Smith* [1995] IRLR 464, in both of which provisions in primary legislation were declared to be incompatible with Community law without a reference to the ECJ having first been made.

source, was an open question, as was whether Lord Diplock's general principle of construction in *Garland* was sufficiently broad to require courts to interpret domestic law so as to be consistent with non-directly effective Community law.

The question became unavoidable for UK courts, however, when the ECJ, in order to enhance the effectiveness of directives in the face of their non-implementation or misimplementation by member states, developed an "interpretive obligation" requiring national courts to interpret national law consistently with non-directly effective directives. This has led to the emergence of a new Community law principle, widely referred to in the literature as the principle of "indirect effect", whereby Community law which is not directly effective must be taken into account by national courts when interpreting national law. The implications of that interpretive obligation for UK courts, and in particular for the constitutional accommodation between domestic and Community law in the UK, are clearly considerable, especially in view of the fact that, unlike the Community law principles of direct effect and supremacy, it could not have been in the contemplation of the legislature when it enacted the ECA in 1972.[24]

The interpretive obligation was first articulated by the ECJ in *Von Colson*.[25] There the Court held that, when applying national law, and in particular the provisions of a national law specifically introduced in order to implement a directive, national courts are required to interpret that law in the light of the wording and the purpose of the relevant directive.[26] The Court founded this obligation on the status of national courts as national authorities of the member state, in which capacity they bore responsibility for the fulfilment of Community obligations. In particular, the obligation under Art. 189 on a Member State arising from a directive, to achieve the result envisaged by that directive, and their duty under Art. 5 of the Treaty to take all appropriate measures to ensure the fulfilment of that obligation, were said to be "binding on all the authorities of Member States including, for matters within their jurisdiction, the courts."[27]

Although the basis of the interpretive obligation was made clear in *Von Colson*, both the scope of its application, and the strength of it when it applied, remained uncertain. In particular, as far as the scope of its application was concerned, the judgment of the Court was ambiguous as to whether

---

[24] For accounts of the principle of indirect effect from the perspective of Community law, see eg. Craig & de Búrca, *EC Law: Text, Cases and Materials* (Oxford: Clarendon Press, 1995) at 189–97; Hartley, *The Foundations of European Community Law*, 3rd edn., (Oxford: Clarendon Press, 1993) at 222–5; Weatherill & Beaumont, *EC Law: The Essential Guide to the Legal Workings of the European Community* 2nd edn.(London: Penguin Books, 1995) at 355–8. For consideration of the interpretive obligation generally, and in particular its implications for UK courts, see de Búrca, "Giving Effect to European Community Directives" (1992) 55 MLR 215.

[25] Case 14/83, *Von Colson and Kamann* v. *Land Nordrhein-Westfalen* [1984] ECR 1891.

[26] Ibid. at para. 26. Whether the duty so expressed applied to *any* national law, or was confined to implementing legislation, is returned to below.

[27] Ibid.

it applied to the interpretation of all national law, or only legislation specifically enacted to give effect to a directive. The case itself concerned the adequacy of the remedies provided by a German law designed to implement the Equal Treatment Directive, but in one passage of its judgment the Court did not seem to confine the scope of the interpretive obligation to implementing measures, referring to national law generally, and in particular national law specifically introduced in order to implement a directive.[28] In this part of the judgment, the obligation to construe implementing legislation in the light of the relevant directive appeared to be seen by the Court as merely an *a fortiori* case of a more general obligation rooted in the need to ensure that the purposes of Community measures are achieved. However, in a later passage the Court appeared to confine the obligation to implementing legislation.[29] Inevitably, the result of this ambiguity at the heart of the *Von Colson* judgment gave rise to two competing views as to the scope of the interpretive obligation, one wide, the other narrow. According to the wide view, it was clear from the nature of the reasoning deployed in *Von Colson* that the duty on national courts was a general one which applied whenever they applied national law in an area covered by a directive.[30] On the narrower view, the obligation was confined to implementing legislation, or at the very least did not require national courts to construe a pre-existing statute in order to comply with a subsequent non-directly effective directive.[31]

As for the strength of the interpretive obligation, whether it applied to all national law or only implementing legislation, it was not clear from the judgment in *Von Colson* how far national courts were required to go in order to comply with the duty. Would, for example, the national courts of a member state with a dualist tradition be permitted to continue applying an ambiguity requirement before reference could be made to sources outside the statute as an aid to its interpretation? Similarly, how far would a national court be required to go in departing from the ordinary meaning of domestic law in order to read it so as to be in conformity with non-directly effective directives? The question essentially was whether some modification of national interpretive techniques would be required in order to comply with the obligation. The decision in *Von Colson* itself appeared to allow for such national differences in interpretive techniques, in a passage apparently qualifying the obligation to interpret and apply national law in conformity with Community law by adding "in so far as it is given discretion to do so under national law".[32] However, this qualification offered little in the way of guidance to

---

[28] Ibid. The Advocate General, on the other hand, did confine her formulation of the obligation to national measures intended to implement a directive: ibid. at 1915–16.

[29] Ibid. at para. 28.

[30] See eg. A. Arnull, "The *Duke* Case: An Unreliable Precedent" [1988] PL 313 at 316–17.

[31] See eg. E. Szyszczak, "Sovereignty: Crisis, Compliance, Confusion, Complacency?" (1990) 15 ELR 480 at 484–5; Advocate General Slynn in Case 152/84, *Marshall* v. *Southampton and South West Hampshire Area Health Authority (Teaching)* [1986] ECR 723; [1986] QB 401 at 411.

[32] [1984] ECR 1891 at para. 28.

national courts and in any event it soon disappeared from the Court's formulations of the obligation.[33]

These uncertainties about the scope and strength of the *Von Colson* obligation were a matter of particular importance in the UK where, it will be
recalled, the tradition of parliamentary sovereignty was responsible for a very
narrow, positivist conception of statutory interpretation as a quest for the historical intention of Parliament at the time it enacted the particular measure in
question. Moreover, the connected tradition of dualism had led to an equally
narrow approach to the relevance of instruments emanating from non-
domestic or "international" sources unless it was first established that there
was ambiguity or uncertainty in the statute itself which could only be resolved
by recourse to such outside sources. Indeed, the decision of the majority of
the Court of Appeal in *Macarthys*, that even directly effective Community law
would only be taken into account in construing domestic legislation in cases
of ambiguity or doubt, had been a salutary reminder of the continued vitality
of this tradition notwithstanding the UK's membership of the Community. A
strong requirement to interpret non-implementing national law, the "natural"
meaning of which was otherwise clear, so as to conform with a later, unim-
plemented, non-directly effective directive would undoubtedly require
modification of traditional methods of statutory interpretation if UK courts
were to comply.

In any event, the development by the ECJ of such an interpretive obligation
on national courts in relation to non-directly effective Community law was
bound to cause difficulties for UK courts, whatever its scope or strength. By
the date of the *Von Colson* judgment, UK courts had only recently begun to
use such interpretive techniques as the guise under which to accord supremacy to directly effective Community law. The prospect of their ready co-
operation in being enlisted by the ECJ to do the same in relation to non-
directly effective Community law therefore seemed remote. A frosty UK reception for this latest constitutional development in the jurisprudence of the ECJ
was made all the more likely by the tendency, seen above, to base that construction approach on nothing more than the terms of sections 2(1) and 2(4)
of the ECA 1972. If UK courts were to be consistent in their view that
Community law owed its effect in the UK entirely to the ECA, they would
have to justify their acceptance of the *Von Colson* obligation either by interpreting sections 2(1) and 2(4) as applying to non-directly effective as well as
directly effective Community law, or by relying on the instruction to courts
in s. 3 of the ECA to treat any question as to the effect of any Community
instrument as a question of law to be determined in accordance with the principles laid down by and any relevant decision of the European Court.
However, as will be seen below, the language and structure of s.2 make it
inapt to cover non-directly effective Community law. And as for s.3, this has

---

[33] See eg. Case 222/84 *Johnston* v. *Chief Constable of the RUC* [1986] ECR 1651 at 1690.

only rarely been relied on by UK courts as the sole justification for their acceptance of the ECJ's principles of direct effect and supremacy, and there was
nothing qualitatively different about the emerging interpretive obligation. It
therefore seemed unlikely that the ECA would provide the basis for the acceptance by UK courts of the new Community principle of indirect effect.

4. RESISTANCE TO THE OBLIGATION BY UK COURTS

The anticipated reluctance of UK courts to follow the *Von Colson* interpretive obligation materialised in the decision of the House of Lords in *Duke*.[34]
The case concerned the construction of the same statutory provision as that
in issue in *Garland*, namely the exception in s. 6(4) of the Sex Discrimination
Act 1975 providing that the Act's prohibition of discrimination on grounds of
sex does not apply to "provision in relation to . . . retirement". Mrs. Duke
was compulsorily retired by her employers after she reached the age of 60, in
accordance with the employers' policy to enforce retirement of women
employees when they reached 60 and men when they reached 65. The ECJ had
already held in *Marshall* that requiring women to retire at an earlier age than
men was contrary to the Equal Treatment Directive.[35] However, that ruling
only assisted those in public sector employment, because in the same case the
Court had also ruled that directives cannot have direct effect between private
parties.[36] Since Mrs. Duke had been employed by a private sector company,
she could not rely directly on the directive, as interpreted in *Marshall*, because
it did not have direct effect. Nor could she rely on the Sex Discrimination Act
1986, passed in order to comply with the ruling in *Marshall*, which prohibited discrimination in relation to retirement for both state and private employees, because it came into force after her dismissal and did not apply
retrospectively. She had to rely on the unamended s. 6 of the SDA 1975, complete with the express exception in s. 6(4) for provision in relation to retirement.

Mrs. Duke's argument was essentially that s.6(4) of the SDA 1975 had to
be read alongside Community law and construed in such a way as to har-
monise the two. Three distinct foundations were offered for the obligation on
municipal courts to have regard to Community provisions when construing
national law and to adopt that interpretation which accorded with
Community law where the language of the national law admitted of two interpretations.[37] First, it was argued that the combined effect of s. 2(1) and 2(4)

---

[34] *Duke* v. *GEC Reliance Ltd.* [1988] AC 618.

[35] Case 152/84, *Marshall* v. *Southampton and South West Hampshire Area Health Authority
(Teaching)* [1986] ECR 723; [1986] QB 401.

[36] That is, so-called "horizontal direct effect", as opposed to "vertical direct effect" against
organs of the state.

[37] [1988] AC 618 at 623D–E.

of the ECA 1972 required the SDA 1975 to be construed in accordance with the Equal Treatment Directive. Second, reliance was placed on the general principle of construction, articulated by Lord Diplock in *Garland*, that municipal law should, where possible, be construed in conformity with international obligations. Third, Mrs. Duke invoked the *Von Colson* principle, requiring national courts to seek to interpret their national law in accordance with relevant directives of Community law.[38] The respondent employers relied on the exception in s. 6(4) SDA 1975, arguing that a British court which accepted their construction of that provision as a matter of domestic law was bound to give effect to it. They argued that, since the language of the statutory section contained no ambiguity, the argument based on Community law simply did not arise.[39]

The response of the House of Lords to the appellant's Community law arguments exemplifies the continuing judicial resistance in the UK to making the constitutional accommodation necessitated by Community membership. Lord Templeman, invited to construe a 1975 statute in the light of a 1976 directive as interpreted in a decision by the ECJ in 1986, clung to the traditional notion of the judicial interpretive role as uncoverer of Parliament's historic state of mind at the time the statute was passed. Not surprisingly, given that uncompromising premise, he rejected outright the argument for the recognition of a general obligation on UK courts to construe national law so as to conform with Community law.

> "Of course a British court will always be willing and anxious to conclude that UK law is consistent with Community law. Where an Act is passed for the purpose of giving effect to an obligation imposed by a directive or other instrument a British court will seldom encounter difficulty in concluding that the language of the Act is effective for the intended purpose. But the construction of a British Act of Parliament is a matter of judgment to be determined by British courts and to be derived from the language of the legislation considered in the light of the circumstances prevailing at the date of enactment."[40]

Having considered at length the circumstances in which the 1975 Act was passed, including the White Paper which preceded the enactment of the SDA,[41] Lord Templeman was satisfied that, as a simple matter of historical fact, it was not passed to give effect to the Equal Treatment Directive, but was intended to preserve discriminatory retirement ages.[42]

Fortified by the historical certainty that emerged from this reconstruction of the circumstances existing at the time the SDA was enacted in 1975, Lord Templeman rejected each of the arguments put forward as reasons why the

[38] Lord Diplock's judgment in *Garland* was said to support, directly or indirectly, all three arguments.
[39] [1988] AC 618 at 627G.
[40] Ibid. at 638G–H.
[41] *Equality for Women*, Cmnd. 5724 (1974).
[42] [1988] AC 618 at 639A.

UK courts should construe the Act so as to be in conformity with Community law. Section 2(4) ECA was said to apply only where Community provisions were directly applicable. It neither enabled nor constrained a British court to distort the meaning of a British statute in order to enforce against an individual a Community directive which has no direct effect between individuals.[43] Lord Diplock's approach in *Garland* was expressly not followed, not because the general principle of construction which he articulated was not accepted, but if anything because, as a mere presumption of interpretation, it had been rebutted by the evidence of the circumstances in which the Act had been passed. That evidence, unsurprisingly, had satisfied Lord Templeman that it was not intended to give effect to the later Equal Treatment Directive as subsequently construed in *Marshall*, and that the words of s. 6(4) were therefore not reasonably capable of being limited in the way contended for by the appellant.[44] Finally, Lord Templeman gave short shrift to the argument that the court was required to construe the domestic statute in a way which gave effect to the directive by the interpretive obligation in *Von Colson*. That case was said to be

> "no authority for the proposition that a court of a member state must distort the meaning of a domestic statute so as to conform with Community law which is not directly applicable. . . . The EEC Treaty does not interfere and the European Court of Justice in the *Von Colson* case did not assert power to interfere with the method or result of the interpretation of national legislation by national courts."[45]

Having thus disposed of each of the suggested foundations for an obligation to construe domestic law consistently with Community law, Lord Templeman invoked what amount to considerations of legal certainty and legitimate expectation as other reasons for not acceding to the interpretation urged upon him by the retired employee. It would, he said, be "most unfair" to the respondent employer to "distort" the construction of the 1975 SDA in order to accommodate the 1976 Equal Treatment Directive as construed by the ECJ in *Marshall* in 1986. The directive was not directly effective as between Mrs. Duke and her employer, and the latter could not reasonably be expected to reduce to precision the "opaque" language of Community legislation. The House of Lords therefore concluded that, as the employer was not liable under Community law, it should not be held liable under British law.

The House of Lords' defiant assertion of national interpretive techniques in *Duke* was widely criticised, in particular by European Community lawyers.[46]

---

[43] Ibid. at 639H–640A.

[44] Ibid. at 639H.

[45] Ibid. at 641C, F.

[46] A. Arnull, (above n. 30); E. Ellis, "EEC Law and the Interpretation of Statutes" (1988) 104 LQR 379; E. Szyszczak, (above n. 31); Fitzpatrick, "The Significance of EC Directives in UK Sex Discrimination Law" (1989) 9 OJLS 336. For a defence of the reasoning in *Duke* from the perspective of a traditional understanding of the relationship between UK courts and Parliament, see eg. C. Greenwood [1988] All ER Rev. 122 at 125.

A good deal of the criticism was directed at Lord Templeman's view that s.2(4) ECA only applies where Community provisions are directly effective. In an attempt to ground English judicial acceptance of the interpretive obligation in the underlying statutory authority of the ECA 1972, many commentators argued that s.2(1) should be interpreted as including non-directly effective Community law, and that s.2(4) provides the basis for construing national law so as to conform with Community law.[47] Even on its own terms, however, this argument seems unconvincing. The language of s.2(1), in particular the use of the words "without further enactment", and the fact that the section goes on to provide separately in s.2(2) for the implementation of non-directly effective obligations by delegated legislation, seem clearly to suggest that s.2(1) applies only to directly effective Community law. Similarly, the language of s.2(4), in particular the words "construe and take effect subject to", seems inappropriate when applied to the interpretation of national law in the light of Community law, as opposed to the supremacy of Community law.

Such responses, using traditional techniques of statutory interpretation to rebut the argument, might be thought to miss the point, since manifestly Parliament could not have had the principle of indirect effect in mind in 1972 as it did not then exist. Rather the argument is that, as Weatherill and Beaumont put it, s.2 of the ECA should be interpreted in accordance with the spirit of the evolving Community rather than in accordance with the letter of the statute.[48] But, as with all such attempts to justify domestic judicial acceptance of constitutional developments in the European Community by reference to some underlying statutory authority, this achieves only the most formal and utterly transparent reconciliation with sovereignty theory.

More telling, however, was the criticism of Lord Templeman for failing to appreciate the clear implication in *Von Colson* that, by laying down an interpretive obligation on national courts, the ECJ had indeed interfered with their freedom to interpret national law according to national techniques of interpretation.[49] Lord Templeman's assertion of national interpretive autonomy was motivated by two principal considerations. First, he was determined to preserve the distinctively British conception of statutory interpretation as the discovery of an original legislative intent, to which it was the duty of the courts, as Parliament's constitutional subordinates, to give effect. Second, he was concerned about what he perceived to be the unfairness wrought on individuals or other private parties by the inevitable retrospectivity of assigning a meaning to statutory words which is other than the "ordinary, plain or natural meaning" they might otherwise be expected to bear. Those premises inevitably influence what counts as a "distortion" of statutory language, and,

---

[47] N. Foster, "The Effect of the European Communities Act 1972, s. 2(4)" (1988) 51 MLR 775; Ellis, (above n. 46) at 383; Lewis, "EEC Law in the United Kingdom: Marshalling Arguments in Reliance on Directives" [1989] CLJ 6; Fitzpatrick, (above n. 46) at 347–8.

[48] Weatherill & Beaumont, (above n. 24) at 366.

[49] See eg. Arnull, (above n. 30) at 317.

likewise, whether particular statutory words are "reasonably capable" of bearing a particular interpretation. The sense in which the statutory words were "not capable" of bearing the meaning which would comply with the directive in *Duke*, or would be "distorted" if they were made to bear such a meaning, was not that they could not bear that meaning in a purely linguistic sense. They manifestly could. Rather it was that, in view of the evidence of Parliament's historic intention and the unfairness which it was thought would be caused to the employer by changing their meaning retrospectively, they could not, in a normative sense, be given that meaning by a court which professes its allegiance to the will of the UK Parliament and purports to respect the principle of legal certainty by applying a plain and natural meaning rule when construing statutory language.

By jealously preserving national techniques of statutory interpretation in this way, Lord Templeman may well have thought that, far from defying the ECJ's ruling in *Von Colson*, he was merely applying its own qualification on that obligation, that national courts are only obliged to interpret and apply national law in conformity with Community law "in so far as it is given discretion to do so under national law". On this view, Lord Templeman in *Duke* was merely recognising that UK courts simply do not have discretion under national law to interpret non-implementing legislation in a way which is at odds with what Parliament demonstrably intended, or which in the national court's view causes unacceptable unfairness to those relying on the ordinary meaning of the statutory language.

However, to suggest that UK courts are prevented in this way from construing non-implementing domestic legislation so as to conform with non-directly effective Community law is unconvincing for a number of reasons. First, as has been seen above, the supposed enslavement of UK courts to Parliament's historical intention is a legal fiction which has nowhere been more systematically exposed as such than in the context of Community law. The suggestion that courts have no interpretive latitude in cases where there is little room for doubt about Parliament's intention is therefore incorrect. The constitutional accommodation of the Community law doctrine of supremacy, to give but one example, has demonstrated the ability of the courts to modify traditional understandings of the sovereignty of Parliament where political reality is reflected in shifting conceptions of judicial obligation.

Second, the implication that, to give statutory words a meaning other than their natural or ordinary meaning is inevitably unfair to those affected by the legislation, is too simple. It is true that such concerns with legal certainty and the protection of reasonable reliance have supplied one of the main rationales behind the traditional UK approach of interpreting statutes according to their "plain and natural" meaning. But, even on its own terms, could it really be reasonable for a private party to expect, so long after the UK became a member of the Community, that the meaning of domestic law was to be derived from the statutory words alone, construed in isolation from relevant

Community law?[50] A similar legitimate expectation argument in *Macarthys* drew a robust response from Lord Denning.[51] There the employers argued, having lost the litigation, that they ought not to be liable for costs because they had been entitled to go by the English statute on equal pay and not by the Treaty. Lord Denning rejected this argument, holding that the employers had no right to look at the English statute alone, but ought throughout to have looked at the Treaty as well.[52] That case concerned directly effective Community law, to which, it is true, the attention of employers is at least drawn by s.2(1) ECA 1972, but there seems no reason in principle why, at this advanced stage of European legal integration, the same ought not to be said of non-directly effective Community law. Employers and others affected by the subject-matter of such law have been aware since *Von Colson* was decided that the ECJ requires national courts to interpret domestic legislation so as to conform with Community law, and therefore, to adapt Lord Denning's words, have no right to look at the English statute alone, but ought also to look at relevant Community law, whether directly effective or non-directly effective.

The third, and most telling, reason for scepticism about Lord Templeman's justifications for not accommodating the *Von Colson* obligation is that there is judicial interpretive discretion inherent in the interplay between the very premises Lord Templeman invokes to resist that obligation. The two principles of parliamentary sovereignty and legal certainty on which Lord Templeman implicitly relies, far from pulling in the same direction, are often themselves in fundamental tension. A literal interpretation of statutory words, in the interests of legal certainty, may sometimes operate to defeat the manifest purpose underlying legislation, and, by the same token, a purposive interpretation, in order to give effect to Parliament's manifest purpose, may involve a departure from or addition to the literal or ordinary meaning of the words used. The fact that the history of statutory interpretation in the present century has largely been a story of the battles between purposive and literal approaches is itself evidence of the interpretive leeway that is available even to UK judges. Indeed, this scope for judicial choice between literal and purposive approaches to statutory interpretation lay at the heart of two subsequent cases, in which the House of Lords appeared to show that it was willing to accept at least the narrower version of the *Von Colson* obligation, that is, in relation to national implementing legislation.

5. THE INTERPRETIVE OBLIGATION ACCEPTED?

In *Pickstone*, the case turned on the construction of a statutory provision which had been demonstrably inserted in order to bring the national legisla-

---

[50] See de Búrca, (above n. 24) at 229–31 for a general consideration of how to reconcile the interpretive obligation with legal certainty and the protection of legitimate expectations.

[51] *Macarthys Ltd.* v. *Smith* [1981] 1 QB 180 at 200H-201B.

[52] Ibid. at 201B–C.

tion into line with the requirements of a Community law directive as interpreted by the European Court.[53] Art. 119 of the EC Treaty, it will be recalled,
requires that men and women should receive equal pay for equal work. The
Equal Pay Directive, adopted in 1975, made clear that Art. 119 required both
equal pay for equal work and equal pay for work of equal value. The Equal
Pay Act 1970, as amended by the Sex Discrimination Act 1975, provided in
s.1(2)(a) for women to bring a claim for equal pay "where the woman is
employed on like work with a man in the same employment", in other words,
for equal pay for equal work. The Act also provided, in s.1(2)(b), for an equal
pay claim to be brought "where the woman is employed on work rated as
equivalent with that of a man in the same employment", that is, for equal pay
for work of equal value. However, the statutory scheme impeded the practical effectiveness of this latter right, because a woman's work could only be
rated as equivalent with that of a man after a job evaluation study, which
could only be carried out with the employer's consent.[54]

In 1982 the European Court declared the UK to be in breach of its obligations under the Treaty for failing to introduce into its national legal system
the necessary measures for the implementation of the Equal Pay Directive.[55]
The UK Government chose to correct the defect in its equal pay legislation by
regulations made under s.2(2) of the ECA 1972 which empowers ministers to
make regulations for the purpose of implementing any Community obligation
or of enabling any such obligation to be implemented.[56] The amending regulations added a new s.1(2)(c) to the Equal Pay Act 1970, providing for a claim
for equal pay to be made

> "where a woman is employed on work which, not being work in relation to which
> paragraph (a) or (b) above applies, is, in terms of the demands made on her . . . of
> equal value to that of a man in the same employment."

The minister introducing the amending regulations in the House of Commons
made clear in his speech that the purpose of the amendment was to close the
gap identified by the European Court, namely, to allow a woman to claim
equal pay with a man for work of equal value where the jobs are not covered
by a job evaluation study.[57]

The applicant, Mrs. Pickstone, was a "warehouse operative" who claimed
that her work was of equal value with that of a man employed as a "checker
warehouse operative", relying on the newly inserted provision. The employers, however, argued that, because they employed one man as a warehouse
operative, doing the same work as Mrs. Pickstone for the same pay, her case

---

[53] *Pickstone* v. *Freemans plc* [1989] AC 66. For comment see A. Bradley, "The Courts,
Community Law and Equal Pay: A Constitutional Case?" [1988] PL 485.

[54] Equal Pay Act 1970, s.1(5).

[55] Case 61/81, *Commission of the European Communities* v. *United Kingdom* [1982] ECR 2601;
[1982] ICR 578 at 599.

[56] The Equal Pay (Amendment) Regulations 1983 (SI 1983 No. 1794).

[57] H.C. Deb., Vol. 46, col. 479 (July 20, 1983).

was covered by s.1(2)(a) (equal pay for equal work), and the exclusionary words in the new s.1(2)(c) therefore operated to bar her claim. If the employers' construction of the new section was right, it would mean that the amending regulations had failed to implement the UK's obligations under Art. 119 and the Equal Pay Directive, as interpreted by the European Court.

The employers' construction of the legislation succeeded before the industrial tribunal, the Employment Appeal Tribunal[58] and the Court of Appeal, although the Court of Appeal went on to hold that the applicant was entitled to pursue her equal value claim under Art. 119 directly.[59] The House of Lords, however, was prepared to take a less literal approach to the interpretation of the provision and unanimously rejected the employers' construction. All those who gave reasoned judgments adopted a "purposive" approach to the construction of the statutory provision, in the sense that they had regard to the purpose for which it was introduced by the amending regulations, but the justifications offered for doing so differed. Lord Keith's was the broadest approach, for he seemed to think that the manifest purpose of the provision was sufficient to justify rejecting the employers' literal construction. To accede to that construction, he held, would leave a large gap in the legislation, which could be exploited by employers employing one token man on the same work as a group of potential women claimants for equal pay for work of equal value.[60] Such a consequence would mean that the UK had yet again failed fully to implement its obligations under Art. 119 of the Treaty and the Equal Pay Directive and failed to give full effect to the ECJ's decision, and it was plain that Parliament could not possibly have intended such a failure when it resolved to adopt the amending regulations. So confident was he that the employers' narrow construction of the statutory words was wrong that he did not even think it mattered what precise terms were to be implied into the provision to modify its literal meaning. It was sufficient to say that the words must be construed purposively in order to give effect to the manifest broad intention of the maker of the regulations and of Parliament, and that the employers therefore were not entitled to rely on the statutory words to bar the claim for equal pay.

Lord Templeman took a similar purposive approach, relying heavily on a detailed account of the background and legislative history of the regulations, including extracts from Hansard revealing the minister's reasons for introducing the amending regulations, in order to establish the intention behind the regulations as an historical fact.[61] Lord Oliver was the most reluctant convert

---

[58] [1986] ICR 886.

[59] [1989] AC 66 at 73–97, considered by Bradley, (above n. 53) at 489–91. The Court of Appeal adopted the same approach as that taken by the majority in *Macarthys* v. *Smith* [1979] ICR 785, considered above, in that they first interpreted the statute in isolation from Community law, before turning to see what Community law required. This mistaken approach appears to have been based on the agreement between counsel that Community law was material to the construction of the statute only if the words in question were ambiguous: [1989] AC 66 at 83A–B.

[60] Ibid. at 111G–H.

[61] Ibid. at 122H–123A.

to the necessity for a purposive construction of the regulations. He emphasised that so to construe a provision which, on its face, was unambiguous involved a departure from a number of well-established rules of construction: the rule that the intention of Parliament is to be ascertained from the words which it has used; that those words are to be construed according to their plain and ordinary meaning; that even a treaty being implemented by legislation cannot be referred to as an aid to construction in the absence of ambiguity in the implementing Act; and that what is said in Parliament cannot be used as an aid to construction.

Nevertheless, Lord Oliver recognised that a statute passed in order to implement the UK's Community obligations fell into a special category and had to be construed in the light of that purpose. In his view,

> "a construction which permits the section to operate as a proper fulfilment of the UK's obligation under the Treaty involves not so much doing violence to the language of the section as filling a gap by an implication which arises, not from the words used, but from the manifest purpose of the Act and the mischief it was intended to remedy."

However, it is difficult to draw many firm conclusions about the basis on which Lord Oliver was persuaded to depart from what he regarded to be the usual practice and take a purposive approach to the interpretation of the statute, because no clear distinction was drawn by him between directly effective Community law in the shape of Art. 119 and the non-directly effective Equal Pay Directive. He spoke generally of "the necessity – indeed the obligation – to apply a purposive construction which will implement the UK's obligations under the Treaty",[62] but was not specific about the foundation for that obligation. At some points in the judgment it appeared to be founded in the ECA, for example where he explained that the reason implementing legislation falls into a special category is that the UK's Community obligations have been incorporated into English law by s.2(1) ECA,[63] and, elsewhere, in his references to "the compulsive provision of s.2(4)".[64] Yet, in other places, he appeared to found his approach on the general principle of interpretation enunciated by Lord Diplock in *Garland*, asking whether the statutory provision was reasonably capable of bearing a meaning which complied with the obligations imposed by the Treaty.[65] The general tenor of his judgment, however, suggests that Lord Oliver's approach was more an attempt to respect the supremacy of Art. 119 than an acceptance of any general obligation to construe domestic law in conformity with non-directly effective Community law.

Of the three reasoned judgments in *Pickstone*, only Lord Templeman's referred expressly to the *Von Colson* obligation. The fact that he referred to

[62] Ibid. at 125H.
[63] Ibid. at 126D.
[64] Ibid. at 125B and 128C.
[65] Ibid. at 127C–128A.

it in order to distinguish this case from his judgment in *Duke* in which he had held, in effect, that the obligation did not apply because the Act was not implementing legislation, suggests that he considered *Pickstone* to be a case in which the obligation applied.[66] His conclusion that in this case there was no difficulty in construing regulations in a way which gave effect to the declared intention of the UK Government as well as being consistent with the objects of the Treaty, the directive and the decision of the ECJ, suggests that he was accepting the narrow version of the *Von Colson* obligation, but he did not provide any more specific justification for being bound even by such a limited obligation.

The same willingness to construe implementing legislation in the light of its historical purpose was again shown by the House of Lords in *Litster*.[67] The Transfer of Undertakings (Protection of Employment) Regulations 1981[68] were also made under s.2(2) of the ECA 1972, for the express purpose of implementing the Acquired Rights Directive.[69] The express object of the directive was to provide for the protection of the rights of employees in the event of a change of employer. It required that, on the transfer of a business from one employer to another, the benefit and burden of a contract of employment between the old owner and the new owner should devolve on the new owner, and that the transfer shall not in itself constitute grounds for dismissal by either the old or the new owner.[70] The implementing regulations provided for the necessary transfer of contractual rights and obligations to the new owner, and for the dismissal of an employee by either the old or new owner to count as unfair dismissal if the transfer, or a reason connected with it, was the reason for the dismissal.[71] By Regulation 5(3), however, the beneficiaries of the protection were defined as those persons employed in the business "immediately before the transfer". That definition appeared to be at odds with the ECJ's subsequent interpretation of the directive, in which it had held that the workers entitled to the protection of the directive included not only those employed at the date of the transfer, but those whose employment had been terminated on a date before the transfer in breach of the directive's prohibition on dismissal by reason of the transfer.[72]

The point of construction arose in *Litster* because the respondent employer sought to take advantage of what, on a literal interpretation, was clearly a loophole in the UK Regulations' definition of those entitled to benefit from the protection they introduced. The receivers of an insolvent business agreed to sell its assets and, at the request of the new owner, dismissed the work-

---

[66] [1989] AC 66 at 123B–D.

[67] *Litster* v. *Forth Dry Dock & Engineering Co. Ltd.* [1990] 1 AC 546.

[68] SI 1981 No. 1794.

[69] Council Directive 77/187/EEC.

[70] Ibid., Arts. 3 and 4.

[71] Regulations 5(1) and 8(1) respectively.

[72] Case 101/87, *P. Bork International A/S* v. *Foreningen af Arbejdsledere i Danmark* [1988] ECR 3057 at 3077; [1989] IRLR 41 at 44.

force one hour before the transfer took place. The new owner continued the business but employed only three of the former employees, replacing the remainder of the workforce with new employees at lower wages. The new owners contested their liability for damages for unfair dismissal on the basis that the applicants were not employed "immediately before the transfer" within the meaning of Regulation 5(3) because they had been dismissed an hour beforehand.

As in *Pickstone*, the House of Lords were not prepared to countenance the manifest frustration of legislative purpose which such a literal interpretation inevitably produced, and were unanimous in holding that words ought to be implied into the relevant regulation in order to achieve the purpose of giving effect to the directive. Regulation 5(3) was therefore to be construed by implying words indicating that the protection applied not only to those who were employed "immediately before the transfer", but also those who would have been so employed had they not been unfairly dismissed before the transfer for a reason connected with it.[73] So there was unanimity in the House of Lords that domestic primary and subordinate legislation designed to give effect to the UK's Community law obligations should be construed not literally but purposively, in the sense that it should be given a meaning which achieves Parliament's historical intention to implement Community law.

As in *Pickstone*, however, the basis for adopting such a "purposive" approach was less than clearly articulated in any of the three reasoned judgments.[74] Lord Keith expressly considered it to be the "duty" of the court to give Regulation 5(3) a construction which accorded with the decisions of the ECJ interpreting the directive to which the regulation was intended by Parliament to give effect,[75] but relied primarily on the precedent of *Pickstone* to explain why such an approach was necessary, rather than supplying any independent justification for why the duty arose in such cases. As in *Pickstone*, Lord Templeman was alone in appearing to found the duty on the *Von Colson* interpretive obligation, but again he did not make clear on what basis he considered that case to impose an obligation on UK courts. He held that UK courts were under a duty to follow the practice of the ECJ by giving a purposive construction to directives and to regulations issued for the purpose of complying with directives.[76] To conflate the interpretive duties on national

---

[73] Lord Keith, [1990] 1 AC 546 at 554H; Lord Templeman at 558H. As in *Pickstone*, Lord Oliver, at 577C, was the only Law Lord who thought it necessary to formulate in precise terms the words which were to be implied into Regulation 5(3) in order for the regulations to fulfil their purpose.

[74] The other two members of the House of Lords, Lords Brandon and Jauncey, each agreed with the reasons given by the other three.

[75] [1990] 1 AC 546 at 554G.

[76] Ibid. at 558C–E. Weatherill & Beaumont, (above n. 24) at 365 n. 124, suggest that Lord Templeman's omission of the words in *Von Colson* qualifying the interpretive obligation ("in so far as the national court is given discretion to do so under national law"), which he had cited in both *Duke* and *Pickstone*, may indicate a willingness to follow the ECJ's subsequent case-law omitting the let-out clause. For the reasons explained below, however, it is most unlikely that Lord Templeman considered himself to be going any further than he had gone in *Pickstone*.

courts in this way, however, is to elide the bases on which those duties rest. The duty to follow the ECJ's approach to construing directives could, if necessary, be justified by reference to s.3 ECA 1972, but a duty to construe implementing regulations is a different matter. Since it concerns the interpretation of national law, it demands separate justification. As in *Pickstone*, Lord Templeman therefore proceeded by asserting the existence of the duty rather than explaining the basis on which it arose.

Lord Oliver, whose judgment in *Pickstone* had clearly accepted an interpretive obligation on UK courts but failed to make clear whether he considered that obligation to exist only in relation to directly effective Community law, dispelled any doubts on that score by unequivocally accepting such an obligation in relation to the non-directly effective Community law at issue in *Litster*. Indeed, Lord Oliver's judgment comes closest to providing a justification for the recognition of such an obligation. Although not expressly referred to, it is quite clear that the foundation of Lord Oliver's approach is Lord Diplock's general principle of construction in *Garland*. This is apparent, for example, in his formulation of the question to be decided: whether the regulations are so framed as to be capable of being construed in conformity with the ECJ's interpretation of the directive.[77] He clearly proceeded on the basis that a greater latitude in construction was permissible in the case of legislation designed to give effect to the state's Treaty obligations, and therefore, while the employer's literal construction would be correct if the regulation fell to be construed by reference to the ordinary rules of construction applicable to a purely domestic statute, the court was entitled to supply by implication the words necessary to ensure compliance with those obligations.[78]

To what extent do the decisions in *Pickstone* and *Litster* indicate that the House of Lords was now more favourably disposed towards the *Von Colson* interpretive obligation than it had been in *Duke*? It is certainly noteworthy that in *Litster* not one of the judgments relied on ss.2(1), 2(4) or 3 of the ECA 1972 to justify their purposive approach, suggesting that there was unanimity that, whatever the scope and strength of the interpretive obligation on UK courts to construe Acts of Parliament consistently with non-directly effective Community law, its origins are to be found in something quite independent of Parliament's intentions in enacting the ECA 1972. It is also true that, in both cases, the House of Lords distinguished between "ordinary canons of construction" and the "purposive" approach to be applied in the case of legislation implementing Community law.[79] However, it is easy to exaggerate the

---

[77] [1990] 1 AC 546 at 575H. See also his statement, at 563A–C, that for the parties to the transfer to be at liberty to avoid the manifest purpose of the directive was not a conclusion which would be willingly embraced "in the absence of the most compulsive context rendering any other conclusion impossible."

[78] Ibid. at 576D–577B. Like the ECJ in *Von Colson*, Lord Oliver, at 576G, explicitly had in mind not only the purpose of the directive but also what he regarded as "the mandatory obligation to provide remedies which are effective and not merely symbolic".

[79] As was seen above, in both cases the contrast was most clearly articulated by Lord Oliver.

extent to which the approach taken in *Pickstone* and *Litster* was a modification of traditional techniques. It should not be forgotten that both cases concerned the interpretation of statutory instruments passed under s. 2(2) ECA and therefore it was clear on their face that they were intended to implement Community law obligations.[80] Implying words into legislation in order to give effect to the manifest but inadequately expressed intention of Parliament is a well-established technique, particularly where not to do so would facilitate the ready evasion of the legislative measure and thus frustrate the legislative purpose. The modern trend away from traditional techniques of literal interpretation towards a more "purposive" approach is well documented, and the relaxation in *Pepper* v *Hart* of the exclusionary rule forbidding reference to *Hansard* in the construction of statutes is a sure indication of the advanced stage that evolution has reached.[81]

The point, however, is not simply that the courts already adopt a purposive approach to interpretation generally, and do not confine their use of that approach to the Community law context. More significant is the fact that "purposive" interpretation in this sense is perfectly compatible with the traditional theory of parliamentary sovereignty. It is still premised on it being the courts' constitutional duty when interpreting statutes to discover Parliament's intention as a matter of historical fact and arrive at a construction which gives effect to that reified intention. Indeed, *Pepper* v *Hart* itself was justified by reference to this conception of the courts' constitutional duty. *Pickstone* and *Litster* can therefore hardly be seen as the welcome embrace by the House of Lords of European methods of interpretation or of the *Von Colson* obligation. Rather, the cases are better seen as the reception of such an obligation to the extent that it not only was consistent with, but could also be justified by, what the UK courts continued to insist was their paramount constitutional duty, to implement the will of the sovereign UK Parliament.[82]

There was one respect, however, in which the two cases go rather beyond what can be justified by this conception of the courts' role. That is by accepting that the implementing regulations are to be interpreted not only in the light of the directive being implemented but in light of the ECJ's interpretation of that directive, which may post-date the implementing measure and reveal a meaning not apparent at the time the implementing regulations were made. This is less apparent in *Pickstone* than in *Litster*, in which 1981

---

[80] Indeed, Lord Oliver in *Pickstone* [1989] AC 66 at 128D, had thought the purpose of the amending regulations to be manifest, and did not see the need to refer to the minister's statement to Parliament as evidence of what Parliament intended.

[81] [1993] AC 593.

[82] The persistence in the UK of a view of the judicial function according to which courts are mere implementers of the latest expressed will of the political branches is shown by the recent recommendation of the UK Government to the 1996 Intergovernmental Conference. It proposes that the Council have the power to amend legislation where it considers that the ECJ has interpreted it contrary to the Council's policy: *Memorandum by the United Kingdom on the European Court of Justice* (London, July 1996).

Regulations implementing a 1977 directive were interpreted in the light of a 1988 decision of the ECJ. However, none of the members of the House of Lords addressed how this could be reconciled with the courts' professed role as loyal implementers of Parliament's historically discoverable intention.

6. CONTINUED RESISTANCE

The extent to which the apparent judicial acceptance of the *Von Colson* obligation was reconcilable with traditional conceptions of the judicial role meant that hopes expressed by some, that the apparent preparedness to modify traditional canons of construction in *Pickstone* and *Litster* would lead the House to reconsider *Duke*, were almost bound to be disappointed.[83] Despite the preponderance of critical academic commentary, arguing that the decision in *Duke* was "a thoroughly unreliable precedent",[84] a differently constituted House of Lords unanimously approved of and applied it in *Finnegan*.[85] The issue was identical to that in *Duke*, only the provisions in the SDA 1975 were contained in the Sex Discrimination (Northern Ireland) Order 1976 (SI 1976 No. 244) which, unlike the SDA, was made *after* the adoption of the Equal Treatment Directive. The compulsorily retired employee succeeded in the industrial tribunal, which held that the equivalent to s. 6(4) SDA 1975 in the Northern Ireland Order had to be given an interpretation which was consistent with the Equal Treatment Directive, but that decision was overturned by the Court of Appeal in Northern Ireland.

Before the House of Lords the employee argued that the fact that the Northern Ireland Order was made after the adoption of the Equal Treatment Directive, whereas the SDA 1975 was enacted before, was a crucial distinction from *Duke*, and brought the case within the scope of the obligation in *Von Colson* to interpret national implementing legislation in the light of the directive to which it was intended to give effect.[86] Alternatively, the employee invited the House of Lords to depart from its own decision in *Duke*, on the ground that Lord Templeman had adopted the wrong approach to the construction of the SDA 1975, by not construing it in the light of Community law.[87] Finally, if those arguments failed, the employee argued that the issue should be treated as a question of European law, being a matter of the UK's obligations under the EC Treaty, which therefore required a reference to the ECJ.[88]

---

[83] See eg. Fitzpatrick, (above n. 46) 336 at 355.
[84] Arnull, (above n. 30) at 320.
[85] *Finnegan* v. *Clowney Youth Training Programme Ltd.* [1990] 2 AC 407.
[86] Ibid. at 410B–D.
[87] Ibid. at 410E.
[88] Ibid. at 410F.

The House of Lords, however, held unanimously that the *Von Colson* obligation was of no application.[89] Relying, as in *Duke*, on the legislative history and the chronology of the relevant measures, Lord Bridge held that it would be wholly artificial to treat the 1976 Order as having been made with the purpose of implementing Community law, merely because, unlike the SDA, it was made after the directive. In his view it was quite clear, as a matter of history, that until the decision in *Marshall* neither the UK Parliament nor the UK Government perceived there to be any conflict between the exception for retirement and the Equal Treatment Directive, and it could not therefore be said that the 1976 Order was introduced in order to amend the law so as to bring it into line with the directive. It was not made in order to implement Community law in the same sense as the Regulations at issue in *Pickstone* and *Litster*. He expressly agreed with the reasoning in *Duke* and, like Lord Templeman in that case, considered that to hold otherwise would be "most unfair" to employers in that it would, in effect, be giving retrospective effect to the post-*Marshall* legislative amendments and would also effectively eliminate the distinction between directly effective Community law and that which requires implementation by legislation. In also rejecting the employee's argument that a reference should be made to the ECJ in order to answer what was essentially a question of European law, the House of Lords showed itself to be deaf to the considerable volume of academic criticism of the failure of the House of Lords in *Duke* to make a reference on the question of the scope of the *Von Colson* obligation.[90] In refusing the request to do so in *Finnegan*, Lord Bridge showed that he was every bit as hostile to the ECJ's interpretive obligation, by pointedly observing that the interpretation of the 1976 Order was for the UK courts, not the ECJ.[91]

In *Duke* and *Finnegan*, no fewer than nine Law Lords had unanimously taken the view that the ECJ's interpretive obligation did not require them to effect any change in the way UK courts interpret statutes in the Community law context.[92] The narrow version of the *Von Colson* obligation could safely be accepted in *Pickstone* and *Litster*, because it was consistent with traditional techniques of statutory interpretation, but it was clear that English courts remained reluctant to depart from their traditional conception of their role as seekers of an historical intention when interpreting national legislation, and as upholders of the interests of legal certainty. Soon, however, a further development of constitutional importance in Community law would require UK courts to articulate the basis on which it interpreted domestic law in the light of Community law, when the ECJ took the interpretive obligation a stage further by expressly preferring the wide view of *Von Colson*.

---

[89] Ibid. at 416D–H.
[90] See eg. Fitzpatrick, (above n. 46) 336 at 353–4; Lewis, (above n. 47) at 7; Arnull, (above n. 30) 313 at 319–20.
[91] [1990] 2 AC 407 at 416H–417A.
[92] Only Lord Oliver sat in both cases.

7. THE STRENGTHENED OBLIGATION AND ITS RECEPTION

In *Marleasing* the ECJ finally removed the uncertainty which had surrounded the scope of the *Von Colson* obligation.[93] It held that

". . . in applying national law, whether the provisions in question were adopted before or after the directive, the national court called upon to interpret it is required to do so, as far as possible, in the light of the wording and the purpose of the directive . . .".[94]

The ECJ thereby made clear that the obligation to construe national law in the light of the wording and purpose of non-directly effective Community law was not confined to national implementing legislation, but applied equally to national law which pre-dated the relevant Community provisions. Doubt inevitably remained, however, about the strength of the obligation. On the one hand, there was the qualification that national courts must read national law so as to conform with a relevant directive "as far as possible", the equivalent of the qualifying words in the original formulation of the *Von Colson* obligation. On the other, in the case itself the Court appeared to go a long way towards prescribing the interpretation which would achieve the necessary conformity,[95] suggesting that the obligation was of such strength as to leave very little room for a national court to decide that the language of the national provision was not reasonably capable of bearing the meaning necessary to conform.

Even assuming that the interpretive obligation articulated in *Marleasing* is not of such strength as to require national courts to read national law so as to give effect to a directive regardless of the ability of the national law to bear such a meaning, its extension to non-implementing legislation, including earlier national law, had major implications for UK courts. As was seen above, the narrow view of the *Von Colson* obligation could be accommodated by UK courts consistently with their traditional commitment to implementing the supreme will of Parliament, but the stronger *Marleasing* obligation, requiring as it did the interpretation of legislation in the light of later non-directly effective Community law, could not be so reconciled, nor, for the reasons explained above, could it be justified on the basis of s.2 of the ECA. If UK courts were to comply with the wider and apparently stronger interpretive obligation, they would not only have to revisit *Duke* and *Finnegan*, but would surely have to acknowledge the independent common law basis for their acceptance of this latest Community law development of constitutional significance.

---

[93] Case C-106/89, *Marleasing SA* v. *La Comercial Internacionale de Alimentacion SA* [1990] ECR I-4135.

[94] Ibid. at para. 9.

[95] Ibid. See de Búrca, (above n. 24) at 223; Hartley, (above n. 24) at 223–4.

When the opportunity to do so arose in *Webb*, the House of Lords not only accepted unquestioningly the *Marleasing* obligation to interpret earlier legislation in the light of a later non-directly effective directive,[96] but also showed eventually that it was prepared to go to the limits of interpretive flexibility in order to give the English statute a meaning consistent with the directive as interpreted by the ECJ.[97] The case raised the question of the compatibility of the comparative approach to eliminating sex discrimination, on which the UK's Sex Discrimination Act is based, with the emerging ECJ jurisprudence on pregnancy discrimination. In *Dekker*[98] and *Hertz*,[99] the ECJ had held that, since only women can be refused employment on the ground of pregnancy, such a refusal therefore constitutes direct discrimination on the grounds of sex for the purpose of the Equal Treatment Directive, and a refusal of employment on account of the financial consequences of absence due to pregnancy must be regarded as based, essentially, on the fact of pregnancy. Comparison with the treatment of a real or hypothetical male employee was not necessary in order to establish such discrimination. A comparative exercise, however, is central to the relevant provisions of the principal UK statute, the Sex Discrimination Act 1975. By s.1(1)(a), a person discriminates against a woman in any circumstances relevant for the purposes of the Act if on the ground of her sex he treats her less favourably than he treats or would treat a man. By s.5(3), a comparison of the cases of persons of different sex under s.1(1) must be such that the relevant circumstances in the one case are the same, or not materially different, in the other. Such a comparator-based approach obviously has its limitations when it comes to using the law against sex discrimination for the protection of pregnant women.[100]

The question which arose in *Webb* was whether it was direct discrimination contrary to s.1(1)(a) of the Sex Discrimination Act for an employer to dismiss a woman employed on an indefinite contract, but recruited initially to cover for another employee due to take maternity leave, on discovering that she too was pregnant and due to have her baby at about the same time as the woman for whom she had been recruited to cover. The industrial tribunal dismissed her claim, holding that the real reason for her dismissal was her anticipated inability to carry out the primary task for which she had been recruited, and that a man recruited for the same purpose would have been treated

---

[96] *Webb* v. *EMO Air Cargo (UK) Ltd.* [1993] ICR 175.

[97] *Webb* v. *EMO Air Cargo (UK) Ltd. (No. 2)* [1995] ICR 1021.

[98] Case C-177/88, *Dekker* v. *Stichting Vormingscentrum voor Jonge Volwassenen (VJV-Centrum) Plus* [1990] 1 ECR 3941 at para. 12; [1992] ICR 325.

[99] Case C-179/88, *Handels-og Kontorfunktionaerernes Forbund i Danmark* v. *Arbejdsgiverforening* [1990] ECR I-3979; [1992] ICR 332.

[100] For a detailed account of the limitations of the comparator approach, see S. Fredman, "A Difference with Distinction" (1994) 110 LQR 106. See also N. Bamforth, "The Changing Concept of Discrimination" (1993) 56 MLR 872, commenting on the first House of Lords decision in *Webb*.

similarly if he had required to be absent during the critical period.[101] The EAT dismissed her appeal, following the same reasoning.[102]

In the Court of Appeal, the applicant relied on *Von Colson* and *Marleasing* to argue that the court was required to interpret the 1975 Act in the light of the Equal Treatment Directive and in particular the ECJ's interpretation of it in *Dekker*.[103] She argued that since the interpretation of the Act she contended for was at the very least possible, the court was under an obligation to adopt that interpretation in order to achieve the aim of the Equal Treatment Directive. The Court of Appeal held that, on a proper interpretation of the 1975 Act, a comparison had to be made with a man with a condition as nearly comparable as possible which had the same practical effect on his ability to do the job, and that, since such a man would also have been dismissed, on the facts there was no direct discrimination. Significantly, however, the Court of Appeal seemed prepared to accept the *Marleasing* obligation on national courts to construe the 1975 Act, so far as possible, consistently with Community law, including the Equal Treatment Directive and its subsequent interpretation by the ECJ.[104] The court thereby appeared to abandon the view of the House of Lords in *Duke* that non-implementing legislation could not be construed in the light of a later directive consistently with the constitutional role of the UK courts. Nevertheless, when it came to deciding whether the applicant's construction was possible, the court still took its cue from Lord Templeman in *Duke*, holding that they were not constrained by the *Marleasing* principle to "distort" the meaning of the British statute.[105] The terms in which they expressed that conclusion gives cause to doubt the extent to which the Court of Appeal was really departing from the premises underlying the *Duke* decision.[106]

The House of Lords also accepted the *Marleasing* obligation, albeit again with a *Duke*-type gloss that it does not require national courts to "distort" the meaning of national legislation.[107] It noted that, although the Equal Treatment Directive does not have horizontal direct effect,

"nevertheless it is for a UK court to construe domestic legislation in any field covered by a Community Directive so as to accord with the interpretation of the Directive as laid down by the European Court of Justice, if that can be done with-

---

[101]   [1993] ICR 175 at 178F–G.

[102]   [1990] ICR 442.

[103]   [1992] ICR 445. See A. Arnull, "When is pregnancy like an arthritic hip?" (1992) 17 EL Rev 265.

[104]   See eg. Balcombe LJ, [1992] ICR 445 at 464G. This was said to be common ground between the applicant and the *amicus curiae* (the respondent employer being unrepresented).

[105]   Ibid. at 461A, 464H–465B, 468D–E and 469D.

[106]   Glidewell LJ, ibid. at 460G–H, agreed that the correct approach to adopt was that contained in a passage from Lord Templeman's speech in *Duke* which included reference to the SDA being non-implementing legislation, and Balcombe LJ, ibid. at 60j, cited both *Duke* and *Finnegan* in support of his view that the court was not required to distort the meaning of the 1975 Act.

[107]   [1993] ICR 175.

out distorting the meaning of the domestic legislation . . . . This is so whether the domestic legislation came after or, as in this case, preceded the Directive."[108]

In this passage, the House of Lords quietly departed from its own decision in *Duke* by accepting that the interpretive obligation now applied to non-implementing legislation, but at the same time retained the qualification that UK courts could not be required to "distort" the meaning of Acts of Parliament.[109] As it read *Marleasing*, the qualification that a national court is only required to construe a domestic law to accord with a directive if it is possible to do so, meant that the domestic law must be open to an interpretation consistent with the directive, otherwise the national court is entitled and bound to give effect to the national law notwithstanding the terms of the directive.

The House of Lords' view of the proper construction of the national legislation, considering it first in isolation, was that the dismissal did not in the circumstances constitute direct discrimination.[110] It reached this conclusion on the basis of a narrow view of causation. The applicant was not dismissed simply because she was pregnant, Lord Keith held, but because her pregnancy had the consequence that she would not be available for work at the critical period.[111] The "relevant circumstance" for the purpose of the comparison which the Act required to be made was therefore said to be her expected unavailability at the material time. The precise reason for that unavailability was not a relevant circumstance, nor was it relevant that the reason was a condition which was capable of affecting only women.[112] But despite reaching this view as to the proper construction of the domestic legislation, the House of Lords was prepared to make a reference to the ECJ to establish whether, for the purposes of the Equal Treatment Directive, the Court would regard the fundamental reason for the dismissal of the woman in such circumstances as being her unavailability for the job and not her pregnancy. In making such a reference, the House of Lords explicitly envisaged that, in the event of the ECJ deciding the latter, it would be "necessary for this House to consider whether it is possible to construe the relevant provisions of the 1975 Act in such a way as to accord with such decision."[113]

The ECJ held that there could be no question of comparing the situation of a woman who finds herself incapable, by reason of pregnancy, of performing the task for which she was recruited with that of a man similarly

---

[108] Ibid. at 186D–E.

[109] The acceptance of the interpretive obligation in relation to non-implementing legislation is now taken for granted. In *Meade-Hill* v. *British Council* [1995] ICR 847 at 854D-E, for example, the respondent employer did not dispute that the provisions of the SDA 1975 were to be construed in order to give effect to the Equal Treatment Directive.

[110] [1993] ICR 175 at 182D.

[111] Ibid. at 181C.

[112] Ibid. at 182A–B.

[113] Ibid. at 187G.

incapable for medical or other reasons.[114] Pregnancy was not comparable with a pathological condition, and Community law's protection for a woman during pregnancy and after childbirth could not be dependent on whether her presence at work during maternity was essential to the proper functioning of the undertaking in which she was employed. In the ECJ's view, the Equal Treatment Directive therefore precluded dismissal of an employee in the circumstances of the applicant.

There now existed a direct conflict between the ECJ's interpretation of the requirements of the Equal Treatment Directive and the "proper construction" of the 1975 Act arrived at by the industrial tribunal, the EAT, the Court of Appeal and the House of Lords. The obvious difficulty of accommodating the ECJ's approach within a statutory framework premised on a comparison between a male and female employee led some commentators to think that the applicant faced an uphill task in persuading the House of Lords not only to depart from its earlier interpretation, but also that the 1975 Act was capable of being interpreted consistently with the requirements of the Equal Treatment Directive at all.[115] The likelihood seemed to be that the House of Lords would consider that what was required in order to comply with the ECJ's ruling went beyond the bounds of legitimate judicial interpretation, and refuse to "distort" the meaning of the legislation, preferring to leave it to the legislature to amend the legislation in order to comply with the UK's Community law obligations.

Yet in fact, on the case's return from the ECJ, the House of Lords demonstrated the extent to which Community membership has encouraged interpretive flexibility hitherto unknown in the UK.[116] Lord Keith accepted that the House of Lords now had to endeavour to construe the 1975 Act so as to accord if at all possible with the ruling of the ECJ.[117] The problem, as he saw it, was how to fit the more precise terms of the statutory test for unlawful discrimination in the Sex Discrimination Act into the ECJ's interpretation of the broad principles dealt with in the Equal Treatment Directive. The only way to do so was, still within the statute's comparative framework, to hold that the reason for her unavailability, ie. pregnancy, was after all a circumstance relevant to her case, and was a circumstance which could not be present in the case of the relevant man.[118] By this feat of interpretive dexterity, the House of Lords not only avoided a conflict between domestic law and Community law as interpreted by the ECJ, but also gave its sanction to the

---

[114] Case C-32/93, *Webb* v. *EMO Air Cargo (UK) Ltd.* [1994] ECR I-3567, paras. 24–9; [1994] QB 718. See S. Fredman, "Parenthood and the Right to Work" (1995) 111 LQR 220.

[115] See eg. E. Szyszczak, "The Status to be Accorded to Motherhood" (1995) 58 MLR 860.

[116] *Webb* v. *EMO Air Cargo (UK) Ltd. (No. 2)* [1995] ICR 1021. See E. Szyszczak, "Pregnancy Discrimination" (1996) 59 MLR 589.

[117] Ibid. at 1026E.

[118] Ibid. at 1027B. This way of giving effect to the ECJ's ruling, whilst still retaining the comparison test inherent in the legislation, had been suggested as a possibility by Szyszczak, (above n. 115) at 865, but even she thought it seemed "a distortion of the domestic legislation".

adoption by English courts of an approach to interpretation of English statutes whereby the question asked is not whether construing the statutory words so as to conform with Community law would "distort" their meaning, but whether such a construction is linguistically possible.

8. THE JUSTIFICATION FOR RECOGNISING THE PRINCIPLE OF INDIRECT EFFECT

The significance of the House of Lords decision in *Webb* is not to be underestimated. In *Duke* and *Finnegan*, it will be recalled, the House of Lords set its face firmly against any compromise of national rules of statutory interpretation, insisting that the *Von Colson* obligation did not interfere with the method or result of the interpretation of national legislation by national courts. The apparently warmer reception given to the interpretive obligation in *Pickstone* and *Litster* was entirely explicable by the fact that what fell to be interpreted in those cases was manifestly implementing legislation, and to give it a broad and purposive construction was therefore perfectly compatible with the traditional conception of the judicial role when interpreting statutes, and caused no unfairness. In *Webb*, however, by interpreting legislation in the light of later directives, the House of Lords has finally, if silently, let go of the notion of statutory interpretation as the implementation of an actual legislative intention with a real historical existence. By the lengths to which it was prepared to go to accommodate the ECJ's ruling in the fundamentally incompatible national statutory framework, it also demonstrated that it considered that obligation to be of such strength that courts must do their utmost to find an interpretation of the national law which is consistent with Community law. *Webb* could therefore justifiably be said to mark the point of departure from the earlier reconciliation of the interpretive obligation with traditional sovereignty theory, which *Marleasing* had made impossible, and the unqualified acceptance of the full interpretive obligation articulated by the ECJ.

What, though, is the justification for UK courts accepting the interpretive obligation as wholeheartedly and unquestioningly as they now appear to have done?[119] As was seen above, when UK courts finally acknowledged the supremacy of directly effective Community law over national law, they purported to justify the development by basing it on Parliament's own intention in the ECA 1972. One might have expected the courts to do the same by relying on s.3 of the ECA to justify the recognition of the ECJ's full interpretive obligation.[120] The argument has frequently been made in academic

---

[119] See R v. *Secretary of State for the Environment, ex p. Greenpeace* [1994] 4 All ER 352 at 365j–368h for another example of a UK court complying with the *Marleasing* obligation by reading words into national legislation, without pausing to consider the justification for so doing.

[120] The argument that ss.2(1) and 2(4) ECA provide the basis for the recognition of the principle of indirect effect was considered above.

commentaries seeking to explain the judicial acceptance of the principle of indirect effect. Campbell, for example, argues that the judicial response of UK courts to the ECJ's interpretive obligation is "authorised" by s.3. The artificiality of appealing to s.3 in this way is acknowledged, but it is said to be "in theory sufficient" to justify the change in interpretive approach.[121]

However, just as the so-called "underlying statutory authority" of the ECA cannot justify the judicial accommodation of the supremacy and direct effect of Community law, nor can it justify the fundamental change of interpretive approach required by the interpretive obligation as formulated in *Marleasing*. Even on its own terms the justification is inadequate, since the principle of indirect effect only began to be developed by the ECJ in 1984. Nor does relying on an evolutionary approach to interpreting s.3[122] achieve anything more than the most formal reconciliation with parliamentary sovereignty.[123]

In any event, it is surely not without significance that the courts themselves have not sought to justify their acceptance of the interpretive obligation in terms of the ECA at all. Section 2 was expressly ruled out in *Duke* as a possible basis for an obligation on UK courts to interpret national law in the light of non-directly effective Community law, and it seems that no court has ever relied on s.3 as the justification for doing so. The better explanation of the judicial acceptance of the ECJ's interpretive obligation is that it represents a further stage in the evolution of Lord Diplock's common law principle of construction in *Garland*.[124]

Just as UK courts accepted the supremacy of European Community law over domestic law by degrees, in a gradual process which in some respects is still taking place, so they have only very gradually accepted the normativity of non-directly effective Community law. Once it became clear that the interpretive context in which UK courts operated as Community law courts had been irreversibly reconfigured by the European Court of Justice, the courts recognised the impossibility of resisting the development consistently with the political reality of the UK's membership of the Community, and embraced what undoubtedly amounts to a significant modification of traditional interpretive techniques. It was therefore by a judicial evolution of the common law, rather than the effect of any statutory provision, that the principle of indirect effect came to be accepted by UK courts.

---

[121] A. Campbell, "National Legislation and EC Directives: Judicial Co-operation and National Autonomy" (1992) 43 NILQ 330 at 337, 353.

[122] See eg. Weatherill & Beaumont, (above n. 48) at 366.

[123] See de Búrca, (above n. 24) at 226–7 on the superficiality of the reconciliation which is thereby achieved with sovereignty theory.

[124] This view is supported by Arnull, "The Incoming Tide: Responding to *Marshall*" [1987] PL 383 at 392, n. 38, who refers to the *Von Colson* duty on national courts being "reinforced for English courts by the remarks of Lord Diplock in *Garland*."

9. CONCLUSION

The aim of this chapter has been to demonstrate the way in which judicial responses to the constitutional challenges posed by European Community membership have exposed the inadequacy of traditional sovereignty theory, whether continuing or self-embracing. Chapter 2 explained why Community membership poses difficulties for sovereignty theory and chronicled the early judicial attempts to avoid confronting the hard questions of how the UK constitution could accommodate all the demands which necessarily come with membership of a larger political and legal entity. The present chapter has sought to complete the picture by showing how the eventual acceptance by UK courts of the supremacy of directly effective Community law, and of the indirect effect of non-directly effective Community law, cannot be satisfactorily explained in terms of traditional understandings of sovereignty theory. The House of Lords' acceptance of the supremacy of Community law in *Factortame* and *EOC*, and of indirect effect in *Webb*, go far beyond anything which can plausibly be justified in terms of the ECA 1972, or indeed in terms of any version of sovereignty theory.

It has been argued that what has taken place in relation to both supremacy and indirect effect is best understood as a common law development, an evolution of the judiciary's sense of its own constitutional obligations. The common law principle of construction articulated by Lord Diplock in *Garland*, that domestic law is to be interpreted in the light of international obligations, has steadily evolved in the Community law context. It has, as Allan puts it, been accorded "special moral force" in relation to Community obligations, reflecting "the important political role which UK membership of the Community has come to assume'.[125] Membership of the European Community has forced English judges to focus on the interpretive nature of their constitutional function, as opposed to their traditionally conceived function of discovering and applying Parliament's historical intention. Ironically, the historic predominance of sovereignty theory in English judicial thinking may even have contributed to its own decline, by driving English courts to discover ever greater interpretive flexibility when interpreting domestic legislation, so as to avoid finding an inconsistency or conflict between domestic law and Community law. As has been seen in the course of the last two chapters, if courts could find a meaning which was consistent with Community law, they could avoid having to confront the constitutionally embarrassing prospect, in the UK's legal culture, of judicially invalidating primary legislation.

Inevitably, as the common law principle of interpretation has acquired greater strength in relation to Community law, so the sovereignty of Parliament in this context has become attenuated by degrees. Gradually, the

---

[125] T.R.S. Allan, *Law, Liberty and Justice* (Oxford: Clarendon Press, 1993) at 279.

courts have increased the principle's strength in relation to directly effective Community law, until the point has been reached where an Act of Parliament which cannot be interpreted consistently with such Community law will be disapplied to the extent of the inconsistency. Where the relevant Community law is not directly effective the principle has less force, but still requires a conscientious attempt to reach an interpretation of domestic law which is consistent with the Community law provision. The point may now have been reached where, while the courts would still almost certainly obey a statute by which the UK withdrew from the European Community altogether, it is no longer clear whether the courts would give effect to a statute expressed to override a particular Community law obligation. It is by no means fanciful that UK courts would hold in such a case that, so long as the UK remains a member of the Community, it cannot be selective about the obligations with which it chooses to comply.

What has come about, therefore, is nothing short of a common law development of a constitutional kind, in recognition of the inescapable fact that acceptance of the requirements of Community membership is inconsistent with the traditional view of the sovereignty of Parliament. As was seen in chapter 2, it was self-evident from the outset that the task for the UK was not so much how to accommodate Community law within the national legal system as how to accommodate the national legal system to Community law. That is now much more explicitly acknowledged than it was at the time of the parliamentary debates about accession. Then, it will be recalled, Parliament was frequently reassured that its sovereignty remained unaffected by anything in the European Communities Bill and would not be threatened by membership. In the wake of the ECJ's ruling in *Factortame*, however, the Attorney General told the House of Commons that "when a country joins the Community, it is obliged to reconcile its constitution, whether written or unwritten, with Community membership."[126]

That constitutional reconciliation has been a gradual process of common law evolution, in which the accommodation has gradually been made by the courts, rather than by Parliament. While the ECA 1972 undoubtedly had a role to play in that evolution, it is largely to the judicial development of common law principles of construction, assisted by that statutory provision, that Community law owes the status it has today attained in domestic courts. What this story reveals about the nature of Parliamentary sovereignty must be faced. It is fully appreciated by those writers who acknowledge the common law foundation of the doctrine of sovereignty and therefore anticipate that the nature of sovereignty is likely to evolve over time.[127] None has captured the

---

[126] HC Deb., Vol. 175 WA 141 (26 June 1990).

[127] See eg. Allan, (above n. 125), who sees sovereignty changing as the nature of the political community changes; Bradley, above ch. 2, n. 4, who argues that the orthodox doctrine of the sovereign Parliament is not immutable and is likely to continue to change in the future; and Craig, above n. 21, who argues that the justification for parliamentary sovereignty must be found in arguments of principle which may change (or even disappear) over time.

idea quite as vividly as de Smith, however. Writing before the UK's accession to the European Community, he observed prophetically

> "If, however, with the passage of time, the Community develops characteristics of a political federation, and if the incongruity of the orthodox doctrine of parliamentary sovereignty becomes increasingly apparent in a context of expanding Community law, then a climate of opinion will doubtless develop in which heterodoxy will thrive and eventually prevail. The legal concept of parliamentary sovereignty may then drift away into the shadowy background from which it emerged."[128]

As the last two chapters have sought to demonstrate, in the community law context heterodoxy has been thriving for some time and the drift into the shadowy background is at an advanced stage.

At the beginning of chapter 2, it was explained that this digression into a lengthy account of the domestic status of Community law was justified because of its relevance to this book's principal concern, the domestic status of international human rights norms. The important developments which have taken place in the doctrine of Parliamentary sovereignty as a result of the UK's membership of the European Community inevitably raise much wider questions about the changing nature of sovereignty. Many writers have considered the implications of these developments in the Community law context for the more effective protection of human rights in domestic law. Most of these contributions have considered whether the experience in giving domestic effect to Community law throws any new light on the old debate about whether or not a domestic Bill of Rights or incorporation of the European Convention is a good idea, and in particular whether such human rights legislation could be entrenched against future repeal.[129]

This book, however, seeks to draw rather different lessons from the Community law experience in accommodating Community law, lessons which are both of more immediate relevance to the question of the domestic status of unincorporated international human rights standards, and which in any event will remain equally relevant even if human rights legislation is enacted. It asks what lessons are to be learned from that experience concerning the nature of the judicial function and the basis on which courts may legitimately have regard to legal norms emanating from sources other than the domestic Parliament.[130] Throughout the last two chapters it has been argued that Lord

---

[128] Above ch. 2 n. 5 at 614. See also Lloyd, above ch. 2 n. 5 at 192: "A time might eventually come when even the lawyers would recognise that a change had imperceptibly been wrought in the actual law itself and that Parliament could not, even if it wished, and *even as a matter of strict law*, legislate in defiance of such overriding matters as . . . the EEC Treaty" (emphasis in original).

[129] See eg. Wade, above ch. 2, n. 3 at 4; Bradley, above ch. 2, n. 5 at 98–105; Craig, above n. 21 at 253–5.

[130] Cf. Allott's speculation about whether, after *Factortame*, the courts will now take the next step and "recognise that fundamental rights are already contained in the structure of the British legal system, limiting the power of the Queen in Parliament": "Parliamentary Sovereignty: From Austin to Hart" (1990) 49 CLJ 377 at 380.

Diplock's common law basis for according effect and supremacy to community law, as opposed to Lord Denning's statutory basis, is to be preferred, not only because it better describes the gradualist way in which Community law has acquired greater normative force in UK courts, but because it captures an important truth about the interpretive nature of the judicial function which is of general application outside the particular Community law context. The remainder of this book draws on that insight to construct an analogy between the constitutional accommodation of Community law and the changing domestic status of international human rights norms, and to argue that, just as the *Garland* principle of construction has come to have special moral force in relation to Community law, so the time has come to recognise that it is also of particular strength in relation to international human rights law.

4

The Early Domestic Career of International Human Rights Law

1. INTRODUCTION

While the UK's membership of the European Community has undoubtedly produced the most focused challenge to the traditional account of its constitutional arrangements, the ratification of international human rights treaties poses equally fundamental questions about the extent to which those constitutional underpinnings have been transformed by this particular aspect of the post-War trend towards globalisation and interdependence. In particular, the UK's accession to the European Convention on Human Rights and full participation in its enforcement machinery have led to the assimilation of the European constitutional standards now clearly emerging from the inevitably harmonising process of Convention adjudication and enforcement. As the number of human rights instruments has steadily increased, and the jurisprudence interpreting the older instruments become more established, so the frequency of judicial reference to such instruments in domestic cases has increased. Indeed, as appears from the Table in Appendix I, of more than 450 cases in which judicial reference has been made to unincorporated international human rights law since the UK's ratification of the ECHR in 1953, well over half have been in the last five years alone.

As will be seen, however, so deeply ingrained is the sovereigntist habit of mind that it is still commonly thought that the question of the precise domestic status of such unincorporated human rights law is relatively uncontroversial. Although there is a growing awareness that the answer to the question is becoming increasingly fluid,[1] it is fair to say that most practitioners would still regard the answer to be axiomatic: that, although sources of human rights law such as the ECHR or ICCPR, as unincorporated international treaties, are not themselves part of our law, nevertheless, where either statute or common law is uncertain or ambiguous, resort may legitimately be had to such treaties to help a court resolve the uncertainty or ambiguity in domestic law.[2] This and the following two chapters seek to demonstrate, through a detailed historical

---

[1] See eg. M.J. Beloff and H. Mountfield, "Unconventional Behaviour? Judicial Uses of the European Convention in England and Wales" [1996] EHRLR 467.

[2] The authority most frequently cited for this proposition is *R* v. *Secretary of State for the Home Department, ex p. Brind* [1991] 1 AC 696. As will be seen, the law reports are replete with formulations to this effect.

evaluation of the role played by international human rights law in English law, that, like most axioms, this simple statement obscures far more than it reveals.[3]

As the most cursory glance at the Table of cases at Appendix I reveals, the vast majority of judicial references to unincorporated international human rights law has been to the ECHR. Given that this is the UK's regional human rights instrument, and that the right to petition the UN Human Rights Committee under the ICCPR has not been accepted, this is not surprising. It is equally unsurprising that most writing about the domestic status of international human rights norms in the UK has been concerned with the ECHR. Amongst those writers who have very usefully surveyed the domestic status of the ECHR, it has been common to divide up their treatment of the increasingly frequent judicial utterances according to the different uses to which the Convention has been put by English courts.[4] It is usual to consider the Convention's use in four broad categories: first, as an aid to statutory interpretation; second, in the development of the common law; third, in the law of judicial review; and, fourth, as part of EC law.[5] These categories are acknow-

---

[3] See also the argument in ch. 1 that the "ambiguity" precondition is a fallacious requirement derived from an over-expansive and outdated theory of sovereignty.

[4] The principal studies of the subject are to be found in P.J. Duffy, "English Law and the European Convention on Human Rights" (1980) 29 ICLQ 585; A. Drzemczewski, *The European Convention on Human Rights in Domestic Law* (Oxford: Clarendon Press, 1983), at 177–87; N. Bratza, "The Treatment and Interpretation of the European Convention on Human Rights" in J.P. Gardner (ed.), *Aspects of Incorporation of the European Convention on Human Rights into Domestic Law* (London: British Institute of Human Rights, 1993), ch. 6; A. Clapham, *Human Rights in the Private Sphere* (Oxford: Clarendon Press, 1993), Part I ("The Different Ways in which the European Convention on Human Rights is Relevant, or may become Relevant, in United Kingdom Courts", esp. chs. 1 and 2); A.J. Cunningham, "The European Convention on Human Rights, Customary International Law and the Constitution" (1994) 43 ICLQ 537; Lord Lester, "European Human Rights and the British Constitution" in J. Jowell & D. Oliver (eds.), *The Changing Constitution*, 3rd ed. (Oxford: Clarendon Press, 1994), ch.2; D. Beyleveld, "The Concept of a Human Right and Incorporation of the European Convention on Human Rights" [1995] PL 577; M.J. Beloff and H. Mountfield above n. 1. See also A.E. Boyle, "Sovereignty, Accountability and the Reform of Administrative Law" in Richardson and Genn (eds.), *Administrative Law and Government Action* (Oxford: Clarendon Press, 1994), ch. 4 at 96–101; McCrudden and Chambers, *Individual Rights and the Law in Britain* (Oxford: Clarendon Press, 1994), at 570–81; Loveland, *Constitutional Law* (London: Butterworths, 1996) at 583–604; Lester, "The Impact of European Human Rights Law" [1996] JR 21.

[5] It is interesting to compare the analyses of the principal authors in more detail. Duffy, (above n. 4), identifies four "factors" which mitigate the full rigours of the rule that the Convention is not justiciable in English courts: (i) statutory interpretation; (ii) the *ultra vires* rule; (iii) the Convention as part of the common law (as customary international law, as an element of public policy and where no clear precedent exists); (iv) European Communities Law. Bratza, (above n. 4) at 66, identifies three main "areas" in which regard has been had to the Convention: (i) as an aid to statutory interpretation; (ii) as guidance in the development of the common law; (iii) in the field of judicial review. Clapham, (above n. 4) at 14, identifies seven "situations" in which the Convention may be relevant: (i) as an aid to statutory interpretation; (ii) as part of the common law; (iii) as part of European Community law; (iv) as a factor to be taken into consideration by administrative bodies when exercising their discretion; (v) due to a pending application in Strasbourg; (vi) due to the case-law of the European Court of Human Rights; (vii) due to a friendly settlement under the Convention. Cunningham, (above n. 4) at 553, identifies five "situations" in which English courts have had regard to human rights treaties : (i) in resolving ambiguity in statutory language; (ii) in reviewing the exercise of executive discretion; (iii) in resolving

ledged to overlap and to conceal significant sub-categories. For example, the "development of the common law" category for some authors covers not just instances where the common law is unclear on a particular matter, but includes cases in which regard is had to the Convention in the exercise of a judicial discretion and in the judicial development of "public policy".

While the undoubted advantage of such a categorising approach is that it achieves an admirable clarity of exposition, and thus brings a semblance of order to what might otherwise appear to be a bewildering variety of cases from disparate contexts, it risks obscuring the theoretical basis on which any role at all is being accorded to the Convention. It seems curious, for example, that the use to which the Convention has been put in judicial review, and in particular in the judicial control of administrative and executive discretion, should be treated in a separate category, as if what the courts do in the law of judicial review is something quite distinct from the interpretation of statutes or the development of the common law. As has been made increasingly explicit in recent years, the courts' judicial review jurisdiction is an inherent, common law jurisdiction, involving a blend of statutory interpretation and common law development which is the very essence of its constitutional nature. Indeed, its treatment by commentators as a category in its own right for the purposes of analysing the use which has been made of the Convention may be a reflection of the discomfort which this causes for more traditional constitutional theory, with its emphasis on the legislative monopoly of the sovereign Parliament. Judicial review therefore straddles the statutory interpretation and common law development categories. Even outside of judicial review, these categories cannot be kept separate from each other, since it is in the nature of statutory interpretation that it takes place in the context of common law values.[6] One needs only to recall that the international treaty presumption is itself a product of the common law, and its more recent evolution equally a common law development,[7] to realise the limited utility from a theoretical point of view in drawing a rigid distinction between the use of international human rights law as an aid to statutory interpretation and its use as a guide in the development of the common law.

This book therefore does not follow the approach of analysing the use which has been made of international human rights norms in the different

uncertainty in equity and the common law; (iv) in the exercise of judicial discretion; (v) in developing concepts of public policy. Beloff and Mountfield, (above n. 1), identify no fewer than twelve (admittedly overlapping) "uses" to which the Convention has been put judicially. Lord Bingham, in his first speech as Lord Chief Justice, told the House of Lords that there were six ways in which the ECHR can have an influence in domestic proceedings: (i) where a UK statute is capable of two interpretations; (ii) where the common law is uncertain, unclear or incomplete; (iii) where construing implementing legislation; (iv) where the courts have a discretion to exercise; (v) when courts must decide what public policy demands; (vi) where matters are covered by EC law.

[6] For an example of a judicial attempt to keep the two categories separate, see McCullough J. in *R* v. *Radio Authority, ex p. Bull* [1995] 4 All ER 481 at 500h: "we are not here in the realm of the common law; we are interpreting a statutory provision."

[7] See ch. 1.

categories of situation in which they may today be relevant before an English court. Instead, a more historical approach is taken, tracing the gradual evolution in the varying uses to which international human rights law has been put, from its first appearance in domestic judgments in the 1970s to the present day. This approach is adopted in the hope that, while it may be analytically less satisfying, it enables a larger picture to emerge from which the increasing use which is being made of international human rights law by domestic courts can be seen in the broader context of the overall transformation of English public law from a sovereignty-derived system of rules to a more rights-based constitutionalism.

For convenience of exposition, the development of the case-law is divided into three phases. Although these are broadly chronological, the dividing line between one phase and another is marked by a shift in attitude towards the domestic status of international human rights norms, so there is inevitably a degree of overlap. In the brief Phase I, the courts approached international human rights treaties such as the ECHR assuming that they were under an obligation to interpret domestic law in such a way as to achieve conformity with the UK's obligations under those instruments. This was the fleeting moment in English legal history when human rights instruments were treated as being within the scope of a generally applicable treaty presumption and as such were, in effect, a mandatory relevant consideration in the exercise of administrative discretion. In Phase II, however, sovereignty and dualism reasserted themselves, for a variety of reasons. This was a period of judicial schizophrenia, as the courts repeatedly invoked the ambiguity device to shore up domestic administrative law against invasion by the international law of human rights, and in particular the ECHR, at the same time as referring to the ECHR relatively freely in the course of interpreting and developing the common law, and even when interpreting statutes in contexts other than administrative law.

In Phase III, which extends to the present day and is the subject of chapters 5 and 6, a number of different developments have combined to break down the sovereigntist walls which had been erected around administrative law during Phase II. For example, the use which is being made of the ECHR in the development of the common law has reached the point where to continue to insist on its irrelevance to the exercise of statutory discretion appears absurd. The growing recognition of the common law foundation of the judicial review jurisdiction has made the distinction between the role of international human rights law in interpreting statutes and its role in developing the common law increasingly unsustainable. And international human rights standards, again particularly those of the ECHR, are increasingly reflected in government policy documents or internal guidance to civil servants, making it ever more difficult for courts to maintain a dualist stance. As a result of these and other developments, English courts have increasingly considered themselves to be under a duty to interpret domestic law so as to be in conformity with international human rights law, so that the evolution from Phase II to Phase III, it will be argued, is a story of the gradual judicial acceptance of a full interpretive obligation in relation to international human rights standards.

2. INTERPRETING DOMESTIC LAW IN THE LIGHT OF INTERNATIONAL HUMAN RIGHTS LAW

(a) A General Presumption of Statutory Interpretation

For more than twenty years following the entry into force of the ECHR, on 3rd September 1953, it had no domestic impact whatsoever. Its sole appearance in the Law Reports during that time was in *Zoernsch* v. *Waldock*, a case well known to public international lawyers but more for its contribution to the law of sovereign immunity, than for any use which was made of the Convention.[8] A disappointed German applicant, whose petition against the Federal Republic of Germany had been rejected by the European Commission of Human Rights, brought an action alleging "negligence and corruption" against Sir Humphrey Waldock, the British President of the Commission, and its Secretary. The validity of the delegated legislation purporting to make the officers immune from suit[9] depended on whether the Commission was an organ of the Council of Europe, which was treated by the Court of Appeal as a "question of fact", to be resolved by considering the provisions of the Convention.[10] The case is therefore an example of the Convention being treated as an object of factual inquiry, as if it were foreign law, rather than an example of its use as an interpretive guide to the meaning of domestic law.

It was not until 1973, in *R* v. *Miah*, that Stephenson LJ became the first English judge to make what could properly be described as *use* of international human rights law, as an aid to the interpretation of a statute.[11] In deciding whether penal provisions of the Immigration Act 1971 had retrospective effect, he referred to the fact that retrospective legislation of a penal character was "in general, forbidden" by Article 7 of the ECHR and Article 11(2) of the Universal Declaration of Human Rights (UDHR).[12] This passing reference to international human rights treaties was made as if to reinforce the common law's own presumption against retrospectivity, which was stated in the form of a general rule that all statutes, other than those which are merely

---

[8] [1964] 1 WLR 675.

[9] Articles 11 and 12 of the Council of Europe (Immunities and Privileges) Order 1960, (SI 1960 No. 442), made under s.1 of the International Organisations (Immunities and Privileges) Act 1950.

[10] [1964] 1 WLR 675 at 682. The decision that the writ be set aside on the ground that both defendants were within the immunity conferred by the Order was upheld.

[11] [1974] 1 WLR 683 at 690H–691A. Slightly earlier, Lord Kilbrandon in *Broome* v. *Cassell & Co. Ltd*. [1972] AC 1027 at 1133A had fleetingly referred to the Convention in what could be described as an interpretive way, when interpreting the scope of the courts' common law power to award punitive damages. The case is considered further below.

[12] Both Article 7 ECHR and Article 11(2) UDHR prohibit retrospective criminal liability.

declaratory or which relate only to matters of procedure or evidence, are *prima facie* prospective, and retrospective effect is not to be given to them unless by express words or necessary implication that appears to have been the legislature's intention. Lord Reid, in the House of Lords in the same case, followed suit, citing the same two articles of the ECHR and UDHR as evidence of the strong and longstanding feeling against retrospective criminal legislation and as a reason why "it is hardly credible that any government department would promote or that Parliament would pass" such legislation.[13]

What was the significance of this first use of international human rights law in the interpretation of a domestic statute? It is true that there is a striking coincidence of subject matter between the guarantee in Articles 7 and 11(2) of the ECHR and UDHR and one of the common law's strongest presumptions, that against retrospective penal legislation, which suggests that the reference to the two treaties made no difference to the outcome of the case. It is also true, as Clapham points out, that Article 7 of the ECHR lends itself to relatively unproblematic application by a domestic court, being more in the nature of a rule, with only one narrow exception, than of a broad general principle such as those articulated in Articles 8 to 11, which require weighing against other broad principles.[14] This made it relatively uncontroversial for the court to invoke Article 7, and could be taken to suggest that no general conclusions about the status of international human rights norms in general can be drawn from the case.

To read the case in this narrow way would be mistaken, however. Lord Reid's comments in particular seem to be of quite general import, and although he did not expressly say that the courts would presume that both the executive and Parliament *always* intended to act consistently with international treaty obligations, it seems clear that he had some such general presumption in mind. His comments do not seem to be in any way conditional on there being a coincidence between a common law presumption and the content of the international obligation in order for that obligation to be relevant, nor was there any explicit mention of statutory ambiguity being a precondition of reference to the international human rights instruments, nor indeed any express consideration of whether there was any such ambiguity in the statute which fell to be interpreted in the case itself. It would seem then that for Lord Reid, *Miah* was not a case of applying a presumption of parliamentary intention to comply with a particular international obligation where domestic law was unclear, but a case in which the court applied a more general presumption that Parliament did not intend to legislate inconsistently with *any* of its obligations under international human rights law.[15]

[13] *Waddington* v. *Miah* [1974] 1 WLR 683 at 694B–E. As will be seen, judicial references to the Universal Declaration have been relatively rare.

[14] Clapham, *Human Rights in the Private Sphere* (above n. 4) at 14.

[15] It should be recalled that Lord Reid had already indicated his belief in such a general presumption, without a preliminary requirement of ambiguity, in relation to international law generally in *Smith* v. *East Elloe Rural District Council* [1956] AC 736 at 765.

Why was it that in the mid-1970s, after an interlude of more than two decades, international human rights law suddenly began to appear in counsel's arguments before domestic courts? The timing of the development was undoubtedly related to the slowly dawning awareness of the potential significance of the ECHR system. In 1966 the UK had recognised the competence of the Commission to receive individual petitions, and by 1973 the first applications against the UK were beginning to be heard by the Commission and the Court. By the time Sir Leslie Scarman delivered his important Hamlyn Lectures in September 1974,[16] *Golder's* case[17] was already before the Court and the *Sunday Times* case[18] and *Ireland* v. *UK*[19] were also pending before the Commission. Not surprisingly, Scarman identified the international human rights movement as one of the principal challenges from overseas which then confronted England's common law system, and to which in his view that system was going to have to adapt if it was to survive.[20]

With the far-sightedness which was his judicial trademark, Scarman clearly sensed the importance of the sea-change which had taken place in international law since the end of the Second World War, and the implications of that change for the domestic legal system. Recognising that international law was no longer exclusively the business of sovereign states, but was now concerned with the protection of individual citizens, he predicted that the ECHR was merely a reflection of a groundswell of public demand for the protection of individual rights which one way or another would have to be accommodated in the English legal system.[21] If that growing demand were to be met, and the UK to honour its international obligations, Scarman saw no alternative but for there to be a fundamental constitutional resettlement, in which provisions protecting the fundamental rights of the individual were entrenched against even legislative encroachment. Such a resettlement, in his view, would merely return the common law to its earlier attitudes.

Although Scarman's diagnosis of the challenge was persuasive, his prescription for responding to it was arguably more questionable. He appeared to see only two options facing the UK, either to continue as before, ignoring the international human rights movement, or to arrive at a new constitutional settlement by entrenching protections for certain rights against legislative encroachment. In fact, in a series of judicial decisions in the mid-1970s, certain English judges, including Lord Scarman himself, demonstrated that there was a third option available, which was for the common law itself to respond to the challenges presented by developments on the international plane, without the need for fundamental constitutional change of the sort envisaged by Scarman. All that was necessary was for courts to recognise an obligation

---

[16] *English Law—The New Dimension*, Hamlyn Lectures, 26th Series (London: Stevens, 1974).
[17] *Golder* v. *UK* (1975) 1 EHRR 524.
[18] *Sunday Times* v. *UK* (1979) 2 EHRR 245.
[19] (1978) 2 EHRR 1.
[20] *English Law—The New Dimension* at 10–21.
[21] Ibid. at 14.

always to take into account any relevant provisions of international human rights law when interpreting domestic law.

In *Birdi*, for example, in which an illegal entrant sought *habeas corpus* on the ground that his detention was in breach of Articles 5, 6 and 13 of the ECHR, Lord Denning MR said that courts "could and should take the Convention into account in interpreting a statute. An Act of Parliament should be construed so as to conform with the Convention".[22] The case is probably more famous for Lord Denning's surprising statement that "if an Act of Parliament did not conform to the Convention I might be inclined to hold it invalid".[23] This was an exorbitant claim, and even sounded so coming from the habitually extravagant Master of the Rolls. It should be seen as testimony to the novelty of the use of the Convention in domestic courts at this time, and ought not to detract from the importance of Lord Denning's recognition of the presumptive relevance of the Convention whenever a court is interpreting a domestic statute.

If international human rights treaties could legitimately be used by the courts as an aid to statutory interpretation, as Stephenson LJ and Lords Reid and Denning seemed to think, the potential for their use in administrative law, much of which of course involved statutory interpretation, was obviously enormous. In particular, they seemed to offer a constraint on the exercise of wide statutory discretions, which were notoriously difficult to challenge by way of judicial review due to the inherently deferential *Wednesbury* standard applied by courts when reviewing such discretions.[24] Applicants' lawyers were not slow to realise this, particularly in the context in which international human rights law had made its first appearance, immigration. Perhaps realising the enormous implications for domestic administrative law if such treaties could legitimately be used as an aid to statutory interpretation, the Government fought a rearguard action, predictably invoking the logic of parliamentary sovereignty to argue that, as an unincorporated international treaty, the ECHR was of no domestic legal relevance and should therefore be ignored by English courts.

In *Bhajan Singh*, for example, an illegal entrant detained with a view to deportation challenged the Secretary of State's refusal to provide him with facilities to marry, on the ground that he had failed to take into consideration Article 12 of the ECHR, which protects the right to marry and found a family.[25] By this time the European Court of Human Rights had delivered its first

---

[22] *Birdi* v. *Secretary of State for Home Affairs*, Bar Library Transcript No.67B, reported only at [1975] SJ 322.

[23] This heretical thought was later described by Lord Denning as "a very tentative statement" and retracted in *R* v. *Secretary of State for the Home Department, ex p. Bhajan Singh* [1976] 1 QB 198, considered below. In ch. 7 it will be seen that in fact developments in European Community law and domestic law in the space of just two decades have turned heresy into orthodoxy as far as legislation in the sphere of Community law is concerned.

[24] *Associated Provincial Picture Houses Ltd.* v. *Wednesbury Corporation* [1948] 1 KB 223.

[25] *R* v. *Secretary of State for the Home Department, ex p. Bhajan Singh* [1976] QB 198.

judgment in a case against the UK, *Golder*,[26] in which it was found that the requirement in the English Prison Rules that a prisoner obtain the leave of the Secretary of State before communicating with a lawyer violated Articles 6 and 8 of the Convention. Not surprisingly, in view of the public attention the ruling against the UK had engendered, considerable reliance was placed upon it by the applicant as an example of the seriousness of Britain's international obligations under the Convention.[27] The Home Secretary conceded that the government always endeavours to comply with the Convention, but argued that "a treaty even if it has been signed has no effect so far as the courts are concerned until it has been made an Act of Parliament."[28] Reliance was placed on *Blackburn* v. *Attorney General*[29] and *McWhirter* v. *Attorney General*,[30] in both of which, it will be recalled from chapter 1, Lord Denning MR's Court of Appeal had, in rejecting challenges to the executive's negotiation and signing of the Treaty of Accession to the European Communities, invoked the pure dualism which was said to flow from the premise of parliamentary sovereignty, that an international treaty has no effect, as far as the domestic courts are concerned, until it has been incorporated by Act of Parliament.

This attempt by the Government to invoke the supposedly hard and fast distinction between domestic law and unincorporated international law, so as to exclude the ECHR from domestic judicial view entirely, was implicitly rejected by both the Divisional Court and the Court of Appeal in *Bhajan Singh*. Lord Widgery CJ, in the Divisional Court, was in "no doubt that the terms of the Convention are properly to be regarded in this country where an issue in this country makes them relevant."[31] Similarly, Lord Denning MR in the Court of Appeal was unequivocally of the view that courts can and should take the Convention into account whenever interpreting a statute which affects the rights and liberties of the individual; they should, he said, seek to solve problems concerning human rights in the light of the Convention and in conformity with it. Following Lord Reid in *Miah*, Lord Denning's use of the Convention was in the form of a general presumption of interpretation: it was to be assumed that the Crown, in taking its part in legislation, would not do anything which conflicted with treaties.[32]

Lord Denning in *Bhajan Singh* was, however, careful to correct his statement in *Birdi*, that he might hold an Act of Parliament invalid if it did not

---

[26] (1975) 1 EHRR 524. Judgment was given on 21 February 1975.
[27] [1976] 1 QB 198 at 206E.
[28] Ibid. at 205B.
[29] [1971] 1 WLR 1037.
[30] [1972] CMLR 882.
[31] [1976] QB 198 at 202E, citing *Birdi*, above n. 22, as authority. Although Widgery LCJ's view of when a court is entitled to look at the Convention was broad, his interpretation of the relevant provision shows the inappropriateness of traditional English techniques of literal interpretation when applied to the broad provisions of the Convention. He held that the "and" in Article 12 was conjunctive, so that the right to "marry and found a family" covered only those who intended to do both!
[32] Ibid. at 207D–208B.

conform to the Convention, as going too far. He restated the orthodox position that a treaty does not become part of English law except and in so far as it is made so by Parliament and that if a statute contained any provisions contrary to the Convention, the Act would prevail.[33] But in another important respect he went even further than Lord Reid had gone in *Miah*, by spelling out the consequences of the general presumption for the exercise of statutory administrative discretion. In his view, both the Secretary of State and immigration officials ought to have regard to the principles in the Convention when carrying out their duties, since those principles were only a statement of the principles of fair dealing and, as Lord Denning's Court of Appeal had recently been instrumental in establishing, it was their public law duty to act fairly.[34] By thus asserting a coincidence of content between the Convention's principles and the common law duty to act fairly,[35] at the same time as saying that the Convention is a factor which must be taken into account by officials and ministers when exercising their statutory powers, Lord Denning appeared to hold out the prospect of the Convention becoming in its own right a ground of challenge to the exercise of executive or administrative discretion.

The same prospect seemed also to be held out by Lord Scarman, whose first judicial reference to the Convention, following his Hamlyn Lectures, was in *Phansopkar*.[36] He was the only member of the Court of Appeal to give detailed consideration to the argument of the wives of two patrials that their refusal of entry by the immigration officer, on the ground that they had to return to their country of origin to apply for the necessary certificate of patriality, was in breach of Article 8 of the ECHR.[37] Lord Scarman's methodology was to secure judicial protection for fundamental rights by adopting a particular approach to statutory interpretation. He treated the ECHR alongside Magna Carta as a reason why the Secretary of State's power to impose conditions on applicants for a certificate of patriality should be strictly construed. The hallowed principle, "justice delayed is justice denied", enshrined in Magna Carta, was said to be reinforced by the Convention, to which it was now the "duty" of public authorities administering the law, and of courts interpreting and applying the law, to have regard.[38]

---

[33] [1976] QB 198 at 207G.

[34] Ibid. at 207F. The duty to act fairly had recently emerged in cases such as *In re H.K. (An Infant)* [1967] 2 QB 617; *R v. Liverpool Corporation, ex p. Liverpool Taxi Fleet Operators' Association* [1972] 2 QB 299.

[35] An assertion that ignored the difficulties pointed out by counsel for the Secretary of State, [1976] QB 198 at 205E, that the precise content of the Convention's provisions is a matter for argument.

[36] *R v. Secretary of State for the Home Department, ex p. Phansopkar* [1976] QB 606.

[37] Lord Denning MR mentioned the applicants' reliance on the ECHR, ibid. at 616F, but along with Lawton LJ based his decision on Magna Carta: a reminder that, despite the breadth of his dicta in *Birdi* and *Bhajan Singh*, Lord Denning's use of the Convention was erratic. Even in his strong dissent in *Hubbard v. Pitt* [1976] QB 142, for example, in which he mounted a robust defence of the right of protest as one aspect of the right of free speech, he did not take up the defendants' argument, ibid. at 164H, that in the light of Articles 10 and 11 of the Convention the injunction restraining their protest ought to be discharged.

[38] [1976] QB 606 at 626C–D, citing *Bhajan Singh* as authority for this "duty".

In adopting this strict constructionist approach in favour of fundamental rights, Scarman LJ was careful to acknowledge the ultimate sovereignty of Parliament. The significance of his words merit their quotation in full:

> "It may, of course, happen under our law that the basic rights to justice undeferred and to respect for family and private life have to yield to the express requirements of a statute. But in my judgment it is the duty of the courts, so long as they do not defy or disregard clear unequivocal provision, to construe statutes in a manner which promotes, not endangers, those rights. Problems of ambiguity or omission, if they arise under the language of an Act, should be resolved so as to give effect to, or at the very least so as not to derogate from the rights recognised by Magna Carta and the European Convention."[39]

The first sentence of this passage is reminiscent of Scarman's concern, so eloquently articulated in his Hamlyn Lectures, about the courts' impotence in the face of Parliament's ultimate sovereign power to override fundamental rights simply by using sufficiently express language.[40] The second sentence, however, and his actual disposition of the case itself, suggest a capacity in the common law to protect the rights contained in the Convention by way of judicial interpretation, without the need for the entrenchment of rights against legislative invasion. Here Scarman was demonstrating the ability of the courts to achieve much of what he had desired in his lectures, merely by adapting the common law which formed the background against which statutes fell to be interpreted.[41]

Of particular significance in Scarman LJ's formulation of the construction approach in *Phansopkar* was his comment that the courts should strive to reach results consistent with the ECHR not just when questions of ambiguity arose under statutory language, but in cases of *omission* as well. To ask whether there has been a legislative omission, rather than whether there is simply a legislative ambiguity, is to adopt an entirely different approach to statutory interpretation. The "ambiguity" approach proceeds, ostensibly at least, on the assumption that legislation is an expression of Parliament's historical intention, and statutory interpretation an exercise in discovering that intention. On this view, imperfectly expressed ("ambiguous") intentions are perfectible by courts by reference to other sources which help to uncover the "true" intention behind the legislation. A court which asks whether there has been a legislative omission, on the other hand, is likely to have a broader

---

[39] Ibid. at 626F–G.

[40] In Lord Scarman's memorable words: "When times are normal and fear is not stalking the land, English law sturdily protects the freedom of the individual and respects human personality. But when times are abnormally alive with fear and prejudice, the common law is at a disadvantage: it cannot resist the will, however frightened and prejudiced it may be, of Parliament"; *English Law—The New Dimension* (above n. 16) at 15.

[41] Although the third and last sentence of the passage quoted seems to come close to the retention of ambiguity as a precondition to reference to the Convention, which was criticised in ch. 1, it is significant that Scarman talks not of "ambiguity or uncertainty" in domestic law, but of "ambiguity or omission", on which see further below.

conception of the judicial function when interpreting statutes, extending to the filling of gaps in legislation. Whereas "ambiguity" tends to operate as a pre-condition which must first be satisfied before reference can be made to the interpretive "aid", to ask whether there has been a legislative omission immediately makes the question of conformity with the international obligation a part of the overall context in which the meaning of the provision has to be interpreted.

The difference is easily demonstrated by reference to *Phansopkar* itself. There, the issue on which the court looked to see whether the statute spoke was itself defined by the right at stake: did the Secretary of State have the power to compel the wives of patrials, who had a statutory right to enter "without let or hindrance", to return to their country of origin to apply for their certificate of patriality and wait in the same queue as those with no such right? Not surprisingly, put like that, Scarman LJ found that neither the statute nor the rules expressly authorised such an interference with the applicants' fundamental rights. It can be seen then how, in practice, an approach which admits the possibility of legislative omission is more likely to make the relevant fundamental rights constitutive of the context in which the interpretive exercise takes place. An approach which confines itself to ambiguity, by comparison, may encourage courts to find clarity in the very generality of the statutory words conferring the Secretary of State's discretion, so that the rights in the international instrument never even become relevant.

Although Scarman LJ in *Phansopkar* treated the ECHR on an equal footing with Magna Carta in his reasoning, as both being instruments which recognise and protect rights, his use of the Convention as an aid to the interpretation of the Immigration Act needs separate justification because, unlike Magna Carta, it is not a domestic statute and therefore not, in the strict sense, a "part of" English law. The fact that it originates from an external source demands an explanation as to why it is relevant at all in the exercise of interpreting the domestic statute. Although this was not to be found in *Phansopkar* itself, it was forthcoming from Scarman LJ in a case decided very shortly after, *Pan-American World Airways Inc. v. Dept. of Trade*.[42] Although this case did not directly concern the ECHR, Scarman LJ cited the courts' recent practice of interpreting the Immigration Act 1971 in the light of the Convention as authority for the existence of an exception to the general rule that the courts take no notice of unincorporated treaties. He said that it was proper for the courts to take note of an international convention in a situation where two courses were reasonably open to the court, only one of which would lead to a decision consistent with international obligations. If the courts had to construe statutory words or formulate a legal principle in an area where the government had accepted international obligations, the courts would have regard to the international convention "as part of the full content

---

[42] [1976] 1 Lloyds LR 257, at 261 col.2–262 col.1.

or background of the law", even though there was no statute expressly or impliedly incorporating that convention into domestic law. This was said to be especially the case with multilateral conventions.[43]

Scarman in *Pan-Am* therefore showed his clear preference for an approach to the relevance of international instruments which dispenses with ambiguity as a condition on which the legitimacy of any reference rests. On the approach he articulated, the international obligation forms part of the very context in which the court decides the possible meanings of the provision, instead of being artificially kept out of sight until the court has decided, as a separate preliminary matter, whether there is an ambiguity which the instrument could help to resolve. This explains then why in *Phansopkar* Scarman LJ had treated the ECHR as being as relevant as Magna Carta in the court's exercise of construing the statutory language, notwithstanding the lack of any statute which could be said to incorporate it.

(b) International Human Rights Law and the Common Law

The initial judicial enthusiasm for interpreting domestic law in the light of the ECHR was by no means confined to the interpretation of statutes. There were some early signs that certain judges considered themselves obliged to interpret the common law as well in a such a way as to achieve conformity with the Convention, even where the question of interpretation arose in the context of a private law dispute. Lord Kilbrandon's comment in *Broome* v. *Cassell & Co. Ltd.*, for example, that free speech was to be seen as a "constitutional right" since ratification of the Convention, was made in the context of deciding the proper scope of the court's common law jurisdiction to award punitive damages.[44]

There was a similar foretaste of the ECHR's future relevance in private law disputes in *Blathwayt* v. *Baron Cawley*, in which Lord Wilberforce considered the Convention in the course of deciding whether a testamentary disposition with a disinheritance provision, disentitling any legatee who became Roman Catholic, was void as being contrary to public policy.[45] Significantly, rather like Lords Denning, Reid and Scarman in the cases already considered, Lord Wilberforce clearly thought the Convention to be of some relevance in deciding this question of common law, for he accepted that conceptions of public

---

[43] This passage was invoked by Kerr LJ in support of his approach to the relevance of unincorporated international law in *Rayner* [1989] Ch. 72 at 165D–G, considered in ch. 1.

[44] [1972] AC 1027 at 1133A.

[45] [1976] AC 397 at 425H–426C. The relevance of international law to a court's determination of the contents of "public policy" has long been accepted by English courts, although, as Mann points out, *Studies in International Law* (Oxford: Clarendon Press, 1973) at 340, it is often "difficult in theory and immaterial in practice" to draw a clear distinction between a treaty referred to because it expresses a rule of customary international law and one referred to because it constitutes a head of public policy.

policy were dynamic rather than static, and that widely accepted treaties such as the Convention may show the direction in which such conceptions ought to move. However, although the relevance of the Convention was acknowledged, Lord Wilberforce was in little doubt about how English courts should resolve a clash between the values protected by the Convention and those prioritised by the common law: even if disinheritance provisions were becoming inconsistent with widely accepted standards, it was held that as a competing conception of public policy it was not strong enough to override the freedom, "firmly rooted in our law", of testamentary disposition.[46]

3. THE FLIGHT FROM HUMAN RIGHTS IN ADMINISTRATIVE LAW

By the end of 1975 it therefore seemed as if the courts were prepared to take considerably more notice of human rights treaties, and of the ECHR in particular, than of any other unincorporated treaties. Most significantly of all, the cases from the immigration context, *Miah, Birdi, Bhajan Singh* and *Phansopkar*, had potentially wide implications for domestic administrative law, suggesting as they did that executive and administrative statutory discretions had to be exercised consistently with the Convention. This latter development came to an abrupt halt, however, in *Salamat Bibi*.[47] The retrenchment seems to have been at least in part a response to what was probably too bold an argument by the applicant, providing a salutary reminder to advocates that adventurous arguments in the wrong case often make bad law. The wife of a Commonwealth citizen settled in the UK, who, along with her two children, had been refused leave to enter to visit her husband, made two arguments based on the ECHR. First, she argued that the immigration officer had exercised his discretion without taking into account her right to respect for family life under Article 8, an argument which seemed merely to invite the court to follow the authorities already considered. Second, however, she argued in the alternative that Article 8 was directly enforceable in the English courts and had to be read in conjunction with the provisions of the Immigration Act 1971. The argument was that, as a consequence of the UK's acceptance of the right of individual petition to the European Commission of Human Rights, domestic courts must now recognise and enforce the provisions of the Convention.[48]

The applicant's second argument was inviting the court to go well beyond any position it had hitherto adopted on the domestic status of the Convention,

---

[46] Indeed, the tension between the new age of public intervention for the protection of human rights and the private ordering of the old common law world is neatly captured in Lord Wilberforce's observation, [1976] AC 397 at 426C, that "[d]iscrimination is not the same thing as choice . . . neither by express provision nor by implication has private selection yet become a matter of public policy".

[47] R v. *Chief Immigration Officer, Heathrow Airport, ex p Salamat Bibi* [1976] 1 WLR 979.

[48] Ibid. at 982B and 984F.

or indeed of any unincorporated international instrument, and it is scarcely surprising that it was rejected in the strongest terms by each member of the Court of Appeal. All three judges reiterated as axiomatic that the Convention was not part of English law and could not become so until it was made law by Parliament.[49] The courts could look to the Convention to clear up any ambiguity or uncertainty in domestic statute or common law, "seeking always to bring them in harmony with it",[50] but that position was far short of the Convention being part of domestic law, and it certainly could not have the effect of overriding clear statutory rules with which it was in conflict.[51]

This much was not surprising, but the Court of Appeal went on to reject also the applicant's other argument that the immigration officer should have exercised his discretion having regard to Article 8, thus retreating from the ground it had previously occupied on this question in earlier cases. Lord Denning expressly retracted his comment in *Bhajan Singh* that immigration officers ought to bear in mind the principles of the Convention, and Roskill LJ expressly agreed with that retraction.[52] Both judges thought that it was asking too much of such officers to expect them to know or to apply the Convention. It was said to be enough if they went simply by the immigration rules laid down by the Secretary of State. Roskill LJ also thought that Scarman LJ had gone too far in his statement of the position in *Phansopkar* and *Pan-Am*, when he had talked in terms of a duty or obligation on both courts and administrators to have regard to the Convention when interpreting statutes.

This wholesale rejection of the argument that the immigration officer should have had regard to the Convention appears to have been based on wholly practical concerns rooted in a new scepticism about the practical applicability of the Convention's broadly drafted provisions, with their vague statements of principle and their wide exceptions, by busy administrative officers. Roskill LJ, for example, was clearly concerned with over-burdening immigration officers, which he thought would be the inevitable result of forcing them to consider the application of the Convention on every occasion when they exercised discretion. Lord Denning MR, showing a similar concern with the practicalities of applying the ECHR, thought the drafting of Article 8 to be so wide as to be incapable of practical application.[53] The very different drafting style of the Convention was offered as a reason why it was better to confine it to a purely residual role, relevant only to the court when there was doubt over the meaning of domestic law.[54]

---

[49] Lord Denning MR, ibid. at 984H; Roskill LJ at 986A–B; Geoffrey Lane LJ at 988C.

[50] Lord Denning MR, ibid. at 984G–H; Geoffrey Lane LJ at 988C.

[51] Roskill LJ, ibid. at 986H; Geoffrey Lane LJ at 988C.

[52] Lord Denning MR, ibid. at 984H; Roskill LJ at 986G; Geoffrey Lane LJ at 988D–E.

[53] Ibid. at 985B. See Geoffrey Lane LJ at 988E to the same effect.

[54] Contrast Lord Denning's views on the Convention in *Salamat Bibi* with his praise for the virtues of the modern "European way" of interpretation in Community law compared with the English literalist tradition: see *The Discipline of Law* (London: Butterworths, 1979) at 15–22; and see *Bulmer Ltd.* v. *Bollinger SA* [1974] Ch. 401 at 411.

However, to reject the applicant's argument on practical grounds alone hardly seems satisfactory, especially as it had the support of previous Court of Appeal authority, and, in some cases at least, on carefully reasoned legal grounds. Although the Court had unequivocally rejected the suggestion that the ECHR was part of English law, that was not enough to dispose of the applicant's discretion argument, since the court had also accepted that the Convention was relevant in the event of ambiguity or uncertainty. It was therefore incumbent on the Court of Appeal to explain why the presumption which it acknowledged to exist did not apply where a discretion of wide and therefore necessarily uncertain scope had been statutorily conferred on administrative officers. Indeed, Lord Denning's formulation of his understanding of the domestic relevance of the Convention showed that he was still drawn to a general presumption of intended conformity with the Convention, rather than one triggered by ambiguity. The courts, he said, would assume that when Parliament was enacting a statute, or a Secretary of State framing rules, they had regard to the Convention and intended to make the enactment accord with the Convention, and the courts would interpret them accordingly.[55] On this view, the Convention was surely relevant to the exercise of the immigration officer's discretion, even though it was not, strictly speaking, "part of" English law in the sense that the applicant could directly found her case upon it.

Could the decision be explained on the basis that the presumption, if applicable, was rebutted by practical considerations in the particular context? In other words, did the perceived impracticality of immigration officers having regard to the Convention form the basis for an inference by the court that Parliament could not have had such an intention, an inference that rebutted the presumption that they did so intend? A conclusion in these terms might have been more intellectually defensible, but it seems clear that it does not describe the Court of Appeal's reasoning. The objections made to the practicability of applying the Convention's provisions were not specific to the immigration context, or the particular Convention Article in issue, but were of general import, being based on the drafting style of the Convention. The clear implication of the decision, then, is that statutory discretions never have to be exercised consistently with the Convention for the simple reason that the Convention was not "part of" English law. As such, the Court of Appeal's decision in *Salamat Bibi* is of profound significance for the role of international human rights law in administrative law, but it rests on a most unsatisfactory theoretical basis. In particular, no attempt was made to reconcile this conclusion with the existence of the international treaty presumption, according to which, in its strongest form, international treaties, while not in the strict sense "part of" domestic law, nevertheless have some relevance in the interpretation of that law.

---

[55] [1976] 1 WLR 979 at 984H.

The determination of the Court of Appeal in *Salamat Bibi* to keep the ECHR out of judicial review of administrative discretion threatened to undermine the emerging status of the treaty presumption as a general presumption, rather than one triggered by ambiguity, or at least to exclude international human rights instruments such as the ECHR from the scope of that general presumption. The common distinguishing feature of *Miah, Birdi, Bhajan Singh, Phansopkar* and *Pan-Am* was that in each case it had been taken for granted that the presumption that Parliament intended to legislate consistently with treaty obligations, including the Convention, was general in the sense that it did not require ambiguity in statutory language to make the international obligation relevant to the exercise in construction of statutory language. Now, in *Salamat Bibi*, the Court of Appeal had seized on the quintessentially sovereigntist device of ambiguity to reject the argument that the ECHR was a relevant factor to be taken into account in the exercise of administrative discretion, and the generality of its reasoning was such that it risked marginalising the domestic status of international human rights treaties in contexts other than the review of administrative discretion.[56]

4. THE CONTINUING USES OF HUMAN RIGHTS LAW OUTSIDE ADMINISTRATIVE LAW

(a) Statutory Interpretation in Other Contexts

It soon became clear, however, that it was really only in the context of judicial review of administrative discretion that the courts were concerned to limit the scope of the treaty presumption in order to keep international human rights law at bay in administrative law. In an employment case, *Ahmad* v. *ILEA*, for example, decided within a year of *Bibi*, the Court of Appeal made no insistence on there being ambiguity in the relevant statutory language before reference could legitimately be made to the ECHR as an aid to the interpretation of statutory language.[57] A teacher who was a devout Muslim claimed unfair dismissal, arguing that his employer had forced him to resign by refusing to allow him to miss forty-five minutes of classes once a week in order to attend prayers. The central question in the case was the meaning to be given to the statutory protection for freedom of religion in s.30 of the Education Act 1944, which provided, so far as relevant,

---

[56] In *Allgemeine* v. *Customs and Excise Commissioners* [1980] QB 390 at 394E (considered in ch. 7 below) it was argued before the Court of Appeal that *Salamat Bibi* was wrong and ought to be overruled in so far as it decided that public officers were not obliged to have regard to the provisions of the ECHR in the exercise of a discretion conferred on them by domestic legislation, but the point was not taken up in the judgments.

[57] [1978] QB 36.

"no teacher . . . shall . . . receive any less emolument or be deprived of, or disqualified for, any promotion or other advantage by reason of his religious opinions or of his attending or omitting to attend any religious worship."

No reliance was placed on the Convention by the applicant in his grounds of appeal, but Scarman LJ, inhabiting a world with broader horizons, drew attention to Article 9 in the course of argument,[58] and each member of the court proceeded to consider the ECHR in the course of their judgment.

It is particularly noteworthy that, in contrast to *Salamat Bibi*, virtually no time was spent considering the legal status of the ECHR in domestic courts or the legitimacy of referring to it in the interpretation of a statute. This is all the more remarkable when it is remembered that the statute which fell to be interpreted, the Education Act 1944, pre-dated the existence, let alone the ratification, of the Convention, so that strictly speaking any reference which was made to the Convention as a "guide to interpretation" could not be justified in traditional terms as an exercise in discovering Parliament's historical intention.

Whereas in *Salamat Bibi* Lord Denning appeared to equivocate between treating the treaty presumption as a general presumption and treating it as merely a presumption triggered by ambiguity, at least where the treaty concerned was the ECHR, in *Ahmad* he reverted to an unqualified statement of a general presumption, saying "The Convention is not part of our English law, but, as I have often said, we will always have regard to it. We will do our best to see that our decisions are in conformity with it."[59] He went on to express the same reservations about the vagueness of its language as he had expressed in *Salamat Bibi*, and to voice concerns about it being invoked to support unmeritorious claims and vexatious litigation. Nevertheless, he proceeded to make, as he saw it, a conscientious attempt to bring its high-sounding principles down to earth and give them content in the particular context in which it was sought to rely on them.

Although his judgment can be justly criticised for giving too little weight to freedom of religion, nevertheless he carried out a balancing exercise very similar to that required by the Convention, weighing the right to exercise one's religion on the one hand against the protection of the rights of others (the education authority and the children) on the other. It is hard to imagine that he would have carried out such an explicit balancing exercise in interpreting the statutory provision had the entire exercise not been conducted in the light of Article 9. Similarly, Orr LJ did not directly consider the question of the status of the Convention in domestic law, or whether there was ambiguity in the statutory language, but simply addressed the Article 9 argument on its merits, noting that the Convention itself expressly made freedom of religion subject to limits, before concluding that s.30 could not be construed as entitling

---

[58] [1978] QB 36 at 38D; and see Lord Denning MR at 41D.
[59] Ibid. at 41D.

an employee to absent himself, for the purpose of religious worship, from his place of work during working hours and in breach of his contract of employment.[60]

It is in Scarman LJ's dissent, however, that the continuation of the pre-*Bibi* approach to the status of international human rights law can be most clearly seen. Undaunted by Roskill LJ's criticisms in *Bibi*, Scarman LJ showed unswerving consistency with his position in *Phansopkar* and *Pan-Am*, that there was an obligation on judges to interpret domestic law consistently with international obligations, without requiring them first to go through an ambiguity gateway. It was, he said, no longer possible to argue that because international treaty obligations do not become law unless enacted by Parliament, courts paid no regard to them. On the contrary, they paid very serious regard to them: they would interpret statutory language and apply common law principles, wherever possible, so as to reach a conclusion consistent with international obligations.[61] The statutory provision protecting teachers from religious discrimination had to be given a construction which reflected changes both in society and in the legal background since the statute was enacted, and those background changes included the UK's acceptance of various international obligations, including the Convention, designed to protect human rights and freedoms. Taking this broad approach to the construction of the section, Scarman LJ held that the teacher had been unfairly dismissed in breach of the statutory protection.[62]

Ahmad is significant, not just for the continuity between Scarman LJ's dissent and the pre-*Bibi* case-law, but for the way in which it demonstrates in even the majority's approach the relative lack of judicial preoccupation with the status of the ECHR when interpreting statutes outside of the context of reviewing administrative discretion. Although neither Lord Denning nor Orr LJ found anything in Article 9 which required a broad interpretation of the statutory provision, the fact that both were prepared to take the Convention into account at all, without any obvious qualms about the legitimacy of doing so, is significant in itself. The same willingness was in evidence in Lord Denning's judgment in *Panesar*, another employment case concerning indirect religious discrimination.[63] A Sikh applicant for a job in the employer's chocolate factory invoked Article 9 ECHR in support of his claim that he was indirectly discriminated against by the application to him of the employer's rule requiring workers in the factory to be "clean shaven". As in *Ahmad*, Lord

---

[60] Ibid. at 45E–F.

[61] Ibid. at 48E, citing *Salomon* [1967] 2 QB 116 and *Post Office* v. *Estuary Radio* [1968] 2 QB 740, considered in ch. 1 above.

[62] Scarman LJ's dissent is an excellent example of the approach to statutory interpretation advocated throughout this book. The section fell to be construed and applied "not against the background of the law and society of 1944 but in a multi-racial society which has accepted international obligations and enacted statutes designed to eliminate discrimination on grounds of race, religion, colour or sex", ibid. at 48D.

[63] *Panesar* v. *Nestlé Co. Ltd.* [1980] ICR 144.

Denning proceeded on the basis that, although it was not part of English law, "we have much regard to it".[64]

Such willingness to have regard to the ECHR in the employment context was in stark contrast to the reluctance even to consider it in administrative law. In *Chahal*, for example, a Sikh who had been convicted for driving a motorbike without wearing protective headgear challenged the regulation under which he was convicted by way of judicial review.[65] One of the grounds on which it was alleged that the regulation was *ultra vires* was that it contravened Art. 9 ECHR. The argument was ignored altogether by the court.[66]

(b) International Human Rights and the Common Law

Not only did courts post-*Bibi* continue to apply a general presumption of conformity with the ECHR when interpreting statutes in non-administrative law contexts, but they also continued to expound the common law against what seemed to be a similar background presumption. This often took the form of judicial assertion of an identity between the common law and the Convention. For example, in *Associated Newspapers Group* v. *Wade*, Lord Denning held it to be implicitly accepted as a fundamental principle of English law that the press shall be free, and that in this respect English law corresponded with Art. 10 ECHR.[67] Similarly, in *UKAPE* v. *ACAS*, in the context of a union recognition dispute, Lord Denning asserted that Article 11 of the Convention, protecting the right to freedom of assembly and association, including the right to form and join trade unions, did no more than state a basic principle of English law, for the common law had always recognised that everyone has the right to freedom of association and, as a corollary, the right to form and join trade unions.[68] The consequence of such recognition was that when Parliament enacted legislation on trade unions it was to be taken not to intend

---

[64] [1980] ICR 144 at 147F–H. As in many of the early cases in which the ECHR was considered, however, it made little difference. Lord Denning merely held that the employer's "no beards" rule would be saved by Art. 9(2) as being justified on grounds of health. He treated this as a purely factual question, without carrying out a proportionality-type exercise by asking, for example, whether there was a less restrictive way of achieving that objective, such as by requiring beards to be covered at all times in the factory.

[65] *R* v. *Aylesbury Crown Court, ex p. Chahal* [1976] RTR 489.

[66] The reasoning supporting the dismissal of the application shows just how badly a human rights dimension was needed. Widgery LCJ held that the application had no substance, as no one was bound to ride a motorbike, and the cause of the impact on the Sikh community was their religion not the regulation.

[67] [1979] 1 WLR 697 at 708H–709A. According to Lord Denning, the common law's protection of the freedom of the press went even further than Art. 10 ECHR, for it required that there should be no interference by private individuals, including trade unions, and not merely by public authority.

[68] [1979] 1 WLR 570 at 582H–583C. In *Express Newspapers* v. *Keys* [1980] IRLR 247 at 249 col. 2 Griffiths J. followed Lord Denning's approach in *UKAPE* v. *ACAS*, finding that the common law, like the ECHR, recognises freedom of assembly.

to contravene that basic right. In the House of Lords, Lord Scarman agreed with Lord Denning that both Article 11 and the common law recognised and protected the right of association, including the right to join a trade union, but held that it did not follow from the existence of that right that every trade union which can show that it has members employed in a particular company or industry has a right to recognition for the purposes of collective bargaining.[69] In his view, neither the common law nor the Convention compelled a conclusion which would cause such chaos in industrial relations.

Although Lords Denning and Scarman reached very different conclusions, they were united in their adoption of the judicial technique of treating the ECHR as merely the articulation of rights already immanent in the common law.[70] Such a technique obviously comes very close to recognising and giving effect to the Convention as customary law,[71] especially in cases such as this where the extent of the common law's recognition of the right in question was at best doubtful, so that the identification of the common law right with the Convention right is really a development of the common law. Moreover, in a case such as this where what was at stake turned on the interpretation of a statutory provision, the identification of the Convention right with a common law right protected against statutory encroachment by a presumption of interpretation is tantamount to the recognition of a general presumption of conformity with the particular Convention right.

During this same period, the ECHR also came to play a more explicit role in the development of the common law, by judicial reference to it where the common law was unclear. In *R* v. *Lemon*, for example, the famous private prosecution of Gay News by Mary Whitehouse for blasphemous libel, the question for the court was whether the *mens rea* of the common law offence of blasphemous libel was an intent to blaspheme.[72] Lord Scarman saw the issue as "one of legal policy in the society of today" and proceeded to interpret the common law in the same teleological way as he had interpreted s.30 of the Education Act 1944 in his dissent in *Ahmad*.[73] Taking up again his Hamlyn theme of the importance of protecting rights and freedoms in modern pluralistic societies, he thought that the movement in recent statutes, such as the Obscene Publications Act and the Race Relations Act, towards a focus on the objective nature of the words or material published, rather than the

---

[69] [1981] AC 424 at 445F–446A. As Clapham points out, *Human Rights in the Private Sphere* (above n. 4) at 26, Lord Scarman's conclusion is more consistent with Article 11 jurisprudence, but neither judge made reference to such case-law.

[70] See, to similar effect, Lord Denning in *Cheall* v. *APEX* [1983] QB 126 at 136B–D, identifying Article 11 ECHR with the basic common law principle of freedom of association.

[71] In *Cheall* v. *APEX*, ibid. at 137C, Lord Denning MR concluded that Article 11(1) ECHR "is part of the law of England or at any rate the same".

[72] [1979] AC 617.

[73] Ibid. at 664F Lord Scarman was alone among the Law Lords in referring to the ECHR. Contrast the centrality of the Convention in the most recent judicial consideration of the law of blasphemy in *R* v. *Chief Metropolitan Stipendiary Magistrate, ex p. Choudhury* [1991] 1 QB 429, considered in ch. 5 below.

intention of the author or publisher, made legal sense in a plural society which recognised the human rights and fundamental freedoms of the ECHR. He read Article 9 as imposing, by implication, a duty on everyone to refrain from insulting or outraging the religious feelings of others, and he noted that the right of free speech under Article 10 carried with it duties and responsibilities and was subject to legitimate restrictions. Lord Scarman therefore upheld the convictions, holding intent to be irrelevant, but criticised the law of blasphemous libel for protecting only the Christian faith and expressed the hope that it would be legislatively extended to protect other faiths.

A similar use of the Convention in the development of the common law was made in *Gleaves* v. *Deakin*, in which Lord Diplock spent most of his judgment discussing the criminal offence of defamatory libel in terms of its conformity with Article 10, expressing the view that the offence had aspects which involved serious departures from accepted principles upon which the modern criminal law was based and which were difficult to reconcile with the obligations accepted under the Convention.[74] His recommendation that the law be reformed by requiring the consent of the Attorney-General to be obtained before a prosecution for criminal libel could be brought, to avoid the risk of failing to comply with the UK's international obligations under the Convention, is an interesting example of an unsolicited advisory declaration on the compatibility of domestic law with the Convention.[75]

The limits to the use which could be made of the ECHR in developing the common law were, however, demonstrated in *Malone* v. *Metropolitan Police Commissioner*.[76] The plaintiff in that case sought a declaration that, in the absence of legislative authorisation and strict controls, tapping his telephone was an infringement of his right to privacy under Art. 8 ECHR. He argued, *inter alia*, that the ECHR should have a significant effect in determining what the law was on a point which was devoid of direct authority. In the absence of a common law right to privacy, Megarry V-C declined to extend the common law by reference to the ECHR, holding that it was difficult for the Court to lay down new rules of common law that would carry out the Crown's treaty obligations. However, before reaching this conclusion, he accepted that the Convention ought to be taken into account in deciding what the law ought to be, and gave it due consideration in his judgment. He even found it impossible to see how, in the light of the Court's judgment in *Klass* v. *Germany*,[77]

---

[74] [1980] AC 477 at 482G–484C. Like Lord Scarman in *Lemon*, Lord Diplock was the only Law Lord to mention the Convention. The lack of consistency amongst judges in the use they made of the Convention at this early stage in the history of its domestic career is well shown by the fact that in *R* v. *Lemon* Lord Scarman gave extensive consideration to the Convention while Lord Diplock gave it none, while in *Gleaves* v. *Deakin*, decided a matter of weeks later, the converse was the case.

[75] Ibid. at 484B–C. The other Law Lords agreed with the recommendation but made no reference to the Convention.

[76] [1979] Ch 344.

[77] (1978) 2 EHRR 214.

English law could be said to satisfy the requirements of the Convention. To award a declaration to that effect, however, would be going far beyond any possible function of the Convention in influencing English law, and he declined to make a declaration on a matter which was not strictly speaking justiciable in English courts.

Other decisions from this period confirmed that, outside of administrative law, the presumption of the consistency of domestic law with international obligations continued to apply, and was not merely a presumption of statutory interpretation, but applied equally to judicial interpretation of the common law. When, for example, only shortly after the decision of the European Court of Human Rights in the *Sunday Times* case,[78] a different question concerning the scope of the courts' common law contempt jurisdiction fell to be decided by the House of Lords, in *AG* v. *BBC*, Lord Scarman again demonstrated how English common law could be (and in his view was required to be) interpreted in the light of the ECHR, notwithstanding that neither it nor the decisions of the Court of Human Rights were part of English law.[79] He held that in deciding whether the common law contempt jurisdiction of the High Court extended to a local valuation court, which was not a court of law but a court discharging administrative functions, the potential impact on the UK's international obligations, as interpreted by the European Court of Human Rights, had to be borne in mind.[80] If the UK was to comply with its obligations under the Convention, he said, the House of Lords had to ask itself whether it was satisfied that there was a pressing social need for the law of contempt to cover such bodies.[81] However, the precise status of the presumption was left in doubt by the fact that Lord Fraser appeared to introduce into the common law context the same precondition of ambiguity in domestic law which had been allowed to creep into statutory interpretation in the administrative law context. Courts, he said, should have regard to the Convention and to decisions of the Court of Human Rights in cases where domestic law is "not firmly settled."[82]

Another common law context in which courts have relatively freely referred to the ECHR without pausing for too long to consider the basis on which they did so is where there exists a judicial discretion to be exercised. In *Spycatcher No. 1*, for example, in which the issue was whether interlocutory injunctions granted to restrain publication of Peter Wright's notorious book should continue until trial, Lord Templeman proceeded directly to a consideration of the compatibility of the continuation of the injunctions with Article 10 ECHR as if that provision were a directly applicable part of domestic law, without any

[78] *Sunday Times* v. *UK* (1979) 2 EHRR 245.
[79] [1981] AC 303.
[80] Ibid. at 354B–F. Although Lord Scarman was again alone in referring to the ECHR, others were clearly influenced in reaching their conclusion by considerations of freedom of speech and of the press.
[81] Ibid. at 362C–D.
[82] Ibid. at 352.

discussion of why such a course was either permitted or required.[83] It was simply asserted that determination of the appeal involved consideration of the Convention because the case involved "a conflict between the right of the public to be protected by the Security Service and the right of the public to be supplied with full information by the press."[84] The unarticulated assumption appeared to be that when courts are required to balance competing public interests in this way they are exercising "a judicial discretion in conformity with the Convention".[85]

The basis on which it was considered proper to take the ECHR into account in such circumstances was made clearer at the trial of the main action, *Spycatcher No. 2.*[86] Scott J. held that the courts, in determining disputes as to the relative weight to be given to competing public interests, ought to try to strike the balance in a way that is consistent with treaty obligations accepted by the government, because there was "a clear analogy with the well-known rule of construction of statutes that requires statutes to be construed, if possible, consistently with the government's treaty obligations."[87] In making explicit this important analogy, Scott J., like Lord Scarman in *AG* v. *BBC*, was in effect acknowledging the ultimate common law foundation of the notice taken of the ECHR by English courts: the presumption that domestic law is consistent with international obligations is not, nor should it be, confined to the interpretation of statutes, but applies equally where the court is required to interpret or develop the common law, or to weigh competing public interests in the exercise of a judicial discretion. The rule of statutory construction is but one manifestation of a more general presumption about the consistency of domestic law with international obligations. Moreover, the nature of that presumption is not merely permissive but obligatory. Courts are not merely entitled to have regard to international human rights instruments when interpreting statutes, interpreting the common law or exercising a judicial discretion, but are *required* to carry out those functions consistently with such instruments in so far as they are not prevented from doing so by unambiguous domestic law to the contrary.

A further and different reason for the legitimacy of referring to the ECHR was also apparent in both the Court of Appeal and the House of Lords in *Spycatcher No. 2*. In a passage which has subsequently been much cited, Lord Donaldson MR confidently declared that he could find no inconsistency

---

[83] *AG* v. *Guardian Newspapers Ltd.* [1987] 1 WLR 1248 at 1296F–1299G. The dissentients Lords Oliver and Bridge did not proceed on the same assumption. Indeed the latter, ibid. at 1286C–D, in his now famous dissent, declared his confidence in the ability of the common law to protect fundamental rights and freedoms, unassisted by the Convention, to have been undermined by the majority's decision.

[84] Ibid. at 1296F–G.

[85] Ibid. at 1299F.

[86] *AG* v. *Guardian Newspapers Ltd. (No. 2)* [1990] 1 AC 109.

[87] Ibid. at 157H–158A. Scott J. also made clear, at 159B–D, that the court should have regard not only to the terms of the Convention itself but to decisions of the European Court of Human Rights interpreting its provisions.

between domestic law and the Convention: the substantive right to freedom of expression in Article 10 was subsumed within the universal freedom of action of every citizen in domestic law.[88] Under both domestic law and the Convention, courts had the power and the duty to assess the pressing social need for the proportionate maintenance of confidentiality against the right to freedom of expression. In the House of Lords, Lord Goff similarly could see no inconsistency between English law on confidentiality and Article 10 of the Convention.[89] The difference was said to be merely one of approach and there was no reason to believe that English law did not equally require that interference with freedom of expression should be no more than is proportionate to the legitimate aim pursued. Significantly, however, Lord Goff went further than the Court of Appeal in stating what he clearly believed to be an interpretive obligation:

"I conceive it to be my duty, when I am free to do so, to interpret the law in accordance with the obligations of the Crown under this treaty."[90]

5. KEEPING HUMAN RIGHTS OUT OF ADMINISTRATIVE LAW

The distinguishing characteristic of this second phase in the history of international human rights law in domestic courts, however, is that, notwithstanding the relatively liberal use which was being made of the ECHR in the interpretation and development of the common law, and the Privy Council's adoption of a "broad and generous" approach to the interpretation of Commonwealth constitutional documents which were based on the Convention,[91] English courts maintained throughout this period their firm resistance to the ECHR becoming a ground on which the exercise of administrative discretion could be challenged. Occasions on which the Convention or its case-law, or any human rights instrument, were referred to and made a difference to the outcome in an administrative law case were rare, and tended to be confined to situations in which the Court of Human Rights had already found a violation in closely analogous circumstances,[92] or cases concerning

[88] Ibid. at 178F–H. See to similar effect Dillon L.J. at 203F–G and Bingham L.J. at 219G–220C.
[89] Ibid. at 283E–284A.
[90] Ibid. at 283G. The tenor of the statement, and in particular the fact that it is couched in terms of an interpretive "duty", suggests that the qualification "when I am free to do so" was not meant to import any ambiguity precondition, but rather was a reference to the situation in which there is no irreconcilable conflict between domestic law and the international obligation.
[91] See eg. *Minister of Home Affairs* v. *Fisher* [1980] AC 319 at 328F–H and 330B–C; *Thornhill* v. *AG Trinidad and Tobago* [1980] 2 WLR 510 at 516A–B. For a critical account of the Privy Council's overall record, see K.D. Ewing, "A Bill of Rights: Lessons from the Privy Council" in W. Finnie, C.M.G. Himsworth & N. Walker (eds.), *Edinburgh Essays in Public Law* (Edinburgh: Edinburgh University Press, 1991) at 231.
[92] See eg. *Raymond* v. *Honey* [1983] AC 1 and *R* v. *Secretary of State for the Home Department, ex p. Anderson* [1984] QB 778. In both cases the applicants' argument was greatly assisted by the existence of decisions of the European Court of Human Rights in similar cases against the UK (*Golder* v. *UK* (1979) 1 EHRR 524 and *Silver* v. *UK* (1983) 5 EHRR 347).

the interpretation of legislation introduced in order to comply with such a judgment. Those cases aside, a more or less straight line can be drawn from *Salamat Bibi* to the well known House of Lords decision in *Brind*, which, it will be argued, represents the epitome of this second phase.[93] This judicial resistance was made possible only by a reassertion of sovereignty in the shape of the reinstatement of the ambiguity gateway to use of international human rights law, notwithstanding that this went very much against the grain of contemporary developments, and in particular the gradual strengthening of the treaty presumption chronicled in chapter 1.

It was noted above that the consequences of *Salamat Bibi* for administrative law were potentially far-reaching. In effect the decision meant that, notwithstanding the existence of a presumption of statutory interpretation that Parliament always intends to legislate consistently with its international obligations, a presumption that arguably had already by judicial development acquired full constitutional status, there is no requirement that delegated power must be exercised in conformity with international human rights law such as the ECHR. This consequence was spelled out of *Bibi* in *Fernandes*, in which the Court of Appeal rejected an argument that the Secretary of State was under an obligation to take the ECHR into account in deciding whether or not to suspend a deportation order, where an application to the Commission of Human Rights was actually pending and the government had been asked for its observations, but had not been requested by the Commission to stay deportation.[94] The Convention could be resorted to in order to resolve some ambiguity or uncertainty in municipal law, the court held, but the Secretary of State was under no legal obligation to take account of the Convention when making his decision and the only test the court could apply was whether it was *Wednesbury* unreasonable. As in *Bibi* itself, which was heavily relied upon, the concern seemed to be primarily one of administrative efficiency, a fear that if the courts imposed a requirement that the Convention be taken into account whenever discretion is exercised, the administration would be brought to a grinding halt.[95]

The inflexibility of the courts' insistence that international human rights treaties do not constitute a relevant consideration to which the Secretary of State or administrative officials must have regard was demonstrated by *Kirkwood*, in which an argument that the ECHR was relevant where a much more fundamental right was at stake was rejected.[96] A prisoner who was awaiting extradition to the US for trial on a murder charge mounted a *Wednesbury* unreasonableness challenge to the Secretary of State's decision to

[93] R v. *Secretary of State for the Home Department, ex p. Brind* [1991] 1 AC 696.

[94] *Fernandes* v. *Secretary of State for the Home Department* [1981] Imm AR 1.

[95] See eg. Ackner LJ, ibid. at 7. Clapham, *Human Rights in the Private Sphere* (above n. 4) at 40, considers *Fernandes* to be an "unfortunate extension" of *Bibi*, because the impracticability argument ought not to apply to decisions taken by the Secretary of State rather than immigration officers.

[96] R v. *Secretary of State for the Home Department, ex p. Kirkwood* [1984] 1 WLR 913.

proceed with his extradition, in total disregard of his application to the European Commission in which he complained that extradition would infringe his right not to be subjected to inhuman and degrading treatment under Article 3. He sought to get round the obstacle of *Fernandes* by claiming that there must be some obligation on the Secretary of State where the consequences for the applicant were much more serious than a breach of Article 8. Mann J. held that *Fernandes* was indistinguishable, and that there was no obligation on the Secretary of State to have any regard to the ECHR when exercising his discretion.[97]

Despite the theoretical weakness of this position, in light of the status of the treaty presumption, and the fact that the justification was growing progressively weaker the more use the courts were making of the ECHR in the development of the common law, the line was held, perhaps even reinforced, in *Chundawadra*.[98] The case concerned a challenge to the Secretary of State's exercise of his wide statutory discretion to deport a person who was not a British citizen if he "deems his deportation to be conducive to the public good."[99] The applicant argued that both the Secretary of State in making the deportation decision and the Immigration Appeal Tribunal in reviewing it should have had regard to Article 8 of the ECHR, since the applicant had strong family ties in this country and no relations in the country to which he was being returned. Taylor J. had rejected that argument, following *Bibi* and *Fernandes* in holding that the extent to which the Convention was relevant or could be used was in interpreting statute law if there was any ambiguity or doubt, but that it could not provide a proportionality test as an alternative to *Wednesbury* unreasonableness where the domestic legislation was "perfectly clear."[100] He held that there was therefore no obligation on either the Secretary of State or the IAT to take the Convention into account.

In the Court of Appeal the applicant argued that the use of the words "conducive to the public good" in the statutory definition of the Secretary of State's discretion entitled him to have regard to whether he should fulfil his international obligations in deciding what is conducive to the public good, and that, where there is an international convention laying down a test, the Secretary of State, in the exercise of his discretion, ought to have regard to a convention to which the Government of which he is a member has

---

[97] Compare the position taken by the House of Lords in *R v. Secretary of State for the Home Department, ex p. Khawaja* [1984] AC 74 and *Bugdaycay v. Secretary of State for the Home Department* [1987] AC 514, both considered in ch. 6 below, that the level of scrutiny ought to be responsive to the nature of the right at stake; and *R v. Secretary of State for the Home Department, ex p Shah*, unreported decision of the Divisional Court of 9th April 1990 (available on LEXIS), in which the question of whether the Secretary of State was under a duty to take into account the fact that an application had been made to the Commission was expressly left open as being arguable either way.

[98] *Chundawadra v. Immigration Appeal Tribunal* [1988] Imm AR 161.

[99] Immigration Act 1971, s.3(5)(b).

[100] [1987] Imm AR 227 at 232.

adhered.[101] Failure to do so meant that he and the Tribunal were in breach of their *Wednesbury* obligation to have regard to all relevant considerations, or alternatively in breach of the requirement in the Immigration Rules that the decision-maker take into account "the relevant circumstances" and "every relevant factor known to him."[102]

For the Court of Appeal, the answer to the argument that the Secretary of State was obliged to take account of the ECHR flowed from the fact that the Convention was not part of English law. Glidewell LJ invoked the dualist-sounding part of Lord Diplock's judgment in *Salomon* as an exposition of the reasoning which underpinned the decisions in *Salamat Bibi* and *Fernandes*. However, no mention was made of Lord Diplock's reservation later in the same judgment about going through the artificial stage of construing the domestic provision in isolation before considering the international convention, nor was any mention made of *Garland* or any of the other post-*Salomon* cases concerning the domestic status of international law, in which the requirement of preliminary ambiguity had been quietly abandoned by, amongst others, Lord Diplock himself. Moreover, not content with following *Salamat Bibi* and *Fernandes*, Glidewell LJ went even further than those cases by holding that the Secretary of State and the IAT were obliged *not* to have regard to the Convention, because it was only in cases of ambiguity or doubt that they were *entitled* to have regard to it.[103] In other words, in the absence of statutory ambiguity, the ECHR was not even a permissive relevant consideration, let alone a mandatory one.

The case which stands as the embodiment of judicial resistance to the infiltration of international human rights law into domestic administrative law and which epitomises this second phase in the history of that process is, of course, *Brind*.[104] Since this is the decision which has become the first refuge of any respondent faced with the barest mention of any international human rights instrument by an applicant, the reasoning on which it is based merits detailed consideration. The case concerned a challenge by journalists to what became known as the Northern Ireland broadcasting ban. The ban was in the form of directives issued by the Home Secretary to the broadcasting authorities, requiring them to refrain from broadcasting any matter consisting of any words which were either spoken by a person who represents or purports to represent certain specified organisations, which included lawful as well as pro-

---

[101] Before the Court of Appeal, [1988] Imm AR 161 at 170, the applicant also tried an entirely new argument in an attempt to circumvent the *Bibi* and *Fernandes* obstacles to a relevant considerations argument, namely that he had a legitimate expectation that the Secretary of State and the IAT would take into account the test derived from Article 8 of the ECHR. As will be seen in ch. 6 below, like the far-reaching argument in *Bibi* itself, that the ECHR was directly enforceable as part of domestic law (to which in fact it was tantamount), the legitimate expectation argument in *Chundawadra* produced a remarkably dualist response from the Court of Appeal.

[102] Immigration Rules, paras. 156 and 159.

[103] [1988] Imm AR 161 at 173.

[104] R v. *Secretary of State for the Home Department, ex p. Brind* [1991] 1 AC 696.

scribed organisations, or, in their content, supported or solicited or invited support for such organisations. The directives, which received subsequent parliamentary approval by a resolution of each House, were issued in the exercise of a discretionary power conferred in wholly open-ended terms by a section of the Broadcasting Act 1981,[105] giving the Secretary of State power to issue a notice at any time requiring the broadcasting authorities to refrain from broadcasting any matter or class of matter specified in the notice. There was no express limitation on the discretion thus conferred.

One of the principal grounds on which relief was sought was that the Home Secretary had acted unlawfully in that he had exercised his discretion in breach of Article 10 of the ECHR.[106] In making this argument the applicants sought to draw on the growing number of instances in which courts had found the common law and the Convention to be identical in order to persuade the court of the artificiality involved in continuing to insist that the Convention was irrelevant to the exercise of administrative discretion. On their face, the statutory words were absolutely clear: the discretion was unlimited. According to the doctrine of parliamentary sovereignty, courts should have no role in supervising the exercise of such a power, because by refraining from imposing any limits on its scope Parliament has indicated its intention that the power is to be unconstrained. But the courts had long since rejected the possibility of unrestricted delegated power, and shown their allegiance to a substantive conception of the rule of law, by asserting a common law jurisdiction to impose limits on discretions conferred in open-ended terms. Discretions, however open-ended the terms in which they were conferred, were always limited by the well-known public law principles of *Padfield* and *Wednesbury*, that the power must be used so as to promote and not frustrate the policy and objects of the enabling legislation, and that it must not be exercised so unreasonably that no reasonable minister could have exercised it in that way.[107] As McCowan LJ put it in the Court of Appeal, summarising this part of the applicants' argument, though the words appeared clear they could not mean what they said, "because if they did the power given by them to the Secretary of State would be unrestricted, whereas there clearly ought to be some restriction."[108]

Given that it was well established that the apparently unlimited power was to be subject to implied limitations, one of those limitations, the applicants

---

[105] Section 29(3) (in the case of the IBA). In the case of the BBC, the power was contained in Clause 13(4) of the "licence and agreement" made between the BBC and the Secretary of State in 1981. Although the language of the two provisions differs slightly, their effect is the same.

[106] The question of the effect of the Convention was said by Lord Donaldson MR, [1991] 1 AC 696 at 717F, to be "in the forefront of the argument". The other grounds of challenge were that the directives were disproportionate to the mischief they were seeking to control, and that they were *Wednesbury* unreasonable.

[107] See *Wednesbury* (above n. 24) and *Padfield* v. *Minister of Agriculture, Fisheries and Food* [1968] AC 997.

[108] [1991] 1 AC 696 at 727E.

argued, should be Article 10 ECHR, because it must be presumed that Parliament did not intend to authorise the minister to exercise the discretion in breach of the Convention. This argument was put in a number of different ways by the applicants. First, the applicants argued that it was well established that the common law recognised a constitutional right to freedom of expression, and that Parliament must therefore be presumed not to have intended to confer power on the Secretary of State to make directives that conflicted unnecessarily with that common law principle. By this argument the applicants were seeking to invoke a generic common law presumption of the sort which, it will be seen below in chapter 5, has recently been advocated by Lord Browne-Wilkinson, that Parliament must be presumed not to have intended to authorise unjustified interferences with certain fundamental rights recognised at common law, amongst which is the right to freedom of expression.[109]

The applicants' second argument, although closely related to the first, was that Parliament must also be presumed not to have intended to legislate inconsistently with international treaty obligations and therefore, in this case, not to have intended to authorise infringements of the Convention. By this argument the applicants were relying on the general presumption of intended conformity with international obligations which, as has already been seen, evolved in cases such as *Miah* and *Garland*, into a presumption of general application, rather than one triggered by ambiguity. The courts' attention was drawn to the enormous overlap between the general common law presumption and the general treaty presumption arguments by pointing out the large number of cases in which courts had said that the common law already protects the rights secured by the Convention, and in particular Article 10, and to the government's own reliance on this supposed identity as a reason for not incorporating the Convention.

Lest the arguments based on general presumptions failed, the applicants also argued that resort to the Convention was in any event justified by the need to resolve an ambiguity in domestic law. The source of that ambiguity was said to be the uncertain width of the statutory power. Determining the limits which were to be implied into that power involved the court in an exercise of statutory interpretation against the background of common law principles limiting discretionary power, and that was said to be an exercise in the resolution of uncertainty to which the Convention was highly relevant. Finally, the applicants sought to couch their Convention argument in terms of the conventionally accepted grounds on which discretionary powers can be challenged, arguing for example that Article 10 was a relevant consideration that the minister was obliged to take into account. The applicants even tried, before the House of Lords at least, the argument which had so conspicuously failed in the Court of Appeal in *Chundawadra*, that the applicants, like all

---

[109] Lord Browne-Wilkinson, "The Infiltration of a Bill of Rights" [1992] PL 397.

citizens of the UK, had a legitimate expectation, based on the UK's ratification of the Convention, that each of the three branches of the state would comply with the provisions of the Convention.[110] However, the success of any of these more conventional arguments depended entirely on how receptive the courts would be to what was really the essence of the applicants' case, to which all their more detailed arguments could be said to boil down: that the content of Article 10 of the Convention was the same as that of the common law of England, and as such constituted a substantive limitation on the exercise of administrative discretion which the courts would enforce on judicial review.

The applicants' reliance on the Convention in *Brind* therefore neatly confronted the courts with the question of how the line of authority from *Salamat Bibi* through *Fernandes* to *Chundawadra* could be reconciled with the courts' steadily increasing willingness to find the common law and the Convention to be identical, and their increasingly explicit acceptance of the ultimate common law foundation of the judicial review power. Before the Divisional Court,[111] the applicants' argument that the limits of the Home Secretary's statutory power must be defined by reference to Article 10 of the Convention succeeded, but the basis on which it did so is revealing. The Divisional Court rejected the argument based on the general common law presumption that Parliament must not have intended to authorise unnecessary infringements of free speech, and the identity of that presumption with Article 10. Watkins LJ accepted the minister's response to that argument that, even though there may exist at common law certain such presumptions which apply to construing primary legislation, a minister was not required "to exercise his statutory powers so as to conform with the common law or existing rights created by the common law".[112] Therefore, even supposing the common law and Article 10 were identical, as the applicants argued, that could not help their case.

This was a surprisingly sweeping ground on which to reject the applicants' argument, for it rejects even Dicey's account of how the executive "even when armed with the widest authority" is nevertheless still "under the supervision . . . of the courts".[113] For Dicey, it will be recalled, even powers conferred in unlimited terms were "confined by . . . the interpretation put upon the statute by the judges", who, in so doing, were said to be influenced by the general spirit of the common law and to construe statutory exceptions to common law principles much more strictly than would either those who exercise or conferred them.[114] While Watkins LJ's basis for rejecting the argument was probably inadvertently wide, sweeping away as it did any possible justification for a substantive review jurisdiction, his judgment in this respect exemplifies the tendency of sovereigntist judges to reassert the logical certainties perceived

---

[110] [1991] 1 AC 696 at 733H.

[111] (1989) 139 NLJ 1229 (also available on LEXIS).

[112] Ibid. at 1230 col. 2.

[113] A.V. Dicey, *An Introduction to the Study of the Law of the Constitution*, 10th edn. with introduction by E.C.S. Wade (London: Macmillan, 1959), at 413.

[114] Ibid., at 414.

to flow from a sovereignty premise when confronted with arguments from the common law which they consider to be constitutionally unacceptable.

The basis on which the applicants' Convention argument succeeded in the Divisional Court was the treaty presumption. The Secretary of State's sovereigntist counter-argument, that recourse could only be had to Article 10 if there was some ambiguity in the statutory language, and that there was no such ambiguity present in this statute, was rejected by Watkins LJ, who held that

> "where Parliament has created for a minister a statutory power in terms which place no limitation on that power, but it is accepted, as in this case, that there must be and are limitations upon that power then reference may be made to Article 10 by a court when deciding what are the limitations to be placed on the use of that power".[115]

The Divisional Court's judgment in *Brind* does not make clear whether it accepted the treaty presumption argument on the basis that *Garland* embodies a general presumption which had not been rebutted by clear statutory language, or on the basis that it is a presumption triggered by ambiguity which had been triggered in this case by the very lack of express limitation on the power. If anything, the court's emphasis on the minister's concession that there must be and are limitations on the power suggested that it took the latter view of the *Garland* presumption, and found ambiguity to reside in the combination of the open-endedness of the discretion on its face and the acknowledged existence of common law limits on such discretions. The difference is of importance because, on the more limited view of the scope of the treaty presumption, the infinitely malleable device of ambiguity is retained, with all its potential to be used by the courts as a valve to regulate reference to international human rights law in an instrumental way.

The applicants' Convention argument did not fare so well in the Court of Appeal or House of Lords, however. In both courts it produced the very reassertion of parliamentary sovereignty that Watkins LJ had invoked in response to the argument based on a presumption in favour of fundamental common law rights. This retreat into sovereignty theory took two forms. First, there was the "no ambiguity" argument, which sought to meet the applicants' statutory construction argument on its own terms. Lord Donaldson MR and McCowan LJ in the Court of Appeal, and Lord Ackner in the House of Lords, all expressly gave as a reason for rejecting the applicants' argument that there was no ambiguity in the statutory provision conferring the discretionary power on the Home Secretary.[116] The existence of the *Garland* presumption was acknowledged, but in the absence of such an ambiguity, they held, it simply did not apply, since there was no uncertainty in domestic law which needed settling.

---

[115] (1989) 139 NLJ 1229, relying on *Garland* [1983] 2 AC 751 and *AG v. BBC* [1981] AC 303.
[116] Lord Donaldson MR [1991] 1 AC 696 at 718G ("[w]hatever the width of the authority conferred . . ., there is . . . no ambiguity"); McCowan LJ at 728C ("no force in the argument that because on the face of [it] it is unlimited but ought to be limited, therefore it is ambiguous"); Lord Ackner to similar effect at 761F.

Second, there was the "backdoor incorporation" argument, which more openly relied for its justification on the consequences of accepting the applicants' argument. According to this argument, the treaty presumption could not be relied on where the effect of it succeeding would be to incorporate the treaty into domestic law, since that would be using a principle of statutory interpretation to subvert the very purpose it was supposed to serve, namely the discovery and implementation of the supreme will of Parliament. Lord Donaldson MR, for example, "unhesitatingly and unreservedly" rejected the argument that an open-ended bestowal of authority to take executive action should be limited by the requirement that it be exercised consistently with the terms of the Convention, "because it involves imputing to Parliament an intention to import the Convention into domestic law by the back door, when it has quite clearly refrained from doing so by the front door".[117] Similarly Ralph Gibson LJ and Lord Bridge held that to apply the *Garland* presumption to the interpretation of an apparently unlimited discretion was to go far beyond the resolution of an ambiguity and was instead to incorporate the treaty into domestic law, which would be a judicial usurpation of the legislative function.[118]

Neither type of judicial response to the applicants' argument is satisfactory. First, the "no ambiguity" argument treats the *Garland* treaty presumption as a presumption triggered by ambiguity, when in fact, as has been argued in chapter 1, it has long since evolved into a much stronger presumption of general application which is not contingent on ambiguity, particularly where the subject-matter of the international treaty concerns human rights. In any event, even if it were necessary to prove ambiguity, for the courts to say that there is no ambiguity in an open-ended conferral of power surely proves too much. If Parliament's failure to stipulate express limits on the discretion conferred is sufficient to rebut the *Garland* principle of statutory interpretation, it is hard to see why it does not also rebut all the other presumptions and principles of statutory interpretation on which the courts rely to justify their control of statutory discretion, including the long-established requirements that discretions be exercised reasonably, in good faith, for proper purposes and in conformity with the policy and objects of the Act. Out with the *Garland* bathwater go babies *Padfield* and *Wednesbury*.

Second, the "backdoor incorporation" argument illustrates well the temptation for English courts to resort to the binary metaphors of dualism when presented with an argument that threatens to make the substantive nature of their constitutional jurisdiction too explicit. As was pointed out in chapter 1,

---

[117] Ibid. at 718F.

[118] Lord Bridge, ibid. at 748C; Ralph Gibson LJ at 726C–D; Lord Ackner, at 762A–B made the same backdoor incorporation argument, although in his case this response was directed not at the applicants' argument on the *Garland* presumption, which he disposed of with the "no ambiguity" argument, but at their argument that the minister was obliged to have proper regard to the Convention.

the various ways in which pure dualism is compromised in practice, including the courts' recognition of customary international law as part of the common law and the application of the treaty presumption, make it wholly inappropriate to talk in simple terms about international law becoming part of domestic law through a legitimate front door (legislative incorporation) and an illegitimate back door (judicial incorporation). Indeed, the entire dualist metaphor of front doors and back doors through which international law is legitimately or illegitimately admitted is fundamentally flawed, because it lacks the conceptual sophistication necessary to reflect the many ways in which international norms may be legally relevant to domestic judges performing their interpretive function.

Only Lord Templeman in the House of Lords in *Brind* came close to accepting the applicants' argument that the ECHR is relevant to an English court's determination of the limits against which the minister's exercise of his discretionary power is to be measured.[119] In his short and rather opaque speech, he neither expressed agreement with any other member of the court nor expressed his own opinion on the applicants' Convention argument. Instead, he made ambiguous references to the Convention which suggest at least a sneaking sympathy with the view that the Convention is already a part of the common law as customary international law. However, a judicial philosophy of *sub silentio* incorporation such as Lord Templeman appeared to adopt in *Brind* is no substitute for an articulated basis on which references to unincorporated international human rights law can or must be made and will not help to legitimate the exercise of a perfectly defensible jurisdiction.[120]

6. CONCLUSION

This chapter has sought to trace the domestic career of international human rights law through its first two phases. During Phase I, in the mid-1970s, domestic judges displayed not only a willingness to interpret domestic law in the light of international human rights instruments, but often considered themselves under an obligation to do so. Under the influence of Lords Denning, Reid and Scarman, both statute and common law were interpreted so as to be consistent with international human rights norms, and no exception was made for statutes conferring administrative discretions.

During Phase II, however, the question of the domestic status of international human rights law became curiously bifurcated. On the one hand, some judges clearly continued to consider themselves under an obligation to inter-

---

[119] [1991] 1 AC 696 at 750–751.

[120] See Lord Templeman's similar approach in *Spycatcher No. 1* [1987] 1 WLR 1248 at 1296F–1299G; but for evidence of the judicial inconstancy encouraged by sovereignty theory, contrast his view of the domestic status of international treaties in *Rayner* [1990] 2 AC 418 at 476F–477A.

pret domestic law so as to achieve consistency with such norms, particularly those contained in the ECHR, and recognised that for this purpose it was necessary to have regard to such instruments and, in the case of the ECHR at least, to the international jurisprudence interpreting them. This was fully in accord with the general trend towards a greater receptiveness to customary international law and the related strengthening of the international treaty presumption, trends which, it has been argued in chapter 1, were themselves manifestations of the acceptance by English courts of their emerging role in a new constitutionalism.

On the other hand, however, the vast majority of judges have been unable to accept what they mistakenly consider to be the dramatic consequences of that trend for their traditional role in administrative law. Sensitivity to the political delicacy of the balance of power between the judiciary and the democratically accountable executive and legislative branches has led courts to maintain their traditionally deferential stance towards the review of executive and administrative discretions, particularly where they are statutorily conferred in broad terms, notwithstanding the enhanced domestic status being accorded to international human rights norms outside of administrative law. Rather than grapple with the difficult theoretical questions of how to reconcile such democratic concerns with the legitimate constitutional role for judges which is presupposed by human rights instruments such as the ECHR, most during this phase preferred the easy refuge of dualistic certainties, selectively invoking the sovereigntist premise to deny the existence of any interpretive obligation in those contexts involving judicial review of executive or administrative discretions. The vehicle permitting such selectivity was the classic sovereigntist device of "ambiguity", permitting judges to retain, in effect, a discretion as to whether international norms are relevant at all to a question of interpretation of domestic law.

It is this selectivity in the invocation of the old dualist premises that is the distinguishing feature of Phase II in the history of using international human rights law in English courts. To insist on applying an "ambiguity" precondition in administrative law, however, has appeared increasingly indefensible as more and more regard has been paid to international human rights norms, particularly those in the ECHR, in the interpretation of the common law and as, at the same time, the common law foundation of the courts' judicial review jurisdiction has become more explicitly acknowledged. Statements such as Lord Goff's in *Spycatcher No. 2*, acknowledging what amounts to an interpretive obligation on judges to construe domestic law consistently with the ECHR,[121] foreshadowed a transition to a distinct third phase, the subject of chapters 5 and 6, in which the presumptive relevance of international human rights law has gradually come to be more openly acknowledged, even, though falteringly, in the context of administrative discretions.

---

[121] [1990] 1 AC 109 at 283G.

5

The Emergence of a Common Law
Human Rights Jurisdiction

1. INTRODUCTION

The astonishingly dualist statements with which both the Court of Appeal and the House of Lords rejected the European Convention argument in *Brind* inspired little confidence that England's highest courts were capable of responding with imagination to what, by now, could scarcely still be called English law's "new dimension". The striking image of "back-door incorporation"[1] undoubtedly expresses a genuine concern about the proper division of constitutional responsibility between judiciary and Parliament, but at another level it betrays a cruder, almost patriotic concern to shore up the island fortress of the English legal system against the alien influences of Europeanisation. There is a manifest insularity in Lord Donaldson MR's conclusion in the Court of Appeal, for example, that "in most cases the English courts will be wholly unconcerned with the terms of the Convention",[2] and in Lord Ackner's statement in the House of Lords that, the treaty not having been incorporated, the question whether the Secretary of State had acted in breach of Article 10 did not arise.[3] Such judicial sentiments certainly fall foul of Kerr LJ's gentle rebuke in *Rayner*, that to prohibit reference to underlying international instruments is "excessively insular, and perhaps in these times almost absurd".[4] *Brind*, surely, was the last stand of legally and constitutionally conservative judges with a Canute-like scorn for the tides of history.

In fact, notwithstanding the irresistible momentum behind the legal, historical and intellectual trends underlying European integration, and the constitutional imagination unleashed by the need to acknowledge not only the supremacy and direct effect of European Community law but its indirect effect too,[5] the attraction of the sovereigntist bolt-hole from arguments invoking

---

[1] For an earlier example of judicial resort to this dualist metaphor see *Chundawadra* [1988] Imm AR 161 at 174, rejecting the attempt to use the administrative law doctrine of legitimate expectation as the "back door" by which to introduce the ECHR into English law. See Chapter 6, section 8 below.

[2] [1991] 1 AC 696 at 718B.

[3] Ibid. at 762B. See also Lord Ackner's view, ibid. at 762H–763A, that the "European test" of whether the interference complained of corresponds to a pressing social need must inevitably involve the courts in a forbidden review of the merits of the decision.

[4] [1989] Ch. 72 at 165C–D.

[5] See chs. 2 and 3.

international human rights norms has proved remarkably durable. Confronted increasingly frequently by such arguments, and in particular arguments relying on the ECHR, English courts have continued to find comfort in the reassuring certainties of dualist dogma, and *Brind* has proved to be more than the mere finger in the dyke that many had hoped it was at the time it was delivered.[6] The key to its longevity, it will be suggested, is that at the same time as appearing to slam the door firmly shut on domestic use of international human rights law in public law other than where domestic law is ambiguous, the House of Lords sanctioned what amounts to an evolution of the common law of judicial review, by approving a more rigorous scrutiny of decisions affecting fundamental rights.[7] By this limited concession to historical inevitability, English courts have asserted an indigenous, common law human rights jurisdiction in public law whilst ostensibly preserving their commitment to parliamentary sovereignty, both by resisting attempts to incorporate human rights treaties judicially, and by retaining domestic control over the degree of scrutiny of administrative decisions so as to ensure that it does not go beyond that which they consider compatible with their constitutional position as subordinates to Parliament. The decision in *Brind* therefore stands as a splendid monument to the curious bifurcation which characterised the second phase in the history of the domestic career of international human rights law.

In the remainder of this book it will be argued that the domestic status of unincorporated human rights law has now entered a new phase (Phase III), in which the approach to its status in *Brind*, quite apart from being misconceived in the narrow sense of having questionable foundation in legal authority,[8] has latterly become intellectually indefensible in the light of recent judicial practice. This new phase in the history of the domestic career of international human rights law can be seen as the product of a number of separate but intimately related developments, chief among which are the following three. First, and the principal concern of this chapter, the judicial tendency to assert an identity between the common law and the ECHR, already increasingly evident in Phase II, has shaded into a new-found willingness to *develop* the common law in order to achieve that identity. Second, and the subject of chapter 6, the courts' increasingly explicit recognition of the independent, common law nature of their supervisory jurisdiction, and the corresponding decline in the explanatory power of parliamentary sovereignty and its derivative, *ultra vires*, have undermined the basis for isolating public law from the influence of international human rights law. And third, as will be seen in chapter 7, European Community law has provided a new route for the reception of human rights law, and in particular the ECHR, into English law.

---

[6] See in particular *R v. Secretary of State for the Environment, ex p. NALGO* (1993) 5 Admin LR 785 and *R v. Ministry of Defence, ex p. Smith* [1996] QB 517 (DC & CA), both considered in ch. 6 below.

[7] See section 4 below.

[8] See ch. 1.

Of course, there is no clear line of demarcation between the second phase of bifurcation and the third phase of common law development, but, as will be argued in chapters 6 and 7, the combination of these trends has led to increasing judicial awareness of the absurdity in according a high degree of judicial recognition to the ECHR, both in the development of the common law and in areas of domestic law which are within the field of Community law, whilst continuing to insist on its irrelevance in the context of judicial review of administrative discretion. If this third phase of development were pursued to its logical conclusion, the result would be the unqualified judicial recognition of a full interpretive obligation, an acceptance by courts of a constitutional requirement that they must conscientiously strive to interpret all domestic law (common law and statute alike, and in all contexts) so as to achieve consistency with international human rights law. Progress towards that destination has inevitably been uneven, however, and Phase III is necessarily a transitional phase. The remaining chapters are therefore to a large extent a chronicle of the undoing of *Brind* as the courts gradually grope their way towards the recognition of such an obligation. If what is argued for in what follows seems to some dangerously novel, it should not be forgotten that, were courts to follow through the trends identified here to their logical conclusion, nothing more dramatic would have come about than a return to that brief phase in the mid-1970s when courts, led by the constitutionalists Lords Reid and Scarman, applied a general presumption of conformity with international human rights law whenever domestic law fell to be interpreted, even where that law conferred an executive or administrative discretion, and subject only to Parliament's assertion of its sovereignty in the ultimate sense described in chapter 2.

2. TOWARDS PHASE III: A CLEAR SHIFT IN EXTRA-JUDICIAL OPINION

The advent of a new phase in the history of the domestic status of international human rights law was presaged by a sudden upsurge in the number of senior members of the profession and, in particular, the judiciary who were prepared to venture their opinions on the subject in public lectures and the pages of the law journals; a sure measure of how pressing the question has become in everyday practice.[9] These ruminations, which have concentrated on the domestic relevance of the ECHR in particular, pre-date the decision of the House of Lords in *Brind*. In 1988, for example, in a paper presented to the Bar Conference, John Laws, still at the time standing Junior Counsel to

[9] So frequent and bold have judicial contributions become that the question of judicial participation in public controversy has become an issue in its own right: see eg. the House of Lords debate on the subject initiated by the Shadow Lord Chancellor Lord Irvine, HL Deb., Vol. 572, col.s 1254–313 (5 June 1996); the Lord Chancellor Lord Mackay's lecture to the Citizenship Foundation, "Parliament and the Judges—A Constitutional Challenge?" (8 July 1996); and Lord Chief Justice Bingham's lecture to the City of London (17 July 1996).

the Crown, detected a "recent judicial enthusiasm for perceiving a harmony between common law and Convention law" and permitted himself to "wonder whether the process of making the Convention effective in domestic terms may not be achieved by judicial development, short of legislative incorporation."[10] Significantly, although Laws had particularly in mind the recent judgments in the *Spycatcher* litigation,[11] which had concerned the compatibility of the common law with Article 10, he was not merely speculating on the general question of the domestic status of the ECHR, but was expressly considering the possibility of judges finding "a window through which to require government decision-makers to keep faith" with the Convention. There could be no doubt, then, that he was contemplating a judicially engineered role for the ECHR in administrative law.

Since becoming a Justice of the High Court, Laws J. has warmed to his theme. Released at last from the constraints of daily representing the executive, gamely advocating arguments designed mainly to check the onward march of judicial review, Laws J. used his lecture to the Administrative Law Bar Association in 1992 to pose the question "is the High Court the guardian of fundamental constitutional rights?".[12] As its author pointed out, it was a question the answer to which was too obvious to be worth asking in most other jurisdictions; but in the UK, with its nostalgic attachment to Parliamentary sovereignty and the associated hostility of its legal culture to the language of fundamental rights, it had, even in 1992, the appearance of being revolutionary.

The question Laws explored was the one he had fleetingly referred to in his paper to the Bar Conference four years earlier: whether, without recourse to legislative constitutional change, the common law was nevertheless able to accord a priority to fundamental rights comparable to their entrenchment in written sets of norms, and to do so by the characteristically common law methodology of developing principles which, while apparently new, in fact belong to a continuum whose starting point is uncontentious and well-established.[13] Laws's thesis, in short, is that the judicial protection of fundamental rights and freedoms is within the reach of interpretive development of the common law. In his view, the effective protection of basic rights such as those found in the main provisions of the ECHR need not await the legislative incorporation of that instrument or the adoption of a written constitution, because the courts themselves can secure a high degree of priority for those rights by building on existing public law principles. All that is required to achieve that end is for the courts to adopt an approach to judicial review whereby "the greater the intrusion proposed by a body possessing public

---

[10] J. Laws, "The Ghost in the Machine: Principle in Public Law" [1989] PL 27 at 31.
[11] Considered in ch. 4 above.
[12] J. Laws, "Is the High Court the Guardian of Fundamental Constitutional Rights?" [1993] PL 59.
[13] Ibid. at 59.

power over the citizen into an area where his fundamental rights are at stake, the greater must be the justification which the public authority must demonstrate."[14] On this approach, a governmental interference with a citizen's fundamental rights will only survive judicial scrutiny if it can be demonstrated to rest on a distinct justification in the public interest.

Laws did not shrink from the implications of such a development for the traditional doctrines of administrative law.[15] For the common law of judicial review to be developed in the way he was suggesting, it was necessary for the courts to refine the *Wednesbury* doctrine, by swapping its monolithic standard of irrationality for differential standards of review sensitive to the nature of the subject-matter. This would involve applying, for example, a more exacting standard where fundamental rights are at stake than in cases concerning, say, national economic policy. Indeed, Laws frankly admitted that if the courts were to lay claim to a jurisdiction as guardians of fundamental rights, it would be necessary for the law of judicial review to recognise the concept of proportionality as something distinct from conventional *Wednesbury* unreasonableness, and for courts to resist being seduced by the exaggerated claim that such a concept is inherently inconsistent with the secondary or supervisory nature of the review jurisdiction. Without the recognition of such a concept, courts will not be equipped to ensure that decision-makers accord the first priority to fundamental rights unless they can show a substantial, objective, public justification for overriding them. The well-known *Padfield* rule of statutory construction, that statutory power may not be used save for the purpose for which it was conferred, could be turned into a presumption that a statute's purpose could not include any interference with fundamental rights, rebuttable only by the respondent showing that the only possible interpretation of the statute was to permit the interference. And the rule that public decision-makers owe no duty to give reasons would have to give way to the requirement that a decision-maker whose decision has interfered with a fundamental right must justify the interference to the satisfaction of the court.

For present purposes, however, the true significance of Laws's contribution in this lecture lies in the way in which it identifies and addresses the traditional objections to judicial reference to international human rights norms and in particular the ECHR. He does this in two ways. The first is by making central to his argument the distinction which, it was pointed out at length in chapter 1, has largely been absent from English judicial reasoning due to the historical prevalence of dualism in the approach of our courts to the domestic status of international law. That is the distinction between, on the one hand, incorporation of the ECHR in the literal sense of making it a part of the law of England, on which individuals can found their case, and, on the other, judicial reference to the ECHR as a source of norms or values which

---

[14] J. Laws, "Is the High Court the Guardian of Fundamental Constitutional Rights?" [1993] PL 59 at 69.

[15] Ibid. at 71–8.

are either already inherent in our law or, to the extent that they are not, may legitimately be integrated into it by the judges in their development of the common law.[16] Laws makes this incorporationist disclaimer to neutralise the objection from the old constitutional fundamental, which he accepts as a "legal fact", that international treaties are not part of domestic law because the Crown cannot be a source of law.[17] For courts to have regard to the ECHR as a text to inform the content of the common law was no more a subversion of that old and elementary rule, he argued, than was the well-established practice of courts deriving comparative assistance by referring to cases decided in other jurisdictions.[18]

The second means deployed by Laws to counter the anticipated objections from traditional defenders of sovereignty, dualism and *ultra vires* is the classic common lawyer's technique of stressing the essential continuity, at the level of abstract principle, between what has gone before and what is being proposed. Pointing out that the significant developments in judicial review over the last 20 years had largely been brought about by judicial development of the common law anyway, that even the conventional *Wednesbury* principles involved imposing a judge-made standard on the decision-maker, and that the courts already imposed a more exacting standard on decision-makers where particularly important interests were at stake,[19] Laws concluded that the judicial approach he advocated is "conceptually no different from what the courts have already done in evolving standards of administrative conduct within the four corners of conventional judicial review".[20] Moreover, the courts had already been deploying the ECHR to inform the content of private law concepts where questions of fundamental rights arose, and there was no inherent reason why similar development of public law by reference to the ECHR would necessarily upset the constitutional balance between the courts and decision-makers exercising statutory powers.[21]

[16] Ibid. at 61. As will be seen in ch. 7, the very same distinction has been drawn by the European Court of Justice, to justify its drawing on the ECHR as a "source of inspiration" for its fundamental rights jurisprudence, notwithstanding that the Community has never incorporated it into Community law.

[17] But see ch. 1 for arguments against this "fundamental rule" applying to international human rights instruments, particularly Lauterpacht's argument that, since the purpose of the rule is to protect citizens' rights against the executive, it cannot be relied on by the executive to the detriment of the citizen: "International Law and Her Majesty's Judges", 1993 F.A. Mann Memorial Lecture (unpublished).

[18] Equating the ECHR and its case-law with other "comparative" material, however, understates the normative reasons why courts should have regard to it. As was seen in ch. 1, there are strong theoretical arguments for treating the ECHR and its jurisprudence as more than merely comparative material.

[19] Relying in particular on passages from Lord Bridge's judgments in *Bugdaycay* [1987] AC 514 at 531 and *Brind* [1991] 1 AC 696 at 748, considered in section 4 below.

[20] Above n. 12 at 71.

[21] As will be seen below, Laws J. has given practical effect to his views in his judicial capacity in cases where he has sought to find in the common law those rights, such as the right to freedom of expression and the right to life, which occupy a central place in the ECHR: see eg. *R v. Advertising Standards Authority, ex p. Vernons* [1992] 1 WLR 1289 and *R v. Cambridge District Health Authority, ex p. B* [1995] 1 FLR 1055.

Laws's article has been extremely influential,[22] not least because it caught the mood of a significant change in attitude towards the ECHR on the part of some judges at the beginning of the present decade. That shift was also noted and welcomed by Lord Woolf, who, in his 1990 Hamlyn Lectures, expressed regret that the courts had not done more to develop English law in accordance with the ECHR.[23] It was clearly his view that the new-found willingness to consider the ECHR was a development which was long overdue and that in the past the courts had taken an unnecessarily blinkered view. Lord Woolf considered that hesitation to be understandable in terms of the courts' unfamiliarity with the general approach to adjudication under the ECHR, but he clearly thought that there was no fundamental theoretical objection to the ECHR playing a much larger role in domestic law. He thought that its principles were in any event already largely part of the common law tradition and he clearly subscribed to the view that the courts should therefore not shrink from all the consequences of recognising a general presumption of conformity with the ECHR when interpreting legislation, including statutes conferring administrative discretions.

> "In reviewing the exercise of discretionary powers on *Wednesbury* grounds the courts could justifiably assume that ministers and their officials do not wish to act inconsistently with this country's treaty obligations under the Convention and the reasonableness of their actions could be judged against the background of that assumption."[24]

Since that was very similar to the argument subsequently rejected by the House of Lords in *Brind*, however, Lord Woolf has in more recent writings[25] favoured the approach of Lord Browne-Wilkinson, who, in his 1991 Harry Street lecture, took a rather different route from that subsequently taken by Laws to arrive at the same destination of greater domestic judicial protection for fundamental rights.[26] Whereas Laws J. urged that more reference be made to the ECHR by domestic courts in their development of the common law, and in particular in their development of the common law of judicial review, Lord Browne-Wilkinson argued for the rediscovery of an indigenous human rights jurisdiction on the back of traditional English principles of statutory interpretation. He took as his starting point the refusal by the House of Lords in *Brind* to permit the ECHR to infiltrate domestic public law *via* the pre-

---

[22] Crown Office judges tell of applications for judicial review in which the only "authority" cited was a certain Administrative Law Bar Association lecture.

[23] Lord Woolf, *Protection of the Public: A New Challenge*, Hamlyn Lectures (London: Stevens, 1990) at 120–2.

[24] Ibid. at 121–2. Although it has been common to refer to the presumed intention of the executive in exercising discretionary powers, see eg. Lord Reid in *Miah* and Lord Denning in *Bhajan Singh*, it is strictly speaking not clear why the executive's intention, rather than Parliament's, should be relevant to a court's interpretation of the scope of statutory powers.

[25] See eg. Lord Woolf's 1994 F.A. Mann Lecture, "Droit Public—English Style" [1995] PL 57 at 69–70.

[26] Lord Browne-Wilkinson, "The Infiltration of a Bill of Rights" [1992] PL 397.

sumption of statutory interpretation that Parliament intends to legislate consistently with the UK's international treaty obligations. That apparent closure of the more direct route of construing the scope of broad statutory discretions so as to give effect so far as possible to the ECHR prompted Lord Browne-Wilkinson to ask whether there was not a more general presumption of statutory interpretation, protecting precisely the fundamental freedoms which the ECHR protects, and the recognition of which would secure the protection of individual freedom without the need for constitutional change authorising judges to refer to the ECHR.

In Lord Browne-Wilkinson's view, debate over whether or not to incorporate the ECHR, or adopt a domestic bill of rights, had diverted attention from the principles of the indigenous common law, which, if only judges would revert to them, would provide the means by which courts could prevent unjustified infringements of fundamental rights and freedoms. Such a reversion to long established principles of statutory construction could provide much of the protection of what he called a "half-way bill of rights", in which certain fundamental human rights are declared to exist, and infringement of them by the executive constitutes a legal wrong, but courts do not have the power to invalidate an Act of Parliament.[27] All that was required was simply a development of judicial consciousness beyond the traditional solicitousness of the common law for freedom of the person or the sanctity of property rights to a concern for other fundamental rights and freedoms such as those protected by the ECHR. On this view, much the same level of protection as that provided by a half-way bill of rights could be achieved if the judges merely up-dated the common law's catalogue of rights which it already protects by way of presumptions of interpretation and reverted to strictly construing statutes conferring general powers capable of interfering with those rights.[28]

Like Laws J., who argued that his suggested approach would involve only a "modest" change in judicial practice, Lord Browne-Wilkinson was anxious to stress the historical continuity of his recommended approach, claiming that it amounts to no more than a rediscovery of "the principles of our indigenous common law".[29] The adoption of his strict constructionist approach, he argued, involved no discontinuity in judicial practice, but would simply amount to a recognition by the courts that their familiar strict construction of penal, taxation and confiscatory provisions were merely particular manifestations of a more general presumption against interference with individual freedom.

---

[27] Ibid. at 399. A "half-way bill" was to be contrasted to a "full bill" in which courts had power to strike down legislation which infringed protected rights.

[28] As will be seen in ch. 8 below, however, the price to pay for the development of an indigenous human rights jurisdiction may be the forfeiting of the comparative insights afforded by the ECHR case-law.

[29] Above n. 26 at 404.

The significance of Lord Browne-Wilkinson's recommended approach is that it offers courts a constitutionally more palatable way of reviewing the exercise of broad statutory discretions for conformity with fundamental rights and freedoms, without falling foul of the strictures in *Brind* against illegitimately incorporating international treaties which Parliament has deliberately not incorporated. Lord Browne-Wilkinson's suggested presumption is intended to be a strong rule of statutory construction of general application, and therefore applicable to powers conferred in general words. Unlike many of the courts which have considered arguments that general powers must be exercised within ECHR limits, Lord Browne-Wilkinson is alive to the crucial distinction between a general presumption rebutted by clear words or necessary implication, and a presumption triggered only by ambiguity.[30] A presumption triggered by ambiguity is obviously weaker than one rebuttable only by clear words or necessary implication. In Lord Browne-Wilkinson's view, general words which are not ambiguous but which on their face appear to authorise action interfering with basic freedoms should not be so construed, notwithstanding their lack of ambiguity. They should only be so construed if Parliament has made clear by express provision or necessary implication that it intended to authorise such interference. The Browne-Wilkinson general presumption would therefore serve to fill the gap left by the House of Lords' rejection of the argument in *Brind* that domestic law, including general powers, should be construed so as to give effect as far as possible to the ECHR.

More recently, Sedley J. has added his voice to those calling for a reinvigorated common law to acknowledge the legitimacy of its role in the protection of fundamental values.[31] Sedley's contribution to this development can be said, without exaggeration, to be unique. He comes from an intellectual tradition whose central insight seems indisputable: that the unavoidable lesson of history is that judges have not been reliable upholders of the moral and political principles underlying democracy, because of their blindness to the crucial relationship between liberty and the distribution of power.[32] From that central conviction springs a healthy scepticism for the rhetoric of human rights and an acute awareness of the gap which too often exists between the high-sounding ideals espoused by judges and their realisation in practice, a consciousness which is conspicuously lacking from most of the calls to arms

---

[30] See ch. 1.

[31] See, in particular, his 1995 Paul Sieghart Memorial Lecture, "Human Rights: a Twenty-First Century Agenda" [1995] PL 386 and the important decision in *R v. Secretary of State for the Home Department, ex p. McQuillan* [1995] 4 All ER 400, considered in ch. 7 below.

[32] See eg. Sedley, "Administrative Law: A Tsar is Born" in Marxism Today, March 1984; "Law and State Power: A Time for Reconstruction" (1990) J. Law & Soc. 234; Review of Michael Mandel: *The Charter of Rights and the Legalisation of Politics in Canada* (1990) 18 Int. J. Soc. L. 500; "Hidden Agendas: The Growth of Public Law in Britain and Canada" Institute of Comparative Law, Waseda University (ed.), *Law in East and West: On the Occasion of the 30th Anniversary of the Institute of Comparative Law, Waseda University* (1988) 417.

from other members of the judiciary. It leads Sedley to dissociate himself from those who profess their faith in the existence of a higher-order law which protects fundamental human rights by setting them on a pedestal above the political fray and entrusting to judges their protection against "political" interference.[33] This is the credo of classical liberal rights theory and Sedley quite rightly challenges it for its conceit in making ahistorical assumptions about the primacy and universality of what are, in some cases at least, essentially contingent values, and for its related assumption about the neutrality of constitutional adjudication by judges.[34]

Sedley's advocacy of a judicial role in the protection of fundamental values is derived from an altogether more pragmatic outlook. Although he rejects the metaphysical concept of a higher-order law, he accepts the legitimacy of a distinctively "constitutional" role for judges, but it is a role which rests on the more modest foundation of judicial recognition of society's contingent but fundamental needs. Sedley therefore arrives at much the same destination as the other writers considered above, in terms of his acceptance of a judicial role in constitutional adjudication, but he does so by a very different route. Not for him Laws's higher order law and the judicial supremacism it entails; not for him either Browne-Wilkinson's more nostalgic call for a return to the bygone days of a robust common law protecting the rights of the individual. Sedley's cautious embrace of constitutional and human rights adjudication is grounded in the less romantic, indeed, admirably pragmatic appreciation that the problem in western democracies today is "how to ensure that as a society we are governed within a law which has internalised the notion of fundamental human rights."[35] Despite his many and well-founded reservations, Sedley is therefore ultimately prepared to part company with those writers of the traditional left, such as Griffith, Ewing and Gearty, who have consistently maintained their opposition to any judicial role in the protection of fundamental rights on the principal ground, crudely put, that in the long run the judges are less to be trusted than the people as guardians of society's fundamental values.[36]

What are the implications of Sedley's scepticism of liberal constitutionalism for the domestic status of international human rights norms? Consistently with his appreciation of the contingency of fundamental values, he describes

---

[33] Laws's credentials as such a theorist have become increasingly apparent as he has publicly articulated his thoughts in further lectures and articles. See, in particular, "Law and Democracy" [1995] PL 72; and his 1996 Mishcon Lecture.

[34] Above n. 31 at 390–1.

[35] Ibid. at 391.

[36] See eg. J.A.G. Griffith, *The Politics of the Judiciary*, 4th edn. (London: Fontana, 1991) and *Judicial Politics Since 1920: A Chronicle* (Oxford: Blackwell, 1993); K.D. Ewing, "A Bill of Rights: Lessons from the Privy Council" in Finnie, Himsworth & Walker (eds.), *Edinburgh Essays in Public Law* (1991) at 231; C.A. Gearty, "The Cost of Human Rights: English Judges and the Northern Irish Troubles" (1994) 47 CLP 19; K.D. Ewing and C.A. Gearty, *Freedom Under Thatcher: Civil Liberties in Modern Britain* (Oxford: Oxford University Press, 1990) at 262–75.

the human rights protected by the ECHR, and by other instruments such as the Universal Declaration, as

> "the Enlightenment's values of possessive individualism, derived from the historic paradigm . . . of the conscious human actor whose natural enemy is the state—a necessary evil—and in whose maximum personal liberty lies the maximum benefit for society."

As a statement of the historical limitations of the ECHR's catalogue of rights, this is undeniable, but it might be thought to be unduly pessimistic. It surely ought to be recognised that these statements of the Enlightenment's values of possessive individualism include at least some of the values prized also by those who take a more optimistic view of the possibilities of state action to redress the inequalities which inevitably result from private ordering. Under-inclusive its protections may be, but many of the rights it recognises would figure in any account of the minimum standards required by common human-ity.[37] Were it otherwise, it is unlikely that there would be the emerging social consensus around the incorporation of the ECHR which, on Sedley's own theory of what legitimates a judicial role in protecting fundamental values, justifies judges having regard to the values it protects. Nor is there anything in that theory which precludes judges from having regard to other interna-tional instruments, such as the Social Charter or the various anti-discrimina-tion conventions, which more often require positive state action to make effective the values they protect.

Although there are significant differences of emphasis between these extra-judicial pronouncements, and in particular between those of Sedley and the rest, common amongst them is a belief in the ability of the common law to adapt itself in order to achieve a greater level of protection in domestic law for fundamental rights and freedoms.[38] Most significantly, there appears to be emerging a remarkable level of judicial consensus on the inappropriateness of continuing to insulate public law from the influence of fundamental rights jurisprudence. It is true that, to the extent that Lord Browne-Wilkinson's

---

[37] Sedley accepts a universalist foundation to the extent that the values he recognises as fun-damental are rooted in considerations of common humanity: see eg. *R v. Wealden District Council ex. p. Wales*, The Times, 22 September 1995 and his view that human rights are *human* rights and as such should not be enjoyed by corporations. See also Higgins' response to the cultural rel-ativists' critique of universal human rights, *Problems and Process—International Law and How We Use It* (Oxford: Clarendon Press, 1994) at 96–8, arguing from a profound belief in "the uni-versality of the human spirit."

[38] See eg. Sedley, "The Sound of Silence: Constitutional Law Without a Constitution" (1994) 110 LQR 270, arguing that the common law has both the capacity and the obligation to move towards a principled constitutional order. Compare the views of the former Lord Chief Justice and Master of the Rolls, who both consider legislative incorporation to be necessary in order for the courts to be able to give full domestic effect to the ECHR: Lord Taylor CJ, Dimbleby Lecture, 29 November 1992 and H.C. Deb. Vol. 560 cols. 1142–4 (25 January 1995); Sir Thomas Bingham MR, "The European Convention on Human Rights: Time to Incorporate?" (1993) 109 LQR 390 and "International Conventions and Domestic Law" in Markesinis (ed.), *The Gradual Convergence—Foreign Ideas, Foreign Influences and English Law on the Eve of the Twenty-First Century* (1994) at 165.

recommended return to an indigenous human rights jurisdiction is treated as an alternative to developing English law in the light of international human rights law, it carries with it the danger that English courts will be deprived of a rich source of guidance for the development of the common law.[39] But, on the whole, the marked shift in attitude charted in this section marks a welcome shift, from the tendency in Phase II merely to *assert* that the ECHR and the common law are identical, to a new willingness to *develop* the common law in light of the ECHR. As such, it represents a willingness to abandon the transparent pretence of courts that they are merely "finding" or "declaring" some metaphysically pre-existent common law, in favour of a more proactive development of the common law in response to modern conditions. Such a development surely heralds the arrival of a new and distinct phase in the domestic life of international human rights law. By explicitly acknowledging both the fact and the legitimacy of judicial law-making, it also puts a greater onus on judges to justify their development of the law by sound reasoning, and should therefore enhance their public accountability for legal change.[40]

The practical realisation of these extra-judicial speculations that English courts already possess an indigenous human rights jurisdiction, quite independently of the ECHR or any other international human rights treaties, has gathered pace in recent years as more and more judges have acknowledged the special nature of the judicial role in cases where fundamental rights are at stake. The judicial assertion of such a jurisdiction has taken a number of different forms. The first has been by Lord Browne-Wilkinson's preferred route of recognising a general presumption of statutory interpretation in favour of fundamental rights, particularly when construing the scope of powers conferred in wide and general terms. The second has been by Laws J.'s favoured approach of refining the common law principles of judicial review, especially by lowering the *Wednesbury* threshold and applying a more exacting standard of review to discretionary decisions interfering with fundamental rights. The third has been by judicial development of the common law in non-public law contexts, such as the law of libel. And the fourth has been by exercising judicial discretions in the light of international human rights norms, for example when deciding whether or not to grant an injunction.

Since each of these is merely a particular manifestation of the same development in different contexts, namely the emergence of a common law human rights jurisdiction, there is a certain artificiality in treating them separately as if each were a distinct development in its own right. However, as the courts themselves have yet to acknowledge explicitly the connection between them, it will be necessary to consider each in turn before returning at the end of the chapter to ask what, at a more theoretical level, is the nature of the

[39] See ch. 8 below for consideration of the early signs that this risk is materialising.
[40] See S. Sedley, "Governments, Constitutions and Judges" in G. Richardson and H. Genn (eds.), *Administrative Law and Government Action: The Courts and Alternative Mechanisms of Review* (Oxford: Clarendon Press, 1994), ch. 2 at 42.

development taking place, and on what basis international human rights law is being accorded a role in that development.

3. THE EVOLUTION OF A COMMON LAW PRESUMPTION OF STATUTORY INTERPRETATION

One of the various means by which English courts have asserted an indigenous human rights jurisdiction is by deploying the technique of statutory interpretation similar to that recommended by Lord Browne-Wilkinson, that is, interpreting the extent of wide statutory powers against a strong background presumption that the grant of such wide powers was not intended to authorise interference with fundamental freedoms. Lord Browne-Wilkinson has himself helped to blaze this trail in practice. In his dissent in *Wheeler*, for example, in which members of a rugby club challenged the local authority's decision to ban the club from using its recreation ground because of its failure to condemn the national team's tour of South Africa, Browne-Wilkinson LJ saw the case as one involving the use of public powers to interfere with the fundamental right of the club and its members to freedom of speech and conscience.[41] The question to be decided, in his view, was whether general powers conferred on elected public bodies for the administration of public property or money could lawfully be used to punish those who lawfully and reasonably declined to support the views held by the public body.[42] He held that it was undoubtedly part of the constitution of this country that, in the absence of express legislative provision to the contrary, each individual has the right to express and hold his own views, and general statutory powers such as those relating to public open spaces could not be lawfully exercised by discriminating against those holding particular lawful views or refusing to express certain views.[43] Parliament itself could, by legislation, interfere with such basic freedoms, but, in the absence of express words, it could not be taken to have intended to confer on others such a right to interfere.[44]

Similar use of a strong presumption against interference with individual freedom was made by Browne-Wilkinson, this time sitting as Vice-Chancellor, in *Marcel*, in which the question was for what purpose the police may use documents compulsorily seized pursuant to statutory powers.[45] The statute conferring the powers of seizure (the Police and Criminal Evidence Act 1984)

---

[41] *Wheeler* v. *Leicester City Council* [1985] AC 1054.

[42] The general powers relied on were those under the Open Spaces Act 1906, the Public Health Acts and s.71 of the Race Relations Act 1976, requiring local authorities to carry out their functions having due regard to the need to eliminate unlawful racial discrimination and to promote good race relations.

[43] [1985] AC 1054 at 1063D–E.

[44] Ibid. at 1064H–1065E. The House of Lords, at 1079D–E, upheld Browne-Wilkinson LJ's conclusion, but expressly did not follow the "wider ground" on which he based his dissent.

[45] *Marcel* v. *Commissioner of Police of the Metropolis* [1992] Ch. 225.

contained no express provision regulating the purposes for which documents, once seized, could be lawfully used, but Browne-Wilkinson V.-C. held that there clearly must be *some* limit on the purposes for which they could be used.[46] Starting, as in *Wheeler*, from the premise that search and seizure constituted fundamental infringements of the individual's immunity from interference by the state with his privacy and property, which he described as "fundamental human rights", he held that, in the absence of clear words, Parliament could not be assumed to have legislated so as to interfere with the basic rights of the individual to a greater extent than was necessary to secure the protection of the public interest for which the power was conferred. He therefore held that the statutory authorisation only extended to using seized documents for police purposes related to the investigation and prosecution of crime.

In his lecture, Lord Browne-Wilkinson collected a number of older examples of courts strictly construing wide statutory powers in accordance with a presumption in favour of fundamental rights. In *Morris v. Beardmore*, for example, the House of Lords strictly construed a police constable's statutory power to require a person to submit to a breath test, so as to render unlawful a request made by a constable who was at the time trespassing on that person's private property.[47] The presumption was said to be that, in the absence of express provision to the contrary, Parliament did not intend to authorise tortious conduct. There was no express power or right of entry on private property in the relevant statutory provision and, in the words of Lord Scarman, it was not the task of judges, exercising their ingenuity in the field of implication, to go further in the invasion of fundamental private rights and liberties than Parliament has expressly authorised.[48]

It is in a trilogy of decisions concerning a prisoner's right of access to a court, however, that Lord Browne-Wilkinson's theoretical approach of protecting fundamental rights through strict construction of wide discretionary powers has been best exemplified in practice.[49] The Home Secretary enjoys a wide statutory discretion to make rules for, among other things, the regulation and management of prisons and the discipline and control of persons required to be detained therein.[50] Rule 33(3) of the Prison Rules 1964, made by the Secretary of State under that general rule-making power, gave a prison governor power to read or examine every correspondence to or from a

---

[46] Ibid., at 234C–H.

[47] [1981] AC 446. The statutory power was contained in s. 8(2) of the Road Traffic Act 1972.

[48] Ibid. at 463G. Lord Scarman explained, at 464C–E, that he deliberately described the right of privacy as "fundamental", partly because it aptly describes the importance attached by the common law to the privacy of the home, and partly because the right enjoys the protection of the ECHR. Cf. Lord Diplock, ibid. at 455F–G, who said that the presumption owed nothing to the ECHR.

[49] *Raymond v. Honey* [1983] 1 AC 1; *R v. Secretary of State for the Home Department, ex p. Anderson* [1984] QB 778; *R v. Secretary of State for the Home Department, ex p. Leech (No. 2)* [1994] QB 198.

[50] Prison Act 1952, s. 47(1).

prisoner and to stop any correspondence on the ground that its contents are "objectionable" or "of inordinate length".[51] That power to read or stop correspondence was qualified by rule 37A(1), which provided that it was not to be exercised over correspondence between a prisoner who was a party to any legal proceedings and his legal adviser in connection with the proceedings, unless the governor had reason to suppose that it contained matter not relating to the proceedings.[52]

In *Raymond* v. *Honey*, the decision relied on by Lord Browne-Wilkinson as the exemplar of the approach he recommends, a prison governor stopped a prisoner's application to the High Court to commit the governor for contempt for stopping a letter to the prisoner's solicitor in connection with pending legal proceedings.[53] The governor stopped the application on the ground that, under the "prior ventilation rule" then contained in the Prison Rules, allegations against a prison officer had first to be investigated in the prison. In deciding whether in doing so the governor had committed any contempt, the House of Lords did not confine itself to the narrow question of whether the governor had reasonably exercised his powers under the Prison Rules, but expressly preferred to deal with the case on broader grounds,[54] which involved going back to the question of how the regulation-making power in the primary legislation itself was to be construed. The way in which they approached that question of the construction of statutory words expressed in general terms is the embodiment of the half-way bill of rights approach now advocated by Lord Browne-Wilkinson.[55]

Instead of starting with a textual analysis of the statutory words, or of the statute in which they were found, the House of Lords' starting point was to articulate the common law principles which were in play. The relevant basic principles were that to obstruct or interfere with an individual's "constitutional right" to have unimpeded access to courts of law for the ascertainment and enforcement of their legal rights and obligations was a contempt of court,[56] and that a convicted prisoner, despite being imprisoned, retains all civil rights which are not taken away expressly or by necessary implication.[57]

Proceeding from that premise, Lord Wilberforce asked whether there was anything in the statutory rule-making power which authorised the making of

---

[51] SI 1964 No. 388, as subsequently amended.

[52] Rule 37A was added as a result of the decision of the European Court of Human Rights in *Golder* v. *UK* (1975) 1 EHRR 524.

[53] [1983] 1 AC 1.

[54] Lord Wilberforce, ibid. at 12H.

[55] Ibid. at 12H–13C.

[56] Ibid. at 10D–G. This was said to be a principle which had been strongly affirmed by the European Court of Human Rights in *Golder* above n. 52.

[57] Ibid. at 10G–H. Lord Bridge, ibid. at 14G, added a third basic principle, that a citizen's right to unimpeded access to the courts can only be taken away by express enactment, relying on *R & W Paul Ltd.* v. *The Wheat Commission* [1937] AC 139 (also relied on by Lord Browne-Wilkinson in his lecture, (above n. 26) at 406).

regulations which would deny or interfere with a prisoner's right of unimpeded access to court. The general power to make rules for the regulation and management of prisons and the discipline and control of prisoners was held to be "quite insufficient" to authorise interference with so basic a right, and the Prison Rules had to be construed in accordance with the scope of the statutory power to make them if they were to be *intra vires*.[58] The governor's stopping of the prisoner's application to the High Court was therefore an unauthorised interference with the right of access to court and as such constituted a contempt.

This approach to statutory construction, which meets with the approval of Lord Browne-Wilkinson as the "proper approach" in cases where fundamental rights are at stake,[59] was taken a stage further by the Divisional Court in *Anderson*.[60] The case concerned a challenge by a prisoner to the "simultaneous ventilation rule", whereby both correspondence with and visits by a prisoner's legal adviser were restricted in so far as they related to complaints about treatment in prison which had not also been made through the appropriate internal procedure.[61] The applicant, who had been refused permission to receive a visit from his legal adviser to advise him about contemplated legal proceedings against a prison officer, invited the court to find that the standing orders containing the simultaneous ventilation rule were *ultra vires*.

Following the approach of the House of Lords in *Raymond* v. *Honey*, the Divisional Court approached the construction of the rule-making power by considering first the rights of the prisoner at common law. In articulating the relevant common law principles, it went further than the House of Lords in *Raymond*, holding that unimpeded access to a solicitor for the purpose of receiving advice and assistance in connection with the possible institution of civil proceedings formed an inseparable part of the right of access to the courts themselves.[62] Having held that the common law guarantees a right of access to a solicitor, it went on to find that the simultaneous ventilation rule constituted an impediment to that right by imposing a precondition on such access. It was inherent in the logic of *Raymond* v. *Honey* that a prisoner's right of access to a solicitor, with a view to taking advice about starting proceedings, should be as unimpeded as the right of access to court itself. It was held to be proper, and indeed inevitable, that there must be *some* regulation of the circumstances in which prisoners may have access to solicitors, but the

---

[58] [1983] 1 AC 1 at 13A. Lord Bridge at 15D–E went further, in keeping with his view that a citizen's right to unimpeded access to court could only be taken away by express enactment, holding that the rules in question were therefore *ultra vires*.

[59] Above n. 26 at 403.

[60] R v. *Secretary of State for the Home Department, ex p. Anderson* [1984] QB 778.

[61] The simultaneous ventilation rule, contained in Standing Orders 5A 34 and 5B 34, was introduced following the condemnation of the prior ventilation rule by the European Court of Human Rights in *Silver* v. *UK* (1981) 3 EHRR 475.

[62] [1984] QB 778 at 793E–F. The court cited *Golder* (above n. 52) in support of this proposition.

simultaneous ventilation rule constituted such an impediment on prisoners' right of access to courts that it was *ultra vires*.[63]

The final case in this trilogy of cases concerning a prisoner's right of access to court has probably now superseded *Raymond* v. *Honey* as the paradigm example of Lord Browne-Wilkinson's approach of delivering a common law half-way bill of rights through statutory construction, and the significance of its reasoning is such that it merits detailed attention. In *Leech (No.2)* the Court of Appeal handed down a skilfully crafted refinement of the Browne-Wilkinson approach which, properly understood, delivers a highly effective common law bill of rights without a single mention of *Brind*, *Wednesbury* or even "proportionality".[64] The applicant, who was contemplating legal proceedings but had not actually instituted them, argued that the power in Prison Rule 33(3) was *ultra vires* the regulation-making power in the Prison Act insofar as it purported to authorise the governor to read and stop correspondence between prisoners and their legal advisers where no legal proceedings were actually pending. The main ground of challenge was that there was nothing in the primary legislation which conferred the power to alter the basis of the privileged relationship between solicitor and client, a privilege which did not depend on whether proceedings had actually been instituted.

A comparison between the way in which the challenge was disposed of at first instance and on appeal demonstrates nicely the truth in an observation made by Lord Browne-Wilkinson in his lecture. He pointed out that a court which asks the *Wednesbury* question, whether a reasonable minister could have reached the view that a certain rule was necessary, is likely to reach a different conclusion from a court which asks whether the statutory provision granting the power to make rules, on its true construction, authorised the making of a rule which interfered with so fundamental a human right.[65] Webster J., at first instance, concluded that there was no power to make rules which were different from or more extensive than those which were reasonably necessary to carry out the statutory purpose, but regarded the question whether the rule was reasonably necessary to carry out that purpose as a matter for the minister, subject only to review for unreasonableness or irrationality. Since he was satisfied on the evidence that no case of irrationality or unreasonableness had been made out, he dismissed the application.

The Court of Appeal expressly thought that the matter should be approached rather differently,[66] and proceeded to conduct what was ostensibly an inquiry into *vires* (was the relevant Prison Rule within the scope of the rule-making power in the statute?) but in substance was tantamount to the

---

[63] The decision in *Anderson* condemning the simultaneous ventilation rule is a rare example of English courts going even further than is required by the Strasbourg case law: the European Commission of Human Rights in *Silver* (1981) 3 EHRR 475 at 502–3 had appeared to indicate that it would have been satisfied with a simultaneous ventilation rule.

[64] R v. *Secretary of State for the Home Department, ex p. Leech (No.2)* [1994] QB 198.

[65] Above n. 26 at 402–3.

[66] [1994] QB 198 at 207A..

exercise of a fundamental rights juridiction under a "half-way bill of rights". Instead of asking whether the minister had acted reasonably in the *Wednesbury* sense when he formulated the relevant Prison Rule, the question as far as the Court of Appeal was concerned was whether the general power in the statute by necessary implication authorised the making of a rule of the width and scope of Prison Rule 33(3). To answer that question, the Court of Appeal took as its focus the impact of the subordinate rule on certain fundamental rights of the prisoner, making the answer to the *vires* question rest on the "objective" justifiability of that impact, rather than on the reasonableness of the Secretary of State's judgment of the necessity for the rules.

The Court's basic premise was that there is a general presumption against statutory interference with vested common law rights, which must entail also a presumption against a statute authorising interference with such rights by subordinate legislation.[67] A statutory rule-making power conferred in general terms should therefore be strictly construed against a background presumption that it is not intended to authorise the making of rules which infringe fundamental rights, unless such infringement is authorised expressly or by necessary implication. Moreover, where, as here, the primary legislation does not expressly authorise the making of the rule, and the question of *vires* therefore turns on whether the power to make such a rule arises by necessary implication, it had to be remembered that "the more fundamental the right interfered with, and the more drastic the interference, the more difficult becomes the implication."[68]

From this starting point, the Court proceeded to identify the vested common law rights of the prisoner which were affected by rule 33(3), and with respect to each it asked whether the rule-making power could be interpreted as authorising an interference with that right. The least important civil right implicated was that of every citizen to the confidentiality of their correspondence. It was said to be "obvious" that a power to make rules to regulate prisons must include a power to make some rules about prisoners' correspondence, and therefore by necessary implication the provision was said to confer power to make rules which may limit this right.[69] More important was the civil right arising from the duty on all professional people, including solicitors, to keep confidential all communications between themselves and their clients. It was said by the court to be "not unreasonable" to interpret the rule-making power as authorising by necessary implication some interference with this general right of confidentiality.[70] Also at stake, however, was a principle

---

[67] Ibid. at 209G–H.

[68] Ibid., at 209D. This was in fact the same argument as was made by the Secretary of State in *Anderson* [1984] QB 778 at 791C–D. Curiously, the Divisional Court in that case, at 793D, read *Raymond* v. *Honey* as leaving no room for the type of balancing operation proposed by the Secretary of State. In *Leech*, counsel for the Secretary of State disavowed any argument that the court should embark on a balancing exercise on the *ultra vires* issue.

[69] Ibid., at 209E–F.

[70] Ibid., at 209H.

considered to be of even greater importance, the right of unimpeded access to a court. This was described as, "even in our unwritten constitution . . . a constitutional right."[71] Inseparable from this right of access to court was a prisoner's right of unimpeded access to a solicitor for the purpose of receiving advice and assistance in connection with possible civil proceedings in the courts. These rights were clearly part of domestic jurisprudence following the decisions in *Raymond* v. *Honey* and *Anderson*. Finally, buttressing these "cardinal principles" of unimpeded access to a court and to legal advice was the important "auxiliary principle" of legal professional privilege between solicitor and client.[72]

Although it was accepted that the citizen's right of unimpeded access could in principle be taken away by necessary implication,[73] it was said that it would be a rare case in which it could be held that a right as fundamental as the right to privileged communication with a lawyer had been by necessary implication abolished or limited by statute. And it would be an even rarer case in which it could be held that a statute authorised by necessary implication the abolition or limitation of so fundamental a right by subordinate legislation.[74]

Having identified the basic rights at stake, and placed them in a hierarchy of importance reflected in the ease with which they may be impliedly displaced by statute, the Court of Appeal went on to consider whether the respondent had demonstrated an "objective need" for a rule as wide as that which had been made in rule 33(3). The question was said to be whether there was a self-evident and pressing need for an unrestricted power to read letters between a prisoner and a solicitor and a power to stop such letters on the ground of prolixity and objectionability.[75] In seeking the answer to this question, the Court clearly proceeded on the basis that the onus was on the Secretary of State to demonstrate that such a need existed. To establish whether that onus had been discharged, the Court considered the affidavit evidence put in on the minister's behalf purporting to explain the rationale behind the relevant regulation. The Court accepted that the rule-making power must be interpreted as conferring by necessary implication power to make rules to prevent escapes and disturbances, to detect and prevent criminal or disciplinary offences, or in the interests of national security, but it held that no objective need had been established for a rule which distinguished between correspondence depending on whether litigation was actually pending or merely contemplated. The evidence of the Secretary of State had demonstrated no more than the need for

[71] Anderson [1984] QB 778 at 210A–B.

[72] For a similar reference to legal professional privilege as "an auxiliary principle buttressing the constitutional right of access to justice", again by Steyn LJ, see *Oxfordshire County Council* v. *M* [1994] Fam 151 at 163D.

[73] Ibid. 210D not following Lord Bridge's stricter approach in *Raymond* requiring express words.

[74] Ibid., at 212D.

[75] Ibid., at 212F.

prison authorities to have the power to ascertain that purported exchanges between a prisoner and a solicitor are genuine communications between client and solicitor and to stop letters which fail such scrutiny.[76]

The Court of Appeal also took into account the *extent* of the interference with the applicant's basic rights. An unrestricted right to read correspondence between prisoner and solicitor was a "considerable disincentive" and a "substantial impediment" to the exercise of the prisoner's basic rights of access to a court and to legal advice and assistance, and the existence of a power to stop such correspondence meant that those rights could be denied altogether.[77] The Court concluded that while s.47(1) of the Prison Act by necessary implication authorised *some* screening of correspondence between a prisoner and a solicitor, the authorised intrusion must be the minimum necessary to ensure that the correspondence is in truth *bona fide* legal correspondence. Rule 33(3) was therefore *ultra vires* so far as it purported to apply to correspondence between prisoners and their legal advisers.[78]

This trilogy of cases concerning prisoners' right of access to court and to legal advice demonstrate the progress that has been made towards the recognition of a general presumption in favour of fundamental rights. It is a measure of that progress that, in the latest edition of his Code on Statutory Interpretation, Bennion devotes an entire Part to what he describes as "the principle against doubtful penalisation".[79] This is said to be much wider than the long-established presumption requiring strict construction of criminal statutes, extending to "any form of detriment", including interferences with various rights protected under the ECHR.[80] Thus it is said to be only a particular manifestation of the general principle against doubtful penalisation that life, health, freedom of the person, family rights, religion, free assembly and association, free speech, property and other economic interests, status or reputation, privacy, rights of legal process, and a residual category of "rights as a citizen" are not to be interfered with except under clear authority of law.[81]

4. DEVELOPING THE COMMON LAW OF *WEDNESBURY* REVIEW

The emergence of a general common law presumption of statutory interpretation in favour of fundamental rights will inevitably affect the approach of

---

[76] Ibid., at 213H, 214D–E.

[77] Ibid., at 216H–217A.

[78] Ibid., at 218C–D.

[79] F.A.R. Bennion, *Statutory Interpretation: A Code*, 2nd ed. (London: Butterworths, 1992), Part XVII.

[80] Ibid. at 571.

[81] There are of course many other examples of courts recognising more specific rights: see eg. *In re O* [1991] 2 WLR 475 at 480F (only clear statutory words, or even clearer implication, can overrule so old and fundamental a freedom as the privilege against self-incrimination).

the courts to illegality as a ground of judicial review, as both *Anderson* and *Leech* demonstrate, but there is nothing inherent in the nature of that development to confine it to judicial review. The emerging presumption applies generally, whenever a court is called on to interpret a statute which has the potential to infringe fundamental rights. Another means by which English courts have asserted a fundamental rights jurisdiction in recent years, however, has been more specific to the law of judicial review. That is the development of the common law of judicial review itself, by lowering the *Wednesbury* threshold of unreasonableness and applying a more exacting standard of review to discretionary decisions by public bodies which interfere with fundamental rights.[82] Undoubtedly the two most frequently cited examples of this approach to enhancing judicial protection for fundamental rights are the passages from Lord Bridge's judgments in *Bugdaycay*[83] *and Brind*, in both of which he clearly presupposed that the intensity of review, or how hard a court will look at the decision, will vary according to the subject matter of the decision under challenge.

In *Bugdaycay*, the challenge was to a decision of the Secretary of State refusing the applicant asylum as a refugee from Uganda and directing that he be removed to Kenya, the safe country from which he had arrived in the UK. The Secretary of State had made those decisions without seeking to verify the applicant's claim, confirmed by a senior diplomatic representative of Kenya, that he was unlikely to be allowed to re-enter Kenya and was likely to be removed to Uganda where he feared he would be killed. The fact that, quite literally, the applicant's life might depend on the Secretary of State's decision prompted Lord Bridge to articulate a significant refinement of the usual *Wednesbury* principles of review. The court's power of review of any exercise of discretion in relation to asylum applications was acknowledged to be limited, but

> "[w]ithin those limitations the court must . . . be entitled to subject an administrative decision to the more rigorous examination, to ensure that it is in no way flawed, according to the gravity of the issue which the decision determines. The most fundamental of all human rights is the individual's right to life and when an administrative decision under challenge is said to be one which may put the applicant's life at risk, the basis of the decision must surely call for the most anxious scrutiny."[84]

Lord Templeman expressly agreed with Lord Bridge that "where the result of a flawed decision may imperil life or liberty a special responsibility lies on the court in the examination of the decision-making process."[85]

---

[82] The role of human rights in the law of judicial review since the decision in *Brind* is given separate and more detailed treatment in ch. 6, but it is necessary to anticipate that discussion to a certain extent in order to give a full account in this chapter of the common law developments which are manifestations of the broader assertion of an indigenous human rights jurisdiction.

[83] *R* v. *Secretary of State for the Home Department, ex p. Bugdaycay* [1987] AC 514. Strictly speaking the relevant passage was uttered in disposing of the separate appeal of *In re Musisi*.

[84] Ibid. at 531E–G.

[85] Ibid. at 537H. Lords Griffiths and Goff agreed with Lord Bridge; Lord Brandon agreed with both Lord Bridge and Lord Templeman.

Lord Bridge accordingly proceeded to subject to a "detailed examination"[86] the evidence relating to the way in which the immigration authorities had dealt with the application for asylum. Following a rigorous analysis of the reasons contained in the respondent's affidavit evidence, Lord Bridge concluded that, since, when assessing the danger of the applicant being sent home to Uganda, the Secretary of State had not taken into account the evidence that Kenya had in the past returned Ugandan refugees to Uganda in breach of its international obligations, his decision could not be allowed to stand.

Lord Bridge returned to the same theme in *Brind*.[87] Having rejected the applicants' arguments that the Secretary of State's power could only be exercised in accordance with Article 10 of the ECHR, for the reasons recounted in chapter 4, he nevertheless went on to lay claim to a domestic jurisdiction over the protection of human rights. The fact that courts could not presume that Parliament intended unlimited statutory discretions to be exercised within ECHR limits did not mean that courts were powerless to prevent the exercise by the executive of such discretions in ways which infringed fundamental human rights, he said. In deciding whether the Secretary of State could reasonably impose the restriction he did on the broadcasters, the courts were

> "perfectly entitled to start from the premise that any restriction of the right to freedom of expression requires to be justified and that nothing less than an important competing public interest will be sufficient to justify it. The primary judgment as to whether the particular competing public interest justifies the particular restriction imposed falls to be made by the Secretary of State to whom Parliament has entrusted the discretion. But we are entitled to exercise a secondary judgment by asking whether a reasonable Secretary of State, on the material before him, could reasonably make that primary judgment."[88]

As in *Bugdaycay*, Lord Bridge was not alone in his refinement of the *Wednesbury* standard of unreasonableness to accommodate the human rights dimension. While his approach implicitly lowered the *Wednesbury* threshold,[89] Lord Templeman was more explicit in his recognition of *Wednesbury*'s inadequacy in modern conditions. He commented that the subject matter and

---

[86] Ibid. at 527A.

[87] [1991] 1 AC 696 at 748F–749G. That Lord Bridge considers the threshold of unreasonableness to vary according to the context is also implicit in his judgment in *R v. Secretary of State for the Environment, ex p. Hammersmith LBC* [1991] 1 AC 521, in which he held that decisions concerning the formulation and implementation of national economic policy are not open to challenge on grounds of irrationality, short of the extremes of bad faith, improper motive or manifest absurdity. The clear implication is that the ground of irrationality embraces lesser standards than the extreme of "manifest absurdity" which may be appropriate in a different context.

[88] [1991] 1 AC 696 at 748H–749B.

[89] The view that Lord Bridge's approach in *Bugdaycay* is a refinement of *Wednesbury* is supported by the fact that "the very experienced counsel appearing [at first instance] expressly disclaimed any challenge to the decision of the Secretary of State on *Wednesbury* principles", [1987] AC 514 at 526H. The ground on which the applicant succeeded was argued for the first time in the House of Lords.

date of that case[90] could not make it either necessary or appropriate for the courts to judge the validity of an interference with human rights by asking themselves whether the Home Secretary has acted irrationally or perversely.[91] In his view, the courts could not escape from asking themselves "whether a reasonable minister, on the material before him, could reasonably conclude that the interference with freedom of expression . . . was justifiable".[92]

Since Lord Roskill expressed his entire agreement with Lord Bridge, there was in fact a majority of the House of Lords in *Brind* who effectively rejected *Wednesbury* in favour of a test formulated in such a way that courts are likely to intervene more readily in cases concerning fundamental rights. The headnote writer's claim that this was a case in which *Wednesbury* was "applied" is therefore somewhat misleading.[93] In fact only Lords Ackner and Lord Lowry purported to apply the traditional *Wednesbury* test, and even they effectively lowered the threshold of that test by acknowledging that in cases concerning rights of fundamental importance, "close scrutiny" must be given to the reasons provided as justification for interfering with that right.[94]

Neither of these first two techniques for asserting a domestic human rights jurisdiction, that is, a strong presumption of statutory interpretation and a variable threshold of *Wednesbury* review, constitute dramatic new departures for the common law. They do, however, represent important *developments* of the common law so as to bring up to date the range of values protected by old techniques.[95] Take the presumption of statutory interpretation in favour of individual rights and freedoms. As Lord Browne-Wilkinson himself pointed out in the lecture that helped to revive awareness of this particular strand in the common law's tradition, the courts have long adopted a strict construction of statutory powers which interfere with more traditional rights such as property or the freedom of the person from physical restraint. This is evident, for example, in the many cases establishing that wide discretionary powers cannot include the power to levy a charge because no tax can be imposed

[90] *Wednesbury* was a case concerning local authority licensing of cinemas and was decided in 1948, before the post-War international human rights movement had really gathered momentum. The Universal Declaration of Human Rights, for example, was proclaimed by the UN General Assembly on 12 December 1948.

[91] [1991] 1 AC 696 at 751E–F.

[92] That Lord Templeman thought that courts should apply a different test in fundamental rights cases was equally manifest in his *obiter dictum* in R v. *Independent Television Commission, ex p. TSW Broadcasting Ltd.* (unreported decision of the House of Lords, 26 March 1992), in which, having rejected the challenge on grounds of irrationality, he said "this is not a case in which TSW can . . . require a close scrutiny of possible threats to human rights or fundamental freedoms."

[93] [1991] 1 AC 696 at 697E. This may seem pedantic but it can be of practical importance. For an example of a court relying on the headnote in *Brind* to dispose of an applicant's argument, see R v. *Secretary of State for the Home Department, ex p. Togher,* unreported decision of CA, 1 February 1995 (available on LEXIS).

[94] [1991] 1 AC 696 at 757C and 763G.

[95] Consideration of the more general significance of these developments for administrative law, in particular their embodiment of a concept of proportionality, is postponed until ch. 6.

without express parliamentary language.[96] Cases such as *Raymond* v. *Honey*, *Anderson* and *Leech* represent the modern application of that judicial technique to reflect the changing catalogue of rights considered "fundamental", and therefore worthy of presumptive protection, by the common law today.[97]

By the same token, the variable intensity of judicial scrutiny in public law in accordance with the gravity of the issue which the decision under challenge determines, acknowledged explicitly by Lords Bridge and Templeman, has, in reality, always been a feature of the law of judicial review. There are numerous examples of courts adopting a more rigorous approach to the review of administrative discretions where the interests at stake were those to which the common law traditionally attached greater value, such as the right to property and other economic interests.[98] The significant development is in Lord Bridge's implicit acknowledgment that cases involving fundamental human rights require the courts to be more rigorous in their scrutiny of the decision being challenged. This not only marks an unusually candid recognition that review of discretionary powers is not constrained by a monolithic and inherently deferential *Wednesbury* standard, but marks also an equally welcome evolution in the kinds of interests which the common law recognises as worthy of judicial protection in public law, from the traditional narrow cluster of property rights and personal liberty, to a more modern catalogue of civil and political rights.[99]

5. COMMON LAW DEVELOPMENT OUTSIDE ADMINISTRATIVE LAW

It will be recalled from chapter 4 that one of the features of the second phase in the domestic career of international human rights law was a tendency for judges to avoid difficult theoretical questions about the exact domestic status of the ECHR by asserting an identity between the protection offered by the common law and that provided by the ECHR. That tendency was both adverted to and exemplified by Lord Donaldson MR in the Court of Appeal in *Brind*, when he observed that in most of the cases in which the ECHR had featured in the judgments,

"the reference has been fleeting and usually consisted of an assertion, in which I would concur, that you have to look long and hard before you can detect any

---

[96] See eg. *AG* v. *Wilts United Dairies* (1921) 19 LGR 534.

[97] As will be seen, the catalogue of rights recognised by the common law as "fundamental" is steadily expanding. Indeed, it would appear from the speeches of the House of Lords in *R* v. *Khan* [1996] 3 WLR 162, considered in section 7 below, that English law is on the verge of explicitly recognising a common law right to privacy, but it was held not to be necessary for disposing of the appeal to determine whether such a right yet existed.

[98] See eg. *Bromley LBC* v. *GLC* [1983] 1 AC 768 and other cases in which the courts have invented the concept of a fiduciary obligation owed by local authorities to ratepayers.

[99] As will be seen, however, the common law's recognition of economic, social and cultural rights, or "third generation" rights such as the right to a clean environment, has been much more limited.

difference between the English common law and the principles set out in the Convention."[100]

Lord Browne-Wilkinson in his lecture agreed, considering it to be "now inconceivable" that any English court would hold that the individual freedoms of a private person are any less extensive than the basic human rights protected by the ECHR.[101] This asserted identity between the common law and the ECHR, which has been frequently relied on by the UK government as a reason for not incorporating the Convention,[102] increasingly found favour with the judiciary, because it provided a convenient way of dealing with ECHR arguments without having to answer the difficult question of its precise domestic status. Either the ECHR could be said to be irrelevant because it added nothing to domestic law, or consideration of it could be made legitimate, since it was no different from domestic law.

Although it is true, as was seen in chapter 1, that the drafting of the ECHR was clearly influenced by English attempts to articulate common law values, is it realistic to suppose, as so many judges have consistently asserted, that there is such a happy coincidence between the common law and the ECHR? Quite apart from the obvious difficulty in asserting an identity between the common law and a set of general principles subject to evolutionary development in their interpretation and application by the Strasbourg organs, the judges' frequent claim that the common law has been a trusty protector of fundamental rights without need of constitutional reinforcement is dubious, at least in relation to certain of the rights contained in the ECHR. As Fleming has observed in the context of free speech and defamation,[103]

> "the truth of the matter is, quite frankly, that English law has long been at odds with the law of many other Anglo-American jurisdictions in continuing to subordinate speech on matters of public concern to what English courts still perceive to be the tender sensibilities of public officials and institutions."

Much the same could be said for many of the other rights and freedoms protected by the ECHR. The supposed identity of common law and ECHR is surely a modern manifestation of the ancient myth that judges are not lawmakers. The perceived need to perpetuate that myth largely explains the nostalgic attachment to sovereignty theory with its fiction that Parliament is the only legitimate law-maker. Even the most ardent defender of the sovereignty of Parliament would find it hard to deny that what the courts have in fact been busy doing, during this period of common law revival, is *developing* the common law, extending it to cover rights and interests not previously valued

---

[100] [1991] 1 AC 696 at 717E–F.
[101] Above n. 26 397 at 405.
[102] See eg. HL Deb, Vol. 560, cols. 1164–5 (25 January, 1995).
[103] (1993) 109 LQR 12 at 14, commenting on *Derbyshire County Council v. Times Newspapers* [1993] AC 534, considered below.

by a conservative common law which privileged above all property-based or personal liberty interests.[104]

Occasionally, however, courts have been prepared to be explicit about their use of the ECHR to develop the common law, usually in those areas outside of administrative law where the prohibition articulated in *Brind* and its predecessors was thought not to bite. A good example of such a decision is that of the Divisional Court in *Choudhury*, in which judicial review was sought of the magistrate's refusal to issue summonses for blasphemous and seditious libel against Salman Rushdie and the publishers of the *Satanic Verses*.[105] The application was refused, principally on the ground that the scope of the common law offence of blasphemy was clearly confined to protection of the Christian religion, and it was the function of the legislature not the court to extend it. Significantly, however, the Divisional Court did not merely accept the argument that, because the common law position was clear, it was unnecessary to pay any regard to the ECHR. On the contrary, the court expressly agreed that it was necessary for it to be satisfied that the UK was not in breach of the ECHR for so confining the scope of the offence of blasphemy,[106] and proceeded to carry out one of the most extended considerations of ECHR provisions and case-law ever conducted by an English court, before concluding that to refuse to extend the common law of blasphemy to protect the Muslim faith would not be a breach of the ECHR.[107]

This would have been an exercise in futility had the court not thought that it would be legitimate for it to "extend" what appeared, apart from any consideration of the ECHR, to be the clear scope of the common law offence. It can therefore be inferred that, just as Watkins LJ in the Divisional Court in *Brind* had held that general words in a statute were not to be read literally but subject to the implied limits of the ECHR, so in *Choudhury* the same judge thought that even where domestic common law is clear it is still legitimate, and may even be necessary, for the court to go on to consider the substantive question of whether that "clear" common law position complies with the ECHR. The case could therefore be said to stand for the proposition that the ECHR is still relevant to a domestic court's determination even where the common law is clear. As was the case with courts accepting the relevance of the ECHR to the construction of statutory powers, this can be seen in one of two ways.[108] Either it can be seen as acknowledging that ambiguity may arise

---

[104] See Lester, "English Judges as Law Makers" [1993] PL 269, a timely update of Lord Reid's famous essay "The Judge as Law Maker" (1972) 12 JSPTL 22, in which Lord Reid condemned the notion that judges simply declare the law as a fairy-tale which nobody any longer believes.

[105] *R v. Chief Metropolitan Stipendiary Magistrate, ex p. Choudhury* [1991] 1 QB 429.

[106] Ibid. at 449G. The court's agreement was however expressed to be "in the context of this case."

[107] Ibid. at 449H–452C. See Clapham, *Human Rights in the Private Sphere* (Oxford: Clarendon Press, 1993) at 314–22 for criticism of the Court's use of the ECHR case-law and regret at the need for courts to rely so heavily on counsel to make up for its deficit of knowledge and experience.

[108] See ch. 1.

from the very existence of the ECHR obligation. Or, preferably, it could be read as saying that there is no requirement that domestic law (domestic common law at least) must be ambiguous before reference may be made to the ECHR. Although not made explicit in *Choudhury*, the judgment seems to rest on the assumption that the court is under a constitutional responsibility to interpret domestic law so as to make it consistent with the ECHR. If this is correct, it amounts to an abandonment of the requirement introduced by Lord Fraser in *AG* v. *BBC*, that the common law, like a statute, must be ambiguous, or "not firmly settled", before resort can legitimately be had to the ECHR.[109]

This important feature of the Divisional Court's judgment in *Choudhury* was picked up by two members of the Court of Appeal in *Derbyshire*, a decision even more remarkable than *Choudhury* for the lengths to which the court went, both in the extent of its use of the ECHR and its case-law, and in its formulations of when and in what sense the ECHR becomes relevant to an issue before a domestic court.[110] The issue in the case was whether a local authority had the right at common law to maintain an action for damages in defamation in respect of its governmental and administrative reputation. One of the grounds on which the defendant newspaper sought to have the action struck out was that the right to free speech, whether as a common law right or under Article 10 of the ECHR, prevented a public authority from bringing such an action.

Morland J. had given the defendants' ECHR argument short shrift, adopting Lord Ackner's *Brind* formulation of the basis on which a court may have regard to the ECHR, and holding that as there was no ambiguity or uncertainty in English law over the extent to which local authorities may sue for libel, no explicit regard to Article 10 was required.[111] Each member of the Court of Appeal, however, found that there was uncertainty about the common law position, and each had regard to the ECHR and its case-law in order to resolve it, although there were subtle differences between their approaches to the status of the ECHR. Balcombe LJ proceeded from the premise that "Article 10 does not establish any novel proposition under English law", accepting the view of both Lord Donaldson MR and Lord Goff in *Spycatcher (No.2)*, that Article 10 is in effect the same as English common law. However, whereas in previous cases, including *Spycatcher (No.2)* itself, such an assertion of the identity of the common law and the ECHR had always been a prelude to the court ignoring or paying scant regard to the ECHR, Balcombe LJ drew the opposite conclusion: if the two really were the same, then rather than proceeding to ignore the ECHR, why should the court not decide the issue in

---

[109] [1981] AC 303 at 352.

[110] *Derbyshire County Council* v. *Times Newpapers* [1992] QB 770. As will be seen below, the House of Lords decided the case on a rather different basis.

[111] Ibid. at 785E–786E. For good measure he added that in any event the English civil law of defamation was within the "margin of appreciation" allowed to a state under the ECHR.

terms of the ECHR? He found it "convenient" to consider the question at stake by reference to Article 10 alone, giving as his reason that it states the right to freedom of expression and the qualifications to it "in precise terms".[112] Instead of merely asserting the identity of the common law and the ECHR and moving on, an analysis in ECHR terms is at the very forefront of Balcombe LJ's judgment.

It is difficult to extract a straightforward formulation of the status of the ECHR from any one member of the Court of Appeal in *Derbyshire*, let alone the Court as a whole. Balcombe LJ acknowledged the fact of the unincorporated status of Article 10 and repeated Lord Ackner's *Brind* formulation, that it may nevertheless be resorted to in order to help resolve some uncertainty or ambiguity in municipal law. However, later in his judgment he appeared to cast doubt over whether ambiguity or uncertainty was required at all and whether reference to the ECHR is a matter of discretion or *obligation* for the national court. He began by saying that Article 10 may be used to resolve an ambiguity in English primary or subordinate legislation, when considering the principles on which a court should act in exercising a discretion, and when the common law (including the doctrines of equity) is uncertain. However, to this list of situations in which Article 10 could legitimately be referred to by an English court, notwithstanding that it had not been incorporated into domestic law, he added "[e]ven if the common law is certain the courts will still, when appropriate, consider whether the UK is in breach of Article 10", citing *Choudhury* in support of this proposition.[113] Although no indication was given as to when such consideration may or may not be "appropriate", and the comment was strictly speaking *obiter* in any event because he went on to find that there was here uncertainty in the common law, nevertheless the dictum shows that Balcombe LJ, like the Divisional Court in *Choudhury*, was prepared explicitly to concede a role to the ECHR in the development of the common law even where it was otherwise clear. Similarly Butler-Sloss LJ found that reference to the ECHR was justified because the law was not clear, but added that, even if it were clear, *Choudhury* was authority for it still being *necessary* to refer to the ECHR.[114]

At times both judges also formulated the position of the ECHR in domestic law in terms of courts being under a *duty* to have regard to it rather than having a discretion, power or entitlement to do so in certain situations. For example, Balcombe LJ went on to say "where the law is uncertain, it must be right for the court to approach the issue before it with a predilection to ensure

---

[112] Ibid. at 812B. Compare the concerns voiced about the breadth and vagueness of the ECHR's terms in the early case-law such as *Bibi*, and still relied on by the UK Government as a reason for not incorporating the ECHR.

[113] Ibid. at 812E–F.

[114] Ibid. at 830F. For an unsuccessful attempt to argue, in reliance on these dicta, that regard should be had to the Convention even where the common law was clear, see *R v. Mid-Glamorgan Family Health Services Authority, ex p Martin* [1995] 1 WLR 110.

that our law should not involve a breach of Article 10."[115] And Butler-Sloss LJ, as well as talking of Article 10 "applying"[116] and of the "duty" of English courts to take account of it,[117] said "where there is an ambiguity, or the law is otherwise unclear or so far undeclared by an appellate court, the English court is not only entitled but . . . *obliged* to consider the implications of Article 10."[118] Taken together with their preparedness to refer to the ECHR even where the common law is clear, this would suggest that Balcombe and Butler-Sloss LJJ considered the court to be under a general obligation to construe domestic law so as to be in conformity with the ECHR. However, their judgments were ultimately equivocal on this. Butler-Sloss LJ, for example, said elsewhere in her judgment that "where the law is clear and unambiguous, either stated as the common law or enacted by Parliament, recourse to Article 10 is unnecessary and inappropriate."[119]

Only Ralph Gibson LJ, who had been a member of the Court of Appeal in *Brind*, formulated the circumstances in which regard could legitimately be had to the ECHR in terms of a preliminary requirement of ambiguity or lack of clarity in the common law. He was quite unequivocal that if, by established principles of law, it was clear that the local authority had the right to sue for libel, the court had no option but to let the action proceed, even if there was no doubt that subsequently that would be held to be a violation of the ECHR.[120] Unlike the other two members of the court, he made no mention of *Choudhury* or of the possibility of referring to the ECHR even where the common law was clear. However, even he chose the language of obligation rather than permission to describe the sense in which the ECHR was relevant, saying that where the law was not clear the court "must" have regard to the principles stated in the ECHR.[121]

The Court of Appeal's willingness in *Derbyshire* to find uncertainty or ambiguity in the common law is also worthy of note. The members of the court seem to have based their finding of "uncertainty" on the fact that there was no authority on the point which was binding on the Court of Appeal, nor any legislation on the issue, so that, in Balcombe LJ's words, the court was "in a position to define the extent of this common law tort in such a way as

---

[115] [1992] QB 770 at 813B. See also 813H ("we both can and should consider the effect of Article 10").

[116] Ibid. at 829D.

[117] Ibid. at 830A.

[118] Ibid. at 830B (emphasis added).

[119] Ibid. at 830A–B. However, as with the qualification expressed in *Spycatcher (No. 2)* [1990] 1 AC 109 at 283G by Lord Goff, who considered it to be his duty to interpret domestic law in accordance with treaty obligations "when I am free to do so", these words can be taken to be merely an acknowledgment that, in cases of irreconcilable conflict, courts must give precedence to the domestic norm. As was explained in ch. 1, section 9, that is quite different from imposing an ambiguity precondition on reference to unincorporated international norms.

[120] [1992] QB 770 at 818F.

[121] Ibid. at 819B.

not to require a positive amendment of the law by Parliament."[122] This is a very expansive notion of uncertainty, which will be of great importance for the domestic relevance of international human rights norms so long as ambiguity remains a precondition of legitimate reference to unincorporated international instruments.

Having found the law to be uncertain, each judge proceeded to carry out a balancing exercise of precisely the sort required by Article 10 ECHR, in which the right to freedom of expression was weighed against the competing public interests, and the unanimous conclusion was reached that for the common law to permit a local authority to maintain a libel action in respect of its governing reputation would impose greater restrictions on freedom of expression than are necessary in a democratic society. In carrying out the balancing exercise, the judges borrowed the concepts and methodology from the Strasbourg case-law: balancing competing interests, pressing social need, proportionality to the legitimate aim, necessity in a democratic society.

The Court of Appeal's decision in *Derbyshire* left little room for doubt that the status of international human rights in domestic law had moved into another phase. Although the reasoning of the judgments is cast in terms of using the ECHR to resolve an uncertainty in the common law, it is difficult to avoid the conclusion that the ECHR was here being used by the Court of Appeal to *develop* the common law rather than merely as a supposed aid to uncovering what it had always been.[123] Moreover, it seems clear that a majority of the court considered themselves under a general obligation to strive to interpret the common law so as to conform with the ECHR, while the third member considered himself to be under such an obligation where there was ambiguity, and all three were prepared to take a generous approach to what counts as the requisite uncertainty in the state of the law.[124]

6. JUDICIAL DISCRETION AND INTERNATIONAL HUMAN RIGHTS LAW

The final means by which English courts have asserted a common law human rights jurisdiction is by accepting the relevance of international human rights law, or developing the common law in the light of it, when deciding how to

---

[122] Balcombe, however, LJ, ibid. at 813H. See also Ralph Gibson LJ at 822E–F; Butler-Sloss LJ at 830E, 835B. Compare the willingness of Scarman LJ. in *Phansopkar* [1976] QB 606 (above ch. 4, n. 41) to refer to the ECHR in cases of legislative omission as well as ambiguity. Contrast the reluctance of Megarry V.-C. in *Malone* v. *Metropolitan Police Commissioner* [1979] Ch. 344 at 379B–C to "lay down new rules of common law or equity that will carry out the Crown's treaty obligations, or . . . discover for the first time that such rules have always existed."

[123] Though Butler-Sloss LJ [1992] QB 770 at 835B–C, whilst acknowledging that the court was "ventur[ing] into relatively unchartered waters", still characterised the exercise as one of "declar[ing] the present state of the law".

[124] As will be seen in ch. 8, the House of Lords in *Derbyshire* [1993] AC 534 reached the same conclusion as the Court of Appeal but found it unnecessary to enlist the assistance of the ECHR in doing so.

exercise an inherent judicial discretion.[125] This tendency, it will be remembered from chapter 4, was already in evidence during Phase II. Lord Templeman in *Spycatcher No. 1*, for example, had considered the compatibility with Article 10 ECHR of restraining publication when deciding whether, in the court's discretion, the interlocutory injunctions restraining breach of confidence should be continued.[126] Since *Spycatcher*, courts have been prepared to take the ECHR into account when exercising their discretion in a growing number of areas.[127] In *R v. Advertising Standards Authority, ex p Vernons Organisation*, for example, in which the applicant for judicial review sought an interim injunction restraining the publication of the Authority's adverse report which it sought to quash in the main proceedings, Laws J. announced that "there is a general principle in our law that expression of opinion and the conveyance of information will not be restrained by the courts save on pressing grounds", and freedom of expression was said to be "as much a sinew of the common law as it is of the . . . Convention."[128] Since no such "pressing ground" was found to exist, the court exercised its discretion to refuse the interim restraint on publication.

The relevance of the ECHR to the exercise of common law judicial discretion was similarly asserted in *Middlebrook Mushrooms*, in which the Court of Appeal discharged an interlocutory injunction restraining the defendant union from distributing leaflets to intending customers at supermarkets supplied by the employers with whom the union was in dispute.[129] Although Article 10 of the ECHR was not specifically relied on by the union, in Neill LJ's view it was relevant to bear in mind that in all cases which involve a proposed restriction on the right of free speech the court is concerned, when exercising its discretion, to consider whether the suggested restraint is "necessary".[130]

One area of judicial discretion in which courts have gone a very long way in seeking to exercise that discretion consistently with the ECHR has been when deciding, pursuant to their inherent wardship jurisdiction, whether to

---

[125] Again, there is an obvious overlap between this judicial technique and the other common law developments so far considered. Its treatment as a separate category is justified only by the fact that courts have treated the exercise of judicial discretions as a discrete function when referring to international instruments. Consideration of the role of the ECHR in the exercise of judicial discretions conferred by statute is postponed until the following section, for reasons which will become apparent.

[126] *A-G v. Guardian Newspapers (No. 1)* [1987] 1 WLR 1248 at 1296F–1297F.

[127] In *A-G v. Blake* [1996] 3 All ER 903 at 909f–g, for example, Sir Richard Scott V.-C. held that the treaty obligation contained in Art. 10 ECHR "must be borne in mind" when considering the nature and breadth of the continuing duty binding ex-members of the intelligence and security services."

[128] [1992] 1 WLR 1289 at 1293A–B.

[129] *Middlebrook Mushrooms v. Transport and General Workers' Union* [1993] ICR 612.

[130] Ibid. at 620C–D. Since the question of the exercise of discretion did not arise in the case itself, Neill LJ's remarks are entirely *obiter*. Contrast the conspicuous lack of any mention of the ECHR in the Court of Appeal's decision in the earlier analogous case of *Hubbard v. Pitt* [1976] QB 142.

impose restrictions on publicity where the interests of the child require some protection of confidentiality.[131] The growing judicial awareness of the importance of the freedom of the press had led to a number of decisions in which courts had tried to set out an approach which ensured that appropriate weight was accorded to that freedom when deciding whether to restrain publicity.[132] The first such case in which the ECHR was referred to, however, was *In re W*, in which a local authority had obtained an injunction restraining a newspaper from publishing an article about a male ward of court who was known to have been involved in homosexual activities with older men and had been placed by the authority with two male foster parents who had had a stable gay relationship with each other for many years.[133] The newspaper argued that the effect of the injunction was to prevent the public from being informed of a matter that was plainly of public interest.

Neill LJ sought to extract some guidelines from recent developments in the judicial recognition of the freedom of the press, the relevant principles of the ECHR and the recent cases concerning the publication of stories about wards of court. When considering whether or not to make an order restraining publication in the exercise of its inherent discretion, the court would attach great importance to the freedom of the press and would also take account of Article 10 of the ECHR, he said. However, the freedoms protected by Article 10 were subject to exceptions, including restrictions on publication for the protection of children, and it was therefore necessary to carry out a balancing exercise, in which the welfare of the child was not the paramount consideration. The guidance Neill LJ proceeded to offer on how to carry out that balancing exercise, although couched in different vocabulary, bears a striking resemblance to the proportionality analysis that the European Court of Human Rights would carry out in determining whether there has been a breach of Article 10.

The balancing exercise involved the court in weighing the need to protect the ward from harm against the right of the press to publish or comment. An important factor in striking the balance would be the nature and extent of the public interest in the matter. Curiosity, for example, was to be distinguished from genuine public interest. Usually the public interest in publication could be satisfied without identification of the ward, but the risk of some wider identification may have to be accepted. Finally, and most reminiscent of the Strasbourg proportionality test, any restraint had to be in clear terms and be

---

[131] The granting of such injunctions in the exercise of the wardship jurisdiction is a relatively recent phenomenon, as is pointed out by Hoffmann LJ in *R v. Central Independent Television plc* [1994] 3 WLR 20 at 31D, where, in a judgment hostile to the development, he asks by what authority the courts have assumed a power to create by injunction a right of privacy for children.

[132] Most notably in *In re M and N (Minors) (Wardship: Publication of Information)* [1990] Fam. 211, in which Butler-Sloss LJ established at 223H that when balancing the interests of the ward of court against the freedom of the press, "the welfare of the child is not the paramount consideration". The Court of Appeal in that case recognised the need to strike a balance, giving the newspaper the right to publish the story but at the same time imposing certain safeguards protecting privacy.

[133] *In re W (A Minor) (Wardship: Restrictions on Publication)* [1992] 1 WLR 100 at 103A–G.

no wider than was necessary to achieve the purpose for which it was imposed. Applying those guidelines to the facts of the case, Neill LJ held that the newspaper should be able to publish the story, because the placement of a boy with homosexual foster parents was a matter of genuine public concern, but subject to the newspaper taking steps to avoid any risks that the article would lead to identification of the ward.

The contrast with *Brind*, decided a matter of months earlier, could not be starker. In the one case, concerning judicial review of *administrative* discretion, the ECHR was an irrelevance because it had not been legislatively incorporated into English law. In the other, concerning the exercise of *judicial* discretion, not only would the ECHR be expressly taken into account, but an approach would be adopted which is close to if not the same as that applied under the ECHR itself.

The essentially constitutional nature of the balancing exercise to be carried out by the courts in such cases gained further recognition in the case of *In re H*, in which the Court of Appeal considered the question to be of sufficient importance to require that in future when an injunction was sought the effect of which was to restrain the press, the matter should be transferred to the High Court.[134] In that case an injunction had been granted by a county court judge restraining a male to female transsexual father with custody of his three children from exposing them to any form of publicity until the youngest child reached the age of majority in ten years time. The Court of Appeal again demonstrated the courts' willingness in exercising its discretion to take into account the provisions of the ECHR, this time not only Article 10, but Article 8 as well.[135] The balance to be struck between the competing and conflicting matters of public interest was acknowledged to be always a delicate one, and the court demonstrated its sensitivity to the competing interests in the way in which it disposed of the appeal. It held that the facts of the case did disclose a matter of public interest, namely the fact that the court, with the support of the local authority, had approved of young children being and remaining in the care of a parent who was a transsexual and who had undergone a sex-change operation. However, public interest was said to turn to public curiosity once information was sought as to the identity of the parties, and at that point the public interest in the protection of the children became the greater public interest. The terms of the injunction were accordingly varied so as to require the transsexual father not to pursue any dealings with the media from the property at which she and the children lived, in order to ensure that the children's privacy was respected.

Concern that the judicial discretion to restrain publicity in the exercise of its wardship jurisdiction was paying too little heed to the interests of press freedom surfaced in *R v. Central Independent Television*.[136] An injunction had

---

[134] *In re H-S (Minors) (Protection of Identity)* [1994] 1 WLR 1141.
[135] Ibid. at 1148C–E.
[136] [1994] 3 WLR 20.

been granted restraining the broadcast of a programme about a convicted pae-dophile without his image being obscured, because of a mother's concern that pictures of the paedophile, who was her five year old child's father, would lead to her and her daughter being identified. Article 10 of the ECHR featured prominently in Hoffmann LJ's robust judgment reasserting the importance of freedom of speech and of the press and doubting the wisdom of any judge-made exceptions to it. In his view, freedom of speech was subject only to clearly defined exceptions laid down by common law or statute, and the judi-cial impulse to multiply those exceptions by balancing freedom of speech against other interests was to be resisted. Outside of the established excep-tions, there could be no question of balancing interests: freedom of speech was a trump card which always wins. In support of these trenchant views, Hoffmann LJ invoked Article 10 of the ECHR, asserting that "in order to enable us to meet our international obligations under the Convention", it was necessary that exceptions should be necessary in a democratic society and fall within certain permissible categories as required by Art. 10(2).[137] Hoffmann LJ was clearly of the view that Article 10 ECHR ought to be considered by a domestic court whenever a judicial discretion of any sort is being exercised.[138]

Why have the courts so readily accepted that international human rights norms should be considered when there is a judicial discretion to be exercised? No court has yet articulated the reason why judges should exercise judicial discretions so as to conform with the ECHR, or why they are not equally caught by the supposedly constitutional reasons which underpin the reason-ing in *Brind*. Hoffmann LJ, for example, was in no doubt in the *Central Independent Television* case that Article 10 of the ECHR was highly relevant, but did not suggest why judges must justify their decisions restricting freedom of speech in terms of the ECHR when government ministers and administra-tors are not so required.

As was seen in chapter 1, however, there is a good reason, in terms of inter-national law, why courts should do so, but it has never been articulated by an English court. It is quite simply that, in international law, the courts, as public authorities, are as much a part of the state as the executive government, with equal responsibility for ensuring that the rights protected by interna-tional law are secured in the domestic legal system, so far as it is within their power to do so. The closest any English court has come to articulating this

---

[137] For recent reiteration of the ruling in *Central Independent Television*, that the balancing of freedom of the press against the interest of the child is only necessary where the threatened pub-lication touches matters which are of direct concern to the court in its supervisory role over the care and upbringing of the ward, see *Re W (Wardship: Discharge: Publicity)* [1995] 2 FLR 466.

[138] Although it was acknowledged by Hoffmann LJ, [1994] 3 WLR 20 at 31G, that privacy may be a legitimate exception to free speech, it is clear that for him Article 8 did not have the same importance as Article 10 when deciding what was necessary in order to meet the UK's inter-national obligations under the ECHR. This suggests that, when it comes to determining the domestic relevance of an international human rights norm, there is a hierarchy coinciding with the extent of the common law's recognition of a particular right.

position is probably Lord Diplock's intervention in argument in *Salomon*, where he referred to the courts construing domestic statutes in conformity with the Crown's treaty obligations, so that the Crown in its judicial capacity does not sleep while in another capacity it watches.[139] *Salomon*, of course, did not concern the exercise of judicial discretion, but Lord Goff in *Spycatcher (No. 2)* may well have had the same thought in mind when he declared it to be his "duty" to interpret domestic law in accordance with the Crown's treaty obligations.[140]

However, as will be seen in greater depth in chapter 8, this explanation requires much more of the courts than that they exercise their own discretions consistently with international human rights law. It requires them also to interpret and develop the common law to achieve such consistency, and there is no logical reason why it should not also require them to adopt the same approach to the interpretation of statutes. It may be the width of these implications which has so far prevented any English court from giving this explanation of why they automatically look to the ECHR when exercising a judicial discretion, without any of the usual reservations which attend referring to it when reviewing an exercise of administrative discretion.

7. THE OVERLAP BETWEEN COMMON LAW DEVELOPMENT, JUDICIAL DISCRETION AND STATUTORY INTERPRETATION

It is hard to see how, given the growing willingness of courts to develop the common law and to be guided in the exercise of their own discretion by reference to the ECHR, English courts can continue to isolate statutory interpretation from the influence of international human rights law other than in cases where the judicially stipulated precondition of ambiguity is met. As has already been observed, it is not as if interpreting statutes is a discrete part of the judicial function, quite separate from the judges' interpretive role in relation to the common law. On the contrary, all statutory interpretation takes place in the context of the common law, as Lord Browne-Wilkinson's revival of the common law presumptions makes explicit, and therefore the more the courts have regard to the ECHR in their interpretation and development of the common law, the more artificial it seems for courts to continue to insist on the preliminary ambiguity requirement when interpreting statutes. This inter-relationship of common law development, judicial discretion and statutory interpretation is most explicit in cases concerning the exercise of a statutorily conferred judicial discretion, and cases concerning the exercise of such discretions are therefore particularly revealing of the nature of the development which is taking place.

---

[139] [1967] 2 QB 116 at 132D–E.
[140] [1990] 1 AC 109 at 283G.

Rantzen, for example, concerned the interpretation of a judicial discretion which was conferred by statute, but which implicitly referred to the previous common law.[141] A newspaper, appealing against a jury award of libel damages of £250,000, argued that the award was so high as to amount to a restriction or penalty on the right to freedom of expression which was neither prescribed by law nor necessary in a democratic society. It contended that the court should therefore exercise its new statutory power to interfere with a jury's award of damages in a defamation action by substituting a lower award.[142] For that power to arise, the case had to be one in which the Court had power to order a new trial on the ground that the damages awarded were "excessive", and whether this was a case in which the power should be exercised therefore turned on the interpretation to be given to the word "excessive". Before the power to order a new trial had been given statutory recognition, it had existed at common law, but the established practice had been to exercise it sparingly, and to treat awards as "excessive" only in exceptional cases where they were so high as to be divorced from reality. The newspaper now invoked the recent cases asserting that the common law was consistent with Article 10 to argue that the common law approach of setting a high threshold to judicial interference with jury awards ought to be re-examined. Therefore, although the argument was, strictly speaking, about the interpretation of a statutory term, that exercise in statutory interpretation necessarily involved the court in reassessing the courts' exercise of their common law power to order a new trial.

The Court of Appeal paid lip-service to *Brind* by reiterating that the ECHR had not become part of English law and that Article 10 therefore could not be applied directly, but held that it was necessary to examine the powers of the court to order a new trial and substitute a lower award "in the light of the guidance recently given by the House of Lords as to the relationship between the common law and Article 10 of the ECHR and also in the light of the guidance as to the proper scope of Article 10 given by the European Court of Human Rights."[143] The Court of Appeal clearly thought that the effect of recent authorities was to expand the role of the ECHR in domestic law beyond the resolution of an ambiguity in primary or subordinate legislation or the exercise of a judicial discretion, so that "[w]here freedom of expression is at stake . . . Article 10 has a wider role and can properly be regarded as an articulation of some of the principles underlying the common law."[144] The Court concluded that it "must" interpret its power to order a new trial, and the word "excessive" in the statute, so as to give proper weight

---

[141] *Rantzen* v. *Mirror Group Newspapers* [1994] QB 670.

[142] Section 8(1) and (2) Courts and Legal Services Act 1990 and RSC Ord 59 r.11(4).

[143] [1994] QB 670 at 687F–G.

[144] Ibid. at 691C–D, citing Lord Goff's now familiar dictum in *Spycatcher (No.2)* [1990] 1 AC 109 at 283G, and Lord Keith's satisfaction with the consistency of the common law and the Convention in *Derbyshire* [1993] AC 534 at 550.

to the guidance given by the House of Lords and the European Court of Human Rights.[145] To interpret them restrictively, so as to grant an almost limitless discretion to a jury, would fail to provide a satisfactory measurement for deciding what is necessary in a democratic society or justified by a pressing social need. The high barrier to jury awards therefore had to be lowered, and replaced by a new test: "Could a reasonable jury have thought that this award was necessary to compensate the plaintiff and to re-establish his reputation?" The Court of Appeal was relatively open about this being a development of the common law, saying that subjecting large awards to a more searching scrutiny than has been customary in the past was required by the common law "if properly understood."[146]

Rantzen demonstrates well the extent to which Lord Goff's dictum in *Spycatcher* may be used as the basis for interpreting domestic law so as to achieve consistency with the ECHR. The Court of Appeal not only interpreted the statutory provision and common law power in the light of the requirements of the ECHR, but also went on to consider whether the present absence of guidance for juries on the assessment of damages conflicted with the ECHR requirement that restrictions on freedom of expression must be "prescribed by law".[147] In its view, unless in future juries were referred to awards made by the Court of Appeal under its new power to intervene to substitute a different sum, the English practice of allowing juries to set the level of damages would conflict with the principle that restrictions on freedom of expression should be "prescribed by law".[148] It is hard to see how such an approach differs from direct application or enforcement of the Article 10 right.[149]

The Court of Appeal in *Rantzen* does not seem to have shared the ambivalence towards the ECHR displayed by the House of Lords in *Derbyshire*. As in the Court of Appeal's decision in that case, it made extensive use of the ECHR terminology and concepts and made lengthy reference to its case-law. Moreover, it is impossible to see the Court as doing anything other than developing the common law in this case. Indeed, it was quite open about the fact that it was interpreting the statutory power against the background of a common law position re-examined in the light of the House of Lords' recent statements about the relationship between the common law and the ECHR. Once the courts have taken this important step, it becomes impossible to avoid the

---

[145] [1994] QB 670 at 692D. The language of obligation is reminiscent of the Court of Appeal in *Derbyshire* (above n. 115).

[146] Ibid. at 692G–H.

[147] Ibid. at 693G.

[148] Ibid. at 694C.

[149] In reaching this decision, the Court of Appeal anticipated the decision of the European Court of Human Rights in *Tolstoy Miloslavsky* v. *UK* (1995) 20 EHRR 442, holding that the Court of Appeal's power to interfere with libel awards was so constrained that it could not offer adequate and effective safeguards against a disproportionately large award and therefore the award of £1.5 million was not necessary in a democratic society and was in breach of Article 10. See *John* v. *MGN* [1996] 2 All ER 35 for a post-*Tolstoy* reconsideration of the approach to jury awards in libel cases.

question of how to reconcile the revival of the common law presumptions, and their development in the light of international human rights norms, with the relaxation of the *Hansard* rule in *Pepper* v. *Hart*.[150] The rationale for permitting reference to parliamentary material is that it is the courts' primary constitutional duty to give effect to Parliament's intention, and therefore where statutory language is ambiguous or obscure the courts can seek historical evidence of that intention. The potential conflict arises because Lord Browne-Wilkinson's strong "half-way bill of rights" presumption, which the Court of Appeal in *Rantzen* appeared to adopt, is of *general* applicability: it does not require the statutory language to be ambiguous or obscure in order to be triggered.

The decision in *Rantzen* provides a good example of just such a clash. In an attempt to overcome the ambiguity as to the meaning of the word "excessive" in the statute, recourse was had to *Hansard*. It was quite clear from the statement of the Lord Chancellor, introducing the relevant amendment in the House of Lords, that the new provision was intended only to give the Court of Appeal the new power to substitute a different award; it was expressly not intended to alter the grounds on which it would be right to interfere with a jury's verdict.[151]

According to the constitutional premises from which *Pepper* v. *Hart* is derived, the availability of such an unequivocal statement from the Lord Chancellor, stating that the new section was not intended to affect the test for when the Court of Appeal could order a new trial, ought to have resolved any ambiguity in the legislation against the freedom of expression argument. Yet the Court effectively ignored the evidence of the Lord Chancellor's intention, saying only that it did not lend any support to the defendants' propositions and going on, undeterred, immediately to say that the terms of the power must be examined in the light of Article 10. The fact that the Court of Appeal chose to resolve the ambiguity in favour of the fundamental right in this case is a particularly stark example of the exercise by the courts of an independent jurisdiction which does not depend for its justification on Parliamentary intention, real or presumed. How could it be "presumed" that Parliament did not intend to leave damages awards in the hands of juries except in the most exceptional cases, when there was evidence of that very intention before the court? In choosing effectively to ignore *Hansard*, the Court of Appeal in *Rantzen* was expressing a clear preference for a conception of the judicial role in which judges have a constitutional responsibility to uphold certain fundamental values, entirely independently of Parliament's will.[152]

---

[150] [1993] AC 593.

[151] [1994] QB 670 at 687B–D. Lord Mackay described the amendment as "a useful although not a major change in the law": HL Deb. Vol. 516 (20th Feb. 1990) cols. 170–1.

[152] The question of the proper relationship between *Hansard* and the ECHR as aids to the construction of legislation arose in *R* v. *Broadcasting Complaints Commission, ex p. Barclay* (unreported decision of Sedley J., 4 October 1996). Although it was not necessary to decide the point, Sedley J. did not accept the respondent's submission that resort to the Convention was

The extent to which the interpretation of statutory provisions or delegated legislation in the light of the ECHR can amount to a derogation from legislative intention, as that concept is understood in sovereignty theory, can be shown by comparing the Lord Chancellor's statement in *Hansard* with the statement of Hirst LJ in *Houston* v. *Smith*, that the reform of the law of defamation by the new rule of court had had a "profound effect."[153]The Court of Appeal's decision in that case in fact went further than *Rantzen*, by adopting the identical approach of interpreting the law in the light of the ECHR, in the context of an action for slander between two private individuals.[154] The same broad principles were said to apply, even though the case did not concern the freedom of the press, and a jury award of £150,000 in respect of sexual harrassment allegations was reduced to £50,000 by applying the new ECHR-inspired test formulated in *Rantzen*.

The decision of the House of Lords in *Khan* has further highlighted the contrast between the courts' approach to the relevance of the ECHR in cases concerning the exercise of statutory administrative discretions and their approach in cases involving the exercise of a statutory *judicial* discretion.[155] The case concerned the admissibility in a criminal trial of evidence obtained by an electronic listening device illegally attached to the outside of a property. Unlike the use of such devices by the security services or the interception of public communications, both of which were governed by statute,[156] the use by police of secret listening devices on private property was not authorised either by statute or at common law. It was admitted that the attachment of the device involved a civil trespass by the police and a certain amount of damage to the property, and that without the evidence of the conversations thus obtained there was no case against the accused. At his trial for the importation of controlled drugs, the accused argued that the evidence should be excluded in the exercise of the judge's discretion under s.78 of the Police and Criminal Evidence Act 1984, which provides:

> "In any proceedings the court may refuse to allow evidence on which the prosecution proposes to rely to be given if it appears to the court that, having regard to all the circumstances, including the circumstances in which the evidence was obtained, the admission of the evidence would have such an adverse effect on the fairness of the proceedings that the court ought not to admit it."

He relied on the decision of the European Court of Human Rights in *Malone*, arguing that in the absence of any legal regime governing the use of such

unnecessary if the "true purpose" of the legislature was apparent from *Hansard*; in his view, if both *Hansard* and the Convention had something to say on the obscure point it was necessary to look at both.

[153] Unreported decision of the Court of Appeal, 16 December 1993 (available on LEXIS).

[154] The Convention of course has no direct application as between private parties, although the court is an organ of the state for Convention purposes, even when administering private law.

[155] *R* v. *Khan* [1996] 3 WLR 162.

[156] The Security Service Act 1989 and the Interception of Communications Act 1985 respectively.

devices, the interference with privacy was not "prescribed by law", as required by Article 8(2), and for that reason alone ought to have been ruled inadmissible.[157] The case therefore raised directly the question whether a criminal court must have regard to the ECHR and its jurisprudence when exercising its broad statutory discretion.[158]

On the *voir dire* into the admissibility of the evidence, the trial judge accepted that there was an arguable breach of Article 8 of the ECHR, because in the absence of statutory authority the situation was riddled with ambiguities and was therefore closely analogous to the situation in *Malone*, but concluded that, even allowing for there being such an arguable breach, that came nowhere near allowing him to exclude the evidence. On appeal against conviction in the Court of Appeal, it was argued that the evidence ought to have been excluded in the exercise of the judge's statutory discretion to exclude, because it had been obtained in breach of Article 8.[159]

In the Court of Appeal Lord Chief Justice Taylor appeared to take a quite different approach from the trial judge to the question of the relevance of the ECHR to the exercise of the s. 78 judicial discretion.[160] He said that it was clear from *Chundawadra* and *Pan-Am* that it was permissible to have regard to the ECHR, which was of persuasive assistance, in cases of ambiguity or doubt, but that in the circumstances of this case the position was neither ambiguous nor doubtful.[161] Nor, he said, was it incumbent on the court to consider whether there was a breach of Article 8, and he did not propose to do so. On the face of it, therefore, he was effectively saying that the ECHR was irrelevant, or even that it was impermissible to have regard to it, when a trial judge was exercising the statutory discretion to exclude otherwise admissible evidence under s. 78. This was a surprisingly dualist stance for the Court of Appeal to take in a non-administrative law context where what was in issue was the exercise of a judicial discretion, particularly in light of the growing number of cases at Court of Appeal level and above in which the reasoning clearly proceeded on the premise that the ECHR was presumptively relevant wherever there was a judicial discretion to be exercised, notably *Spycatcher No. 1*, *Middlebrook Mushrooms* and *Rantzen*.

However, having thus imported into the law concerning the exercise of judicial discretions the ambiguity device for keeping the ECHR at bay in

---

[157] *Malone* v. *UK* (1985) 7 EHRR 14.

[158] Alongside the statutory discretion there still exists a common law discretion to exclude evidence where necessary to secure a fair trial for the accused, but the statutory discretion was treated by both the Court of Appeal and the House of Lords as being at least as wide as that conferred by the common law.

[159] It was also argued that the evidence should have been excluded as being inherently inadmissible as a matter of law, and that there was a domestic law analogy with the prohibition in s.9 of the Interception of Communications Act 1985 on the admissibility in evidence of intercepted communications. For present purposes, however, only those parts of the case concerning the relevance of the ECHR to the exercise of the s.78 discretion are considered.

[160] [1995] QB 27.

[161] Ibid. at 40E–F.

administrative law, Lord Taylor proceeded to conduct an explicit balancing exercise very similar to that which would be carried out by a court deciding whether there had been a breach of Article 8.[162] Taking into account the fact that the police had followed Home Office guidelines which circumscribed the use of such devices, that the criminal conduct under investigation was of a type of great gravity, and that the trespass and damage were slight, he concluded that the invasion of privacy was outweighed by other considerations and should not be regarded as having such an adverse effect on the fairness of the proceedings that the court ought to exclude the evidence. In reaching this conclusion, it was even pointed out that Article 8 itself recognises that there are circumstances in which such intrusion is necessary and therefore justifiable in a democratic society. So having begun by stating general propositions of law the import of which appeared to make the ECHR irrelevant to the trial judge's exercise of discretion under s. 78, Lord Taylor then went on to adopt an approach very similar to that required by the ECHR in deciding whether the trial judge had exercised his discretion correctly.[163]

In the House of Lords, the civil liberties organisation Liberty was granted leave to put in a written submission arguing that the Court of Appeal was wrong to hold that Article 8 was irrelevant to a court's exercise of its discretion under s.78. It argued that the court's duty under that section to have regard to the circumstances in which the evidence was obtained required it to have regard to the fact that the evidence was apparently obtained in circumstances which amounted to a breach of Article 8. As Liberty was careful to point out in its written intervention, the requirement in Article 13, that individuals have an effective remedy for violations of their rights under the ECHR, did not mean that evidence obtained in breach of the ECHR must necessarily be excluded, but it did mean that national law had to provide an effective means of reviewing the admissibility of the evidence in light of the provisions of the ECHR. To satisfy the requirements of Article 13, Liberty argued, the trial judge must consider the alleged breach of the ECHR when deciding whether to exercise its power to exclude under s.78. The Government, for its part, argued that Lord Taylor had been right to regard the ECHR as irrelevant to the exercise of the s.78 discretion.

The House of Lords, however, thought that the arguments of both Liberty and the Government proceeded on a wrong assumption about Lord Taylor's judgment.[163a] The Lord Chief Justice, in Lord Nolan's view, had not said that Article 8 was "irrelevant". On the contrary, he had gone on to refer to it twice in the passage immediately following that in which he set out the circumstances in which a domestic court can have regard to it. According to the

---

[162] [1995] QB 27 at 40G–41C.

[163] A comparison of some of Lord Taylor's judgments dealing with the Convention reveals that he often proceeded in this way, first finding there to be no ambiguity or uncertainty, then proceeding anyway as if dealing directly with a Convention argument: see eg. *R v. Taylor*, [1996] 2 Cr. App. Rep. 64 at 69C–70F; *R v. Cowan* [1995] 3 WLR 818 at 825 C–H.

[163a] [1996] 3 All ER 289.

House of Lords, Lord Taylor was merely saying that Article 8 formed no part of English law, that this was not a case of ambiguity or doubt in which it could be invoked as an aid to construction, and that it was no part of the Court of Appeal's function to consider whether there was a breach of the Article, as that was solely a question for the European Court of Human Rights. Then in a passage of some significance for the general status of international human rights law in domestic courts, Lord Nolan said:

> "That is not to say that the principles reflected in the Convention on Human Rights are irrelevant to the exercise of the section 78 power. They could hardly be irrelevant, because they embody so many of the familiar principles of our own law and of our concept of justice. In particular, of course, they assert the right of the individual to a fair trial".

It is clear from this passage and what follows that what the House of Lords considers to be presumptively relevant to the exercise of the s.78 discretion is Article 6(1) and its case-law on the requirements of a fair trial. It "noted with interest" the decision of the European Court of Human Rights in *Schenk*, in which it said that the admissibility of evidence was primarily a matter for regulation under national law, and rejected the proposition that unlawfully obtained evidence was necessarily inadmissible.[164]

To this extent, the House of Lords in *Khan* appears to have accepted, as Lord Taylor in the Court of Appeal may have accepted but certainly did not make explicit, that since the content of Article 6(1) and English law on the requirements of a fair trial are perceived to be the same, that provision of the ECHR and its case-law are relevant to the exercise of a trial judge's s.78 discretion. Unlike in the Court of Appeal, there was no mention of any precondition of ambiguity or doubt in the statutory words which had first to be established before reference to the ECHR was even permissible. For the House of Lords, reference to Article 6(1) and its case-law were justified, it seems, simply by virtue of the fact that English law and the ECHR on the subject of a fair trial were already perceived, in the words of Lord Nicholls, to "march hand in hand". As Emmerson has pointed out, the generality of this justification is such that Article 6 and its case-law are now presumptively relevant to the exercise of *any* judicial discretion exercised in the course of a criminal trial.[165] Indeed, since a large number of judicial discretions are vested in the criminal trial judge, the decision in *Khan* represents an important first step in the constitutionalisation of the law of criminal procedure. This significant extension into the criminal sphere of the presumptive relevance of the ECHR to the exercise of judicial discretions therefore serves to point up

---

[164] *Schenk* v. *Switzerland* (1991) 13 EHRR 242. Lord Slynn similarly asked himself whether there was a breach of the right to a fair trial "based on an analogy with Article 6 of the Convention", and concluded that, looking at the trial as a whole as the European Court of Human Rights had done in *Schenk*, there was not.

[165] Editorial, [1996] EHRLR 345 at 347.

once again the disparity in judicial approaches to the relevance of the ECHR in the exercise of judicial as opposed to administrative discretions.

Though undoubtedly of great significance, this is as far as *Khan* goes in accepting the relevance of the ECHR to the exercise of judicial discretion. Unlike the Court of Appeal in *Rantzen*, which, it was seen above, went to great lengths in order to interpret its new statutory discretion so as to achieve consistency with Article 10,[166] the House of Lords was not prepared to require the s.78 discretion to be exercised in a way which sought to achieve conformity between domestic law and other ECHR rights such as those protected by Article 8. Liberty's argument, that s.78 should be interpreted as requiring the trial judge to consider whether the evidence had been obtained in breach of Article 8, was not accepted.[167] Lord Nolan was prepared to accept that such a consideration *may* be relevant to the exercise of the discretion ("for what it is worth"), but he clearly thought that whether or not to refer to such case-law was a matter entirely for the discretion of the trial judge concerned. In this part of his judgment, dealing with the relevance of a possible breach of Article 8 to the question of admissibility, Lord Nolan equated the relevance of a breach of the ECHR with a breach of the law of a foreign country, which is conspicuously different from his earlier willingness to equate the principles of the ECHR with "the familiar principles of our own law" when considering Article 6. In similar vein, Lord Nicholls thought the ECHR jurisprudence could have a valuable role to play in light of the identity between the English law concerning fair trial and the ECHR, but its relevance seemed to be no more than that of any other comparative material from other jurisdictions dealing with similar problems. Moreover, the fact that possible breaches of other Articles *could* be relevant to the exercise of the discretion to exclude did not mean that the trial judge was obliged to decide whether or not there had been a breach of the ECHR. Indeed, Lord Nolan went further, and said it would be inappropriate for a trial judge to do so.[168]

It is clear from these comments that the House of Lords in *Khan* did not consider itself to be under the same strong interpretive obligation as have other courts when considering the exercise of judicial discretions. Even in the context of considering Article 6 of the ECHR, which the House of Lords did appear to treat as being presumptively relevant, Lord Nolan still seemed to treat the case-law of the ECHR as an optional extra for the domestic court. For example, although he attached considerable significance to the Court's decision in *Schenk* in so far as it supported his decision that the trial had not

[166] Including, in effect, the ignoring of clear evidence of ministerial intention in *Hansard*.

[167] Only Lord Browne-Wilkinson appeared to think that it was *necessary* to consider possible breaches of the Convention in the obtaining of the evidence, and even this is a matter of inference from his statement that the trial judge had "properly taken into consideration any possible breach of Article 8."

[168] Compare the similar stance taken by some courts in administrative law, considered in ch. 6 below, that, even where the ECHR is a relevant consideration, it is not for the decision-maker to decide whether a decision is in breach of the Convention.

been rendered unfair by the admission of evidence potentially obtained in breach of the Convention, when it came to dealing with Liberty's argument that the European Court might have reached a different conclusion on the facts of the present case, he said

> "we are not concerned with the view which the European Court of Human Rights might have taken of the facts of the present case. Its decision is no more a part of our law than the Convention itself."

8. CONCLUSION

The detailed analysis of judicial reasoning in this chapter has been necessary to make good the claim made at its outset that, from about the beginning of the 1990s, a new and distinct phase was entered in the domestic history of human rights law. The chapter has shown the way in which the extra-judicial articulation of various theoretical bases on which English courts could provide greater judicial protection for fundamental rights has been followed by the practical realisation of a common law human rights jurisdiction, as courts have rediscovered strong presumptions of statutory interpretation, refined *Wednesbury* review, developed the common law and exercised judicial discretions so as to give a measure of protection for human rights.

The precise nature of these developments has not always been made clear, however, and for convenience of exposition the courts' own, often rather artificial dividing lines between the different judicial techniques have been observed. But this should not be permitted to conceal the reality of what has been taking place, which is nothing short of the emergence of a common law human rights jurisdiction. The common feature which underpins each of the four categories of development outlined above is a judicial willingness to develop the common law in a way which provides recognition for and greater protection of fundamental rights. The precise basis on which international human rights law, and in particular the European Convention on Human Rights, has a role to play within that emerging jurisdiction, has never been made satisfactorily explicit, and is a question to which this book returns in chapter 8. Suffice it to say for present purposes that English courts' treatment of the ECHR's principles as being identical in content to the common law provides an interesting illustration of the dynamic process whereby customary norms acquire the force of law. As was seen in chapter 1, English common law presumptions influenced the rights articulated in the ECHR at its inception, and now the ECHR's provisions are in turn feeding back into the English common law, along with the Strasbourg institutions' elaboration of their meaning.

But there still remains the unspoken question. With such fundamental changes taking place in the common law, and sovereignty theory also undergoing evolutionary change under the influence of European Community membership, how could administrative law, and in particular judicial review of broad statutory discretions, continue to be insulated from the changes taking place around it? It is to the courts' attempts to grapple with that question that we turn in chapter 6.

6

Human Rights in
Administrative Law

1. INTRODUCTION

What are the implications of the recent emergence of a common law human
rights jurisdiction for the role of human rights norms in administrative law?
It will be recalled from chapter 4 that the distinguishing feature of what has
been described as Phase II in the domestic career of international human rights
law was the courts' determined resistance to its influence in public law,
notwithstanding the relative equanimity with which an emerging interpretive
obligation appeared to be accepted in the interpretation and development of
the common law in other areas outside of administrative law. Although, as
was seen in chapters 4 and 5, ECHR arguments enjoyed a measure of success
in judicial review proceedings in the prisons context even during Phase II, due
largely to some notable early successes by prisoners before the European
Court of Human Rights, in other subject matter areas, particularly immigration, the courts maintained their resolute stand against the ECHR or any
human rights instrument having *any* role to play in judicial review.[1] The purpose of the present chapter is to examine the extent to which the developments in the common law charted in the previous chapter have undermined
the courts' ability to maintain their resistance to international human rights
law having a role in public law.

2. ORTHODOXY REASSERTED

The decision in *Brind*, it will be recalled, is very much a double-edged sword.
On the one hand, as was seen in chapter 4, the clear rejection by all but Lord
Templeman of the relevance of the ECHR in judicial review of the exercise of
broad administrative discretions provided respondents with an easy answer to
any argument deploying the ECHR or other international human rights
norms. Such unincorporated law was irrelevant, they argued, unless the applicant could jump the ambiguity hurdle by showing that there was some

---

[1] See in particular *Brind*'s forebears in *Bibi* [1976] 1 WLR 979, *Fernandes* [1981] Imm AR 1,
and *Chundawadra* [1988] Imm AR 161, all considered in ch. 4. For an account of judicial hostility to human rights instruments in the immigration context, see S. Legomsky, *Immigration and
the Judiciary: Law and Politics in Britain and America* (Oxford: Oxford University Press, 1987).

independent ambiguity in the relevant statutory language authorising the power being challenged, and the mere width of the power conferred was not itself a source of ambiguity. Not surprisingly, there are countless examples from the administrative law context, and immigration in particular, of *Brind* being used by courts for precisely this purpose.[2] On the other hand, as was demonstrated in chapter 5, there was a clear majority in *Brind* in favour of refining the traditional approach in fundamental rights cases by lowering the *Wednesbury* threshold and scrutinising the justification for the decision more rigorously than in cases where fundamental rights are not engaged. Not surprisingly, the case has subsequently been relied on by both respondents and applicants, the former seeking to rely on the House of Lords' rejection of the relevance of the ECHR, and the latter invoking the passages from the judgments of Lords Bridge and Templeman in particular where the "close scrutiny" approach was most clearly articulated.

The unenviable task of seeking to make sense of these contradictory trends embodied in the case-law fell to the Court of Appeal in *NALGO*.[3] The unhappy result, after a careful review of the recent authorities, was a constitutionally conservative reassertion of all the orthodoxies: sovereignty, dualism, *ultra vires* and an unreconstructed and universally applicable *Wednesbury* test. However, what is particularly interesting about the decision in *NALGO* is that, confronted with the practical reality of the various common law developments charted in chapter 5, the court was driven more than in any previous case to abandon sweeping theoretical objections to the relevance of the ECHR, and to rely instead on the special nature of judicial review proceedings, and in particular of judicial review of decisions of the executive, as its justification for rejecting the applicant's reliance on the ECHR and domestic fundamental rights jurisprudence. Although the challenge itself failed, it is quite evident from the reasoning deployed to defeat it that maintaining judicial review as a fortified island, untouched by the wider developments taking place in the common law, was becoming an increasingly transparent exercise with little theoretical credibility.

The challenge in *NALGO* was to the validity of the Local Government Officers (Political Restrictions) Regulations 1990 (SI 1990 No. 855), which imposed, as deemed conditions of employment, restrictions on the political activities of local government employees holding politically restricted posts. The Regulations were made by the Secretary of State under a very broadly worded rule-making power.[4] The applicant union argued, among other

---

[2] See, as just a few (reported) examples, *R* v. *Secretary of State for the Home Department, ex p. Chinoy* [1992] 4 Admin LR 457; *R* v. *Secretary of State for the Home Department, ex p. Jibril* [1993] Imm AR 308; *Kwapong* v. *Secretary of State for the Home Department* [1994] Imm AR 207.

[3] *R* v. *Secretary of State for the Environment, ex p. NALGO* (1993) 5 Admin LR 785.

[4] Section 1(5) of the Local Government and Housing Act 1989 (terms of appointment or conditions of employment of persons holding politically restricted posts deemed to incorporate "such requirements for restricting his political activities as may be prescribed for the purposes of this subsection by regulations made by the Secretary of State").

things, that because the regulations invaded fundamental rights of freedom of expression, the court was entitled to test the validity of the regulations by reference to the principles enshrined in Article 10 of the ECHR, and the right approach was therefore to consider whether the restrictions were "necessary in a democratic society."[5]

Reviewing the recent case-law on the domestic status of the ECHR, Neill LJ noted that although the courts had no power to enforce ECHR rights directly, and had no choice but to enforce domestic law if it conflicted with the Convention, nevertheless it could be relevant in at least three circumstances.[6] First, in order to resolve an ambiguity in English primary or subordinate legislation.[7] Second, when considering how a discretion is to be exercised.[8] And third, when the relevant rules of the common law or equity are uncertain.[9] However, instead of asking by what principles reference to the ECHR was justified in these three sets of circumstances, Neill LJ fell into the error of treating judicial review as if it involved some judicial function quite separate from interpreting ambiguous statutes, exercising judicial discretion and developing the common law where it was uncertain. To discover the relevance of Article 10 in judicial review proceedings, he turned, not to the fast developing common law recognition of the ECHR's principles, but to the speeches in the House of Lords in *Brind*, from which he claimed to distil a number of principles said to be relevant to an application for judicial review of a decision of a Government minister.[10]

Since Article 10 was not part of domestic law, he said, it was not necessary for the Minister, when exercising an administrative discretion conferred on him by Parliament, to exercise that discretion in accordance with Article 10, nor even to have regard to its provisions as a relevant matter to be taken into account. Nevertheless, where fundamental human rights including freedom of expression were being restricted, the Minister would need to show that there was an important competing public interest which was sufficient to justify the restriction. The primary judgment as to whether the competing public interest justified the particular restriction was for the Minister. The court was only entitled to exercise a secondary judgment by asking whether a reasonable Minister, on the material before him, could reasonably make that primary judgment. However, Neill LJ concluded that, as the law stood at present, it was clear that, though the Minister was required to justify the restriction imposed by reference to an important and sufficient competing public interest, the reviewing court was not entitled to lower the threshold of unreasonableness. Although Lord

---

[5] As will be seen below n. 24, the union also argued that the regulations offended against the principle of proportionality, because their restrictions on political activities constituted a disproportionate interference with freedom of expression.

[6] (1993) 5 Admin LR 785 at 794D–799A.

[7] Citing Lord Ackner in *Brind* [1991] 1 AC 696 at 760.

[8] Citing Lord Templeman in *AG* v. *Guardian Newspapers Ltd.* [1987] 1 WLR 1248 at 1296–7.

[9] Citing *Derbyshire County Council* v. *Times Newspapers Ltd.* [1992] QB 770 (CA).

[10] (1993) 5 Admin LR 785 at 798A–H.

Templeman in *Brind* had admittedly said that the test of unreasonableness was less stringent than the classic *Wednesbury* test of irrationality, Neill LJ claimed to be unable to extract from the other speeches any real support for the view that "the latitude to be given to a Minister is to be confined within tighter limits when his decision impinges on fundamental human rights."

Thus was the distinct fundamental rights jurisdiction which had begun to emerge from the shadows of *Wednesbury* review re-absorbed within the traditional, high threshold test of perversity, supposedly insensitive to the nature of the interest affected by the decision under challenge. All that is required of the decision-maker to survive the "close scrutiny" required by the House of Lords in *Brind* is to identify a public interest which, in the decision-maker's judgment, justifies the restriction on fundamental rights. The high *Wednesbury* threshold, far from being lowered, is reintroduced at the stage of reviewing the decision-maker's judgment of the justification for the measure, and crude, context-blind deference is preserved.

Neill LJ's ultra-orthodox reading of *Brind* in *NALGO* was endorsed by the Divisional Court in *Smith*, the challenge to the government's policy prohibiting gays from serving in the armed forces, which raised equally starkly the same question of the proper relationship between the indigenous human rights jurisdiction, the domestic status of the ECHR and the traditional grounds of judicial review.[11] The principal ground on which the policy was challenged was that it was irrational, but its legality was also questioned on the ground that it breached Articles 8 and 14 of the ECHR. Service personnel who happened to be gay, it was argued, had a clear *prima facie* right under the ECHR to serve in the armed forces, and not to be discharged merely on the grounds of their sexual orientation. The question of the relevance of the ECHR to the issue in the case was argued at length before the Divisional Court, which was taken to decisions such as *Spycatcher*, *Rantzen* and *McQuillan*,[12] but Simon Brown LJ was content to rely on Neill LJ's distillation of the *Brind* principles in *NALGO* as an accurate statement of the legal position.[13] In his view, the ECHR, or the fact that the case concerned the restriction of fundamental human rights, had only a relatively limited impact on judicial review. The dicta in cases such as *Bugdaycay*, that where fundamental human rights were restricted by the decision, the minister needed to show that there was an important competing public interest sufficient to justify the restriction, did not mean that the threshold of unreasonableness was lowered in those cases.[14] As

---

[11] *R v. Ministry of Defence, ex p. Smith* [1996] QB 517. The decision of the Court of Appeal in the same case is considered in section 6 below.

[12] *R v. Secretary of State for the Home Department, ex p. McQuillan* [1995] 4 All ER 400, considered in detail in ch. 7 below.

[13] [1996] QB 517 at 536C–537C. The other member of the Court, Curtis J., ibid. at 546D–E, rejected the applicants' ECHR argument by deploying the trusty "no ambiguity" response legitimated by the House of Lords in *Brind*.

[14] Ibid. at 538B–C, relying on Lord Ackner's assertion in *Brind* [1991] 1 AC 696 at 763A that any lowering of the threshold must inevitably involve the court in an illegitimate review of the merits of the decision.

Simon Brown LJ understood the close or anxious scrutiny which, according to such dicta, courts were supposed to carry out in such cases, it meant that

> "within the limited scope of review open to it the court must be scrupulous to ensure that no recognised ground of challenge is in truth available to the applicant before rejecting his application. When the most fundamental human rights are threatened, the court will not, for example, be inclined to overlook some perhaps minor flaw in the decision-making process, or adopt a particularly benevolent view of the minister's evidence, or exercise its discretion to withhold relief."[15]

The human rights dimension was of no more significance than that and left the well established grounds of review unchanged.

3. THE CHANGING NATURE OF JUDICIAL RESISTANCE

The Court of Appeal's decision in *NALGO* and the Divisional Court's in *Smith* demonstrate not only the continued judicial resistance to international human rights law having any role to play in judicial review, but also the way in which the precise nature of that resistance has gradually changed over time as English courts' own fundamental rights jurisdiction has become increasingly explicit. In the early cases such as *Salamat Bibi* and *Fernandes*, in which the courts first took flight from using the ECHR in administrative law, the legal reason given for holding that immigration officers did not have to have regard to the ECHR when exercising their discretion was that it had not been made part of English law, but the reasoning seemed principally motivated by practical concerns. The Court of Appeal in *Bibi*, for example, was concerned about over-burdening immigration officers, who would not only have to be aware of the existence of relevant human rights provisions, but would have to apply in practice provisions that were drafted in such a way as to make them "incapable of practical application".[16] Ackner LJ in *Fernandes* was similarly concerned with making immigration control "impractical" if decision-makers had to have regard to unincorporated treaty provisions.[17] In *Brind*, by comparison, there was no mention of such practical difficulties, and ostensibly both the Court of Appeal and the House of Lords were mainly concerned with the implications for the separation of powers between courts and legislature. As Lord Bridge put it in the House of Lords, for courts to hold that generally worded administrative discretions must be exercised in conformity with the ECHR would be "a judicial usurpation of the legislative function."[18]

---

[15] Ibid. at 537H–538A. As will be seen below, however, Simon Brown LJ ultimately hedged his bets on the correct approach to take, appearing to concede in the very next paragraph that fundamental rights cases are characterised by a more intensive review process and a greater readiness to intervene.

[16] [1976] 1 WLR 979 at 984H, 985B and 988E.

[17] [1981] Imm AR 1 at 7.

[18] [1991] 1 AC 696 at 748F.

As was seen above in the account of the decision in *NALGO*, however, the more use is made of the ECHR by the courts in other ways, the less persuasive that reason sounds. A court which has to set out a large variety of situations in which the ECHR is relevant domestically, as Neill LJ did in *NALGO*, cannot very well proceed to explain its irrelevance in the judicial review context by relying solely on the fact that Parliament has chosen not to incorporate it. So it was inevitable that the more the courts laid claim to a common law human rights jurisdiction, informed by international human rights instruments, the more the true nature of their resistance to the use of such instruments in public law would emerge.

That resistance is indissociable from their resistance to the recognition of the principle of proportionality as a part of administrative law. Both are products of a judicial fear that any stricter test than *Wednesbury* is incompatible with the supervisory nature of the courts' role in public law. The unusual feature of international human rights instruments such as the ECHR, compared to other international treaties, is that the question of their domestic status engages not merely questions of the respective roles of executive, courts and legislature in making law, but also questions of the proper balance of power between courts on the one hand and the executive and administration on the other. For courts to review executive and administrative decisions for conformity with an instrument such as the ECHR would transform the entire methodology of public law adjudication, at least in cases where fundamental rights are at stake.

This book is not the place in which to enter on a detailed discussion of the nature of the concept of proportionality or to consider the history of its career in English public law since Lord Diplock's tentative suggestion in *GCHQ* that the principle of proportionality might possibly be adopted at some time in the future as an additional ground of review.[19] However, some consideration of it cannot be avoided, since judicial resistance to the use of human rights law goes hand in hand with suspicion about the implications of recognising a principle of proportionality as a part of domestic administrative law. The principal reason for the reluctance of most English judges to countenance proportionality as a ground of review in its own right is that, in their view, it would inevitably collapse the crucial distinction between a supervisory and an appellate jurisdiction, on which the legitimacy of judicial review is presumed to depend. This fear of judicial usurpation of executive or administrative functions was very much in evidence in the judicial responses to the attempt to rely on proportionality as a separate ground of challenge in *Brind*.

The argument there was that the Secretary of State had acted unlawfully because the directives to the broadcasters were disproportionate to the mischief at which they were aimed. With the exception of Lord Templeman in

---

[19] *Council of Civil Service Unions* v. *Minister for the Civil Service* [1985] AC 374 at 410E. On proportionality generally, see De Smith, Woolf & Jowell, *Judicial Review of Administrative Action*, 5th edn. (London: Sweet and Maxwell, 1995) at 593–607.

the House of Lords, who appeared to apply a proportionality test,[20] the argument was rejected by every judge who considered it. It prompted, however, two types of rejection: one general, the other particular. Those judges who thought acceptance of proportionality as a ground of review would inevitably result in the courts substituting their own decision for that of the minister, and would thereby inevitably undermine the crucial distinction between review and appeal, absorbed proportionality within the high-threshold *Wednesbury* test.[21] The notion of proportionality as anything more than a facet of *Wednesbury* unreasonableness, requiring courts to take a closer look at the justification for a decision, was emphatically rejected by these judges in terms which precluded any possibility of its future adoption. Lord Ackner, for example, found no formulation of the principle as a ground of review satisfactory, because the question they all posed for the court to answer ultimately boiled down to "is the particular decision acceptable?", the answer to which necessarily involved the court in reviewing the merits of the decision.[22] In this way, proportionality was acknowledged to be a principle of administrative law, but having no independent existence outside of the already established but extremely narrow ground of substantive unreasonableness.

Lords Roskill and Bridge, however, rejected the argument in less general terms, expressly preserving the possible future adoption of proportionality as an independent ground of review. Lord Roskill in particular was at pains to respond to the attempt to absorb proportionality within *Wednesbury* unreasonableness, by reminding the House of Lords that Lord Diplock in *GCHQ* had clearly envisaged its adoption as a separate category and not merely as a possible reinforcement of one or more of the three stated categories such as irrationality.[23] Since Lord Bridge's rejection of the argument was also particular rather than general, and Lord Templeman had no compunction about applying a proportionality test in any event, the possibility of proportionality's future adoption in fact commanded a majority in the House of Lords in *Brind*.

Nevertheless, the same fears of judicial overreaching permeate the Court of Appeal's response to the proportionality argument made by the applicant union in *NALGO*.[24] As an alternative to its argument that the regulations restricting political activities violated Article 10 ECHR, the union argued that they offended against the principle of proportionality, because their

---

[20] [1991] 1 AC 696 at 751F ("the interference with freedom of expression must be necessary and proportionate to the damage which the restriction is designed to prevent.")

[21] See eg. Watkins LJ in the Divisional Court (unreported); in the Court of Appeal, Lord Donaldson MR ibid. at 722F and 723C; McCowan LJ at 729G; in the House of Lords, Lord Ackner at 762E; Lord Lowry at 766D–E.

[22] Ibid. at 763A–B. See, to similar effect, Lord Lowry, ibid. at 767G (very little room for judges to operate an independent judicial review proportionality doctrine in the space which is left between conventional judicial review doctrine and the forbidden appellate approach).

[23] Ibid. at 750D–E.

[24] (1993) 5 Admin LR 785 at 799A–801D.

restrictions on political activities constituted a disproportionate interference with freedom of expression. Just as the ECHR had been accepted as being relevant in a variety of circumstances, but was said to be wholly irrelevant when it came to judicial review of ministerial decisions, so the Court of Appeal had no choice but to acknowledge the advance of the principle of proportionality in various areas of English law, but again found that it stopped short of the citadel: judicial review of the executive remained insulated from its influence. The Court recognised that the principle of proportionality would be applied by an English reviewing court where some rule of European Community law was in play, for example, or by an appellate court considering the exercise of a judicial discretion or the appropriateness of a particular penalty, but there were said to be greater difficulties in a court applying the principle of proportionality when exercising its function of judicial review. Although Lord Diplock in *GCHQ* and Lords Bridge and Roskill in *Brind* had clearly countenanced the possibility of proportionality becoming in time a ground of review, separate from the traditional *Wednesbury* ground, and Lord Templeman in the latter case had gone even further by appearing actually to apply a proportionality test, Neill LJ was

> "quite satisfied that it is not open to a court below the House of Lords to depart from the traditional *Wednesbury* grounds of reasonableness when reviewing the decision of a Minister of the Crown who has exercised a discretion vested in him by Parliament."[25]

Neill LJ saw the virtue of all courts in the European Community applying common standards in administrative law, and was explicitly prepared to countenance the future development of proportionality as a separate ground of intervention in judicial review of decisions made at below ministerial level, but he could not entertain a lower threshold test being applied to decisions by the government.[26] The reason given for the court's caution was that the constitutional balance between courts and executive was a delicate one which made judges reluctant to lower the threshold of unreasonableness where decisions at government level were being reviewed. Although the "margin of appreciation" afforded to decision-makers by courts applying a principle of proportionality was acknowledged, as Neill LJ understood it that doctrine did not afford as great a degree of latitude to the decision-maker as that afforded by *Wednesbury*.[27]

The convergence of these concerns about the doctrine of proportionality, giving domestic effect to the ECHR, and giving closer scrutiny to decisions affecting fundamental rights was made explicit in *Smith* in the Divisional

---

[25] (1993) 5 Admin LR 785 at 800E, agreeing with Lord Lowry's impeccably orthodox statement in *Brind* [1991] 1 AC 696 at 767G (see above, bracketed text in n. 22).

[26] Though *Wednesbury* itself, of course, concerned review of a local authority's rather than a minister's decision.

[27] (1993) 5 Admin LR 785 at 801B–C. See ch. 8 below for comment on the appearance of the "margin of appreciation" doctrine in English judgments.

Court. Simon Brown LJ was concerned that the effect of accepting the applicants' argument about the relevance of the ECHR, or their argument that decisions infringing fundamental human rights warranted more rigorous scrutiny, would carry the courts beyond the bounds of their constitutional role in relation to the executive.[28] Although he accepted that the courts had an undoubted responsibility for the protection of human rights, he considered the judicial role under the ECHR to be of quite a different kind from that which could legitimately be exercised under present constitutional arrangements. If the ECHR were part of English law and the courts therefore free to apply a full proportionality test, in his view a shift in the constitutional balance would come about, because the court would then be carrying out the primary judgment instead of the secondary judgment which is its more limited role under domestic law as it currently stood. Simon Brown LJ's judgment highlights the close relationship between the judicial determination to keep human rights law out of administrative law and the longstanding judicial resistance to proportionality.

These judicially expressed concerns about judges overstepping the constitutional bounds of their role have recently found a new champion in the Shadow Lord Chancellor, Lord Irvine, whose lecture to the Administrative Law Bar Association,[29] and speech in similar vein to the House of Lords,[30] amount to a shot across the bows of judges with ideas beyond their station. Lord Irvine's self-styled "back-to-basics" contribution urges judicial self-restraint as a "constitutional imperative", so as not to usurp the discretion left to decision-makers in the exercise of their decision-making powers. The *Wednesbury* formulation of the permissible grounds on which courts can interfere with discretionary decisions is said to be merely shorthand for the constitutional imperative of judicial self-restraint, and Lord Irvine condemns in no uncertain terms attempts to modify them. In particular, he sets out to resist the argument for lowering the *Wednesbury* threshold in fundamental rights cases. This he sees as an attack on the *Wednesbury* principles which will inevitably lead judges astray into illegitimate territory for decision-makers lacking the democratic legitimacy of being elected.

To the extent that Lord Irvine's views ignite a debate about the need for a more worked out doctrine of judicial deference to administrative decision-making, they are to be welcomed. The principled development of English public law has long been hampered by the absence of a theory of deference. Unfortunately, Lord Irvine's doctrine of judicial self-restraint is derived from an outmoded theory of the sovereignty of Parliament, and the way in which

---

[28] *R v. Ministry of Defence ex p. Smith* [1996] QB 517 at 541A–D.

[29] "Judges and Decision-Makers: The Theory and Practice of *Wednesbury* Review" [1996] PL 59.

[30] HL Deb., Vol. 572, cols. 1254–1313 (5 June 1996). The irony of a Lord Chancellor-in-waiting initiating a debate about "judicial activism" under the guise of a concern about judicial impartiality was not lost on Lord Rodgers, who wryly observed, at col. 1264, that the greater threat to the public's confidence in the impartiality of the judges was "if they failed to apply the same rules to the decisions of an incoming government as they have applied to those of the present one."

he proposes to give it effect is by preserving a monolithic *Wednesbury* standard with a high threshold to be crossed, regardless of the context. Such a course is open to a number of criticisms. It proceeds on the false assumption that a monolithic *Wednesbury* test offers the only means of preserving a meaningful distinction between the primary judgment of the decision-maker and the secondary judgment of the court. But throughout Lord Irvine's lecture that is a matter of assertion rather than argument. It has always been an exaggerated and unimaginative claim to allege that abandoning *Wednesbury* inevitably transforms the judicial review function into a usurpation of the primary decision-maker's role. The appearance of the concepts of lowering the threshold of unreasonableness in human rights cases and raising it even higher (so-called "super-*Wednesbury*") in cases concerning, say, national economic policy, is evidence of the pressure on courts to develop differential review, sensitive to the multiplicity of factors which go to the question of how hard a court should look at the challenged decision. Indeed, Lord Irvine's own implicit approval of the application of a "super-*Wednesbury*" test in cases such as *Notts County Council*[31] and *Hammersmith*[32] appears to acknowledge that differing degrees of judicial self-restraint are appropriate according to the type of case.[33] Finally, Lord Irvine's argument ignores the fact that, in all but name, proportionality has already arrived in English law, as the following section will attempt to show.

4. THE COMMON LAW HUMAN RIGHTS JURISDICTION AND JUDICIAL REVIEW:
PROPORTIONALITY IN ALL BUT NAME

In the review in chapter 5 of the various techniques by which courts have asserted a common law human rights jurisdiction, it was seen that two in particular have a direct impact on the law of judicial review: the developments in the common law of *Wednesbury* review, and the rediscovery of strong presumptions of statutory interpretation in favour of fundamental rights. In each of these developments in the law of judicial review, it will be argued, the courts have already in effect recognised proportionality as being part of English public law, but without, so far, daring to speak its name.[34]

[31] *R v. Secretary of State for the Environment, ex p. Nottinghamshire County Council* [1986] 1 AC 240.

[32] *R v. Secretary of State for the Environment, ex p. Hammersmith LBC* [1991] 1 AC 521.

[33] For a similarly puzzling insistence that the *Wednesbury* test is both monolithic, in the sense of comprising a single, universal standard, and yet "sufficiently flexible to cover all situations", see the decision of the Court of Appeal in *R v. Ministry of Defence ex p. Smith* [1996] QB 517 at 556C.

[34] For the debate as to whether proportionality is already implicitly recognised in English law, see J. Jowell and A. Lester, "Beyond *Wednesbury*: Towards Substantive Principles of Administrative Law" [1987] PL 386 and "Proportionality: Neither Novel Nor Dangerous" in J. Jowell and D. Oliver (eds.), *New Directions in Judicial Review* (London: Stevens, 1988) at 51; J. Jowell, "Is Proportionality an Alien Concept?" (1996) 2 Eur. Pub Law 401.

Take first the development which has been described as the lowering of the *Wednesbury* threshold. According to this common law development, in a case involving what is recognised by the common law to be a fundamental right, a reviewing court will require the decision-maker to show an important competing public interest sufficient to justify the interference. Although in *NALGO* and, to a lesser extent, *Smith*, this has now been re-absorbed into *Wednesbury* unreasonableness in the way explained above, in fact, as Laws has consistently argued, this development can quite easily be shown to represent a real conceptual shift away from *Wednesbury*, and towards the judicial recognition of a general principle of proportionality.[35] The significant part of the development, which Lord Bridge articulated in *Brind*, was the explicit introduction of the concept of "justification" into the review of discretion on substantive grounds. Until that point, substantive review under *Wednesbury* had been conventionally articulated in terms of *manifest* unreasonableness or absurdity, that is, unreasonableness or arbitrariness which appeared on the face of the decision. As reviewing courts consistently held, an applicant who challenged a decision on the ground that it was *Wednesbury* unreasonable could not be entitled to reasons for the decision, or discovery of documents which might reveal such reasons, since if it was *Wednesbury* unreasonable that would be obvious to the court on the face of the decision, without having to look into the decision-maker's justification for reaching it.

Once reviewing courts accept that they have a role in ensuring that decisions are "justified", however, they have inescapably accepted a role in the evaluation of the reasoning supporting a decision, and this inevitably involves them in a balancing or weighing exercise which is precisely what a constitutional or human rights court does when it applies a proportionality test to assess the justifiability of an infringement with a presumptively protected right. Indeed, one need look no further than the language used by Lord Bridge in *Bugdaycay* and *Brind* to show that the very concept of justification involves the reviewing court in such a balancing exercise. The key phrase is that "nothing less than an important competing public interest will be sufficient to justify" the restriction. The unavoidable relativity of the concepts of "importance" and "sufficiency" import an evaluative dimension into the reviewing court's role which, even if present in practice before, has never been so explicitly acknowledged. The reviewing court cannot meaningfully decide whether a particular public interest relied on by a decision-maker is "important" without having a view of its own as to the relative importance of a range of public interests. Similarly, to assess whether the public interest relied on is "sufficient" to justify the interference necessarily involves the court taking a view as to the relative importance of the right interfered with and the seriousness of the particular infringement of it. Indeed, Lord Bridge's reference to

---

[35] J. Laws, "Is the High Court the Guardian of Fundamental Constitutional Rights?" [1993] PL 59 at 69. In the interests of emphasising doctrinal continuity, Laws is equally happy to label the development a "significant refinement" of *Wednesbury*, rather than a departure.

"the most anxious scrutiny" in cases where the right to life is at stake suggests that he envisaged a variable standard according to the importance of the right, so that the intensity of review will depend in part on where in the hierarchy of rights the particular right falls.

In short, a reviewing court adopting Lord Bridge's approach must carry out an exercise which involves assessing the importance of the right, the seriousness of the interference and the weight of the competing public interest before it can reach a sensible view as to the sufficiency of the justification offered. As Sedley J. put it in *Quijano*[36]

> "The test propounded by Lord Templeman in *Brind* may best be viewed as a refinement of the *Wednesbury* test for the purpose of ensuring, not merely that account is taken of the UK's treaty obligations in the field of human rights, but that the decision-maker in doing so consciously addresses the question whether any interference which the decision may involve is justified."

The approach of the reviewing court is, in other words, qualitatively different from looking at a decision to see whether it is, on its face, "so unreasonable that no reasonable decision-maker could have reached it". Indeed, this much seemed ultimately to be conceded by Simon Brown LJ in *Smith*. Having concluded that, even where fundamental human rights are being restricted, the threshold of unreasonableness was not lowered, he went on to add

> "On the other hand, the minister on judicial review will need to show that there is an important competing public interest which he could reasonably judge sufficient to justify the restriction and he must expect his reasons to be closely scrutinised. Even that approach, therefore, involves a more intensive review process and a greater readiness to intervene than would ordinarily characterise a judicial review challenge."[37]

So, for all his protestations that to lower the *Wednesbury* threshold would necessarily be to trespass on the merits of the decision, Simon Brown LJ eventually arrived at something of a hybrid, which he described as "the conventional *Wednesbury* basis adapted to a human rights context."[38]

A proportionality doctrine is equally immanent in the other significant common law development affecting public law, the revival of strong presumptions of statutory interpretation, though here it is necessary to look slightly harder to uncover it. In chapter 5 it was noted that one effect of adopting a "strict construction" approach to the interpretation of discretionary powers is to afford presumptive protection to certain rights recognised at common law which would otherwise have been trumped by a generally worded statutory power. But if the presumption is merely that Parliament does not intend to interfere with fundamental rights, the protection this device can afford to such

---

[36] *R* v. *Secretary of State for the Home Department, ex p. Quijano* (unreported), 12 May 1994.
[37] [1996] QB 517 at 538C–D. The rather different approach taken by the Court of Appeal is considered in the following section.
[38] Ibid. at 540F.

rights will inevitably be limited because, as De Smith, Woolf and Jowell point out, at least *some* interference with fundamental rights is often integral to a statute's aims.[39] Where the clear purpose of legislation is to authorise interference with such rights, the presumption would be easily rebutted. It might be thought that this is made all the more likely by the fact that Lord Browne-Wilkinson, perhaps anticipating the criticism that a strong presumption rebuttable only by express language might too often operate to defeat Parliament's intention where it had failed to make its intention sufficiently clear, diluted the requirement of express authorisation by clear words by allowing the presumption to be rebutted by "necessary implication".[40] A presumption against *any* interference with fundamental rights, rebuttable by necessary implication from a statute's general purpose, would offer very little protection for fundamental rights.

In practice, however, the courts have applied a presumption of a rather more sophisticated kind. Instead of merely presuming against *any* interference with fundamental rights, they have presumed against any *unnecessary* interference. This is a most significant qualification, because it imports into the presumption the concept of proportionality. According to this version of the presumption, where legislation confers a general power which clearly contemplates *some* interference with fundamental rights, the courts will presume that Parliament did not intend that power to be exercised in a way which infringes fundamental rights or freedoms any more than is necessary in order to achieve the aim for which the power was given. As Lord Browne-Wilkinson put it, courts applying the general presumption

> "would not limit general powers so as to exclude interference with individual freedom to the extent that such interference was by necessary implication part of the intention of Parliament."[41]

Such a limitation on the scope of the presumption is said to be analogous to the "provisos" in the ECHR which make the rights contained in it "yield to the necessary requirements of good democratic government".[42]

In this respect, Lord Browne-Wilkinson's approach in *Marcel*, where he applied just such a presumption when construing legislation which clearly contemplated *some* interference with property and privacy,[43] was an important refinement of his approach in *Wheeler*, in which, when interpreting the scope of a Council's statutory powers, he needed only presume that the

---

[39] Above n. 19, at 588, giving as obvious examples immigration legislation restricting entry or authorising deportation, and planning legislation authorising extensive interference with property rights. The authors also point out, ibid. at 589, that if general words conferring a discretion rebut the presumption of conformity with treaty obligations, as was held in *Brind*, they should just as surely rebut a presumption against interference with domestic fundamental rights.

[40] Lord Browne-Wilkinson, "The Infiltration of a Bill of Rights" [1992] PL 397 at 408.

[41] Ibid., at 408.

[42] Ibid.

[43] [1992] Ch. 225.

legislation did not intend to authorise *any* interference with freedom of speech or conscience.[44] Similarly, the Court of Appeal in *Leech*, confronted with a general statutory power which by necessary implication authorised *some* interference with correspondence between a prisoner and his legal adviser, applied a presumption that the authorised intrusion must be the minimum necessary to achieve the purposes of the broad rule-making power.[45]

The unavoidable consequence of recognising a presumption of statutory interpretation that Parliament did not intend to infringe certain fundamental rights or freedoms more than to the minimum extent necessary to achieve the legislative purpose is to give effect to a principle of proportionality, because the very notion of "necessity" presupposes a consideration of the relationship between end and means. One need only look at the approach of the Court of Appeal in *Leech* to see the inevitability of applying a proportionality test when conducting such an inquiry. As was seen in chapter 5, the Court's inquiry was into the *vires* of the Prison Rule in form only. In substance, the inquiry was into the justification for the impact on the fundamental rights of the prisoner. First, the Court identified the rights of the prisoner which were interfered with and assessed their importance relative to each other. Second, it considered the public interests which the rule-making power could legitimately serve. Third, it considered the extent to which the prisoner's rights were actually affected by the rule. Finally, it placed the two sets of interests in the scales and, weighing them, concluded that the intrusion on the prisoner's basic rights were not the minimum necessary to achieve the legitimate purposes of the rule-making power. A clearer application of a "proportionality" test than this it is difficult to imagine. Proportionality is thus converted into a principle of statutory interpretation. In all but name the concept of proportionality, the introduction of which as a substantive principle of administrative law has been resisted for so long, has been quietly introduced into domestic public law as an uncontroversial matter of statutory interpretation, at least in contexts where fundamental rights recognised at common law are at stake, without, on the face of it, causing too much disturbance to the traditional constitutional justification of the judicial review power.[46]

Not surprisingly, in light of the extent to which the notion of proportionality had already taken root in English public law, the apparent reassertion of public law orthodoxy by the Court of Appeal in *NALGO* and the Divisional Court in *Smith* has not succeeded in arresting the common law developments

---

[44] The flaw in the authority's decision in *Wheeler* [1985] AC 1054, in other words, was not that it had a disproportionate impact on freedom of speech and conscience, but that, given the purposes for which the statutory powers were conferred, the ban served an illegitimate aim. In terms of the traditional grounds of review, it is better understood as a case of improper purpose than of *Wednesbury* unreasonableness.

[45] [1994] QB 198 at 217G.

[46] That this was the effect of accepting the applicant's argument in *Leech* was pointed out by counsel for the Secretary of State, who argued that the applicant was "seeking to rely on the doctrine of proportionality, which was no part of English law": [1994] QB 198 at 200E.

which have brought about a significant infusion of the substance of human rights norms into the law of judicial review. The remainder of this chapter considers the ways in which this gradual but steady evolution has manifested itself in the various grounds of review.

5. HUMAN RIGHTS AND THE CONSTRUCTION OF STATUTORY POWERS

As *Leech* itself demonstrated, the protection of human rights through common law presumptions of statutory interpretation opens up the possibility of challenging decisions of public bodies on the ground of illegality (in the sense of lack of jurisdiction), arguing that the scope of their powers, properly construed, does not extend to the unnecessary infringement of fundamental rights. Moreover, if courts were prepared to have regard to international human rights law when determining the content of the common law presumptions, this promised a way of giving some effect to such instruments when interpreting the scope of statutory powers, notwithstanding their non-incorporated status.

This potential for human rights law to infuse the "illegality" ground of judicial review was very much in evidence in a decision concerning the extent of the jurisdiction of the Broadcasting Complaints Commission.[47] The BBC challenged the jurisdiction of the Commission to entertain a complaint from the National Council for One Parent Families on behalf of the 1.3 million single parents who the Council alleged were unfairly treated by a television programme called "Babies on Benefit". Under the Commission's enabling statute, complaints to the Commission could be made by an individual or a body of persons, but they were not to be entertained by the Commission unless made by the person affected or a person authorised by the person affected.[48] "Person affected" was defined in the statute to mean a participant in the programme who was the subject of the unfair or unjust treatment complained of, or a person who had "a direct interest" in the subject matter of that treatment.[49] The Commission's jurisdiction to entertain the Council's complaint therefore turned on the proper construction of the statutory expressions "person affected" and "direct interest".

In a most significant passage of his judgment, Brooke J. held that, in construing the statutory wording, he was entitled to have recourse to Article 10 ECHR as a guide to its meaning, not only if there was ambiguity, in which case the long established treaty presumption applied, but *"a fortiori* when Article 10 mirrors the common law of England". Since this was plainly a case concerned with broadcasters' freedom of expression, and Lord Keith in

---

[47] *R v. Broadcasting Complaints Commission, ex p. British Broadcasting Corporation, The Times,* 24 February 1995.

[48] Broadcasting Act 1990, s.144(2).

[49] Ibid., s.150.

Derbyshire had made clear that the common law on freedom of expression mirrored Article 10, he proceeded to consider that article and some of the case-law thereunder at some length. His consideration of the ECHR, he said, led him to conclude that it would need very clear language to identify a parliamentary intention that a national body should be permitted to complain to the Broadcasting Complaints Commission about the treatment in a broadcast programme of very large numbers of unidentified people. When the statutory language was properly construed in the light of Article 10, the interest of the National Council for One Parent Families was clearly "indirect" and the Commission had therefore misdirected itself in law in concluding that it had jurisdiction to entertain its complaint.

The significance of Brooke J.'s judgment in the *Broadcasting Complaints Commission* case is not merely that he appears to have been genuinely influenced by his consideration of Article 10, but that he was prepared to construe the statutory words in the light of the ECHR without first determining whether they were independently ambiguous. He was prepared to do this because the statute concerned freedom of expression and it was established by high authority that the common law background on that subject, against which the statute fell to be interpreted, was identical to the relevant provision of the ECHR. This is a welcome judicial recognition of the confluence of common law development and statutory interpretation noted at the end of chapter 5,[50] and is of potentially great significance for the role of international human rights law in domestic judicial review. The common law of England has now been held to be identical to many of the rights contained in the Convention, and the ECHR and its case-law ought, therefore, to be presumptively relevant to the construction of any statute concerning such rights. Indeed, if, as Lord Browne-Wilkinson asserts in his lecture, it is now inconceivable that any court in this country would hold that the individual freedoms of a private person are any less extensive than the basic human rights protected by the ECHR,[51] Brooke J.'s approach to statutory interpretation would mean that the ECHR is *always* relevant as a guide to the meaning of statutory language in cases concerning any of the rights contained in the ECHR.[51a]

---

[50] Contrast the more compartmentalised approach of McCullough J. in *R* v. *Radio Authority, ex p. Bull* [1995] 3 WLR 572 at 591E, considered below n. 57.

[51] Above n. 40 at 405.

[51a] For an even more clearly articulated example of this approach, see Brooke LJ's judgment in *R* v. *Radio Authority, ex p. Bull* (decision of the Court of Appeal, 17 December 1996). There he observed that, although Lord Goff's dictum in *Spycatcher* was uttered in a case concerned with the principles of the common law, the well known canons of statutory interpretation whereby courts presume that Parliament intends neither to take away common law rights nor to breach international obligations, "make his words equally relevant when the courts are concerned with the interpretation of a statute in the field where this country has bound itself by international treaty obligations." See also Brooke LJ in *R* v. *Secretary of State for Transport, ex p. Richmond upon Thames LBC (No. 4)* [1996] 4 All ER 903 at 907j–908d where he held, again in the context of statutory discretionary powers, "ministers must be presumed to have intended to comply with its [the Convention's] requirements when exercising powers conferred on them by Parliament unless there is evidence of a clear Parliamentary intention to contrary effect."

An example of an applicant urging a narrow construction of a power by invoking a presumption against disproportionate interference with fundamental rights occurred in *Bull*, in which British Amnesty challenged the decision of the Radio Authority that radio advertising by it was unacceptable.[52] The Authority was required by a provision in the Broadcasting Act not to include any advert by or on behalf of any body whose objects are wholly or mainly of a political nature.[53] The statute itself contained no definition of "political", but the Authority's own Code of Advertising Standards explained in a practice note that the term "political" was here being used in a wider sense than party political and precluded issue campaigning for the purposes of influencing legislation or executive action by local or national government.

The principal ground on which Amnesty challenged the authority's decision was that it had misconstrued the meaning of the word "political" in the legislation and thereby misdirected itself in law. Since the statute plainly contemplated curtailment of freedom of speech, which was a fundamental freedom recognised by both the English common law and the ECHR, it was argued the statute should be construed in such a way as to limit so far as possible the inroad which it made on the recognised freedom.[54] Restrictively construed in this way, it was claimed, British Amnesty would not have fallen foul of the statutory prohibition on political advertising on commercial radio.

The Divisional Court, however, dismissed the application and in doing so missed an ideal opportunity to articulate the approach which, it was seen above, is implicit in cases such as *Marcel* and *Leech*. Nevertheless, the ECHR was not treated as irrelevant to the question of statutory construction. One member of the court in particular, Kennedy LJ, conspicuously declined to follow the course urged upon it by the respondent, which was ritually to invoke the *Brind* response that Article 10 cannot be regarded as a source of rights and obligations, because that would amount to backdoor incorporation. One of Kennedy LJ's reasons for dismissing Amnesty's construction argument relied directly on the provisions of Article 10, without dwelling at all on the precise reasons for its relevance. He held that the provision in the Broadcasting Act was part of a licensing system for which Article 10 specifically provided, and therefore that Article was unlikely to have any significant part to play in the construction of the section.[55] However unconvincing that might be as an interpretation of Article 10, it is significant precisely because it is such an interpretation. In contrast to Kennedy LJ's use of the text of Article 10, McCullough J. preferred the easy answer provided by *Brind*. He held that the statutory provision was not ambiguous and where that was the case the

---

[52] *R v. Radio Authority, ex p. Bull* [1995] 3 WLR 572.

[53] Broadcasting Act 1990, s. 92(2)(a)(i).

[54] Relying on the views of Lord Keith in *Derbyshire* and Lord Goff in *Spycatcher* that the common law and Article 10 are identical.

[55] [1995] 3 WLR 572 at 585E. Article 10(1) provides "This Article shall not prevent states from requiring the licensing of broadcasting television or cinema enterprises."

ECHR had no part to play in the interpretation of a statutory provision.[56] He also rejected Amnesty's reliance on the identity between Article 10 and the common law by distinguishing *Spycatcher* on the basis that the court was here concerned with the interpretation of a statutory provision and the court was therefore "not here in the realm of the common law."[57]

Both judges, however, having for different reasons dismissed the relevance of the ECHR to the question of construction, and declined to apply a "minimum interference necessary" presumption, nevertheless proceeded to dispose of this ground of challenge in the balancing terms reminiscent of a court adjudicating under a human rights instrument. McCullough J., for example, said he did not regard the provision as a significant interference with freedom of speech, that the rights of the unwilling listener had also to be considered, and that there was much to be said in the public interest for confining within strict limits such freedom to communicate unsolicited political opinions.[58] Similarly, Kennedy LJ said that a balance had to be struck between freedom of communication on the one hand and the other rights to be protected, such as freedom from being forced to listen to unsolicited information of a contentious kind and the danger of the wealthy distorting the democratic process.[59] Both judges also expressed the view that a large of measure of discretion, or a wide margin of appreciation, should be left to the Authority in assessing the need for interference.[60] So although both members of the court disavowed any reliance on Article 10 in construing the statutory provision, in fact it is quite clear thay they both had a very clear view that, on the merits, there was no breach of that Convention article.[60a]

In *JCWI*, there was a more successful attempt to invoke what in effect is a presumption that Parliament does not intend to authorise disproportionate interferences with fundamental rights.[61] The Secretary of State made regulations to remove all entitlement to benefit from two categories of asylum-seeker: those who submit their claims for asylum other than immediately on arrival in the UK, and those whose claims have been rejected by the Home Secretary but who then appeal against that refusal.[62] The Regulations were made pursuant

---

[56] Ibid. at 591D.

[57] Ibid. at 591D–E contrast the approach of Brooke LJ in the Court of Appeal, above n. 51a.

[58] [1995] 3 WLR 572 at 591E–592A.

[59] Ibid. at 585F–G.

[60] McCullough J., ibid. at 592A; Kennedy LJ, ibid. at 585G.

[60a] Although the Court of Appeal dismissed Amnesty's appeal, the argument that the Authority's powers should be restrictively construed in the light of the ECHR was more favourably received. Lord Woolf MR held that the words "wholly or mainly" in s. 92(2)(a)(i) were ambiguous and, since the provision constituted a restriction on freedom of communication, it should be construed restrictively, in a way which limits the application of the restriction to bodies whose objects are substantially or primarily political. Brooke LJ agreed that the words should be given a restricted meaning, but adopted an approach which effectively dispenses with the need for a prior finding of "ambiguity": see above n. 51a.

[61] R v. *Secretary of State for Social Security, ex p. Joint Council for the Welfare of Immigrants*, [1996] 4 All ER 385.

[62] The Social Security (Persons From Abroad) Miscellaneous Amendment Regulations 1996 (SI 1996 No. 30).

to an enabling power in primary legislation in very wide terms, empowering the Secretary of State to make regulations specifying the persons who were or were not entitled to receive income support and other income-related benefit.[63] The purpose of the regulations was clear: to discourage economic migrants from claiming asylum, thereby speeding up the system for processing such claims, and to save the taxpayer an estimated £200 million a year in benefit payments. The effect of the regulations, however, was to give asylum-seekers what Simon Brown LJ described as "a bleak choice": to remain in the UK destitute and homeless until their claims are finally determined, or to abandon their claims and return to face the very persecution they had fled.

The applicants argued that the regulations were *ultra vires* because, however widely drawn the enabling power, it could not have been intended to permit this degree of interference with statutory rights or with fundamental human rights. The statutory rights interfered with were the rights of access to the refugee determination procedures established by the Asylum and Immigration Appeals Act 1993. The effect of withdrawing subsistence benefits from asylum seekers would be to cause many of them, including inevitably those whose claims might eventually be upheld, to forgo their claims, and to substantially impede the ability of others to pursue their claims. The applicants relied in part on the well established principle that specific statutory rights are not to be cut down by subordinate legislation passed under the *vires* of a different Act, and in part on *Leech*, arguing that this was an even stronger case for finding the regulations *ultra vires*, since they had an even more direct effect on an even greater human right. The respondent minister, on the other hand, sought to persuade the court, as in *Smith*, that this was an appropriate case for the application of the so-called "super-*Wednesbury*" test, embodying an even greater reluctance than usual to interfere with governmental decisions, because the regulations had been made within a carefully defined system of parliamentary scrutiny and control in an important area of the national economy and with the legitimate aim of removing an unwarranted burden on public funds.

The Court of Appeal, by a majority, held that the regulations were *ultra vires*.[64] In doing so, Simon Brown LJ was fully aware that he was going further than the court had gone in *Leech*, in which there was a direct interference with unquestioned basic rights. He recognised that, whereas that was a case of courts restraining the state from interfering by positive action with rights to be free of such interference, this was a case of a court imposing on the Secretary of State, in effect, a positive duty to maintain the provision of benefits to asylum seekers so as not to render nugatory their right to have their

---

[63] Under the Social Security (Contributions and Benefits) Act 1992, ss. 135, 137 and 175.

[64] Neill LJ dissented, holding that the Secretary of State had to strike a balance and could not be said to have acted illegally in making the Regulations. Although he held *Leech* to be "plainly distinguishable", he nevertheless applied an explicit proportionality test to determine the *vires* of the Regulations. A court was only entitled to intervene, he said, when the interference with other statutory or common law rights is disproportionate to the objects to be achieved. Contrast Neill LJ's attitude to proportionality in *NALGO* (1993) 5 Admin LR 785, considered in section 3 above.

claims for asylum determined. It was also different in that, unlike in the case of the Prison Rules, Parliament had been closely involved in the making of the regulations under attack.[65] Nevertheless, he was still prepared to hold the regulations *ultra vires* in view of their drastic effect on asylum seekers. Either they inevitably rendered nugatory rights which were necessary implicit in the 1993 Act, or they "necessarily contemplate for some a life so destitute that no civilised nation could tolerate it."

Although Simon Brown LJ expressed his conclusion as resting on the ground that statutory rights were being inevitably overborne, his reasoning goes considerably further and is clearly grounded in considerations of the nature of the human rights at stake.[66] Indeed, so basic were those human rights, in his view, that it could not be necessary to resort to the ECHR to take note of their violation. He preferred to rely on the English common law, and his judgment appears to recognise an independent common law right to be treated with common humanity in the sense of having one's fundamental needs taken into account.[67] Whether interference with that common law right alone would have been sufficient for Simon Brown LJ to invalidate the regulations had there been no statutory rights in play cannot be known. But it is quite clear from his trenchant comments, that the regulations were "uncompromisingly draconian in effect", and that the effects they contemplate could not be tolerated in a civilised society, that he regarded the common law as embodying some minimum standards in respecting individuals' fundamental needs which are relevant to determining the *vires* of regulations. Moreover, his judgment seems to contemplate that such considerations may justify a finding of *ultra vires* even where to do so may impose positive and costly obligations on the state. The *JCWI* decision therefore represents not only an important application of the common law approach of protecting human rights by strictly construing the scope of wide statutory powers in favour of common law rights, but an important reorientation of the kinds of rights capable of being recognised at common law as basic or fundamental.[68]

---

[65] The regulations had been the subject of consultation with the Social Security Advisory Committee and of a reasoned response by the minister to their adverse report; debated in both Houses of Parliament; reported on by the all-party Social Security Committee of the House of Commons; and debated again in the Commons before coming into force.

[66] Waite LJ, who agreed with Simon Brown LJ, also based his judgment on the inconsistency between the Regulations and the statutory rights of asylum seekers under the Asylum and Immigration Appeals Act 1993. However, since what rendered those statutory rights impossible to exercise was the deprivation of the basic means of sustaining life itself, it is suggested that there was in practice no material distinction between the applicants' fundamental rights and statutory rights arguments.

[67] He cited Lord Ellenborough CJ in *R v. Inhabitants of Eastbourne* (1803) 4 East 103, who said of poor foreigners "the law of humanity, which is anterior to all positive laws, obliges us to afford them relief, to save them from starving."

[68] The subsequent passage of the Asylum and Immigration Act 1996, achieving by primary legislation what, in the Court of Appeal's view, no civilised nation could tolerate, provides a forceful reminder of the present ineffectiveness of Parliament, as compared to the courts, in defending the fundamental rights of unpopular minorities.

6. HUMAN RIGHTS LAW AS "BACKGROUND" TO IRRATIONALITY

In the Court of Appeal in *Smith*, the Master of the Rolls, having observed that the UK's obligation to respect and secure compliance with Article 8 of the ECHR was not enforceable by domestic courts, did not go on to say that the ECHR was therefore irrelevant.[69] Rather, he said that the relevance of the ECHR was "as background to the complaint of irrationality."[70] This can only have been a reference to his consideration, earlier in his judgment, of the approach to be adopted to irrationality challenges in cases concerning fundamental human rights. There he had accepted the following formulation as an accurate distillation of the principles laid down in *Bugdaycay* amd *Brind*:

> "The court may not interfere with the exercise of an administrative discretion on substantive grounds save where the court is satisfied that the decision is unreasonable in the sense that it is beyond the range of responses open to a reasonable decision-maker. But in judging whether the decision-maker has exceeded this margin of appreciation the human rights context is important. The more substantial the interference with human rights, the more the court will require by way of justification before it is satisfied that the decision is reasonable in the sense outlined above."[71]

This formulation, which was expressly adopted by each member of the Court of Appeal,[72] is unquestionably a refinement of the *Wednesbury* test. Unlike the Divisional Court, the Court of Appeal did not seek to express itself in the unhelpful language of whether or not such an approach amounted to "lowering the *Wednesbury* threshold". It preferred to recognise the special importance of the human rights context, and to acknowledge explicitly not only that, in that context, a balancing exercise must be carried out by the court, but that, in carrying out that balancing exercise, the court will require more or less justification according to the seriousness of the interference.[73] As was noted in section 4 above, the introduction of the notion of a variable standard of justification depending on the seriousness of the interference is undeniably a conceptual shift away from the monolithic *Wednesbury* test towards some sort of proportionality test which unavoidably involves judicial balancing.

In the light of this formulation of the irrationality test, the sense in which human rights law such as the ECHR is relevant as "background" to an irrationality complaint becomes clear. When asked to interfere with an exercise of administrative discretion on the ground that it is irrational, the court must

---

[69] *R v. Ministry of Defence, ex p. Smith* [1996] QB 517.

[70] Ibid. at 558E.

[71] Ibid. at 554E–G.

[72] Henry LJ, ibid. at 563A; Thorpe LJ, ibid. at 565A ("sensible and not inconsistent with the speeches in *Brind*").

[73] Although the formulation does not expressly refer to the importance of the right, this can be assumed to be implicit in the reference to "the more substantial the interference with human rights".

decide whether the decision is one which has been taken in a "human rights context". The common law obviously provides that context but according to the Court of Appeal in *Smith* the ECHR is also relevant. This is hardly surprising in view of the convergence between the common law and the ECHR which was detailed in chapter 5. An important feature of the formulation accepted by the Court of Appeal in *Smith* is that it appears to accept that the common law of judicial review for irrationality is informed not only by the rights contained in the relevant international instrument, but by the adjudicative methodology which has been adopted in their enforcement.

This notion of human rights law as "background" to irrationality captures nicely the use which has recently been made of the ECHR in a number of judicial review cases. In *Togher*, for example, the Court of Appeal acknowledged that the courts nowadays increasingly recognise that, where they have to consider a case which raises a question of *Wednesbury* irrationality, the rights of the person affected are thrown increasingly into prominence, and although the ECHR had not been adopted into English law, the courts tended to pay greater attention to it as reflecting English common law principles.[74] A woman remand prisoner suspected of conspiracy to import drugs challenged her security classification as provisional Category A, which was the only security category which prevented her from breast-feeding her young baby. She argued that the Secretary of State had failed to balance properly the factors relied on as justifying her security status against the human rights of which she was being deprived by being separated from her child. Relying on Articles 3 and 8 of the ECHR, she argued that the courts should scrutinise with greater care and be readier than hitherto to criticise the Secretary of State's balancing exercise.

Although the Court of Appeal dismissed the application, it proceeded on the assumption that the ECHR reflected common law principles. Thus it concluded that there could not possibly be said to be an infringement of Article 3 "or its equivalent standard of common law". And as for Article 8 "or its equivalent in common law", the woman prisoner's right not to be separated from her young child was unquestionably an extremely important aspect of family life which had to be fully respected, but, as Article 8 itself expressly acknowledged, it had to be balanced against other interests, and as the Secretary of State had rested his decision on a distinct and positive justification in the public interest, his approach could not be faulted.[75]

Undoubtedly the high water mark of using human rights law as background to irrationality was in the well-known case of Child B, in which Laws J. sought to give practical effect to his views on the appropriate standard of

---

[74] R v. *Secretary of State for the Home Department, ex p. Togher*, unreported decision of CA, 1st February 1995 (available on LEXIS).

[75] For criticism of the emphasis in this and other cases on the Secretary of State's *approach*, rather than on whether the substance of the decision has a disproportionate impact on a protected right, see section 7 below.

review in fundamental rights cases.[76] The challenge was to a decision of the respondent health authority not to provide funding for further treatment for a 10-year old child suffering from life-threatening leukemia. Laws J., seeing the fundamental right, the right to life, as being engaged in the case, doubted whether the touchstone for the legality of the decision was "the crude *Wednesbury* bludgeon", and drew counsel's attention to the passages from Lord Bridge's judgments in *Bugdaycay* and *Brind*. Those passages, in Laws J.'s view

> "pointed the way . . . to a developing feature of our domestic jurisprudence relating to fundamental rights which should now I think be regarded as having a secure home in the common law . . . . The principle is that certain rights, broadly those occupying a central place in the ECHR and obviously including the right to life, are not to be perceived merely as moral or political aspirations nor as enjoying a legal status only upon the international plane of this country's Convention obligations. They are to be vindicated as sharing with other principles the substance of the English common law."

According to Laws J., English law required that where a public body enjoys a discretion whose exercise may infringe such a right, it is not to be permitted to perpetrate any such infringement unless it can show a substantial objective justification on public interest grounds. The public body was said to be the first judge of the question whether such a justification exists, but the court has a secondary role in ensuring that only those infringements are allowed that can be justified by an objection of substance put forward in the public interest. Such reasoning was said not to amount to incorporation of the ECHR, which could be deployed by judges, not as a statutory text, but as persuasive legal authority to resolve outstanding uncertainties in the common law. Applying this approach, Laws J. held that the decision not to fund further treatment had interfered with Child B's right to life, and the reasons put forward by the health authority did not constitute substantial public interest grounds justifying the infringement of B's right. Where what was at stake was the life of a 10 year old child, the authority "had to do more than toll the bell of tight resources." It had to provide an adequate explanation of the priorities that had led it to decline to fund the treatment.

Laws J.'s decision was reversed later the same day by the Court of Appeal, which made no mention of the ECHR and conspicuously did not adopt Laws J.'s approach to fundamental rights cases.[77] In particular it thought it unrealistic to impose on health authorities the burden of justifying to courts the allocation of its budget. It may well be that Laws J.'s enthusiasm for the new approach he has been championing carried him unwittingly into the realms of the non-justiciable in the case of Child B, but his judgment demonstrates very clearly the steps in the reasoning of a court which recognises international human rights law as background to the law of irrationality. Even the Court

---

[76] R v. *Cambridge Health Authority, ex p. B* [1995] 1 FLR 1055.
[77] [1995] 1 WLR 898.

of Appeal, whose approach was much more conventionally based on a rigid distinction between legality and merits, expressly recognised that a very high value is put on human life in our society, and that no decision affecting human life could be regarded with other than the greatest seriousness.[78]

7. HUMAN RIGHTS LAW AS A RELEVANT CONSIDERATION

(a) From Irrelevant to Permissive to Mandatory Consideration?

As will be recalled from chapter 4, when the brief Phase I was brought to a close by the reaction against the use of the ECHR in administrative law, there followed a series of cases in which the courts consistently held that decision-makers were under no public law duty to have regard to the ECHR as a relevant consideration.[79] Indeed, so keen were the courts to keep international human rights norms out of administrative law during Phase II, that they even pursued dualist logic to the bizarre conclusion that an administrative decision-maker was obliged *not* to refer to the ECHR other than in a genuine case of ambiguity or doubt about the meaning of statutory words.[80] This was in stark contrast to the position in other jurisdictions, where ratified but unincorporated treaty obligations were considered permissive relevant considerations, which a decision-maker exercising a statutory discretion was perfectly entitled, but not obliged, to have regard to.[81]

In more recent cases, courts have been less concerned to insist on the irrelevance of human rights norms to the exercise of administrative discretion, but have consistently refused to treat them as a mandatory consideration to which the decision-maker must have regard on pain of having the decision quashed for failure to take into account all relevant considerations. In *Brind*, it was accepted that the Secretary of State had considered the ECHR, but argued that he should have had "proper regard" to it, by which was presumably meant he should have correctly construed it and exercised his discretion in conformity with it. Lord Ackner rejected that argument, as inevitably resulting in the backdoor incorporation of the ECHR, because it would oblige the courts to ask in each case whether the restrictions were "necessary in a democratic society."[82] Lord Templeman was alone in regarding the ECHR as a relevant

---

[78] For a defence of Laws J.'s more rigorous scrutiny of the health authority's decision-making process, see R. James and D. Longley, "Judicial Review and Tragic Choices" [1995] PL 367.

[79] See eg. *Salamat Bibi* [1976] 1 WLR 979; *Fernandes* [1981] Imm AR 1; and *Kirkwood* [1984] 1 WLR 913.

[80] *Chundawadra* [1988] Imm AR 161 at 173, considered in ch. 4 above.

[81] Compare *Chundawadra* with the approach to relevant considerations in *Minister for Immigration and Ethnic Affairs* v. *Teoh* (1995) 128 ALR 353 at 360, l.30 (considered in section 8 below), where the High Court of Australia examined the legislation conferring the discretion for any indication that an otherwise relevant international convention had been excluded as a permissory consideration.

[82] [1991] 1 AC 696 at 761G–762B. In *Teoh* (1995) 128 ALR 353 at 365 l.30, the High Court of Australia refused to treat an unincorporated treaty obligation as a mandatory relevant consider

matter which the Secretary of State had to take into account in exercising his discretion.[83] The Court of Appeal in both *NALGO* and *Smith* was in no doubt that the fact that a decision-maker failed to take account of ECHR obligations when exercising an administrative discretion was not of itself a ground for impugning that exercise of discretion.[84]

Notwithstanding the apparently clear statement in *Brind*, *NALGO* and *Smith* that the ECHR need not be taken into account as a relevant matter by administrators, a number of dicta suggest a growing judicial sympathy for the relevance of the ECHR to the exercise of administrative discretion. In the immigration context in particular, *Brind*'s explicit rejection of the attempt to make the ECHR a mandatory relevant consideration has not prevented judges in subsequent cases from making clear their expectation that appropriate regard will be had by the Secretary of State to relevant Articles of the ECHR. This expectation has manifested itself in different ways. In its weakest form it takes the shape of a judicial plea to the minister to reconsider the case in the light of the ECHR in cases where the court is sympathetic to an applicant's ECHR argument but feels unable to grant relief.

An example, decided very shortly after *Brind*, is the factually unusual case of *Zibirila-Alassini*, in which the applicant claimed to have a genuine fear that if he were returned to his native country he would be selected as a sacrificial victim due to his Muslim faith.[85] Rose J. held that the Secretary of State's decision to refuse political asylum was not open to challenge as being in breach of the ECHR when that argument had not been made before the Secretary of State himself, but took the unusual step of suggesting at the end of his judgment that, in light of the applicant's Article 3 argument, the Secretary of State might wish to look at the matter again, and consider whether this was a case for exceptional treatment outside the rules.[86] A similar course was taken in *Wells*, in which the Court of Appeal, "recognising the limited function of this court", rejected the argument that a deportation order was disproportionate because it fell foul of the test of necessity enshrined in Article 8 ECHR, but all three members of the Court made a strong plea to the Secretary of State to look again at all the circumstances of the case.[87]

---

ation for the same reason; though if the unincorporated principle had had a common law counterpart it would have been regarded as a mandatory consideration (ibid. at 366 l.25).

[83] [1991] 1 AC 696 at 751D.

[84] Neill LJ in *NALGO* (1993) 5 Admin LR 785 at 798B–C; Sir Thomas Bingham MR in *Smith* [1996] QB 517 at 558E. In *Britton* v. *Secretary of State for the Environment* (unreported decision of His Honour Judge Rich QC, sitting as a Deputy High Court Judge, 24 October 1996), it was held that it was irrational for the Secretary of State to say on the one hand, in a policy document, that international obligations must be taken into account, and on the other hand, in a decision letter, that it was not necessary for him to decide whether his decision would be a violation of Art. 8 ECHR.

[85] *R* v. *Secretary of State for the Home Department, ex p. Zibirila-Alassini* [1991] Imm AR 367.

[86] Ibid. at 369–370.

[87] *R* v. *Secretary of State for the Home Department, ex p. Wells*, unreported decision of CA, 10 May 1995 (available on LEXIS).

In other immigration cases, the judicial expectation that the ECHR will be taken into account has taken the form of the new-found willingness to discover a happy coincidence between the common law and the ECHR. In *Sinclair*, for example, in which an extradition order was quashed on the ground that it would be unjust and oppressive to extradite the applicant in the circumstances, Watkins LJ doubted whether Article 8 of the ECHR was strictly speaking applicable, but nevertheless found the principle underlying it "very much to the point."[88] Again, in *Dawit Teame*, it was said that, irrespective of the European Convention, the principles in Article 8 were understood and valued in the UK and could be said to be axiomatic.[89] Every Secretary of State exercising power under immigration legislation was said to be aware of those principles and, "whenever he has a relevant discretion to exercise, he must give them proper attention." The same view appeared to be taken by Potts J. in *Chahal*, where he said that, although the ECHR was not part of domestic law, he would expect the Secretary of State to take the relevant provisions into account.[90] The connection between this new judicial expectation and the trend towards identifying the common law with the ECHR was made explicit by Staughton LJ in *Dibia*.[91] Relying on Lord Donaldson's now familiar observation that there was no great difference between the ECHR and the common law, he regarded Article 8 as reflecting what the Home Office ought to bear in mind when deporting the parent of a child who was entitled to remain in the country. According to Staughton LJ, "the common law, common sense and common humanity" required the Home Office to carry out a balancing exercise between the interests of the child on the one hand and the interest in maintaining a proper system of immigration control on the other.

As it has become clear that the courts are beginning to treat Article 8 in the immigration context as a relevant consideration to be taken into account in the exercise of discretion, so decision-makers have responded by attempting to make their decisions review-proof on this ground. In *Zighem*, for example, in which an illegal entrant challenged the decision to order his removal on the basis that to do so would prevent or impede contact between him and his daughter, the Secretary of State's decision letter reassured the applicant that the Article 8 arguments made on his behalf had been very carefully considered, but informed him that the Secretary of State remained firmly of the opinion

---

[88] *R v. Secretary of State for the Home Department, ex p. Sinclair* [1992] Imm AR 293 at 300.

[89] *R v. Secretary of State for the Home Department, ex p. Dawit Teame*, unreported decision of Judge J., 11 February 1993 (available on LEXIS).

[90] *R v. Secretary of State for the Home Department, ex p. Chahal* [1993] Imm AR 362 at 380. See also *R v. Secretary of State for the Home Department, ex p. Akhtar*, unreported decision of May J., 14 December 1995 (available on LEXIS), in which it was held that Article 8 ECHR was not a matter of substantive law within UK courts, but accepted that the concepts it enshrines are matters which the Secretary of State should take into account in an appropriate case in exercising his discretion.

[91] *Dibia v. Chief Immigration Officer, Heathrow Airport*, unreported decision of CA, 19 October 1995 (available on LEXIS).

that removal would not constitute a breach of Article 8.[92] Latham J. held that a mere assertion by the Secretary of State that removal would not breach the ECHR was "unintelligible", because it did not enable the court to say with certainty precisely what the reasons for decision were.[93] It did not, for example, identify whether the Secretary of State had decided that there would be no interference with family life under Article 8(1) or that the interference with family life was justified under Article 8(2). Such preparedness to quash an immigration decision for inadequate reasoning suggests that the emerging judicial recognition of Article 8 as a relevant consideration has the potential to make a very real difference in practice to the way in which such decisions are made.[94]

(b) Policy Guidance on Human Rights as a Relevant Consideration

It is common for public decision-makers, and in particular central government departments, to prepare and circulate to decision-makers guidance as to how to go about making particular decisions, or as to current government policy in a particular area. It is also well established as a matter of administrative law principle that such policy guidance may be treated by the courts as a mandatory relevant consideration in appropriate circumstances, or may give rise to a legitimate expectation that the guidance will be followed.[95] Not surprisingly, then, government policy documents, instructions or administrative guidance notes are usually very careful to avoid any express mention of unincorporated international human rights law, as a precaution against courts finding that the mere mention of the relevant treaty turns it into a mandatory consideration or gives rise to a legitimate expectation that decisions will be made in conformity with it.

---

[92] *R* v. *Secretary of State for the Home Department, ex p. Zighem*, unreported decision of Latham J., 1 November 1995 (available on LEXIS). The applicant made an argument that he was entitled to the benefit of Home Office Policy DP/2/93 (see below), but the case was decided on the basis of the applicant's independent argument that the removal order was in breach of Article 8 ECHR, which the Secretary of State either failed to take into account or misconstrued. The central issue in the case was said to be whether or not the respondent had considered the case properly in the light of Article 8.

[93] The use of such standard form responses in decision-letters suggests that heed is not being paid to the advice in *Judge Over Your Shoulder – Judicial Review: Balancing the Scales*, 2nd edn. (London: Cabinet Office, 1994) at 15, warning decision-makers either to avoid using phrases such as "I have considered all other arguments you have raised but they are not sufficient to affect the decision I have reached", or, if they are used, to be prepared to justify the statement to the courts.

[94] Compare, however, the cases concerning Home Office Policy DP/2/93 considered in sub-section (c) below.

[95] On policy guidance as a relevant consideration, see De Smith, Woolf & Jowell, (above n. 19) 354–5. On statements of policy and legitimate expectation, see *A-G of Hong Kong* v. *Ng Yuen Shiu* [1983] 2 AC 629, *R* v. *Home Secretary, ex p. Khan* [1984] 1 WLR 1337, *R* v. *Secretary of State for the Home Department, ex p. Ruddock* [1987] 1 WLR 1482. The role of the doctrine of legitimate expectation in the protection of human rights is considered in section 8 below.

The most striking example of this governmental caution is the well-known *Judge Over Your Shoulder* pamphlet, designed by the Treasury Solicitors Department to give administrators at all levels an introduction to the basic principles of administrative law and judicial review.[96] References to the ECHR, or any other international human rights instrument, are conspicuously absent. There is a section called "What about Europe?", but this deals exclusively with EC law, and the only fundamental rights or freedoms of which civil servants are made aware are the four freedoms of movement (capital, goods, persons and services), and the right not to be discriminated against on grounds of sex or nationality.[97] There is not even any mention of the ECHR as a source of rights and freedoms in EC law, let alone any mention that administrators must, as a matter of Community law, act consistently with the ECHR when they are acting within the field of EC law.[98]

There are, however, some notable exceptions, where policy guidance or departmental advice does refer explicitly to international obligations. In the planning context, for example, Planning Policy Guidance Notes ("PPGs"), which contain departmental advice on government policy, are material planning considerations to which regard must be had by local planning authorities and the Secretary of State when making decisions pursuant to their wide statutory powers, and PPG1 makes quite clear the relevance of international obligations. It states that the planning system must take account of such obligations, and elsewhere it expressly envisages that departures from the Development Plan may be justified because of the particular contribution the proposal will make to fulfilling an international commitment.[99] Although no court has yet considered the point, those references arguably make provisions such as Article 8 ECHR and Article 1 of the First Protocol mandatory relevant considerations where they are relevant to the determination of a planning question, which may be of considerable assistance to gypsies and others whose lifestyle is not adequately provided for by the current planning system.

Rather more significant in terms of enhancing the domestic status of the ECHR was the escape into the public domain of an internal Home Office document providing guidance to immigration officers on cases involving marriage and children, and explicitly taking into account the effect of the ECHR.[100] Since the publication of that policy, Article 8's creeping advance into judicial review of immigration decisions has accelerated considerably. Significantly, the guidance in policy DP/2/93 not only made express reference to the ECHR itself, but drew attention to the trend in recent European Court cases that

---

[96] Now in a 2nd edition, (see above n. 93) and D. Oliver, "The Judge Over Your Shoulder— Mark II" [1994] PL 514.

[97] *Judge Over Your Shoulder* (above n. 93) at 20–1.

[98] See ch. 7 below.

[99] PPG1, paras. 4 and 30 respectively.

"*however unmeritorious the applicant's immigration history*, the Court is strongly disposed to find a breach of Article 8 where the effect of an immigration decision is to separate an applicant from his/her spouse or child."[101]

Although not expressed in as many words, it is clear that the purpose of the instruction is to ensure that enforcement action in cases involving marriage and children does not conflict with Article 8 of the ECHR, as interpreted by the European Court of Human Rights.[102] To this end, the instruction identifies broad categories of case and sets out the approach to be taken in making enforcement decisions in that type of case. For example, in one of its most significant provisions, the policy sets out, in effect, a presumption not to proceed with enforcement action in deportation and illegal entry cases where the subject has a genuine and subsisting marriage to a person settled in the UK, provided certain other specified conditions are also satisfied.[103] Once it has been established that the marriage is genuine and subsisting, the person's immigration history is said to be of little relevance. Similarly, the test for removing a person with criminal convictions but family ties here is said to be whether removal can be justified as "necessary in the interests of a democratic society", and immigration officers are advised that in determining necessity minor offences or a poor immigration history do not carry much weight.[104]

The internal guidance was never intended to be a public document. As every administrator knows, failure to follow criteria set out in a published policy document may well lead to successful challenges in the courts on the basis of failure to take into account a relevant consideration or disregard of a legit-imate expectation engendered by the policy itself.[105] Its existence, however, seems to have come to light in the course of proceedings in *Hlomodor*, which involved a challenge to a deportation order on the grounds that to deport the

[100] *Home Office Enforcement Policy Group Instruction to Immigration Enforcement Section*, DP/2/93, January 1993. The text is in Appendix VI. From March 1996, the policy has been with-drawn and replaced by policy DP/2/96 which makes only one mention of the ECHR.

[101] Policy DP/2/93, Introduction, para. 1 (emphasis in original). The significance of the under-lining was noted by Hidden J. in *R v. Secretary of State for the Home Department, ex p. Hastrup*, unreported, 28 November 1995 (available on LEXIS).

[102] The policy does not mention any cases by name, but it is clear which decisions have influenced its contents. The factors articulated in para. 6, for example, which are to be consid-ered in deciding whether it is reasonable for the child of divorced or separated parents to accom-pany the parent to live abroad, reflect the criteria to be applied in weighing the right to respect for private and family life against the countervailing public interests under Article 8: see eg. *Berrehab v. The Netherlands* (1989) 11 EHRR 322, paras. 27–9.

[103] Policy DP/2/93 para. 2. The other conditions are (a) that the marriage predates enforce-ment action and (b) has lasted two years or more, or (c) the settled spouse has lived here from an early age or it is otherwise unreasonable to expect him or her to accompany on removal, or (d) one or more of the children of the marriage has the right of abode in the UK.

[104] Policy DP/2/93, para. 8. See eg. *R v. Secretary of State for the Home Department, ex p. Iye* [1994] Imm AR 63.

[105] See eg. *R v. Secretary of State for the Home Department, ex p. Khan* [1984] 1 WLR 1337. For criticism of the use of unpublished informal instructions in the immigration context, see S.S. Juss, *Immigration, Nationality and Citizenship*, (London: Mansell, 1993) at 166–9.

applicant would be a breach of the Article 8 rights of the applicant's child.[106] The existence of the internal guidance giving general advice about Article 8 was disclosed in correspondence from the Secretary of State, but he refused to disclose the guidance itself in the proceedings, and Popplewell J. rejected the applicant's argument that he was entitled to its disclosure. Nor, as an internal document, could it give rise to a claim of legitimate expectation.[107] Indeed, if anything, the existence of the document worked against the applicant in *Hlomodor*, as Popplewell J. regarded its mere existence as evidence that the Secretary of State had considered Article 8.[108]

The potential for the existence of the internal guidance to make a substantive difference to the outcome of applications for judicial review has, however, become apparent in subsequent cases. In *Amankwah* the applicant, who had been an overstayer for five years by the time of his marriage to a wife with indefinite leave to remain, challenged the Secretary of State's decision to deport him following refusal of his application for leave to remain on grounds of his marriage.[109] The Immigration Rules under which the Home Secretary had to consider the exercise of his statutory discretion to deport[110] provided that the public interest in deportation was to be balanced against any compassionate circumstances of the case, and that deportation would normally be the proper course where the person had remained without authorisation.[111] Not surprisingly, then, Popplewell J. indicated that the challenge would ordinarily have fallen short of the high *Wednesbury* standard which it was necessary to meet in order to persuade a court to interfere with the exercise of such a wide discretion.[112]

The existence of the internal policy document, however, made all the difference. Accepting that it did not give rise to a legitimate expectation on the part of the applicant, because it was not a published document, and recognising that the policy set out in the document was neither an Act of Parliament, nor "fixed in tablets of stone", Popplewell J. held that it was nevertheless a policy to which the Secretary of State had to have regard in

---

[106] *R v. Secretary of State for the Home Department, ex p. Hlomodor*, unreported decision of Popplewell J., May 14 1993 (available on LEXIS).

[107] See eg. *R v. Secretary of State for the Home Department, ex p. Akyol* [1990] Imm AR 571.

[108] Earlier in his judgment Popplewell J., in keeping with the emerging judicial expectation charted above, had held that the Secretary of State "should" consider Article 8 when dealing with this sort of application. In the Court of Appeal, it was conceded by the Secretary of State that Article 8 should be regarded as a relevant factor but, typically, that concession was said to be only "for the purposes of the hearing": *Hlomodor v. Secretary of State for the Home Department* [1993] Imm AR 534 at 536.

[109] *R v. Secretary of State for the Home Department, ex p. Amankwah* [1994] Imm AR 240. Leave was given by Brooke J. expressly to give an opportunity to settle the question whether applicants in immigration cases can base challenges on internal Home Office guidance which explicitly takes into account the effects of the Convention.

[110] Under s.3(5)(a) Immigration Act 1971.

[111] Immigration Rules, HC 251, paras. 162 and 166 respectively.

[112] [1994] Imm AR 240 at 242.

exercising his discretion.[113] There was nothing in the reasons given by the Secretary of State to indicate that any factor, other than the mere fact that the applicant was an overstayer, had been taken into account to take the case outside of the general rule laid down by the Secretary of State's policy document, and to the extent that the decision was not in conformity with the policy document, it was held to be not fair and therefore perverse.

The uneasiness of the Home Office at having unwittingly provided applicants with a long awaited peg on which to hang ECHR arguments was manifest. In *Hlomodor*, it will be recalled, it refused to disclose the guidance to the applicant, despite having referred to it in correspondence, and at the leave stage in *Amankwah* it argued that since the policy had never been published or made public, but had been leaked in an unauthorised way, it could not give rise to a case founded on legitimate expectation. In *Iye* the Secretary of State was reprimanded for his evasiveness by a judge of the Court of Appeal, who expressed his dissatisfaction that the Secretary of State had not made clear whether he acknowledged any duty on his part to comply with policy DP/2/93 and whether it was intended or not to give effect to Article 8 of the ECHR as interpreted by the European Court.[114] And, no doubt fearing a flood of legal challenges relying on the policy, the Home Office refused to make a copy of it available to the editor of the Immigration Appeal Reports for publication.[115]

Once the substance of the policy was in the public domain, however, the courts were not too concerned with how it had got there, and there have been other cases since *Amankwah* in which the courts have shown their readiness to hold the Secretary of State to his stated policy. In *Hastrup*, in which an illegal entrant married to a British citizen and with a British child challenged the decision to remove him, the Secretary of State sought to limit the effect of the policy by arguing that it was not appropriate for a reviewing court to construe the policy to decide its true meaning in order to see whether the Secretary of State had misinterpreted it or misdirected himself as to its proper meaning as if it were a statute.[116] Rather, it was argued, since the policy was the Secretary of State's own policy, it was for him to decide what it meant, and his interpretation of it could only be challenged for *Wednesbury* unreasonableness. This attempt to confine the role of the reviewing court within traditional *Wednesbury* bounds was rejected by Hidden J. who upheld the challenge on the basis that the Secretary of State had not carried out a proper and adequate balancing exercise between compassionate circumstances on the one hand and the public interest on the other. The argument that this was a case where the applicant's immigration history was so bad that it justified a

---

[113] Ibid. at 245.
[114] R v. *Secretary of State for the Home Department, ex p. Iye* [1994] Imm AR 63 at 67 (Evans LJ).
[115] Ibid. at 66, footnote.
[116] R v. *Secretary of State for the Home Department, ex p. Hastrup*, unreported decision of Hidden J., 28 November 1995 (available on LEXIS).

departure from the general rule of non-enforcement contained in the policy, and that that decision could not be described as being *Wednesbury* unreasonable, was rejected by Hidden J., showing how far some judges are prepared to go in ensuring that the Secretary of State's decisions are in conformity with his policy.[117] The Court of Appeal, however, disagreed, reverting to more orthodox doctrines to hold that the policy document provided guidance only, and could not fetter the Home Secretary's discretion.[118]

Even in cases in which reliance on the policy has not succeeded, its very existence has produced some innovative approaches to the status of the ECHR. In *Ozminnos*, for example, an uncle who was refused leave to enter the UK to settle with his niece, a British citizen with whom he maintained a sexual relationship, argued that the Secretary of State had failed to follow his own internal policy guidance by concluding that the policy did not apply because of the permanent legal impediment to their marriage due to their consanguinity.[119] The applicant's argument was that the Secretary of State had acted irrationally by failing to conclude that the relationship was a common law relationship within the terms of the guidance.[120] Although the argument failed, Auld J.'s judgment is noteworthy for his conflation of the domestic status of the ECHR with Lord Bridge's indigenous approach in *Brind*.

He said that while the ECHR was not directly applicable in English courts, nor was there any presumption that the Secretary of State's discretion had to be exercised in accordance with the ECHR, nevertheless restrictions on the rights upheld by it needed to be justified. He read Lord Bridge in *Brind* to be saying that where ECHR matters are raised, the courts were entitled to exercise a secondary judgment by asking themselves whether a reasonable Secretary of State, aware that the UK was a signatory to the ECHR, could reasonably disregard its provisions.[121] This is a novel reading of *Brind*, in which Lord Bridge talked of the courts' jurisdiction to make a secondary judgment on the justification of measures infringing fundamental rights as something quite independent of the ECHR. Its significance is therefore that it brings the ECHR back into the indigenous human rights jurisdiction asserted by Lord Bridge as an alternative to the forbidden route of giving domestic status to the ECHR as a mandatory relevant consideration. On Auld J.'s reading of the approach indicated by the House of Lords in *Brind*, articles of the ECHR "have at least some role as relevant factors in the taking of a decision."[122]

---

[117] Contrast, however, the cases considered in sub-section (c) below in which some courts have been more reluctant to interfere with the Secretary of State's decisions under the policy.

[118] *The Times*, 15 August 1996.

[119] *R* v. *Secretary of State for the Home Department, ex p. Ozminnos* [1994] Imm AR 287.

[120] Policy DP/2/93, para. 7.

[121] [1994] Imm AR 287 at 291. Even the Secretary of State's formulation of the question appeared to concede the relevance of Article 8. He argued, ibid. at 292, that the approach to adopt was to ask whether, *having regard to the considerations of Article 8*, the decision to interpret and apply his policy in the way he did was *Wednesbury* unreasonable.

[122] Ibid. at 293. For a similar hybrid formulation, reintroducing the Convention into Lord Bridge's indigenous human rights jurisdiction, see Brooke J. in *R* v. *Secretary of State for the*

The decisions in these cases demonstrate the way in which internal policy guidance, intended to bring Home Office practice into line with the latest interpretation of the ECHR by the Strasbourg organs, can interact with ordinary administrative law principles governing the review of discretion to provide remedies which would not otherwise be available, thus giving a measure of indirect effect to the ECHR in domestic law. In each case great care was taken to make clear that the ECHR was not being directly applied by the court and that the policy was not to be interpreted as if it were a statute.[123] However, in quashing the decisions for not being in conformity with policy guidance intended to bring administrative practice into line with the ECHR, the judgments in *Amankwah* and *Hastrup* are as good as a finding that there had been a violation of the ECHR. The cases are therefore good examples of the indirect ways in which the ECHR can penetrate domestic administrative law without being formally incorporated.

In these recent decisions, the courts have clearly retreated from their earlier position during Phase II that Article 8 was of no relevance in judicial review of immigration decisions because the ECHR was not "part of" domestic law. They have undoubtedly been greatly assisted in doing so by the existence of the internal policy document DP/2/93, but cases such as *Sinclair*, *Dawit Teame* and *Chahal* show that the trend had already begun before the existence of that document came to light, and other such as *Dibia* and *Zighem* show that the continuation of the trend is by no means dependent on the existence of the policy. Moreover, where the policy does apply, cases such as *Amankwah* and *Hastrup* at first instance show that some courts are prepared to scrutinise the decision-making process of the Secretary of State more rigorously than ever *Wednesbury* allowed, to ensure that a proper balancing exercise has been conscientiously carried out. With these decisions, then, the wheel seems to be turning full circle, back towards those cases from Phase I, such as *Miah*, *Bhajan Singh* and *Phansopkar*,[124] in which the courts effectively treated the ECHR as a mandatory relevant consideration in the exercise of administrative discretion.

Home Department, ex p. Patel [1995] Imm AR 223 at 229: when making the secondary judgment, the national court "is not standing in the shoes of the European Court of Human Rights and judging whether there has been a breach of the Convention; rather, it is looking at the approach of the Secretary of State and asking itself: could any rational Secretary of State, reasonably reminding himself of the provisions on the European Convention on Human Rights by which this country is bound, have reasonably formed the view that he did when he took his administrative decision in this matter?"

[123] In *Amankwah* [1994] Imm AR 240 at 243 Popplewell J. noted that he was not being asked to decide whether the decision to deport was in breach of the European Convention and at 244 that the policy was not an Act of Parliament nor fixed in tablets of stone; in *Ozminnos* [1994] Imm AR 287 at 291 Auld J. pointed out that although the policy document referred expressly to Article 8 of the Convention, it could not and did not purport to incorporate that Article in the guidance that it went on to give, but was merely providing that Article 8 was a provision to which immigration officers should have regard when exercising their discretion in accordance with the policy set out; and in *Hastrup The Times*, 15 August 1996 Hidden J. agreed that the policy was not to be subjected to fine analysis and interpreted as if it were a statute.

[124] Considered in ch. 4 above.

(c) Does it Make Any Difference to Outcomes?

It was seen above how, in a number of recent cases in the immigration context, the courts have shown a new readiness to scrutinise the Secretary of State's justification for a particular decision and to intervene if not satisfied that he has conducted a proper balancing exercise between the right to private and family life on the one hand and the public interest in immigration control on the other.[125] Part of the explanation for this change in attitude was the existence of policy DP/2/93, which was deliberately formulated to give advice to those administering immigration laws in light of the UK's obligations under the ECHR. However, this trend has been subject to two important checks, both of which provide grounds for asking whether even the full acceptance of the status of the ECHR as a mandatory relevant consideration would make any difference in practice to the outcomes of cases.

The first limit is in the shape of a narrowly legalistic approach to interpreting policy DP/2/93 itself. In a series of cases, the courts have shown their reluctance to adopt a purposive approach to its interpretation, which might be thought surprising bearing in mind that it was after all intended to bring administrative practice into line with the requirements of the ECHR. The Strasbourg case-law on Article 8 makes no distinction as between different types of case as far as the applicability of the Article is concerned, yet English courts have refused to allow arguments by analogy with the policy in cases to which strictly speaking it does not apply. In particular, applicants challenging refusal of leave to enter, who married or had children during their temporary admission, have not been permitted to rely on the existence of policy DP/2/93 by analogy. In *Comfort Henry*, Harrison J. held that it was quite clear that the policy was expressed to relate to deportation and illegal entry cases, and was therefore of no application to a case concerning refusal of leave to enter.[126] The Court of Appeal approved of that approach in *Abu Shahed*, saying "it would be quite wrong to apply policy statements to situations or circumstances other than those they are expressly stated to be applied to".[127] As a result a refused asylum seeker with a British wife and British child could not claim the benefit of the policy when challenging his removal. The consequence of such a pedantic refusal to take a purposive approach to the interpretation of the Home Office's marriage and children policy is the "curious irony" noted by Simon Brown LJ in *Jackson*, which is that "under the present policy guidance an applicant may be better off the worse their immigration history and the more plainly they have offended immigration control."[128] The absurdity

---

[125] See in particular *Zighem*, *Amankwah* and *Hastrup* at first instance.

[126] *R v. Secretary of State for the Home Department, ex p. Comfort Henry* [1995] Imm AR 42.

[127] *R v. Secretary of State for the Home Department, ex p. Abu Shahed* [1995] Imm AR 303 at 308.

[128] *R v. Secretary of State for the Home Department, ex p. Jackson*, unreported decision of CA, 30 November 1995 (available on LEXIS).

was manifest in *Jackson* itself, in which the applicant, who was an asylum seeker who had married a British citizen during her temporary admission, sought to argue that she was within the statutory definition of "illegal entrant" so that she could claim the benefit of the policy, notwithstanding that characterising herself in this way risked prejudicing her future immigration status. Nevertheless, as the Court of Appeal in *Jackson* observed, whether there was a justifiable basis for denying the benefit of policy DP/2/93 to those such as asylum seekers who are temporarily admitted but ultimately refused leave to enter could now, after *Abu Shahed*, only be settled by the House of Lords.

In *Mirza* an equally legalistic approach was taken to interpreting policy DP/2/93. Notwithstanding the various reminders that the policy was not to be treated as if it were a statute, the Court of Appeal assumed that there was an analogy between an ambiguity in a policy document and an ambiguity in a statute, and that in either case the Court may have regard to the ECHR to help resolve the ambiguity.[129] However, it held that as there was no ambiguity in the policy, there was no need to resort to the ECHR. Since DP/2/93 is in effect an administrative implementing measure, to scrutinise it for ambiguity before recourse could be had to the ECHR is reminiscent of the similar approach to implementing legislation in *Ellerman Lines* v. *Murray* during sovereignty's heyday.[130]

The second check on the development noted in section (b) above has been the tendency to subsume review in the light of Article 8 within a monolithic and inherently deferential *Wednesbury* standard, with the result that recognising the ECHR as a mandatory relevant consideration to be taken into account when making immigration decisions makes very little if any difference in practice. In *Iye*, for example, the Court of Appeal accepted that disregard of the guidance in DP/2/93 would be a valid reason for saying that the decision was wrongly made, but if the court was satisfied that the Secretary of State had in substance considered what he was required to consider by the guidance, the only question was whether no sensible Secretary of State could ever have reached the decision that was arrived at.[131] In other words, so long as the guidance was not disregarded, the balancing exercise that was required to be carried out was for the Secretary of State, subject only to review for *Wednesbury* unreasonableness; the existence of the guidance did not change the standard to be applied by the court on review.

In *Kuteyi*, the applicants sought to confront the court with the manifest absurdity of maintaining an inflexibly high threshold of review at the same time as acknowledging the relevance of the ECHR to the lawful exercise of discretion.[132] The applicants, who were challenging their deportation, had

---

[129] *R* v. *Secretary of State for the Home Department, ex p. Mirza*, [1996] Imm AR 314.

[130] [1931] AC 126.

[131] *R* v. *Secretary of State for the Home Department, ex p. Iye* [1994] Imm AR 63 at 66.

[132] *R* v. *Secretary of State for the Home Department, ex p. Kuteyi*, unreported decision of Popplewell J., 20 July 1995 (available on LEXIS).

received a decision letter containing the increasingly common assertion that the Secretary of State had considered their submission about Article 8 but did not consider that their removal would breach that Article. Relying on Lord Bridge's judgment in *Brind*, as interpreted by Auld J. in *Ozminnos*, they argued that if, as the Secretary of State accepted, he had to have regard to Article 8, then he must decide whether his decision breaches it, because otherwise he might well have misunderstood the effect of it. It was not enough for him to say that he had considered it and was satisfied that there was no breach; he must show by his reasoning that he has properly understood it.

The argument clearly made good sense: what, after all, would be the point of requiring the Secretary of State to have regard to Article 8 of the ECHR if the courts were then prepared to defer to the Secretary of State's judgment of whether or not his decision would breach that Article, provided he could show that he had taken it into account? The argument was rejected, however, by Popplewell J., who held that it was not for the Secretary of State to decide whether Article 8 had been breached or not. All he had to do was to look at all the facts and "have regard to" Article 8. Provided he did that, he was entitled to make up his mind, without deciding, as a matter of law, whether Article 8 was breached or not.[133] It further followed that it did not matter that the Secretary of State had not set out the reasoning by which he had concluded that Article 8 had not been breached.

8. LEGITIMATE EXPECTATION AND INTERNATIONAL HUMAN RIGHTS LAW

(a) An Australian Precedent

A recent decision of the High Court of Australia has set English public lawyers wondering whether it might be possible to use legitimate expectation as the vehicle for giving indirect effect to unincorporated international human rights instruments in English law. The case of *Teoh* raised the question of the relevance of unincorporated international law to the exercise of a broad administrative discretion.[134] Mr. Teoh was a non-Australian citizen who had married an Australian citizen whilst on a temporary entry permit, and subsequently had three children in addition to the wife's four other children by previous relationships. Whilst his application for a grant of resident status was

---

[133] See to similar effect Brooke J. in *Patel* [1995] Imm AR 223 at 230, referring to the jurisdiction described by Lord Bridge in *Brind* as a "residual jurisdiction"; and both Popplewell J. and the Court of Appeal in *R v. Secretary of State for the Home Department, ex p. Egueye-Ghemre*, unreported decision of Popplewell J., 3rd August 1995 and of CA, 9th November 1995 (both available on LEXIS), in which, despite the fact that the applicant was clearly within the terms of policy DP/2/93, it was still held to be the applicant's task to show that the Secretary of State's decision that his was an exceptional case was perverse.

[134] *Minister for Immigration and Ethnic Affairs v. Teoh* (1995) 128 ALR 353. See M. Taggart, "Legitimate Expectation and Treaties in the High Court of Australia" (1996) 112 LQR 50; R. Piotrowicz, "Unincorporated Treaties in Australian Law" [1996] PL 190.

pending, he was convicted of serious offences relating to the importation and possession of heroin, to which his wife was addicted, and sentenced to six years' imprisonment. His application for resident status was subsequently refused on the ground that, in light of his criminal record, he was not of good character.[135] He sought a review of the refusal, relying principally on the hardship that his deportation would cause for his wife, young children and step-children. The Immigration Review Panel found that, although Teoh's family faced a very bleak and difficult future if resident status were refused, nevertheless the compassionate grounds were not sufficiently compelling to outweigh the policy against serious criminal offending. The refusal was upheld and a deportation order subsequently made.

On Teoh's application for judicial review of those decisions, two judges of the Federal Court quashed the refusal to grant resident status on the ground that the relevant statutory discretion had been exercised inconsistently with a legitimate expectation that the decision-maker would treat the application in a manner consistent with the terms of the UN Convention on the Rights of the Child, which Australia had ratified but not incorporated into Australian law.[136] Article 3(1) of the Convention requires decision-makers in all actions concerning children to treat the best interests of the child as a primary consideration. Lee J. considered that the executive's ratification of the Convention was a statement to both the national and the international community that Australia recognised and accepted the principles of the Convention.[137] Carr J. held that the Convention formed part of the context in which Australian decision-makers have to determine how to carry out their duty to act fairly.[138] Both held that, notwithstanding its non-incorporation, ratification of the Convention gave rise to a legitimate expectation that actions concerning children would be conducted in a manner which respected the principles of the Convention. In this context, this meant that there was a legitimate expectation that the decision-maker would determine Mr. Teoh's application on the basis that the best interests of the children would be treated as a primary consideration. Having thus found that the ratification of the Convention

---

[135] The scope of the statutory discretion to grant or refuse resident status, under the Migration Act 1958, was "unconfined" other than by the usual requirement that it must not be exercised for any objects other than those the legislature could have had in mind: ibid. at 360. The "good character" condition was a policy requirement contained in departmental instructions, which also indicated that one of the bases of assessment was whether the applicant had a criminal record, and that the nature, number and "recency" of the offences were relevant.

[136] (1994) 121 ALR 436, Lee and Carr JJ.. The third member of the court, Black CJ, also quashed the decision, but on the basis that the decision-maker had not given proper consideration to the effect of the break-up of the family, which was conceded by the minister to be a relevant consideration. The Convention was not irrelevant to Black CJ's decision, however: as a reflection of the standards to which Australia was seen by the international community to aspire, it formed "part of the general background" against which decisions affecting children are made (ibid. at 443). Cf. the recent use of the ECHR by English courts as "background" to allegations of irrationality in section 6 above.

[137] Ibid. at 449.

[138] Ibid. at 466.

generated a legitimate expectation that decisions would be taken in accordance with its terms, the two Federal Court judges went further and held that procedural fairness placed the decision-maker under an obligation to initiate appropriate inquiries and obtain reports as to the future welfare of the children in the event that the father were deported. The failure to do so meant that the power had not been exercised consistently with the expectation aroused by ratification of the Convention.

No doubt alarmed by the far-reaching implications of this doctrinal innovation,[139] the minister appealed to the High Court of Australia. The Government relied primarily on the quintessentially dualist argument that a ratified but unincorporated convention could never give rise to a legitimate expectation, because it was axiomatic that international treaties cannot give rise to individual rights and obligations in municipal law until the treaty has been incorporated by statute. The High Court had no difficulty accepting that unincorporated treaties do not become part of domestic law unless incorporated by legislation and cannot be a direct source of individual rights and obligations in municipal law. Indeed, they vigorously reasserted it as a proposition well established by a wealth of authority and rooted in the constitutional separation of powers between the executive and Parliament.[140] The majority, however, refused to be seduced by the Government's invitation to conclude from that premise that unincorporated treaties therefore have no role to play in the exercise by the executive of broad statutory discretions. The mere fact that a treaty had not been incorporated did not mean that it was of no significance for domestic law. Statutes, for example, were to be interpreted and applied, so far as their language permits, so as not to conflict with Australia's international obligations, and unincorporated conventions, especially those declaring universal fundamental rights, could be used by courts as a legitimate guide in their development of the common law. The fact that unincorporated treaties enjoyed even this much domestic status showed that there was no *intrinsic* reason for excluding the provisions of such treaties from consideration by decision-makers merely because of their unincorporated status.[141] It was therefore no answer for the Government to argue, as it did, that the Convention on the Rights of the Child was simply irrelevant to the question of whether the minister's statutory discretion had been unlawfully exercised.[142]

The majority did not stop at pointing out that it was well established in judicial practice that ratification of unincorporated treaties had *some* legal

---

[139] The argument was not one of the grounds of appeal to the Federal Court and seems to have emerged in the course of argument before that court.

[140] Mason CJ and Deane J. (1995) 128 ALR 353 at 361, 1.40 to 362, 1.5, with whom Gaudron J. agreed at 375, 1.20; Toohey J., ibid. at 370, 1.40. Amongst the authorities cited in support of the orthodox rule was Lord Oliver in *Rayner* v. *DTI* [1990] 2 AC 418 at 500, considered in ch. 1 above.

[141] Mason CJ and Deane J. ibid. at 363, 1.12; Toohey J. ibid. at 371, 1.1 ("it does not follow that the Convention has no role in the present case").

[142] Toohey J., ibid. at 371.

significance in domestic law, but went on to venture their clearly held view that there was a good reason why that was so. Ratification of international conventions was "not to be dismissed as a merely platitudinous or ineffectual act". On the contrary, ratification was a positive statement by the executive government to the world and to the Australian people that the executive government and its agencies will act in accordance with the relevant treaty.[143] As the New Zealand Court of Appeal had observed in *Tavita*, this made it unattractive for the minister to argue that no regard at all need be paid to Australia's acceptance of international obligations by ratifying a convention.[144] The Australian High Court, however, was prepared to go further than merely comment on the unattractiveness of the Government's argument, and hold that the positive statement inherent in ratification of a treaty provided an adequate foundation for a legitimate expectation that administrative decision-makers will act in conformity with the treaty. It therefore held that Australia's ratification of the Convention had created a legitimate expectation in Teoh and his children that the decision about his deportation would be made in accordance with the Convention principle that the best interests of the child must be treated as a primary consideration.[145] It was irrelevant that none of them had relied on, or was even aware of, the terms of the Convention. The expectation was objective in the sense that it was whatever expectation might reasonably be engendered by the mere fact of ratification. Applying this approach to the facts of the case, the majority held that there had been a want of procedural fairness in the refusal of resident status to Mr. Teoh, because the decision-maker had not regarded the best interests of the children as a primary consideration, but had treated the policy requirement that applicants be of good character as *the* primary consideration which could only be displaced by other considerations of sufficient weight.[146]

Surely to invest the mere fact of ratification with this new legal significance as the progenitor of a legitimate expectation was to subvert the traditional rule that unincorporated treaties are not part of domestic law, and to countenance the back door incorporation of the treaty into municipal law via

---

[143] Ibid. at 365, l.5 per Mason CJ and Deane J. See also, to similar effect, Toohey J at 373, l.25 ("a solemn undertaking to the world at large"); Lee J. in the Federal Court (1994) 121 ALR 436 at 449, l.10 ("a statement to the national and international community") . Cf. McHugh J., dissenting, (1995) 128 ALR 353 at 385, l.5: ratification of a treaty is, by its very nature, a statement to the international not the national community.

[144] *Tavita* v. *Minister of Immigration* [1994] 2 NZLR 257. The court observed that there should at least be hesitation about accepting an argument by the Government which apparently implied that New Zealand's adherence to international instruments was "at least partly window-dressing."

[145] Mason CJ and Deane J, [1995] 128 ALR 353 at 365 and Toohey J at 373. Gaudron J. reached the same conclusion by the rather different route of finding an identical right in the common law, the existence and significance of which was evidenced by Australia's ratification of the Convention: see below.

[146] Ibid. at 365–6, and 374. The High Court, however, disagreed with the view of the Federal Court that the legitimate expectation required the initiation of appropriate inquiries and obtaining of reports as to the children's future welfare: ibid. at 363–4.

an illegitimate use of legitimate expectation? This was one of the principal objections in McHugh J.'s strongly worded dissent,[147] but the criticism was emphatically denied by the majority, who relied largely on the nature of a legitimate expectation as being something other than a "binding rule of law". The existence of a legitimate expectation that a decision-maker would act in a particular way did not necessarily compel the decision-maker to act in that way. Ratification only gave rise to a legitimate expectation in the absence of statutory or executive indications to the contrary. And if a decision-maker proposed to make a decision inconsistent with a legitimate expectation, all that was required by procedural fairness was that the persons affected should be informed in advance and given an adequate opportunity to argue against the decision-maker acting inconsistently with the terms of the treaty. The rule that unincorporated treaties cannot give rise to enforceable rights and obligations therefore remained intact.

It is interesting to note as a footnote to this consideration of *Teoh* that there was a glimpse in some of the majority judgments of the approach which has now gathered considerable momentum in England, namely the discovery or development of a common law principle which matches exactly that contained in the unincorporated treaty. Mason CJ and Deane J., for example, speculated that the decision might also have been flawed for failure to apply a relevant principle, in that the "best interests of the child" principle relied on may have a "counterpart" in the common law, applicable in cases where the welfare of a child was relevant to the determination to be made.[148] Gaudron J. was more explicit, basing her entire judgment on the existence of a common law right on the part of children and their parents to have a child's best interests taken into account, at least as a primary consideration, in all discretionary decisions by governments and government agencies which directly affect that child's individual welfare.[149] Precisely where she derived this right from, however, is less than clear. It seems to be distilled from a combination of particular obligations owed to children in need of protection, as recognised in the existence of the *parens patriae* jurisdiction of the courts; the ordinary incidents of citizenship; what any reasonable person would assume to be the position; and what is required of a civilized democratic society.[150] The significance of the Convention for Gaudron J. was not that it gave rise to a legitimate expectation that its terms would be complied with, but that its ratification by the Australian Government confirmed that the right was valued and respected within Australian society. She used it, in other words, to help legitimate her

---

[147] (1995) 128 ALR 353 at 376–89. That undertakings to other states in international agreements could not give rise to legitimate expectations in Australian citizens was said to be "a basic consequence of the fact that conventions do not have the force of law within Australia" (ibid. at 385, l.10).

[148] Ibid. at 366 l.25. Cf. the references in *Togher*, above n. 74, to the "equivalent standard of common law".

[149] Ibid. at 375–6.

[150] Cf. Simon Brown LJ in *JCWI* [1996] 4 All ER 385, considered above n. 61.

development of the common law to embrace precisely the unincorporated principle relied on.[151]

(b) An English Version?

Has the High Court of Australia in *Teoh* blazed a trail which should be followed in England? Even assuming, for the time being, that such a course would be desirable, there is an immediate obstacle: it would only be open to the House of Lords to do so, because the Court of Appeal in *Chundawadra* has already dismissed precisely the argument which succeeded in *Teoh*.[152] By a curious coincidence, the case raised virtually exactly the issue which arose in *Teoh*, namely whether in deciding to deport a convicted drug offender whose wife and young daughter were unlikely to accompany him abroad, the Secretary of State and the Immigration Appeal Tribunal had gone wrong by failing to take account of the provisions of an unincorporated treaty. In the English case, however, the relevant international provision relied on was not the Convention on the Rights of the Child, but Article 8 of the ECHR.

In *Chundawadra* it was argued that the appellant had a legitimate expectation that the Secretary of State and then the appeal tribunal would apply to his case the test to be derived from Article 8, namely was it necessary in a democratic society for the prevention of crime to deport this appellant?[153] The legitimate expectation, it was argued, was that they would apply their minds properly to the provisions of the ECHR, as interpreted by the Commission and the Court of Human Rights, and would only act in breach of the ECHR where some rational reason for frustrating the expectation existed. The appellant did not shrink from the width of the submission being made: he accepted that, not being based on anything the government had said or done other than sign the Convention, the effect of the argument was that every citizen has a legitimate expectation that, if part of the ECHR is relevant to a matter under consideration, the minister will take that article of the ECHR into account.[154]

The Court of Appeal rejected the argument in no uncertain terms. Glidewell LJ, after lengthy consideration of the case-law on legitimate expectation, was prepared to accept that, if a minister made a clear statement of Government

---

[151] Curiously, having found that the common law already contained precisely the principle contained in the unincorporated Convention, Gaudron J. still limited her intervention to the imposition of a requirement of procedural fairness, notwithstanding that on her approach she was not constrained in the same way as the other members of the majority perceived themselves to be.

[152] *Chundawadra* v. *Immigration Appeal Tribunal* [1988] Imm AR 161. The argument that citizens of the UK have a legitimate expectation, based on ratification, that each of the three branches of government will comply with the provisions of the Convention, also appears to have been run before the House of Lords in *Brind* [1991] 1 AC 696 at 733H, but was not addressed in any of the judgments.

[153] [1988] Imm AR 161 at 168.

[154] Ibid. at 170, in response to a question from Slade LJ in argument.

policy as to how some matter was to be dealt with in future, that in itself, while not giving rise to any legal rights, may give rise in particular circumstances to an expectation that, until the policy was altered and announced to be altered, it will be followed. But that was said to be wholly different from the situation where the Government had acceded to an international treaty but not embodied it in domestic legislation. Because it was unincorporated, it could not be looked at or prayed in aid at all in relation to matters in domestic courts save when a question of ambiguity in a statute or other legal text arose, and it followed that there could be no legitimate expectation that the ECHR would be looked at.[155] To accede to the argument would be to introduce the ECHR into the law of England by the back door of legitimate expectation when the front door was firmly barred.[156] The English Court of Appeal, in other words, had wholeheartedly accepted in 1987 the very same argument unsuccessfully advanced by the Australian Government in *Teoh* eight years later.[157]

The decision in *Chundawadra*, however, has not caused English lawyers to give up hope that the doctrine of legitimate expectation might provide a route into English law for unincorporated human rights treaties such as the ECHR. Lord Lester, in particular, has been attempting to lay the foundations for a legitimate expectation argument which does not rely solely on the fact of ratification, by extracting parliamentary answers from Government representatives in the House of Lords which might serve as the representation or statement of policy on which to found a general legitimate expectation of governmental compliance with unincorporated but ratified international human rights treaties. The Government, however, no doubt wise to Lord Lester's intentions, have met these questions with evasive answers, blandly reiterating the outdated dualist orthodoxy that whether there has been a breach of a ratified but unincorporated treaty is a question which arises on the international not the domestic plane. So when, for example, Lord Lester asked whether the Government considered that Ministers and civil servants,

---

[155] [1988] Imm AR 161 at 174. See also, to similar effect, Caulfield J at 175 (applicant could not expect, legitimately or otherwise, that the Tribunal would so approach its task as to resort to a treaty which was no part of the law of this country) and Slade LJ at 176 (could not accept that the Government, simply by ratifying the Convention, gave rise to any legitimate expectation). See section 7 above on the ECHR as a relevant consideration.

[156] The Court of Appeal also rejected the argument that the cases which barred direct reliance on the Convention, *Salamat Bibi* and *Fernandes*, pre-dated the full flowering of the concept of legitimate expectation: ibid. at 169. Both those cases were said by the Court to have been preceded by two important early decisions on legitimate expectation, *Schmidt* v. *Secretary of State for Home Affairs* [1969] 2 Ch 149 and *R* v. *Liverpool Corporation, ex p. Liverpool Taxi Fleet Operators' Association* [1972] 2 QB 299 (though in fact the phrase "legitimate expectation" does not feature in the judgments in the latter case).

[157] The decision in *Chundawadra* should serve as another warning of how instrumentalist arguments, which do not directly confront the exaggerated influence of dualist premises, can ultimately be counterproductive, because they tend to drive a culturally resistant court back to the most extreme dualist position that the Convention is simply irrelevant because not "part of" domestic law.

in discharging their public functions, have a duty to comply with the ECHR and the ICCPR, the answer was:

> "International treaties are binding on states and not on individuals. The UK is party to both treaties and it must comply with its obligations under them. In so far as acts of Ministers and civil servants in the discharge of their public functions constitute acts which engage the responsibility of the UK, they must comply with the terms of the treaties."[158]

Although the opening reference to treaties being binding on states not individuals is, in the context, rather obscure,[159] this seems to be an unequivocal acceptance that ministers and civil servants are under a duty to comply with the terms of the treaties. The statement is more equivocal, however, as to the nature of the duty which is acknowledged to exist. Even if the duty to comply which is referred to is claimed to be a duty in international law only, such a statement sits uneasily with the Government's repeated assertion in judicial review proceedings that the ECHR or ICCPR are not relevant considerations when ministers or civil servants are exercising broad statutory discretions.[160] It will often be self-evident to ministers and civil servants that their acts or decisions "engage the responsibility" of the UK under human rights treaties, at least in the sense that there is an overlap of subject-matter, and it is difficult to see how any minister or civil servant can purport to be fulfilling even an internationally owed duty to comply with those treaties if they regard the terms of the international treaty as irrelevant.

Pressed further as to whether the Government considered that local authorities and judges also had a duty to comply with those treaties, a more explicitly dualist response was forthcoming:

> "The acts or omissions of public officers or authorities may engage the international responsibility of the UK in so far as they raise issues in respect of the fulfilment of the UK's obligations under the treaty. The position in international law in this regard is no different for the treaties referred to . . . than for other treaties. In the cases of the ECHR and the ICCPR, the determination whether a particular act or omission does engage the responsibility of the UK is specially entrusted . . . to the supervisory bodies established by those treaties."[161]

This time, then, the Government was careful to make clear that the duty to comply with the terms of the treaties was an *international* responsibility. This at least purports to explain why those international treaties are irrelevant to the exercise of discretion by ministers and civil servants. Acts or omissions which "engage the responsibility of the UK", it seems, are not merely those

---

[158] Baroness Chalker of Wallasey, *Hansard*, HL Deb., Vol. 559, WA col. 84 (7 December 1994).

[159] Presumably what is meant by the reference to individuals is that ministers and civil servants, *as individuals*, are not bound by unincorporated international treaties.

[160] Cf. Cooke P.'s observation in the Court of Appeal of New Zealand in *Tavita* [1994] 2 NZLR 257 at 266, l.1, that it was "unattractive" of the Minister and the Immigration Service to ignore international instruments.

[161] Baroness Chalker of Wallasey, *Hansard*, HL Deb., Vol. 560, WA col. 1 (9 January 1995).

which self-evidently affect rights or interests protected by the treaties, but those which *breach* those treaties, and whether or not they do so is a question for the international mechanisms established by the treaties themselves.

Lord Lester's question as to how, in the absence of incorporating legislation, victims of failures to comply with the ECHR and ICCPR could obtain effective domestic remedies against the Crown, met an equally dualist response. The obligation to provide an effective domestic remedy was said to be a treaty obligation, and therefore whether the UK had complied with it fell to be determined in the same way as whether it had complied with any of the other obligations under the treaties, that is, under the mechanism especially so provided.[162] The case-law of the European Court of Human Rights under Article 13, to the effect that the ECHR did not require any particular method for giving effect to its provisions in national law, was also prayed in aid.[163]

Such dualistic purity as is evident in these answers is seriously out of kilter with the developments concerning the domestic status of international treaties, and in particular of the ECHR, which this book has attempted to show have been taking place in recent years. To insist on treaties being relevant on the international plane only overlooks the many and various ways in which they are already acknowledged to be of relevance to issues in domestic courts. These answers, with their predictable incantations, yielded nothing on which a legitimate expectation argument could be hung.

Undeterred, Lord Lester has argued that such a basis can be found in the combination of recently available parliamentary and governmental material, in particular the new Civil Service Code and Questions of Procedure for Ministers, and parliamentary answers given by Government representatives concerning the duties resting on ministers and civil servants under those codes.[164] The new Civil Service Code, which came into effect on January 1 1996, expressly refers to the "duty" of ministers and civil servants to "comply with the law, including international law and treaty obligations".[165] In response to Lord Lester's question whether that duty meant that individuals in the UK could reasonably expect that ministers and civil servants would discharge their public functions in accordance with their obligations undertaken by ratifying the ECHR and ICCPR, the Government replied, evasively, that the duty to comply with the law "was a duty owed by Ministers, civil servants and citizens alike".[166] Asked further whether British citizens may reasonably expect that ministers and civil servants will comply with the terms of

---

[162] Baroness Chalker of Wallasey, *Hansard*, HL Deb., Vol. 560, WA col. 1 (9 January 1995).

[163] See ch. 8 below for consideration of the Article 13 case law on effective domestic remedies.

[164] Lester, "Government Compliance with International Human Rights Law: A New Year's Legitimate Expectation" [1996] PL 187.

[165] *The Civil Service Code*, paras. 3 and 4. The Government has stated its intention to bring the next revision of Questions of Procedure for Ministers into line with the new Civil Service Code: *Hansard*, HL Deb., Vol. 569, WA, col.s 44–45 (29 November 1995), Baroness Blatch.

[166] *Hansard*, HL Deb., Vol. 566, WA, col. 195 (7 November 1995), Lord Chesham; *Hansard*, HL Deb., Vol. 566, WA, col. 213 (8 November 1995), Baroness Blatch.

Questions of Procedure for Ministers and the new Civil Service Code, the Government answered, again rather obscurely, "It is expected that Ministers and civil servants will comply."[167] Lord Lester considers it to be "strongly arguable" that the government, by their conduct in publishing the two codes and by their answers to Parliamentary Questions, have created a legitimate expectation that ministers and civil servants will comply with international human rights norms, and that this is an argument which should be pursued in an appropriate case in the interests of securing effective domestic remedies for governmental violations of those norms.[168]

(c) Why Legitimate Expectation is not the Way Forward

Lord Lester has truly been a pioneer in designing imaginative ways of giving domestic effect to international human rights instruments, but using legitimate expectation as the vehicle is probably not the best way forward. The objection is not of course to the end which the argument seeks to achieve. Enhanced domestic protection of the rights and freedoms contained in the unincorporated human rights treaties is the very same goal which is sought to be achieved by the recognition of the interpretive obligation for which this book argues. It follows that the purely practical objections to the majority's decision in *Teoh* are not amongst the reasons advanced here for objecting to the use of legitimate expectation. As was seen above, the purely practical objections to giving domestic effect to human rights treaties, which were most commonly heard during the retreat from judicial use of the ECHR in administrative law which marked the end of Phase I, are now hardly ever heard in English courts. Lord Denning's concerns in *Salamat Bibi*, that the ECHR's drafting style was very different from English legislation and that it might be asking too much of administrative officials to know and apply its principles, were relied on by McHugh J. in his dissent in *Teoh*,[169] but have virtually disappeared from English judgments.[170]

As for the warnings of calamitous practical consequences for administratve decision-making in view of the large number of treaties to which the country is a party,[171] that objection would no more seem to lie in the mouth of the executive than the argument that ratified but unincorporated treaties are irrelevant to the exercise of executive and administrative discretion. Since it is the

---

[167] *Hansard*, HL, WA col. 57 (30 November 1995), Baroness Blatch.

[168] Above n. 164 at 189.

[169] (1995) 128 ALR 353 at 388, l. 10. See also Taggart, (above n. 134) at 53.

[170] Partly no doubt reflecting the extent to which, in the intervening two decades, English administrators have been forced to grow accustomed both to the different drafting style of European Community law and to the ever-growing body of Strasbourg case-law interpreting and applying the Convention's broad provisions.

[171] In *Teoh* the Government pointed out to the court that Australia was a party to about 900 treaties: McHugh J., (1995) 128 ALR 353 at 385, l. 20.

executive which enters into international treaty obligations, it does not seem too much to ask that it makes those who make decisions on its behalf aware of those obligations it has undertaken which are relevant to their particular area of decision-making. Indeed, it is consistent with the spirit of *Teoh* that it should be incumbent on the executive to do so, if it is doing anything more than "window-dressing" when it ratifies an international agreement. At the very least this should be the case with human rights treaties, the number of which is relatively small. Although the reasoning of the majority in *Teoh* is expressed to be of general application, it was clearly considered to be of particular relevance to human rights treaties.[172] Indeed, the special significance of such treaties is already recognised by Australian law, which has a mechanism for the Attorney General to make a declaration that a particular treaty is an international instrument relating to human rights and freedoms in order to identify it as a guide to the Human Rights and Equal Opportunity Commission in fulfilling its functions of inquiring into and reporting on any act or practice that may be inconsistent with or contrary to human rights declared in the instrument.[173]

These practical concerns, then, are not the objections to the proposed use of legitimate expectation, since they are objections of general application to any method for giving greater domestic effect to unincorporated international obligations. The principal objections concern, first, whether the argument is likely to succeed before an English court on the current state of the law and, second (and sadly not necessarily related), whether using this particular administrative law doctrine is in the longer term interests of developing a coherent body of judicial review principles.

At the purely pragmatic level of the practical likelihood of the argument achieving its aim, there are a number of doctrinal obstacles which are likely to stand in the way of its acceptance by English courts or which, even if it is accepted, may limit its effectiveness as a means of securing greater respect for fundamental rights. The matters which an applicant has to prove in order to make good a claim that a representation-based legitimate expectation has arisen were recently summarised by Stuart-Smith LJ in *RAM Racecourses*.[174] The applicant must satisfy the court that there has been a clear and unambiguous representation, that the applicant was within the class of persons entitled to rely on it, that they did rely on it and that they did so to their detriment. The material relied on by Lord Lester as giving rise to a legitimate expectation of compliance must be in danger of falling at the very first hurdle. The statement in the new Civil Service Code that ministers and civil

---

[172] See eg. Mason CJ and Deane J., (1995) 128 ALR 353 at 365 l.6 (ratification not to be dismissed as purely platitudinous, "particularly when the instrument evidences internationally accepted standards to be applied by courts and administrative authorities in dealing with basic human rights affecting the family and children.")

[173] Such a declaration was in fact made in relation to the Convention on the Rights of the Child, but only after the decisions in *Teoh*'s case had been taken.

[174] *R v. Jockey Club, ex p. RAM Racecourses* [1993] 2 All ER 225 at 236j.

servants are under a duty to comply with the law, including international law and treaty obligations, hardly seems to pass the test of a clear and unambiguous representation. Like the answers to Lord Lester's earlier Parliamentary Questions, it is ambiguous as to whether the "duty" referred to is a duty owed in international law only, and its lack of specificity, in particular its lack of specific reference to human rights treaties, makes it unlikely to be regarded as a statement capable of engendering a legitimate expectation of governmental compliance with such treaties. Nor do the opaque answers to Lord Lester's questions about the effect of the new Code take matters much further. A ministerial expectation that ministers and civil servants will comply with their duty to comply with the law, which is what Baroness Blatch's answer amounts to, hardly seems to be a foundation for a citizen's legitimate expectation that the government will make discretionary decisions in accordance with human rights treaties.

Even assuming that any representation could be said to inhere in the parliamentary and governmental material relied upon, the courts appear reluctant to broaden the class of people entitled to rely on governmental statements beyond more individuated contexts, as is evident in Lord Keith's recent statement in the *Fire Brigades Union* case that "the doctrine of legitimate expectation cannot reasonably be extended to the public at large, as opposed to particular individuals or bodies who are directly affected by certain executive action."[175] The broad statement of a duty to comply in the codes and the unhelpful parliamentary answers in reality go little further than the mere fact of ratification. Although that fact alone was found to be a sufficient statement in *Teoh*, as Taggart points out, to equate ratification of a treaty with a promise or representation to the citizenry is a large leap from the previous case-law.[176] As for the requirement of detrimental reliance, although it is still a matter for debate whether an applicant relying on a legitimate expectation must be able to show such detrimental reliance on the governmental statement giving rise to the expectation, in so far as it is it would rule out the "objective" expectation relied on by the majority in *Teoh*. Even in the case of an applicant who knew of the existence of the relevant international treaty and of the Government's statements of its duty to comply, it may often be hard to demonstrate that they had relied to their detriment on their expectation that a decision affecting them would be made consistently with that treaty. In short, English courts are unlikely, at the present stage of development of the law on legitimate expectation, to hold that citizens have a legitimate expectation that ministers and civil servants will act in accordance with unincorporated international treaties.

Even if courts could be so persuaded, the doctrine of legitimate expectation hardly provides a very secure foundation on which to build greater domestic protection for human rights. In *Teoh* itself, because Australian law does not

---

[175] [1995] 2 AC 513 at 545H.
[176] Above n. 134 at 51.

yet recognise the substantive protection of legitimate expectations, the expectation of the citizenry that decision-makers would exercise their powers in conformity with ratified but unincorporated international law was entitled to only procedural protection. Hence the decision-maker was free to act inconsistently with the expectation in a particular case provided those likely to be affected by the decision were informed that it was intended not to apply the relevant international norm and given an opportunity to persuade the decision-maker otherwise. English law, by comparison, has indisputably recognised substantive protection of legitimate expectations in the past,[177] but it remains a matter of fierce debate whether judicial protection of substantive expectations can be justified or is beyond the legitimate judicial role.[178] So long as that uncertainty over the proper scope of the legitimate expectation doctrine remains, it could not be guaranteed that English courts would not consider themselves constrained to confine their protection of a citizen's legitimate expectation of governmental compliance to procedural protection only, as in *Teoh*, entitling them merely to be informed in advance and heard as to whether the decision-maker should take the relevant treaty approach or not.

Moreover, even in a jurisdiction which protects substantive legitimate expectations, the protection provided by the doctrine is subject to the ultimate insecurity that whether any expectation arises at all is in the hands of the executive, since there is nothing in the doctrine to prevent the Government from precluding any expectation, substantive or procedural, from arising in the future, by declaring generally that no reliance should be placed by citizens on the mere ratification of international treaties, or on governmental codes and parliamentary answers. Indeed, this is precisely what happened in Australia, where, following the decision in *Teoh*, the Government issued a statement that the mere fact of entering into an international treaty, past or future, did not raise any expectation that government decision-makers would act in accordance with that treaty if the relevant provisions had not been enacted into Australian law.[179] The protection afforded by the doctrine of legitimate expectation is therefore easily defeated by the very party it is sought to constrain.

The objections outlined so far are all essentially doctrinal limitations which are likely to limit the attractiveness and effectiveness of the legitimate expectation argument proposed by Lord Lester. The most fundamental objection of all, however, is an objection of principle concerning the appropriateness of

---

[177] See eg. *R.* v. *Home Secretary, ex p. Asif Khan* [1984] 1 WLR 1337; *R* v. *Secretary of State for the Home Department, ex p. Ruddock* [1987] 1 WLR 1482; *R* v. *Ministry of Agriculture, Fisheries and Food, ex p. Hamble Fisheries* [1995] 2 All ER 714.

[178] See eg. Laws J. in *R* v. *Secretary of State for Transport, ex p. Richmond LBC* (No. 1) [1994] 1 WLR 74. The state of the debate is surveyed by Irvine, [1996] PL 59 at 70–2.

[179] See Piotrowicz (above n. 134) at 193–194; Taggart (above n. 134) at 51. It is interesting, however, that the Australian Government did not consider the issuing of this statement to be sufficient, and also introduced legislation to reverse the decision. The Administrative Decisions (Effect of International Instruments) Bill 1995, however, fell with the Government in the 1996 elections.

using legitimate expectation as the vehicle for giving indirect effect to unincorporated treaties. The attraction of the *Teoh* case to English lawyers is no doubt due in part to the possibilities it appears to open up in a jurisdiction where courts have been prepared to enforce the substance of an expectation, because it appears to offer a way of requiring decision-makers not only to give a hearing before not complying with a treaty, but actually to exercise their powers consistently with international treaties. Closer analysis of the majority's reasoning, however, reveals that, far from being constrained by the limited protection afforded to legitimate expectation in Australian law, it presupposes, and is entirely dependent on, legitimate expectations being given only procedural rather than substantive protection. It was the ultimate unenforceability of a legitimate expectation, the fact that it was different from a binding rule of law and subject to statutory or executive indications to the contrary, that enabled the majority to claim that it was not subverting the traditional rule that no enforceable rights or obligations can arise in domestic law from an unincorporated treaty. If, according to the Australian law on legitimate expectation, ratification had given rise to a legitimate expectation that could only be fulfilled by the decision-maker actually applying the relevant principle or approach set down in the treaty, it is clear that the High Court would have regarded this as illegitimate backdoor incorporation. This much is apparent in the High Court's disapproval of the approach of the two judges in the court below who had also recognised a legitimate expectation arising from ratification. They were said to have erred in requiring that the decision-maker initiate inquiries and obtain reports as to the children's future welfare, because that was based on the wrong assumption that the decision-maker was *bound* to exercise the statutory discretion in conformity with the UN Convention on the Rights of the Child as if it was already part of domestic law. In imposing such a requirement on the decision-maker, those judges had given effect to a substantive rather than a merely procedural expectation.

The weakness of the judicial protection available for legitimate expectations, being confined to procedural protection only, was therefore essential to the exercise. It offered a way of requiring decision-makers to pay some regard to the provisions of unincorporated treaties, whilst leaving them the apparent option of overriding the expectation, provided an opportunity was given to persuade the decision-maker not to depart from the international standard. By this means, unincorporated treaties have *some* relevance to the judicial review of administrative discretions, but decision-makers are not bound to observe the unincorporated norm in the way they would be if it were fully incorporated into domestic law. In other words, the decision in *Teoh* is a wholly instrumental use of the doctrine of legitimate expectation in order to give some indirect effect to unincorporated international instruments.[180]

---

[180] Taggart, (above n. 134) at 53, goes so far as to describe this use of legitimate expectation as a "disingenuous" use of procedural fairness to circumvent the traditional rule about the status of unincorporated treaties.

This dependence of the majority's reasoning on the limited procedural protection available for legitimate expectation in Australian law has a double significance. First, it should be borne in mind by those who would advocate that English courts follow the *Teoh* approach, because the fact that English law, unlike Australian law, *does* recognise substantive protection for legitimate expectations, means that, on *Teoh*'s own terms, a decision giving substantive protection to an expectation that a decision-maker will act in a particular way would amount to illegitimate backdoor incorporation.

Second, it raises the question whether the entirely instrumental use of the doctrine of legitimate expectation as the only administrative law doctrine which could do service as a means of giving some effect to unincorporated treaties in domestic administrative law without giving rise to enforceable rights and obligations in the way forbidden by the traditional rule, achieves that aim at too high a price in terms of the law's development. For some, no doubt, doctrinal distortion is a small price to pay for the long awaited prize of making human rights treaties relevant to the exercise of administrative discretion. But such nakedly instrumental use of the doctrine of legitimate expectation may do damage to the appropriate use of that doctrine. It results in a high degree of artificiality, such as the notion of an "objective" expectation, which need not actually be held by anyone, and the concept of a hearing at which those likely to be affected by a decision have an opportunity to make representations as to why the treaty approach should be followed.[181] More seriously, as with all instrumentalism, it threatens to detach the doctrine from the rationale which has only recently begun to emerge as underlying the judicial recognition and protection of legitimate expectations. The courts have developed that protection as a flexible means of enforcing a number of overlapping principles of good administration, including legal certainty and security, consistency and non-discrimination in administrative decision-making and non-retroactivity.[182] To use it now as the vehicle for giving a degree of domestic effect to unincorporated international treaties would be to stretch it artificially in a way which threatens its genuine utility in the service of those other principles.

Such doctrinal distortion need not be necessary, however, if the right lessons are learned from the central insight in *Teoh*. The surprising use of legitimate expectation in that case sprang from a laudable judicial reluctance to accept the executive's invitation to deduce a supposedly inevitable conclu-

---

[181] One need not share the legally conservative premises of McHugh J., dissenting in *Teoh*, to agree with many of his well aimed criticisms that the majority's approach is an unwarranted extension of the doctrine of legitimate expectation. There is much force in his view, (1995) 128 ALR 353 at 383, 1.40, that "it seems a strange, almost comic, consequence if procedural fairness requires a decision-maker to inform the person affected that he or she does not intend to apply a rule that the decision-maker cannot be required to apply, has not been asked or given an undertaking to apply, and of which the person affected by the decision has no knowledge."

[182] See eg. Lord Fraser in *A-G of Hong Kong* v. *Ng Yuen Shiu* [1983] 2 AC 629 at 638E–F; *R* v. *Inland Revenue Commissioners, ex p. MFK Underwriting Agents* [1990] 1 WLR 1545.

sion from an incontrovertible premise: that unincorporated international treaty obligations are irrelevant to the exercise of administrative discretions because unincorporated treaties do not give rise to enforceable rights and obligations in domestic law. The majority in *Teoh* baulked at drawing that conclusion because it seemed to give judicial sanction to the executive's cavalier attitude to the significance of ratification. Their decision sends an important signal to the executive that its members will not be heard by courts to say that treaties, to which the Government of which they are a member purports to adhere, are irrelevant to their decision-making. This is something which, so far, no English court has been prepared to say to the executive when confronted, as they invariably are, with the wholly unattractive argument that international treaties such as the ECHR and the ICCPR are of no relevance to executive or administrative decision-making pursuant to broad discretionary powers.

It is clear that this important insight in *Teoh* in turn stems from an underlying acceptance by the majority judges of a general judicial obligation to interpret domestic law consistently with international law. Indeed, their resistance to the Government's argument that unincorporated international law was irrelevant to the exercise of administrative discretion can best be understood as a particular manifestation, in the context of administrative law, of the more general obligation. The existence of such an interpretive obligation to interpret domestic law so as to achieve consistency with international obligations was at least implicitly recognised by Mason CJ and Deane J. in the course of their consideration of the status of international treaties in Australian law.[183] Having set out the conventional rendering of the international treaty presumption, that where a statute or subordinate legislation is ambiguous the courts should favour that construction which accords with Australia's international obligations, these two judges went on expressly to prefer a more general formulation of the principle, shorn of any reference to ambiguity, and amounting to a recognition of a strong interpretive obligation on domestic courts:

> "If the language of the legislation is susceptible of a construction which is consistent with the terms of the international instrument and the obligations which it imposes on Australia, then that construction should prevail."[184]

Significantly, Mason CJ and Deane J. thought that this more general formulation of the principle, which is more in the nature of an interpretive obligation than a presumption of interpretation triggered by statutory ambiguity, was still no more than a mere canon of construction which did not import the

---

[183] (1995) 128 ALR 353 at 361–2.
[184] Ibid. at 362, l.25. The judges do not go quite so far as to say that ambiguity is irrelevant, preferring to say instead that "in this context, there are strong reasons for rejecting a narrow conception of ambiguity." Cf. Lord Diplock's formulation in *Garland*, [1983] 2 AC 751 at 711A–B considered in ch. 1 above.

terms of the unincorporated treaty into municipal law as a source of individual rights and obligations. They cited Lord Bridge's dictum in *Brind* in support of this proposition,[185] but in fact Lord Bridge uttered those words in relation to a more narrowly formulated presumption which applied only to assist courts in the resolution of an independently established ambiguity. Moreover, along with the rest of the House of Lords in *Brind*, Lord Bridge rejected the more broadly formulated interpretive obligation approved in *Teoh*, at least in so far as it required the scope of broad statutory discretions to be construed consistently with the unincorporated ECHR, precisely because in his view that amounted to the judicial importation of the ECHR and its jurisprudence into domestic administrative law.[186] When considering the domestic status of international law in the abstract, Mason CJ and Deane J. had no such concerns that their recognition of an interpretive obligation on judges to construe statutes consistently with international obligations would inevitably subvert the traditional rule against judicial incorporation of unincorporated treaties. Here, then, is a potentially significant point of departure between the Australian High Court in *Teoh* and the decision in *Brind*.

However, when it came to giving more concrete doctrinal expression to that interpretive obligation, and to the crucial insight which flows from it that the executive cannot be heard to say a ratified treaty is irrelevant to the exercise of executive discretion, the majority in *Teoh* fought shy of reading implied limitations into the scope of the superficially unconfined power, or requiring the decision-maker to have regard to the unincorporated Convention as a mandatory relevant consideration. To give effect to the interpretive obligation by those means, it was clearly thought, would be tantamount to treating the unincorporated international provision as a binding rule of law and would thus fall foul of the prohibition on unincorporated treaties giving rise to domestically enforceable rights and obligations. Instead, they chose the law of procedural fairness, and within that the weak protection offered by the law on legitimate expectation, as the vehicle by which to give practical effect to the interpretive obligation which underpinned their crucial insight that the executive cannot be allowed to ignore solemnly undertaken international obligations.

Where the High Court of Australia erred, then, was in translating their important insight into a recognition of a legitimate expectation of compliance with international norms. That insight might have led them to revisit the rationale behind the traditional rule that unincorporated treaties cannot give rise to enforceable rights and obligations in domestic law. There is, after all, a considerable overlap between the view that the executive cannot deny the relevance of obligations it has itself incurred for the benefit of the citizen, and Lauterpacht's estoppel-type argument that the executive ought not to be permitted to be the beneficiaries of a rule the purpose of which was to prevent

---

[185] [1991] 1 AC 696 at 748C.
[186] Ibid. at 748D–F.

the citizen being disadvantaged, as opposed to empowered, by executive law-making.[187] This would have enabled them to translate their concerns about executive insouciance into some other administrative law doctrine with more teeth, for example by holding that unincorporated international treaties are a mandatory relevant consideration to be taken into account by executive and administrative decision-makers exercising broad discretionary powers, or that the scope of such powers must be construed so as to ensure they are exercised consistently with treaty obligations. In this way, provided courts recognise the limits of their interpretive obligation by following domestic law in cases of clear conflict, the *ultimate* sovereignty of Parliament is preserved, yet the more extravagant claims made in its name are rightly dispensed with.

In short, as this chapter has sought to show, there are better ways of securing more effective domestic protection for international human rights norms than by pressing into service a doctrine which is ill-fitted for the task and which in any event has only been used elsewhere precisely because of the very weakness of the protection it provides. Other methods, such as strictly construing statutes conferring broad discretions in light of international treaties, or by treating ratified but unincorporated treaties as mandatory relevant considerations in the exercise of administrative discretion,[188] have both a better chance of success in pragmatic terms, and will do less damage in the longer term to the development of a principled approach to judicial review. This is not to say of course that the material assembled by Lord Lester does not have a valuable role to play in the task. But it is suggested that it would be better deployed as further evidence of UK state practice, accepting the binding nature of the norms contained in those treaties, helping to reinforce the common law's recognition of the customary status of those norms, and thereby to strengthen the case for the recognition of a general interpretive obligation on domestic courts to give domestic law a meaning which achieves compliance with international obligations.

9. CONCLUSION

The question posed at the outset of this chapter was to what extent the emergence of a common law human rights jurisdiction had undermined the courts' ability to maintain their resistance to international human rights law having a role in public law. It was seen that, despite the apparent reassertion of public law orthodoxy, an embryonic doctrine of proportionality was beginning to manifest itself in the law of judicial review, in response to the growing pressures for administrative law to accommodate a fundamental rights dimension.

---

[187] See ch. 1 n. 119.

[188] Cf. Taggart, (above n. 134) at 54, who suggests that the decision may provide "a wobbly stepping stone to a position where unincorporated treaty obligations are treated as mandatory relevant considerations in appropriate circumstances".

The lesson to be derived from the chapter's survey of attempts to use human rights law under the various heads of review is that there are serious practical limits to any approach which simply seeks to graft human rights law and concepts onto unmodified concepts of English public law. For the most part those concepts are derived from a theoretical account of the relationship between the courts and the political branches which presupposes a minimal, deferential role for judges in the review of executive and administrative discretions. So even if the courts accept, as they now seem to have accepted in the immigration context, for example, that the European Convention on Human Rights is, in the language of the conventional grounds of review, a mandatory relevant consideration, that will avail applicants nothing so long as all that courts are prepared to require is that the decision-maker has "had regard to" or "considered" or "taken account of" the relevant provision of the Convention. So long as courts are satisfied with bare assertions that the ECHR has been taken into account, and hold back from requiring that the decision-maker's reasoning process be set out so as to demonstrate to the court's satisfaction that a conscientious effort has been made to decide whether any infringement is justified, English courts cannot be said to be truly exercising a human rights jursidiction. Similarly, so long as courts consider themselves to be reviewing only the approach of a decision-maker, rather than the substance of its decision, no amount of recognition of human rights as "background" to irrationality challenges will secure more effective protection for those rights.

The problem is one of legal culture, and in particular the predominant tendency of English judges to absorb any external influences into familiar habits of mind. On the whole, despite an increasing willingness to concede the relevance of international human rights law, and the ECHR in particular, the courts have been reluctant to modify their traditional approach to reviewing discretions, no matter how inappropriate that seems. The courts' preoccupation with the "approach" of the Secretary of State, as opposed to the substance of decisions, is a remnant of the old substance/procedure distinction which still shows remarkable vitality as a trusty prop for the legitimacy of the judicial review jurisdiction. So long as courts persist in exercising their review function by asking whether the Secretary of State has gone about his decision in the right way, courts are likely to defer to the Secretary of State's judgment wherever he can show that some sort of balancing exercise was carried out, without scrutinising the outcome of that balancing exercise for disproportionality as a proper human rights court would do.

It is for this reason that it is important not merely to see the relevance of the international human rights norms in terms of traditional administrative law concepts. In the brief Phase I, judges such as Reid and Scarman were not merely looking at administrative decisions to see whether the decision-maker had said that the ECHR had been taken into account. They were driven by their premise, the presumption of conformity with international obligations, to make a conscientious attempt to decide whether a particular interpretation of the scope of the power would involve a breach of the ECHR. Clearly it is not possible to interpret law so as to be in conformity with international obligations unless the court is also prepared to take a view as to what is and what is not required by the international obligation, an exercise which must involve a consideration of the jurisprudence interpreting the obligation where such jurisprudence exists. If the recent progress towards a more pervasive role for international human rights norms in public law is to make any difference to the outcomes of cases, it is therefore vital that each doctrinal development be properly understood as a particular manifestation of a more general acceptance of an interpretive obligation to construe domestic law consistently with international commitments.

7

The Reception of International Human Rights Law via *European Community Law*

1. INTRODUCTION

With characteristic prescience, Lord Scarman in his 1974 Hamlyn Lectures remarked casually "[i]t may be that since the passing of the European Communities Act 1972 the Convention already has, or will, without further enactment by the British Parliament, become part of English law."[1] His subsequent comment, however, that the ECHR could be made part of the municipal law of the UK "only by Act of Parliament (or, conceivably, by legislative action of the EEC)", suggests that Lord Scarman did not foresee the extent to which the infiltration of the ECHR into UK law as an incident of Community membership would be a product of judicial action by the ECJ rather than of legislative action by the Community's political institutions.[2] In the two decades since Lord Scarman's aside was uttered, developments in the case-law of the European Court of Justice and in the attitude of domestic courts to Community law[3] have combined to achieve what is in effect an indirect incorporation of the ECHR and other international human rights instruments into domestic law in those ever-widening subject-matter areas which are within Community competence.

This chapter will consider the implications of these developments for the domestic status of international human rights law, and the extent to which English judges have so far shown themselves aware of these implications in actual cases before domestic courts.[4] It will be suggested that there are two

---

[1] *English Law—The New Dimension* (London: Stevens, 1974) at 12–13.

[2] Ibid. at 14. To have anticipated the development would have required remarkable foresight, since, as will be seen below, the ECJ's fundamental rights jurisprudence was still very much in its infancy at the time of Lord Scarman's lectures.

[3] See ch. 3 above.

[4] The amount of writing on the specific question of the ECHR's status in the UK through Community law (as opposed to the more general question of its status in Community law) is still relatively small and mainly consists of A. Clapham, *Human Rights in the Private Sphere* (Oxford: Clarendon Press, 1993), at 33–9; Lord Browne-Wilkinson, "The Infiltration of a Bill of Rights" [1992] PL 397 at 399–402 and "The Impact of European Law on English Human Rights and Public Law" in Markesinis (ed.), *The Gradual Convergence* (Oxford: Clarendon Press, 1994) at 202–4; N. Grief, "The Domestic Impact of the European Convention on Human Rights as

separate reasons why the status of fundamental rights in European Community law is of interest to the UK practitioner concerned with the domestic status of such norms. First, the process by which the European Court of Justice has derived fundamental rights from the constitutional and legal traditions common to the member states provides an interesting precedent for the process on which English courts have now embarked, namely the "discovery" of the fundamental rights immanent in a constitutional order purporting to be founded on the "rule of law". Second, the fact that the ECJ has taken that course is itself a reason why English courts should also embark on that process, not, it will be argued, because of anything in the European Communities Act 1972 compelling such a move, but in recognition of the UK's progressive integration into an emerging European constitution.

2. THE STATUS OF FUNDAMENTAL RIGHTS IN EUROPEAN COMMUNITY LAW

The European Community has never acceded to the ECHR, nor do the EC's founding treaties contain any charter of fundamental rights and freedoms.[5] Like so many important features of the Community legal order, the role played by the ECHR and fundamental rights generally in Community law has been almost entirely judge-made and has come about in the incremental way typical of Court-led developments.[6] Originally the Court was resistant to challenges to Community measures based on fundamental rights arguments,

Mediated through Community Law" [1991] PL 555; J. McBride & L. Neville Brown, "The United Kingdom, the European Community and the European Convention on Human Rights" (1981) YEL 167; P.J. Duffy, "English Law and the European Convention on Human Rights" (1980) 29 ICLQ 585 at 614–15.

[5] Incorporation of the ECHR was proposed in the attempts to establish a European Political Community in the early 1950s, but these were abandoned: see Craig & de Búrca, *EC Law: Text, Cases and Materials* (Oxford: Clarendon Press, 1995) at 283–4. The present state of the debate as to whether the European Community should accede to the Convention is considered below.

[6] The literature on the role of fundamental rights generally in EC law is extensive. More recent writing on the role of human rights in the post-Maastricht European Union is considered below. For more comprehensive accounts of the earlier development of fundamental rights protection by the ECJ, see Craig & de Búrca, (above n. 5), ch. 7; G. de Búrca, "Fundamental Rights and the Reach of EC Law" (1993) 13 OJLS 283; A. Clapham, *Human Rights in the Private Sphere* (above n. 4), ch. 8 and "A Human Rights Policy for the European Community" [1990] YEL 309; J. Coppell & A. O'Neill, "The European Court of Justice: Taking Rights Seriously?" (1992) 12 LS 227; J.H.H. Weiler and N.J.S. Lockhart, "'Taking Rights Seriously' Seriously: The European Court and Its Fundamental Rights Jurisprudence" (1995) 32 CML Rev. 51 and 579 (a reply to Coppel & O'Neill); F.G. Jacobs, "The Protection of Human Rights in the Member States of the European Community: The Impact of the Case Law of the Court of Justice" in J. O'Reilly (ed.), *Human Rights and Constitutional Law* (Dublin: Round Hall Press, 1992), 243–50; D.R. Phelan, "Right to Life of the Unborn v Promotion of Trade in Services: the European Court of Justice and the Normative Shaping of the European Union" (1992) 55 MLR 670. For useful earlier analyses, see A. Drzemczewski, *European Human Rights Convention in Domestic Law: A Comparative Study* (Oxford: Clarendon Press, 1983), ch.9 ("The Domestic Application of the Convention and European Community Law"); S. Ghandi "Interaction Between the Protection of Fundamental Human Rights in the European Community and under the European Convention on Human Rights" [1982] *Legal Issues of European Integration* 1.

perceiving that the supremacy and uniformity of Community law was in danger of being undermined if Community measures could be invalidated for inconsistency with national constitutional norms. On the other hand, the supremacy and efficacy of Community law seemed equally threatened by the courts of Member States refusing to accord priority to Community law, because of their concern that national constitutional guarantees provided better protection than Community law. The Court's solution to this dilemma was to forge an autonomous Community law notion of fundamental rights as part of the general principles of law it recognised, and it was careful to root those rights in the "constitutional traditions common to the Member States." Thus in *Internationale Handelsgesellschaft*, the ECJ reiterated that supremacy of Community law required that the validity of Community measures could not be impugned for incompatibility with fundamental rights protected by national constitutions, before going on to declare that ". . . respect for fundamental rights forms an integral part of the general principles of Community law protected by the Court of Justice."[7]

From this first appearance of the language of fundamental rights in the reasoning of the ECJ, the Court has gradually expanded its role in the Community legal order. In *Nold*, for example, it expanded the sources of the rights to which it would have regard beyond the constitutional traditions of the Member States, saying "international treaties for the protection of human rights on which the Member States have collaborated or of which they are signatories, can supply guidelines which should be followed within the framework of Community law".[8] The progression was taken a step further in *Rutili* when the Court expressly mentioned the ECHR for the first time.[9] The limitations imposed by Community law measures[10] on the Member States' power to derogate from the Treaty right of free movement were said to be a specific manifestation of the more general principle enshrined in Articles 8–11 and Article 2 of Protocol 4 of the ECHR, that restrictions on those rights in the interests of national security or public safety are only permissible in so far as they are necessary for the protection of those interests in a democratic society. The reference, in other words, was merely by way of analogy at the level of general principle.

In these early cases, the Court was careful to make clear that it was not judicially incorporating the ECHR as a source of rights directly enforceable against the Community institutions, but that it was merely drawing inspiration or guidance from it in the development of an independent notion of fun-

---

[7] Case 11/70, *Internationale Handelsgesellschaft* v. *Einfuhr-und-Vorratstelle für Getreide und Futtermittel* [1970] ECR 1125, at 1134 para. 4. The development was presaged in Case 29/69, *Stauder* v. *City of Ulm* [1969] ECR 419, at para. 7, in which the Court interpreted a provision in a Community measure in such a way as not to prejudice "the fundamental human rights enshrined in the general principles of Community law and protected by the Court."

[8] Case 4/73, *Nold* v. *Commission* [1974] ECR 491, at para. 13.

[9] Case 36/75, *Rutili* v. *Minister for the Interior* [1975] ECR 1219, at para.32.

[10] Principally Council Directive 64/221/EEC, considered further below.

damental rights which was part of the Community's autonomous "general principles".[11] By appealing to international standards which had gained the acceptance of all the Member States, in the form of their signature to the ECHR, the Court was seeking to establish a legitimate basis for a fundamental rights jurisdiction of its own in order to head off the challenge to its supremacy from national constitutional courts, while at the same time avoiding the allegation that it was going beyond its authority in giving the ECHR direct effect against Community institutions. Clearly there are very close parallels between this early stage in the development of the ECJ's fundamental rights jurisdiction and the current phase of development of domestic law described in chapter 5. There it was seen that English courts are currently attempting to legitimate a home-grown fundamental rights jurisdiction by developing the common law in a variety of ways, such as rejuvenating the common law presumptions, scrutinising the exercise of administrative discretion more closely, and exercising judicial discretion with greater sensitivity to fundamental rights. They have called in aid the ECHR, and occasionally other instruments, when they assist in that process, but, just as the ECJ in these early cases was scrupulous to make clear that it was merely referring to the ECHR for guidance in establishing the general principles of Community law, so domestic courts have been equally anxious to point out that any use they may make of the ECHR is not as a source of rights as such, but as an "aid to interpretation".[12]

Although the ECJ began by accepting that measures of the Community institutions could be challenged before the Court on the ground that they infringed fundamental rights, including rights protected by the ECHR,[13] as the Court's case-law has developed, so it has become increasingly clear that the Court also considers Member States to be constrained by the ECHR when they act within the sphere of Community law. In a series of cases, the Court made clear that Member States must abide by the ECHR in their implementation of Community law. While this could be said to have been at least implicit in *Rutili* as early as 1975,[14] it has been made more explicit in cases

---

[11] See eg. the Opinion of Advocate General Trabucchi in Case 118/75, *Watson and Belmann* [1976] ECR 1185 at 1207.

[12] See Laws J. in particular for this determination to distinguish "incorporation" from interpretive "guidance": "Is the High Court the Guardian of Fundamental Constitutional Rights?" [1993] PL 59 at 61.

[13] For other examples of cases in which Community measures have been reviewed by the ECJ for their compatibility with the Convention, see Case 130/75, *Prais* v. *Council* [1976] ECR 1589; Case 136/79, *National Panasonic* v. *Commission* [1980] ECR 2033; Case 374/87, *Orkem* v. *Commission* [1989] ECR 3283; Joined Cases 46/87 and 227/88, *Hoechst AG* v. *Commission* [1989] ECR 2859; Case 44/79, *Hauer* v. *Land Rheinland-Pfalz* [1979] ECR 3727; Case C-331/88, *R* v. *Ministry of Agriculture, Fisheries and Food, ex p. Fédération Européenne de la Santé Animale* [1990] ECR I-4023.

[14] Case 36/75, [1975] ECR 1219. In Case 118/75, *Watson and Belmann* [1976] ECR 1185 at 1207 Advocate General Trabucchi thought that it followed from *Rutili* that the requirement of respect for fundamental rights applied even against Member State action within the sphere of application of Community law, but his reasoning was not taken up by the Court.

from the mid-1980s, including two in which UK delegated legislation implementing Community obligations has been found to be contrary to Community law when that law was interpreted in the light of the ECHR.[15]

Even more significantly, the Court has made the ECHR into an even greater constraint on Member State action by gradually extending the scope of what counts as "acting within the field of Community law". It has done this by gradually accepting the argument that Member States' action can be scrutinised for compliance with the ECHR when it is derogating from a Community law obligation, for example by invoking one of the derogations in the Treaty or, possibly, by relying on one of the Court-made exceptions by which it is permitted to justify a restriction on a Community requirement. This evolution in the Court's definition of the circumstances in which it will consider the compatibility of a national measure with the ECHR can be traced through three decisions in particular.

First, in *Cinéthèque*, the Court accepted that it was its duty to ensure observance of fundamental rights in the field of Community law, but appeared to reject the argument that a Member State was acting within the field of Community law when it adopted measures which, but for the existence of an exception in the Treaty or the Court's jurisprudence, would be in breach of a Community obligation.[16] Such a situation was said to fall within the jurisdiction of the national legislator, and therefore the Court had no power to examine the compatibility of the national law with the ECHR. Second, in *Demirel*, the Court described the limits on its power to scrutinise national measures for compatibility with general principles in slightly different terms.[17] Instead of saying that it had no such power in respect of national measures which fell "within the jurisdiction of the national legislator", the Court said that it had no power to examine the compatibility with the ECHR of national legislation "lying outside the scope of Community law". By this subtle change of wording, the Court appeared to entertain the possibility of reviewing national measures for compatibility with the ECHR even in areas of overlapping jurisdiction.[18] Third, the expansionist trend was taken a significant stage further in *ERT*, in which the Court held that a national derogating measure could only fall within a Treaty exception if it was compatible with the fundamental rights which, it was reiterated, form an integral part of the general

---

[15] Case 222/84, *Johnston* v. *Chief Constable of the RUC* [1986] ECR 1651 and Case 63/83, *R* v. *Kirk* [1984] ECR 2689. Other examples of Member State implementing action being reviewed for compatibility with the Convention are Case 249/86, *UNECTEF* v. *Heylens* [1987] ECR 4097; Case 249/86, *Commission* v. *Germany* [1989] ECR 1263; Case 5/88, *Wachauf* v. *Germany* [1989] ECR 2609.

[16] Joined Cases 60 & 61/84, *Cinéthèque* v. *Fédération Nationale des Cinémas Français* [1985] ECR 2605, at para. 26.

[17] Case 12/86, *Demirel* v. *Stadt Schwäbisch Gmund* [1987] ECR 3719, at para. 28.

[18] Coppel and O'Neill (above n. 6) at 235 first drew attention to this change of emphasis, which in their view "may . . . have revolutionised the impact of fundamental rights considerations on national administrative and legislative action."

principles of law and the observance of which the Court ensures.[19] By the beginning of the 1990s, then, the ECJ had clearly asserted a jurisdiction to review any national derogation from Community law for compatibility with fundamental rights, at least where the derogation relied on was based on an express exception provided for in the Treaty.[20]

For the Court to move in this way, from reviewing the Community institutions' observance of fundamental rights to reviewing acts of the Member States for observance of those rights, within a vaguely defined and ever-expanding "sphere of Community law", was a controversial development, not least because it obviously had the potential to increase significantly the domestic impact of the ECHR, particularly in those Member States such as the UK which have not legislatively incorporated the ECHR into domestic law. By this extension of the Court's fundamental rights jurisdiction, the ECJ had not only arrogated to itself a constitutional jurisdiction over the actions of Member States which was nowhere contemplated in the founding Treaties, but it had given the domestic courts in those states (indeed, *required* them to exercise) a jurisdiction to review national measures for conformity with the ECHR which they otherwise lacked, albeit one confined to the sphere of Community law.[21]

Despite the controversy surrounding the development, the Court's arrogation of a fundamental rights jurisdiction has been repeatedly affirmed by the political branches of the Community and by the Member States themselves. As early as 1977 the use to which the Court was already at that stage putting the ECHR was approved by the Parliament, Council and Commission, which issued a Joint Declaration on Fundamental Rights, stressing the "prime importance they attach to the protection of fundamental rights, as derived in particular from the constitutions of the Member States and the European Convention" and declaring that "[i]n the exercise of their powers and in pursuance of the aims of the European Communities they respect and will continue to respect these rights."[22] This at least provided some endorsement from

---

[19] Case C-260/89, *Elliniki Radiophonia Tilorassi AE* v. *Dimotiki Etairia Pliroforissis and Sotirios Kouvelas* [1991] ECR I-2925 at para. 43. For a proposal which would extend the Court's jurisdiction to review national measures for compliance with fundamental rights even further, see the Opinion of Advocate General Jacobs in Case C-168/91, *Konstantinidis* v. *Stadt Altensteig* [1993] ECR I-1191, at para. 46.

[20] When the derogation relied on is not expressly provided for in the Treaty but is a Court-made exception, as in *Cinéthèque* itself, it remains an open question whether the Court will hold that the derogating measure is outside the scope of Community law so that it has no power to examine the measure for compatibility with the Convention. The reasoning in *ERT*, however, that the Court should examine limitations on Community rights in the light of the Convention because the justification for such limitation is "provided for by Community law", seems wide enough to cover such a case.

[21] It is for precisely this reason that the UK Government has consistently opposed the Community's accession to the ECHR. In 1992 the Report of the House of Lords Select Committee on the European Communities, *Human Rights Re-examined* (3rd Report, HL Paper 10), was against Community accession: see HL Deb Vol. 540 cols. 1087–118 (26 November 1992). The Government's present stance is considered below.

[22] OJ 1977 C 103/1.

the political institutions of the legitimacy of the Court's practice of interpreting Community acts presuming that they were intended to be consistent with fundamental human rights, including those protected by the ECHR. Community law's recognition of fundamental rights was further restated in the preamble to the Single European Act, in which the Member States declared their determination

> "to work together to promote democracy on the basis of the fundamental rights recognised in the constitutions and laws of the Member States, in the Convention for the Protection of Human Rights and Fundamental Freedoms and the European Social Charter, notably freedom, equality and social justice."[23]

The Member States' acceptance of the ECJ's continued expansion of its fundamental rights jurisdiction, including even its more recent decisions which force the ECHR into the domestic legal sphere to an unprecedented degree, can arguably be inferred from certain provisions in the Treaty on European Union. In the Preamble to that Treaty, for example, the Member States confirmed "their attachment to the principles of liberty, democracy and respect for human rights and fundamental freedoms and of the rule of law."[24] Article F(2), however, provides perhaps the most explicit endorsement of the Court's use of the European Convention as a source of rights, using as it does the very language which the ECJ has used since its first assertion of such a jurisdiction. It provides:

> "The Union shall respect fundamental rights, as guaranteed by the European Convention for the Protection of Human Rights and Fundamental Freedoms . . . and as they result from the constitutional traditions common to the Member States, as general principles of Community law."

Article K.2(1) TEU also provides that various matters identified as matters of common interest for co-operation in the fields of justice and home affairs, including asylum and immigration policy, "shall be dealt with in compliance with the European Convention". However, Articles F(2) and K.2 were expressly made non-justiciable by Article L TEU, so as to preclude the ECJ from adjudicating on them, reflecting perhaps the reluctance of the Member States to countenance any firmer basis for the protection of fundamental rights in the Community's constitutional order.[25] Notwithstanding the gradual progress which has been made towards a more explicit recognition of a fundamental rights dimension to the constitution of the European Community and Union, the lack of a firmer foundation

---

[23] Single European Act 1986 (Cmnd. 9758). This reference by the Member States to the Social Charter as a source of fundamental rights is particularly noteworthy, since this instrument is hardly ever referred to by courts, including the ECJ.

[24] As will be seen in section 5 below, in *R* v. *Secretary of State for the Home Department, ex p. Adams* [1995] All ER (EC) 177, Steyn LJ attached considerable significance to this particular recital in the preamble.

[25] The non-justiciable status of TEU's human rights provisions has not, however, prevented the ECJ from referring to them, eg. in Opinion 2/94, considered below.

for such protection has continued to attract much criticism. Twomey, for example, has criticised the TEU's failure to deal in more detail with human rights issues, arguing that "the proponents of integration have underestimated the extent to which enumerated human rights form the constitutional bedrock of a legal order, be it national or transnational."[26] Neuwahl has similarly argued that the provisions of the TEU neither constitute nor provide the basis for a real step forward, in practical terms, in the protection of human rights, which is only likely to be achieved by Community accession to the ECHR.[27] More fundamentally still, Ward has criticised the Court's jurisprudence, and the recognition of human rights in the Treaties, as exemplifying the limited modernist conception of human rights derived from the ideology of economic liberalism on which the Community legal order has largely been built.[28]

Dissatisfaction with the post-Maastricht position ensured that interest in the Community's full accession to the ECHR did not diminish and in 1994 the Council sought the Opinion of the Court on the compatibility of accession with the EC Treaty. The European Court of Justice, in its Opinion, has now ruled that the Community cannot accede to the ECHR without Treaty amendment.[29] The Court reviewed the various ways in which respect for human rights is presently secured in the Community legal order, such as through the general principles of law, the observance of which the Court ensures, and the many references to and declarations of respect for fundamental rights in the Community Treaties and other documents, and it reiterated that respect for fundamental rights is a condition of the lawfulness of Community acts.[30] However, it concluded that accession to the ECHR would amount to such a modification of the system for the protection of human rights, with equally fundamental institutional implications for the Community and for the Member States, as to amount to a change "of constitutional significance", and therefore beyond the scope of Art. 235 of the EC Treaty. That provision was

---

[26] P. Twomey, "The European Union: Three Pillars without a Human Rights Foundation" in O'Keeffe and Twomey (eds.), *Legal Issues of the Maastricht Treaty* (Chichester: Wiley, 1994) at 121.

[27] N. A. Neuwahl, "The Treaty on European Union: A Step Forward in the Protection of Human Rights?" in N.A. Neuwahl and A Rosas (eds.), *The European Union and Human Rights* (The Hague: Martinus Nijhoff, 1995), ch. 1.

[28] I. Ward, *The Margins of European Law* (London: Macmillan, 1996), ch. 8. Ward's "reconstructive alternative" is to urge the Community and Union to embrace a rather elusive postmodern conception of human rights which aims to prevent the exclusion of the marginalised "other". For other arguments advocating both a more inclusive catalogue of rights and a better articulated foundation for the protection of such rights in the Community legal order, see eg. G. de Búrca, "The Language of Rights and European Integration" in J. Shaw and G. More (eds.), *New Legal Dynamics of European Integration* (Oxford: Oxford University Press, 1995); S. O'Leary, "Aspects of the Relationship between Community Law and National Law" in Neuwahl & Rosas (eds.), (above n. 27), ch. 2; J.H.H. Weiler, "Fundamental Rights and Fundamental Boundaries: On Standards and Values in the Protection of Human Rights", ibid., ch. 3.

[29] Opinion 2/94, March 28 1996. See S. O'Leary, "Accession by the European Community to the European Convention on Human Rights—The Opinion of the ECJ" [1996] EHRLR 362.

[30] Ibid. at para. 34.

said to be designed to fill the gap where powers needed to be implied to enable the Community to pursue its Treaty objectives, but the very nature of the Community meant that it could not provide a legal basis for widening the scope of Community powers beyond those conferred upon it by the Treaties.

As a result of the ECJ's Opinion, the question of whether to amend the Treaty to enable accession is under discussion during the 1996/97 Inter-governmental Conference ("the IGC"), as is the suggestion that the Community might adopt its own charter of rights. Predictably, the UK Government's stance at the IGC is one of total opposition to any strengthening of the protection for fundamental rights in the European Union, on the ground that the European Union is "not the right context for the protection of fundamental human rights".[31] Given that opposition, it seems unlikely that any measures to improve the protection of fundamental rights in the European Union will emerge from the IGC, and that, in the absence of action at the political level, responsibility for the continued evolution of the status of fundamental rights in Community law will continue to rest with the ECJ.

3. THE IMPLICATIONS FOR THE DOMESTIC STATUS OF INTERNATIONAL HUMAN RIGHTS LAW

As a result of these developments in the case-law of the ECJ, it is now clear beyond doubt that, as a matter of Community law, national courts must not only interpret provisions of Community law in the light of international human rights agreements, and in particular the ECHR, but must also take such instruments into account when construing domestic primary or delegated legislation, or reviewing administrative action, which is within the scope of Community law in the sense that it is implementing Community obligations or derogating from them. Moreover, not only must domestic courts take international human rights agreements into account in such cases, but they must refuse to apply any such implementing or derogating provision which cannot be interpreted consistently with them, or refuse to uphold any such administrative action which is inconsistent with them. For a domestic court to apply such a provision or uphold such action would be a breach of Community law because it would be inconsistent with the general principles of Community law, of which the rights protected by international human rights treaties form an integral part.

---

[31] *A Partnership of Nations: The British Approach to the European Union Intergovernmental Conference 1996* (Cmnd. 3181, 1996), paras. 54–8. Behind the rather transparent concerns about duplication and confusion of jurisdictions (para. 56), lies the more fundamental concern articulated at para. 58: "The EU . . . is not a state and should take care not to develop ideas which feed people's fear that it has a vocation to become one." The implicit identification of human rights protection with citizenship of sovereign nation-states is hard to reconcile with the UK Government's equally determined resistance to the incorporation into English law of the ECHR.

In view of the unincorporated status of the ECHR and other instruments in UK domestic law, and in particular the longstanding judicial reluctance to countenance any role for international human rights law in judicial review, the constitutional implications of this development for the UK are clearly of considerable significance. Even according to the conventional account, that Community law owes its status in domestic law entirely to the European Communities Act 1972, the developments in the case-law of the ECJ result in at least a degree of incorporation of otherwise unincorporated international treaties, because UK courts are required by s.3(1) ECA to determine any question as to the meaning, effect or validity of a Community law provision, on which they decide not to make an Article 177 reference, "in accordance with the principles laid down by and any relevant decision of the European Court". This traditional and essentially sovereigntist explanation of the reception of international human rights law into domestic law *via* EC law was the one preferred by the Lord Chief Justice, Lord Bingham, in his maiden speech in the House of Lords during a recent debate on the Constitution:

> ". . . laws derived from the Convention are incorporated as part of the law of the Community. That of course is a law which the courts in this country must apply since we are bound by Act of Parliament to do so."[32]

This book prefers a rather different explanation of why developments in the fundamental rights jurisprudence of the ECJ have profound significance for the domestic status of international human rights norms in the UK. It will be recalled from chapters 2 and 3 that English courts have recently accepted the full implications of the Community law doctrines of supremacy, direct effect and the effective protection of Community law rights, so that domestic legislation will now be disapplied where it cannot be interpreted consistently with directly effective Community law and will be interpreted consistently with non-directly effective directives in so far as it is possible to do so. Those developments, it was argued, had gone far beyond anything which could plausibly be justified by reference to the ECA 1972 or the sovereignty of Parliament, and were better explained in terms of an evolution in the common law principle of construction that domestic law is to be interpreted in the light of international obligations. The same explanation, it will be argued, justifies the acceptance by English courts of their obligation, as a matter of Community law, to take international human rights law into account when considering the compatibility of domestic measures with Community law.[33]

On either view, the combined effect of recent developments in the case-law of the ECJ and in the status accorded to Community law by domestic courts is that international human rights instruments such as the ECHR have attained a new status in domestic law. The steadily growing importance of

---

[32] HL Deb, Vol. 573 cols. 1466–7 (3 July 1996).

[33] The question of the precise basis on which international human rights law has been received *via* Community law is returned to in sections 5 and 6 below.

fundamental rights, and in particular the ECHR, in both the jurisprudence and constitutional documents of the Community not only sidesteps the *Brind* prohibition on the use of the ECHR as a ground of review of executive or administrative rule-making power or other discretion, but goes even further by effectively conferring on courts a jurisdiction to review even primary legislation for conformity with basic human rights.[34] The only constraint is that the national measure falls within the scope of application of Community law.

Just how big is the area of domestic law which falls within the sphere of application of Community law for this purpose cannot be said with any certainty. As was indicated above, the ECJ has been steadily expanding the sphere in which national courts are expected to review national measures for compatibility with fundamental rights, so that national measures derogating from as well as implementing Community obligations are now clearly within the field of Community law.[35] The areas of national life now subject to regulation by Community law have steadily increased, now extending well beyond areas of pure economic activity, and are likely to continue to do so as European integration proceeds with each round of Treaty amendment. As a result, the extent to which domestic law is permeated by international human rights law via Community law is only likely to increase. As Lord Browne-Wilkinson observes, "the closer our links with Europe, the nearer we will get to the protection of a full Bill of Rights."[36]

Surprisingly, despite the undoubted potential significance of the development of a human rights jurisdiction by the ECJ for the domestic law of the UK, and in particular for the constitutional foundations of its public law, its practical impact has so far been remarkably slight.[37] Ironically, one of the most extensive considerations given by an English court to the ECJ's fundamental rights jurisprudence occurred in a case to which there was manifestly no Community law dimension. In *Jones* v. *Miah*, landlords appealed against an award of damages for the tort of unlawful eviction under the Housing Act

---

[34] Lord Browne-Wilkinson, "The Infiltration of a Bill of Rights" [1992] PL 397 at 401, slightly overstates the case when he says that "in those areas affected by the EEC Treaties, the ECHR is already indirectly incorporated into English domestic law [and] . . . is directly enforceable in our courts". As was seen above, the ECJ itself has been careful to avoid the language of incorporation and enforceability when developing the role of international human rights treaties as part of Community law's general principles, preferring to use such instruments as a strong interpretive guide to the meaning of Community law.

[35] Less clear, however, is whether national measures which neither implement nor derogate but merely overlap with Community law in their regulation of a particular subject-matter area are within the sphere of application of Community law for the purposes of ensuring compatibility with fundamental rights.

[36] Above n. 34 at 402. Lord Browne-Wilkinson made the observation to explain the likely future expansion of the area in which the ECHR is relevant through Community law, but, as should by now be apparent from this book's central argument, his comment is of much wider significance.

[37] As will be seen below, the important decision in *ERT* appears to have been cited in only one English case, *R* v. *Secretary of State for the Home Department, ex p. McQuillan* [1995] 4 All ER 400.

1988, in respect of an eviction which had taken place before the Act had received the royal assent.[38] The relevant statutory provisions providing for the award of damages for unlawful eviction were expressed to apply to evictions which had taken place before the passage of the Act. The landlords argued that the relevant legislative provisions imposed penal consequences with retrospective effect which was alleged to be contrary to EC law and invalid, on the ground that the ECJ had adopted the ECHR, to which all Member States of the Community were party, and in particular Article 7, as part of the common law of the Community which was binding on all Member States.[39]

Dillon LJ noted that it had been held many times that international human rights treaties of which the Member States are signatories, such as the ECHR, can supply guidelines which should be followed within the framework of Community law, and he cited *Nold*, *Hauer* and *Kirk* as specific examples. Particular reliance had been placed on *Kirk* by the landlords, since in it the ECJ had treated Article 7 as applying to "penal provisions" rather than the narrower category of criminal provisions, and had also explicitly said that the principle enshrined in Article 7 takes its place among the general principles of law whose observance is ensured by the European Court. However, Dillon LJ held that he could not read those comments in *Kirk*

"as legislating, in the absence of any Act of Parliament, to make the provisions of the European Convention, and Article 7 in particular, part of the domestic law of England, directly enforceable in the English courts even in a case which has no EEC element."[40]

Although this statement is not without ambiguity, it could be inferred from its closing words, *"even in a case which has no EEC element"*, that Dillon LJ fully accepted that the consequence of the ECJ case-law he had cited was that where there *is* an EEC element in a case, the ECHR is directly enforceable in English courts, and that it is only where the context is entirely one of domestic law, as it was in *Jones* itself, that the *Brind* test of textual ambiguity must be satisfied before the ECHR has any relevance at all. Therefore, although in the case itself the ECHR was irrelevant because the issue was one of domestic English law and not of European law, Dillon LJ's comments may provide some *obiter* recognition of the direct enforceability of the ECHR in English courts, even without any Act of Parliament, in a case which has an EC element.

An equally unsuccessful attempt to rely on international human rights law through Community law was made in *Stedman* v. *Hogg Robinson Travel*. A shopworker who had been dismissed for refusing to work on Sundays and who could not meet the statutory requirement of two years' continuous employment applicable to a claim for unfair dismissal,[41] sought to have the

---

[38] [1992] 33 EG 59.
[39] Ibid. at 62 col.1.
[40] Ibid. at 62 col.2.
[41] Employment Protection (Consolidation) Act 1978, s.64(1)(a).

statutory qualification period disapplied as being contrary to Community law.[42] Her argument was essentially that Sunday working was a matter which fell within the scope of Community law and that, since Community law endowed her with certain rights with regard to working on a Sunday, and any national regulation of Sunday working must respect those rights, national courts were under a Community law obligation to disapply any jurisdictional provisions such as the statutory qualification period which prevented the effective protection of those rights. Amongst a number of provisions from international agreements in which the applicant sought to ground her right not to work on a Sunday, she invoked Articles 8 and 9 of the ECHR, guaranteeing respectively the right to privacy and family life and freedom of religion.

The EAT dismissed the argument, being unable to find anywhere, whether in the Treaty, secondary legislation, the decisions of the ECJ, the ECHR or any of the other international human rights agreements referred to, any recognition of a right not to work on a Sunday, either as a Community right or as a fundamental right relevant to the interpretation of Community rights. Dismissal for refusal to work on a Sunday simply was not a matter within the scope of Community law, and the domestic provision restricting industrial tribunals' unfair dismissal jurisdiction to claims brought by applicants with two years' continuous employment therefore applied to bar the shopworker's claim.

Jones v. *Miah* and *Stedman* serve as useful reminders that arguments relying on international human rights law through Community law can only be made where the relevant national measure falls within the scope of application of Community law.[43] Within that area, commentators have generally expected that the greatest impact is likely to be felt in the judicial review of implementing measures, particularly of delegated legislation adopted under s.2(2) ECA 1972.[44] In fact, it transpires from a survey of the cases to date that the question of the domestic status of human rights law through Community law has mainly arisen in cases concerning national derogations from Community law rights.

---

[42] Unreported decision of EAT of 23 May 1994 (available on LEXIS).

[43] For another speculative attempt to rely on the ECHR through Community law, see *Sanders* v. *Chichester*, *The Times*, 2 December 1994, in which the unsuccessful Liberal Democrat candidate in the European elections challenged the decision of the Returning Officer to register a "Literal Democrat" candidate, arguing, *inter alia*, that Article 3 of the First Protocol to the ECHR, providing for free elections "under conditions which will ensure the free expression of the opinion of the people in the choice of the legislature", should have been taken into account by the Returning Officer when making his decision whether or not to register the candidate. The court did not take up the argument.

[44] See eg. Grief, (above n. 4) at 566–7.

4. HUMAN RIGHTS LAW AND NATIONAL DEROGATIONS FROM RIGHTS
OF FREE MOVEMENT

(a) National Measures Derogating from Free Movement of Goods

In what appears to be the earliest English case to raise the question of the interrelationship between a domestic statutory provision, Community law and the ECHR, *Allgemeine Gold-und Silberscheideanstalt* v. *Customs and Excise Commissioners*, the English courts took a predictably narrow approach to the role of the ECHR in domestic law *via* Community law.[45] A German firm, which had been fraudulently induced to part with 1500 Krugerrand, sued for the return of the gold coins, which had remained the firm's property at the time when they were seized by the English Customs and Excise Commissioners after being found concealed in the spare tyre of a car entering the UK. Whether the firm was entitled to the return of their confiscated property turned on whether the coins were liable to forfeiture under a statutory provision in an Act of 1952 which provided in broad terms that imported goods were liable to forfeiture where they were concealed in a manner which appeared to be intended to deceive a customs officer.[46] Clearly inspired by the recent appearance of the language of fundamental rights protection in the case-law of the ECJ, in cases such as *Handelsgesellschaft*, *Nold* and *Rutili*, the firm argued that the provision of domestic law providing for liability to forfeiture was inconsistent with the Treaty of Rome, and sought an Article 177 reference to ask the ECJ whether the free movement of goods provisions of the Treaty imposed on Member States an obligation not to confiscate the property of a Community national without compensation. No specific Article of the Treaty was relied upon as having this effect, rather the argument was that all matters concerning the free movement of goods between Member States were governed by the relevant provisions of the EC Treaty, into which there had to be read an implied guarantee for the respect of fundamental human rights.[47]

At first instance, Donaldson J. declared himself satisfied that the rights enshrined in the ECHR were relevant to a consideration of the rights and duties of the Community institutions, and that they may be part of the background against which the express Treaty provisions had to be interpreted.[48] Drzemczewski sees in these comments the possibility of an implicit acceptance

---

[45] [1978] 2 CMLR 292. See Clapham, (above n. 4) at 35–7; Drzemczewski, (above n. 6) at 237–9.

[46] Section 44(f) Customs and Excise Act 1952.

[47] [1978] 2 CMLR 292 at 294.

[48] Ibid. at 294–5. However, Donaldson J. dismissed an argument that Advocate General Trabucchi's comments in *Watson and Belmann*, above n. 14, supported the view that the Treaty contains implied Articles guaranteeing fundamental human rights, saying that those observations had to be considered in the context of an argument about the meaning of specific provisions of the Treaty.

by Donaldson J. that the ECHR's substantive norms are an integral part of EC law which domestic courts are obliged to consider in situations where specific Treaty provisions need elucidation.[49] However, the case may be of even more significance for the breadth of Donaldson J.'s reasons for refusing to make a reference to the ECJ, for they offer a glimpse of a deep-seated cultural resistance to any attempt to use Community law as the vehicle for making the ECHR relevant to the interpretation of a domestic statute.

The explanation which Donaldson J. gave for finding the firm's fundamental rights submission not arguable, and therefore not an appropriate matter to refer to the ECJ, was in sweeping terms, and makes it hard to imagine any situation in which the ECHR, *via* Community law, could ever be of relevance to the interpretation of domestic law. He thought it a good question, for example, why so many distinguished people were wasting so much time debating the need for a new Bill of Rights incorporating the provisions of the ECHR if the UK already had one in the Treaty of Rome and the relevant British legislation giving effect to that Treaty.[50] He accepted the submission that there were no implied Articles protecting fundamental rights in the Treaty, and that the "clear" domestic provision was therefore quite unaffected by the EC Treaty. Any complaint that the domestic provision was in breach of the ECHR, he said, should be pursued in Strasbourg, not the domestic courts.[51]

The decision on appeal in the same case serves as a useful reminder that such a thoroughgoing dualist response to the domestic relevance of the ECHR through Community law should have come as no surprise at this stage in the development of the domestic courts' jurisprudence on the general question of the domestic status of the ECHR. Before the Court of Appeal, the firm abandoned its argument based on the relevance of the ECHR through Community law, and instead mainly sought to make it relevant by invoking the *Salomon* presumption as part of a more general statutory interpretation argument.[52] It argued that when Parliament enacted the forfeiture provision it must be presumed not to have intended to breach international law principles, including the well-settled principle enshrined in Article 1 of the First Protocol, that the property of an alien will not be confiscated without proper compensation.[53]

That argument was unanimously rejected by the Court of Appeal, in terms which clearly resonate with Donaldson J.'s response to the attempt to introduce fundamental rights into the interpretation of the provision via Community law in the court below. Bridge LJ, for example, said

[49] Above n. 6 at 239.
[50] [1978] 2 CMLR 292, at 295.
[51] See, to similar effect, the Scottish case of *Surjit Kaur* v. *Lord Advocate* [1980] 3 CMLR 79.
[52] [1980] QB 390.
[53] For the persistence of judicial resistance to such arguments in this context, see *Customs and Excise Commissioners* v. *Air Canada* [1991] 2 QB 446, where a similar argument about the construction of forfeiture provisions was rejected by the Court of Appeal in a case without a Community law dimension.

"if I were satisfied, which I am not, that there were such a principle of international law [that private property was not to be confiscated without compensation] . . . I should still be wholly unconvinced that it would be open to us to write into the Customs and Excise Act 1952 the extensive amendments which it would be necessary to introduce in order to give effect to that principle".[54]

Sir David Cairns took an equally restrictive view of the room for interpretive flexibility in the exercise of statutory interpretation. He could not see how it was possible "so to construe the Act as to exclude from the forfeiture provision" goods belonging to an alien innocent of any complicity in the smuggling.[55]

Were facts similar to the *Allgemeine* case to arise again today, a domestic court would now be obliged to take a quite different approach to the arguments raised by the plaintiff firm. If the smuggled goods were articles which counted as "goods" for the purposes of Article 30,[56] the domestic forfeiture provision would, after the decision in *ERT*, be within the scope of Community law as a derogation made under Article 36 and the domestic court would be obliged to review the derogation for compatibility with the right not to have property confiscated without compensation, as protected by the ECHR.[57] The court would therefore be required to interpret the forfeiture provision in the light of Article 1 of the First Protocol, and, if it found forfeiture without compensation to be a breach of that right[58] and the domestic provision incapable of being interpreted so as to admit an exception, it would be required as a matter of Community law to refuse to apply the domestic statutory provision. That such a consequence might flow from EC membership was clearly beyond the wildest imagination of the judges who decided the original *Allgemeine* case, all of whom, unlike Lord Scarman, had not yet awoken to the implications of the "new dimension" to English law, and were therefore still receptive to the sovereigntist arguments of the Customs Commissioners, invoking the judicial obligation to obey the "unambiguous" provisions of a municipal Act.

Surprisingly, in view of the developments taking place at this time in the fundamental rights jurisprudence of the ECJ, it seems to have been almost a full decade after *Allgemeine* before an argument seeking to rely on the ECHR

---

[54] [1980] QB 390 at 406E.

[55] Ibid. at 407B–C. The odd judge out was Lord Denning MR, ibid. at 403G–404B, who, having observed that the ECHR was not part of English law, characteristically went on to consider the argument on its merits, holding that, in view of the broad exceptions in Article 1 of the First Protocol, there was nothing in the ECHR that impaired a state's right to forfeit property which had been imported in breach of its custom laws.

[56] In an earlier reference made in the course of the criminal proceedings against the smugglers, Case 7/78, *R* v. *Johnson* [1978] ECR 2247, the ECJ had held that the coins were not "goods" for the purposes of Article 30.

[57] See eg. Case C-62/90, *Commission* v. *Germany* [1992] ECR I-2575, [1992] 2 CMLR 549.

[58] In fact, in a subsequent application to Strasbourg, the Commission found a violation of Article 1 of the First Protocol, but the Court found no violation: *Allgemeine Gold und Silberscheideanstalt* v. *UK* (1986) 9 EHRR 1.

via Community law was again advanced before an English court, in *AG* v. *Observer Ltd.*[59] Following the grant of the interlocutory injunctions against the newspapers in the *Spycatcher* litigation,[60] Derbyshire County Council applied to court to have determined the question whether the council, in its capacity as library authority for the county, could lawfully buy copies of *Spycatcher* from any Member State of the European Community, import them into the jurisdiction and make them available to members of the public through its public libraries. The council relied on the guarantee of free movement of goods in Article 30 of the EC Treaty, arguing that it was to be interpreted as incorporating the rights conferred by the ECHR, and that the Treaty should therefore be construed taking into account, in particular, Article 10.[61]

Knox J. held that this argument was prevented from succeeding by the fact that Article 10 had already been taken into account by Lord Templeman when the House of Lords in *Spycatcher* decided to continue the interlocutory injunctions until trial, and that the court was bound by his conclusion that the interference with freedom of expression which the injunctions constituted was "necessary" within the meaning of Article 10(2).[62] The significant feature of his judgment, however, is that he came to this conclusion on the assumption that the council's submission that Article 10 of the ECHR was to be taken into consideration was right. Here, then, would appear to be at least an implicit acceptance by an English court that Member State derogations from Community obligations must be considered by national courts in the light of the ECHR, even before the *ERT* case had made this explicit in the ECJ's own case-law.[63]

However, it may not be possible to draw such a strong conclusion from the case, for two reasons. First, both the form in which the argument was made and the court's response to it indicate a lack of familiarity with the ECJ's case-law on fundamental rights and the status of the ECHR, none of which was cited either by the court or, it seems, in argument. In *Allgemeine*, it will be recalled, it was argued that the ECHR was relevant because there had to be read into the Treaty an implied guarantee of the rights protected by the ECHR. In the *Observer* case, the argument seems to have been put in terms

---

[59] [1988] 1 All ER 385. In the intervening decade, the question of the ECHR's status in Community law appears to have arisen only once before an English court, when in *Ostreicher* v. *Secretary of State for the Environment* [1978] 1 All ER 591 one of the decisions of the ECJ in which the ECHR was used as a constraint on the Community institutions, Case 130/75, *Prais* v. *Council* [1976] ECR 1589, was cited by the court. However, this was purely because, as a case concerning an inability to keep an appointment for religious reasons, it was factually very similar to the case at hand, which, as a challenge to the validity of a compulsory purchase order, lacked any EC dimension.

[60] See Ch. 3.

[61] [1988] 1 All ER 385 at 398c–d.

[62] Ibid. at 398e–g.

[63] As in *ERT* itself (above n. 19), the case concerned a derogation that was likely to be justified under express treaty provision: as a derogation from the Community obligation to ensure the free movement of goods, it was likely to be justified in terms of Article 36.

of the EC Treaty "incorporating" the ECHR. Neither of these reflect the nature of the development which had been taking place in the ECJ's case-law. It will be recalled that the ECJ had been careful to make clear that the effect of its decisions in which reference had been made to the ECHR was not to incorporate it into Community law as such, but rather to draw analogies, at the level of general principles, between the rules of Community law and those of the ECHR, and to use the ECHR as a guideline rather than a binding source of law giving rise to directly enforceable rights.[64] As Knox J. noted, the matter had not been fully argued, and he merely commented that there may be some guidance to be derived from decisions of the ECJ in relation to permissible derogations under Article 36.

Second, the fact that the compatibility of the injunctions with Article 10 of the ECHR had already been considered by the House of Lords in the *Spycatcher* litigation itself meant that for the court to hold that it was right to take the ECHR into consideration did not appear to be a particularly revolutionary step.[65] These factors make it unlikely that Knox J. thought that by making the assumption he did he was accepting as a general proposition that national courts must always scrutinise any national derogation from a Community obligation for compatibility with the ECHR.

In the more recent decision of *R* v. *Uxbridge Justices, ex p. Webb*, the Court of Appeal did, briefly, consider an ECHR argument on its merits in a matter which was clearly within the scope of Community law provisions on free movement of goods, but it did not articulate the basis on which the ECHR was directly relevant to its decision.[66] As in *Allgemeine*, the case concerned a challenge to forfeiture provisions in the customs legislation. Customs had seized sexually explicit videos from the director of the National Campaign for the Reform of the Obscene Publications Acts on his return to the UK from the Netherlands. Having failed in proceedings contesting the material's liability to forfeiture under the customs legislation providing for forfeiture of obscene imported articles, he sought judicial review to compel the magistrates to state a case for the opinion of the High Court on their liability to forfeiture.

The applicant, who appeared in person, relied on both Article 30 of the EC Treaty and Article 10 of the ECHR, although he does not appear to have

---

[64] See eg. Opinion of Advocate General Trabucchi in *Watson and Belmann* [1976] ECR 1185 at 1207.

[65] Knox J.'s view that he was bound by the decision of the House of Lords in *Spycatcher No.1*, that the injunctions were "necessary", is questionable, however. He was required to decide, not whether restraining newspapers from publishing extracts from *Spycatcher* was necessary in a democratic society, but the quite different issue of whether the interlocutory injunctions covered a library's import of books from a Member State, which required a new inquiry in terms of Article 10(2). The failure to draw this distinction exemplifies the reluctance of English judges to carry out a meaningful proportionality test and their tendency to conclude that an infringement is justified as soon as it can be shown to serve one of the public interests articulated in Article 10(2).

[66] Unreported decision of the Divisional Court, 9 June 1993 (available on LEXIS).

argued explicitly that the court was obliged as a matter of Community law to scrutinise the forfeiture provisions for compatibility with the right to freedom of expression contained in the ECHR. The Divisional Court dealt with these arguments consecutively but entirely separately, holding, first, that the provisions of the customs legislation were within the exceptions contained in Article 36 of the Treaty,[67] and, second, that those provisions did not contravene Article 10 of the ECHR, because they were within the scope of the exceptions contained in Article 10(2). No explicit connection was made, however, between the court's consideration of Article 36 of the Treaty and of Article 10 of the ECHR, and the conclusion that the provisions were in conformity with Article 10 was more a matter of assertion than the product of any genuine scrutiny. This suggests that there may have been little improvement in judicial awareness of developments in the ECJ since the decision in *Allgemeine*.

(b) National Measures Derogating from Free Movement of Persons

In more recent years, questions of the interrelationship of domestic law, the ECHR and Community law have arisen more frequently in the context of national measures derogating from Community law rights to the free movement of persons within the territory of the Member States. The most fertile sources of litigation raising this issue have been deportation and exclusion orders, which raise questions as to the scope of the public policy and security derogations respectively.[68]

English courts' relative unfamiliarity with such questions is illustrated by the decision of the Court of Appeal in *Cilloni* which, like *Rutili*, concerned the guarantee of freedom of movement for workers in Article 48 and the directive on the exceptions to the free movement of workers, Council Directive 64/221/EEC.[69] An EC national challenging the IAT's decision to uphold the deportation order made against him by the Home Secretary, alleged that it was in breach of Article 3 of the ECHR, because it would be degrading treatment or punishment to deport him when he was responding well to drug rehabilitation treatment. The Court of Appeal dismissed this argument on the

---

[67] Glidewell LJ relied on *R* v. *Bow Street Metropolitan Stipendiary Magistrate, ex p. Noncyp Ltd.* [1990] 1 QB 123, in which the Court of Appeal held that the prohibition on the importation of obscene articles contained in the customs legislation was permitted by Article 36 of the EC Treaty. No mention was made of the ECHR in that case (although it did predate the ECJ's decision in *ERT*).

[68] On derogations from rights of free movement generally, see Craig & de Búrca, (above n. 4), ch.17. On derogations on grounds of public policy, see Hall, "The European Convention on Human Rights and Public Policy Exceptions to the Free Movement of Workers under the EEC Treaty" [1991] EL Rev 466.

[69] *R* v. *Immigration Appeal Tribunal, ex p. Cilloni*, unreported decision of the Court of Appeal of 8th November 1991 (available on LEXIS).

basis that the decision could not be made to fall within any interpretation which could be made of that Article.

The significant feature of the judgment is that the court considered the ECHR argument on its merits, without any discussion of whether such direct reliance on the provisions of the ECHR was legitimate. Although the court was right to do so, since *Rutili* makes clear that in such a case the national court must ensure that the public policy derogation is consistent with the ECHR, the Court of Appeal skipped that stage in the reasoning, and in fact appears to have addressed the argument on the basis that the ECHR was a "community law provision."[70] No mention was made of *Rutili* in the judgment. The case therefore represented something of a missed opportunity for an English court to make clear the basis on which it considers the ECHR to be relevant to a domestic court through Community law. Since the case was a renewed application for leave to apply for judicial review, however, it is perhaps not surprising that the opportunity was not taken.

In *Marchon* an attempt was made to persuade an English court that it was now obliged under Community law to scrutinise a derogation from the Community right of free movement for its compatibility with the affected individual's fundamental rights, including rights under the ECHR.[71] The case concerned a challenge to a deportation order against an EC national, a consultant psychiatrist, who had been convicted of importing heroin and sentenced to a long custodial sentence. No recommendation of deportation had been made by the court, but the Secretary of State made a deportation order in the exercise of his statutory power to deport any person whose continued presence in the country he deemed not to be conducive to the public good.[72] Under the relevant EC directive, as interpreted by the ECJ, the public policy ground of derogation from the Community law right of freedom of movement could only be invoked to justify the deportation of an EC national where there was a propensity to re-offend or, alternatively and exceptionally, where the serious nature of the offence was such as to constitute a present threat to public policy.[73] The Secretary of State made no allegation concerning propensity to re-offend, but relied solely on the nature of the applicant's past conduct as constituting a present threat to public policy. The deportation order was upheld by the Immigration Appeal Tribunal.

The applicant argued that, in the light of the case-law of the ECJ,[74] both the Secretary of State and the IAT were required to carry out, in addition to the balancing exercise required by the relevant directives and the Immigration Rules, a further balancing exercise similar to that required under Articles 8–11

---

[70] The ECHR was also referred to at one point in the judgment as "a statute of European Community law".

[71] *R v. Immigration Appeal Tribunal, ex p. Marchon* [1993] Imm AR 98.

[72] Immigration Act 1971 s.3(5)(b).

[73] Council Directive 64/221/EEC, Articles 3.1 and 3.2, as interpreted by the ECJ in Case 30/77, *R v. Bouchereau* [1977] ECR 1999.

[74] Including *Rutili* (above n. 9).

of the ECHR, to determine whether deportation of the applicant was "necessary in a democratic society".[75] The applicant was not therefore relying
expressly on a particular ECHR right in an attempt to limit the scope of the
derogation, but rather was indirectly invoking developments in the ECJ's fundamental rights case-law by analogy in the hope of achieving a stricter interpretation of the public policy derogation.

Henry J. rejected the argument, on the basis that a second balancing exercise of the sort advocated, assessing the proportionality of the threat to public policy in relation to the impact on the applicant's fundamental rights, was
not required by EC law. In his view, all that was required was the balancing
involved in the application of the *Bouchereau* test and there was no need to
over-complicate that question by grafting on an ECHR-style test of necessity
when scrutinising a derogation for justification on grounds of public policy.[76]
The applicant's argument could have raised the *ERT* point more directly had
he argued that the application of the public policy derogation to his case must
be construed in the light of a specific ECHR right, for example Article 8's protection for family life. However, the tenor of the court's response suggests
that, even had he done so, English judicial hostility to the very notion of proportionality would still have led the court to confine itself to ensuring that the
Secretary of State and tribunal had applied the test required by *Bouchereau.*

Signs of continuing judicial resistance to recognising that the ECHR has a
role in domestic law through Community law were also evident in *Tejinder
Singh,* in which an illegal entrant of Indian nationality who had married a
British citizen whilst awaiting the determination of his claim to political asylum sought judicial review of the Secretary of State's decision to refuse him
indefinite leave to remain on the basis of his marriage.[77] The applicant, who
clearly sought a ruling that the Secretary of State should have had regard to
the marriage, argued that a reference should be made to the ECJ for interpretation by that court of the application to Community law, and hence to
UK domestic law, of Article 8 of the ECHR.[78] The argument had no prospect
of success as there was clearly no Community law element on the facts of the
case, but some comments of the court made *obiter* in dismissing the application suggest that the court would have been reluctant to recognise any role
for the ECHR even if it had been clearly within the scope of Community law.

Auld J. said that, even supposing that the applicant could, by way of a reference, properly invite the ECJ to consider the application of Article 8 of
the ECHR to Community law and thence to domestic law, there were still a

---

[75] [1993] Imm AR 98 at 106. The applicant also argued that the Secretary of State and the tribunal were also obliged to consider whether deportation was disproportionate to the present
threat which he allegedly posed to public policy, and whether that threat was sufficiently serious
to justify interfering with his fundamental right of free movement as an EC national.

[76] Ibid. at 107.

[77] *R* v. *Secretary of State for the Home Department, ex p Tejinder Singh,* unreported decision
of 2 February 1993 (available on LEXIS).

[78] The applicant sought to rely on *Surinda Singh* [1992] Imm AR 565.

number of difficulties in the applicant's way. First, there were said to be considerable difficulties in the interpretation of Article 8 of the ECHR and its application to domestic law for the purpose of modifying the Secretary of State's usual approach in such cases. Implicit here was a judicial reluctance to disturb settled administrative practices by introducing the ECHR into this area of discretionary power. Second, it was said to have been established by *Brind* that the ECHR was not part of domestic law and, third, its terms were said to be not relevant considerations in the *Wednesbury* sense. Although the case may well have been an inappropriate one in which to make the Community law argument, this judicial response strongly suggests that, even in an appropriate case which is clearly within the scope of Community law, the familiar judicial determination to immunise administrative discretion from the effect of the ECHR might remain an obstacle.

5. THE EFFECT OF EUROPEAN CITIZENSHIP

In chapter 1, passing reference was made to the advent of European citizenship as one of the developments symbolising the contemporary transition from a constitutionalism presupposing a sovereign nation-state to a new, transcendent constitutionalism in which individual citizens are the bearers of rights which have their source on the international plane. On 1st November 1993, when the Treaty on European Union ("TEU") came into force, every person holding British nationality became also a citizen of the European Union, entitled to enjoy the rights conferred by the Treaty and subject to the duties imposed by it.[79] The reality of overlapping legal systems is now matched by the advent of overlapping citizenship.[80]

The aim of this section of the present chapter is to consider, first, the nature of the change that has taken place, or potentially may take place, as a result of the advent of European citizenship and, second, the response of English courts to that development. It will be suggested that the significance of European citizenship for the domestic status of international human rights law is twofold. First, to the extent that citizenship brings with it substantive new Community rights, it further extends the sphere of application of Community law and, since national measures which interfere with those Community rights must be assessed by national courts for their compatibility with international agreements concerning human rights, it thus enlarges the area of domestic law permeated by international treaties such as the ECHR through the medium of Community law.[81] Second, less tangibly but equally

---

[79] Treaty on European Union, Article 8. See Craig & de Búrca, (above n. 4) at 707–11.

[80] Or rather, as Ward points out, "Dualism and the Limits of European Integration" (1995) 17 Liv. LR 29 at 30–1, we are now "subjects of the Crown and citizens of Europe."

[81] Article 8 definitely confers a number of new political rights on citizens of the Union, such as the right to vote and to stand for election in municipal elections and elections to the European

significantly, the concept of European citizenship is of immense symbolic significance, not merely as another staging post in the process of European integration, but as a compelling reason in its own right for harmonising the protection of fundamental rights throughout the European Union.[82]

(a) The Nature of European Citizenship

Much has been written about the precise nature of the concept of European citizenship.[83] The Commission, in its Report on Citizenship, hailed the advent of Union citizenship as creating a direct political link between the people of Europe and the European Union, of immense significance in the constitutionalisation of the European Union.[84] On this view, the provisions of the TEU on citizenship mark the transition from an economic to a political community.[85] How far the provisions themselves go in giving substance to that notion, however, is a matter of debate. Almost all commentators are agreed that the significance of Union citizenship lies not so much in the present substance of citizenship rights but in its power as a symbol of the evolution of a European constitution and in its potential as a dynamic concept for future development.[86] Many commentators are more sceptical, however. Lyons, for example, clearly considers citizenship to be more rhetoric than reality,[87] and d'Oliveira has argued that European citizenship is, so far at least, "a symbolic plaything without substantive content".[88] For these commentators, Article 8 TEU was a

---

Parliament, the right to diplomatic and consular assistance and the right to apply to the Ombudsman (Arts. 8b–e), but, as will be seen below, the more difficult question is whether Art. 8a(1) has extended rights of residence and free movement to Community nationals who are not economically active, or to nationals within their own Member State.

[82] The harmonising potential of the idea of European citizenship was appreciated by Advocate General Jacobs before citizenship of the Union was formally established by the TEU. In *Konstantinidis*, Case C-168/91, [1993] ECR I-1191 at 1211–12, he expressed the view that Community nationals exercising their Community rights in another Member State were entitled to say "civis europeus sum" and to invoke that status in order to oppose any violation of their fundamental rights. This would have led to a significant extension of the Community's human rights jurisdiction over the Member States, but the Court did not take up the suggestion.

[83] See, as a sample of the extensive literature, D. O'Keeffe, "Union Citizenship", in D. O'Keeffe & P. Twomey (eds.), *Legal Issues of the Maastricht Treaty* (1994), 87; C. Closa, "Citizenship of the Union and Nationality of Member States", ibid. at 109, and "The Concept of Citizenship in the Treaty on European Union" (1992) 29 CMLRev. 1137; U.K. Preuss, "Problems of a Concept of European Citizenship" (1995) 1 ELJ 267; M. Newman, *Democracy, Sovereignty and the European Union* (London: Hurst, 1996), ch. 6.

[84] Commission Report on Citizenship, COM (93) 702.

[85] The TEU also renamed the EEC Treaty the "EC Treaty", symbolically omitting the "economic" from the title.

[86] See eg. O'Keeffe in O'Keeffe & Twomey, (above n. 83) at 106–7.

[87] C. Lyons, "Citizenship in the Constitution of the European Union: Rhetoric or Reality?" in R. Bellamy (ed.), *Constitutionalism, Democracy and Sovereignty: American and European Perspectives* (Aldershot: Avebury, 1996), ch. 7.

[88] H.U.J. d'Oliveira "Union Citizenship: Pie in the Sky?" in A. Rosas & E. Antola (eds.), *A Citizens' Europe: In Search of a New Order* (London: Sage, 1995), 58 at 82; "European Citizenship: Its Meaning, Its Potential" in R. Dehousse (ed.), *Europe After Maastricht: An Ever Closer Union?* (Munchen: LBE, 1994), ch.6.

cynical exercise in superficial legitimation of the Union rather than a substantive reorientation of the legal order around the rights of individuals.[89]

The greatest debate over the significance of Union citizenship has revolved around the scope of the rights "to move and reside freely within the territory of the Member States", conferred by Article 8a(1). On their face, those provisions appear to extend the rights to reside and move freely to Community nationals who are not economically active. On the other hand, those rights are expressly subject to "the limitations and conditions laid down in this Treaty and by the measures adopted to give it effect."[90] The Community had already adopted Directives conferring rights of free movement and residence on Community nationals not economically active, subject to various limits and conditions,[91] and it is an open question whether Art. 8a(1) confers any rights additional to those which already existed prior to the TEU. It is also an open question whether Art. 8a(1) confers any rights on nationals within their own Member States.[92]

As will shortly be seen, the question of the scope of Art. 8a(1) has yet to be considered fully by the ECJ, and the English case-law thus far reflects this uncertainty as to the scope of that provision and the significance of Union citizenship. Although in *Adams*[93] and *McQuillan*[94] it was felt that there was a serious question deserving of an Art. 177 reference to the ECJ as to whether Art. 8a had created new rights of movement and residence, in *Vitale*, *Phull* and *Castelli* the courts were confident that Art. 8a did not create any new rights of residence for the various applicants in those cases.

(b) European Citizenship and Fundamental Rights in English Courts

The rights contained in Art. 8a(1) have been relied upon as the basis of challenges to exclusion orders made by the Home Secretary under the prevention of terrorism legislation. The legislation confers a very broad discretion on the Secretary of State to make exclusion orders excluding from Great Britain any person who he is satisfied is or has been concerned in the commission, preparation or instigation of acts of terrorism in relation to the affairs of Northern Ireland, or is attempting to enter Great Britain with a view to being concerned

---

[89] Much of the literature is also highly critical of the exclusiveness of a concept of citizenship based on nationality of a Member State. See eg. M. Everson, "The Legacy of the Market Citizen" in Shaw & More (eds.), *New Legal Dynamics of European Union* (above n. 28), at 73; Ward, *The Margins of European Law* (above n. 28), chs. 5 & 6; Ferrajoli, "Beyond sovereignty and citizenship: a global constitutionalism" in R. Bellamy (ed.), *Constitutionalism, Democracy and Sovereignty* (above n. 87) at 151.

[90] See in particular *R v. Secretary of State for the Home Department, ex p. Vitale* [1996] All ER (EC) 461 and *R v. Westminster City Council, ex p. Castelli* (1996) HLR 125.

[91] Directives 90/364–6 (the "Residence Directives").

[92] *Phull v. Secretary of State for the Home Department* [1996] Imm AR 72.

[93] *R v. Secretary of State for the Home Department, ex p. Adams* [1995] All ER (EC) 177.

[94] *R v. Secretary of State for the Home Department, ex p. McQuillan* [1995] 4 All ER 400.

in the same.[95] The Secretary of State may exercise the power to exclude "in such a way as appears to him expedient to prevent acts of terrorism".[96] In *Adams*, the President of Sinn Fein challenged by way of judicial review an exclusion order made against him by the Home Secretary.[97] The challenge was based in part on domestic law, the argument being that the Secretary of State had exercised his power for an improper purpose in the *Padfield* sense, and that his decision was unreasonable or irrational in the *Wednesbury* sense. The principal basis for the challenge, however, was that, by preventing the applicant from entering Great Britain, the order infringed the applicant's alleged Community law right, as a citizen of the European Union, to move freely within the territory of the Union under Article 8a.[98]

Assuming Article 8a(1) to be applicable, the applicant argued that, under Community law, the Secretary of State was obliged to give reasons for the exercise of his statutory discretion to make an exclusion order, and that, as the Secretary of State could have allowed the applicant to enter the country for a few hours to address MPs, a three year blanket exclusion order fell foul of the Community law principle of proportionality. The Secretary of State argued that Art. 8a(1) did not apply because it was merely declaratory of the specific economic categories of free movement, or, if it had a wider scope, because it was not directly effective, or because the applicant's movement was a matter internal to the UK. If, contrary to the Secretary of State's main argument, the applicant could rely on Art. 8a(1), the Secretary of State argued that the matter was covered by an express derogation under Article 223 of the Treaty, which provides that "no Member State shall be obliged to supply information the disclosure of which it considers contrary to the essential interests of its security", or alternatively that a derogation to the same effect had to be implied by way of analogy into Article 8a(1).[99]

The Divisional Court agreed to refer to the ECJ various questions concerning the scope of Art. 8a(1), including whether it was merely declaratory of existing Community law rights, whether the rights under it were directly applicable, and whether it applied to situations which were wholly internal to a Member State.[100] While too much cannot be read into a court's willingness to make a reference, the terms in which Steyn LJ accepted the arguability of the applicant's construction of Art. 8a(1) strongly suggest that he was sympathetic towards what was described above as the wide view of Art. 8a(1).

---

[95] Prevention of Terrorism (Temporary Provisions) Act 1989, s.5(1)(a).

[96] Ibid., s.4(1).

[97] *R* v. *Secretary of State for the Home Department, ex p. Adams* [1995] All ER (EC) 177. See S. Douglas-Scott & J.A. Kimbell, "The Adams exclusion order case: new enforceable civil rights in the post-Maastricht European Union?" [1994] PL 516.

[98] Ibid. at 182j–183a. The applicant also argued that the exclusion order interfered with his right to provide and receive services in another Member State under Article 59 of the EC Treaty, but that argument received short shrift from the Divisional Court: ibid. at 187a.

[99] Ibid. at 187e–g.

[100] Ibid. at 192c–e.

This much is apparent from his clear acceptance throughout his judgment that the process of European integration has now reached a stage where it has gone beyond a mere economic community and become a political community, united by a common attachment to principles of liberty, democracy and respect for human rights and fundamental freedoms and the rule of law.[101] He appeared equally prepared to accept that there now existed a direct political link between citizens of the member states and the European Union which, prior to the TEU, did not exist.[102] He drew on the Commission's Report on Citizenship, in which the Commission observed that Art. 8a(1) refers to all persons, whether or not they are economically active, and emphasised that the status of rights of free movement in Community law had now been fundamentally altered.[103] All this suggests that Steyn LJ would have preferred the broad interpretation of Art. 8a(1) had he been required to make the decision himself,[104] but as there was not yet a decision of the ECJ on the scope of the new Article, a reference was thought the more appropriate course.

Equally significant, and no doubt intimately related to its apparent view of the significance of European citizenship, the Divisional Court in *Adams* took an enlightened view of the domestic court's role in scrutinising a national derogation from a Community right for conformity with fundamental rights. The extent of its agreement with the applicant's analysis in terms of fundamental rights is striking.[105] Assuming Art. 8a(1) to be applicable, it agreed that the right to move freely within the European Union was a fundamental right. It agreed that the right which the applicant sought to enter Great Britain to exercise, namely his right of free speech, was also a fundamental right, which, it noted, was protected by Article 10 of the ECHR as well as being enshrined in the preamble of the TEU. It also noted that the Commission's Report on Citizenship stated that "the rights flowing from citizenship are in effect granted constitutional status." The court further agreed that it is a principle of Community law that rights under Community law must be protected by an effective means of resort to judicial review, and that without reasons for the making of an exclusion order the rights of a citizen to apply

---

[101] Ibid. at 186f. See also Steyn LJ's invocation of a common European heritage to justify his statement of a proportionality principle in *Giles* v. *Thompson* [1993] 3 All ER 321 at 336d: "In our European democracy it is the first imperative of enlightened government in the broad sense that individual liberty ought not to be constrained unless there are clear, present and compelling reasons to do so in the interests of the collective welfare"; and his 1996 ALBA lecture: *The Weakest and Least Dangerous Department of Government*; "we live in a liberal European democracy based on values of justice, liberty, equality and humanity. Judges are therefore entitled to assume, unless a Statute makes crystal clear provision to the contrary, that Parliament would not wish to make unjust laws'.

[102] Ibid. at 188b–c and 189a.

[103] *Report on Citizenship of the Union*, COM (93) 702, December 21 1993.

[104] The broad construction was referred to as "at the very least . . . arguable", [1995] All ER (EC) 177 at 188d and "seriously arguable", at 189a.

[105] Ibid. at 189d–e.

for judicial review will in practice, in the vast majority of cases, be ineffective.[106]

Nevertheless, the court accepted the inevitability of the existence of derogations in respect of the interests of security of Member States. The fact that the right in Article 8a(1) was expressed to be subject to the limitations and conditions laid down in the Treaty and by measures adopted to give effect to it was held to bring the express derogation in Article 223 into play. In any event, the court held, if Article 8a(1) was to be given a broad interpretation, it was subject to an implied derogation in respect of the interests of security of Member States. However, in its explicit recognition that those derogations "must be narrowly construed", the court appeared to accept that it was for the court to scrutinise the derogation from the Community law right for its compatibility with fundamental rights. In what followed, though, there was a curious divergence in the reasoning, which inevitably meant that the full implications flowing from that premise were not followed through.

On the one hand, the court rejected the argument that, as a matter of Community law, the Secretary of State was under an obligation to give reasons for the making of an exclusion order, and refused to refer this question to the ECJ, holding in effect that the existence of the derogations was a complete answer to the argument that there was a duty to give reasons.[107] Whether the relevant derogation was the express Treaty derogation in Article 223, the implied Treaty derogation in Article 8a(1) itself, or the derogation to be found in secondary legislation,[108] the result was the same: the Secretary of State was under no duty to give reasons if there was evidence that the interests of state security were at stake. Since the Secretary of State's affidavit evidence comprehensively asserted that it would be contrary to the interests of the state to reveal the grounds on which his decision was based, the court held that there was no obligation under Community law to give such reasons.[109]

On the other hand, however, the court was more receptive to the applicant's other Community law argument concerning the proportionality of the restric-

---

[106] Cf. Steyn LJ's strong championing of the right of access to court as a constitutional right in *R* v. *Secretary of State for the Home Department, ex p. Leech* [1994] QB 1, considered in ch. 5 above, and *Oxfordshire County Council* v. *M* [1994] 2 All ER 269.

[107] [1995] All ER (EC) 177 at 190h–191d. See the contrary argument of O'Leary, (1996) CMLRev 777 at 790 (Case Comment on Case C-175/94, *R* v. *Secretary of State for the Home Department, ex p. Gallagher* [1996] 1 CMLR 557), that the lack of reasons for an exclusion raises serious questions about the compatibility with Community law of the exercise of exclusion powers in the terms provided in the PTA with Community law.

[108] Article 6 of Council Directive 64/221/EEC, providing an "interests of the security of the state" exception to the right to be informed of the grounds on which the right of free movement has been derogated from.

[109] The court found the decision of the European Court of Human Rights in *Fox, Campbell & Hartley* v. *UK* (1990) 13 EHRR 157 to be not of great assistance, but as Sedley J. pointed out in *R* v. *Secretary of State for the Home Department, ex p. McQuillan* [1995] 4 All ER 400, considered below, one thing which is clear from that decision is that, at least for the purposes of Article 5(1) of the Convention, the mere *ipse dixit* of the executive as to the interests of national security was not enough.

tion on his freedom of expression, and agreed to refer to the ECJ a question about the precise meaning of the proportionality principle in the particular context of this case.[110] The reason for doing so was to seek guidance from the ECJ as to how that principle, which was acknowleded to be a part of domestic law through Community law,[111] was to be applied in a case where a limitation on the Community right of free movement involved a conflict between freedom of speech and national security, a matter on which there was no ECJ authority. It noted that the explanations of the principle were not in harmony, but spanned a spectrum of views from a narrow doctrine not unlike *Wednesbury* unreasonableness at one end, to *de novo* review at the other, and the court wondered whether there were better explanations of the principle placing it somewhere between these two extremes, and acknowledging the need to adapt the principle to the circumstances of a particular case. It therefore agreed to refer to the ECJ the question

> "What are the precise requirements of the principle of proportionality in a case such as the present, which, in relation to limitations on rights of free movement, involves freedom of speech and national security?"

The court's reasoning on the derogations aspect of the case therefore displays a puzzling asymmetry. In the case of the Community law principle of proportionality, the court was clearly prepared to examine the derogation in the light of the fundamental right of freedom of expression which stood to be affected. In the case of the Community law right to reasons, however, the court effectively permitted the derogation to operate as a trump, by failing to bring to bear any scrutiny for compatibility with fundamental rights. Ultimately, the court accepted the wholly unsupported assertions in the Secretary of State's affidavit evidence that the interests of security prevented the giving of reasons for the decision to make the order. Yet, if the court accepts the state's *ipse dixit* on why reasons should not be given, why should it not also accept its *ipse dixit* that the impact of the measure on free speech and free movement is proportionate to the interests of protecting state security?

This inconsistency is all the more surprising in view of the court's acknowledgment elsewhere in its judgment that effective judicial control depends on the availability of the reasons behind the decision. This is evident not only in the court's explicit agreement with the submissions of the applicant to this effect, but in the express ground on which the court dismissed the applicant's domestic law claims.[112] It held that no meaningful *Padfield* or *Wednesbury* review could be carried out without access to the Secretary of State's reasons

---

[110] As will be seen below, there is a certain artificiality in separating the right to reasons argument from the proportionality argument.

[111] [1995] All ER (EC) 177 at 191j.

[112] Ibid. at 185d–h. The short shrift given to the applicant's *Padfield* and *Wednesbury* arguments highlights again the absurd contrast of approaches between a court applying purely domestic law and the same court applying Community law, informed by human rights treaties such as the ECHR and the approach taken thereunder.

for making his decision. Yet, when it came to considering the applicant's Community law claims, the court appeared to think that a meaningful proportionality test could be carried out without the reviewing court having available to it at least the gist of the reasons on which the Secretary of State based his decision.

Such inconsistency may be purely the result of domestic judges' inexperience of the nature and operation of the proportionality principle. It is hard to see how the domestic court is going to carry out a meaningful proportionality test if it does not have access to the Secretary of State's reasons for decision. In applying a proportionality test, the court will inevitably have to consider questions such as whether there was a rational connection between the means chosen and the end pursued, and whether there was any less restrictive alternative available to the Secretary of State which would still have achieved his aim. It will be difficult to scrutinise the decision in these terms without access to the information before the Secretary of State when he made the decision.

The Divisional Court in *Adams* ought to have examined in light of the ECHR the derogation from the otherwise applicable right to reasons for the infringement of a Community law right. In particular, it ought to have scrutinised the derogation in light of the guarantees in Articles 6(1) and 13 of a right of access to an effective judicial remedy, on which the right to freedom of speech in Article 10 was dependent. The court's misgivings about imposing a duty to give reasons may be understandable in the national security context, given the strong public interest in preserving the safety and confidentiality of intelligence sources. But the court's acquiescence in the bare assertion of the state's right to derogate from the individual's right of access to an effective remedy surely impairs the substance of the rights guaranteed in Articles 6 and 13, because it enables the court's constitutional review jurisdiction to be effectively ousted at the say-so of the state. Therefore, although the decision in *Adams* is significant for its recognition of the extent to which the ECHR can indirectly penetrate administrative law through the medium of Community law, it still amounts to only a partial recognition of the full implications of the development in Community law that requires national derogations from Community rights to be scrutinised by national courts for compatibility with international human rights norms.

6. COMMON LAW DEVELOPMENT AND THE EMERGING EUROPEAN CONSTITUTION

Probably the highwater mark of domestic law's permeability by the ECHR through Community law is to be found in Sedley J.'s decision in *McQuillan*.[113] Like *Adams*, the case concerned a challenge to an exclusion

---

[113] R v. *Secretary of State for the Home Department, ex p. McQuillan* [1995] 4 All ER 400.

order made under the Prevention of Terrorism (Temporary Provisions) Act 1989. However, whereas Adams had merely wanted to visit Britain to address a meeting of MPs at Westminster, McQuillan wanted to take up residence and work in Britain because, as a formerly active member of the Irish Republican Socialist Party, he had been the target of terrorist assassination attempts and feared for the life of himself and his family if he remained in Northern Ireland. Since the applicant also had dual British and Irish nationality, his challenge to the exclusion order raised questions under Article 48 of the EC Treaty, guaranteeing free movement of workers, as well as under Article 8a(1), guaranteeing the the rights of Union citizens to move and reside freely within the territory of the Member States.

The applicant's argument was essentially that, by virtue of his citizenship of Britain, Ireland and the European Union, he had the right to move freely within the UK and the territory of the Union, and any derogation from that right had to be a rational, proportionate and sufficiently reasoned decision in the context of the risk to his life and liberties arising from his effective confinement to Northern Ireland. The provisions of the ECHR which the applicant argued were relevant to the court's review of the legality of the derogation which the exclusion order constituted were Article 2, guaranteeing that everyone's right to life shall be protected by law, and Article 3, providing that no-one shall be subjected to inhuman or degrading treatment. Both of these were non-derogable guarantees under the ECHR by virtue of Article 15.

The applicant made full use of the ECJ's jurisprudence by which the ECHR had become an increasingly important source of Community law. He invoked *Rutili*, as requiring strict interpretation of any use of public policy to justify derogation from any of the fundamental principles of Community law such as free movement for workers, and *Johnston* as demonstrating the principle of effective judicial control that underpinned the other fundamental principles such as free movement or equal treatment.[114] Moreover, it was argued, it was not only a matter of logic that the English common law ought to follow the example of Community law by incorporating the principles, as opposed to the text, of the European Convention, but it was now, after the decision in *ERT*, a *requirement* of Community law that English courts do so. It was on the basis of this formidable analysis in terms of fundamental rights that the applicant sought to persuade the court to carry out a proportionality review of the derogation in the circumstances of the case.

Sedley J.'s response to these arguments can fairly be said to amount to the most explicit recognition to date of the extent to which the ECHR now permeates domestic law through Community law. Even more significantly, his judgment combines that development with the parallel domestic development of a common law human rights jurisdiction in a most distinctive and refreshingly candid way. Like Steyn LJ in *Adams*, Sedley J. in *McQuillan* accepted

---

[114] Case 36/75, *Rutili v. Minister for the Interior* [1975] ECR 1219; Case 22/84, *Johnston v. Chief Constable of the R.U.C.* [1986] ECR 1651.

much of the applicant's analysis in terms of fundamental rights, but he was much more explicit in finding those rights to be the articulation of values grounded in the common law. Freedom of movement, for example, was said to be "a fundamental value of the common law", with the result that the courts would subject the reasoning underlying any limitation of it to close scrutiny. Similarly the common law had historically shown its concern to protect the right to life, a concern which had manifested itself as subjecting to the most anxious scrutiny administrative decisions which affected the right, such as in *Bugdaycay*.[115] A concern to ensure that executive action should subject nobody to inhuman treatment was also said to be included "in the common law's priorities".

By finding these fundamental Community and ECHR rights to be protected by the common law, Sedley J. was giving practical effect to the significant shift in judicial opinion described at the beginning of chapter 5.[116] For many, such judicial creativity will give cause for concern. Sedley J., however, was careful to attempt to dissociate this exercise in creative judicial interpretation from the old conceit that, in making statements about the common law, judges are merely declaring what the law has always been. In his recognition of the common law's concern to prevent executive action inflicting inhuman treatment, for example, he expressly acknowledged that such recognition enlarged the statutory prohibition against cruel and unusual punishments contained in the Bill of Rights of 1688. Like some other judges before him, Sedley J. is not afraid to be overt about developing the common law where he thinks that this can be justified on the present state of the legal materials.

Whereas some judges have been attracted to the idea of an indigenous human rights jurisdiction in order to neutralise resort to unincorporated international human rights treaties, and avoid having to refer to such instruments or the jurisprudence in which they have been interpreted, Sedley J. was careful to make clear that to find a coincidence between the rights protected at common law and those protected by the ECHR does not render the ECHR otiose. On the contrary, the role of the ECHR in the larger scheme of European integration was explicitly recognised by him as an important factor in the development of the common law.

"Through the jurisprudence of the European Court of Justice the principles, though not the text of the Convention now inform the law of the European Union. If, as the UK government has accepted in *Vilvarajah*, an irrationality challenge can be mounted where a real risk of infringement of Article 3 can be shown to have been ignored; and if on the wider scale it is for the courts of the UK to apply principles of European law wherever appropriate; the principles and standards set out in the Convention can certainly be said to be a matter of which the law of this country now takes notice in setting its own standards. . . . Once it is accepted that the

---

[115] [1987] AC 514. See ch. 5 above for consideration of this common law development.
[116] Indeed, he expressly acknowledged his debt to the reasoning of Laws J. in "Is the High Court the Guardian of Fundamental Constitutional Rights?" [1993] PL 59.

standards articulated in the European Convention are standards which both march with those of the common law and inform the jurisprudence of the European Union, it becomes unreal and potentially unjust to continue to develop English public law without reference to them."[117]

This passage reveals a rich understanding of the dynamics of domestic constitutional change in the wider context of an integrating Europe. Drawing together developments in the jurisprudence of the ECJ, the attitude of domestic courts to such developments in Community law and the UK government's own practice in acknowledging the appropriateness of judicial review for putative violations of fundamental rights under the ECHR, Sedley J. constructs a forceful justification for developing the English common law in light of the standards articulated in the Convention. The consequence for the law of judicial review was that reviewing courts should apply differential legal standards reflecting the distinction between rights recognised as fundamental and those which do not enjoy such a pre-eminent status. To arrive at this point was to recognise that the standard of justification of infringements of rights and freedoms by executive decision inevitably varies in proportion to the significance of the right at issue. Sedley J. was fully aware that such an approach might amount to the recognition of a doctrine of proportionality, but wisely avoided being drawn into the ultimately semantic game of labelling his approach as proportionality or not. As he rightly observed, even if his approach was tantamount to such a doctrine, he was merely making explicit what had long been implicit in the common law in *Bugdaycay* and even *Brind* itself.[118]

All this availed the applicant nothing, however, for although Sedley J. thought it clearly his task to carry out a rigorous scrutiny of the rationality of the making of the exclusion order, in view of the fundamental values affected by it, he ultimately held that he was prevented from doing so. This was because he was bound by Court of Appeal authority to accept that what he had earlier described as the "laconic" formula used by the Secretary of State in his affidavit evidence, to assert that the interests of national security were at stake, was sufficient to preclude any further inquiry by the court.[119] He also refused to make an Art. 177 reference, on the basis that the questions as to the rights conferred by Art. 8a(1) and the requirements of the principle of proportionality would be decided by the ECJ in the *Adams* reference.[120]

[117] [1995] 4 All ER 400 at 422e–j.

[118] See ch. 5 above for the same argument.

[119] The Court of Appeal in *R v. Secretary of State for the Home Department, ex p. Gallagher* [1994] 3 CMLR 295 had upheld the principle that the subject of an exclusion order could not be informed of the reasons why the order is made or why it cannot be revoked, beyond the mere recitation of the statutory formula, because to do so might lead to the discovery of sources of information and so compromise police operations or put the lives of informants or their families at risk.

[120] The proceedings were stayed pending the outcome of the *Adams* reference, which was subsequently withdrawn following the revocation of the exclusion order being challenged. As a result, the ECJ has still not considered directly the scope of Art. 8a.

This ultimate inability to give effect to his carefully articulated approach to fundamental rights cases ought not to be allowed to detract from the general significance of Sedley J.'s judgment. That significance lies in its transcendence of the so-called indigenous approach to protecting fundamental rights, by locating the common law's development of a human rights jurisdiction in the wider context of the harmonisation of constitutional standards in an integrating Europe. It is an approach born of an appreciation of the constitutionalising effect of the integration process.[121] Unlike Lord Bingham, for whom, it will be recalled, the domestic effect of the ECHR through Community law is owed to s. 3 of the European Communities Act 1972, Sedley J. made no mention of that Act in *McQuillan*. Instead, he clearly considered himself to be developing the English common law in the light of the UK's progressive integration into an emerging European constitution.[122]

7. CONCLUSION

This chapter has sought to show the extent to which the reception of international human rights law into domestic law *via* Community law has now become not only theoretically possible but a practical reality. The dynamic evolutionary process by which the ECJ has gradually derived fundamental rights and principles from international instruments such as the ECHR and the constitutional traditions of the Member States, turned them into an integral part of the Community legal order, and by that route into a more integral part of domestic legal orders, demonstrates the increasing permeability and interpenetration of European legal systems in this age of legal and political integration.[123] The acceptance in turn by English courts of an obligation

---

[121] For another example of Sedley J.'s receptiveness to fundamental rights arguments placed in the wider context of European integration, see R v. *Secretary of State for the Home Department, ex p. Payne* [1995] Imm AR 48. There, at 50–1, he was prepared to accept as arguable in an appropriate case the "interesting and by no means fanciful" argument that the immigration authorities must now have regard to the ECHR in exercising their discretion because, since the TEU, it has become a Community task to co-operate in the field of immigration in accordance with the ECHR, and by Art. 5 of the EC Treaty, which is incorporated into UK law, Member States must facilitate the achievement of Community tasks.

[122] There have recently been much debate about the extent to which Europe already has, or needs, a constitution: see eg. N. Walker, "European Constitutionalism and European Integration" [1996] PL 266; P. Eleftheriadis, "Aspects of European Constitutionalism" (1996) 21 EL Rev 32; T.C. Hartley, "The European Court, Judicial Objectivity and the Constitution of the European Union" (1996) 112 LQR 95; J.H.H. Weiler, "Does Europe Need a Constitution? Demos, Telos and the German Maastricht Decision" (1995) 1 ELJ 219; D. Grimm, "Does Europe Need a Constitution?" (1995) 1 ELJ 282; I. Harden, "The Constitution of the European Union" [1994] PL 609. See also A. O'Neill, *Decisions of the European Court of Justice and their Constitutional Implications* (London: Butterworths, 1994) at 100–2 on the emergence of "a common European law' and J. Shaw, *Law of the European Union*, 2nd edn. (London: Macmillan, 1996) ch. 3.

[123] See Case 155/79, *A.M. & S. Europe Ltd.* v. *Commission* [1982] ECR 1575 at para 18 ("Community law . . . derives from not only the economic but also the legal interpenetration of the Member States").

to have regard to such international instruments when considering the compatibility of national laws or measures with Community law, notwithstanding the unincorporated status of those instruments in domestic law, has conspicuously not been justified by reference to the European Communities Act 1972. Rather it appears to rest on the increasing acceptance, by at least some English judges, of the political legitimacy of the Community legal order.

A short but sweeping passage from the judgment of Lord Browne-Wilkinson in *Hamilton* v. *Naviede* exemplifies the integrationist dynamic by which this gradual convergence of constitutional standards has come about.[124] Considering the relationship between statutory provisions in financial regulation legislation and the privilege against self-incrimination, Lord Browne-Wilkinson demonstrated his preferred technique of restoring common law rights to a quasi-constitutional status by asserting that "[o]ne of the basic freedoms secured by English law is that (subject to any statutory provisions to the contrary) no one can be forced to answer questions or produce documents which may incriminate him in subsequent criminal proceedings". However, the evolution of this fundamental principle of the privilege against self-incrimination was traced from its ancient roots in the common law, through its adoption by other common law countries where it enjoys constitutional status, to its present recognition in the case-law of the ECJ and the ECHR. He cited three recent ECHR cases in which a demand to produce self-incriminating documents had been held to be a breach of Article 6, demonstrating that the privilege was one of the basic rights protected by the ECHR,[125] and two ECJ cases in which the same right had been recognised as part of the general principles of Community law.[126] As European integration proceeds, the opportunities for courts to forge common constitutional standards in this way can only increase.

In the meantime, however, there remains the bizarre bifurcation in English courts between human rights cases with an EC dimension and those without. In the former case, the court must not only have regard to international instruments, and in particular the ECHR, but must apply the Community law (and ECHR) doctrine of proportionality when doing so. In the latter case, such international instruments are often held to be irrelevant if unincorporated, and even if regard is had to them, seldom do courts go further and apply what amounts to a proportionality test to determining the justification for any infringement. It is true that, as in other areas, the acceptance of obligations

---

[124] [1994] 3 WLR 656 at 662F–H.

[125] *Funke* v. *France* (1993) 16 EHRR 297, *Miailhe* v. *France* (1993) 16 EHRR 332 and *Cremieux* v. *France* (1993) 16 EHRR 357.

[126] Case 374/87, *Orkem* v. *Commission* [1989] ECR 3283 and Case C-60/92, *Otto Bank* v. *Postbank NV* [1993] ECR I-5683, paras. 11 & 12. Note however that in these cases the ECJ said that no general principle against self-incrimination could be derived from the Convention or International Covenant or the national laws of Member States, but that nevertheless as a matter of Community law the Commission could not require an answer or document to be supplied which would provide evidence on a matter which it was for the Commission to prove.

and doctrines in Community law has had an inevitable spillover effect, as courts strive to avoid what has been called the "drifting apart" of national laws governing similar situations,[127] depending on whether they fall within or without the sphere of Community law.[128] But the courts' continued resistance to the explicit recognition of proportionality as a principle of English administrative law has led to the curious spectacle of the same court declaring itself constitutionally unable to review for disproportionate impact on fundamental rights in one breath, before doing precisely that, as a matter of Community law, in the next.[129] Not only does the growing experience of operating a proportionality doctrine as a matter of Community law render implausible the objection that courts lack the competence to do so, but whether or not a particular case has a Community law dimension may be completely fortuitous. Only when more courts appreciate that, as Sedley J. put it in *McQuillan*, it is not only unreal but potentially unjust to carry on in this way, will better progress be made in the UK towards the reception of the emerging common constitutional law of Europe.

---

[127] See eg. M v. *Home Office* [1994] 1 AC 377; *Woolwich Equitable Building Society* v. *IRC* [1993] AC 70.

[128] See eg. D. Williams, "The Influence of European Union Law upon United Kingdom Administration" in Richardson and Genn, (eds.), *Administrative Law and Government Action* (Oxford: Clarendon Press, 1994); Himsworth, "Legitimately expecting proportionality?" [1996] PL 46. See also the Law Commission's view, *Administrative Law: Judicial Review and Statutory Appeals*, Law Com No. 226 (1994), para. 2.10, that "differences between the judicial review procedure in domestic English cases and in EC cases need to be justified."

[129] Compare the treatment of the domestic *Wednesbury* challenge in *Adams* with that of the Community law challenge on the ground of disproportionate impact on the applicant's fundamental rights.

8

Towards an Interpretive Obligation

This book's thesis is that the time has come for the judicial recognition of an obligation to construe domestic law in conformity with international human rights norms. The foregoing chapters have sought to chart the domestic career of such norms against the backdrop of the fundamental changes taking place in the nature of the international and supranational legal orders. The domestic impact of the paradigm shift at the international level has so far been most keenly felt through the UK's membership of the European Community, which has exposed the inadequacy of traditional constitutional theory in today's conditions. The emergence of a constitutionalism on both a global and a regional scale, which transcends national boundaries, has inevitably had its influence on a national legal system which, for reasons largely of historical accident, had remained rooted in the pre-modern sovereignty paradigm.[1] Community membership, and participation in other supranational and inter-governmental structures of a kind which have only come into being in the post-War years, have gradually rendered the traditional account increasingly obsolete, as both external (national) sovereignty and internal (parliamentary) sovereignty have in reality become divisible and subject to limitations not formerly entertained by judges and theorists raised on the old Diceyan certainties.

However, despite the fact that the law of international human rights has been one of the principal causes of this paradigm shift at the international level, domestic courts have been slow to accord it recognition. In particular, with the exception of a shortlived period in the 1970s when a small contingent of constitutionalist judges held sway (Phase I), English public law long remained insulated from the influence of international human rights law, cut off by the judges themselves for fear that to concede the domestic relevance of such norms would undermine the foundation on which the legitimacy of judicial review was believed to depend. That foundation was the sovereignty

---

[1] See R.C. Van Caenegem, *An Historical Introduction to Western Constitutional Law* (Cambridge: Cambridge University Press, 1995) for an illuminating historical perspective on the contemporary debate about constitutional reform.

of Parliament, together with its various administrative law derivatives, such as the *ultra vires* doctrine and a generally deferential stance towards review of the executive and administration.

In more recent years, however, and in particular since the late 1980s, we have witnessed in the UK the emergence of a common law human rights jurisdiction, manifesting itself in a variety of techniques whereby the judiciary has contrived to provide a degree of protection for the rights and freedoms typically contained in the international human rights treaties, or at least in the older of those treaties protecting traditional civil and political rights. Latterly, even the citadel of administrative law, the relative sanctity of which was the distinguishing feature of Phase II, has begun to be breached, so that now the standards of judicial review have begun to be infused with the substance of international human rights norms, and the courts have in some instances silently adopted the adjudicative technique of judicial balancing which necessarily attends adjudication on constitutional rights. This trend has been reinforced by the growing importance of international human rights treaties, and in particular the ECHR, in the constitutional order of the European Community and Union. This development indeed marks the coming together of arguably the two most profound influences responsible for the transformation of domestic public law.

As a result of these developments, and true to the usual dynamic of incremental legal change, judicial practice long ago left behind the theoretical framework in which courts purport to operate, but the vocabulary of that framework has survived, as the only language the courts consider to be legitimate. The failure of the courts to modify their conceptual and linguistic tools to reflect the reality of the modern developments which they themselves have helped to bring about, renders those developments constantly vulnerable to atavistic lapses which deny the very basis on which such recognition of international human rights norms has been accorded. In this final chapter it will be argued that the only way to avoid such lapses in the future is to recognise a full interpretive obligation on domestic courts to construe domestic law in such a way as to achieve consistency with the UK's obligations under international human rights treaties. Drawing together the various themes which have pervaded the foregoing account of the changing domestic status of international human rights norms, the chapter aims to show, not only that the commonly imagined obstacles to the recognition of such an interpretive obligation are not in fact obstacles at all, but that the normative force of the argument for such recognition is, at this particular point in political and constitutional history, irresistible. First, however, it is necessary to consider the precise nature of the development which has been taking place over the last decade, for one of the consequences of the common law's conceptual and linguistic conservatism is that there has yet to emerge a satisfactory account explaining or justifying the increasing resort in practice to unincorporated international human rights norms.

2. THE NATURE OF THE DEVELOPMENT TAKING PLACE

Drzemczewski's argument in the 1970s, that the rights contained in the ECHR, or some of them, are already part of English law in so far as they are declaratory of customary international law, was considered in chapter 1. The argument, it will be recalled, was criticised by Duffy for being over-optimistic about the extent to which English courts were prepared to find that norms of international law were already part of English law as being declaratory of customary international law, particularly where there already exists a domestic precedent to the contrary.[2] It is now apparent, having considered in detail the nature of judicial responses to arguments invoking the ECHR and other unincorporated human rights instruments, that Duffy's prediction has proved correct, in so far as English courts have yet to recognise a provision of the Convention as being customary international law and thereby automatically a part of English law in the sense that it can be directly enforced against the state without the need for any further act of incorporation.

The debate has recently been revisited by Cunningham, however, in the light of English courts' new willingness to extend the circumstances in which they will refer to human rights treaties and in particular to the ECHR.[3] Cunningham's argument is that in many of the recent decisions in which judicial resort has been made to the ECHR and its case-law, courts have effectively been recognising the norms contained therein as customary international law, even though they are not articulating their use of it in those terms. He suggests that the justification for English courts' increasingly frequent reference to the ECHR is that they are implicitly recognising it as influential in the dynamic process whereby rules of customary international law are generated by a combination of treaty negotiation and ratification together with the subsequent practice of states party to the treaty. There being no reason in principle why such generation of customary norms should not take place at the regional level, Cunningham effectively revives Drzemczewski's argument that English courts are, implicitly at least, applying the ECHR as customary international law which is already, by virtue of that status, part of the English common law.[4]

The difficulty with Cunningham's thesis, as he himself acknowledges, is that there is so far no evidence of any English court expressly accepting that parts of the ECHR are declaratory of customary international law and therefore applicable as part of the common law.[5] It is certainly true that on

---

[2] Duffy, "English Law and the European Convention on Human Rights" (1980) 29 ICLQ 585 at 599–605.

[3] A.J. Cunningham, "The European Convention on Human Rights, Customary International Law and the Constitution" (1994) 43 ICLQ 537.

[4] Although Cunningham's conclusion, ibid. at 567, is that neither Drzemczewski's argument nor its critique is proven, the thrust of his argument is quite clearly that English courts are effectively applying the ECHR as customary international law.

[5] Ibid. at 564.

occasion certain courts have come close to doing so. Arguably the closest the courts have come is in the status accorded to Article 3 ECHR in *Williams*[6] and *Nahar*.[7] In both cases the common law was held, in effect, to supply a "cruel and unusual treatment" clause into a statutory provision which was otherwise without standards, so as to impose an irreducible minimum below which the court, reflecting public standards of morality, would not allow conditions of detention or treatment of prisoners to fall. In neither case, however, did the court articulate its approach in terms of recognising Article 3 ECHR as customary international law. Indeed, the continued insistence in the more recent cases that the use to which the ECHR is being put by courts does not amount to "incorporation" suggests that courts emphatically do not consider that instrument or any part of it to be "part of" the common law in the sense that it can be enforced directly in domestic courts.[8]

Cunningham has undoubtedly marshalled an impressive case for saying that the approach of English courts to international human rights treaties, and in particular to the ECHR, has undergone a significant evolution in the last few years. However, his ability to provide an explanation of that development is limited by the fact that he takes as his starting point the traditional constitutional picture painted by the courts. Proceeding from the dualist premise, which he regards as a "constitutional principle",[9] he seeks to demonstrate that the conventional criteria for the recognition of customary international law are satisfied in the case of the ECHR, or at least some of its provisions, with the result that it has become an integral part of English law. This makes it inevitable that he reaches the ultimately disappointing conclusion that "there must remain some legitimate doubt whether such an increase can be justified in terms of strict constitutional principle".[10] In fact, what Cunningham has described is nothing short of an evolution in the constitutional principle itself. To ask whether what has been taking place satisfies traditional criteria of a norm's eligibility for membership of the domestic legal system is therefore to ask the wrong question. Not merely the criteria themselves but the very notion of two distinct legal systems which the question presupposes have been superseded by developments in the judicial conception of the courts' interpretive function.

The better way to characterise the increasing use which is being made of international human rights instruments by domestic courts is to accept that they are not being applied or enforced as if they were customary international law in the conventional sense, but are being accorded a new role which is a product of the evolution which has come about in the constitutional function

---

[6] *Williams* v. *Home Office (No. 2)* [1981] 1 All ER 1211 at 1244j–1245e.

[7] *R* v. *Metropolitan Police Commissioner, ex p. Nahar, The Times* 28 May 1983.

[8] See eg. Laws's incorporationist disclaimer, 'Is the High Court the Guardian of Fundamental Constitutional Rights?" [1993] PL 59 at 61–2.

[9] Above n.3 at 551 and 563–4.

[10] Ibid. at 564.

of the judiciary. In the increasingly interdependent world of international agreements regulating how states behave towards their own citizens, the ways in which states "internalise" international norms have become more sophisticated. There are many ways of describing the development which has been taking place. Some talk in terms of the "indirect incorporation" of international human rights law.[11] Some say that courts are "infusing" the normative content of international human rights norms into their own interpretation of domestic norms, by altering the content of the latter to reflect the former.[12] Others talk of international human rights instruments being used as a text to "inform" the common law, or provide "guidance" for its development.[13] As will be argued below, although it is seldom heard it could equally well be said that the international human rights norms are being given "indirect effect", analogous to the indirect effect accorded to non-directly effective Community law.

Whatever description is preferred, the basic idea is the same. International human rights law has attained a domestic status which is greater than that of other international treaties but still short of full incorporation, a status that cannot be explained in terms of the traditional premises of sovereignty and dualism. The development reflects the distinction between "hard" and "soft" law which has emerged in recent years as old conceptions of law and state have been reconceived in the light of modern developments. The ECHR may not be accepted as customary law in the "hard" sense that it gives rise to rights and obligations which can be directly enforced in domestic courts. But it at least furnishes norms which courts increasingly consider themselves bound to take into account when deciding on the meaning of domestic law. The development of the common law which has been taking place could therefore be said to amount to an acceptance of the ECHR as "soft" customary international law.

Moreover, if, as has been argued here, the normativity of international human rights law from different sources is a matter of degree, and precisely where on the spectrum between irrelevance and full enforceability a particular norm falls will depend on a variety of factors strengthening or weakening the domestic normative force of a particular norm, there is nothing "illogical" about courts distinguishing between one international instrument and another, or even one provision and another within the same instrument.[14] There is, for example, a stronger argument for the recognition of the ECHR

---

[11] See Beyleveld, "The Concept of a Human Right and Incorporation of the European Convention on Human Rights" [1995] PL 577.

[12] On using international human rights law to infuse constitutional and statutory standards in the US, see R.B. Lillich, "The Role of Domestic Courts in Enforcing International Human Rights Law" in H. Hannum (ed.), *Guide to International Human Rights Practice*, 2nd ed. (Philadelphia, University of Pennsylvania Press, 1992) at 239–41.

[13] See eg. Laws, (above n. 8) at 61, considered in ch. 5 above.

[14] Cunningham, (above n. 3) at 566 suggests that the distinction between the ECHR and other international instruments is "illogical".

by English courts because of the importance of that instrument as a regional human rights instrument, and in view of the progress which has been made towards European integration, and in particular the role played by the ECHR in the Community legal order.[15]

What we are witnessing in the recent trend towards asserting an identity between the common law and the ECHR is a characteristically English process of legal change. National law is effectively being brought into line with international human rights norms by a subtle process of interpretive development which preserves the national law's distinctive character as "national". In this way, the courts avoid having to confront the difficult separation of powers concerns which mainly underpin the traditional rule about the domestic status of unincorporated treaties, although ironically in avoiding the clash with Parliament over its legislative monopoly, courts are increasingly brought into conflict with the executive and the administration against which the international human rights norms are enforced.

In chapter 2, it was noted that the UK's lack of a written constitution, and the consequent lack of any formal mechanism for constitutional change other than ordinary legislation, was both a source of weakness and a source of strength when it came to acceding to the European Communities. The disadvantage was that there was no ready means of amending the constitution in order to meet the minimum requirements of Community membership, such as the direct effect and supremacy of Community law. On the other hand, as Mitchell noted, it had the potential advantage that constitutional concepts can respond more readily to changes in the broad framework of ideas, as judges adapt domestic law according to their perception of the changing pattern of evolution of the Communities.[16] The same holds true of the development of human rights protection. The informal and pragmatic nature of the British constitution has, paradoxically, facilitated the reception of international human rights law by the courts by enabling them to adapt their approach to their interpretation of domestic norms so as to give indirect effect to those unincorporated international norms the normative force of which they consider to warrant such effect.[17]

If this understanding of the nature of the development taking place is correct, it is legitimate to ask why it is necessary, as this book argues, for English courts to recognise a full interpretive obligation in relation to international human rights norms, given the pace at which they are now developing the common law so as to accord recognition and protection to fundamental

---

[15] Note that, although Cunningham at the end of his article, ibid. at 567, raises the question of how "ever closer union" through the European Community will affect the relationship between the general principles of law common to the Member States, customary international law and the ECHR, he expressly does not consider what he describes as the issue of the "incorporation" of the ECHR by way of s. 3 of the European Communities Act 1972 (ibid. at 538 n. 7).

[16] Mitchell, "What do you want to be inscrutable *for*, Marcia?" (1967–8) CMLRev 112 at 125.

[17] See McCrudden & Chambers, *Individual Rights and the Law in Britain* (Oxford: Clarendon Press, 1994) at 583–6.

rights. Before turning to the positive reasons for the recognition of such an obligation, it is necessary to provide a fuller account of the shortcomings of the present approach.

3. THE INADEQUACY OF THE PRESENT APPROACH

(a) Marginalising the Sources of International Human Rights Law

One of the principal reasons for the recognition of an interpretive obligation is that the "indigenous" approach of rejuvenating the common law presumptions risks marginalising international human rights law as a source of guidance for the English courts, as they develop the common law. If, as Lord Browne-Wilkinson believes, all that is required is the reassertion by courts of their traditional concern to protect individual freedom against unjustified infringement, and if the ECHR is really no more than the articulation of values already recognised and protected at common law, there is a danger that the "rediscovery" of the common law's constitutional dimension will serve only to marginalise international human rights norms and the jurisprudence interpreting them, instead of according them a central role in the development of the common law as envisaged, for example, by Laws J.[18]

That danger is already becoming apparent in a number of cases in which English courts have made reference to the ECHR or its case-law, but only at the very end of the reasoning, supposedly to "reinforce" or "buttress" a conclusion already arrived at in the light of supposedly settled principles of domestic law.[19] The decision of the House of Lords in *Derbyshire* illustrates the danger well.[20] The Court of Appeal, it will be recalled, made extensive reference to the ECHR and its case-law in the course of reaching its conclusion that the common law does not permit a local authority to maintain a libel action in respect of its governing reputation. That decision was upheld by the House of Lords, but the role played by the ECHR in reaching that conclusion was significantly different. Lord Keith, who gave the only judgment, concluded that at common law a local authority did not have the right to sue for libel, but was careful to add that he had reached his conclusion "upon the common law of England, without finding any need to rely upon the European Convention."[21] Agreeing with Lord Goff's *Spycatcher (No.2)* dictum that

---

[18] Lord Browne-Wilkinson himself in his dissent in *Wheeler* v. *Leicester City Council* [1985] AC 1054 at 1064B said that the ECHR did not extend freedoms of conscience and speech any further than domestic law.

[19] Mitchell, considering the likely judicial approach to European Community law in the event of the UK's accession, commented on "the general habits of judges in national courts to assume the identity of other systems of law with that with which they are most familiar": "What do you want to be inscrutable *for*, Marcia?" (1967–8) 5 CMLRev 112 at 117. The observation certainly holds true in the context of judicial approaches to the ECHR.

[20] *Derbyshire County Council* v. *Times Newspapers* [1993] AC 534.

[21] Ibid. at 551F

there was no difference in principle between English law on freedom of speech and Article 10, he merely noted that he found it "satisfactory to be able to conclude that the common law of England is consistent with the obligations assumed by the Crown under the Treaty in this particular field."[22] Although Lord Keith noted that the Court of Appeal had reached the same conclusion principally by reference to Article 10, and summarised that Court's analysis in terms of Article 10,[23] he did not carry out his own analysis and it is clear that he thought it quite unnecessary even to consider the Convention when the answer could be "found" in the common law itself.

A similar contrast is to be found by comparing the decision of the Court of Appeal in *Rantzen*[24] with the subsequent decision of the same court on essentially the same point in *John* v. *MGN Ltd*.[25] In the former case, it will be recalled from chapter 5, the Court of Appeal made extensive use of the concepts and terminology derived from the ECHR and also made lengthy reference to the jurisprudence in which Article 10 had been interpreted and applied by the European Court of Human Rights, in reaching its conclusion that jury awards of libel damages were to be subjected to more rigorous scrutiny than in the past. In *John*, by comparison, Sir Thomas Bingham MR, having already held that libel damages should never exceed the minimum necessary to achieve the underlying purpose of such damages, went on to observe that the same result was achieved by the application of Article 10 of the ECHR, which, whilst not a free-standing source of domestic law, was not in any way in conflict with the common law, but reinforced and buttressed the conclusion reached independently of the Convention.[26] He was anxious to make clear that this conclusion would have been reached in any event, even if the ECHR did not exist. The coincidence in timing of this common law development and the decision of the European Court of Human Rights in *Tolstoy*, in which the limits on the Court of Appeal's power to interfere with jury libel awards was held to be a breach of Article 10, suggests that the Master of the Rolls was rather understating the influence of the developing law of international human rights on this subject.[27]

The same risk, that relying on the rejuvenation of the common law for the effective protection of fundamental rights will marginalise the rich body of international human rights law, was even apparent in *Leech*, the case in which, it will be recalled from chapter 5, the Court of Appeal effectively

---

[22] *Derbyshire County Council* v. *Times Newspapers* [1993] AC 534 at 550. For an example of subsequent reliance on Lord Keith's assertion that Article 10 is coextensive with the English law of freedom of expression, see *Watts* v. *Times Newspapers* [1996] 1 All ER 152 at 167e–f, where it was held that the placing of the onus of proof on the defendant in establishing qualified privilege was not an infringement of freedom of expression.

[23] [1993] AC 534 at 550E–551F.

[24] *Rantzen* v. *Miror Group Newspapers Ltd.* [1994] QB 670.

[25] [1996] 2 All ER 35.

[26] Ibid. at 58j.

[27] *Tolstoy Miloslavsky* v. *UK* (1995) 20 EHRR 442.

adopted Lord Browne-Wilkinson's common law bill of rights approach.[28] The applicant in that case invoked a recent decision of the European Court of Human Rights, *Campbell*, in which the practice complained of had been held to be a violation of Article 8, arguing that the decision could be used to resolve any uncertainty in the common law on the question of interference with solicitor-client confidentiality and as a guide to the minimum interference with that fundamental right that was necessary and justifiable in the prison context.[29] The Court of Appeal, however, preferred to approach the case "from the point of view of settled principles of our domestic law",[30] and referred to *Campbell* only at the very end of the judgment, noting that it "reinforces a conclusion that we have arrived at in the light of the principles of our domestic jurisprudence."[31] Such an approach, referring to the relevant international human rights instrument only as a postscript, is to be contrasted with the approach adopted by the House of Lords in the earlier cases concerning prisoners' correspondence, in which the ECHR was referred to at the stage of articulating the common law principle at stake.[32]

The formula that a conclusion has been reached purely on the basis of the common law, without needing to resort to the ECHR or any other international instrument, is now appearing with remarkable regularity at the end of judgments in which courts have interpreted domestic law in an unusually creative way. Lord Mustill, for example, dissenting in *R* v. *Brown*, thought that the European decisions were a source of valuable guidance on the approach the English courts should adopt to the question of criminalising consensual sado-masochistic conduct. He took heart from the fact that the decisions of the European Court of Human Rights clearly favoured the appellants' right to privacy, but made sure to add that this was "a conclusion at which I have independently arrived".[33] And in *In re D*, Lord Mustill again (this time with the agreement of the rest of the House of Lords) held that on the view he had reached of the English law, which was "entirely consistent" with the principles to be derived from the ECHR cases, there was no need to engage what he described as "the important general question" which would have arisen if it had differed from ECHR jurisprudence.[34]

---

[28] *R.* v. *Secretary of State for the Home Department, ex p. Leech* [1994] QB 198.

[29] *Campbell* v. *UK* (1992) 15 EHRR 137.

[30] [1994] QB 198 at 217B.

[31] Ibid. at 217F. As was seen in ch. 5, however, the proportionality-type methodology deployed in reaching this conclusion makes it inconceivable that "the principles of our domestic jurisprudence" were not influenced in their application by Steyn LJ's evident familiarity with the ECHR and the adjudicative approach of the Court of Human Rights.

[32] See Lord Wilberforce in *Raymond* v. *Honey* [1983] 1 AC 1 at 10E–F and Lord Goff in *Anderson* [1984] QB 778 at 793E–F.

[33] *R* v. *Brown* [1994] 1 AC 212 at 272G.

[34] *In re D (Minors) (Adoption Reports: Confidentiality)* [1996] AC 593 at 613H–614C. In both cases Lord Mustill expressed scepticism about the value of a vocabulary of "rights". See also Lord Oliver in *Re KD* [1988] 1 All ER 577 at 588.

Even in cases in which it is apparent that the common law has been interpreted, often very creatively, in the light of the Convention, courts continue to insist that the Convention has not played any part in the reasoning. In *Merrick*, for example, the applicant, who had been denied access to his solicitor whilst in custody on remand at a magistrates' court, invoked Article 6(1) of the ECHR in his challenge to the legality of the police's policy of restricting access to specified times.[35] It has long been established in the Convention's jurisprudence that the right of access to court includes the right of access to a lawyer,[36] but the Divisional Court merely recited the applicant's argument to that effect and placed no reliance on either the Convention or its case-law in justifying its decision that the policy was unlawful. Instead, it found there to be a common law right to consult a solicitor as soon as reasonably practicable.[37] It is inconceivable that the court was not influenced in making this important development of the common law by the Strasbourg jurisprudence and the domestic decisions which have in turn been expressly influenced by that jurisprudence.[38]

This trend represents an unfortunate reversion to the judicial tendency which was prevalent in Phase II, whereby the identity of the common law and the Convention is asserted but not substantiated by analysis. It is a worrying development for a number of reasons. First, it appears to undermine to some extent the view which, it has been argued, is implicit in both the Divisional Court's decision in *Choudhury* and the Court of Appeal's decision in *Derbyshire*, that the courts are under an obligation to interpret domestic law so as to be in conformity with the Convention.

Second, it threatens to deprive the courts of the benefit of consideration of the Convention jurisprudence, a repository of years of experience of human rights adjudication by the Strasbourg organs.[39] It is a notable feature of the House of Lords decision in *Derbyshire* that more extensive consideration was given to US and South African authorities than to ECHR case-law. Whilst every sign of judicial comparativism is to be welcomed and encouraged, the relative neglect of the case-law of a legal system of which the UK is an integral part is regrettable.[40]

Third, inherent in the House of Lords approach in *Derbyshire* is a risk that the courts will adopt an interest-balancing approach to adjudication which

[35] *R* v. *Chief Constable of South Wales, ex p. Merrick* [1994] 1 WLR 663.

[36] *Golder* v. *UK* (1975) 1 EHRR 524.

[37] [1994] 1 WLR 663 at 675H–676B.

[38] Eg. *Raymond* v. *Honey* [1983] 1 AC 1 and *R* v. *Secretary of State for the Home Department, ex p. Anderson* [1984] QB 778.

[39] In *In re Z (A Minor) (Freedom of Publication)* [1995] 4 All ER 961, Leggatt J. at first instance, at 966f–j, considered Article 10 ECHR and found the restriction on publication to be justified under Article 10(2); the Court of Appeal did not consider Article 10 at all.

[40] By no means all judges are guilty of such neglect. In *R* v. *Secretary of State for the Home Department, ex p. Norney* [1995] Admin LR 861, for example, Dyson J. at 871D added almost as an afterthought that there was no conflict between the common law and the ECHR, but that did not stop him giving proper consideration to the relevant Article (5(4)) and the case-law relied on.

undervalues the Convention right.[41] Lord Keith's reasoning was that, not only was there no public interest favouring the right of organs of government to sue for libel, but it was contrary to the public interest that they should have such a right, because that would place an undesirable fetter on freedom of speech.[42] Such a characterisation of the nature of Convention rights is likely to lead to a utilitarian balancing exercise which is quite different from the structured proportionality exercise conducted by the Convention organs, and is not likely to lead to the effective protection of Convention rights at the domestic level.

This development means that English courts will not be sensitive to developments in the Strasbourg jurisprudence when they make their decision, thus making it more likely that a decision will be reached which does not conform to the requirements of that case-law and which will ultimately have to be remedied by the long and expensive trip to Strasbourg, the necessity for which, it is often heard, is an indictment of our legal system.

(b) The Danger of Selectivity

In addition to the danger that English courts will deprive themselves of the benefit of substantial and evolving international jurisprudence interpreting international human rights norms as a source of guidance in their development of the common law, the development of an indigenous human rights jurisdiction also carries with it the risk of a very selective recognition of rights which the common law regards as "fundamental". In particular, there is a danger that reliance on judicial development of the indigenous common law may be inherently backward looking. In other words, the rights which the common law is prepared to regard as fundamental are those classical liberal rights, such as the right to property and associated freedom interests, which the common law has traditionally prioritised and against which so much regulatory legislation has been deliberately directed by the administrative state. Indeed, as Sedley has observed, it is no coincidence that one of the main areas in which considerable progress has been made in the domestic recognition of international human rights norms has been that of free speech, which is now, in the age of mass media, a commercially valuable commodity.[43]

The danger of reversing the progress made by the administrative state this century should not be underestimated. There are very real concerns that the

---

[41] See C. Warbrick, "Rights, the European Convention on Human Rights and English Law" (1994) 19 ELR 34 for this criticism. Warbrick makes the same criticism of the reasoning of the House of Lords in *Wynne* v. *Secretary of State for the Home Department* [1993] 1 WLR 115, in which it was held, at 122F–123E, that the conflict between a prisoner's interest in appearing in court in civil proceedings and the public interest in keeping the prisoner secure was best resolved by practical means. Despite the fact that the case clearly concerned the scope of a prisoner's right of access to court, the case was not considered to raise any issue of constitutional principle.

[42] [1993] AC 534 at 549C.

[43] Sedley, J. "Human Rights: A Twenty-First Century Agenda' [1995] PL 386 at 395–6.

ECHR, which is the international human rights instrument most frequently referred to, is not a suitable statement of fundamental values for a modern democratic state, being very much a product of its times and pre-dating the many international treaties now recognising social, cultural and environmental rights. The almost total absence of housing or homelessness cases from the Table in Appendix I, despite the fact that this is one of the most important areas of judicial review,[44] is a reflection of this fact. Similarly, with the occasional exception there is little sign that the courts consider themselves capable of developing a common law principle of equality.[45] It is of the utmost importance that the true basis on which the courts are now giving indirect effect to international human rights law is articulated, so that other international agreements protecting human rights other than those contained in the ECHR or ICCPR, can also begin to permeate national law.

What is needed, then, is the articulation of a stronger legal basis to underpin the status of international human rights law in domestic law.

4.   THE REASONS FOR RECOGNISING AN INTERPRETIVE OBLIGATION

It was commented in chapter 5, when considering Laws's argument that having regard to the ECHR as a text to inform the content of the common law was no less legitimate than referring to cases decided in other jurisdictions,[46] that to equate the ECHR and its case-law with other comparative material was to understate the normative reasons why courts should have regard to it. Many of the reasons why courts should now recognise an interpretive obligation in relation to international human rights law have been stated throughout this book. They embrace a wide range of considerations, from relatively contingent considerations such as the inadequacy of present mechanisms for political accountability to more universalist claims about the special significance of human rights instruments as containing values derived from the lowest of common denominators, common humanity.[47]

One reason for recognising the enhanced normativity of international human rights law, however, has been only fleetingly referred to, and that is

---

[44] See research undertaken by the Public Law Project, *Judicial Review in Perspective* (London: Cavendish Publishing, 1995). Note however that the ECJ in Case 249/86 *Commission* v. *Germany* [1989] ECR, 1263 ruled that the right to respect for family life in Article 8 of the ECHR was relevant in the context of German housing policy.

[45] Lord Scarman's dissent in *Ahmad* v. *ILEA* [1978] QB 36 is a notable exception, in which he was prepared to develop the common law in the light not only of international standards, but domestic positive law passed in order to implement those standards, including the anti-discrimination legislation.

[46] Above n. 13 at 63.

[47] Kirby, "The Role of the Judge in Advancing Human Rights by Reference to International Human Rights Norms" (1988) 62 Austr. LJ 514 has provided a useful summary of many of the arguments both for and against a more proactive judicial role in the protection of fundamental rights.

the unbroken custom of professing adherence to such norms. The normativity of international human rights norms is inevitably increased in the eyes of domestic courts if there is evidence of consistent state practice indicating an acceptance by the state of the binding nature of those norms.[48] What evidence is there of UK state practice indicating such acceptance as far as international human rights instruments are concerned? Inevitably the strongest evidence of such state practice exists in relation to the ECHR. There are numerous ways in which the ECHR influences the national political system, which in turn feed into the legal system. There is a consistent state practice, for example, of passing amending legislation or changing administrative practice to bring domestic law into line with the Convention as interpreted by the European Court of Human Rights where there has been an adverse ruling against the UK Government, or a decision of the Committee of Ministers or a friendly settlement.[49] The ECHR is often taken into account by Parliament when debating legislation,[50] and at the earlier stage of drafting legislation.[51] Indeed, there is even now an established practice that the Law Commission will consider the implications of any proposals for reform in the light of the UK's international obligations under human rights treaties.[52] Similarly, it affects the drafting of delegated legislation and of administrative rules and policies.[53] Sometimes internal administrative guidance is issued aimed deliberately at bringing administrative practice into line with the latest requirements of the ECHR as interpreted by the European Court of Human Rights. Immigration enforcement policy DP/2/93 is probably the most famous example of such a policy.[54]

---

[48] Inevitably there is a considerable overlap between the traditional criteria for recognition of customary international law, and the factors which influence the weight to be given to an international norm in the new paradigm. However, to look for evidence of "state practice" as evidence of the normativity of norms is not the same as applying criteria to determine whether or not a particular norm qualifies for membership of the domestic legal system.

[49] Examples of implementing legislation were given in ch. 4.

[50] During the passage of the Intelligence Services Bill, for example, Lord Lester sought the Lord Chancellor's assurance that the Government fully accepted the principles contained in an amendment he was supporting, the effect of which was to ensure that the Intelligence Services would always act in accordance with the ECHR: HC Deb., Vol. 551 col. 252 (13 January 1994). The Lord Chancellor assured Lord Lester that the principles contained in the amendment had been taken into account in the preparation of the Bill and were embodied in its provisions: ibid., at cols. 252–4.

[51] Though for a criticism of the inadequacy of the present system of pre-legislative scrutiny, see D. Kinley, *The European Convention on Human Rights: Compliance without Incorporation* (Aldershot: Dartmouth, 1993).

[52] See eg. *Law Commission Report on Judicial Review and Statutory Appeals*, Law Comm. No. 226 para. 2.8; Law Commission Consultation Paper No 134, *Consent and Offences Against the Person*, para. 32.4.

[53] See eg. C. Symons, "The Effect of the European Convention on Human Rights on the Preparation and Amendment of Legislation, Delegated Legislation and Administrative Rules in the United Kingdom" in M.P. Furmston, R. Kerridge and B.E. Sufrin (eds.), *The Effect on English Domestic Law of Membership of the European Communities and of Ratification of the European Convention on Human Rights* (The Hague: Martinus Nijhoff, 1983).

[54] See ch. 6 above.

In addition to these influences on the political system evidencing an acceptance of the binding nature of the norms contained in the ECHR and its case-law, there are many examples of statements by government officials indicating such acceptance. There are Baroness Chalker's replies to Lord Lester's questions concerning the Civil Service Code considered in chapter 6 above. The UK Government has itself relied on the increasing domestic impact of international human rights standards when seeking to satisfy the respective enforcement bodies of the ECHR and ICCPR of English law's compatibility with the obligations enshrined in those instruments. In the last two periodic reports to the UN Human Rights Committee under the ICCPR, for example, the Government has stressed the increased influence of the ECHR in domestic courts and even gone so far as to state that international human rights obligations are "part of the legal context in which judges consider themselves to operate."[55] Similarly, in Strasbourg the UK Government has argued before the European Court of Human Rights that judicial review satisfies the requirement in Article 13 ECHR that there be an effective remedy for violations of the Convention, claiming that the grounds of judicial review are sufficiently broad to enable the substance of a Convention claim to be tested before a national authority.[56]

Finally, no amending legislation was passed when the ECHR was ratified, nor when the ICCPR was ratified, suggesting that the Government was content at the time that UK law complied with all the international obligations undertaken.[57] Moreover, the Government has repeatedly asserted, when arguing against the need for incorporation of the ECHR or ICCPR, that incorporation is unnecessary because English law already complies with the requirements of those instruments.[58] In *Kolpinghuis Nijmegen*, the Advocate-General took the view that when a member state decides that the position under national law renders any implementing measures unnecessary, it is clearly for the national court to interpret and apply the national laws in accordance with the requirements of Community law.[59] The same argument, it is suggested, has equal force in relation to the ECHR and other international human rights instruments in respect of which the Government has asserted that no amendment of domestic law is necessary. This is necessary if the executive is to be made to take its international commitments seriously and not be allowed to get away with the sort of "window-dressing" which so offended the High Court of Australia in *Teoh*.

---

[55] 1989 Report to the UNHRC, para. 5; 1994 Report, para. 5 (cited by Klug, Starmer and Weir, *The Three Pillars of Liberty: Political Rights and Freedoms in the UK* (London: Routledge, 1996) at 105).

[56] *Vilvarajah* v. *UK* (1992) 14 EHRR 248.

[57] See F. Klug, K. Starmer and S. Weir, "The British Way of Doing Things: The United Kingdom and the International Covenant on Civil and Political Rights, 1976–94" [1995] PL 504

[58] See eg. Baroness Blatch, HL Deb., Vol. 560 cols. 1164–5 (25 January 1995).

[59] Case 80/86, *Officier Van Justitie* v. *Kolpinghuis Nijmegen* [1987] ECR 3969 at para. 21.

If the case for according greater normative weight to unincorporated international human rights norms is made out, there remains the question how English courts can accommodate that enhanced normativity. A convenient answer to that question is to be found in the analogy with European Community law.

5. THE ANALOGY WITH COMMUNITY LAW

In chapters 2 and 3, extended consideration was given to the question of what justifies the judicial recognition of the direct effect and supremacy of Community law, and the indirect effect of non-directly effective Community law. There it was argued that Community law can no longer be said to owe its status in English courts, in any meaningful sense, to the European Communities Act 1972. Rather, it owes that status to the steady evolution of the common law principle of construction, articulated at an earlier stage in its development by Lord Diplock in *Garland*, that domestic law is to be interpreted in the light of international obligations, an evolution assisted by, but by no means solely attributable to, the ECA 1972. That principle, it was argued, although formulated in relation to international treaties generally, was capable of acquiring greater strength in relation to particular types of international obligations, and had come to have what Allan has called "special moral force" in the case of Community law, reflecting judicial perceptions of the political realities of European integration.[60] The courts, recognising the significance of the UK's participation in a new political entity with its own legal system, have gradually increased the strength of that general principle in relation to Community law. Indeed, in relation to directly effective Community law they have imbued it with such strength as to lead them to "disapply" an Act of Parliament which cannot be rescued from irreconcilable conflict by interpretive ingenuity. In the case of non-directly effective Community law, the principle is weaker, permitting irreconcilable conflict where unavoidable, but is still of sufficient strength to require them to strive conscientiously to give domestic law a meaning which will avoid such conflict.

This book draws on the analogy provided by the constitutional accommodation of Community law to argue that, just as the *Garland* principle of construction has acquired special moral force in relation to Community law, so also it should be recognised as having special moral force in relation to international human rights law.[61] It is not argued, at least not at this stage in the

[60] T.R.S. Allan, *Law, Liberty and Justice: The Legal Foundations of British Constitutionalism* (Oxford: Clarendon Press, 1993) at 276, 279.

[61] Wade, in his comment on the decision in *Factortame (No. 2)*, "What has Happened to the Sovereignty of Parliament?" 107 LQR 1 at 4, also seeks to draw an analogy, asking whether there might be any lessons to be learnt from what he sees as the constitutional revolution in relation to Community law as far as the future domestic status of the European Convention on Human Rights is concerned. However, remaining steadfastly loyal to his continuing sovereignty premise,

UK's constitutional development, that the principle should be of the same strength as that which is now applied in relation to directly effective Community law. That would be not only to make international human rights law directly effective, but to recognise its supremacy over domestic law where the two are in conflict. This, on the present state of the law, would be too great a departure from present practice. All that is argued for is an acceptance that the principle is of equivalent force to that now recognised in relation to non-directly effective Community law, that is, of such strength as to amount to an obligation on domestic courts to construe domestic law in such a way as to achieve consistency with the relevant international norms, if such consistency can be achieved.

Even if, however, one accepts the premise of this argument, that Community law owes its special status in the UK, not solely to the ECA 1972, but to an evolution in the courts' perceptions of political reality, it might still be retorted that the analogy with international human rights law is a weak one because such law does not form part of a distinct legal order which claims supremacy over national legal orders, nor emanate from political institutions enjoying anything like the significance of the European Community. It is certainly true that none of the international systems for the protection of human rights makes quite the same demands on national legal systems as those made by the European Community legal system. As was seen in chapter 2, it is, in effect, a condition of membership of the Community that member states make any necessary constitutional changes to be able to accommodate the ECJ's integrationist creations of direct effect and supremacy, to which should now be added the interpretive obligation in relation to non-directly effective Community law. However, to rely on these obvious differences between the nature of the Community and the international systems for the protection of human rights as political and legal entities is to overlook a fundamental requirement of those systems which, it is suggested, is crucial to establishing the analogy. That requirement is the obligation on member states to provide effective remedies for the protection of the rights and achievement of the goals for which the member states brought the system into existence in the first place.

It will be recalled from chapters 2 and 3 that the common thread running through the reasoning of the ECJ in its landmark constitutional decisions establishing the doctrines of direct effect, supremacy and indirect effect was the principle of the practical effectiveness of Community law. In *Van Gend en Loos, Costa, Simmenthal, Factortame, Von Colson* and *Marleasing* the Court, in one form or another, stressed the importance of ensuring that Community law had practical effect throughout the member states if the Community's goals were to be achieved. Indeed, the Court consistently relied on this as one of the principal justifications for the significant developments which those

he is only prepared to speculate about the possibilities which are thereby opened up for "entrenching" the ECHR or a bill of rights by legislative means.

cases represent. For the ECJ, such a principle flowed inexorably from the very nature of the entity which had been created, but a Treaty foundation for the principle of *effet utile*, or practical effectiveness, was also found in Article 5 of the EC Treaty, containing the obligation to take all appropriate measures to ensure the fulfilment of Community obligations and to facilitate the achievement of the Community's tasks.[62] It is the UK courts' eventual acceptance of this ultimate foundation for the doctrines of supremacy and direct and indirect effect, it is suggested, that is the real basis for Community law's current status.

6. THE PRINCIPLE OF PRACTICAL EFFECTIVENESS IN INTERNATIONAL HUMAN RIGHTS LAW

The same general principle of practical effectiveness finds expression in all the main international human rights instruments. Article 8 of the Universal Declaration, for example, provides that "everyone has the right to an effective remedy by the competent national tribunals for acts violating the fundamental rights granted him by the constitution or by law". Under the ICCPR, each State Party undertakes, by Article 2(2), to take the necessary steps to adopt such legislative or other measures as may be necessary to give effect to the rights recognised in the Covenant, and, by Article 2(3), to ensure that any person whose rights and freedoms are violated shall have an effective remedy. In the ECHR, Article 1 requires the Contracting Parties to secure to everyone within their jurisdiction the Convention rights and freedoms[63] and Article 13 imposes an obligation on member states to provide an effective national remedy for violations of the Convention.[64]

The European Court of Human Rights, constrained no doubt by its perception that the Council of Europe is of a more intergovernmental nature than the European Community, has been less bold than the ECJ in its elaboration of the principle underlying this provision.[65] There is no *Van Gend en Loos* in

[62] Advocate General Tesauro in Case C-213/89, *R* v. *Secretary of State for Transport, ex p. Factortame Ltd* (No. 2) [1991] 1 AC 603 at 627C, for example, described Art. 5 EC as "the real key to the interpretation of the whole system".

[63] See Robertson and Merrills, *Human Rights in Europe* 3rd edn. (Manchester: Manchester University Press, 1993), ch.1, for the significance of a last-minute amendment to the text of Article 1 making it clear that the member states already recognised the rights set out in the Convention, rather than merely undertook to recognise them in future.

[64] See Harris, O'Boyle & Warbrick, *Law of the European Convention on Human Rights* (London: Butterworths, 1995), ch. 14; Van Dijk & Van Hoof, *Theory and Practice of the European Convention on Human Rights*, 2nd edn., (Dordrecht: Kluwer, 1990) at 520–32; Robertson & Merrills, (above n. 63) at 167–71; S. Farran, *The UK Before the European court of Human Rights: Case Law and Commentary* (London: Blackstone Press, 1996) ch. 13.

[65] For criticism of the Court's Article 13 jurisprudence for not requiring more of member states, see Van Dijk and Van Hoof, (above n. 64) at 528–31; Thune in D. Gomien (ed.), *Broadening the Frontiers of Human Rights: Essays in Honour of Asbjorn Eide* (Oslo: Scandinavian University Press, 1993) at 79.

the Strasbourg jurisprudence; it was established early in the life of the Convention that neither Article 13 nor anything else in the Convention imposes an obligation on member states to give direct effect to its provisions by incorporation into the national legal system.[66] That having been established, there could be no question of a *Costa* or a *Simmenthal*; without an obligation to incorporate, there could obviously be no obligation to make convention law supreme. Article 13 has therefore been interpreted as not requiring the availability of a remedy for violation of the Convention by primary legislation,[67] nor for legislative violation of equivalent domestic norms.[68] It follows that, so long as the present interpretation of Article 13 prevails, the Strasbourg organs will not require an ECHR equivalent of *Factortame* in English courts.

What Article 13 has been interpreted as requiring is the possibility of "canvassing the substance" of the Convention argument before a national authority.[69] So, not only is there no obligation to incorporate the Convention into domestic law, and no requirement to give a remedy for legislative violations of the Convention, but Article 13 does not even require national courts to take it expressly into account when interpreting their domestic law. It is enough for national law to provide a procedure which gives the applicant an opportunity to make the substance of the argument that would be made if the Convention could be relied on directly. It is fair to say, then, that the principle of indirect effect recognised by the Strasbourg jurisprudence is considerably weaker than the obligation imposed on national courts by the ECJ in relation to non-directly effective Community law. Just as there is no *Van Gend en Loos* or *Costa*, so there is no direct equivalent of *Marleasing* or *Von Colson*, requiring national courts to do their best to construe domestic law in a way which is consistent with the ECHR.

Notwithstanding the timidity of the Court and Commission in their enunciation of the general principles said to underlie Article 13, the provision remains of crucial importance in the overall scheme of rights protection under the ECHR. As Steiner and Alston usefully remind us, human rights violations occur *within* a state, principally in relations between a government and its own citizens, and, ultimately, effective protection must come from within the state.[70] All international systems of human rights protection therefore rely on the domestic legal system as the first line of defence against violations of inter-

---

[66] *Ireland* v. *UK* (1978) 2 EHRR 25. The ICCPR similarly has not been interpreted by the UN Human Rights Committee as requiring state parties to incorporate the Covenant into domestic law, nor to adopt a Bill of Rights. Indeed, Article 2(2) expressly provides that the steps required to be taken to give effect to the rights in the Covenant may be such as are in accordance with its constitutional processes.

[67] *Young, James and Webster* v. *UK* (1981) 4 EHRR 38.

[68] *Leander* v. *Sweden* (1987) 9 EHRR 433, at para. 77.

[69] *Soering* v. *UK* (1989) 11 EHRR 439 at 481 (para. 121).

[70] H.J. Steiner and P. Alston, *International Human Rights in Context: Law, Politics and Morals* (Oxford: Clarendon Press, 1996) at 709.

national norms.[71] As a means of encouraging member states to perform that role properly by providing effective national remedies, Article 13 is a potentially powerful instrument in the hands of the Convention organs. In this sense, it is the equivalent of Article 5 of the EC Treaty, for it too plays a central role in the co-operative relationship between the ECHR institutions and the legal systems of the member states.[72] By placing primary responsibility on the national legal system for implementing and enforcing the rights protected by the Convention, Article 13 could be interpreted in a way which emulates the similar approach of the ECJ in providing for the decentralised enforcement of Community rights by requiring national authorities to ensure their effective protection in the national legal system.[73] Unlike the ECJ, however, the European Court of Human Rights has not adopted a teleological approach to Article 13. As O'Boyle *et al* observe, given that one of the main goals of the Convention system is to make recourse to the Strasbourg institutions a matter of last resort, it is surprising that the Court has not been more consistent in interpreting Article 13 in a way which enhances the effectiveness of national remedies.[74]

7. JUDICIAL REVIEW AS AN "EFFECTIVE REMEDY"

Given that the ECHR has no direct effect in the UK due to its non-incorporation, and that the dualist tradition of UK courts has tended to limit the degree to which it enjoys any indirect effect, it is important to ask whether English law complies with even the minimum conditions which the European Court of Human Rights has held Article 13 to impose?[75] Generally this is not a question which can be answered in the abstract,[76] but there are features of certain English procedures which make it valid to inquire whether they can ever provide an effective remedy within the meaning of Article 13.

In light of the determined judicial resistance to the influence of human rights law or thinking on administrative law, demonstrated in chapters 4 to 6 above, it is no surprise that the greatest controversy has arisen over whether the present law of judicial review satisfies even the minimal requirements of

---

[71] As Steiner and Alston also point out, ibid. at 708, states are not only the violators of human rights, but are also "the first-line enforcers of the international human rights system that they have created." See, to similar effect, Robertson and Merrills, (above n. 63) at 27.

[72] See Campbell's analysis of the relationship between national courts and the Community legal system: C. Campbell, "National Legislation and EC Directives: Judicial Co-operation and National Autonomy" (1992) 43 NILQ 330.

[73] O'Boyle *et al.*, (above n. 64) at 461.

[74] Ibid.

[75] As O'Boyle et al point out, ibid. at 461, it is no coincidence that so many of the cases on Article 13 originate in the UK, adding the discretionary or residual nature of much public power and the relatively unintrusive judicial control as other features making Article 13 particularly relevant to the UK.

[76] See *AGOSI* v. *UK*. Series A No. 108 (1986).

Article 13. The problem arises for all the reasons encountered in those chapters when trying to account for the general hostility of English courts to human rights arguments in judicial review cases. The judicial insistence on preserving the supposed distinction between the "manner" in which a decision is made and "the merits"; the preservation of the high threshold *Wednesbury* test for irrationality challenges; and the refusal, so far, to give practical effect to the concept of proportionality as part of English law, or even, in the case of some judges, to countenance the possibility, are all potential obstacles to the effectiveness of judicial review as a remedy for the purposes of Article 13. Whether, in the light of those limitations, the availability of judicial review amounts to a substantively effective remedy as required by that Article has led to a difference of opinion between the Commission and the Court.

In *Soering*, in which the applicant challenged a decision to extradite him to the United States to stand trial for murder, it was argued not only that to do so would violate his rights under Article 3 by exposing him to the risk of inhuman or degrading treatment in the form of death row phenomenon, but that there had also been a violation of Article 13, because he could not make that argument to an English court when challenging the decision by way of judicial review.[77] The Commission accepted the argument and found a violation of Article 13,[78] but the Court held that the substance of the applicant's Article 3 argument could have been put to an English court on judicial review under the head of irrationality. The availability of judicial review was therefore held to be a substantively effective remedy for the purposes of Article 13.

The Court reached the same conclusion in *Vilvarajah*, in which the applicants challenged the decision to deport them on the ground that it violated their right to life under Article 2, and that the inability to make that argument on their unsuccessful judicial review of the decision violated Article 13.[78a] Again the Commission agreed with the applicants and the Court disagreed, holding that judicial review had provided an effective remedy. The Court was clearly influenced in reaching that decision by the fact that English courts professed to carry out a stricter scrutiny in cases where the right to life itself was at stake.[79] Even the House of Lords' very clear contradistinction between a proportionality doctrine and the permissible limits of judicial review in *Brind*[80] failed to persuade the Commission that the scope of judicial review was inadequate for the purposes of Article 13. Notwithstanding that one of the central issues arising in that case was whether the broadcasting ban could be considered to be proportionate to its aim under Article 10(2) of the Convention, and that it was precisely that test of proportionality which the House of Lords declined to apply, the journalists' complaint was declared inadmissible.

[77] *Soering* v. *UK* (1989) 11 EHRR 439 at 480, (para. 116).
[78] Ibid. at 500–2, (paras. 158–68).
[78a] (1991) 14 EHRR 248.
[79] *Bugdaycay* [1987] AC 514 considered in ch. 5 above.
[80] (1994) 18 EHRR CD76 at CD84

The problem with the Court's approach to Article 13 and the adequacy of judicial review is that it is too easily persuaded that the mere ability to make an argument satisfies the requirement that there be an opportunity to canvass the substance of the Convention argument before the domestic court. The fact is that the restrictions on the supervisory jurisdiction of the High Court on judicial review[81] do not permit the court to carry out the balancing exercise which is necessary if the substance of the Convention argument is to be properly "canvassed". The mere fact that there has been (or could have been) an opportunity to put the substance of a Convention argument before a domestic judge is not enough if the grounds of judicial review are so restricted as not to permit a proper balancing exercise to be carried out, in which the justification for the alleged interference with the applicant's right is scrutinised and subjected to a proportionality test. To put an argument before a court which perceives its hands to be tied in this way does not lead to the substance of the Convention argument being "canvassed" in any meaningful sense of that word. It is asserted by the applicant, but not addressed by the court.

The refusal to depart from *Soering* and *Vilvarajah* in *Brind* has led some to conclude that nothing will now persuade the Court of Human Rights that judicial review is anything other than an adequate and effective remedy for the purposes of Article 13.[81a] However, the Court of Appeal has now obligingly provided even more convincing evidence of the manifest ineffectiveness of judicial review than that provided by the House of Lords in *Brind*. In *Smith*, the gays in the military case, all three members of the Court of Appeal candidly pointed out the contrast between the role of an English court in judicial review and the role of the European Court of Human Rights.[82] As Henry LJ put it,[83]

> "If the Convention were part of our law, then . . . the primary judgment on this issue would be for the judges. But Parliament has not given us that primary jurisdiction on this issue. Our present constitutional role was correctly identified . . . as exercising a secondary or reviewing judgment. As it is, in relation to the Convention, the only primary judicial role lies with the European Court of Human Rights at Strasbourg."

---

[81] The same applies to statutory appeals such as those under the Town and Country Planning Act 1990.

[81a] In *Chahal* v. *UK* (decision of European Court of Human Rights, 15 November 1996), however, it was held that there was a violation of Art. 13 in conjunction with the right in Art. 3 not to be subjected to torture or to inhuman or degrading treatment or punishment, in a case in which the UK Government relied on national security grounds to justify its proposed deportation of the applicant. The Court held, at paras. 150–5, that in view of the extent of the deficiencies of both judicial review proceedings and the special "advisory panel" procedure used in national security cases, those remedies, even taken together, could not be said to satisfy the requirements of Art. 13 in conjunction with Art. 3. Although the Court was careful to confine its comments to Art. 13 in the context of Art. 3 rights, to which it attaches special importance, it is arguable that the decision presupposes a notion of "effective remedy" under Art. 13 which requires some independent scrutiny of the Government's justification for interfering with Convention rights.

[82] *R* v. *Ministry of Defence, ex p. Smith* [1996] 1 All ER 257, considered in chapter 6 above.

[83] Ibid. at 272c.

Amongst the reasons the judge gave for not expressing a view as to whether there was in that case a violation of the Convention were that

> "the evidence and submissions before us were directed to our secondary review jurisdiction, and not to the primary jurisdiction. We should not opine on a case not argued before us. If the Convention were . . . part of our domestic law, then in the exercise of the primary jurisdiction the court in, for it, a relatively novel constitutional position, might well ask for more material than the adversarial system normally provides, such as a Brandeis brief. The court could well appear to be taking too narrow a view if it hypothetically answered a different question on limited evidence."[84]

These dicta make abundantly clear the inadequacy of judicial review for the purposes of canvassing the substance of the applicants' Convention arguments. In *Brind*, as was seen in chapter 5, the refusal to apply an overt proportionality test was compensated for by the application of a more rigorous scrutiny looking remarkably similar, which may have satisfied the Commission in the same way as the Court had been satisfied by the *Bugdaycay* presumption in *Vilvarajah*. In *Smith*, however, the inadequacy of judicial review was expressly relied upon by the court as the reason for not taking a view on the substance of the applicants' Convention argument, which will make it that much more difficult for the Court of Human Rights to find that there has been no violation of Article 13.[85]

The combination of the attitude of domestic courts to the limited scope of their judicial review jurisdiction and the attitude of the European Court of Human Rights to Article 13 has trapped those attempting to enforce their Convention rights in a "Catch-22" situation. On the one hand, the UK Government has argued in domestic courts that no special test applies in a fundamental rights case from any other case.[86] On the other hand, it has argued in Strasbourg either that a complainant has failed to exhaust domestic remedies by not applying for judicial review (when to do so would likely be hopeless anyway), or that judicial review was an effective remedy so that there is no violation of Article 13. In *McQuillan*, as was seen in chapter 7, Sedley J. sought to square the circle. He invoked the UK Government's own argument before the European Court of Human Rights in *Vilvarajah*, that a rationality

---

[84] See, to similar effect, Sir Thomas Bingham MR, [1996] 1 All ER 257 at 267d and Thorpe LJ at 273c.

[85] The Human Rights Committee, in its Comments on the UK's Fourth Periodic Report on compliance with the ICCPR, found that the legal system of the UK does not ensure fully that an effective remedy is provided for all violations of the rights contained in the Covenant, as a result of the combined effects of the non-incorporation of the Covenant into domestic law, the refusal to sign the Optional Protocol and the absence of a domestic Bill of Rights: *Comments of the Human Rights Committee: United Kingdom of Great Britain and Northern Ireland*, July 27, 1995, CCPR/C/79/Add. 55, para. 9.

[86] See ch. 6. The practice is exemplified by the arguments in the gays in the military case, in which it was argued not only that no different test applies in fundamental rights cases, but that an even higher standard than usual (so-called "super-*Wednesbury*") should be applied because of the alleged "national security" context.

argument was available to the applicant in that case had he challenged the decision by way of judicial review, to hold that the common law already independently recognised the fundamental right to life as a relevant consideration to be taken into account in the exercise of executive discretion.[87]

One solution would be to recognise a general interpretive obligation in relation to international human rights norms, including those contained in the ECHR. *Von Colson* provides the ideal analogy from the Community law context. There it was recognised by the ECJ that courts are "national authorities" for the purpose of the relevant Treaty Articles, and therefore share responsibility with the political branches for ensuring that Community obligations are carried out. Under the ECHR, not only are courts required under Article 13 to ensure that effective remedies are available for violations of Convention rights, but they are also public authorities for the purpose of all the other rights in the Convention, and are as capable of infringing those rights as are the political branches. As the *Sunday Times* litigation demonstrates, court judgments engage a state's liability under the Convention, in the sense that a judicial interpretation of the common law may infringe the rights protected under the Convention. This fact alone is sufficient to ground an interpretive obligation, as a matter of Convention law, when courts interpret the common law. If they wish to avoid inadvertently interpreting domestic law in a way which itself infringes the Convention, they should take its provisions into account when deciding on the meaning to be given to domestic law.[88] The proposed interpretive obligation would ensure that English law complies with Article 13, as well as enhancing the degree of domestic protection for Convention rights. The emergence of such an obligation in the national courts of states in which the ECHR lacks internal legal validity has been described as an "encouraging tendency" by Bernhardt.[89]

8. WILL AN INTERPRETIVE OBLIGATION MAKE ANY DIFFERENCE?

Even if the courts were to take the step advocated here, and recognise a full interpretive obligation to interpret domestic law so as to be in conformity with international human rights norms, would it make any practical difference to the domestic level of observance of those norms? Bratza, surveying the

---

[87] [1995] 4 All ER 400 at 409f–g, a good example of judicial development of the common law by reference to the state's own account of its practice, bridging the gap between rhetoric and reality in the process.

[88] Since, in Strasbourg, responsibility for defending a judicial interpretation of the common law falls on the Government, it can only be assumed that the Government would prefer the courts to consider the Convention's provisions at the time of reaching its decision on the meaning of the common law, to minimise the likelihood of a conflict arising and being subsequently held to account in Strasbourg.

[89] R. Bernhardt, "The Convention and Domestic Law" in R. St. J. Macdonald, F. Matscher and H. Petzold (eds.), *The European System for the Protection of Human Rights* (Dordrecht, Martinus Nijhoff, 1993) at 26.

cases in which the ECHR had been judicially referred to by 1993, concluded that it had made little or no difference to the result at which the court arrived.[90] McCrudden and Chambers are equally negative about its impact, concluding that indirect use of the Convention in the courts has proved of limited utility so far.[91] According to the Democratic Audit's analysis, the Convention could be said to have affected the outcome in only three of the cases between 1972 and 1993 in which it has been cited in the judgment.[92]

A similar question was asked in chapter 6 in the context of the ECHR's emerging status in certain contexts as a mandatory consideration to be taken into account in the exercise of administrative discretion. There it was observed that, so long as courts regard the "relevant considerations" ground of judicial review as a "procedural" ground only, so that the court's inquiry is exhausted when it is satisfied that the relevant part of the ECHR was in fact taken into account, the Convention's emerging status as a mandatory consideration would make little or no difference to the outcomes of cases. Unless courts were prepared to require evidence of the balancing exercise having been carried out, and to review its outcome for disproportionate impact on the fundamental right or interest affected, it was observed, respondents would simply redraft their decision-letters to make them "judge-proof".

The same general point applies in relation to the proposed interpretive obligation. To recognise an interpretive obligation in relation to international human rights instruments is to do much more than merely "have regard to" a particular catalogue of rights and freedoms when interpreting domestic law. As was demonstrated in chapters 5 and 6, it is also to adopt the methodology of a constitutional court, and in particular to apply a proportionality test to determine the justifiability of any impact on a protected right. As was also seen in those chapters, many courts are already effectively doing this, but recognition of an interpretive obligation would require it to be done explicitly. A reviewing court would be required, not merely to advert to the fundamental right which might be at stake, but to articulate the standard of justification appropriate to the case, making clear the factors, such as the importance of the right, the extent of the impact upon it, or the nature of the subject-matter of the decision, which will affect the stringency of the standard of justification to be applied in the particular case. It will not be sufficient, as many courts in the past seem to have assumed, merely to find that a challenged decision is within the proviso to a particular right just by virtue of some public interest being invoked, without carrying out any balancing exercise of the competing rights and interests at stake.

---

[90] N. Bratza, "The Treatment and Interpretation of the European Convention on Human Rights by the English Courts" in Gardner (ed.), *Aspects of Incorporation of the European Convention on Human Rights into Domestic Law* (London: British Institute of Human Rights, 1993), 65 at 67.

[91] McCrudden & Chambers, *Individual Rights and the Law in Britain* (above n. 17) at 575.

[92] F. Klug, K. Starmer & S. Weir, (above n. 55) at 106.

Another way in which the effectiveness of any interpretive obligation could be thwarted would be by the unthinking adoption by English courts of the Strasbourg concept of the "margin of appreciation."[93] That doctrine embodies the notion of a legitimate area of discretion available to a national decision-maker within which the European Convention organs will not interfere because, within that area, the national decision-maker is better placed than the supranational institutions to make a judgment. The analogy with the notion of an administrative decision-maker's sphere of autonomy with which a reviewing court ought not to interfere is immediately apparent, and the danger is that courts will simply exchange the deferential *Wednesbury* standard for the "margin of appreciation" concept in the Strasbourg jurisprudence, notwithstanding that the reasons why a supranational body should exercise judicial restraint are likely to be different from the reasons why it might be appropriate for a domestic court to defer. The concept has already begun to appear with alarming regularity in recent domestic cases and commentary,[94] and there is a grave risk that judicial enthusiasm for it will prevent the articulation of differential standards of review which are sensitive to the multiplicity of context-dependent factors which determine the appropriate standard of review. That risk will be much enhanced if the UK Government succeeds in its current campaign to persuade other members of the Council of Europe to press for "a wider and more consistent application of the margin of appreciation", which would turn the doctrine into a supranational *Wednesbury* standard of review.[95] Even if the analogy itself were not problematic, the margin of appreciation in the Strasbourg case-law more often than not operates as a conclusory label which precludes a proper consideration of the appropriate intensity of review, and there must be a very real risk of importing those deficiencies in its operation along with the concept itself.

However, these reasons for doubting whether reference to international human rights law by domestic courts makes any difference to outcomes must be weighed against a number of other considerations which give greater cause

[93] Harris, O'Boyle & Warbrick, (above n. 64) at 12–15; Van Dijk & Van Hoof, (above n. 64) at 585–606. See also T.H. Jones, "The Devaluation of Human Rights under the European Convention" [1995] PL 430.

[94] See eg. De Smith, Woolf & Jowell, *Judicial Review of Administrative Action* 2nd edn., (London: Sweet and Maxwell, 1995) at 586; Irvine "Judges and Decision-Makers: The Theory and Practice of *Wednesbury* Review" [1996] PL 59 at 67 and 74; Laws "Law and Democracy" [1995] PL 72 at 92–3. For examples of judicial use of the margin of appreciation concept, see *Derbyshire County Council* v. *Times Newspapers Ltd.* [1992] QB 770 at 786; *R* v. *Ministry of Defence, ex p. Smith* [1996] QB 517 at 566F; *R* v. *Secretary of State for the Home Department, ex p. Mbatube* [1996] Imm AR 184 at 188; *R* v. *Radio Authority, ex p. Bull* [1996] QB 169 at 192F.

[95] In a UK position paper on the European Court and Commission of Human Rights circulated by the Foreign Office in 1996 to other Council of Europe members, the UK Government suggested "a resolution in the Committee of Ministers, drawing on the following points: (a) account should be taken of the fact that democratic institutions and tribunals in Member States are best placed to determine moral and social issues in accordance with regional and national perceptions; (b) full regard should be paid to decisions by democratic legislatures and to differing legal traditions; (c) long-standing laws and practices should be respected, except where these are manifestly contrary to the Convention."

for optimism. The impact of international human rights law where it has been referred to is difficult to quantify, since its influence may often be indirect and, as was seen above, may often play an unacknowledged part in the formulation or development of the common law. Bratza's observation that, more often than not, the ECHR was invoked by the court to reinforce the view which had already been plainly formed by the court as to the outcome of the case, should therefore be treated with caution. The formula now appearing with increasing regularity in English judgments, that a particular conclusion has been reached on the basis of the common law without needing to resort to the ECHR or any other international instrument should not be taken at face value. In fact, as was seen above, it is often very clearly the case that a court's development of the common law has been influenced by an instrument such as the ECHR or the jurisprudence interpreting that development, but courts prefer to couch their reasoning in terms of the indigenous common law in order to confer greater legitimacy on the exercise of infusing human rights standards into domestic law.

That an interpretive obligation is capable of making a very real difference to outcomes in practice can be very briefly demonstrated, by taking two examples from contexts in which the ECHR has recently begun to be used a great deal more than in the past: immigration and planning. In the planning context, the human rights dimension, which is present in many planning decisions affecting minorities such as gypsies and travellers, has traditionally played a very subsidiary role. It has been swept into a narrow personal circumstances exception to a general presumption that planning is concerned with land use in the narrow sense. On the traditional approach, the general principle has been that the test of what is a material consideration in planning terms is whether it serves a planning purpose, and a planning purpose is one which relates to the character of the use of the land.[96] The personal circumstances of an occupier and personal hardship, however, were not to be ignored in the administration of planning control.[97] However, it is quite clear that, even if relevant in a particular case, personal circumstances will seldom outweigh the more general planning considerations.[98] The questions which fell to be decided in the law of planning were primarily questions of land-use, to which personal circumstances were of only peripheral relevance and only likely to make a difference to the outcome in the most exceptional of cases.

Introducing a human rights dimension, however, as recognition of the proposed interpretive obligation would do as a matter of course, requires decision-makers to approach the questions to be determined from a quite different perspective where the decision interferes with a fundamental right. Instead of the onus resting on those adversely affected by planning decisions to show that theirs is one of those most exceptional cases where "personal

[96] See eg. *Westminster City Council* v. *Great Portland Estates* [1985] AC 661 at 670C–D.
[97] Ibid. at 670E–H.
[98] See eg. para. 38 of Planning Policy Guidance Note 1.

circumstances" ought to outweigh planning considerations, the onus transfers to the planning authority to demonstrate that any interference with a presumptively protected right, such as the right to respect for home or family life, can be justified as being proportionate to the aims served by planning control. This switch of onus, once the persons affected have established that the decision engages their fundamental rights, has the potential to make an important difference in practical terms, if properly followed through by the courts. In some recent cases, in which it has been held that planning authorities must have regard to "considerations of common humanity" before exercising their planning enforcement powers, there are signs that some courts are already beginning to introduce a human rights dimension without any reference to international standards. Acceptance of an interpretive obligation would help to hasten this important reorientation of the law of planning around the human dimension.[99]

The other context which provides concrete evidence of the difference which can be made by the introduction of a human rights dimension is immigration which has already been considered in detail in chapter 6. There, again, human rights considerations have traditionally been swept into the category of "compassionate circumstances", to be weighed against the presumptive public interest in immigration control, but only capable of influencing the outcome in the most exceptional of cases.[100] The introduction of policy DP/2/93 in effect displaces that presumption, and in its place introduces presumptions against enforcement in certain categories of case, reflecting the presumptive importance of the fundamental rights at stake in those types of case. Although, as was seen in chapter 6, the existence of the policy is no guarantee that the courts will apply the correct approach, there are some examples of cases in which courts have forsaken the old, deferential approach based on compassionate circumstances, in favour of imposing a heavy onus on the decision-maker to justify with detailed reasons an infringement of a fundamental right.[101]

9. CONCLUSION

This chapter has sought to state the case for the recognition by English courts of a strong interpretive obligation to construe domestic law so as to be consistent with international human rights norms. The Bangalore Principles considered in chapter 1, were an important and timely step in the right direction,

---

[99] See eg. *R* v. *Lincolnshire County Council, ex p. Atkinson*, The Times, 22 September 1995; *R* v. *Kerrier District Council, ex p. Uzell* (1996) 71 P & CR 566.

[100] See eg, para. 364 of the Immigration Rules, under which decision-makers apply a presumption in favour of deportation and ask whether there are compassionate circumstances which outweigh that presumption.

[101] See eg. *R* v. *Secretary of State ex p. Zighem* [1996] Imm AR 194.

but they fall short of recognising an interpretive obligation. In particular, their retention of ambiguity as a precondition of reference to international human rights norms will inhibit the development of domestic law so as to conform with those norms. If the ambiguity precondition is abandoned, it has been argued throughout this book, there is enormous scope for remedying domestically many of the violations of international norms which have recently been identified by thorough research of the UK's present arrangements.[102]

Virtually all commentators on this subject since the early 1970s have agreed that, while there is some evidence of imaginative use made by the courts of international human rights law, there remains ample scope for a bolder use of such law, both in the development of the common law and in the review of administrative decisions.[103] This book has attempted to articulate a legal basis on which to construct arguments which make greater use of such norms. Inevitably, the influence of international human rights law will vary considerably between different judges.[104] Ultimately, as Higgins reminds us, the receptiveness of courts to arguments invoking such law is a matter of legal culture, and as Kirby observes, it will take an act of will on the part of a generation of judges gradually to place domestic law into its international setting.[105] The present generation of English judges has that opportunity, whether or not the European Convention on Human Rights is incorporated into domestic law. If they are to seize it, they must take seriously their special responsibility, as organs of the state, for ensuring the effective protection of the rights enshrined in the international instruments. But above all, if recognition of the interpretive obligation advocated here is to make any difference, they must be prepared to acknowledge the nature of the transformation which has taken place in English legal culture as a result of the variety of international and European influences, and embrace the constitutionalism which embodies the spirit of the times.

---

[102] See Klug et al. (The Democratic Audit, 1996), above, n. 55, and C. Foley (with Liberty), *Human Rights, Human Wrongs: The Alternative Report to the United Nations Human Rights Committee* (London: Rivers Oram Press, 1995).

[103] See eg. Scarman, *English Law—The New Dimension*, Hamlyn Lectures (London: Stevens, 1974) at 85–8 and *The Shape of Things to Come: The Shape of the Future Law and Constitution of the United Kingdom*, Radcliffe Lectures (Warwick: University of Warwick, 1988) at 60–2; Duffy, "English Law and the European Convention on Human Rights" (1980) 29 ICLQ 585; Woolf, *Protection of the Public—A New Challenge*, Hamlyn Lectures (London: Stevens, 1990) at 120–2.

[104] Klug et al., op cit. at 106.

[105] Kirby, "The Role of the Judge in Advancing Human Rights by Reference to International Human Rights Norms" (1988) 62 Austr. LJ 514.

Appendix I

CHRONOLOGICAL TABLE OF ENGLISH CASES IN WHICH
JUDICIAL REFERENCE HAS BEEN MADE TO UNINCORPORATED
INTERNATIONAL HUMAN RIGHTS LAW

Explanatory notes:

1. The unincorporated international human rights instruments covered by the Table are the European Convention on Human Rights ("the ECHR"), the International Covenant on Civil and Political Rights ("the ICCPR") and the Universal Declaration of Human Rights ("the UDHR").

2. Cases in which the report indicates that a relevant human rights instrument was referred to in argument but not in the judgment of the court, or where the reference merely recites the use made of the instrument by the Court below, are not included in the Table. However, the Table does include cases in which reference has been made to international human rights law in the course of, for example, applications for leave to apply for judicial review, even where such reference has been fleeting, in order to give a comprehensive picture of the areas in which such law is most frequently invoked and those in which it most frequently meets judicial resistance.

3. The Table does not claim to be exhaustive in its coverage, but is as comprehensive as current research tools permit.

4. Bold type in column 1 indicates that a case is referred to in the text of the book.

5. ^{EC} in column 1 indicates a case concerning the interrelationship of the ECHR and EC law.

6. ^{LiP} in column 1 indicates a case in which a human rights instrument was relied on by a litigant in person.

7. $^{DP/2/93}$ in column 1 indicates an immigration case concerning Home Office enforcement policy DP/2/93.

8. † in column 3 indicates dissenting judge.

9. * in column 3 indicates the relevant judge where more than one judgment was handed down but not all members of the court made reference to unincorporated international human rights law.

10. The subject-matter categories in column 5 refer to that aspect of the case in which the human rights question arose.

11. ( ) around a treaty article or case name in columns 7 or 8 indicates that the specific Article or case was not expressly referred to in the judgment, but it is clear from the context which Article or case the court had in mind.

12. "Com. Rep." in column 8 indicates that the court referred to the Commission Report in a case which subsequently went to the European Court of Human Rights.

13. Full citations of the ECHR cases referred to in column 8 are set out immediately after the Table.

14. An analysis of the cases in the Table, listing them by subject-matter and by Article of ECHR, can be found at the end of this Appendix.

15. The following abbreviations are used in the Table:

AG	Attorney General
CA (Civ. Div.)	Court of Appeal (Civil Division)
CA (Crim. Div.)	Court of Appeal (Criminal Division)
Com. Rep.	Report of the European Commission of Human Rights
DC	Divisional Court
DPP	Director of Public Prosecutions
EAT	Employment Appeal Tribunal
ECJ	European Court of Justice
Eur. Comm. HR	European Commission of Human Rights
Eur. Ct. HR	European Court of Human Rights
HL	House of Lords
IAT	Immigration Appeal Tribunal
PC	Privy Council
QBD	Queen's Bench Division
SS	Secretary of State

Name of Case & Citation	Date of Judgment	Court	Type of Proceedings	Subject Matter	Treaty cited	Articles cited	Case-law cited	Nature of reference made to unincorporated international human rights law
1. *Zoernsch v Waldock* [1964] 1 WLR 675, 682-3, 687, 690	24.3.64	CA (Civ. Div.) Wilmer*, Danckwerts & Diplock* LJJ	Action for damages (appeal against strike out)	Sovereign immunity	ECHR	21, 24, 25, 30, 31, 35, 37, 58	•	ECHR considered to resolve "question of fact" whether Commission an organ of the Council within meaning of Act conferring immunity
2. *Broome v Cassell & Co. Ltd.* [1972] AC 1027, 1133A	23.2.72	HL Lords Hailsham, Reid, Morris, Dilhorne, Diplock, Wilberforce & Kilbrandon*	Action for damages (appeal against exemplary damages)	Defamation	ECHR	(10)	—	Free speech to be regarded as a "constitutional right" since ECHR was ratified; that right would be seriously hampered if profit motive sufficient to justify punitive damages
3. *R v Miah* [1974] 1 WLR 683, 690H-691A	20.12.73	CA (Crim. Div.) Stephenson LJ*, Chapman & Forbes JJ	Appeal against conviction	Crime/ immigration	ECHR UDHR	7, 11(2)	—	Common law's presumption against retrospectivity applies in general to legislation of a penal character and such legislation is, in general, forbidden by ECHR and UDHR
4. *Waddington v Miah* [1974] 1 WLR 683, 694C-E	3.5.74	HL Lords Reid*, Morris, Dilhorne, Simon & Salmon	Appeal against conviction	Crime/ immigration	ECHR UDHR	7, 11(2)	—	Hardly credible that any government department would promote or that Parliament would pass retrospective criminal legislation in light of provisions against such legislation in ECHR and UDHR
5. *Hubbard v Pitt* [1976] QB 142, 156H	8.11.74	QBD Forbes J	Application for interlocutory injunction	Public protest	ECHR	11	—	Mention of democratic right to public assembly in ECHR cited, but does not give a right to assemble anywhere, particularly not on highway
6. *Birdi v SS Home Affairs* [1975] 119 SJ 322	11.2.75	CA (Civ. Div) Lord Denning MR* Stephenson & Geoffrey Lane LJJ	*Habeas corpus*	Immigration	ECHR	5, 6, 13	—	Acts not conforming to ECHR might be held invalid; in any event Acts could and should be interpreted so as to be in accordance with ECHR
7. *R v SS Home Dept., ex p Bhajan Singh* [1976] QB 198, 202E	2.5.75	QBD (DC) Widgery LCJ*, James LJ & May J	Judicial review	Immigration	ECHR	12, 5(1)(f)	*Golder v UK*	No doubt that terms of ECHR are properly to be regarded in this country where an issue makes them relevant
8. *R v SS Home Dept., ex p Bhajan Singh* [1976] QB 198, 207D-208B	19.5.75	CA (Civ. Div.) Lord Denning MR* Browne & Geoffrey Lane LJJ	Judicial review (appeal)	Immigration	ECHR	12, 5(1)(f)	—	Court can and should take ECHR into account whenever interpreting a statute which affects the rights and liberties of the individual; it is to be assumed that the Crown would do nothing in conflict with treaties; immigration officers and SS ought to bear in mind ECHR's principles in exercising their duties, as part of acting fairly
9. *AG v Antigua Times Ltd.* [1976] AC 16, 24H-25C	19.5.75	PC Lords Fraser*, Dilhorne, Edmund-Davies, Wilberforce & Sir Thaddeus McCarthy	Action for declarations (appeal)	Press regulation	ECHR UDHR	25, Art.1 Prot. 1	—	ECHR referred to in order to determine whether rights and freedoms chapter of Antigua Constitution, based on ECHR, applies to artificial as well as natural persons
10. *Benin v Whimster* [1976] QB 297, 309A-B	5.6.75	CA (Civ. Div.) Lord Denning MR*, Roskill & Ormrod LJJ	Appeal by statutory case stated	Foreign compensation	ECHR	—	—	Practice of having regard to ECHR cited as analogy for construing domestic statutes or delegated legislation in accordance with agreement or treaty being implemented

Case	Date	Court & Judges	Proceeding	Subject		Article	ECHR case	Commentary
11. *R v SS Home Dept., ex p Phansopkar* [1976] QB 606, 616F, 626C–G	11.7.75	CA (Civ. Div.), Lord Denning MR*, Lawton & Scarman* LJJ	Judicial review & *habeas corpus* (appeal)	Immigration	ECHR	8	—	It is now the duty of public authorities in administering the law and of courts in interpreting and applying the law to have regard to ECHR; it is the duty of courts, so long as they do not defy or disregard clear unequivocal provision, to construe statutes in a way which promotes, not endangers, those rights
12. *Mistry v Entry Clearance Officer, Bombay* [1976] Imm AR 54, 57–9	23.7.75	IAT, Dalton, Bonham-Carter & Warburton	Statutory appeal	Immigration	ECHR	8	*Papayianni v UK*	Qualified nature of right to respect for family life in ECHR noted in deciding that provision in Immigration Rules was not *ultra vires*
13. *Pan-American World Airways Inc. v Dept. of Trade* [1976] 1 Lloyd's Rep. 257, 261 col.2–262 col.1	29.7.75	CA (Civ. Div.), Lord Denning MR, Lawton & Scarman* LJJ	Action for declaration (appeal)	Civil aviation regulation	ECHR	—	—	If statutory words have to be construed or a legal principle formulated in an area of law where HM has accepted international obligations, courts will have regard to the obligation as part of full content or background of the law, even though no statute expressly or impliedly incorporates it
14. *Blathwayt v Baron Cawley* [1976] AC 397, 425H–426C	22.10.75	HL, Lords Wilberforce*, Simon, Cross, Edmund-Davies & Fraser	Application for declarations (appeal)	Trusts	ECHR	(9, 14)	—	No doubt that conceptions of public policy should move with the times and that widely accepted treaties such as ECHR may point the direction in which such conceptions ought to move, but testator's freedom outweighed freedom from religious discrimination
15. *R v Chief Immigration Officer, Heathrow Airport, ex p Salamat Bibi* [1976] 1 WLR 979, 984D–985C, 986A–H, 988B–F	11.5.76	CA (Civ. Div.), Lord Denning MR, Roskill & Geoffrey Lane LJJ	Judicial review (appeal)	Immigration	ECHR	8, 25	—	Presumption of conformity is made, but ECHR not part of domestic law; officials under no duty to have regard to ECHR, which is too vague for practical application
16. *Maynard v Osmond* [1977] QB 240, 252B–C	13.7.76	CA (Civ. Div.), Lord Denning MR*, Orr & Waller LJJ	Action for declarations (appeal)	Employment/ civil procedure	ECHR	(6)	—	Principle of entitlement to legal representation agreed by government when signed ECHR, but *prima facie* right subject to Parliamentary will
17. *Ahmad v ILEA* [1978] QB 36, 41B–G, 45E–F, 48B–F, 50E	22.3.77	CA (Civ. Div.), Lord Denning MR, Orr & Scarman* LJJ	Statutory appeal	Employment	ECHR	9	—	† ECHR not part of English law but courts will always have regard to it; ECHR rights must be balanced against rights and interests of others
18. *R v SS Home Affairs, ex p Hosenball* [1977] 1 WLR 766, 779A–C	29.3.77	CA (Civ. Div.), Lord Denning MR*, Geoffrey Lane & Cumming-Bruce LJJ	Judicial review (appeal)	Immigration	ECHR	6(1)	*Agee v UK*	Commission's interpretation of Art.6(1) ECHR confirms that natural justice may have to be modified where national security is at stake
19. *Ostreicher v SS Environment*[BEC] [1978] 1 All ER 591, 593j–595a	5.5.77	QBD, Sir Douglas Frank QC	Statutory review	Planning	ECHR	9	—	ECHR of little assistance because it does not apply and is in vague terms; right outweighed by administrative convenience and interests of other objectors
20. *R v GLC, ex p Burgess* [1978] ICR 991, 995A–F	17.4.78	QBD (DC), Lord Widgery CJ*, Boreham & Drake JJ	Judicial review	Employment	ECHR	9	—	ECHR not part of English law, and "no more than an unadopted convention persuasive in purpose only"; statute therefore prevails in event of contradiction
21. *R v Board of Visitors of Hull Prison, ex p St. Germain* [1979] QB 425, 464H–465A	3.10.78	CA (Civ. Div.), Megaw, Shaw & Waller* LJJ	Judicial review (appeal)	Prisons	ECHR	—	*Kiss v UK*	UK government's submission in case before Commission cited in support of view that visitors are independent with a duty to act judicially and therefore

Name of Case & Citation	Date of Judgment	Court	Type of Proceedings	Subject Matter	Treaty cited	Articles cited	Case-law cited	Nature of reference made to unincorporated international human rights law
22. *Uppal v Home Office* (1978) 21 ECHR YB 979	20.10.78	Ch.D Megarry V-C	Action for declarations	Immigration	ECHR	8, 25	—	International obligations such as ECHR, not enforceable as part of English law, cannot be the subject of declaratory judgments or orders
23. *UKAPE v ACAS* [1979] 1 WLR 570, 582H–583C	17.1.79	CA (Civ. Div.) Lord Denning MR*, Lawton & Brandon LJJ	Judicial review (appeal)	Employment	ECHR	11	—	ECHR only states common law right to freedom of association; Parliament presumed not to intend to contravene that basic right
24. *Patel v University of Bradford Senate* [1979] 1 WLR 1066, 1070A–C	23.1.79	CA (Civ. Div.) Orr*, Ormrod & Geoffrey Lane LJJ	Action for declarations (appeal)	Education	ECHR	—	—	Nothing in ECHR in any way contravened on the facts
25. *R v Lemon* [1979] AC 617, 665B–E	21.2.79	HL Lords Diplock, Dilhorne, Edmund-Davies, Russell & Scarman*	Appeal against conviction	Blasphemous libel	ECHR	9, 10	—	Recognition of both religious freedom and justified limits on free speech in ECHR cited to support view of law on blasphemy fit for a rights-respecting plural society
26. *Malone v MPC (No.2)* [1979] Ch. 344, 351A–C, H–352C, 353E–G, 354D–355D, 356C–E, 362E–366D, 378D–381C	28.2.79	Ch. D. Megarry V-C	Action for declaration	Interception of communications	ECHR	1, 8, 13, 25	*Klass v Germany*	ECHR did not confer rights enforceable in domestic law; court would take it into account if law uncertain, but cannot invent new common law rules; to do so would carry court far beyond any possible function of the ECHR as influencing English law than has ever been suggested
27. *Associated Newspapers Group Ltd. v Wade* [1979] 1 WLR 697, 708H–709A	3.4.79	CA (Civ. Div.) Lord Denning MR*, Lawton & Geoffrey Lane LJJ	Application for interlocutory injunction	Employment	ECHR	10	—	Fundamental principle of the common law, that the press shall be free, corresponds with Art.10 ECHR and a trade union cannot invade it
28. *Gleaves v Deakin* [1980] AC 477, 482G–484C	10.4.79	HL Lords Diplock*, Dilhorne, Edmund-Davies, Keith & Scarman	Judicial review (appeal)	Defamation (criminal libel)	ECHR	10	—	Common law offence of defamatory libel probably inconsistent with ECHR; legislative reform suggested to ensure compliance
29. *Mutasa v A-G* [1980] QB 114, 117F–G	2.5.79	QBD Boreham J	Action for declaration	Sovereign immunity	ECHR	5, 6	—	ECHR not to be regarded as part of the law of the land
30. *Minister of Home Affairs v Fisher* [1980] AC 319, 328F–H, 330B–C	14.5.79	PC Lords Wilberforce*, Hailsham, Salmon, Fraser & Sir William Douglas	Judicial review (appeal)	Immigration	ECHR ICCPR UDHR	8	—	A broad and generous, not legalistic, interpretation, should be given to rights in Bermudan Constitution, reflecting origins in ECHR
31. *Mustafa v SS Home Dept.* [1979–80] Imm AR 32, 37–8	30.5.79	IAT Hooton, Bowman, & Newman	Statutory appeal	Immigration	ECHR	6(1)	—	ECHR "persuasive" only; in any event, UK had accepted principles set out in Art.6 long before it signed ECHR
32. *Science Research Council v Nassé* [1980] AC 1028, 1066E–F	1.11.79	HL Lords Wilberforce*, Salmon, Edmund-Davies, Fraser & Scarman	Interlocutory application for discovery (appeal)	Employment/ civil procedure	ECHR	6	—	Unnecessary to have resort to ECHR to establish right to a fair hearing, which is the whole object of rules on discovery and inspection

	Date	Judges	Action	Subject	ECHR/UDHR	Articles	Case	Notes
33. *Terence Thornhill v A-G of Trinidad and Tobago* [1980] 2 WLR 510, 516A–B	27.11.79	PC Lords Diplock*, Dilhorne, Edmund-Davies, Scarman & Lane	Action for a declaration (appeal)	Police powers	ECHR UDHR	—	—	Statements of broad general principle in Commonwealth constitutions protecting rights and freedoms, like ECHR, not to be construed like Acts
34. *Panesar v Nestlé Co. Ltd.* [1980] ICR 144, 147I–H	27.11.79	CA (Civ. Div.) Lord Denning MR* & Sir George Baker	Application for leave to appeal	Employment	ECHR	9	—	ECHR "not law here, but we have much regard to it"; even if it were regarded as law, impugned practice would be saved by Art.9(2)
35. *Allgemeine Gold- und Silberscheideanstalt v Customs & Excise Commissioners* &c [1980] QB 390, 403F–404B	19.12.79	CA (Civ. Div.) Lord Denning MR*, Bridge LJ & Sir David Cairns	Action for a declaration (appeal)	Customs & excise	ECHR	Art.1 Prot. 1	—	ECHR not part of English law yet, but courts do pay attention to it even as it stands; exceptions in Article made clear that it does not impair a state's right to forfeit property brought into country in breach of its custom laws
36. *UKAPE v ACAS* [1981] AC 424, 438G–H, 445F–446A	14.2.80	HL Lords Wilberforce, Diplock, Edmund-Davies, Keith & Scarman*	Judicial review (appeal)	Employment	ECHR	11	—	Right of association, including right to join a union, recognised and protected by both common law and ECHR, but does not give a right to recognition
37. *Express Newspapers v Keys* [1980] IRLR 247, 249 col.2	7.5.80	QBD Griffiths J	Application for interlocutory injunction	Employment	ECHR	11	—	Common law, like ECHR, recognises freedom of assembly, but that right does not licence unlawful infringement of others' rights
38. *Williams v Home Office (No.2)* [1981] 1 All ER 1211, 1244i–1245e	9.5.80	QBD Tudor Evans J	Action for damages and declaration	Prisons	ECHR UDHR	3	—	ECHR provisions taken into account in considering whether prison regime was "cruel" within meaning of Bill of Rights Act 1688
39. *AG v BBC* [1981] AC 303, 352, 354A–F, 362D	12.6.80	HL Viscount Dilhorne, Lords Salmon, Edmund-Davies, Fraser* & Scarman*	Application for injunction	Contempt of court	ECHR	10	*Sunday Times v UK*	Although neither ECHR nor European Court's decisions are part of English law, UK courts must consider impact of their decisions on UK's obligations under ECHR, as interpreted by Court
40. *Morris v Beardmore* [1981] AC 446, 455G, 464E	17.7.80	HL Lords Diplock*, Edmund-Davies, Keith, Scarman* & Roskill	Appeal against conviction	Crime	ECHR	8, 25	—	Common law, like ECHR, recognises a fundamental right of privacy, in shape of a presumption that, in absence of express provision to contrary, Parliament did not intend to authorise tortious conduct; (per Lord Diplock: that presumption owes nothing to the ECHR)
41. *Fernandes v SS Home Dept.* [1981] Imm AR 1, 5–7	20.11.80	CA (Civ. Div.) Waller*, Ackner* & Watkins LJJ	Judicial review (appeal)	Immigration	ECHR	8, 25	—	Resort may be had to ECHR to resolve ambiguity or uncertainty in domestic law, but does not have force of law; SS under no legal obligation to consider it
42. *Guilfoyle v Home Office* [1981] QB 309, 225G–228G, 228H–229E, 229H–232A	11.12.80	CA (Civ. Div.) Lord Denning MR, O'Connor LJ & Sir John Megaw	Action for declaration (appeal)	Prisons	ECHR	3, 6(1), 8, 25, 27, 28, 31, 32, 48, 50	—	ECHR not relevant to construction of Prison Rules concerning reading of prisoners' correspondence
43. *Schering Chemicals Ltd. v Falkman Ltd.* [1982] QB 1, 18D–H, 20E–F, 21C–F	27.1.81	CA (Civ. Div.) Lord Denning MR*, Shaw & Templeman LJJ	Appeal against injunction	Confidentiality	ECHR	8, 10	*Sunday Times v UK*	ECHR and common law contain same fundamental rights to freedom of the press and privacy; only a "pressing social need" justifies prior restraint
44. *Kynaston v SS Home Affairs* (1981) 73 Cr App R 281, 286–7	18.2.81	CA (Civ. Div.) Lawton* & Eveleigh LJJ, Sir David Cairns	Appeal against refusal of leave to bring action	Mental health	ECHR	5(1)(c)	—	Reference to ECHR not helpful as it gave no specific guide; domestic statute prevails over ECHR

Name of Case & Citation	Date of Judgment	Court	Type of Proceedings	Subject Matter	Treaty cited	Articles cited	Case-law cited	Nature of reference made to unincorporated international human rights law
45. *McGovern v AG* [1982] Ch 321, 325E–G, 349C–H	13.3.81	Ch. D. Slade J	Statutory appeal	Trusts	ECHR UDHR	1, 2, 3, 5, 9, 10	—	ECHR not part of English law; doubted whether court can properly look at it for purpose of construing similarly worded clause in trust deed
46. *In Re S (A Barrister)* [1981] QB 683, 691A–692C	15.4.81	Visitors to the Inner Temple Vinelott*, McNeill & Anthony Lincoln JJ	Appeal against disciplinary ruling	Professional regulation	ECHR	6(1)	*Delcourt v Belgium; Le Compte v Belgium*	Majority opinion in decision of Commission supports visitors' view that constitution of disciplinary tribunal not partial
47. *Haw Tua Tau v Public Prosecutor* [1982] AC 136, 154A–B	22.6.81	PC Lords Diplock*, Fraser, Scarman, Roskill & Sir Ninian Stephen	Appeal against conviction	Criminal procedure	ECHR UDHR	6(2)	—	Art.6(2) ECHR states a fundamental rule of natural justice, not infringed by calling on accused to give evidence on pain of adverse inferences being drawn from refusal
48. *R v Haynes* (1981) 3 Cr App R(S) 330, 331–2	12.11.81	CA (Crim. Div.) Lord Lane CJ, Taylor* & McCullough JJ	Application for leave to appeal against sentence	Mental health	ECHR	5(4)	*X v UK*	Even if effect of European Court decision is that domestic statute is in breach of ECHR, court is bound by it until Parliament alters law
49. *Cheall v APEX* [1982] 3 All ER 855, 871h–872g, 872j–873c, 873h, 874g–h	24.11.81	QBD Bingham J	Action for a declaration and injunction	Employment	ECHR	11	*Young, James & Webster v UK*	Where court presented with alternative formulations of legal principle, regard may be had to fact that one is more consistent with ECHR, but must bear in mind that ECHR is not itself justiciable
50. *Harman v SS Home Dept.* [1983] 1 AC 280, 299F, 311C, 315D, 316H–317G, 318D	11.2.82	HL Lords Diplock*, Roskill, Keith, Scarman† & Simon†	Appeal against committal for contempt	Contempt of court	ECHR	1, 6, 10	*Handyside v UK; Sunday Times v UK*	Consideration of any ECHR provisions not necessary. † Courts should develop English law consistently with protections for open justice and free speech in powerfully persuasive ECHR
51. **Raymond v Honey** [1983] 1 AC 1, 10F–G, 15B–C	4.3.82	HL Lords Wilberforce*, Edmund-Jones, Russell, Lowry & Bridge*	Appeal against committal for contempt	Contempt of court	ECHR	6	*Golder v UK*	Individual's constitutional right to have their legal rights ascertained and enforced by a court strongly affirmed by European Court decision that ECHR protects right of access to court
52. *Mayor and Burgesses LB Hounslow v Perera*	11.3.82	CA (Civ. Div.) Waller*, Fox LJJ & Sir Sebag Shaw	Appeal against order for possession	Employment/landlord & tenant	ECHR	6, 8, 13, 14	—	Litigant in person's argument that ECHR violated based on a complete misunderstanding; nothing had happened which could remotely be a breach of Articles relied on
53. *R v Goldstein* [1982] 1 WLR 804, 813H–814A	2.4.82	CA (Crim. Div.) Lord Lane CJ*, Lloyd & Eastham JJ	Appeal against conviction	Crime	ECHR	10	—	Not necessary to deal with ECHR point; but "freedom of expression does not mean freedom to express yourself on 27 megahertz"
54. *Desmond v Thorne* [1983] 1 WLR 163, 169F	7.4.82	QBD Taylor J	Application for leave to bring prosecution	Defamation (criminal libel)	ECHR	10(2)	—	If ECHR requires AG or DPP to give leave to bring criminal libel cases, a judge performing a similar task must also look at all the circumstances of the case
55. **Cheall v APEX** [1983] QB 126, 136B–D, 137B–D, 146D–147F	18.6.82	CA (Civ. Div.) Lord Denning MR*, Donaldson† & Slade LJJ	Appeal against refusal of declaration & injunction	Employment	ECHR	11	*Young, James & Webster v UK*	Art.11 ECHR only states basic common law principle of freedom of association, to which English law should give effect

Case	Date	Court / Judges	Application	Subject	ECHR / UDHR	Article	Tyrer v UK	Notes
56. *Riley v A-G of Jamaica* [1983] 1 AC 719, 727E, 729H–730A, 734G–H	28.6.82	PC Lords Bridge, Diplock, Hailsham, Scarman*† & Brightman*†	Application for a declaration	Crime	ECHR UDHR	3	—	† Primary purpose of rights chapter of Jamaican Constitution, like ECHR on which it is based, is to protect the individual against abuse of power by the state
57. *Johnson v British Rail Hovercraft Ltd.*	5.7.82	CA (Civ. Div.) Cumming-Bruce* & Eveleigh LJJ	Appeal against refusal to expedite trial	Civil procedure	ECHR	6(1), Art. 1 Prot. 1	—	Having considered Art. 1 of Protocol 1 ECHR, court was not satisfied that the judge's order could be regarded as being a breach of the general principles specified in the Protocol
58. *Taylor v Co-operative Retail Services Ltd.* [1982] ICR 600, 608E–610G	8.7.82	CA (Civ. Div.) Lord Denning, MR, Fox LJ & Sir Sebag Shaw	Statutory appeal	Employment	ECHR	11, 50	*Young, James & Webster v UK*	Even if statutory provisions conflicted with ECHR, court must give effect to them, leaving employee to pursue remedy against government in Strasbourg
59. *R v Immigration Appeal Tribunal, ex p Ali Ajmal* [1982] Imm AR 102, 107	26.11.82	CA (Civ. Div.) Lord Lane CJ* & Sir Roger Ormrod	Judicial review (appeal)	Immigration	ECHR	8, 14	—	ECHR not part of law of UK; if in conflict with domestic law, court cannot take any account of it
60. *R v Barnet LBC ex p Shah* [1983] 2 AC 309, 350A–C	16.12.82	HL Lords Fraser, Scarman*, Lowry, Roskill & Brandon	Judicial review (appeal)	Education/ immigration	ECHR	—	—	Unnecessary to consider possible impact of ECHR, since result contended for on basis of ECHR was same as natural and ordinary meaning of statutory words
61. *R v Immigration Appeal Tribunal, ex p Nessa*	19.1.83	QBD Stephen Brown J	Judicial review (substantive hearing)	Immigration	ECHR	(8)	—	Applicant's arguments that dismissal of appeal against refusal of entry clearance contrary to ECHR because it separated family, and that family unity was a matter of public policy and human rights, recited by court but not addressed
62. *ITC Film Distributors Ltd. v Video Exchange Ltd.*	10.2.83	Ch. D. Warner J	Application to vary injunction	Civil procedure	ECHR	(26)	—	Injunction restraining use of discovery documents varied to permit applicant to use them in application to European Commission of Human Rights; it was for Commission, not domestic court, to decide if domestic remedies exhausted
63. *Cheall v APEX* [1983] 2 AC 180, 190H–191D	24.3.83	HL Lords Diplock*, Brandon, Edmund-Davies, Fraser & Templeman	Appeal against refusal of declaration & injunction	Employment	ECHR	11	—	ECHR not contravened because freedom of association can only be mutual: an individual has no right to associate with others not willing to associate
64. *Wirdestedt v SS Home Dept.* [1982] Imm AR 186, 187, 188–9	25.4.83	IAT Neve, Brown, Torrance	Statutory appeal	Immigration	ECHR	8	—	Applicant not helped by ECHR because "by no construction of the English language" could he be said to be a "close relative" of his homosexual partner
65. *R v MPC, ex p Nahar* The Times, 28 May 1983	27.5.83	QBD (DC) Stephen Brown & McCullough J	*Habeas corpus*	Prisons	ECHR	3	—	Prison conditions must reach some minimum standard to render detention lawful, but ECHR did not assist in defining any precise standard; in any event, on the facts, the applicants had not been subjected to inhuman treatment
66. *Oxley (Collector Of Taxes) v Raynham* (1979–83) 54 TC 779, 780	27.7.83	County Court Judge Sir Ian Lewis	Application for retrial	Revenue	ECHR	9, Art.s 1, 5 of Prot.1	—	ECHR not part of UK law, but may be referred to if any ambiguity or uncertainty; no ambiguity in tax statute, and in any event taxation permitted by first protocol

Name of Case & Citation	Date of Judgment	Court	Type of Proceedings	Subject Matter	Treaty cited	Articles cited	Case-law cited	Nature of reference made to unincorporated international human rights law
67. *R v Immigration Appeal Tribunal, ex p Muruganandarajah* [1983] Imm AR 141, 145, 147–8	14.10.83	QBD Woolf J	Judicial review (substantive hearing)	Immigration	ECHR	—	—	ECHR not part of English law, though proper to have regard to it in cases of doubt or ambiguity; here, statutory language was so clear that alternative construction not possible even if it is more clearly in accord with ECHR
68. *R v SS Home Dept., ex p Tarrant* [1985] QB 251, 282F–G, 295F–296C	8.11.83	QBD (DC) Kerr LJ & Webster J	Judicial review (substantive hearing)	Prisons	ECHR	6(3)(c)	—	Not necessary to deal with ECHR arguments, or permissible to rely on Report of Commission; domestic law leads to same result in practice
69. *Kirmetyaue v The Immigration Appeal Tribunal*	10.11.83	CA (Civ. Div.) Sir John Donaldson MR, May & Dillon LJJ	Judicial review (appeal)	Immigration	ECHR	(8)	—	Applicant's argument, that separation of family which would be result of deportation would be contrary to ECHR, recited but court in no doubt that IAT appreciated the seriousness and importance of the case to the applicant
70. *R v SS Home Dept., ex p Anderson* [1984] QB 778, 789C–79OG, 793E–F	21.12.83	QBD (DC) Robert Goff LJ & Mann J	Judicial review (substantive hearing)	Prisons	ECHR	6(1)	*Golder v UK* *Silver v UK*	European Court decision interpreting ECHR cited to support proposition that unimpeded access to solicitor is an inseparable part of right of access to court
71. *R v SS Home Dept., ex p Kirkwood* [1984] 1 WLR 913, 915F, 916D–F, 918B–919H	10.2.84	QBD Mann J	Application to remove stay	Extradition	ECHR	3	—	No obligation on SS to have any regard to ECHR when exercising his discretion; Commission's indication to SS to take no action pending its consideration of case gave rise to no obligation in either international or domestic law
72. *Hussain v London Country Bus Services Ltd.*	13.3.84	EAT Balcombe J, Ewing & Sirs	Statutory appeal	Employment	ECHR	9	—	ECHR not part of English law but English courts will always have regard to it; nothing in it gave the appellant any right to manifest his religion in derogation of his contract of employment
73. *Lion Laboratories Ltd. v Evans* [1985] QB 526, 536H	26.3.84	CA (Civ. Div.) Stephenson*, O'Connor & Griffiths LJJ	Appeal against interlocutory injunctions	Confidentiality	ECHR	10(2)	—	Both common law and ECHR recognise public interest in maintaining the duty of confidence as a restriction on press freedom; public interest in publication is an inroad on that duty
74. *Traunik v Ministry of Defence* [1984] 2 All ER 791, 798a–f	28.3.84	Ch. D. Megarry V-C	Application to strike out	Civil procedure	ECHR	6(1)	—	ECHR not law, but legitimate to consider its provisions in interpreting the law; given "full weight" in exercise of discretion to strike out proceedings
75. *Sweeney v Maidstone General Commissioners* [1984] STC 334, 334–5	30.3.84	Ch. D. Peter Gibson J	Statutory appeal	Revenue	ECHR	6(3)(b), (c)	—	Trite law that effect of ECHR is not justiciable in the courts; in any event Art.6(3) relates to criminal proceedings, not including appeals against tax penalties
76. *R v SS for Home Dept., ex p Findlay* The Times, 23 May 1984	22.5.84	QBD (DC) Parker LJ* & Forbes J†	Judicial review (substantive hearing)	Prisons	ECHR UDHR	7	—	Accepted that change of policy which would impose a greater penalty than that prevailing at time offence committed would be unlawful, but not accepted that change in parole policy imposed greater penalty
77. *Sakals v United Counties Omnibus Co. Ltd.* [1984] IRLR 474, 477 col.1	28.6.84	EAT Waite J, Ramsay, Webb	Statutory appeal	Employment	ECHR	11	—	References to ECHR permissible to resolve areas of doubt in English statute, but language of statute, properly construed in context, was clear and plain

Case	Court / Judges	Date	Proceeding	Subject	Convention	Article		Commentary
78. *R v SS Home Dept., ex p McAvoy* [1984] 1 WLR 1408, 1414E–G	QBD Webster J	9.7.84	Judicial review (substantive hearing)	Prisons	ECHR	(6(1), 8, 11)	—	ECHR not part of law of England; but general rights in ECHR reflected in rights in particular Prison Rules, which SS obliged to consider in exercising discretion
79. *R v Immigration Appeal Tribunal, ex p Murugananadarajah* [1986] Imm AR 382, 384	CA (Civ. Div.) Donaldson MR*, O'Connor & Griffiths LJJ	16.7.84	Judicial review (appeal)	Immigration	ECHR	—	—	No view expressed as to statute's consistency with ECHR, which is only an aid to construction if there is ambiguity; no ambiguity here
80. *R v SS for Foreign and Commonwealth Affairs, ex p Council of Civil Service Unions* [1984] IRLR 309, 323 col.2–324 col.1	QBD Glidewell J	16.7.84	Judicial review (substantive hearing)	Employment	ECHR	—	—	ECHR relevant where it restates common law or as an aid to construction where domestic law in doubt, but not where no doubt about relevant English law
81. *SS Defence v Guardian Newspapers Ltd.* [1985] AC 339, 361E–F	HL Lords Diplock, Bridge, Fraser†, Scarman*† & Roskill	25.10.84	Appeal against interlocutory order	Contempt of court	ECHR	10	—	† Provision in domestic statute which, like ECHR rights, is formulated as a general rule subject to carefully drawn and limited exceptions, should be approached in same way
82. *R v Immigration Appeal Tribunal, ex p Burhan Aksoy* [1984] Imm AR 171, 174	QBD Nolan J	26.10.84	Judicial review (substantive hearing)	Immigration	ECHR	—	—	Immigration Rule not expressed as clearly as it might have been, but not sufficiently ambiguous or obscure to entitle court to refer to ECHR for guidance
83. *R v Brahmbhatt v Chief Immigration Officer* [1984] Imm AR 202, 209	CA (Civ. Div.) Slade LJ, Neill J & Sir John Megaw	6.12.84	Judicial review (appeal)	Immigration	ECHR	8, 12, 13	—	Reliance on ECHR to support wife's alleged common law right to enter not well founded due to lack of any relevant ambiguity either in the Act or the rules
84. *Re K (Ward: Secure Accommodation)* [1985] FLR 357, 358–9	Fam. Div. Heilbron J	14.12.84	Wardship	Family	ECHR	—	—	Fact that legislation had been passed to bring English law into line with ECHR noted
85. *Wheeler v Leicester City Council* [1985] AC 1054, 1064A–B	CA (Civ. Div.) Ackner & Browne-Wilkinson*† LJJ, Sir George Waller	14.3.85	Judicial review (appeal)	Local government	ECHR UDHR	(9, 10)	—	† ECHR not part of internal law of UK and in any event do not extend freedoms of conscience and speech any further than domestic law
86. *R v Immigration Appeal Tribunal, ex p Bhatia* [1985] Imm AR 39, 42–3	QBD Forbes J	3.4.85	Judicial review (substantive hearing)	Immigration	ECHR	—	—	Permissible to refer to ECHR to resolve ambiguity, but where words are clear and unambiguous courts must give effect to their ordinary and natural meaning
87. *R v SS Education & Science Ex p Talmud Torah Machzikei Hadass School Trust* The Times, 12 Apr 1985	QBD Woolf J	3.4.85	Judicial review (substantive hearing)	Education	ECHR	Art. 2 Prot. 1	—	Art. 2 of First Protocol underlined requirement that in deciding whether efficient and suitable instruction is being provided, SS must take into account the wishes of the parents, notwithstanding UK's reservation
88. *R v Lancashire CC, ex p Huddleston*	QBD Webster J	7.5.85	Judicial review (substantive hearing)	Education	ECHR	Art. 2 Prot. 1	—	ECHR no part of English law and even if it were it had not been shown that the applicant had been denied the right to education; on the contrary she was receiving it, albeit at her own expense
89. *R v HM Customs & Excise, ex p Haworth*	QBD Forbes J	17.7.85	Judicial review (substantive hearing)	Customs & excise	ECHR	—	—	There was no need to go back to Magna Carta or the ECHR: it was an ordinary principle of English law that no government or other agency is entitled to deprive a man of his property without due authority, normally found in statute

Name of Case & Citation	Date of Judgment	Court	Type of Proceedings	Subject Matter	Treaty cited	Articles cited	Case-law cited	Nature of reference made to unincorporated international human rights law
90. *R v Immigration Appeal Tribunal, ex p Siddiqi*	26.7.85	QBD Woolf J	Judicial review (substantive hearing)	Immigration	ECHR	(8)	—	Although, the ECHR could be looked at in situations of doubt, this was not a situation where it could provide any assistance
91. *R v Immigration Appeal Tribunal, ex p Chandawadra*	4.10.85	QBD Mann J	Judicial review (leave application)	Immigration	ECHR	8	—	Immigration Rule requiring SS and IAT to have regard to all relevant circumstances did not require them to consider whether making of deportation order could involve a breach of UK's treaty obligations, a matter relating to the country's foreign affairs
92. *R v SS Environment, ex p Newham LBC* (1986) 84 LGR 639, 654	12.12.85	QBD Taylor J	Judicial review (substantive hearing)	Local government	ECHR	Art. 1 Prot. 1	—	Applicant's argument that ECHR supports common law principle, that in absence of unequivocal statutory language property is not to be taken away without full compensation, recited but not explicitly addressed
93. *Williams & Humbert Ltd v W & H Trade Marks (Jersey) Ltd.* [1986] AC 368, 428A	12.12.85	HL Lords Scarman, Bridge, Brandon, Templeman* & McKay	Appeal against strike out	Compulsory purchase	ECHR	(Art.1 Prot. 1)	—	ECHR's recognition of compulsory acquisition in the public interest cited in support of proposition that such a practice is universally recognised
94. *R v Yorkshire Mental Health Review Tribunal, ex p SS Home Dept.*	21.1.86	QBD Kennedy J	Judicial review	Mental health	ECHR	5	—	Doubtful whether assistance could be derived from Art. 5 ECHR as to proper interpretation of the words of Mental Health Act 1983
95. *R v Oxford Regional Mental Health Review Tribunal, ex p SS Home Dept.* [1986] 1 WLR 1180, 1185D–E	23.4.86	CA (Civ. Div.) Lawton* & Stephen Brown LJJ, Sir John Megaw	Judicial review (appeal)	Mental health	ECHR	(6(1))	—	Role of ECHR cited in account of legislative history of statute which fell to be interpreted
96. *R v SS Home Dept., ex p Herbage* [1987] QB 872, 880A,F	19.5.86	QBD Hodgson J	Judicial review (substantive hearing)	Prisons	ECHR	3	—	Applicant's argument that Prison Act and Prison Rules should be interpreted so as to give effect to rights recognised by ECHR recited
97. **R v Commissioners of English Heritage, ex p Chappell**	19.6.86	CA (Civ. Div.) Dillon* & Croom-Johnson LJJ, Sir Rosaleyn Cumming-Bruce	Judicial review (appeal)	Planning	ECHR	9	—	As a matter of English law, right to manifest religion is subject to reasonable and necessary power of SS to close religious site; no significant difference between ECHR and English law in that respect
98. *R v SS Home Dept., ex p Ruddock* [1987] 1 WLR 1482, 1493F–H	2.9.86	QBD Taylor J	Judicial review (substantive hearing)	Interception of communications	ECHR UDHR	8	*Malone v UK*	Citation of ECHR case-law "of interest", but European Court's own warning against usurping function of national courts cited
99. *R v SS Home Dept., ex p Herbage (No.2)* [1987] QB 1077, 1082B	5.11.86	CA (Civ. Div.) Mayt, Purchas LJJ, Sir David Cairns	Judicial review (appeal)	Prisons	ECHR	(3)	—	†Applicant's argument, that SS and prison governor had acted illegally by infringing ECHR, recited but not addressed
100. *AG v Turnaround Distribution Ltd.* [1989] 1 FSR 169, 177	18.12.86	QBD Simon Brown J	Application to discharge interlocutory injunction	Confidentiality	ECHR	10	—	It does not follow from fact that ECHR is not enshrined in domestic law that it must be ignored by court in exercising discretion to grant injunctive relief or whether to imply contractual term requiring lifelong silence

Case	Date	Court/Judges	Proceedings	Subject	ECHR	Articles	ECHR cases	Commentary
101. *R v Immigration Appeal Tribunal, ex p Chundawadra* [1987] Imm AR 227, 229, 230–5	28.1.87	QBD Taylor J	Judicial review (substantive hearing)	Immigration	ECHR	8, 13	*Silver v UK; Abdulaziz, Cabales & Balkandali v UK*	ECHR relevant only as aid to interpretation in case of ambiguity or doubt but cannot provide test where statute perfectly clear; since no ambiguity, no obligation on SS or IAT to take ECHR into account
102. *R v Chief Immigration Officer Gatwick Airport, ex p Harjendar Singh* [1987] Imm AR 346, 356	28.1.87	QBD Nolan J	Judicial review (substantive hearing)	Immigration	ECHR	—	*East African Asians v UK Sunday Times v UK*	Acknowledged that courts might look to international law more than in the past; but while there is a presumption of conformity, in the event of a conflict the domestic law must apply
103. *R v SS Home Dept., ex p Handscomb* [1987] 86 Cr App Rep 59, 82	2.3.87	QBD (DC) Watkins LJ, Mann & Nolan JJ	Judicial review (substantive hearing)	Prisons	ECHR	5(4)	—	Reference to ECHR not found to be of assistance
104. *R v Immigration Appeal Tribunal, ex p Iqbal*	5.5.87	QBD McCowan J	Judicial review (substantive hearing)	Immigration	ECHR	3, 8, 12, 14	—	ECHR irrelevant because had not been made part of the law of the UK; in any event, nothing had been done which offended ECHR
105. *Re an Inquiry under the Company Securities (Insider Dealing) Act* [1988] AC 660, 684C	6.5.87	CA (Civ. Div.) Slade & Lloyd* LJJ, Sir George Waller	Appeal against decision on statutory inquiry	Contempt of court	ECHR	10	—	Language of statutory provision follows that of ECHR in using word "necessary"
106. *AG v Guardian Newspapers Ltd.* [1987] 1 WLR 1248, 1286B–H, 1288B, 1296f–1299G, 1307B–E	13.8.87	Lords Bridge*†, Brandon, Templeman, Oliver† & Ackner	Appeal against interlocutory injunctions	Confidentiality	ECHR	10	*Sunday Times v UK*	Injunctions satisfied tests of ECHR because justifications for restraint fell within Art. 10(2); † majority's decision undermined confidence in ability of common law to protect freedoms
107. *AG v Observer Ltd.*EC [1988] 1 All ER 385, 396b–c, 398c–g	16.10.87	Ch. D. Knox J	Application for leave to intervene	Contempt of court	ECHR	10	*Sunday Times v UK*	Even if EC Treaty was to be interpreted as incorporating ECHR, interference with freedom of expression was "necessary" within Art.10(2)
108. *Chundawadra v Immigration Appeal Tribunal* [1988] Imm AR 161, 165–70, 172–6	30.10.87	CA (Civ. Div.) Glidewell LJ, Slade & Caulfield JJ	Judicial review (appeal)	Immigration	ECHR	1, 8, 13	—	ECHR not part of English law; since no ambiguity in statute or rules, neither SS nor IAT obliged to have regard to it; nor can it give rise to any legitimate expectation
109. *X v Y* [1988] 2 All ER 648, 658g	6.11.87	QBD Rose J	Application for injunction, disclosure & committal	Confidentiality	ECHR	10(2)	—	Citation of dictum from *Lion Laboratories v Evans*, observing that the public interest in maintaining confidentiality is a restriction on freedom of the press recognised by both domestic law and ECHR
110. *R v Governor of Shepton Mallet Prison, ex p Carroll* [1988]	24.11.87	QBD Nolan J	Judicial review (leave application)	Prisons	ECHR	6, 10	—	Accepted that alleged breaches of ECHR may raise considerations which make case distinguishable from an otherwise applicable precedent; but on the facts, there was no arguable case based on ECHR
111. *Re an Inquiry under the Company Securities (Insider Dealing) Act* [1988] AC 660, 705f–706E	10.12.87	HL Lords Keith, Roskill, Griffiths*, Oliver & Goff	Appeal against order to answer questions	Contempt of court	ECHR	10	*Sunday Times v UK*	In so far as any assistance to be gained from ECHR, it supports the wider construction of "prevention of crime" in s.10 Contempt of Court Act 1981

Name of Case & Citation	Date of Judgment	Court	Type of Proceedings	Subject Matter	Treaty cited	Articles cited	Case-law cited	Nature of reference made to unincorporated international human rights law
112. *In Re State of Norway's Application (No.2)* [1990] 1 AC 723, 777C–F	18.12.87	CA (Civ. Div.) May, Balcombe* & Woolf* LJJ	Application to set aside order to witnesses to attend	Civil procedure	ECHR	6(1)	*Feldbrugge v The Netherlands*; *Deumeland v Germany*	European Court decisions holding "civil rights and obligations" in Art.6(1) ECHR to be an autonomous concept which includes public law rights as well as private rights; illustrate difficulty of finding a uniform recognition of distinction between public and private law
113. *AG v Guardian Newspapers (No.2)* [1990] 1 AC 109, 142A–C, 156E–159D	21.12.87	Ch. D. Scott J	Application for injunctions	Confidentiality	ECHR	10	*Sunday Times v UK*; *Lingens v Austria*	By analogy with the well-known rule of statutory construction, when adjudicating disputes as to the relative weights of competing public interests courts should try to strike a balance consistent with treaty obligations, as interpreted by the European Court; applying Court's test, no pressing social need outweighed press freedom
114. *Re "A" (a Minor)*	21.12.87	CA (Civ. Div.) Purchas*, Dillon & Nourse LJJ	Wardship (appeal)	Family	ECHR	6(1), 8	*O v UK*	In wardship proceedings, welfare of the child is ultimate and paramount consideration, and court would not intervene to protect interests of foster parents even if those interests might justifiably have given rise to claim of breach of ECHR
115. *Smith v SS Environment*	21.12.87	QBD David Widdicombe QC	Statutory appeal	Planning	ECHR	8	—	Appellant's reliance on ECHR recited but not addressed in judgment
116. *Re F (In Utero)* [1988] Fam 122, 132B–C	16.1.88	Fam. Div. Hollings J	Wardship	Family	ECHR	2	—	Decisions showing that right to life does not prevail over mother's own rights said to support court's view of incompatibility of wardship jurisdiction with rights and welfare of mother
117. *R v Board of Visitors of HMP The Maze, ex p Hone* [1988] AC 379, 392G–394F	21.1.88	HL Lords Mackay, Bridge, Ackner, Oliver & Goff*	Judicial review (appeal)	Prisons	ECHR	6(3)(c)	*Engel v The Netherlands*; *Campbell & Fell v UK*	Objective sought to be achieved by English law on natural justice said to be harmonious with Art.6 ECHR as interpreted by European Court; recourse to ECHR did not help applicants because absolute right to legal representation was no more required by ECHR than by English law
118. *Re F (In Utero)* [1988] Fam 122, 142C–G	4.2.88	CA (Civ. Div.) May, Balcombe* & Staughton LJJ	Wardship (appeal)	Family	ECHR	2(1)	*Paton v UK*	ECHR did not help appellant because Art.2, as interpreted by Commission, applies only to persons already born and cannot apply to a foetus
119. *AG v Guardian Newspapers Ltd. (No.2)* [1990] 1 AC 109, 178C–H, 203E–G, 218H–220C	10.2.88	CA (Civ. Div.) Sir John Donaldson MR, Dillon & Bingham LJJ	Application for injunctions	Confidentiality	ECHR	10	*Sunday Times v UK*; *Lingens v Austria*	Common law's protection of free speech asserted to be identical to that of ECHR; substantive right to freedom of expression subsumed within universal freedom of action in domestic law, and courts have both power and duty to assess pressing social need and weigh it against right
120. *R v SS Home Dept., ex p Weeks* The Times, 15 Mar 1988	17.2.88	QBD (DC) Glidewell LJ* & French J	Judicial review (substantive hearing)	Prisons	ECHR ICCPR	5(1),(4),(5), 50	*Weeks v UK*	Court could not give ministerial statement a meaning the words could not bear merely in order to avoid the UK being in breach of its obligations; that was a matter for Strasbourg, not the domestic court

Case	Date	Court / Judges	Type of proceeding		Article	Case	Commentary
121. *Re K D (a Minor) (Ward: Termination of Access)* [1988] AC 806, 811G–812D, 823E–829A	18.2.88	HL Lords Keith, Brandon, Templeman*, Goff & Oliver*	Appeal against termination of access	Family ECHR	6, 8	R v UK	There was no conflict between the approach of the European Court to parents' rights of access to their child and the traditional approach of English courts; any difference was semantic only, because on either approach the parental rights must always give way to the child's best interests
122. *R v Immigration Appeal Tribunal, ex p Singh* [1988] Imm AR 372, 375	26.2.88	QBD MacPherson J	Judicial review (substantive hearing)	Immigration ECHR	(8, 14)	—	ECHR did not compel court to interpret Immigration Act provision so that "wives" could be read as "husbands"; there was no reason why Parliament was not allowed to pass a provision which affected men and women differently
123. *R v SS Home Dept., ex p Rofathullah* [1989] QB 219, 231C–D	13.5.88	CA (Civ. Div.) Purchas*, Woolf & Russell LJJ	Judicial review (appeal)	Immigration ECHR	8	—	British citizen's claim that refusal of leave to enter for his wife was breach of ECHR reserved for argument elsewhere in light of court being bound by *Fernandes* and *Brahmbatt*
124. *Evelyn de Rothschild and Eranda Herds Ltd. v SS Transport* [1989] 1 All ER 933, 935h	12.7.88	CA (Civ. Div.) Slade*, Croom-Johnson & Ralph Gibson LJJ	Judicial review (appeal)	Planning ECHR	Art. 1 Prot. 1	—	Reliance on ECHR in challenge to compulsory purchase order recited but not addressed by court
125. *Champion v Chief Constable of Gwent Constabulary* The Times, 28 Jul 1988	27.7.88	CA (Civ. Div.) Slade, Lloyd & Ralph Gibson LJJ	Judicial review (appeal)	Employment ECHR	8	—	Argument that provision in Police Regs imposing restriction on private life of police officers should be given a liberal construction, in line with Art. 8 ECHR, ie. one which minimises the restriction which may lawfully be imposed on a police officer's private life, accepted, but room for manoeuvre was not great
126. *In Re M and H (Minors) (Local Authority: Parental Rights)* [1990] 1 AC 686, 719B, 721A–722D	28.7.88	HL Lords Brandon*, Elwyn-Jones, Griffiths, Goff & Jauncey	Appeal against refusal of application for custody	Family ECHR	6(1), 8	R v UK	Doubtful whether denial of father's right to have claim for custody adjudicated on the merits by a court was breach of ECHR; even assuming it was, English courts were under no duty to apply ECHR directly, but must give effect to unambiguous statutes even if in breach of ECHR
127. *R v SS Home Dept., ex p Azarmi*	31.8.88	QBD Hutchison J	Judicial review (renewed leave application)	Immigration ECHR	8	—	Decision in *Chundawadra* said to cast very gravest doubt as to whether court ought properly to have regard to ECHR in this context; but even assuming it could, there was nothing in ECHR to suggest that decision to deport was irrational
128. *R v The Nottingham Mental Health Review Tribunal, ex p SS Home Dept.*	15.9.88	CA (Civ. Div.) Balcombe*, Woolf & Russell LJJ	Judicial review (appeal)	Mental health ECHR	—	—	ECHR's role in legislative policy behind mental health legislation and history of mental health review tribunals explained
129. *R v Min. Agriculture, Fisheries & Food, ex p Federation Europeanne de la Sant é Animale*	20.9.88	QBD Henry J	Judicial review (substantive hearing)	Health ECHR	7	—	ECHR ground of challenge to a Community law Directive, in Article 173 proceedings pending before ECJ, recited by court in course of giving reasons for making Art.177 reference to ECJ
130. *AG v Guardian Newspapers (No.2)* [1990] 1 AC 109, 273G, 283E–284A, 291F	13.10.88	HL Lords Keith, Brightman, Griffiths*, Goff* & Jauncey	Application for permanent injunctions	Confidentiality ECHR	10	—	No inconsistency between English law on breach of confidence and ECHR; difference of approach (assumption of freedom subject to established exceptions rather than stated right plus qualifications) does not lead to any different conclusion; in any event, it was duty of courts, wherever free to do so, to interpret law in accordance with Crown's ECHR obligations

Name of Case & Citation	Date of Judgment	Court	Type of Proceedings	Subject Matter	Treaty cited	Articles cited	Case-law cited	Nature of reference made to unincorporated international human rights law
131. *AG v Associated Newspapers Group plc.* [1989] 1 WLR 322, 325G, 328B-G	20.10.88	QBD Mann LJ* & Henry J	Application to commit for contempt	Mental health/ contempt of court	ECHR	5(4)	*X v UK*	Mental health legislation had been amended to bring law into conformity with European Court decision; that decision interpreted as requiring some tribunal independent of the executive, not necessarily a "court" in the strict sense
132. *R v SS Social Services, ex p Darnell*[a]	3.11.88	QBD MacPherson J	Judicial review (substantive hearing)	Employment/ professional regulation	ECHR	(6(1))	(*Le Compte, Van Leuwen & de Meyere v Belgium*)	Doctor's claim that ECHR entitled him to an oral hearing before SS or minister, prior to taking decision to dismiss, rejected as impossible argument in absence of express provision for a hearing
133. *Customs & Excise Commissioners v Air Canada* [1989] QB 234, 247A-D	7.11.88	QBD Tucker J	Condemnation proceedings (preliminary issue)	Revenue/ customs & excise	ECHR	6(1)	—	Court agreed that there is something wrong about a provision entitling customs commissioners to a right of forfeiture *in rem* without recourse to the courts; unlikely that Parliament intended to give such a power without judicial supervision
134. *Singh v SS Environment* [1989] 24 EG 128, 136 col.1	10.11.88	CA (Civ. Div.) Kerr* & Neill LJJ, Sir Denys Buckley	Appeal against refusal of statutory application to quash	Planning	ECHR	Art. 1 Prot. 1	—	Passage from *de Rothschild* mentioning ECHR cited by court
135. *Colman v General Medical Council* The Times, 14 Dec 1988	25.11.88	QBD (DC) Mann LJ & Auld J	Judicial review (substantive hearing)	Professional regulation	ECHR	10	*Sunday Times v UK Lingens v Austria Barthold v Germany*	English courts not bound by ECHR or decisions of European Court but should have regard to them where domestic law uncertain; ECHR jurisprudence, while of some help on broad principles to be applied, of little assistance here, however, because not clear that it requires professional body to demonstrate a pressing social need for its guidance against advertising
136. *Jinnah Rahman v SS Home Dept.* [1989] Imm AR 325, 333	16.12.88	IAT Jackson, Appleby & Allnutt	Statutory appeal	Immigration	ECHR	—	—	English case-law concerning propriety of SS and appellate immigration authorities referring to ECHR cited to help determine question whether they are entitled to and should take into account a different unincorporated treaty
137. *Patel v SS Home Dept.* [1989] Imm AR 246, 252	20.12.88	IAT Neve, Weitzman & Hunte	Statutory appeal	Immigration	ECHR	8	*Berrehab v The Netherlands*	ECHR forms no part of the law of this country
138. *Post Office v Mayers*	27.1.89	EAT Wood J, Boyle & Grieves	Statutory appeal	Employment	ECHR	9	—	Argument that provisions of Art. 9 ECHR should be read into provisions of Employment Protection (Consolidation) Act 1978, so that due weight shall be given to them, rejected
139. *R v Immigration Appeal Tribunal, ex p Patel* [1990] Imm AR 153, 155	12.4.89	QBD Farquharson J	Judicial review (leave application)	Immigration	ECHR	(8)	*Berrehab v The Netherlands*	ECHR not part of the law of this country, and it was therefore not open to court to say that a decision may be reviewed on basis of a decision of the European Court
140. *R v Governor of Pentonville Prison, ex p Naghdi* [1990] 1 All ER 257, 262f	2.5.89	QBD (DC) Woolf LJ* & Saville J	*Habeas corpus*	Extradition/ criminal procedure	ECHR	6(3)(a)	—	Not necessary to refer to ECHR to accept that it is essential that the subject of a request for extradition has a proper opportunity to meet the case for his extradition, which means him being informed of the necessary details of offences

Case	Date	Court / Judges	Application	Subject		Art.	ECHR case	Notes
141. AG v Newspaper Publishing plc. [1989] 1 FSR 457, 475-6	8.5.89	Ch. D. Morritt J	Application to commit for contempt	Contempt of court	ECHR	10	—	ECHR does not form part of our domestic law, but in *Spycatcher* judges did have regard to it in striking a balance between freedom of expression and other public interests; if injunctions themselves were necessary within Art.10(2), *a fortiori* were contempt proceedings against third parties intentionally subverting their purpose
142. R v SS Environment, ex p Davis (1989) 59 P & CR 306, 309, 314	11.5.89	QBD McCowan J	Judicial review (substantive hearing)	Planning	ECHR	6(1), 8(1), Art. 1 Prot. 1	—	No substance in argument that SS's refusal to hear appeal against enforcement notice was violation of ECHR, as applicant could apply for planning permission without an interest in land or challenge notice as *Wednesbury* unreasonable
143. R v Southwark Crown Court, ex p Customs & Excise Commissioners [1990] QB 650, 659E-F	24.5.89	QBD (DC) Watkins LJ* & Brooke J	Judicial review (substantive hearing)	Crime	ECHR	—	—	Use made of ECHR by English courts cited as authority for canon of construction which permits a court to presume, when statutory language gives rise to uncertainty, that Parliament intended compliance with international obligations
144. **R v SS Home Dept., ex p Brind** (1989) 139 NLJ 1229	26.5.89	QBD (DC) Watkins LJ*, Roch & Judge JJ	Judicial review (substantive hearing)	Broad-casting	ECHR	10	—	Even if common law is identical to Art.10 ECHR, minister does not have to exercise statutory powers so as to conform with existing common law rights; but reference may be made to ECHR when deciding limits to be placed on statutory power conferred in unlimited terms
145. R v Inland Revenue Commissioners, ex p TC Coombes & Co. [1989] STC 520, 532b	26.5.89	CA (Civ. Div.) Parker, Bingham*† & Taylor LJJ	Judicial review (appeal)	Revenue	ECHR	8	—	† Importance of protecting a citizen's privacy both recognised by English law and protected by ECHR; any encroachment must be scrutinised to ensure that statutory power is not abused by intrusion going beyond what is reasonably necessary to achieve the public purpose aimed at
146. **Neuton v Neuton** [1990] 1 FLR 33, 48D-49B, 50D-E	9.6.89	CA (Civ. Div.) O'Connor LJ & Sir Roualeyn Cumming-Bruce	Appeal against costs order	Family	ECHR	6(1)	—	Perfectly clear that a breach of ECHR does not impose on a domestic court any right or obligation to make an order inconsistent with the relevant domestic law; aggrieved party must look to Strasbourg to remedy alleged breach of ECHR
147. R v SS Education & Science, ex p MG	29.6.89	QBD (DC) Neill LJ* & Pill J	Judicial review (substantive hearing)	Education	ECHR	Art. 2 Prot. 1	—	Inappropriate to grant declaration as to the regard SS should have to ECHR when rehearing the applicant's case; ECHR does not impose any absolute obligations and it was for SS to decide what it required in context of the applicant's special circumstances
148. R v SS Environment, ex p Rose Theatre Trust Co, The Independent, 4 Jul 1989	3.7.89	QBD Schiemann J	Application to discharge injunction	Planning	ECHR	(Art. 1 Prot. 1)	—	Neither party had sought to rely on the ECHR but developers did rely on the long English tradition that a man is not to be interfered with in use of his property except by due process of law
149. Lord Advocate v The Scotsman Publications Ltd. [1990] 1 AC 812, 822A-D, 823C-H, 826B-C, 828G-829F	6.7.89	HL Lords Keith*, Templeman*, Griffiths, Goff & Jauncey*	Appeal against refusal of interim interdict	Confidentiality	ECHR	10	*Handyside v UK*; *Sunday Times v UK*	Identity of common law approach to restrictions on freedom of expression, noted in *Spycatcher(No.2)*, reiterated; detriment to public interest resulting from disclosure by third party of originally confidential information insufficient to outweigh public interest in freedom of expression

Name of Case & Citation	Date of Judgment	Court	Type of Proceedings	Subject Matter	Treaty cited	Articles cited	Case-law cited	Nature of reference made to unincorporated international human rights law
150. *Re D (A Minor)*	20.7.89	CA (Civ. Div.) Sir Stephen Brown P*, Russell LJ & Sir Michael Kerr	Wardship (appeal)	Family	ECHR	—	—	Alleged failure to act in conformity with ECHR in exercise of High Court's wardship jurisdiction could not possibly weigh as a ground of appeal
151. *R v SS Home Dept., ex p Binbasi* [1989] Imm AR 595, 597, 601–2	25.7.89	QBD Kennedy J	Judicial review (substantive hearing)	Immigration	ECHR	8	*Dudgeon v UK*, *Norris v Ireland*, *Soering v UK*	Not unreasonable for SS, when making an order of deportation, to fail to act upon the speculative possibility that another state may be in breach of ECHR by continuing to criminalise conduct in which applicant might or might not engage
152. *Pickering v Liverpool Daily Post* [1991] 2 AC 370, 380H–381C, 391C	27.7.89	CA (Civ. Div.) Lord Donaldson MR*, Glidewell & Farquharson* LJJ	Appeal against injunction	Mental health/contempt of court	ECHR	5(4)	*X v UK*	If a mental health review tribunal is not a "court" for all purposes, including the law of contempt, the ECHR is not being complied with, since no indication that "court" in ECHR has any different meaning from that which it bears in English law
153. *Re Lonrho plc.* [1990] 2 AC 154, 208E–H	27.7.89	HL Lords Bridge*, Goff & Jauncey	Application to commit for contempt	Contempt of court	ECHR	10	*Sunday Times v UK*	As ECHR is no part of municipal law, courts cannot resort to decisions of European Court as direct authority, but if doubt arises as to construction of legislation passed to conform with such decisions, courts can presume it was intended to avoid future conflicts with ECHR
154. *Somasundaram v Entry Clearance Officer, Colombo* [1990] Imm AR 16, 20	9.8.89	IAT Neve, Farmer & Jackson	Statutory appeal	Immigration	ECHR	8	—	Although there is no power to refer to ECHR where criteria are clearly set out in English law, it may be considered in the exercise of an executive discretion; even assuming its relevance, no evidence that SS had not fully considered it
155. *Marshall v Southampton & SW Hampshire Health Authority (No.2)* [1990] ICR 6, 16H–17A	18.9.89	EAT Wood J*, Lewis & Phipps	Statutory appeal	Employment	ECHR	6, 13	—	Decision of ECJ, taking ECHR into account in interpretation of a provision in a Directive (*Johnston*), cited to support tribunal's interpretation of same provision as requiring a Member State to provide access to the courts but leaving remedies for the state to decide
156. *Re W (A Minor)*	28.9.89	CA (Civ. Div.) Lloyd & Butler-Sloss* LJJ	Wardship (appeal)	Family	ECHR	8	—	Father's argument that court ought to have taken into account ECHR which gave both him and the child the right to form a relationship, recited by court but not expressly dealt with; judge had rightly put child's welfare as paramount
157. *R v SS Home Dept., ex p Ali*	9.10.89	QBD Schiemann J	Judicial review (leave application)	Immigration	ECHR	8	*Berrehab v The Netherlands*	Decision of European Court not binding, but in any event distinguishable because present case concerned recommendation for deportation after conviction, which was probably what framers of Art.8(2) had in mind
158. *R v SS Home Dept., ex p Arora* [1990] Imm AR 89, 97	23.10.89	QBD McCullough J	Judicial review (substantive hearing)	Immigration	ECHR	(8)	—	No breach of ECHR in saying that interests of the child are not paramount but must be balanced against public interest in enforcement of immigration rules; in any event, if ECHR does not accord with statute or rules made thereunder, domestic law prevails

Case	Date	Court/Judge	Proceeding	Area	Instrument	Article	Case cited	Notes
159. *R v SS Home Dept., ex p K* [1990] 1 WLR 168, 177A–178B	23.10.89	QBD McCullough J	Judicial review (substantive hearing)	Mental health	ECHR	S(1)(e), (4)	*Winterwerp v The Netherlands* *X v UK*	It was to be presumed that statute passed after decision of European Court finding previous statute in breach of ECHR was passed with that decision in mind; but concession made by Crown in argument before European Court could not alter meaning of statutory words
160. *W v Egdell* [1990] 1 Ch. 359, 424H–425C	9.11.89	CA (Civ. Div.) Sir Stephen Brown P, Bingham LJ* & Sir John May	Appeal against refusal of injunctions	Mental health/confidentiality	ECHR	8	—	Although no reliance placed on ECHR in argument, court noted of its own motion that its decision, that there was no breach of confidence in the disclosure by a psychiatrist of his report on a detained patient, was in accordance with ECHR, as being within the exceptions in Art.8(2)
161. *R v General Medical Council, ex p Colman* [1990] 1 All ER 489, 499j–500c, 501a–b, e, 504f–507c, 509g	6.12.89	CA (Civ. Div.) Lord Donaldson MR*, Ralph Gibson* & McCowan LJJ	Judicial review (appeal)	Professional regulation	ECHR	10	*Golder v UK* *Sunday Times v UK*	To impute Parliamentary intention to conform with ECHR would be illegitimately to incorporate ECHR by the "back door"
162. *R v SS Home Dept., ex p Brind* [1991] 1 AC 696, 715G, 716H, 717D–718H, 724B–727B, 727C–729F	6.12.89	CA (Civ. Div.) Lord Donaldson MR, Ralph Gibson & McCowan LJJ	Judicial review (appeal)	Broadcasting	ECHR	1, 10	*Ireland v UK* *Lithgow v UK*	You have to look long and hard before you can detect any difference between the English common law and the principles set out in the ECHR. But, the ECHR being unincorporated, in most cases the courts will be wholly unconcerned with its terms. SS is under no obligation to take into account the terms of ECHR. It is to be used as an aid to construction only in the event of an ambiguity, and there was no ambiguity here
163. *Champion v Chief Constable of Gwent Constabulary* [1990] 1 WLR 1, 14C–G	14.12.89	HL Lords Keith, Griffiths, Ackner†, Jauncey, & Lowry	Judicial review (appeal)	Employment	ECHR	8	—	† ECHR can be used as an aid to construction or to illuminate a statute or regulation which is ambiguous or otherwise difficult to construe, since it is desirable that domestic law should accord with ECHR wherever possible; but of no assistance here because no ambiguity/difficulty, and, in any event, not within scope of Art.8
164. *Rance v Mid-Downs Health Authority* [1991] 1 QB 587, 622G	5.2.90	QBD Brooke J	Action for damages	Health	ECHR	2(1)	*Paton v UK*	Decision of European Commission in 1980 of no help to the court in construing statutes passed in 1929 and 1967
165. *AG v Newspaper Publishing plc.* The Times, 28 Feb 1990	27.2.90	CA (Civ. Div.) Fox*, Ralph Gibson & Nicholls LJJ	Appeal against committal for contempt	Contempt of court	ECHR	10	—	Issue of whether application of English law on contempt of court would transgress ECHR nor open to appellants; existing state of English law had been made clear by CA on preliminary issue, and courts must administer English law where it is clear, not water it down by reference to ECHR
166. *R v SS Home Dept., ex p Yassine* [1990] Imm AR 354, 362	6.3.90	QBD Schiemann J	Judicial review (substantive hearing)	Immigration	ECHR UDHR	3	—	Applicants' argument that it was perverse for SS to set in train a process which was likely to result in applicants being shuttled back and forth in conditions which might involve a breach of ECHR recited by court but not addressed
167. *R v Immigration Appeal Tribunal, ex p Singh*	16.3.90	QBD Judge J	Judicial review (substantive hearing)	Immigration	ECHR	(8)	*Berrehab v The Netherlands*	Argument that IAT's decision constituted a breach of ECHR because its effect was to deprive daughter of family life with her father must fail because no question of ambiguity in the relevant Immigration Rules

Name of Case & Citation	Date of Judgment	Court	Type of Proceedings	Subject Matter	Treaty cited	Articles cited	Case-law cited	Nature of reference made to unincorporated international human rights law
168. *Weldon v Home Office* [1990] 3 WLR 465, 477F	28.3.90	CA (Civ. Div.) Fox, Parker & Ralph Gibson* LJJ	Appeal against refusal to strike out	Prisons	ECHR	3	—	Decision (*Nahar*) that Art.3 ECHR does not provide an appropriate standard for application cited
169. **R v Chief Metropolitan Stipendiary Magistrate, ex p Choudhury** [1991] 1 QB 429, 448E–452C	9.4.90	QBD (DC) Watkins* & Stuart-Smith LJJ, Roch J	Judicial review (substantive hearing)	Blasphemous & seditious libel	ECHR	7, 9, 10, 14	*Ahmad v UK*; *Church of X v UK*; *Gay News v UK*; *Sunday Times v UK*	Although scope of common law offence of blasphemy was clear, it was necessary to go on to consider whether that position involved a breach of ECHR; but there was no breach of ECHR in not extending its scope to include non-Christian faiths
170. *R v SS Home Dept., ex p Shah*	9.4.90	QBD (DC) Mustill LJ & Otton J*	Judicial review (application to set aside leave)	Extradition	ECHR	25(1)	—	Question whether SS is under a duty to take into consideration the fact that an application has been made to the European Commission expressly left open as arguable either way
171. *F v Wirral MBC* [1991] Fam 69, 88C–92B, 97D–E, 110D–G	18.5.90	CA (Civ. Div.) Purchas*, Ralph Gibson* & Stuart-Smith LJJ	Action for damages	Family	ECHR	6(1), 8(1)	*R v UK*	Pronouncements of European Court in relation to natural parents' right of access to their child under ECHR did not establish that in domestic law a parent has a cause of action for damages in tort for interference with parental right
172. **Customs and Excise Commissioners v Air Canada** [1991] 2 QB 446, 454B, 463A–466H	14.6.90	CA (Civ. Div.) Purchas* & Balcombe LJJ, Sir David Croom-Johnson	Condemnation proceedings (appeal on a preliminary issue)	Customs & excise	ECHR	6, Art. 1 Prot. 1	*Allgemeine Gold- und Silberscheid- eanstalt v UK*	Argument that where ambiguity shown to exist, court ought to adopt an interpretation of statute consistent with, rather than contrary to, ECHR and judgments of European Court, and that this imported a proportionality requirement into judicial review of discretion, recited by court but not explicitly addressed
173. *R v SS Home Dept., ex p K* [1991] 1 QB 270, 280C–282A	3.7.90	CA (Civ. Div.) Slade, Balcombe & McCowan* LJJ	Judicial review (appeal)	Mental health	ECHR	5(1)(e), (4)	*X v UK*	As statutory words were plain and unambiguous it was not open to court to look to ECHR for assistance in their interpretation; although Parliament was to be presumed to have had decision of European Court in mind when new Act was framed, it had made its intention clear
174. *AG v Ewing*	24.7.90	CA (Civ. Div.) Dillon*, Butler-Sloss & Leggatt LJJ	Appeal against vexatious litigant order	Civil Procedure	ECHR	6, 13	—	An English statute should be interpreted so as to be in conformity with the ECHR if the wording is appropriate; but where wording of statute had statutory predecessors long antedating ECHR, the meaning of that wording could not be different merely because of accession to ECHR
175. *AG v Barker* [1990] 3 All ER 257, 260h–261d	31.7.90	CA (Civ. Div.) Lord Donaldson MR*, Parker & Nourse LJJ	Appeal against injunction	Contract	ECHR	10	—	Art.10 ECHR did not prevent an injunction to restrain publication in breach of contract from having extra-territorial effect; foreign countries would also regard sanctity of contract as central to the necessities of a democratic society

			Habeas corpus		ECHR			
176. *R v Governor of Pentonville, ex p Chinoy* [1992] 1 All ER 317, 325б, 326c–d, 330f, 332a, 333a	9.8.90	QBD (DC) Farquharson LJ & Nolan J*	Habeas corpus	Extradition/ criminal procedure	ECHR	8	—	Any breach of ECHR should be taken into account by judge in exercise of discretion to exclude evidence under s.78 Police and Criminal Evidence Act 1984, as forming part of the circumstances in which evidence was obtained; but in this case, it was sufficient if methods used to obtain evidence were legitimate in English law
177. *Re HIV Haemophiliac Litigation*	20.9.90	CA (Civ. Div.) Ralph Gibson* & Bingham LJJ, Sir John Megaw	Action for damages	Health	ECHR	1, 2, 13	Unpublished Commission Decisions	If there is ambiguity in construction of NHS Act 1977 as to whether it does or does not provide a remedy for breach of duties thereby imposed, courts should apply a presumption that Parliament intended to legislate so as to secure compliance with obligations under ECHR; but not necessary to decide point, in view of strength of plaintiff's case in negligence; Art. 13 would not require a breach of statutory duty action to be available too
178. *R v SS Environment, ex p Davis* (1990) 61 P & CR 487, 492	23.10.90	CA (Civ. Div.) Neill*, Balcombe & Mann LJJ	Judicial review (appeal)	Planning	ECHR	(6(1))	—	Applicant's reliance on ECHR to demonstrate correct approach of the court recited, but not necessary to consider it because there was agreement on the test to be applied by the court in reviewing SS's decision
179. *Marcel v Commissioner of Police of the Metropolis* [1992] Ch 225, 234H–235C	30.11.90	Ch. D. Browne-Wilkinson V-C	Application for injunction	Confidentiality	ECHR	8	—	ECHR of little assistance; it cast no light on whether police were entitled to disclose seized documents to third parties for use in protection of their legal rights, because Art.8(2) expressly permits interference with an individual's privacy for protection of legal rights of others
180. *Re Chinoy*	10.12.90	QBD (DC) Mann LJ* & MacPherson J	Bail application	Extradition/ criminal procedure	ECHR	(8)	—	Pending application before European Commission and prospective domestic challenge to extradition order by way of judicial review on grounds of breach of ECHR both taken into account by court in assessing prospect of delay for purposes of deciding whether to grant bail
181. *Re Osman* The Times, 17 Dec 1990	12.12.90	QBD (DC) Mann LJ* & Garland J	Habeas corpus	Extradition	ECHR	6	*Soering v UK*	Whether risk of denial of a fair trial in requesting country, in breach of ECHR, was a factor to be considered by domestic court when deciding legality of extradition left open; but in any event, no evidence of a risk of a "flagrant denial" of a fair trial such as European Court thought might raise an Art.6 issue
182. *F v S (Wardship: Jurisdiction)* [1991] 2 FLR 349, 354G–355A	21.12.90	Fam. Div. Ward J	Wardship	Family	ECHR	6, 8	—	Well-established that court must strive, when it can, to interpret statutes as conforming with obligations of UK under ECHR; but not possible here because would strain the statutory language too far
183. *Pickering v Liverpool Daily Post plc* [1991] 2 AC 370, 413A–B	31.1.91	HL Lords Bridge* Brandon, Templeman, Goff & Lowry	Appeal against injunction	Contempt/ mental health	ECHR	5(4)	*X v UK*	Role of ECHR in history of mental health legislation recited
184. *R v Ali* The Times, 19 Feb 1991	1.2.91	CA (Crim. Div.) Watkins LJ*, Leonard & Blofeld JJ	Appeal against conviction	Criminal procedure	ECHR	8	—	No need to refer to ECHR because no ambiguity or uncertainty in our law in the context of s.78 Police and Criminal Evidence Act discretion to exclude evidence

Name of Case & Citation	Date of Judgment	Court	Type of Proceedings	Subject Matter	Treaty cited	Articles cited	Case-law cited	Nature of reference made to unincorporated international human rights law
185. **Brind v SS Home Dept.** [1991] 1 AC 696, 747E–748F, 750C, 751C,D,F, 757B–D, 759H–762D	7.2.91	HL Lords Bridge*, Roskill, Templeman*, Ackner* & Lowry	Judicial review (appeal)	Broadcasting	ECHR	10	*Sunday Times v UK*	To presume that a statutory administrative discretion conferred in unlimited terms must be exercised within ECHR limits would be to go far beyond the resolution of an ambiguity, and impute to Parliament an intention that domestic courts should enforce conformity with the ECHR. That would be an illegitimate backdoor incorporation Lord Templeman: Freedom of expression is a principle of every democratic constitution, and interferences with it must be necessary and proportionate to the damage it is sought to prevent
186. *Re S (Minors) (Access: Religious Upbringing)* [1992] 2 FLR 313, 322	5.3.91	CA (Civ. Div.) Butler-Sloss* & Mann LJJ	Appeal against refusal of access	Family	ECHR	—	—	ECHR did not help father seeking access to children and orders concerning their religious and educational upbringing
187. *R v SS Home Dept., ex p Zibirila-Alassini* [1991] Imm AR 367, 368, 369	11.3.91	QBD Rose J	Judicial review (renewed leave application)	Immigration	ECHR	3	*Soering v UK*	ECHR could not be relied on to challenge SS's decision on judicial review when that argument had not been made before SS; but, although SS's decision not open to challenge, court suggested that SS might reconsider decision in light of ECHR
188. **Derbyshire CC v Times Newspapers Ltd.** [1992] QB 770, 783E–786E	15.3.91	QBD Morland J	Application to strike out action for damages	Defamation	ECHR	10	*Lingens v Austria* *Sunday Times v UK*	Court may have regard to ECHR to help resolve ambiguity or uncertainty in municipal law, but no ambiguity or uncertainty in English law about extent to which local authorities may sue for libel; in any event, civil law of defamation is within state's margin of appreciation
189. *R v SS Home Dept., ex p McComb* The Times, 15 Apr 1991	26.3.91	QBD (DC) Taylor LJ* & Rougier J	Judicial review (substantive hearing)	Prisons	ECHR	8	—	Well established law that ECHR not part of the law of England; in any event, ECHR article was not absolute in its terms but clearly involved considerations which may outweigh desirability of moving a prisoner to be close to his family
190. *R v SS Home Dept., ex p Chinoy* [1992] 4 Admin LR 457, 458D–461B, 464A–467C	10.4.91	QBD (DC) Bingham LJ* & McCullough J	Judicial review (application to set aside leave)	Extradition	ECHR	5(1), 8	—	A ground deriving from the ECHR could not be a ground "specified by the law of the requested party" for the purposes of a provision in US–UK extradition treaty entitling SS to refuse to extradite, because after *Brind* it was impossible to hold that ECHR was part of UK law
191. **AG v Times Newspapers Ltd.** [1992] 1 AC 191, 225C–F	11.4.91	HL Lords Keith, Brandon, Ackner, Oliver* & Jauncey	Appeal against committal for contempt	Contempt of court	ECHR	10	—	No breach of ECHR involved in the application of the law of contempt to enforce injunctions, the maintenance in force of which had already been held by HL (in *Spycatcher No.1*) to involve no breach of the ECHR; enforcement clearly necessary for maintaining authority of judiciary
192. *Re C (a Minor)*	16.4.91	CA (Civ. Div.) Glidewell LJ* & Rattee J	Wardship (appeal)	Family	ECHR	—	—	Dictum from *In Re KD (A Minor)*, asserting there to be no inconsistency of principle or application between the English rule of paramountcy and the ECHR rule, cited by court but not addressed

Case	Date	Court/Judge	Type of proceeding	Subject	ECHR	Art.	Case cited	Holding
193. *R v SS Home Dept., ex p Lai*	17.5.91	QBD Henry J	Judicial review (application to set aside leave)	Immigration	ECHR	(8)	—	ECHR not part of English law and on that basis no grounds for judicial review can be founded upon it
194. *AG v Sport Newspapers Ltd.* [1991] 1 WLR 1194, 1206B–C, E	24.5.91	QBD (DC) Bingham LJ* & Hodgson J	Application to commit for contempt	Contempt of court	ECHR	10	—	ECHR did not avail respondents to contempt charge, since the law of contempt, provided it was clear and certain, was directed to an objective which would be accepted as legitimate under ECHR
195. *R v Immigration Appeal Tribunal, ex p Minta* The Times, 24 Jun 1991	3.6.91	QBD Hutchison J	Judicial review (substantive hearing)	Immigration	ECHR UDHR	5(4), 6(1), 13	—	ECHR not relevant because relevant provisions in Immigration Act 1971 held not to be ambiguous
196. *Yorkshire Water Services Ltd. v Hall*	1.7.91	CA (Civ. Div.) Nolan LJ	Application for leave to appeal	Utilities regulation/ contract	ECHR	—	—	ECHR not, at any rate not yet, part of our law and therefore cannot support argument for refusing to pay for Water Board's services
197. *Re A (A Minor) (Wardship: Immigration)* [1992] 1 FLR 427, 430	4.7.91	CA (Civ. Div.) Parker* & Butler-Sloss LJJ	Wardship (appeal)	Family/ immigration	ECHR	6(1), 8	—	ECHR could have no application; if it did, the ramifications would be alarming in the extreme and should not be allowed to be entertained for one moment
198. *R v SS Home Dept., ex p Wynne* The Times, 1 Aug 1991	23.7.91	QBD (DC) Mann & Nolan LJJ, Judge J	Judicial review (substantive hearing)	Prisons/civil procedure	ECHR	6	*Golder v UK*	SS under no obligation to exercise his discretion so as to conform with Art. 6 ECHR
199. *In Re W (A Minor) (Wardship: Restriction on Publication)* [1992] 1 WLR 100, 103C	24.7.91	CA (Civ. Div.) Neill*, Balcombe & Beldam LJJ	Appeal against injunction	Family	ECHR	10	—	Court exercising its discretion to grant an injunction to restrain publication for the protection of the ward in wardship proceedings will take account of Art.10 ECHR, in course of balancing the need to protect the ward from harm against the freedom of the press
200. *R v Parole Board, ex p Wilson*	24.7.91	QBD Simon Brown J	Judicial review (substantive hearing)	Prisons	ECHR	5(4)	*Thynne, Wilson & Gunnell v UK*	Not necessary to decide whether ECHR and its case-law can be invoked to resolve ambiguity or uncertainty in the common law, as well as primary or subordinate legislation, because here common law was not in a state of doubt
201. *R v LB Barnet, ex p Yusuf Islam*	25.7.91	QBD Woolf LJ	Judicial review (substantive hearing)	Local government	ECHR UDHR	9	—	Even ignoring the problems of relying upon the ECHR when it was not part of domestic law, Art.9 could not assist the applicants when the Council was doing no more than refusing to grant them an interest in its property which the applicant wished to use for religious purposes
202. *Akdag v SS Home Dept.* [1993] Imm AR 172, 174, 175	21.10.91	CA (Civ. Div.) Parker*, Scott & Farquharson LJJ	Judicial review (renewed leave application)	Immigration	ECHR	3	*Soering v UK*	ECHR did not assist applicant, since deportation itself could not amount to inhuman or degrading treatment, even if it caused mental or physical disorder, and there was no evidence that the applicant would be subjected to such treatment
203. *Firsoff v The Post Office*	23.10.91	CA (Civ. Div.) Leggatt LJ	Application for leave to appeal	Interception of communications	ECHR	8, 13	—	Because ECHR not part of the law of England, it was not possible for the court to resolve any conflict which might be found to exist between a domestic statute and the ECHR; the party alleging a breach must go direct to Strasbourg

Name of Case & Citation	Date of Judgment	Court	Type of Proceedings	Subject Matter	Treaty cited	Articles cited	Case-law cited	Nature of reference made to unincorporated international human rights law
204. *Dobson v Hastings* [1993] Ch. 394, 405D–406A	8.11.91	Ch. D. Nicholls V-C	Application to commit for contempt	Contempt of court	ECHR	10	*Sunday Times v UK*	ECHR not formally part of English law, but that is not to say that references to the principles enshrined in it may not be valuable, especially when the subject matter is a creature of the common law such as contempt of court
205. *R v Immigration Appeal Tribunal, ex p Cilloni*[n]	8.11.91	CA (Civ. Div.) Scott & Farquharson LJJ, Sir John Megaw*	Judicial review (renewed leave application)	Immigration	ECHR	3	—	ECHR argument addressed on its merits, but held to be no basis for suggesting there had been an infringement of Art.3 ECHR, because impossible to say that decision to deport was degrading treatment
206. *R v Governor of Brixton Prison, ex p Osman (No.4)* [1992] 1 All ER 579, 594e	14.11.91	QBD (DC) Woolf LJ* & Pill J	*Habeas corpus*	Extradition	ECHR	—	—	Fact that applicant for *habeas corpus* had also initiated proceedings in Strasbourg noted
207. *R v SS Home Dept., ex p Westminster Press Ltd.* [1992] 4 Admin LR 445, 453C	2.12.91	QBD (DC) Watkins* & Mann LJJ, Roch J	Judicial review (substantive hearing)	Contempt of court	ECHR	10	—	Court not persuaded that Art.10 ECHR had any relevance to the issues raised in newspaper's claim that Home Office circular to police on effect of the Contempt of Court Act 1981 mis-stated the law in that it was too restrictive of the public's right to know who is being investigated, questioned, arrested or charged
208. *R v Croydon County Court, ex p Alexander*	10.12.91	QBD Hutchison J	Judicial review (renewed leave application)	Debt	ECHR	—	—	ECHR arguments entirely without foundation, and made as a matter of form only in order to pave the way for an application to Strasbourg
209. *R v SS Home Dept., ex p Wynne* [1992] QB 406, 418E–F, 427B–428F	19.12.91	CA (Civ. Div.) Lord Donaldson MR*, Staughton* & McCowan LJJ	Judicial review (appeal)	Prisons/civil procedure	ECHR	6(1),(3) (c)	*Golder v UK*	Notwithstanding that ECHR forms no part of domestic law, it is important to pay attention to it; and the approach adopted in English law to the production of prisoners in court for civil cases was held to be consistent with Art.6(1)
210. *Spring v Guardian Assurance plc.* [1992] IRLR 173, 184 col.2	20.12.91	QBD Lever J	Action for damages	Employment	ECHR	10	—	Defendant employer's claim that to hold the author of a reference subject to a duty of care would impose a new fetter on free speech which falls foul of Art.10 ECHR recited by the court but not addressed
211. *R v SS Environment, ex p NALGO*	20.12.91	QBD Hutchison J	Judicial review (substantive hearing)	Employment/local government	ECHR	10	—	To adopt the ECHR test of proportionality would be to let the ECHR in by the "back door"
212. *Metropolitan Property Realizations Ltd. v Cosgrove*	27.1.92	CA (Civ. Div.) Dillon* & Mann LJJ	Appeal against possession order	Landlord & tenant	ECHR	8, 13	—	ECHR has never been made part of law of UK; it can be taken into account in construing UK statutes, but nothing in relevant legislation on construction of which it can have any bearing; it does not confer rights on individuals which courts can enforce against other private citizens or private corporations
213. *R v SS Home Dept., ex p Sinclair* [1992] Imm AR 293, 300	29.1.92	QBD (DC) Watkins LJ* & Judge J	Judicial review (substantive hearing)	Extradition	ECHR	8	—	Doubtful if, strictly speaking, Art.8 ECHR was applicable to present circumstances, but the principle underlying it was very much to the point

Case	Date	Court	Proceeding	Subject	Treaty	Art.	Strasbourg cases	Commentary
214. *R v Parole Board, ex p Wilson* [1992] QB 740, 75D-F, 751D	30.1.92	CA (Civ. Div.) Nourse, Taylor* & Scott LJJ	Judicial review (appeal)	Prisons	ECHR	5(4)	*Thynne, Wilson & Gunnell v UK*	European Court's decision in favour of this very applicant, and UK government's acceptance of that decision and enactment of legislation to achieve conformity with ECHR, helped constitute formidable case for holding that natural justice required disclosure of reports to applicant, even though reforming legislation not yet in force
215. **Derbyshire County Council v Times Newspapers Ltd.** [1992] QB 770, 803D-E, 810D-817G, 827F, 829C-	19.2.92	CA (Civ. Div.) Balcombe, Ralph Gibson & Butler-Sloss LJJ	Appeal against refusal to strike out	Defamation	ECHR ICCPR	10 19	*Harman v UK; Lingens v Austria; R v UK; Sunday Times v UK; Sunday Times v UK (No.2)*	Balcombe LJ: Where the law is uncertain, the court should approach the issue before it with a predilection to ensure that our law should not involve a breach of Art. 10; even if the common law is certain, the courts will still consider whether the UK is in breach of Art. 10. Butler-Sloss LJ: Where there is an ambiguity, or the law is otherwise unclear or undeclared by an appellate court, the English court is not only entitled but obliged to consider the implications of Art. 10
216. *Re Osman's application* [1992] Crim LR 741	28.2.92	QBD (DC) Woolf LJ & Pill J	*Habeas corpus* & judicial review	Criminal procedure	ECHR	5(1)(f)	—	Argument that Art. 5(1)(f) ECHR contravened recited but not addressed
217. *R v Hereford and Worcester CC, ex p Smith*	11.3.92	QBD MacPherson J	Judicial review (leave application)	Gypsies	ECHR		—	ECHR not part of English domestic law, but can be used in limited circumstances to assist in the interpretation of a statute should ambiguity arise; since no relevant ambiguity here, ECHR has no part to play
218. *Ponsamy Poongavanam v R*	6.4.92	PC Lords Bridge, Templeman, Ackner, Goff & Browne-Wilkinson	Appeal against conviction	Criminal procedure	ECHR	6(1)	*Piersack v Belgium; Sramek v Austria; Hauschildt v Denmark*	ECHR jurisprudence interpreting Art.6(1), which mirrored language of provision in Mauritius Constitution, considered but found not to be in point; neither provision's wording could support a principle that juries must be drawn from a list which is representative of society
219. **Jones & Lee v Miah**[EC] (1992) 24 HLR 578, 586-8	7.4.92	CA (Civ. Div.) Dillon*, Nourse & Leggatt LJJ	Appeal against damages award	Landlord & tenant	ECHR	7		ECHR of no assistance to appellants since there was no ambiguity in relevant statutory provisions having retrospective effect, and in any event they were not penal and therefore outside the article; nor was ECHR directly enforceable as part of general principles of EC law since the case had no EC element
220. *Kwasi Minta v SS Home Dept.* [1992] Imm AR 380, 386	8.4.92	CA (Civ. Div.) Parker, Stuart-Smith* & Beldam LJJ	Judicial review (appeal)	Immigration	ECHR ICCPR			There being no ambiguity in the relevant statutory provision, it was unnecessary to pray in aid the ECHR as an aid to construction
221. *Re A (A Minor)*	30.4.92	CA (Civ. Div.) Balcombe* & Mann LJJ	Wardship (appeal)	Family	ECHR	8	—	Extensive quotations made from judgments in *In Re KD (A Minor)*, in support of proposition that the relevant principle of law is that the welfare of the child is the first and paramount consideration
222. *Balbir Singh v SS Home Dept.* [1992] Imm AR 426, 428, 429	5.5.92	CA (Civ. Div.) Dillon*, Neill & Staughton* LJJ	Judicial review (renewed leave application)	Immigration	ECHR	3	—	No duty on SS to consider whether return of political asylum seekers to first safe country reached, in accordance with UN Convention on Status of Refugees, would involve breach of Art.3 ECHR by exposing refugees to degrading treatment not from authorities but racist groups

Name of Case & Citation	Date of Judgment	Court	Type of Proceedings	Subject Matter	Treaty cited	Articles cited	Case-law cited	Nature of reference made to unincorporated international human rights law
223. *Atkinson v Castan*	3.6.92	CA (Civ. Div.) Neill LJ	Application for leave to appeal	Civil procedure	ECHR	6	*Golder v UK*, *Deweer v Belgium*	Argument that refusal to stay execution of a consent order was a breach of Art.6 ECHR considered on its merits, but held that nothing in circumstances of the case could possibly amount to a breach of Art.6 as presently interpreted
224. *Sujeevan v Cardiff Volkswagen Centre*[a]	15.6.92	CA (Civ. Div.) Parker LJ* & Sir David Croom-Johnson	Application for leave to appeal	Contract	ECHR	—	—	English courts can refer matters to ECJ but does not have power to make references to European Commission of Human Rights
225. *R v Redbourne* [1992] 1 WLR 1182, 1185H–1186E	19.6.92	CA (Crim. Div.) Staughton LJ*, McKinnon & Potter JJ	Appeal against confiscation order	Crime	ECHR	6(2), (3)(d), 7(1)	—	Not necessary to decide Crown's point that previous constructions of the Drug Trafficking Offences Act 1986 put UK in breach of ECHR because they treated the relevant provisions as penal rather than restitutionary
226. *Ahmed v Tower Hamlets Law Centre*	25.6.92	EAT Judge Hargrove QC, Galbraith & Lambert	Appeal against strike out	Employment	ECHR	—	—	Appellant's allegation of breach of ECHR recited but not dealt with
27. *R v Finch* (1993) 14 Cr App R(S) 226, 231	20.7.92	CA (Crim. Div.) Lloyd LJ*, Tudor Evans & Latham JJ	Appeal against confiscation order	Crime	ECHR	—	—	Court recited but declined to deal with Crown's argument (also made in *Redbourne*) that earlier decisions of CA interpreting Drug Trafficking Offences Act 1986 were in breach of ECHR
228. *R v Rochdale Metropolitan Borough Council, ex p Schemet* (1993) 91 LGR 425, 443	24.7.92	QBD Roch J	Judicial review (substantive hearing)	Education	ECHR	Art. 2 Prot. 1	—	Dictum from *Talmud Torah School Trust*, to effect that ECHR underlines SS's duty to take into account parents' wishes when deciding whether or not efficient and suitable instruction is being provided, adopted and followed
229. *R v Advertising Standards Authority Ltd., ex p Vernons Organisation Ltd.* [1992] 1 WLR 1289, 1293A–B	9.9.92	QBD Laws J	Judicial review (application for interim injunction)	Civil procedure	ECHR	(10)	—	Freedom of expression "as much a sinew of the common law" as of the ECHR
230. *Thanapal v General Medical Council*	5.10.92	PC Lords Goff*, Mustill & Woolf	Appeal against suspension	Professional regulation	ECHR	(10)	—	No basis for suggestion that doctor's suspension from practice was a curtailment of his right of freedom of expression in ECHR
231. *AB v John Wyeth & Brother Ltd.* (1992) 12 BMLR 50, 60, 62	13.10.92	CA (Civ. Div.) Balcombe, Steyn & Hoffmann* LJJ	Appeal against interlocutory order	Civil procedure	ECHR	6	*H v France*	There would be much to be said for the argument that the judge's way of constituting the class for the group action was in breach of ECHR if it inevitably deprived all prospective claimants of legal aid and barred them from instituting proceedings, but that was not the inevitable consequence; and even if it delayed their claims, the remedy for that lay elsewhere
232. *R v Immigration Appeal Tribunal, ex p Marchon*[K] [1993] Imm AR 98, 106–7	14.10.92	QBD Henry J	Judicial review (substantive hearing)	Immigration	ECHR	8, 9, 10, 11	—	EC law did not require SS or IAT to carry out an additional balancing exercise similar to that required under ECHR, to determine whether deportation of an EC national was necessary in a democratic society in the interests of public policy, because such balancing was already carried out in applying tests set out in directives

Case	Date	Court	Application	Subject		Art.	ECHR case	Notes
233. *R v Wolverhampton Magistrates' Court, ex p Mould* (1993) 157 JP 1017, 1031C	4.11.92	QBD (DC) Kennedy LJ* & Waterhouse J	Judicial review (substantive hearing)	Local government	ECHR	6	—	No assistance derived from reference to Art.6 ECHR; of course enforcement proceedings under community charge regulations need to be taken within a reasonable time
234. *AG v Associated Newspapers Ltd.* [1994] 2 AC 238, 242C–243F, 246G–H, 247B–248E	12.11.92	QBD (DC) Beldam LJ & Tudor Evans J	Application to commit for contempt	Contempt of court	ECHR	10	*Sunday Times v UK*	Parliament had enacted Contempt of Court Act 1981 mindful of need to comply with ECHR; background to Act and practice of jury trial showed importance attached to complete freedom of discussion in the jury room and that ban on "disclosure" of jury room secrets was not intended to be confined to disclosure by jurors
235. *Re C (Mental Patient: Contact)* [1993] 1 FLR 940, 943H	20.11.92	Fam. Div. Eastham J	Application for declarations	Mental health/family	ECHR	—	—	Access to children is a right guaranteed by both the common law and the ECHR
236. *R v SS Environment, ex p NALGO* [1993] Admin LR 785, 792F, 793G–799A, 802D–E	26.11.92	CA (Civ. Div.) Neill*, Russell & Rose LJJ	Judicial review (appeal)	Employment/local government	ECHR	10	—	Not necessary for a Minister when exercising a statutory discretion to do so in accordance with ECHR; nor can decision be interfered with on ground that Minister did not have regard to ECHR; but Minister must show an important competing public interest to justify a restriction on a fundamental right; the court exercises a secondary reviewing judgment and is not entitled to lower the threshold of unreasonableness
237. *Re Barretto*	30.11.92	QBD Schiemann J	Statutory application for certificate	Crime	ECHR	7(1)	—	The wording of the statute being unclear, the ECHR was relevant as an aid to construction; in light of the principle enshrined in Art.7 combined with the common law presumption against retrospectivity, the statute should not be construed so as to have retrospective effect
238. *Re Hagan* The Times, 28 Dec 1992	15.12.92	QBD (DC) Rose LJ* & Pill J	*Habeas corpus* & judicial review (leave application)	Extradition/criminal procedure	ECHR	5(4)	*Weeks v UK*	Applicants' argument that ECHR requires the courts, not the executive, to review the legality of a citizen's detention, and that evaluation of the effect of delay on the fairness of a trial is better carried out by a court than by SS, recited but not addressed by court, save to observe that ECHR not presently part of English law
239. *Middlebrook Mushrooms Ltd. v Transport and General Workers' Union* [1993] ICR 612, 620C	18.12.92	CA (Civ. Div.) Neill*, Mann & Hoffmann LJJ	Appeal against injunction	Employment/public protest	ECHR	10	—	Relevant to bear in mind that in all cases which involve a proposed restriction on the right of free speech the court is concerned, when exercising its discretion, to consider whether the suggested restraint is necessary
240. *R v Sandwell MBC, ex p Thomas*	22.12.92	QBD Potts J	Judicial review (leave application)	Local government	ECHR	8	—	Applicant's reliance on ECHR as ground on which relief sought recited but not dealt with by court
241. *R v SS Home Dept., ex p Wynne* [1993] 1 WLR 115, 121G–H, 123D–E, 124H	21.1.93	HL Lords Templeman, Goff*, Jauncey, Mustill & Slynn*	Judicial review (appeal)	Prisons/civil procedure	ECHR	6	*Golder v UK*	ECHR case-law supported view that right of access to courts (or, per Slynn, right to appear in person) is not absolute, and that it is not court's function to elaborate a general theory of permissible limitations; practical solutions to balancing competing interests should be found

Name of Case & Citation	Date of Judgment	Court	Type of Proceedings	Subject Matter	Treaty cited	Articles cited	Case-law cited	Nature of reference made to unincorporated international human rights law
242. *SS Home Dept. v Central Broadcasting Ltd.*	26.1.93	CA (Civ. Div.) Bingham MR, McCowan & Hirst* LJJ	Appeal against refusal of interlocutory injunction	Broadcasting	ECHR	10	—	Refusal of English courts to restrain publication or broadcast by interlocutory injunction where impact of article or programme depended on its timing, even if balance of convenience otherwise lay in granting it, said to be fully in line with Art.10 ECHR, though of course that treaty had not been incorporated into domestic law
243. **R v SS Home Dept., ex p Jibril** [1993] Imm AR 308, 309–10	27.1.93	QBD Hutchison J	Judicial review (leave application)	Immigration	ECHR	6(1), 8	—	SS not obliged to give a more fully reasoned decision so as to enable applicant to mount a reasoned challenge to it in the courts, because that would be to give a weight to the ECHR which it is not permissible to give
244. *O'Connor v Mirror Group Newspapers*	1.2.93	CA (Civ. Div.) Ralph-Gibson*, Leggatt & Hoffmann LJJ	Appeal against injunction	Defamation	ECHR	6	—	Unnecessary to decide ECHR point as injunction set aside on other grounds
245. **R v SS Home Dept., ex p Tejinder Singh**^RC	2.2.93	QBD Auld J	Judicial review (leave application)	Immigration	ECHR	8	—	Even assuming that the applicant was entitled to ask the ECJ to rule on the application of the ECHR to Community law and thence to domestic law, applicant could not surmount obstacle that ECHR is not part of domestic law nor a relevant consideration in the exercise of discretion
246. *Saujeen v St. Johns College*^LR	2.2.93	EAT Wood J	Appeal against refusal to extend time	Employment	ECHR	1, 6, 10, 13, 14, 17, 26	—	It may be that appellant has some rights under ECHR, but EAT's task is to apply the time limits and the principles for the extension of time
247. *Airedale NHS Trust v Bland* [1993] AC 789, 863H–864A	4.2.93	HL Lords Keith, Goff*, Lowry, Browne-Wilkinson & Mustill	Appeal against declarations	Health	ECHR ICCPR	2 6	—	Art.2 ECHR & Art. 6 ICCPR evidence that the principle of the sanctity of human life is a principle long recognised not only in our own society but also in most if not all civilised societies throughout the modern world
248. **R v SS Home Dept., ex p Dauit Teame**	11.2.93	QBD Judge J	Judicial review (substantive hearing)	Immigration	ECHR	8	—	Irrespective of ECHR, the principles in Art.8 are understood and valued in UK and treated as axiomatic; every SS acting under immigration legislation is aware of them and must give them proper attention when he has a relevant discretion to exercise
249. *Re T (A Minor)*	11.2.93	CA (Civ. Div.) Butler-Sloss LJ	Appeal against refusal to extend time	Family	ECHR	(8)	—	Mother's argument that it is contrary to the ECHR to remove a child from its mother for no reason recited but not addressed
250. **R v SS Home Dept., ex p Chahal** [1993] Imm AR 362, 373–4, 379–80	12.2.93	QBD Potts J	Judicial review (substantive hearing)	Immigration	ECHR	3	—	Although ECHR not part of domestic law, SS would be expected to take any relevant provisions into account had he not already considered the risk of applicant's being exposed to torture as an aspect of persecution

Case	Date	Court / Judges	Type of action	Subject	Convention	Articles	Cases cited	Conclusion / comment
251. *Derbyshire County Council v Times Newspapers Ltd.* [1993] AC 534, 550E–551G	18.2.93	HL Lords Keith*, Griffiths, Goff, Browne-Wilkinson & Woolf	Action for damages (appeal on a preliminary issue)	Defamation	ECHR	10	*Barthold v Germany*, *Lingens v Austria*, *Sunday Times v UK*	Conclusion that a local authority does not have the right to maintain an action for damages for defamation was reached on the common law of England, without any need to rely on ECHR; the common law is consistent with the obligations assumed by the Crown under the Treaty in the particular field of free speech
252. *Re: S (a Minor) (Parental Rights)* [1993] Fam 572	3.3.93	QBD Judge Phelan	Action for damages	Family	ECHR	—	—	Common law consistent with ECHR
253. *Bryan v SS Environment*	5.3.93	CA (Civ. Div.) Leggatt LJ	Renewed application for leave to appeal	Planning	ECHR	—	—	ECHR not part of domestic law; refusal of application meant applicant had now fulfilled declared intention of exhausting domestic remedies as necessary prelude to applying to European Commission
254. *R v Brown* [1994] 1 AC 212, 237B–F, 247D–E, 256D–E, 271G–272G, 282B–C	11.3.93	HL Lords Templeman, Jauncey, Lowry, Mustill, & Slynn	Appeal against conviction	Crime	ECHR	7, 8	—	Lord Lowry: the Offences Against the Persons Act 1865, being neither post-ECHR nor ambiguous, does not fall to be construed so as to conform with rather than contradict the ECHR. Lord Mustill: ECHR decisions valuable guidance on approach English courts should take. Lord Slynn: not necessary to decide whether invasion of privacy would be justified, even assuming that English law includes a parallel principle to that in Art. 8 ECHR
255. *Rantzen v Mirror Group Newspapers Ltd.* [1994] QB 670, 683C–D,H–686D, 687E–689G, 690E–692H, 693G–694C	31.3.93	CA (Civ. Div.) Neill*, Staughton & Roch LJJ	Action for damages (appeal against damages award)	Defamation	ECHR	10, 13	*Lingens v Austria*, *Sunday Times v UK*, *Sunday Times v UK (No.2)*	ECHR not part of English law and therefore courts have no power to enforce ECHR rights directly, but ECHR may be deployed for purpose of resolving an ambiguity in primary or subordinate legislation or when court is contemplating how a discretion is to be exercised. Where freedom of expression is at stake, Art. 10 has a wider role and can be regarded as an articulation of principles underlying common law
256. *Taylor (Collector of Taxes) v Boughton*	31.3.93	CA (Civ. Div.) Butler-Sloss LJ	Renewed application for leave to appeal	Revenue	ECHR	(9)	—	Appellant's reliance on ECHR to justify withholding of taxes on grounds of conscience rejected as hopeless; courts must enforce tax laws which Parliament passes
257. *Re: W (A Minor) (Residence Order)* [1993] 2 FLR 625, 631E–H	5.4.93	CA (Civ. Div.) Balcombe & Waite LJJ	Appeal against residence order	Family	ECHR	—	—	Dicta from *Re KD (A Minor)* on whether there was any inconsistency between ECHR and English rule about paramountcy of welfare of the child cited; welfare of the child said to be the test, but there was a strong supposition that it is in child's interests to remain with natural parents
258. *L'Office Cherifien des Phosphates v Yamashita-Shinnihon Steamship Co. Ltd.* [1994] 1 AC 486, 494A	7.4.93	CA (Civ. Div.) Sir Thomas Bingham MR*, Beldam† & Kennedy LJJ	Appeal against set aside of arbitration award	Arbitration	ECHR	7	—	Fundamental and longstanding rule that a person should not be held liable or punished for conduct not criminal when committed said to be protected by Art.7 ECHR
259. *R v SS Home Dept., ex p Bateman* The Times, May 10 1993	5.5.93	QBD (DC) Leggatt LJ & McCullough J*	judicial review (substantive hearing)	False imprisonment	ECHR ICCPR	Art. 3 Prot. 7 14.6	Explanatory memorandum to Art. 3 of Prot. 7	Noted that s.133 Criminal Justice Act 1988, on compensation for wrongful imprisonment, derives from Art. 14.6 ICCPR and court's construction of it accorded with Explanatory Memorandum to Art. 3 of Prot. 7 ECHR

Name of Case & Citation	Date of Judgment	Court	Type of Proceedings	Subject Matter	Treaty cited	Articles cited	Case-law cited	Nature of reference made to unincorporated international human rights law
260. *R v Mid Glamorgan Family Health Services Authority, ex p Martin* (1993) 16 BMLR 81, 85, 95–7, 99	14.5.93	QBD Popplewell J	Judicial review (substantive hearing)	Health	ECHR	8	*Gaskin v UK Handyside v UK*	Reference to ECHR of no assistance in the circumstances since the position at common law was quite clear and needed no assistance from Europe: there was no common law right of access to medical records which pre-dated legislation passed to conform with ECHR
261. *R v SS Home Dept., ex p Homodor*^DP1293	14.5.93	QBD Popplewell J	Judicial review (leave application)	Immigration	ECHR	8	—	Although ECHR not part of domestic law, SS considers Art.8, or should do so, when considering applications not to deport; internal Home Office document giving advice about Art.8 did not give rise to any legitimate expectation; on the facts SS had clearly considered Art.8
262. *Hlomodor v SS Home Dept.* DP1293 [1993] Imm AR 534, 536, 539–40	18.5.93	CA (Civ. Div.) Stuart-Smith, McCowan & Kennedy* LJJ	Judicial review (renewed leave application)	Immigration	ECHR	8	*Berrehab v The Netherlands*	Accepted by Crown for purposes of hearing that Art.8 ECHR should be regarded as a relevant factor in exercise of SS's discretion; but Art.8 added nothing to applicant's case
263. *R v SS Home Dept., ex p Leech* [1994] QB 198, 217A–F	19.5.93	CA (Civ. Div.) Neill, Steyn & Rose LJJ	Judicial review (substantive hearing)	Prisons	ECHR	(8)	*Campbell v UK*	Decision of Eur. Ct. HR in *Campbell*, although not directly binding in England, reinforces a conclusion reached in the light of principles of our domestic jurisprudence
264. *AG of Hong Kong v Lee Kwong-Kut* [1993] AC 951, 966F–967A, 968G–969D	19.5.93	PC Lords Keith, Lane, Bridge, Browne-Wilkinson & Woolf*	Appeal against dismissal of information & quashing of indictment	Criminal procedure	ECHR ICCPR	6(2)	*Salabiaku v France*	Decisions of European Court can give valuable guidance as to proper approach to interpretation of Hong Kong Bill of Rights, particularly in relation to provisions in similar terms; and case law contained valuable statement of approach to presumption of innocence which, though not subject to express limitation, had implicit degree of flexibility
265. *R v Uxbridge Justices, ex p Webb*^RC	9.6.93	QBD (DC) Glidewell LJ* & Cresswell J	Judicial review (substantive hearing)	Customs & excise	ECHR	10	—	Domestic legislation providing for the forfeiture of obscene articles imported into the country does not contravene ECHR because Art.10(2) expressly provides that the law may include provisions necessary in a democratic society for the protection of morals
266. *R v SS Home Dept., ex p Kuopong* [1993] Imm AR 569, 573	23.6.93	QBD Macpherson J	Judicial review (application to set aside leave)	Immigration	ECHR	(8, 14)	—	ECHR may be used as an aid to construction, but following *Brind* no argument based on the terms of the ECHR and its place in English law could assist the applicant
267. *Holtom v LB Barnet* The Times, 30 Sep 1993	6.7.93	QBD Judge Oddie	Action for damages	Education	ECHR	—	—	ECHR not considered to directly affect English law or to be of significance in considering if plaintiff had a remedy for breach of statutory duty against local authority in respect of alleged failure to meet her special educational needs
268. *Griffin v Interception of Communications Tribunal*	6.7.93	CA (Civ. Div.) Neill*, Nolan & Evans LJJ	Judicial review (renewed leave application)	Interception of communications	ECHR	—	—	ECHR not part of English law; it is only in certain circumstances that resort can be had, by leave of the court, to provisions of ECHR; there being no ambiguity in the legislation, ECHR could not assist

Case	Date	Court/Judges	Proceeding	Subject	Convention	Article	Cited	Notes
269. R v SS Home Dept., ex p Okoicha	8.7.93	CA (Civ. Div.) Nicholls VC, Butler-Sloss* & Peter Gibson LJJ	Judicial review (renewed leave application)	Immigration	ECHR	8	—	Applicant was right not to raise Art.8 ECHR because there was no evidence of intention to cohabit with husband on a permanent basis
270. Tomlinson v Ridout	22.7.93	CA (Civ. Div.) Balcombe*, Farquharson & Rose LJJ	Appeal against paternity order	Family	ECHR	8	—	Appellant contesting paternity not assisted by argument that requiring him to submit to blood test was a breach of his rights under Art.8 ECHR; while Art.8 undoubtedly requires respect for privacy, it provides an exception for when those rights interfere with rights of others
271. R v SS Home Dept., ex p Iye DP2/93	22.7.93	QBD Auld J	Judicial review (leave application)	Immigration	ECHR	8	—	SS's policy for treatment of illegal entrants with family ties, with its test of whether removal can be justified as necessary in the interests of a democratic society, said to reflect in part Art.8 ECHR; SS had clearly had regard to principles of Art.8 in carrying out his balancing exercise
272. R v Canons Park Mental Health Review Tribunal, ex p A [1994] 1 All ER 481, 485i, 492j–494a	28.7.93	QBD (DC) Mann LJ & Sedley J*	Judicial review (substantive hearing)	Mental health	ECHR	5(4)	Winterwerp v The Netherlands X v UK	In passing new Mental Health Act, Parliament was assumed to have sought to comply with European Court decision holding former legislation in breach of ECHR; a construction which would give a tribunal an original power to determine liability to detention was wrong because would put Act in breach of ECHR
273. Iye v SS Home Dept DP2/93 [1994] Imm AR 63, 65–7	27.8.93	CA (Civ. Div.) Glidewell*, Scott & Evans* LJJ	Judicial review (renewed leave application)	Immigration	ECHR	8	—	ECHR had necessitated internal Home Office guidance, disregard of which would be a valid ground of challenge; but if, as here, it appeared to have been followed, only question on review was whether outcome of SS's balancing exercise was Wednesbury unreasonable
274. R v Guardian Newspapers The Times, 26 Oct 1993	27.8.93	CA (Civ. Div.) Kennedy LJ*, Ognall & Curtis JJ	Application for leave to appeal against in camera order	Criminal procedure	ECHR	10, 13	—	As words of statute clear, unnecessary to seek assistance as to construction from ECHR; in any even there was no inconsistency, since Art.13 neither expressly nor by implication requires an oral hearing and Art.10(2) recognises that restrictions on press freedom may be necessary
275. Chahal v SS Home Dept. [1995] 1 WLR 526, 533H–534A	22.10.93	CA (Civ. Div.) Neill, Staughton* & Nolan LJJ	Judicial review (substantive hearing)	Immigration	ECHR ICCPR	3, 13 7, 13 3	—	ECHR invoked by applicant, but reliance on it unnecessary, since combined effect of Convention on Status of Refugees and Immigration Rules was to require SS to carry out a balancing exercise in which SS was obliged to balance interests of individual as a refugee against interests of national security
276. R v SS Home Dept., ex p T [1994] QB 378, 386F–G, 388F–G	22.10.93	QBD (DC) Kennedy LJ* & Pill J	Judicial review (substantive hearing)	Prisons/mental health	ECHR	(5(4))	Thynne, Wilson & Gunnell v UK X v UK	Role of European Court decisions in history of Mental Health Act 1983 and Criminal Justice Act 1991 recited; and it had to be remembered that the purpose of the provision was to meet the criticism of English law voiced by Eur. Ct. HR
277. Crompton v North Tyneside MBC	29.10.93	QBD (DC) McCowan LJ & Tuckey J*	Appeal against conviction	Criminal procedure	ECHR	6(1)	Hauschildt v Denmark	European Court said to give precisely the same test for bias as English courts
278. R v SS Home Dept., ex p Amankwa DP2/93	2.11.93	QBD Brooke J	Judicial review (leave application)	Immigration	ECHR	8	—	Leave granted to give opportunity to settle point of contemporary public interest, namely whether applicants in immigration cases can base challenges on internal Home Office guidance explicitly taking into account effect of ECHR

Name of Case & Citation	Date of Judgment	Court	Type of Proceedings	Subject Matter	Treaty cited	Articles cited	Case-law cited	Nature of reference made to unincorporated international human rights law
279. *Pratt v AG for Jamaica* [1993] 3 WLR 995, 1012H–1013B, 1014D, F	2.11.93	PC, Lords Griffiths*, Lane, Ackner, Goff, Lowry, Slynn & Woolf	Judicial review (appeal)	Crime	ECHR ICCPR	3	*Soering v UK* *Ireland v UK*	ECHR case-law recognising death-row phenomenon as going beyond Art.3 threshold cited in support of conclusion that period of delay twice as long was an infringement of equivalent provision in Jamaican Constitution
280. *R v Preston* [1994] 2 AC 130, 142D–E, 147G–148B, 167D	4.11.93	HL, Lords Keith, Templeman, Jauncey*, Browne-Wilkinson & Mustill*	Appeal against conviction	Interception of communications	ECHR	8	*Malone v UK*	Role of ECHR in history of Interception of Communications Act 1985 recited; nature of the criticisms made of former law by European Court relied on to support narrow construction of implementing legislation
281. *Re Prankerd*	17.11.93	QBD (DC), Rose LJ* & McKinnon J	Application for leave to appeal against refusal of leave to issue witness summons	Civil procedure	ECHR	(6)	—	Court cannot entertain argument that statutory provision providing for vexatious litigant orders is contrary to ECHR; court is bound by Parliament's enactment and it is the court's duty to deal with application for such an order and all matters ancillary to it
282. *Re Prankerd*	18.11.93	QBD (DC), Rose LJ* & McKinnon J	Application for vexatious litigant order	Civil procedure	ECHR	6, 26	—	Litigant had not been denied a fair hearing in a public court before an impartial tribunal contrary to ECHR, but had had many such hearings; nor would a vexatious litigant order impede his access to the European Court by preventing him from exhausting his remedies in English law
283. *Kuapong v SS Home Dept.* [1994] Imm AR 207, 211–13, 215	25.11.93	CA (Civ. Div.), Ralph Gibson* & Evans* LJJ, Sir David Croom-Johnson	Judicial review (renewed leave application)	Immigration	ECHR	(8, 14)	—	Unarguable after *Brind* to claim that Parliament must be taken to have intended that a rule-making power given to SS can only be exercised consistently with ECHR; there was no ambiguity in the terms of the wide rule-making power given to the minister
284. *R v SS Home Dept., ex p Amankwah* [1994] Imm AR 240, 242, 244	10.12.93	QBD, Popplewell J	Judicial review (substantive hearing)	Immigration	ECHR	8	—	SS's decision held to be unfair and therefore perverse to extent that it was not in conformity with internal policy document taking into account effect of ECHR; basis of judgment was not that the decision was in breach of ECHR but that it did not appear from SS's reasons for decision that he had had regard to his own policy
285. *Houston v Smith*	16.12.93	CA (Civ. Div.), Neill, Beldam & Hirst* LJJ	Action for damages (appeal against damages award)	Defamation	ECHR	10	*Sunday Times v UK*	CA's new power to substitute proper sum of damages for excessive jury award should be interpreted in setting of Art.10 ECHR even in cases not concerning press freedom; question is whether, judged by objective standards of reasonable compensation or necessity or proportionality, jury award was excessive
286. *In re H-S (Minors) (Protection of Identity)* [1994] 1 WLR 1141, 1148B–G	21.12.93	CA (Civ. Div.), Neill LJ & Ward J*	Appeal against refusal to discharge injunction	Family/transsexuals	ECHR	8, 10	—	Where freedoms enshrined in Arts 8 & 10 ECHR were in issue, they must be taken into account by court in its balancing exercise and the welfare of the child was not then the court's paramount consideration; and such balancing should be carried out by the High Court in the exercise of its inherent jurisdiction

	Date	Court		Action	ECHR	No.	Case	Description
287. *Watts v Times Newspapers Ltd.*	21.12.93	QBD Morison J	Action for damages (preliminary issue)	Defamation	ECHR	10	—	Defendant's argument that, in deciding whether publication was made on an occasion of qualified privilege, court should take a modern view of important function of newspapers in a free and democratic society and have regard to Art.10 ECHR, from which English law did not in principle differ, recited but not addressed
288. *Official Solicitor v News Group Newspapers* [1994] 2 FLR 174, 183A–D	28.1.94	Fam. Div. Connell J	Application to commit for contempt	Contempt of court	ECHR	10	*Lingens v Austria*	Insofar as Art.10 was relevant, the statutory provision making it a contempt to publish information relating to Children Act proceedings was prescribed by law, resulted from the pressing social need to protect privacy and was proportionate to the legitimate aim pursued, in view of what else the press could still publish
289. *Re Hayward*	28.1.94	QBD (DC) Ralph Gibson LJ* & Smith J	Judicial review (substantive hearing)	Civil procedure	ECHR	(6)	—	Argument that proceedings for a vexatious litigant order be stayed pending reference to ECJ of question whether statutory provision for making such an order is in breach of ECHR rejected; rights thereunder must be pursued after those proceedings had been determined
290. **Stedman v Hogg Robinson Travel**[BC]	31.1.94	EAT Mummery J, Ferry, Collerson	Statutory appeal (preliminary hearing)	Employment	ECHR	5	—	Appellant's argument that Sunday working comes within Community law doctrine of fundamental rights, referring generally to ECHR, recited
291. *AG v Associated Newspapers Ltd.* [1994] 2 AC 238, 258E–G, 261H–262H	3.2.94	HL Lords Keith, Bridge, Goff, Lowry* & Lloyd	Appeal against committal for contempt	Contempt of court	ECHR	10	*Sunday Times v UK*	If enactment is clear, as here, compliance with ECHR is not in issue, since ambiguity is required for ECHR to be relevant as aid to construction; in any event, absolute prohibition on disclosure of jury room secrets was necessary to maintain courts' authority and impartiality, a justification which permitted no distinction between disclosure by jurors and disclosure by the press
292. *Boddington v Lawton* [1994] ICR 478, 487H–488A	4.2.94	Ch. D. Sir Donald Nicholls V-C	Action for damages (preliminary issue)	Trusts	ECHR	11	—	Art.11 ECHR cited as evidence of general recognition of a person's freedom to join a trade union for protection of their interests
293. *R v SS Home Dept., ex p Ozminno* [DPZP3] [1994] Imm AR 287, 290, 291, 292, 293	4.2.94	QBD Auld J	Judicial review (substantive hearing)	Immigration	ECHR	8	—	ECHR not directly applicable in English courts, nor was there a presumption that SS's discretion should be exercised in accordance with it, nor could internal policy document incorporate Art.8; but restrictions of the rights upheld by it need to be justified and require particular scrutiny, so ECHR articles have at least some role as relevant factors in the taking of a decision
294. **R v Chief Constable of South Wales ex p Merrick** [1994] 1 WLR 663, 671F–G, 673E	9.2.94	QBD (DC) Ralph Gibson LJ* & Smith J	Judicial review (substantive hearing)	Police powers	ECHR	6	*Golder v UK*	Applicant's invocation of ECHR right of access to legal advice as aid to construction of statutory right to a solicitor recited but not relied on by court, which found there to be a common law right to consult a solicitor as soon as reasonably practicable

Name of Case & Citation	Date of Judgment	Court	Type of Proceedings	Subject Matter	Treaty cited	Articles cited	Case-law cited	Nature of reference made to unincorporated international human rights law
295. *R v Central Independent Television plc* [1994] 3 WLR 20, 30C–31D, G	9.2.94	CA (Civ. Div.) Neill, Hoffmann* & Waite LJJ	Appeal against injunction	Broadcasting/ family	ECHR	10	—	To enable us to meet our international obligations under ECHR, it is necessary that any exceptions to freedom of speech should satisfy tests laid down in Art.10(2) ECHR; outside established exceptions, or any new ones enacted in accordance with ECHR, free speech is a trump card, not to be balanced against other interests
296. *R v Canons Park Mental Health Review Tribunal, ex p A* [1995] QB 60, 75C–76B, 77H–78C, 86H–87C	16.2.94	CA (Civ. Div.) Nourse, Kennedy* & Roch† LJJ	Judicial review (appeal)	Mental health	ECHR	5	*X v UK*	Assistance of ECHR can only be invoked as an aid to construction if there is ambiguity or uncertainty in the statute, which there was not here; in any event the construction preferred did not put the legislation in conflict with ECHR
297. *Blackpool and The Fylde College v NATFHE* [1994] ICR 648, 654C–655A	25.2.94	CA (Civ. Div.) Sir Thomas Bingham MR*, Neill & Steyn LJJ	Appeal against interlocutory injunction	Employment	ECHR	8, 9, 10, 11, 13, 14	—	Trite law that ECHR does not form part of our law, but if there were an ambiguity the court would look very sympathetically towards ECHR if it helped in construing the section; but there was no ambiguity here and in any event there was little help to be derived from ECHR
298. *Special Hospitals Service Authority v Hyde* The Times, 18 Mar 1994	3.3.94	QBD Sir Peter Pain	Application for order for disclosure	Confiden- tiality	ECHR	10	*Observer & Guardian v UK*	Common law right to freedom of expression matches that guaranteed by ECHR; an English court will not grant relief to a public authority plaintiff which would interfere with right to information and discussion, unless authority can show that such interference is justified in terms of the tests applied by European Court
299. *Sutton LBC v Davis* [1994] 2 WLR 721, 724H–725A	16.3.94	Fam. Div. Wilson J	Statutory appeal	Local government	ECHR	(3)	*Costello-Roberts v UK*	European Court decision cited to show that corporal punishment of children is not in breach of ECHR unless it reaches a particular degree of severity
300. *Jaramillo-Silva v SS Home Dept.* [1994] Imm AR 352, 358	24.3.94	CA (Civ. Div.) Nourse, Beldam & Simon Brown LJJ	Judicial review (renewed leave application)	Immigration	ECHR	8	—	No arguable case for saying that Art. 8 ECHR could possibly found a challenge to SS's decision to deport; nothing in policy DP/2/93 required SS to invoke s. 3(5)(b) Immigration Act 1971 rather than s. 3(6)
301. *Re T* [1994] Imm AR 368, 373–4	25.3.94	CA (Civ. Div.) Staughton & Hoffmann* LJJ, Sir Roger Parker	Judicial review & appeal against refusal of interlocutory order	Immigration/ family	ECHR	6, 8	—	SS's policy of intervening in Family Court proceedings, where there is evidence that purpose of proceedings is to evade immigration control, understandable in light of desire to fulfil ECHR obligations; reference to Art.6 ECHR reinforced right of unimpeded access to the courts, but SS's immigration powers not qualified by that right
302. *Bremer v Newbury District Council*	19.4.94	CA (Civ. Div.) Glidewell* & Kennedy LJJ, Sir John Megaw	Judicial review (renewed leave application)	Local government	ECHR	8	—	Although ECHR not incorporated into UK law, courts of this country take notice of it, and much of what it contains is no more than a restatement of what is generally regarded as common law; challenge to byelaws on basis of Art.8 unarguable because justification within proviso
303. *Re Coster's Application*	6.5.94	CA (Civ. Div.) Stuart-Smith & Henry LJJ, Sir Ralph Gibson	Judicial review (renewed leave application)	Planning/ gypsies	ECHR	8	—	Art. 8 ECHR did not act to invalidate this nation's planning laws, nor does it prevent a local authority from seeking an injunction to enforce those laws

Case	Date	Court/Judges	Proceeding	Convention	Article	Case cited	Comment
304. *R v SS Home Dept., ex p MacNeill* The Times, 26 May 1994	9.5.94	QBD (DC) Staughton LJ & Buckley J	Judicial review (substantive hearing)	Prisons	ECHR	5(1),(4)	*Weeks v UK*	No breach of ECHR in revoking licence of prisoner detained during HM's pleasure and recalling him to prison; he was still detained in consequence of original court's decision for purposes of Art. 5(1) and Parole Board's consideration of his recall satisfied Art. 5(4)
305. **R v SS Home Dept., ex p Quijano**	12.5.94	QBD Sedley J	Judicial review (leave application)	Immigration	ECHR	8	—	Leave granted on basis that applicant had arguable case that relevant provisions of ECHR had not been taken into account
306. *R v SS Home Dept., ex p Ajayi*[DP293]	12.5.94	QBD Laws J	Judicial review (substantive hearing)	Immigration	ECHR	8	*Berrehab v The Netherlands*	Even assuming (without deciding) that the text of policy DP/2/93 requires SS to make good a legitimate expectation that the ECHR will be regarded in his decisions under the policy, on the facts there was no substance to argument that SS was in breach, as child could accompany mother
307. *R v Lancashire CC, ex p Foster*	16.5.94	QBD (DC) Kennedy LJ & Alliott J	Judicial review (substantive hearing)	Education	ECHR	(Art. 2 Prot. 1)	—	Provisions of Education Act 1980 not ambiguous as to extent of parental preferences and ECHR therefore of no assistance
308. *R v SS Home Dept., ex p Bateman* The Times, 1 Jul 1994	17.5.94	CA (Civ. Div.) Sir Thomas Bingham MR, Farquharson & Simon Brown LJJ	Judicial review (appeal)	Prisons	ECHR ICCPR	Art. 3 Prot. 7 14.6	—	Art. 3 of Seventh Protocol referred to in course of construing s.133 Criminal Justice Act 1988 (compensation for miscarriages of justice), enacted to give effect to Art. 14(6) ICCPR; ECHR provision reproduced language of ICCPR, but protocol not ratified by UK
309. *R v SS Home Dept., ex p McCartney* The Times, 25 May 1994	19.5.94	CA (Civ. Div.) Stuart-Smith, Hoffmann & Saville LJJ	Judicial review (appeal)	Prisons	ECHR	5(4), 7	*Thynne, Wilson & Gunnell v UK*	If SS had a wholly unfettered discretion to set a tariff in light of his own view on deterrence and retribution, it would be contrary to the spirit of decision in *Thynne*, that both parts of sentence be subject to independent judicial control, and probably also contrary to prohibition in Art. 7 on retrospectively imposing heavier penalties
310. **Stedman v Hogg Robinson Travel**[EC]	23.5.94	EAT Mummery J, Ferry & Collerson	Statutory appeal	Employment	ECHR ICCPR	8, 9	—	ECHR did not help appellant to establish recognition of a right not to work on a Sunday on grounds of rights to privacy and family life or freedom of religion, either as a Community right or as a fundamental right relevant to the interpretation of Community rights
311. **R v Khan** [1995] QB 27, 33B, 33G, 35G, 36C & F, 37G, 39B & C, 40E–41C	27.5.94	CA (Crim. Div.) Lord Taylor CJ*, Hutchison & Pill JJ	Appeal against conviction	Crime	ECHR	8	*Malone v UK*	Permissible to have regard to ECHR, which is of persuasive assistance, in cases of ambiguity or doubt; there being no ambiguity or doubt, there was no need to consider whether there was a breach of Art.8; in any event, that Art. recognises that there are circumstances in which intrusion on privacy is justifiable
312. *R v Thames Stipendiary Magistrates, ex p Bates*	29.6.94	QBD (DC) McCowan LJ & Buxton J	Judicial review (substantive hearing)	Criminal procedure	ECHR	6(2)	*Salabiaku v France*	Argument that reverse onus provision in the Dangerous Dogs Act 1991 should be read in light of Art. 6(2) ECHR was unsustainable; in any event, placing onus on the accused in relation to one element of offence was entirely reasonable

Name of Case & Citation	Date of Judgment	Court	Type of Proceedings	Subject Matter	Treaty cited	Articles cited	Case-law cited	Nature of reference made to unincorporated international human rights law
313. *Spring v Guardian Assurance plc* [1995] 2 AC 296, 326G–H, 352E–G	7.7.94	HL Lords Keith, Goff, Lowry*, Slynn & Woolf*	Action for damages	Employment	ECHR	10	—	Freedom of speech at least as important to the common law as it is under international conventions, but protection of it is qualified not absolute and it must be balanced against equally well recognised freedom to earn a livelihood; protection against a negligent reference fully justified any limited intrusion
314. *R v SS Home Dept., ex p Aseidu*	8.7.94	CA (Civ. Div.) Dillon, Hoffmann & Saville LJJ	Judicial review (renewed leave application)	Immigration	ECHR	(8)	—	Argument that decision to deport was *Wednesbury* unreasonable because children's interests were paramount having regard to the ECHR rejected
315. *R v SS Home Dept., ex p Hickey* [1995] QB 43, 52B–C, 54H–55D, 56B–D	19.7.94	CA (Civ. Div.) Butler-Sloss & Rose LJJ, Sir Tasker Watkins	Judicial review (appeal)	Prisons/ mental health	ECHR	5(4)	*Thynne, Wilson & Gunnell v UK* *Wynne v UK*	Criminal Justice Act 1991 was enacted to bring UK into line with ECHR, but there was nothing in procedure laid down by Mental Health Act 1983 which was incompatible with Court's ruling in *Thynne*; discretionary lifers transferred to hospital had regular access to a mental health review tribunal
316. **Hamilton v Naviede (In re Arrows Ltd. (No. 4))** *BC* [1995] 2 AC 75, 95F–H	25.7.94	HL Lords Keith, Jauncey, Browne-Wilkinson*, Lloyd & Nolan	Appeal against order releasing disclosure from undertakings	Criminal procedure	ECHR	6	*Funke v France* *Mialhe v France* *Cremieux v France*	Privilege against self-incrimination, one of basic freedoms secured by English law, was also one of basic rights protected by ECHR, and had also been recognised by ECJ as part of the general principles of Community law of which fundamental rights form an integral part
317. *R v SS Health, ex p LB Hackney*	29.7.94	CA (Civ. Div.) Sir Thomas Bingham MR, Waite & Saville LJJ	Judicial review (appeal)	Civil procedure	ECHR	6	—	Reliance on Art. 6 in support of argument that applicants had not received a fair hearing did not advance the matter any further; under domestic rules and practices, litigants are entitled to such a hearing
318. *R v SS Home Dept., ex p Adams* *BC* [1995] All ER (EC) 177, 189h–190e	29.7.94	QBD (DC) Steyn LJ & Kay J	Judicial review (substantive hearing)	Emergency powers	ECHR	5(1)(c), 10	*Fox, Campbell & Hartley v UK*	Passage relied on in Eur. Ct. HR's judgment in *Fox v UK* not of great assistance in determining whether applicant entitled to reasons for making of exclusion order, because it only imposed a "best endeavours" obligation on the SS when exercising his discretion
319. *R v Mid-Glamorgan Family Health Services, ex p Martin* [1995] 1 WLR 110, 118E–119A	29.7.94	CA (Civ. Div.) Nourse & Evans* LJJ, Sir Roger Parker	Judicial review (appeal)	Health	ECHR	8	*Gaskin v UK*	The fact that the ECHR's provisions did not form part of English law did not mean that they could not be referred to and relied on as persuasive authority as to what the common law is or should be, provided the relevant rules of the common law
320. *R v SS Home Dept., ex p Comfort Henry* *BP293* [1995] Imm AR 42, 43	19.8.94	QBD Harrison J	Judicial review (leave application)	Immigration	ECHR	8	—	Policy DP/2/93 was confined to applications in deportation and illegal entry cases and could not be applied to a leave to enter case; it might be thought that there should be another policy to deal with such cases, but on its face DP/2/93 was meant to deal with deportation and illegal entry

	Date	Court / Judge	Procedure	Subject	Source	Articles	Case references	Argument
321. *R v SS Home Dept., ex p Payne*[EC] [1995] Imm AR 48, 50	24.8.94	QBD Sedley J	Judicial review (leave application)	Immigration	ECHR	8, 12	*Abdulaziz, Cabales & Balkandali v UK*	Argument that since ratification of Maastricht Treaty it has become a Community task to co-operate in field of immigration in accordance with ECHR, and that an administrative authority must now have regard to ECHR in exercising discretion, interesting and by no means fanciful
322. *R v SS Home Dept., ex p McQuillan*[EC] [1995] 4 All ER 400, 409a–411a, 422c–422b	9.9.94	QBD Sedley J	Judicial review (substantive hearing)	Emergency powers	ECHR UDHR	2, 3, 15	*Vilvarajah v UK; Soering v UK; W v UK; X v Ireland; Fox, Campbell & Hartley v UK*	The principles and standards set out in the ECHR are certainly a matter of which the law of this country now takes notice in setting its own standards; once it is accepted that the standards articulated in the ECHR both march with those of the common law and inform the jurisprudence of the EU, it becomes unreal and potentially unjust to continue to develop English public law without reference to them
323. *Re Martin*	21.10.94	QBD (DC) McCowan LJ & Gage J	*Habeas corpus*	Extradition/ interception of communications	ECHR	8	*Malone v UK*	Applicant's argument, that purpose of Interception of Communications Act 1985 was to bring law into line with Art. 8 as interpreted in *Malone*, and it would be absurd if the Act excluded use of such evidence in all proceedings save extradition, recited but not addressed
324. *Johnson v Ministry of Justice, Vienna*[LP]	26.10.94	CA (Civ. Div.) Kennedy LJ & Hale J	Actions for damages	Civil procedure	ECHR	—	—	Insofar as litigant in person wished to make complaints about human rights, the ECHR was not part of English law, and only gave the right to complain to the Commission and Court of Human Rights about alleged breaches by the UK
325. *R v SS Home Dept., ex p Craig*	26.10.94	CA (Civ. Div.) Sir Thomas Bingham MR, Hobhouse & Morritt LJJ	Judicial review (renewed leave application)	Immigration	ECHR	8	*Berrehab v The Netherlands*	The authority of *Berrehab* was muted as a result of the non-incorporation of the ECHR and in any event the rule against separating parents and children is not an absolute one but depends on countervailing factors of which account is taken
326. *Re Chauhan*[LP]	26.10.94	CA (Civ. Div.) Neill, Hoffmann & Henry LJJ	Application for leave to conduct litigation	Civil procedure	ECHR	(6)	—	Litigant in person's argument that ECHR, along with common fairness and statutory purpose of Courts and Legal Services Act 1990, required that he should be allowed to provide legal services, recited but not specifically addressed
327. *Stedman v Hogg Robinson Travel*[EC]	27.10.94	CA (Civ. Div.) Neill, Hoffmann, Henry LJJ	Statutory appeal	Employment	ECHR	8, 9	—	Argument that the principle of protection of fundamental rights in EC law, read in conjunction with Arts. 8 and 9 ECHR, preclude dismissal of employee who refused to work on Sundays rejected because regulation of Sunday working not within the scope of Community law
328. *Tsikata v Newspaper Publishing plc* [1995] EMLR 8, 16	28.10.94	QBD Jonathan Sumption QC	Action for damages (preliminary issue)	Defamation	ECHR	10	*Lingens v Austria; Thorgeirson v Iceland*	No difference of principle between English law on freedom of expression and Art. 10; ECHR case law therefore taken into account in deciding scope of common law defence of qualified privilege
329. *R v Commissioner of Police for the Metropolis, ex p, Bennett* [1995] 2 WLR 598, 604A–C	1.11.94	QBD (DC) Rose LJ*, Potts J	Judicial review (substantive hearing)	Extradition/ criminal procedure	ECHR	5(1)(c), (4)	—	ECHR has not been incorporated into English law, but, assuming that the applicant was entitled to rely on it, there was nothing to prevent him from relying on it before a Scottish court as well as an English one; but it did not advance case

Name of Case & Citation	Date of Judgment	Court	Type of Proceedings	Subject Matter	Treaty cited	Articles cited	Case-law cited	Nature of reference made to unincorporated international human rights law
330. *R v SS Home Dept., ex p Patel* [1995] Imm A.R. 223, 227–9, 230	1.11.94	QBD Brooke J	Judicial review (substantive hearing)	Immigration	ECHR	8	*Berrehab v The Netherlands*	The approach of English courts in judicial review cases where a breach of ECHR is alleged is to ask whether any rational SS, reasonably reminding himself of provisions of ECHR, could have reasonably formed the view that he did, allowing him quite a wide margin of discretion
331. *R v Runnymede BC, ex p Smith* [1995] 70 P & CR 244, 249	10.11.94	QBD Owen J	Judicial review (leave application)	Planning/ gypsies	ECHR	8	—	Applicant's argument, that Council's decisions to apply for an injunction restraining use as a residential caravan site and to institute committal proceedings were in breach of ECHR recited but not specifically addressed
332. *R v SS Home Dept., ex p Anifalje*	22.11.94	CA (Civ. Div.) Steyn & Rose LJJ, Sir Ralph Gibson	Judicial review (renewed leave application)	Immigration	ECHR	6	—	Quite apart from fact that Art. 6 ECHR not part of English law, facts did not give rise to any conceivable breach of Art. 6 even if it did apply; argument that Art. 6 breached because applicant did not know date of hearing therefore rejected
333. *B v Croydon Health Authority* [1995] 2 WLR 294, 299E–F	29.11.94	CA (Civ. Div.) Neill, Hoffmann* & Henry LJJ	Application for injunction and declaration	Mental health	ECHR	8	—	Section 63 Mental Health Act 1983 amply satisfies the requirement in Art.8 that its terms must be sufficiently precise to enable individual to foresee its consequences for him
334. *R v Sheffield Housing Benefits Review Board, ex p Smith* [1995] 93 LGR 139, 158, 160	8.12.94	QBD Blackburne J	Judicial review (substantive hearing)	Social security	ECHR	9	—	Applicants' argument, that in so far as housing benefit regulation was ambiguous or unclear in its content, review board had erred in construing it in a manner inconsistent with rather than in accordance with Art. 9, rejected; Art.9 of no relevance to matters to be decided
335. *Jayetilleke v High Commission of the Commonwealth of the Bahamas*	14.12.94	EAT Mummery J, Lord Gladwin of Clee & Ramsay	Statutory appeal (preliminary hearing)	Employment/ state immunity	ECHR	1, 61, 13	—	ECHR, being unincorporated, could not be relied upon to counteract express provisions of primary legislation in State Immunity Act 1978; no room for a balancing exercise between rights of individuals and the public interest, as Parliament had already carried out that balancing exercise
336. *R v Broadcasting Complaints Commission, ex p Granada Television Ltd.* [1995] EMLR 163, 169	14.12.94	CA (Civ. Div.) Balcombe & McCowan LJJ, Sir Tasker Watkins	Judicial review (appeal)	Broadcasting	ECHR	8	—	Art.8 ECHR referred to as part of the existing jurisprudence showing that the meaning of "privacy" is not confined to matters concerning the individual complainant but extends to the complainant's family
337. *Re K (A Minor)*	15.12.94	CA (Civ. Div.) Sir Stephen Brown (P), Kennedy & Millett LJJ	Application for residence order (appeal)	Family	ECHR	—	—	Dictum from *Re KD (A Minor)* cited: no inconsistency of principle or application between English rule and ECHR rule
338. *Re JL Blackstone*[a]	19.12.94	QBD (DC) Henry LJ* & Kay J	Application for vexatious litigant order	Civil procedure	ECHR	6	—	ECHR not part of the law of England, though courts must take it into account in interpreting affected statutory provisions; Art. 6 borne in mind when construing s.42 Supreme Court Act 1981, but imposition of judicial screening process on vexatious litigant not denial of access to court

Case	Date	Court/Judge	Proceeding	Subject	Convention	Art.	ECtHR case	Commentary
339. *R v SS Home Dept., ex p Tong* [DP29]	21.12.94	QBD Judge J	Judicial review (leave application)	Immigration	ECHR	8	—	Question for court said to be whether SS had overlooked assumption that family life and private life were matters of considerable importance to be given appropriate respect they should enjoy in English law; and SS had not expressly considered child's interests as a British citizen
340. *R v Davey[LJP]*	19.1.95	CA (Crim. Div.) Hobhouse LJ, Pill & Steel JJ	Appeals against conviction	Criminal procedure	ECHR	6(3)	—	Litigant in person's argument that conduct of his trial was contrary to his rights under Art. 6(3) ECHR rejected
341. *Hipwood v Gloucester Health Authority* [1995] ICR 999, 1004	30.1.95	CA (Civ. Div.) McCowan & Simon Brown LJJ	Action for damages (interlocutory appeal)	Civil procedure	ECHR	8	—	Nothing ambiguous about terms of s. 53 County Courts Act 1984 and therefore no need to turn for assistance to Art. 8 ECHR in determining whether defendants entitled to discovery of plaintiff's medical records to their legal advisers
342. *R v SS Home Dept, ex p Togher*	1.2.95	CA (Civ. Div.) Glidewell, Hirst & Hoffmann LJJ	Judicial review (renewed leave application)	Prisons	ECHR	3, 8	—	Although ECHR has not been adopted into English law, the courts tend to pay greater attention to it as reflecting English common law principles, adopting that approach, there were no infringements of ECHR Art.s or the equivalent standards of the common law; SS had carried out the necessary balancing exercise
343. *R v SS Home Dept., ex p Abu Shabid[RP32/93]* [1995] Imm AR 303, 308	8.2.95	CA (Civ. Div.) Nourse & Waite LJJ, Sir Tasker Watkins	Judicial review (renewed leave application)	Immigration	ECHR	8	—	It would be quite wrong to apply policy statements to situations or circumstances other than those they are expressly stated to be applied to, even if it were permissible to use the contents of DP/2/93 by analogy, which was doubtful, SS had in any event used his discretion outside the rules compassionately
344. *R v Southampton Industrial Tribunal, ex p INS News Group Ltd.* [1995] IRLR 247, 250 col. 1	13.2.95	QBD Brooke J	Judicial review (substantive hearing)	Civil procedure	ECHR	10	—	The courts are always anxious to ensure that the needs of the press, which are enshrined in Art. 10 ECHR, are balanced appropriately against the needs of courts and tribunals to do justice in circumstances where witnesses can feel free to give evidence without fear of bad publicity
345. *R v Broadcasting Complaints Commission, ex p BBC* The Times, 24 Feb 1995	22.2.95	QBD Brooke J.	Judicial review (substantive hearing)	Broadcasting	ECHR	10	*Lingens v Austria*	Court entitled to have recourse to Art. 10 ECHR through long-established presumption that Parliament intended to comply with international obligations unless the converse is clearly shown; *a fortiori* when Art. 10 mirrors the common law
346. *McLean v SS Home Dept.*	22.2.95	CA (Crim. Div.) Leggatt, Simon Brown & Ward LJJ	Judicial review (renewed leave application)	Prisons	ECHR	5	*Thynne, Wilson & Gunnell v UK*	Requirement that SS is bound to accept whatever advice Parole Board may tender in connection with a prisoner's early release could not be read into Criminal Justice Act 1991; if a failure to enact such requirement renders UK vulnerable to successful challenge in Strasbourg, so be it
347. *R v Hiley* The Times, 10 Mar 1995	6.3.95	CA (Crim. Div.) Taylor LCJ, Alliott & Owen JJ	Appeal against conviction (renewed leave application)	Crime/ court martial	ECHR	6	—	Argument that trial unfair because tribunal not independent and impartial, and that court martial was convened in contravention of Art. 6 ECHR rejected

Name of Case & Citation	Date of Judgment	Court	Type of Proceedings	Subject Matter	Treaty cited	Articles cited	Case-law cited	Nature of reference made to unincorporated international human rights law
348. **Re W (Wardship: Discharge: Publicity)** [1995] 2 FLR 466, 473H	8.3.95	CA (Civ. Div.) Balcombe, Waite & Hobhouse LJJ	Wardship (appeal)	Family	ECHR	8, 10	—	Dictum of Ward J in *Re H (Minors)* cited: Art.s 8 & 10 ECHR must be taken into account when court balances children's interest in confidentiality against public interest in freedom of the press when deciding whether restraint of publicity is justified
349. **R v Cambridge Health Authority, ex p B** [1995] 1 FLR 1055, 1059E–1061C	10.3.95	QBD Laws J.	Judicial review (substantive hearing)	Health	ECHR	(2)	—	Certain rights, broadly those occupying a central place in the ECHR, are not to be perceived merely as aspirations, nor as enjoying legal status only on international plane, but as part of English common law; ECHR could be deployed, not as a statutory text, but as persuasive legal authority to resolve uncertainties in the common law
350. *R v SS Home Dept, ex p Polat*[2B/2B]	10.3.95	CA (Civ. Div.) Stuart-Smith, Waite & Millett LJJ	Judicial review (renewed leave application)	Immigration	ECHR	8	—	Although marriage did not predate enforcement action, case fell to be considered under guidelines in policy DP/2/93; but decision had been made in light of those provisions, none of which applied, so no error of law or irrationality
351. *Re L (Police Investigation: Privilege)* [1995] 1 FLR 999, 1015D	14.3.95	CA (Civ. Div.) Sir Thomas Bingham MR, Swinton Thomas & Morritt LJJ	Application to be joined as a party	Family/civil procedure	ECHR	(6)	—	The privilege against self-incrimination may, subject to our international obligations under the ECHR, be abrogated by statute, but in the absence of statutory obligation will be respected by the courts
352. *R v SS Home Dept, ex p Singh*	16.3.95	QBD (DC) Pill LJ & Keene J	Judicial review (substantive hearing)	Prisons	ECHR	5(4)	*Singh v UK* (Com. Rep.)	Noted that applicant has ruling in his favour from Eur. Comm. H.R. that UK violated Art. 5(4) ECHR by denying him an oral hearing on revocation of his licence and by permitting SS to veto Parole Board's recommendation for release
353. *A-G's Reference No. 48 of 1994* (1995) 16 Cr App R (S) 980, 985	16.3.95	CA (Crim. Div.) Taylor LCJ, Owen J & the Recorder of London	Reference to review sentence	Sentencing	ECHR	7	—	The Criminal Justice and Public Order Act 1994 could not be interpreted so as to render defendant liable to conviction of an offence which did not exist at time he committed it or to greater penalty than could be imposed at time of its commission because that would be contrary to Art.7 ECHR
354. *R v The Mayor and Commonalty and Citizens of the City of London, ex p Matson*	16.3.95	QBD Latham J	Judicial review (substantive hearing)	Elections	ECHR	6	—	No assistance to be derived from Art. 6 ECHR in deciding whether reasons should have been given; Art. 6 was entirely apposite to exercise on which court was engaged, but had no relevance to ratification process of Court of Aldermen
355. *R v Commissioners of Customs & Excise, ex p MacNamara*	17.3.95	CA (Civ. Div.) Leggatt, Roch & Aldous* LJJ	Judicial review (renewed leave application)	Customs & excise	ECHR	—	—	Argument that ECHR prevents confiscation of indecent or obscene videos on importation rejected; ECHR not part of law of this country, but it has a noble theme which does not include the right to import indecent or obscene videos

Case	Date	Court / Judges	Proceeding	Subject	Convention	Articles	Cases cited	Notes
356. *R v Broadcasting Complaints Commission, ex p Channel 4 Television Corporation*	28.3.95	QBD (DC) Leggatt LJ & Buxton J	Judicial review (substantive hearing)	Broadcasting	ECHR	10	*Lingens v Austria*	No ambiguity in provisions of Broadcasting Act 1990 such as would "make appropriate" (per Leggatt LJ)/"compel or even permit" (per Buxton J) recourse to ECHR; in any event, social need for fairness transcends even freedom of speech
357. *Hambleton DC v Bird*	29.3.95	CA (Civ. Div.) Balcombe & Pill LJJ, Sir Ralph Gibson	Application for injunction (appeal)	Planning/gypsies	ECHR	8	*Buckley v UK* (Com. Rep.)	Commission's ruling in *Buckley* had no bearing on facts or law in case concerning application for injunction to require discontinuance of use of land by gypsies for stationing of caravans
358. *Pelling v Pelling* [LR]	6.4.95	CA (Civ. Div.) Hirst & Aldous LJJ	Appeal against taxation (leave application)	Civil procedure	ECHR	6, 10	—	Litigant in person's argument that ECHR required his appeal to be heard in public rejected; whether an appeal on a taxation matter should be heard in open court or in chambers was a matter for the discretion of the judge on the facts
359. *SS Transport v Persons Unknown* [LR]	26.4.95	CA (Civ. Div.) Balcombe, Henry & Auld LJJ	Appeal against possession order (leave application)	Public protest	ECHR	11, 13	—	Argument that to carry out a peaceful occupation of property in protest is not itself unlawful rejected; has never been held, by European Court of Human Rights or domestic court, that the right to peaceful protest under Art. 11 ECHR includes right to occupy private property
360. *Al-Adsani v The Government of Kuwait*	3.5.95	QBD Mantell J	Action for damages	State immunity	ECHR ICCPR UDHR	3	—	No difficulty in concluding that torture is an offence against public international law and that international law forms part of the law of this country; but where clear language of the statute is to the contrary, as here, statute must prevail
361. *R v SS Home Dept., ex p Wells* [EC]	10.5.95	CA (Civ. Div.) Russell, Hirst & Rose LJJ	Judicial review (renewed leave application)	Immigration	ECHR	8	—	Quite apart from fact that ECHR not part of English law, the evaluation of compassionate circumstances is a matter not for the courts but for the SS
362. *R v SS Home Dept., ex p Sharma* [IR29]	12.5.95	CA (Civ. Div.) Nourse, Millett & Otton LJJ	Judicial review (renewed leave application)	Immigration	ECHR	8	*Beldjoudi v France*	Policy DP/2/93 inapplicable and facts of *Beldjoudi* so wholly different that it was of little assistance; this was a "pure discretion" case in which no ground shown on which it was arguable that court could interfere with decision to deport
363. *R v SS Environment, ex p Friends of the Earth* The Times, 8 Jun 1995	25.5.95	CA (Civ. Div.) Balcombe*, Roch & Pill LJJ	Judicial review (appeal)	Utilities regulation/planning	ECHR	(6, Art.1 Prot. 1)	—	UK's obligation in EC law to implement drinking water Directive did not require SS to override provisions of domestic law, such as requirements of planning law, especially where they protected rights of third parties which may be protected under ECHR
364. *R v Admiralty Board of the Defence Council, ex p Smith* [1995] 4 All ER 427, 432b, 440c–f, 443g–445g, 446j–447d, 447g–449e, 452h–j	7.6.95	QBD (DC) Simon Brown LJ & Curtis J	Judicial review (substantive hearing)	Employment	ECHR ICCPR	8, 13, 14	*Dudgeon v UK* *Norris v Ireland* *Vilvarajah v UK* *Swedish Engine Drivers' Union v Sweden* *B v UK* *Tyrer v UK*	The ECHR, or the restriction of fundamental rights, has a relatively limited impact on judicial review; the court must be scrupulous to see that no recognised ground of challenge is available, but does so within the limited scope of review open to it; only if the ECHR were part of domestic law would the primary judgment, of the proportionality of the restriction, be for the court. In the meantime the court was confined to a secondary review jurisdiction

Name of Case & Citation	Date of Judgment	Court	Type of Proceedings	Subject Matter	Treaty cited	Articles cited	Case-law cited	Nature of reference made to unincorporated international human rights law
365. *R v Immigration Appeal Tribunal, ex p Dhull*[EC]	15.6.95	CA (Civ. Div.) Hirst, Morritt & Auld LJJ	Judicial review (renewed leave application)	Immigration	ECHR	8	—	Seriously arguable point that deportation of wife would be a derogation of ECHR rights as part of EC law
366. *Pelling v Pelling*[LR]	19.6.95	CA (Civ. Div.) Butler Sloss & Aldous LJJ	Application for leave to appeal	Civil procedure	ECHR	(6(1))	—	Litigant in person's reliance on ECHR to support argument that matters of substance should be heard in open court rejected
367. *Sujeeun v Taylor*[LR]	28.6.95	CA (Civ. Div.) Simon Brown & Millett LJJ	Application for leave to appeal	Civil procedure	ECHR	(6(1))	—	Litigant in person's argument that denial of legal aid a breach of ECHR rejected; ECHR not as such part of municipal law
368. *R v Radio Authority, ex p Bull*, [1996] QB 169, 174H, 180F–181C, 181H–182A, 184H, 185C–G	4.7.95	QBD (DC) Kennedy LJ & McCullough J	Judicial review (substantive hearing)	Broadcasting	ECHR UDHR	10	*Casada Coca v Spain* *Informations-verein Lentia v Austria* *Observer & Guardian v UK*	(Kennedy LJ) Art. 10 ECHR unlikely to have significant part to play in construction of provision which was part of licensing system for which Art. 10 specifically provides; and in any event there were other rights to be protected (McCullough J) No ambiguity in statute, and *Spycatcher* dictum not relevant where court interpreting a statutory provision
369. *Mayor & Commonalty & Citizens of City of London v Prince*	6.7.95	CA (Civ. Div.) Neill* & Swinton-Thomas LJJ	Application to suspend warrant for possession	Landlord & tenant	ECHR	6(1)	—	ECHR not part of English law and there was therefore no basis in law on which to suspend warrant for possession pending outcome of applicant's application to European Commission
370. *Hardy v Focus Insurance Co. Ltd. (in liquidation)*	13.7.95	PC Lords Jauncey, Browne-Wilkinson, Slynn, Hoffmann & Sir Roger Parker	Debt action	Civil procedure	ECHR	6(1)	—	Argument that unless order contrary to ECHR dismissed as having no merit
371. *R v SS Home Dept., ex p Choudhry*	17.7.95	CA (Civ. Div.) Balcombe, Peter Gibson & Hutchison LJJ	Judicial review (renewed leave application)	Immigration	ECHR	2, 3, 8	—	Relevance of ECHR merely goes to exercise of SS's discretion and whether or not in reaching his decision SS gave adequate weight to those Articles; decision of SS, with or without consideration of ECHR, not so unreasonable that court should interfere
372. *R v Admiralty Board of the Defence Council, ex p Coupland*	18.7.95	QBD (DC) Stuart-Smith LJ & Butterfield J	Judicial review (substantive hearing)	Court martial/ sentencing	ECHR	6	—	Applicant's argument that both Art. 6 ECHR and the common law required that there should have been an oral hearing of appeal against sentence before the Admiralty Board recited, but not necessary to decide the point
373. *R v SS Home Dept., ex p Kuteyi*	20.7.95	QBD Popplewell J	Judicial review (substantive hearing)	Immigration	ECHR	8	*Marckx v Belgium*	SS does not have to decide, nor the Court investigate, whether or not there has been a breach of Art. 8 ECHR; he has to look at all the facts and have regard to the provisions of Art. 8, and it therefore did not matter that SS had not set out his reasoning why Art. 8 was not breached
374. *Rowan v Canon*[LR]	20.7.95	CA (Civ. Div.) Millett & Schiemann LJJ	Application for transfer of possessions (leave application)	Family	ECHR	(Art.1 Prot. 1)	—	Husband's contention that judge was in breach of ECHR in refusing him leave to apply in relation to transfer of his possessions was understandable as a litigant in person but not the most attractive way of putting his case

	Date	Court/Judges	Proceeding	Subject	Treaty	Art.	Strasbourg case	Notes
375. *R v SS Home Dept, ex p Briggs*, The Independent, 26 Sep 1995	25.7.95	QBD (DC) Kennedy LJ & McCullough J	Judicial review (substantive hearing)	Prisons	ECHR	8	*McCotter v UK*	Accepted that Art.8 can apply to prisoners, with obvious qualification that separation from family inevitable consequence of detention; though not part of domestic law, provisions of ECHR can assist in elucidation of common law or intention of a statute, but no breach of its principles here
376. *Chan Chi-Hung v R* [1995] AC 742, 744B–E	26.7.95	PC Lords Keith, Mustill*, Lloyd, Nicholls & Steyn	Appeal against sentence	Crime	ICCPR	15.1	—	Art. 15.1 referred to in course of interpreting equivalent provision in Hong Kong Bill of Rights; retrospective criminal laws odious to most developed legal systems
377. *Watts v Times Newspapers* [1996] 2 WLR 427, 443C–D	28.7.95	CA (Civ. Div.) Hirst & Henry LJJ, Sir Ralph Gibson	Action for damages (appeal on preliminary issue)	Defamation	ECHR	10	—	Article 10 ECHR coextensive with English law of freedom of expression, but placing of burden of proof on defendant in establishing qualified privilege not an infringement of free expression
378. *R v SS Home Dept., ex p Egueye-Gbemre*[DP/2/93]	3.8.95	QBD Popplewell J	Judicial review (leave application)	Immigration	ECHR	(8)	—	It was for SS not the court to decide whether circumstances of case make an exception to general rule under Policy DP/2.93
379. *R v SS Home Dept., ex p Kumarathasons*	16.8.95	CA (Civ. Div.) Leggatt, Waite & Schiemann LJJ	Judicial review (renewed leave application)	Immigration	ECHR	8	—	Not incumbent on SS when considering granting exceptional leave to remain, in context of a policy which specifically refers to ECHR, to spell out on each occasion the Art. concerned and make reference to it
380. *R v SS Home Dept., ex p Phull*[RC] [1996] Imm AR 72, 73, 79	17.8.95	CA (Civ. Div.) Leggatt, Waite & Schiemann LJJ	Judicial review (substantive hearing)	Immigration	ECHR	8	—	ECHR not available as an adjunct of Community law where applicant had no Community rights to exercise, otherwise ECHR would be incorporated *via* conduit of Community law even in situations not covered by Community law
381. *Saperan v District Judge Locker*[LE]	17.8.95	CA (Civ. Div.) Leggatt & Schiemann LJJ	Application for leave to appeal	Civil procedure	ECHR	(6(1))	—	Litigant in person's argument that judicial immunity from suit would be contrary to ECHR rejected
382. *R v The Mayor and Commonalty and Citizens of the City of London, ex p Matson* [1996] Admin LR 49, 64B	18.8.95	CA (Civ. Div.) Neill*, Waite & Swinton-Thomas LJJ	Judicial review (substantive hearing)	Elections	ECHR	6	—	Not necessary to seek the assistance of Art.6 or any other Art.s of ECHR, important though those Articles are; English law provided a fair solution
383. *In re D (Minors) (Adoption Reports: Confidentiality)* [1996] AC 593, 613H–614C	1.9.95	HL Lords Goff, Browne-Wilkinson, Mustill, Lloyd & Nicholls	Application for adoption	Family/confidentiality	ECHR	6, 8	*Hendriks v Netherlands W v UK McMichael v UK*	On the view reached of the English law there was no need to engage the important general question which would have arisen if it had differed from ECHR jurisprudence; in substance the principles to be derived from ECHR cases were entirely consistent with those proposed
384. *Hughes v SS Environment* (1996) 71 P & CR 168, 171, 174	14.9.95	QBD Christopher Lockhart-Mummery Q.C.	Statutory appeal	Planning/gypsies	ECHR	8, (14)	*Buckley v UK* (Com. Rep.)	Incompatibility of policy with ECHR not raised at planning appeal and therefore not appropriate for Court to consider; in any event, ECHR may be deployed only for purpose of resolving an ambiguity in English primary or subordinate legislation, and there was no ambiguity here
385. *Woolhead v SS Environment* (1996) 71 P & CR 419	21.9.95	QBD Jeremy Sullivan QC	Statutory appeal	Planning/gypsies	ECHR	8	—	The place to raise arguments about Article 8 ECHR was before the Inspector on appeal when full argument could be heard on the facts

Name of Case & Citation	Date of Judgment	Court	Type of Proceedings	Subject Matter	Treaty cited	Articles cited	Case-law cited	Nature of reference made to unincorporated international human rights law
386. **R v SS Home Dept., ex p Norney** [1995] Admin LR 861, 865H–866D, 867F–868A, 868F–G, 870G–871D, 871F–872A	28.9.95	QBD Dyson J.	Judicial review (substantive hearing)	Prisons	ECHR	5(4)	*Thynne, Wilson & Gunnell v UK*; *E v Norway*	Accepted that, as a general rule, the lawfulness of the exercise of executive discretion is not measured by asking whether it infringes ECHR rights, but would be perverse to ignore ECHR where clear that statutory provision was passed to bring domestic law into line with ECHR
387. *Webb v SS Environment* (1996) 71 P & CR 419, 425–7, 425–7	3.10.95	QBD Judge Rich QC	Statutory appeal	Planning/ gypsies	ECHR	8	*Buckley v UK* (Com. Rep.)	Art.8 an unhelpful basis for resolving ambiguities in other documents; and in any event Inspector had directed himself to balance to be struck between rights of occupant and public interest in protection of landscape or countryside amenity
388. *R v SS Home Dept., ex p Mirza*	11.10.95	CA (Civ. Div.) Nourse & Ward LJJ, Sedley J	Judicial review (renewed leave application)	Immigration	ECHR	8	—	Application adjourned pending outcome of petition to HL in *Phull*
389. *R v SS Home Dept., ex p O'Brien* [1996] Admin LR 121, 128G–H	11.10.95	QBD (DC) Rose LJ & Wright J	Judicial review (substantive hearing)	Prisons	ECHR	8	*X v UK*	Art. 8 ECHR could not help applicant in challenge to regime of closed visits by family and lawyer in light of Commission decision
390. *R v Cowan* [1995] 3 WLR 818, 825C–H	12.10.95	CA (Crim. Div.) Taylor LCJ, Turner & Latham JJ	Appeals against conviction	Criminal procedure	ECHR	6	*Murray v UK*	Decisions of Commission and Court of Human Rights not binding, and of assistance to resolve any ambiguity in domestic law, but there was no ambiguity in s.35 Criminal Justice and Public Order Act 1994; nevertheless, Commission's observations in *Murray v UK* were of interest
391. *R v SS Home Dept., ex p Mbatube* [1996] Imm AR 184, 187–9	17.10.95	CA (Civ. Div.) Hirst, Waite & Hobhouse LJJ	Judicial review (renewed leave application)	Immigration	ECHR	8	—	In immigration matters raising Art. 8 problem of respect for family life, the immigration authorities have a wide margin of appreciation
392. **Dibia v Chief Immigration Officer, Heathrow Airport**	19.10.95	CA (Civ. Div.) Staughton*, Auld & Aldous LJJ	Judicial review (renewed leave application)	Immigration	ECHR	8	·	ECHR not part of English law but no great difference between it and common law; Art. 8 reflects what Home Office ought to bear in mind when deporting parent of child entitled to stay
393. *R v Derby Magistrates' Court, ex p B* [1995] 3 WLR 681, 696A	19.10.95	HL Lords Keith, Mustill, Taylor CJ*, Lloyd & Nicholls	Judicial review (appeal)	Criminal procedure	ECHR	(6(1))	—	No doubt that legal professional privilege could be modified, even abrogated, by statute, subject always to the objection that legal professional privilege is a fundamental human right protected by ECHR, as to which no argument was heard
394. *M v SS Home Dept.* [1996] 1 WLR 507, 514H	24.10.95	CA (Civ. Div.) Butler-Sloss, Millett* & Ward LJJ	Statutory appeal	Immigration	ECHR	2, 3	—	To return to country of origin a person who, though not recognised as a refugee, would be in danger of torture, loss of life or inhuman or degrading treatment, would breach ECHR
395. **R v SS Home Dept., ex p Zighem** [1996] Imm AR 194, 195–9	1.11.95	QBD Latham J	Judicial review (substantive hearing)	Immigration	ECHR	8	*Berrehab v The Netherlands*	Secretary of State had not considered the case properly in the light of Art. 8 ECHR, to assert that there would be no breach did not identify whether there would be no interference or whether interference was justified

					ECHR		*Welch v UK*	
396. *In the matter of Re "B"*	2.11.95	QBD McCullough J	Application to appoint receiver	Civil procedure	ECHR	7	*Welch v UK*	If court bound by decision in *Welch*, it would not merely prevent appointment of receiver but would render confiscation order of no effect; but not accepted that decision is a factor which court should take into account when exercising judgment as to extent of realisable property
397. *R v Ministry of Defence, ex p. Smith* [1996] 1 All ER 257, 260j, 263j–264f, 266g–267e, 272a–g, 273b–c	3.11.95	CA (Civ. Div.) Sir Thomas Bingham MR, Henry & Thorpe LJJ	Judicial review (substantive hearing)	Employment	ECHR ICCPR	8, 13	*Vilvarajah v UK Norris v Ireland*	The relevance of the ECHR in the present context is as background to the complaint of irrationality; the fact that a decision-maker failed to take account of ECHR obligations when exercising an administrative discretion is not of itself a ground for impugning that exercise of discretion. Whether any interference satisfied a pressing social need and was proportionate to a legitimate aim could not be answered by a domestic court
398. *R v Legal Aid Board, ex p Shine*	8.11.95	CA (Civ. Div.) Russell & Thorpe* LJJ, Sir Ralph Gibson	Judicial review (renewed leave application)	Legal aid	ECHR	6(3)	—	Argument that refusal of legal aid to appeal against conviction for trading without a licence was in breach of ECHR rejected; the relevant criteria were to be found in Legal Aid Act 1988
399. *R v SS Home Dept., ex p Egueye-Gbemre* [DP293]	9.11.95	CA (Civ. Div.) Russell & Thorpe LJJ, Sir Ralph Gibson	Judicial review (renewed leave application)	Immigration	ECHR	8	—	Decision whether circumstances of applicant's case make an exception to the general rule of non-enforcement in policy DP/2/93 was for SS, unless it could be shown to be in some way perverse or flawed within *Wednesbury* principles
400. *AG v Haywood* The Times, 20 Nov 1995	10.11.95	CA (Civ. Div.) Staughton, Henry* & Pill LJJ	Appeal against vexatious litigant order	Civil procedure	ECHR	6(1)	—	ECHR not part of our law, though regard may be had to it if there is any ambiguity in construing s.42 Supreme Court Act 1981; no such ambiguity and in any event no "human right" to bring actions which are vexatious, frivolous or an abuse of process
401. *R v Boston Justices, ex p Scarborough*	16.11.95	QBD (DC) Staughton LJ*	Judicial review (substantive hearing)	Criminal procedure	ECHR	5(5)	—	Declaration that warrant for arrest unlawfully issued but damages not recoverable from magistrates in absence of bad faith refused because related to private rights and should therefore have been sought by writ action
402. *R v Saunders* [1996] 1 Cr App R 463, 477f–478B	27.11.95	CA (Crim. Div.) Taylor LCJ*, Macpherson & Potter JJ	Appeal against conviction	Criminal procedure	ECHR	6	*Funke v France*	English courts can have recourse to ECHR and decisions thereon only when English law is ambiguous or unclear. Should appellant succeed in Strasbourg, treaty obligations will require consideration to be given to effect of decision here, but court's duty is to apply domestic law which is unambiguous
403. *R v SS Home Dept., ex p Hastrup* [DP293]	28.11.95	QBD Hidden J	Judicial review (substantive hearing)	Immigration	ECHR	8	—	Policy DP/2/93 not to be interpreted as if it were a statute, but by attaching paramount importance to the applicant's bad immigration history, SS had failed to give sufficient weight to his own policy that, in cases to which the policy applied, immigration history was of little relevance
404. *R v SS Home Dept., ex p Jackson* [DP293] [1996] Imm AR 243, 245–6	30.11.95	CA (Civ. Div.) Simon Brown & Auld LJJ, Macpherson J	Judicial review (renewed leave application)	Immigration	ECHR	8	—	Applicants such as asylum-seekers who are temporarily admitted and treated as port refusal cases are not entitled to the benefit of policy DP/2/93; in any event that policy would not avail the applicant as her marriage did not predate enforcement action as required

Name of Case & Citation	Date of Judgment	Court	Type of Proceedings	Subject Matter	Treaty cited	Articles cited	Case-law cited	Nature of reference made to unincorporated international human rights law
405. *R v Taylor* (1996) 2 Cr App R 64, 69C–70F	1.12.95	CA (Crim. Div.) Taylor LCJ, Kay & Smedley JJ	Appeal against sentence	Crime/ sentencing	ECHR	7	*Welch v UK*	No ambiguity or lack of certainty in s.38(4) Drug Trafficking Offences Act 1986 and therefore cannot have regard to European law in interpreting them; in any event, Art. 7 did not avail appellant because he offended at time the Act was already in force and penalties well known
406. *Bennett v Guardian Newspapers Ltd.* The Times, 28 Dec 1995	5.12.95	QBD Sir Michael Davies	Application to strike out qualified privilege defence	Defamation	ECHR	10	*Thorgerson v Iceland* *Sunday Times v UK* *Lingens v Austria*	Accepted that court must have regard to Art. 10; a decision against the defendant, if in accordance with English law, does not infringe Art 10 in any way. There was nothing in cases cited which conflicts with, or requires court to depart from, the common law principles of English law
407. *John v MGN Ltd.* [1996] 2 All ER 35, 47d, 51b–c, 58j	12.12.95	CA (Civ. Div.) Sir Thomas Bingham MR, Neill & Hirst LJJ	Action for damages (appeal)	Defamation	ECHR	10	*Tolstoy Miloslavsky v UK*	ECHR not a free-standing source of law in UK, but no conflict or discrepancy between Art. 10 and the common law; Art. 10 reinforced and buttressed conclusions reached independently of ECHR, and which would have been reached even if the ECHR did not exist
408. *R v DTI, ex p Healaugh Farms* The Times, 27 Dec 1995	13.12.95	QBD Carnwath J.	Judicial review (substantive hearing)	Planning	ECHR	6(1)	—	Unnecessary to consider to what extent the ECHR may be relevant as an aid to construction, as Art. 6(1) did not assist on whether there is a power to award costs at a statutory wayleave hearing, a matter not referred to in the Article
409. *La Compagnie Sucrière de Bel Ombre Ltee v Government of Mauritius*	13.12.95	PC Lords Goff, Jauncey, Woolf, Steyn & Hardie Boys J	Constitutional challenge to validity of legislation	Agricultural regulation	ECHR	Art. 1 Prot. 1	*Sporrong & Lonnroth v Sweden* *Young, James & Webster v UK*	Analogy with ECHR drawn in interpretation of right to property in Mauritius Constitution; the PC, like the Eur. Ct. HR, will extend to the national court a substantial margin of appreciation, and will respect the national legislature's judgment as to what is in the public interest when implementing social and economic policies unless that judgment is manifestly without foundation
410. *R v SS Home Department, ex p Akhtar*	14.12.95	QBD May J	Judicial review (substantive hearing)	Immigration	ECHR	8	—	Art. 8 not a matter of substantive law within UK courts, but accepted that the concepts it enshrines are matters which SS should take into account in appropriate case in exercising discretion
411. *Higgins v Marchant & Eliot Underwriting Ltd.* [1996] 2 Lloyd's Rep 31	21.12.95	CA (Civ. Div.) Leggatt, Rose & Roch LJJ	Appeal against summary judgment	Civil procedure	ECHR	6(1)	—	Argument that RSC Ord. 14 procedure inappropriate because not in conformity with Art. 6 ECHR recited but not addressed
412. *R v SS Home Dept., ex p Dogan*	12.1.96	QBD McPherson J.	Judicial review (leave application)	Immigration	ECHR	(8)	—	Perfectly right that ECHR deals with cases of this kind, but Court does not exist to reconsider and change the decision of the immigration authorities; it can only act if there is unlawfulness, procedural impropriety or perverseness in the making of a decision
413. *R v SS Home Dept., ex p Baran*	18.1.96	QBD Harrison J.	Judicial review (leave application)	Immigration	ECHR	3	—	SS does not have to mention Art. 3 ECHR by name when giving his reasons, but not enough merely to refer to "human rights abuses"

Case	Date	Court & Judges	Action	Subject	ECHR/ICCPR	Art.	Case cited	Notes
414. *R v Registrar of Births, ex p R*	29.1.96	QBD Brooke J	Judicial review (leave application)	Trans-sexuals	ECHR	8	—	In granting leave, court cited female to male transsexual's reliance on Art. 8 in challenge to Registrar's policy of refusing to amend birth certificate
415. *Reid v Chief Constable of Merseyside Police* The Times, 5 Feb 1996	29.1.96	CA (Civ. Div.) Beldam*, Waite & Morritt LJJ	Action for damages for malicious prosecution	Civil procedure	ECHR	6(1)	*Gregory v UK*	Cases on Art. 6(1) ECHR propounded no different test for bias from that propounded by Lord Goff in *R v Gough* [1993] AC 646
416. *R v SS Home Dept., ex p Ghaffar* [DP/2/93]	1.2.96	QBD Tuckey J	Judicial review (substantive hearing)	Immigration	ECHR	8	—	Not necessary to explore precisely how far Art. 8 and policy DP/2/93 affect cases where child of would-be deportee is subject of a residence order under Children Act 1989 and could only accompany parent with leave of the Family Court
417. *R v Registrar of Births, ex p P & G* [1996] 2 FLR 90, 94B-95B, 97G-98B	16.2.96	QBD (DC) Kennedy LJ & Forbes J	Judicial review (substantive hearing)	Trans-sexuals	ECHR	8, 14	*Rees v UK Cossey v UK B v France*	No relevant ambiguity in Births and Deaths Registration Act 1953 which Art. 8 ECHR can help to resolve, and cases so far decided in European Court are indicative of that fact; ECHR argument added nothing to irrationality
418. *Vale of White Horse DC v Treble Parker*	22.2.96	QBD (DC) Otton LJ & Newman J	Appeal by case stated	Planning	ECHR	6(1)	—	No ambiguity and thus not open to Court to look at, or rely upon, the ECHR or any decision made thereunder
419. *British Data Management plc v Boxer Commercial Removals plc* [1996] 3 All ER 707, 712b-j	22.2.96	CA (Civ. Div.) Hirst & Aldous LJJ, Sir Iain Glidewell	Action for *quia timet* injunction	Defamation	ECHR	10	—	Defendant relied on Art. 10 ECHR but sufficient for him to found case on well-established principles of English law to strike out action for injunction where plaintiff cannot prove words which threatened publication is going to contain
420. *R v SS Home Dept., ex p Mirza* [DP/2/93] [1996] Imm AR 314, 318-20	23.2.96	CA (Civ. Div.) Nourse* & Aldous LJJ, Sir John Balcombe	Judicial review (renewed leave application)	Immigration	ECHR	8	—	Assumed that there is an analogy between an ambiguity in a policy guidance document and in a statute, and that in either case the Court may have regard to ECHR; but no ambiguity here and therefore no cause for resorting to ECHR
421. *R v Parole Board, ex p Watson* [1996] 1 WLR 906, 915A, 918B	4.3.96	CA (Civ. Div.) Sir Thomas Bingham MR, Rose & Roch LJJ	Judicial review (appeal)	Prisons	ECHR	(5(4))	—	There was nothing in the decisions of the European Court of Human Rights to suggest that a different test was appropriate in re-release cases from that applied by the Parole Board in cases of initial release
422. *R v Parole Board, ex p Mansell* The Times, 21 Mar 1996	7.3.96	QBD (DC) Otton LJ & Newman J	Judicial review (substantive hearing)	Prisons	ECHR	5(4)	*Singh v UK*	Discretionary lifers and those detained at HM's pleasure are a unique category to whom an oral hearing before Parole Board is granted to bring UK in line with treaty obligations; in any event, not open to applicant to contend before this Court that Respondent has acted in breach of ECHR
423. *Al-Adsani v Government of Kuwait*	16.3.96	CA (Civ. Div.) Stuart-Smith & Ward LJJ, Buckley J	Action for damages	State immunity	ECHR	3	—	Art. 3 ECHR mentioned as one example of an international agreement making torture a violation of a fundamental human right in international law
424. *AG v Limbrick* The Times, 28 Mar 1996	20.3.96	QBD Garland J	Action for injunction	Civil procedure/contempt of court	ECHR	(10)	—	ECHR, which was not part of English law, reflected two conflicting interests: the right to receive information, and corresponding duties and responsibilities which may restrict the right

Name of Case & Citation	Date of Judgment	Court	Type of Proceedings	Subject Matter	Treaty cited	Articles cited	Case-law cited	Nature of reference made to unincorporated international human rights law
425. *Re L (a Minor)* [1996] 2 WLR 395, 407G	21.3.96	HL Lords Jauncey, Mustill†, Lloyd, Nicholls‡ & Steyn	Appeal against order for disclosure	Civil procedure/family	ECHR	6(1), 8	—	†Doubtful whether parent, denied opportunity to obtain legal advice in confidence, is accorded fair hearing to which they are entitled under Art. 6(1). ECHR, read in conjunction with Art. 8; if not so entitled, Parliament should say so expressly
426. *R v SS Home Dept., ex p Theophilus* [1995]	27.3.96	QBD Tucker J	Judicial review (leave application)	Immigration	ECHR	8	—	SS held to be justified in view that deportation would involve no breach of Art. 8 ECHR if family leave together, and that effective immigration control outweighs compassionate circumstances of the case
427. *R v SS Home Dept., ex p Watson* [1995]	2.4.96	QBD Carnwath J	Judicial review (substantive hearing)	Immigration	ECHR	8	*Abdulaziz, Cabales & Balkandali v UK*	Although the ECHR is not part of UK law, the courts now appear to accept that there is a body of recognised human rights to which the courts and other decision makers should have regard. Though not able to be a direct source, the ECHR is a guide to such rights. The courts expect breaches of individual rights to be justified, but mere failure to mention Art. 8 does not invalidate decision. However, if SS relies on a particular interpretation of ECHR, the court may consider whether he has got it right
428. *R v Clerk to South Cheshire Justices, ex p Bold*	16.4.96	QBD Brooke J	Judicial review (leave application)	Criminal procedure/legal aid	ECHR	6	*Benham v UK* (Com. Rep.)	Parliament should be presumed to have intended to comply with its international obligations but if its intention is clear then the fact that it does not comply with ECHR must remain a matter for Strasbourg; Parliament may have to reconsider in due course provisions of national law found to be in breach of Art. 6 by the Commission, but the intention of Parliament in Legal Aid Act 1988 is clear
429. *AG v Blake* [1996] 3 All ER 903, 909e–h	19.4.96	Ch. D. Sir Richard Scott V-C	Action for account of profits	Intellectual property	ECHR	10	—	In considering the nature and breadth of the continuing duty binding ex-members of the intelligence and security services, the treaty obligation in Art. 10 ECHR must be borne in mind
430. *R v Gokal*	24.4.96	QBD Buxton J	Application for leave to appeal against preliminary ruling	Criminal procedure	ECHR	6	*Saunders v UK* (Com. Rep.)	Ambiguity or uncertainty is a precondition of recourse to the ECHR in order to interpret domestic law, but ss.23–26 Criminal Justice Act 1988 are not ambiguous/uncertain so as to justify such recourse; in any event, nothing in Com. Rep. in *Saunders* suggested that an accused who had to consider seriously whether to testify was thereby being forced to incriminate himself
431. *Gilbert v United Parcel Service*	26.4.96	CA (Civ. Div.) Leggatt & Waite LJJ	Application for leave to appeal	Employment	ECHR	8, 9, 10, 14	—	Argument that employer's rule against employees having beards was in breach of ECHR rejected as being without legal merit
432. *R v SS Home Dept., ex p Tella*	29.4.96	CA (Civ. Div.) Stuart-Smith, Peter Gibson & Thorpe LJJ	Judicial review (renewed leave application)	Immigration	ECHR	8	—	Unarguable that SS had not had proper regard to Art. 8 ECHR; it was plain from his decision letter that he had taken the human rights matters into consideration

433. *R v SS Home Dept., ex p Lauerteh*[201,202]	29.4.96	CA (Civ. Div.) Stuart-Smith, Peter Gibson & Thorpe LJJ	Judicial review (renewed leave application)	Immigration	ECHR	8	—	Argument that there would be a breach of Art. 8 ECHR if mother subject to deportation order left behind her British citizen children rejected; that would be her decision, not the SSs
434. *Connelly v RTZ Corporation plc*, The Times, 12 Jul 1996	2.5.96	CA (Civ. Div.) Sir Thomas Bingham MR*, Evans & Ward LJJ	Appeal against refusal to lift stay	Civil procedure	ECHR ICCPR	6(1) (14.1)	—	Whether or not provisions of ECHR and ICCPR are strictly applicable, it is right to bear the UK's international obligations in mind when the court is invited to make an order which would have the practical effect of preventing a plaintiff pursuing his rights anywhere
435. *R v SS Home Dept., ex p Tremayne*	2.5.96	QBD Buxton J	Judicial review (renewed leave application)	Prisons	ECHR	8	—	Argument that random mandatory drug testing in prisons is necessarily in breach of Art. 8 ECHR rejected; the Prison Service's guidelines deliberately sought to balance the interests of the prisoner in not unnecessarily being interfered with on the one hand against the important need effectively to address the problem of drug-taking in the interests of prisoners generally
436. *R v SS Home Dept., ex p Venables*	2.5.96	QBD (DC) Pill LJ & Newman J	Judicial review (substantive hearing)	Sentencing	ECHR	(5(4))	*Thynne, Wilson & Gunnell v UK*	Case-law of ECHR referred to when recounting history of current statutory procedure for release of discretionary life prisoners
437. *Re M (a minor)*	3.5.96	CA (Civ. Div.) Neill & Ward LJJ	Application for stay of order granting leave to take child out of jurisdiction	Family	ECHR	6, 8, 13, 25	*Cruz Varas v Sweden*	The court must give the most careful attention to a request from the Eur. Comm. HR under Rule 36 of its rules of procedure indicating the desirability of interim relief, but the court has its own responsibilities to fulfil; its principal concern must be the welfare of the child, which was best served by being reunited with his natural parents
438. *Hing Fai Tong v SS Home Dept.*[207,208]	7.5.96	CA (Civ. Div.) Neill, Morritt & Hutchison LJJ	Judicial review (renewed leave application)	Immigration	ECHR	8	*Gul v Switzerland*	It would be helpful if, in cases where Art. 8 is of particular relevance, the factors that have been taken into account by SS were spelt out with a little more detail; but it was clear from the decision letter that the necessary balance had been struck
439. *R v Dacorum DC, ex p Cannon*[209] The Times, 9 Jul 1996	17.5.96	QBD (DC) Saville LJ*, Sachs J	Judicial review (substantive hearing)	Planning	ECHR	(6)	—	Argument that ouster clause in s.64 Town and Country Planning Act 1990 offended ECHR, because, through no fault of his own, applicant was now precluded from a determination of his civil rights in any tribunal, rejected; on present state of the law, recourse to ECHR only possible to resolve an ambiguity, and there was no ambiguity in s.64.
440. *Ming Pao Newspapers v AG of Hong Kong* [1996] 3 WLR 272, 276C–277H	20.5.96	PC Lords Keith, Jauncey, Mustill, Nicholls & Sir Ralph Gibson	Appeal against magistrate's ruling of no case to answer	Press regulation	ECHR ICCPR	10 19	*Observer & Guardian v UK; Young, James & Webster v UK; Handyside v UK; Informationsverein Lentia v Austria*	Any restrictions on the guaranteed right of freedom of expression which constitutes one of the essential foundations of a democratic society must be narrowly interpreted and must be proportionate to the aims sought to be achieved thereby, although states enjoy a margin of appreciation in deciding what is necessary to achieve a legitimate aim

Name of Case & Citation	Date of Judgment	Court	Type of Proceedings	Subject Matter	Treaty cited	Articles cited	Case-law cited	Nature of reference made to unincorporated international human rights law
441. *R v Secretary of State for Wales, ex p Emery* [1996] 4 All ER 1, 17f–19e	4.6.96	QBD Louis Blom-Cooper QC	Judicial review (substantive hearing)	Planning	ECHR	6(1)	*Bryan v UK*	Given the European Court's approach to English judicial review in *Bryan*, it was not for this court to do other than acknowledge the conformity of judicial review with Art 6(1) ECHR in the eyes of that Court
442. *Re PB (a minor)* The Independent, 9 Jul 1996	20.6.96	CA (Civ. Div.) Butler-Sloss LJ, Peter Gibson & Thorpe LJJ	Application for residence order (appeal on preliminary issue)	Civil procedure/family	ECHR	6, 10	—	Present procedures in family proceedings, as to when hearing should be held in open court, are in accordance with the spirit of the ECHR; Art. 6 recognises that the right to a public trial is qualified where the interests of juveniles or the protection of the private life of the parties so require; the court in exercising its discretion can take account of the provisions of Art. 6(1) ECHR
443. *R v SS Social Security, ex p Joint Council for the Welfare of Immigrants* [1996] 4 All ER 385, 401e–f	21.6.96	CA (Civ. Div.) Neill, Simon Brown* & Waite LJJ	Judicial review (appeal)	Social security/immigration	ECHR	—	—	So basic are the human rights at issue that it cannot be necessary to resort to the ECHR to take note of their violation
444. *R v Khan* [1996] 3 WLR 162, 165B–D, 165G–166C, 168E–169D, 171E, 172C–175G, 176E–G	2.7.96	HL Lords Keith, Browne-Wilkinson, Slynn, Nolan & Nicholls	Appeal against conviction	Criminal procedure	ECHR	6, 8, 13	*Malone v UK Schenk v Switzerland*	Whether there was a breach of the ECHR was a question solely for the Eur. Ct. HR, but that was not to say that the principles reflected in the ECHR were irrelevant to the exercise of the s.78 PACE discretion; they could hardly be, since they embody so many of the familiar principles of English law, including an individual's right to a fair trial
445. *Buckley v SS Environment*	4.7.96	QBD Malcolm Spence QC	Statutory appeal	Planning/gypsies	ECHR	8	*Buckley v UK* (Com. Rep.)	ECHR is a treaty but it may be useful in the resolution of an ambiguity in the law; Art. 8 ECHR was one reason why planning inspector had to have regard to "the human factor"
446. *R v Clerk to the South Cheshire Justices, ex p Bold* The Times, 15 Jul 1996	9.7.96	CA (Civ. Div.) Nourse, Hobhouse & Aldous LJJ	Judicial review (renewed leave application)	Civil procedure/legal aid	ECHR	6(3)(c)	*Benham v UK*	Decision of Eur. Ct. HR in *Benham*, that parties before magistrates courts in enforcement proceedings which may result in loss of liberty is charged with a criminal offence within Art. 6 ECHR, and therefore entitled to legal aid, of no avail in domestic law because Parliament's intention in Legal Aid Act 1988 was clear
447. *R v SS Home Dept, ex p Urmaza* The Times, 23 Jul 1996	11.7.96	QBD Sedley J.	Judicial review (substantive hearing)	Immigration	ECHR	8	—	It was manifestly the UK Govt's treaty obligation to respect Art. 8 ECHR that led to the introduction of policy DP/2/93, and since seamen deserters are entitled to the protection of Art.8, to interpret policy as excluding them would defeat one of its principal purposes
448. *R v SS Environment, ex p Slot*	16.7.96	QBD Hidden J	Judicial review (substantive hearing)	Planning	ECHR	6(1)	*Bryan v UK*	Art. 6 ECHR could not be relied on in the absence of an ambiguity in relevant legislation, and there was no ambiguity in the clear procedure laid down by Parliament for dealing with diversion of footpaths; in any event Art. 6 not applicable because anticipated benefit of diversion did not affect civil rights and obligations
449. *Neill v Kiam* The Times, 26 Jul 1996	17.7.96	CA (Civ. Div.) Beldam, Evans & Pill LJJ	Action for damages (appeal against damages award)	Defamation	ECHR UDHR	10, 8, 12, 19	*Tolstoy Miloslavsky v UK*	The significance of *Rantzen* and *John v MGN* was that the legal requirements of a valid libel award had been redefined in the light of the recognition as part of the common law of the principles expressed in the ECHR

Case	Date	Court	Type of proceedings	Subject	Court	Article	ECHR case	Notes
450. *R v SS Home Department, ex p Hastrup* DP2/93 The Times, 15 Aug 1996	17.7.96	CA (Civ. Div.) Russell, Peter Gibson & Hutchison LJJ	Judicial review (appeal)	Immigration	ECHR	8	—	Nothing in policy DP/2/93 fettered the SS's discretion; it established a general rule but did not say that immigration history was never significant
451. *R v SS Home Dept., ex p Brezinski*	19.7.96	QBD Kay J	Judicial review (substantive hearing)	Immigration	ECHR	5(4)	—	Reference made to ministerial statement in answer to a parliamentary question concerning the extent to which arrangements for the detention of asylum seekers met the requirements of Art. 5(4) ECHR
452. *R v The Managers of the NW London Mental Health NHS Trust, ex p Stewart,* The Times, 19 Jul 1996	19.7.96	QBD Harrison J	Judicial review (substantive hearing)	Mental health	ECHR	5(4)	—	Although accepted that the interpretation of the relevant provisions of the Mental Health Act 1983 were not free from difficulty, not accepted that the provisions were ambiguous so as to dictate an interpretation in favour of the liberty of the subject
453. *Re R (a minor)*[LR]	22.7.96	CA (Civ. Div.) Stuart-Smith LJ & Bracewell J	Application for leave to appeal against order	Civil procedure/ family	ECHR	6(1), 10	—	The ECHR is not in conflict with the rule that proceedings under the Children Act 1989 are to be held in chambers unless otherwise directed; the ECHR itself provides for the exclusion of the press and public from all or part of a trial on grounds including protection of juveniles
454. *R v SS Transport, ex p London Borough of Richmond (No. 4)* [1996] 1 WLR 1460, 1466A–D	26.7.96	CA (Civ. Div.) Leggatt, Morritt & Brooke LJJ	Judicial review (appeal)	Civil aviation regulation	ECHR	8	*Powell & Rayner v UK*	Although in more overtly rights-based systems of law, such as the ECHR, the balance between the rights of the individual and the rights of the state is achieved through different mechanisms, the final effect is the same; the UK is bound by treaty to observe the ECHR and although not part of national law ministers must be presumed to have intended to comply with its requirements when exercising statutory powers unless there is a clear parliamentary intention to contrary effect
455. *Budd v Colchester BC*	29.7.96	QBD (DC) Schiemann LJ & Smedley J	Appeal by case stated	Criminal procedure	ECHR	—	—	Both our own law and the ECHR indicate that the parameters of a crime should be clearly defined, but it would be introducing undue technicality if a statutory nuisance notice had to specify the number of decibels in relation to barking dogs
456. *R v SS Home Dept., ex p V (a Minor),* The Times, 7 Aug 1996	30.7.96	CA (Civ. Div.) Lord Woolf MR, Hobhouse & Morritt LJJ	Judicial review (appeal)	Sentencing	ECHR	—	—	Development of English law on criminal sentencing has not proceeded from predetermined principles, but has been pragmatic and empirical, including contributions from the Eur. Ct. HR under the ECHR
457. *Foecke v University of Bristol*	30.7.96	CA (Civ. Div.) Saville, Potter & Judge LJJ	Appeal against order of security for costs	Civil procedure	ECHR	6	*Tolstoy Miloslavsky v UK*	The fact that an appeal may be stifled if security for costs is ordered does not mean that no order should be made, any more than it means that the appellant is being deprived of his right of access to court under Art. 6 ECHR
458. *R v SS Home Dept., ex p Launder,* The Times, 29 Oct 1996	6.8.96	QBD (DC) Henry LJ & Ebsworth J	Judicial review (substantive hearing)	Extradition	ECHR	—	—	Although judicial review was a flexible remedy, and could often achieve the same results as could be achieved in the Eur. Ct. HR, it could not be used as a back door for incorporating the ECHR; unless and until the ECHR is incorporated into domestic law, breaches of the ECHR cannot be relied on as such

Name of Case & Citation	Date of Judgment	Court	Type of Proceedings	Subject Matter	Treaty cited	Articles cited	Case-law cited	Nature of reference made to unincorporated international human rights law
459. *R v SS Home Dept., ex p Adebiyi*[DP293]	6.8.96	CA (Civ. Div.) Hobhouse, Millett & Swinton Thomas LJJ	Judicial review (renewed leave application)	Immigration	ECHR	8	—	The general principle of policy DP/2/93 was to have regard to Art. 8 ECHR and the family considerations which that reflects, but each case turns on its own facts and the policy only established a general rule which was not without exception
460. *Re M (a Minor)*	22.8.96	Fam. Div. Johnson J	Wardship	Family	ECHR	1, 3, 8, 25	—	The fact that the ECHR is not part of domestic law did not mean that it was a matter only for Parliament and the UK Govt. and not for the courts; when a court has to exercise a discretion, it will seek to act in a way which does not violate the ECHR. In the exercise of a discretion to grant leave, the fact that the UK by its Govt. has committed itself to the ECHR and the right to petition should outweigh any other matter
461. *R v SS Home Dept., ex p Vidmont*	4.9.96	CA (Civ. Div.) Simon Brown & Morritt LJJ	Judicial review (renewed leave application)	Immigration	ECHR	8, 14	*Berrehab v The Netherlands*; *Abdulaziz, Cabales & Balkandali v UK*	Argument that SS and immigration officers must exercise their discretionary powers so as to protect the relevant ECHR rights to the fullest possible extent held to founder on the rock of *Brind*, according to which discretion does not have to be exercised in accordance with the ECHR
462. *R v Broadcasting Complaints Commission, ex p Barclay* The Times, 11 Oct 1996	4.10.96	QBD Sedley J	Judicial review (substantive hearing)	Broadcasting	ECHR	8, 10, 13	—	Hansard and the ECHR are not to be ranked as aids to construction; the condition of admissibility of both is the same (obscurity in legislation), and if both have something to say on the obscure point, both must be looked at, though if Hansard discloses an intention to breach the ECHR, the ECHR must almost certainly yield; here, though, the language of the statute was plain and unambiguous
463. *R v SS Home Dept., ex p Khan*[DP295]	8.10.96	QBD Turner J	Judicial review (substantive hearing)	Immigration	ECHR	8, 13	*Vilvarajah v UK*; *Abdulaziz, Cabales & Balkandali v UK*	Although the SS had said in policy DP/2/93 that he will have regard to ECHR, he is not bound in national law to apply it, and the cases turning on the interpretation of Art. 8 were therefore of no assistance
464. *R v LB Hammersmith & Fulham, ex p M* The Times, 18 Oct 1996	8.10.96	QBD Collins J	Judicial review (substantive hearing)	Social security/ immigration	ECHR	—	—	If Parliament had expressly said in the Asylum and Immigration Act 1996 that in no circumstances should any assistance other than hospital care be available to asylum seekers who failed to apply immediately on entry, it would certainly put itself in breach of the ECHR; which was another reason for presuming that it did not so intend
465. *Britton v SS Environment*	24.10.96	QBD Judge Rich QC	Statutory appeals	Planning	ECHR	8	—	It was irrational of the Secretary of State to say, on the one hand, in PPG1 para. 4, that the planning system must take account of international obligations and on the other, in a decision letter, that he refuses to express a view as to whether the effect of his decision would be to breach the ECHR

	Date	Court/Judges	Proceeding	Subject	Treaty	Article	Case	Commentary
466. *R v Parole Board, ex p Downing*	24.10.96	QBD (DC) Rose LJ & Maurice Kay J	Judicial review (substantive hearing)	Prisons	ECHR	5(4)	*Hussain v UK*	There was here no scope for any addition to common law principles by reliance on the ECHR because there was no uncertainty or ambiguity in the common law; unless and until the ECHR is incorporated into English law, it is necessary, particularly in judicial review, for the courts to continue to recognise, give effect to and balance the different and distinct roles of Govt, legislature and judiciary. The common law changes direction only slowly
467. *R v SS Foreign and Commonwealth Affairs, ex p Manelfi*	25.10.96	QBD Jowitt J	Judicial review (substantive hearing)	Employment	ECHR	—	—	The applicant could only rely on the breach of this country's international obligations, which are not part of domestic law, in the context of a *Wednesbury* challenge to the content of the relevant rules; and since the content of the rules was non-justiciable, the applicant was unable to argue that they breached international obligations
468. *R v Advertising Standards Authority, ex p City Trading Ltd.*	1.11.96	QBD Ognall J	Judicial review (substantive hearing)	Press regulation	ECHR	10	*Observer & Guardian v UK*	In exercising a supervisory role, the court should not import into the decision-making process the duty to ensure that a measure serves a pressing social need; any failure to apply that test did not make the decision unlawful
469. *R v SS Home Dept., ex p Hargreaves*	20.11.96	CA (Civ. Div.) Hirst*, Peter Gibson & Pill LJJ	Judicial review (appeal)	Prisons	ECHR	8	*X v UK McCotter v UK*	Although not part of English law, the ECHR can assist in the elucidation of common law or in the interpretation of a statute; but any interference with respect for family life was imposed by lawful court sentences and the SS's justifications meet the requirements that a pressing social need must be shown and that restrictions should be no more than is proportionate to the legitimate aim pursued
470. *Olotu v Home Office* The Times, 11 Dec 1996	29.11.96	CA (Civ. Div.) Lord Bingham CJ, Auld & Mummery LJJ	Action for damages (appeal)	False imprisonment	ECHR	5(1)(c),(3),(4),(5)	—	Doubtful if it were permissible to have recourse to ECHR to interpret statutory provisions on compensation for unlawful detention; and in any event excessive detention arose not from UK's failure to afford her her ECHR rights but from her failure to exercise those rights
471. *Abnett v British Airways* The Times, 13 Dec 1996	12.12.96	HL Lords Browne-Wilkinson, Jauncey, Mustill, Steyn & Hope	Action for damages (appeal)	Carrier's liability	ECHR	—	—	The ECHR has no bearing on the interpretation of international conventions such as the Warsaw Convention which are concerned with commerce between countries; not all states are party to both conventions and it cannot be assumed that the principles expressed in the ECHR are common to all those countries party to the Warsaw Convention
472. *O'Hara v Chief Constable of the RUC* The Times, 13 Dec 1996	12.12.96	HL Lords Goff, Mustill, Steyn*, Hoffman & Hope	Action for damages (appeal)	Police powers	ECHR	5(1) (c)	*Fox, Campbell & Hartley v UK*	The drafting technique employed in Art. 5(1)(c) ECHR showed that it contemplated a broader test of whether a reasonable suspicion exists and does not confine it to matters present in the mind of the arresting officer, but the domestic provision could not be approached in this way

Name of Case & Citation	Date of Judgment	Court	Type of Proceedings	Subject Matter	Treaty cited	Articles cited	Case-law cited	Nature of reference made to unincorporated international human rights law
473. *R v Radio Authority, ex p Bull* The Independent, 20 Dec 1996	17.12.96	CA (Civ. Div.) Lord Woolf MR*, Aldous & Brooke* LJJ	Judicial review (appeal)	Broadcasting	ECHR	10	*Observer & Guardian v UK*	Lord Woolf MR: Freedom of communication is protected alike at common law and by the ECHR, and the ambiguous words "wholly or mainly" which in part define the power to interfere should be construed restrictively Brooke LJ: Although Lord Goff's dictum in *Spycatcher* had been said in the context of the common law, it was equally relevant where the courts are concerned with statutory interpretation in a field covered by international obligations

Cases Referred to in Table at Appendix 1

European Commission and Court of Human Rights Cases Referred to in Table

Abdulaziz, Cabales & Balkandali *v*. UK (1985) 7 EHRR 471
Agee *v*. UK No. 7729/76, 7 DR 164 (1976)
Ahmad *v*. UK (1981) 4 EHRR 126
Allgemeine Gold-und-Silberscheideanstalt *v*. UK (1987) 9 EHRR 1

B *v*. France (1993) 16 EHRR 1
B *v*. UK (1988) 10 EHRR 87
Barthold *v*. Germany (1985) 7 EHRR 383
Beldjoudi *v*. France (1992) 14 EHRR 801
Benham *v*. UK (1996) 22 EHRR 293
Berrehab *v*. The Netherlands (1989) 11 EHRR 322
Bryan *v*. UK (1996) 22 EHRR 342
Buckley *v*. UK (1995) 19 EHRR CD20

Campbell *v*. UK (1992) 15 EHRR 137
Campbell & Fell *v*. UK (1985) 7 EHRR 165
Casada Coca *v*. Spain (1994) 18 EHRR 1
Church of X *v*. UK (1968) 29 Coll. Dec. Eur. Comm. HR 70
Cossey *v*. UK (1991) 13 EHRR 622
Costello-Roberts *v*. UK (1995) 19 EHRR 112
Cremieux *v*. France (1993) 16 EHRR 357
Cruz Varas *v*. Sweden (1992) 14 EHRR 1

Delcourt *v*. Belgium (1979–80) 1 EHRR 355
Deumeland *v*. Germany (1986) 8 EHRR 448
Deweer *v*. Belgium (1979–80) 2 EHRR 439
Dudgeon *v*. UK (1982) 4 EHRR 149

E *v*. Norway (1994) 17 EHRR 30
East African Asians *v*. UK (1981) 3 EHRR 76
Engel *v*. The Netherlands (1979–80) 1 EHRR 647

Feldbrugge *v*. The Netherlands (1986) 8 EHRR 425
Fox, Campbell & Hartley *v*. UK (1991) 13 EHRR 157
Funke *v*. France (1993) 16 EHRR 297

Gaskin *v*. UK (1990) 12 EHRR 36
Gay News *v*. UK (1982) 5 EHRR 123
Golder *v*. UK (1979–80) 1 EHRR 524
Gregory *v*. UK No. 22299/93 [1996] EHRLR 204
Gul *v*. Switzerland (1996) 22 EHRR 93

Sporrong & Lönnroth *v*. Sweden (1983) 5 EHRR 35
Sramek *v*. Austria (1985) 7 EHRR 351
Sunday Times *v*. UK (1979–80) 2 EHRR 245
Sunday Times *v*. UK (No. 2) (1992) 14 EHRR 229
Swedish Engine Drivers' Union *v*. Sweden (1979–80) 1 EHRR 617

Thorgeirson *v*. Iceland (1992) 14 EHRR 843
Thynne, Wilson & Gunnell *v*. UK (1991) 13 EHRR 666
Tolstoy Miloslavsky *v*. UK (1995) 20 EHRR 442
Tyrer *v*. UK (1979–80) 2 EHRR 1

Vilvarajah *v*. UK (1992) 14 EHRR 248

W *v*. UK No. 9348/81, 32 DR 190 (1983)
W *v*. UK (1988) 10 EHRR 29
Weeks *v*. UK (1991) 13 EHRR 435
Welch *v*. UK (1995) 20 EHRR 247
Winterwerp *v*. The Netherlands (1979–80) 2 EHRR 387
Wynne *v*. UK Series A No. 294 (1994)

X *v*. Ireland No. 6839/74, 7 DR 78 (1976)
X *v*. UK No. 9054/80, 30 DR 113 (1982)
X *v*. UK (1982) 4 EHRR 188

Young, James & Webster *v*. UK (1983) 5 EHRR 201

Analysis of Cases by Article of ECHR

Note: The numbers indicate the relevant cases in the Table. ( ) around a case number indicates case in which Article not specifically mentioned, but clear from context which Article court had in mind

Article 1
26, 45, 50, 108, 162, 177, 246, 335, 460

Article 2
45, 116, 118, 164, 177, 247, 322, (349), 371, 394, 460

Article 3
38, 42, 45, 56, 65, 71, 96, (99), 104, 166, 168, 187, 202, 205, 222, 250, 275, 279, (299), 322, 342, 360, 371, 394, 413, 423

Article 4

Article 5

6, 7, 8, 29, 44, 45, 48, 94, 103, 120, 131, 152, 159, 173, 183, 190, 195, 200, 214, 216, 238, 272, (276), 290, 296, 304, 309, 315, 318, 329, 346, 352, 386, (401), (421), 422, (436), 451, 452, 466, 470, 472

Article 6

6, (16), 18, 29, 31, 32, 42, 46, 47, 50, 51, 52, 57, 68, 70, 74, 75, (78), (95), 110, 112, 114, 117, 121, 126, (132), 133, 140, 142, 146, 155, 171, 172, 174, (178), 181, 182, 195, 197, 198, 209, 218, 223, 225, 231, 233, 241, 243, 244, 246, 247, 264, 277, (281), 282, (289), 294, 301, 312, 316, 317, (326), 332, 338, 340, 347, (351), 354, 358, (363), (366), (367), 369, 370, 372, (381), 382, 383, 390, (393), 398, (400), 402, 408, 411, 415, 418, 425, 428, 430, 434, 437, (439), 441, 442, 444, 446, 448, 453, 457

Article 7

3, 4, 76, 129, 169, 219, 225, 237, 254, 258, 309, 353, 396, 405

Article 8

11, 12, 15, 22, 26, 30, 40, 41, 42, 43, 52, 59, (61), 64, (69), (78), (82), 83, (90), 91, 98, 101, 104, 108, 114, 115, 121, (122), 123, 125, 126, 127, 137, (139), 142, 145, 151, 154, 156, 157, (158), 160, 163, (167), 171, 176, 179, (180), 182, 184, 189, 190, (193), 197, 203, 212, 213, 221, 232, 240, 243, 245, 248, (249), 254, 260, 261, 262, (263), (266), 269, 270, 271, 273, 278, 280, (283), 284, 286, 293, 297, 300, 301, 302, 303, 305, 306, 310, 311, (314), 319, 320, 321, 323, 325, 330, 331, 333, 336, 339, 341, 342, 343, 348, 350, 357, 361, 362, 364, 365, 371, 373, 375, (378), 379, 380, 383, 384, 385, 387, 388, 389, 391, 392, 395, 397, 399, 403, 404, 410, (412), 414, 416, 417, 420, 425, 426, 427, 431, 432, 433, 435, 437, 438, 444, 445, 447, 450, 454, 459, 460, 461, 462, 463, 465, 469

Article 9

(14), 17, 19, 20, 25, 34, 45, 66, 72, (85), 97, 138, 169, 201, 232, (256), 297, 310, 334, 431

Article 10

(2), 25, 27, 28, 39, 43, 45, 50, 53, 54, 73, 81, (85), 100, 105, 106, 107, 109, 110, 111, 113, 119, 130, 135, 141, 144, 149, 153, 161, 162, 165, 169, 175, 185, 188, 191, 194, 199, 204, 207, 210, 211, 215, (229), (230), 232, 234, 236, 239, 242, 246, 251, 255, 265, 274, 285, 286, 287, 288, 291, 297, 298, 313, 318, 328, 344, 345, 348, 356, 358, 368, 377, 406, 407, 419, (424), 429, 431, 440, 442, 449, 453, 462, 468, 473

Article 11

3, 4, 5, 23, 36, 37, 49, 55, 58, 63, 77, (78), 232, 292, 295, 297, 359

Article 12
7, 8, 83, 104, 321

Article 13
6, 26, 52, 83, 101, 108, 155, 174, 177, 195, 203, 212, 246, 255, 274, 275, 297, 335, 359, 364, 397, 437, 444, 462, 463

Article 14
(14), 52, 59, 104, (122), 169, 246, (266), (283), 297, 364, (384), 417, 431, 434, 461

Article 15
322

Article 25
9, 15, 22, 26, 40, 41, 42, 170, 437, 460

Article 1 of Protocol 1
9, 35, 57, 66, 92, (93), 124, 134, 142, (148), 172, (363), (374), 409

Article 2 of Protocol 1
87, 88, 147, 228, 307

Article 5 of Protocol 1
66

Article 3 of Protocol 7
259, 308

Analysis of Cases by Subject Matter

Note: The numbers indicate the relevant cases in the Table

Agricultural Regulation
409

Blasphemous Libel
25, 169

Broadcasting
144, 162, 185, 242, 295, 336, 345, 356, 368, 462, 473

Civil Aviation Regulation
13, 454

Appendix II

THE BANGALORE PRINCIPLES

REPORT OF JUDICIAL COLLOQUIUM ON THE DOMESTIC APPLICATION OF
INTERNATIONAL HUMAN RIGHTS NORMS, BANGALORE, INDIA

Chairman's Concluding Statement

Between 24 and 26 February 1988 there was convened in Bangalore, India, a high-level judicial colloquium on the Domestic Application of International Human Rights Norms. The Colloquium was administered by the Commonwealth Secretariat on behalf of the Convenor, the Hon Justice P N Bhagwati (former Chief Justice of India), with the approval of the Government of India, and with assistance from the Government of the State of Karnataka, India.

The participants were:

Justice P N Bhagwati (India) (Convenor)
Chief Justice E Dumbutshena (Zimbabwe)
Judge Ruth Bader Ginsburg (USA)
Chief Justice Mohammed Haleem (Pakistan)
Deputy Chief Justice Mari Kapi (Papua New Guinea)
Justice Michael D Kirby CMG (Australia)
Justice Rajsoomer Lallah (Mauritius)
Mr Anthony Lester QC (Britain)
Justice P Ramanathan (Sri Lanka)
Tun Mohamed Salleh Bin Abas (Malaysia)
Justice M P Chandrakantaraj Urs (India)

There was a comprehensive exchange of views and full discussion of expert papers. The Convenor summarised the discussions in the following paragraphs:

1. Fundamental human rights and freedoms are inherent in all humankind and find expression in constitutions and legal systems throughout the world and in the international human rights instruments.

2. These international human rights instruments provide important guidance in cases concerning fundamental human rights and freedoms.

3. There is an impressive body of jurisprudence, both international and national, concerning the interpretation of particular human rights and freedoms and their application. This body of jurisprudence is of practical relevance and value to judges and lawyers generally.

4. In most countries whose legal systems are based upon the common law, international conventions are not directly enforceable in national courts unless their provisions have been incorporated by legislation into domestic law. However, there is a growing tendency for national courts to have regard to these international norms for the purpose of deciding cases where the domestic law — whether constitutional, statute or common law — is uncertain or incomplete.

5. This tendency is entirely welcome because it respects the universality of fundamental human rights and freedoms and the vital role of an independent judiciary in reconciling the competing claims of individuals and groups of persons with the general interests of the community.

6. While it is desirable for the norms contained in the international human rights instruments to be still more widely recognised and applied by national courts, this process must take fully into account local laws, traditions, circumstances and needs.

7. It is within the proper nature of the judicial process and well-established judicial functions for national courts to have regard to international obligations which a country undertakes — whether or not they have been incorporated into domestic law — for the purpose of removing ambiguity or uncertainty from national constitutions, legislation or common law.

8. However, where national law is clear and inconsistent with the international obligations of the State concerned, in common law countries the national court is obliged to give effect to national law. In such cases the court should draw such inconsistency to the attention of the appropriate authorities since the supremacy of national law in no way mitigates a breach of an international legal obligation which is undertaken by a country.

9. It is essential to redress a situation where, by reason of traditional legal training which has tended to ignore the international dimension, judges and practising lawyers are often unaware of the remarkable and comprehensive developments of statements of international human rights norms. For the practical implementation of these views it is desirable to make provision for appropriate courses in universities and colleges, and for lawyers and law enforcement officials; provision in libraries of relevant materials; promotion of expert advisory bodies knowledgeable about developments in this field; better dissemination of information to judges, lawyers and law enforcement officials; and meetings for exchanges of relevant information and experience.

10. These views are expressed in recognition of the fact that judges and lawyers have a special contribution to make in the administration of justice in fostering universal respect for fundamental human rights and freedoms.

Bangalore
Karnataka State
India
26 February 1988

Appendix III

PREAMBLE

Whereas recognition of the inherent dignity and of the equal and inalienable rights of all members of the human family is the foundation of freedom, justice and peace in the world,

Whereas disregard and contempt for human rights have resulted in barbarous acts which have outraged the conscience of mankind, and the advent of a world in which human beings shall enjoy freedom of speech and belief and freedom from fear and want has been proclaimed as the highest aspiration of the common people,

Whereas it is essential, if man is not to be compelled to have recourse, as a last resort, to rebellion against tyranny and oppression, that human rights should be protected by the rule of law,

Whereas it is essential to promote the development of friendly relations between nations,

Whereas the peoples of the United Nations have in the Charter reaffirmed their faith in fundamental human rights, in the dignity and worth of the human person and in the equal rights of men and women and have determined to promote social progress and better standards of life in larger freedom,

Whereas Member States have pledged themselves to achieve, in co-operation with the United Nations, the promotion of universal respect for and observance of human rights and fundamental freedoms,

Whereas a common understanding of these rights and freedoms is of the greatest importance for the full realization of this pledge.

Now, Therefore,

THE GENERAL ASSEMBLY

proclaims

This universal declaration of human rights as a common standard of achievement for all peoples and all nations, to the end that every individual and every organ of society, keeping this Declaration constantly in mind, shall strive by teaching and education to promote respect for these rights and freedoms and by progressive measures, national and international, to secure their universal and effective recognition and observance, both among the peoples of Member States themselves and among the peoples of territories under their jurisdiction.

Article 1

All human beings are born free and equal in dignity and rights. They are endowed with reason and conscience and should act towards one another in a spirit of brotherhood.

Article 2

Everyone is entitled to all the rights and freedoms set forth in this Declaration, without distinction of any kind, such as race, colour, sex, language, religion, political or other opinion, national or social origin, property, birth or other status.

Furthermore, no distinction shall be made on the basis of the political, jurisdictional or international status of the country or territory to which a person belongs, whether it be independent, trust, non-self-governing or under any other limitation of sovereignty.

Article 3

Everyone has the right to life, liberty and security of person.

Article 4

No one shall be held in slavery or servitude: slavery and the slave trade shall be prohibited in all their forms.

Article 5

No one shall be subjected to torture or cruel, inhuman or degrading treatment or punishment.

Article 6

Everyone has the right to recognition everywhere as a person before the law.

Article 7

All are equal before the law and are entitled without any discrimination to equal protection of the law. All are entitled to equal protection against any discrimination in violation of this Declaration and against any incitement to such discrimination.

Article 8

Everyone has the right to an effective remedy by the competent national tribunals for acts violating the fundamental rights granted him by the constitution or by law.

Article 9

No one shall be subjected to arbitrary arrest, detention or exile.

Article 10

Everyone is entitled in full equality to a fair and public hearing by an independent and impartial tribunal, in the determination of his rights and obligations and of any criminal charge against him.

Article 11

1. Everyone charged with a penal offence has the right to be presumed innocent until proved guilty according to law in a public trial at which he has had all the guarantees necessary for his defence.
2. No one shall be held guilty of any penal offence on account of any act or omission which did not constitute a penal offence, under national or international law, at the time when it was committed. Nor shall a heavier penalty be imposed than the one that was applicable at the time the penal offence was committed.

Article 12

No one shall be subjected to arbitrary interference with his privacy, family, home or correspondence, nor to attacks upon his honour and reputation. Everyone has the right to the protection of the law against such interference or attacks.

Article 13

1. Everyone has the right to freedom of movement and residence within the borders of each state.
2. Everyone has the right to leave any country, including his own, and to return to his country.

Article 14

1. Everyone has the right to seek and to enjoy in other countries asylum from persecution.
2. This right may not be invoked in the case of prosecution genuinely arising from non-political crimes or from acts contrary to the purposes and principles of the United Nations.

Article 15

1. Everyone has the right to a nationality.
2. No one shall be arbitrarily deprived of his nationality nor denied the right to change his nationality.

Article 16

1. Men and women of full age, without any limitation due to race, nationality or religion, have the right to marry and to found a family. They are entitled to equal rights as to marriage, during marriage and at its dissolution.
2. Marriage shall be entered into only with the free and full consent of the intending spouses.
3. The family is the natural and fundamental group unit of society and is entitled to protection by society and the State.

Article 17

1. Everyone has the right to own property alone as well as in association with others.
2. No one shall be arbitrarily deprived of his property.

Article 18

Everyone has the right to freedom of thought, conscience and religion; this right includes freedom to change his religion or belief, and freedom, either alone or in community with others and in public or private, to manifest his religion or belief in teaching, practice, worship and observance.

Article 19

Everyone has the right to freedom of opinion and expression; this right includes freedom to hold opinions without interference and to seek, receive and impart information and ideas through any media and regardless of frontiers.

Article 20

1. Everyone has the right to freedom of peaceful assembly and association.
2. No one may be compelled to belong to an association.

Article 21

1. Everyone has the right to take part in the government of his country, directly or through freely chosen representatives.
2. Everyone has the right of equal access to public service in his country.
3. The will of the people shall be the basis of the authority of government; this will shall be expressed in periodic and genuine elections which shall be by universal and equal suffrage and shall be held by secret vote or by equivalent free voting procedures.

Article 22

Everyone, as a member of society, has the right to social security and is entitled to realization, through national effort and international co-operation and in accordance with the organization and resources of each State, of the economic, social and cultural rights indispensable for his dignity and the free development of his personality.

Article 23

1. Everyone has the right to work, to free choice of employment, to just and favourable conditions of work and to protection against unemployment.
2. Everyone, without any discrimination, has the right to equal pay for equal work.
3. Everyone who works has the right to just and favourable remuneration ensuring for himself and his family an existence worthy of human dignity, and supplemented, if necessary, by other means of social protection.
4. Everyone has the right to form and to join trade unions for the protection of his interests.

Article 24

Everyone has the right to rest and leisure, including reasonable limitation of working hours and periodic holidays with pay.

Article 25

1. Everyone has the right to a standard of living adequate for the health and well-being of himself and of his family, including food, clothing, housing and medical care and necessary social services, and the right to security in the event of unemployment, sickness, disability, widowhood, old age or other lack of livelihood in circumstances beyond his control.
2. Motherhood and childhood are entitled to special care and assistance. All children, whether born in or out of wedlock, shall enjoy the same social protection.

Article 26

1. Everyone has the right to education. Education shall be free, at least in the elementary and fundamental stages. Elementary education shall be compulsory. Technical and professional education shall be made generally available and higher education shall be equally accessible to all on the basis of merit.
2. Education shall be directed to the full development of the human personality and to the strengthening of respect for human rights and fundamental freedoms. It shall promote understanding, tolerance and friendship among all nations, racial or religious groups, and shall further the activities of the United Nations for the maintenance of peace.
3. Parents have a prior right to choose the kind of education that shall be given to their children.

Article 27

1. Everyone has the right freely to participate in the cultural life of the community, to enjoy the arts and to share in scientific advancement and its benefits.
2. Everyone has the right to the protection of the moral and material interests resulting from any scientific, literary or artistic production of which he is the author.

Article 28

Everyone is entitled to a social and international order in which the rights and freedoms set forth in this Declaration can be fully realized.

Article 29

1. Everyone has duties to the community in which alone the free and full development of his personality is possible.

2. In the exercise of his rights and freedoms, everyone shall be subject only to such limitations as are determined by law solely for the purpose of securing due recognition and respect for the rights and freedoms of others and of meeting the just requirements of morality, public order and the general welfare in a democratic society.

3. These rights and freedoms may in no case be exercised contrary to the purposes and principles of the United Nations.

Article 30

Nothing in this Declaration may be interpreted as implying for any State, group or person any right to engage in any activity or to perform any act aimed at the destruction of any of the rights and freedoms set forth herein.

Appendix IV

THE EUROPEAN CONVENTION ON HUMAN RIGHTS, 1950: SECTION I AND RELEVANT PROTOCOLS

The Governments signatory hereto, being Members of the Council of Europe,

Considering the Universal Declaration of Human Rights proclaimed by the General Assembly of the United Nations on 10 December 1948;

Considering that this Declaration aims at securing the universal and effective recognition and observance of the Rights therein declared;

Considering that the aim of the Council of Europe is the achievement of greater unity between its Members and that one of the methods by which the aim is to be pursued is the maintenance and further realization of Human Rights and Fundamental Freedoms;

Reaffirming their profound belief in those Fundamental Freedoms which are the foundation of justice and peace in the world and are best maintained on the one hand by an effective political democracy and on the other by a common understanding and observance of the Human Rights upon which they depend;

Being resolved, as the Governments of European countries which are likeminded and have a common heritage of political traditions, ideals, freedom and the rule of law to take the first steps for the collective enforcement of certain of the Rights stated in the Universal Declaration;

Have agreed as follows:

Article 1

The High Contracting Parties shall secure to everyone within their jurisdiction the rights and freedoms defined in Section I of this Convention

Section I

Article 2

1. Everyone's right to life shall be protected by law. No one shall be deprived of his life intentionally save in the execution of a sentence of a court following his conviction of a crime for which this penalty is provided by law.

2. Deprivation of life shall not be regarded as inflicted in contravention of this Article when it results from the use of force which is no more than absolutely necessary:

(*a*) in defence of any person from unlawful violence;
(*b*) in order to effect a lawful arrest or to prevent the escape of a person lawfully detained;
(*c*) in action lawfully taken for the purpose of quelling a riot or insurrection.

Article 3

No one shall be subjected to torture or to inhuman or degrading treatment or punishment.

Article 4

1. No one shall be held in slavery or servitude.
2. No one shall be required to perform forced or compulsory labour.
3. For the purpose of this Article the term 'forced or compulsory labour' shall not include:

(*a*) any work required to be done in the ordinary course of detention imposed according to the provisions of Article 5 of this Convention or during conditional release from such detention;
(*b*) any service of a military character or, in case of conscientious objectors in countries where they are recognized, service exacted instead of compulsory military service;
(*c*) any service exacted in case of an emergency or calamity threatening the life or well-being of the community;
(*d*) any work or service which forms part of normal civic obligations.

Article 5

1. Everyone has the right to liberty and security of person. No one shall be deprived of his liberty save in the following cases and in accordance with a procedure prescribed by law;

(*a*) the lawful detention of a person after conviction by a competent court;
(*b*) the lawful arrest or detention of a person for non-compliance with the lawful order of a court or in order to secure the fulfilment of any obligation prescribed by law;
(*c*) the lawful arrest or detention of a person effected for the purpose of bringing him before the competent legal authority on reasonable suspicion of having committed an offence or when it is reasonably considered necessary to prevent his committing an offence or fleeing after having done so;
(*d*) the detention of a minor by lawful order for the purpose of educational supervision or his lawful detention for the purpose of bringing him before the competent legal authority;
(*e*) the lawful detention of persons for the prevention of the spreading of infectious diseases, of persons of unsound mind, alcoholics or drug addicts, or vagrants;

(*f*) the lawful arrest or detention of a person to prevent his effecting an unautho-
rized entry into the country or of a person against whom action is being taken
with a view to deportation or extradition.

2. Everyone who is arrested shall be informed promptly, in a language which he understands, of the reasons for his arrest and of any charge against him.
3. Everyone arrested or detained in accordance with the provisions of paragraph 1 (*c*)
of this Article shall be brought promptly before a judge or other officer authorized by
law to exercise judicial power and shall be entitled to trial within a reasonable time
or to release pending trial. Release may be conditioned by guarantees to appear for
trial.
4. Everyone who is deprived of his liberty by arrest or detention shall be entitled to
take proceedings by which the lawfulness of his detention shall be decided speedily by
a court and his release ordered if the detention is not lawful.
5. Everyone who has been the victim of arrest or detention in contravention of the
provisions of this article shall have an enforceable right to compensation.

Article 6

1. In the determination of his civil rights and obligations or of any criminal charge
against him, everyone is entitled to a fair and public hearing within a reasonable time
by an independent and impartial tribunal established by law. Judgment shall be pronounced publicly but the press and public may be excluded from all or part of the trial
in the interest of morals, public order or national security in a democratic society,
where the interests of juveniles or the protection of the private life of the parties so
require, or to the extent strictly necessary in the opinion of the court in special circumstances where publicity would prejudice the interests of justice.
2. Everyone charged with a criminal offence shall be presumed innocent until proved
guilty according to law.
3. Everyone charged with a criminal offence has the following minimum rights:

(*a*) to be informed promptly, in a language which he understands and in detail, of
the nature and cause of the accusation against him;
(*b*) to have adequate time and facilities for the preparation of his defence;
(*c*) to defend himself in person or through legal assistance of his own choosing or,
if he has not sufficient means to pay for legal assistance, to be given it free when
the interests of justice so require;
(*d*) to examine or have examined witnesses against him and to obtain the attendance and examination of witnesses on his behalf under the same conditions as
witnesses against him;
(*e*) to have the free assistance of an interpreter if he cannot understand or speak the
language used in court.

Article 7

1. No one shall be held guilty of any criminal offence on account of any act or omission which did not constitute a criminal offence under national or international law at

the time when it was committed. Nor shall a heavier penalty be imposed than the one that was applicable at the time the criminal offence was committed.

2. This article shall not prejudice the trial and punishment of any person for any act or omission which, at the time when it was committed, was criminal according to the general principles of law recognized by civilized nations.

Article 8

1. Everyone has the right to respect for his private and family life, his home and his correspondence.

2. There shall be no interference by a public authority with the exercise of this right except such as is in accordance with the law and is necessary in a democratic society in the interests of national security, public safety or the economic well-being of the country, for the prevention of disorder or crime, for the protection of health or morals, or for the protection of the rights and freedoms of others.

Article 9

1. Everyone has the right to freedom of thought, conscience and religion; this right includes freedom to change his religion or belief, and freedom, either alone or in community with others and in public or private, to manifest his religion or belief, in worship, teaching, practice and observance.

2. Freedom to manifest one's religion or beliefs shall be subject only to such limitations as are prescribed by law and are necessary in a democratic society, in the interests of public safety, for the protection of public order, health or morals, or for the protection of the rights and freedoms of others.

Article 10

1. Everyone has the right to freedom of expression. This right shall include freedom to hold opinions and to receive and impart information and ideas without interference by public authority and regardless of frontiers. This article shall not prevent States from requiring the licensing of broadcasting, television or cinema enterprises.

2. The exercise of these freedoms, since it carries with it duties and responsibilities, may be subject to such formalities, conditions, restrictions or penalties as are prescribed by law and are necessary in a democratic society, in the interests of national security, territorial integrity or public safety, for the prevention of disorder or crime, for the protection of health or morals, for the protection of the reputation or rights of others, for preventing the disclosure of information received in confidence, or for maintaining the authority and impartiality of the judiciary.

Article 11

1. Everyone has the right to freedom of peaceful assembly and to freedom of association with others, including the right to form and to join trade unions for the protection of his interests.
2. No restrictions shall be placed on the exercise of these rights other than such as are prescribed by law and are necessary in a democratic society in the interests of national security or public safety, for the prevention of disorder or crime, for the protection of health or morals or for the protection of the rights and freedoms of others. This Article shall not prevent the imposition of lawful restrictions on the exercise of these rights by members of the armed forces, of the police or of the administration of the State.

Article 12

Men and women of marriageable age have the right to marry and to found a family, according to the national laws governing the exercise of this right.

Article 13

Everyone whose rights and freedoms as set forth in this Convention are violated shall have an effective remedy before a national authority notwithstanding that the violation has been committed by persons acting in an official capacity.

Article 14

The enjoyment of the rights and freedoms set forth in this Convention shall be secured without discrimination on any ground such as sex, race, colour, language, religion, political or other opinion, national or social origin, association with a national minority, property, birth or other status.

Article 15

1. In time of war or other public emergency threatening the life of the nation any High Contracting Party may take measures derogating from its obligations under this Convention to the extent strictly required by the exigencies of the situation, provided that such measures are not inconsistent with its other obligations under international law.
2. No derogation from Article 2, except in respect of deaths resulting from lawful acts of war, or from Articles 3, 4 (paragraph 1) and 7 shall be made under this provision.
3. Any High Contracting Party availing itself of this right of derogation shall keep the Secretary-General of the Council of Europe fully informed of the measures which it

has taken and the reasons therefore. It shall also inform the Secretary-General of the Council of Europe when such measures have ceased to operate and the provisions of the Convention are again being fully executed.

Article 16

Nothing in Articles 10, 11 and 14 shall be regarded as preventing the High Contracting Parties from imposing restrictions on the political activity of aliens.

Article 17

Nothing in this Convention may be interpreted as implying for any State, group or person any right to engage in any activity or perform any act aimed at the destruction of any of the rights and freedoms set forth herein or at their limitation to a greater extent than is provided for in the Convention.

Article 18

The restrictions permitted under this Convention to the said rights and freedoms shall not be applied for any purpose other than those for which they have been prescribed.

PROTOCOLS

First Protocol: Enforcement of Certain Rights and Freedoms not included in Section I of the Convention

The Governments signatory hereto, being Members of the Council of Europe,

Being resolved to take steps to ensure the collective enforcement of certain rights and freedoms other than those already included in Section I of the Convention for the Protection of Human Rights and Fundamental Freedoms signed at Rome on 4th November, 1950 (hereinafter referred to as 'the Convention'),

Have agreed as follows:

Article 1

Every natural or legal person is entitled to the peaceful enjoyment of his possessions. No one shall be deprived of his possessions except in the public interest and subject to the conditions provided for by law and by the general principles of international law.

The preceding provisions shall not, however, in any way impair the right of a State to enforce such laws as it deems necessary to control the use of property in accordance with the general interest or to secure the payment of taxes or other contributions or penalties.

Article 2

No person shall be denied the right to education. In the exercise of any functions which it assumes in relation to education and to teaching, the State shall respect the right of parents to ensure such education and teaching in conformity with their own religious and philosophical convictions.

Article 3

The High Contracting Parties undertake to hold free elections at reasonable intervals by secret ballot, under conditions which will ensure the free expression of the opinion of the people in the choice of the legislature.

Fourth Protocol: Securing certain Rights and Freedoms other than those included in the Convention and in Protocol No. 1

The Governments signatory hereto, being Members of the Council of Europe,

Being resolved to take steps to ensure the collective enforcement of certain rights and freedoms other than those already included in Section I of the Convention for the Protection of Human Rights and Fundamental Freedoms signed at Rome on 4 November 1950 (hereinafter referred to as 'the Convention') and in Articles 1 to 3 of the First Protocol to the Convention, signed at Paris on 20 March 1952,

Have agreed as follows:

Article 1

No one shall be deprived of his liberty merely on the ground of inability to fulfil a contractual obligation.

Article 2

1. Everyone lawfully within the territory of a State shall, within that territory, have the right to liberty of movement and freedom to choose his residence.
2. Everyone shall be free to leave any country, including his own.
3. No restrictions shall be placed on the exercise of these rights other than such as are

in accordance with law and are necessary in a democratic society in the interests of national security or public safety, for the maintenance of 'ordre public', for the prevention of crime, for the protection of health and morals, or for the protection of the rights and freedoms of others.

4. The rights set forth in paragraph 1 may also be subject, in particular areas, to restrictions imposed in accordance with law and justified by the public interest in a democratic society.

Article 3

1. No one shall be expelled, by means either of an individual or of a collective measure, from the territory of the State of which he is a national.

2. No one shall be deprived of the right to enter the territory of the State of which he is a national.

Article 4

Collective expulsion of aliens is prohibited.

Seventh Protocol: Concerning Various Matters

The member States of the Council of Europe signatory hereto,

Being resolved to take further steps to ensure the collective enforcement of certain rights and freedoms by means of the Convention for the Protection of Human Rights and Fundamental Freedoms signed at Rome on 4 November 1950 (hereinafter referred to as 'the Convention'),

Have agreed as follows:

Article 1

1. An alien lawfully resident in the territory of a State shall not be expelled therefrom except in pursuance of a decision reached in accordance with law and shall be allowed:

   (*a*) to submit reasons against his expulsion,
   (*b*) to have his case reviewed, and
   (*c*) to be represented for these purposes before the competent authority or a person or persons designated by that authority.

2. An alien may be expelled before the exercise of his rights under paragraph 1.a, b and c of this Article, when such expulsion is necessary in the interests of public order or is grounded on reasons of national security.

Article 2

1. Everyone convicted of a criminal offence by a tribunal shall have the right to have his conviction or sentence reviewed by a higher tribunal. The exercise of this right, including the grounds on which it may be exercised, shall be governed by law.
2. This right may be subject to exceptions in regard to offences of a minor character, as prescribed by law, or in cases in which the person concerned was tried in the first instance by the highest tribunal or was convicted following an appeal against acquittal.

Article 3

When a person has by a final decision been convicted of a criminal offence and when subsequently his conviction has been reversed, or he has been pardoned, on the ground that a new or newly discovered fact shows conclusively that there has been a miscarriage of justice, the person who has suffered punishment as a result of such conviction shall be compensated according to the law or the practice of the State concerned, unless it is proved that the nondisclosure of the unknown fact in time is wholly or partly attributable to him.

Article 4

1. No one shall be liable to be tried or punished again in criminal proceedings under the jurisdiction of the same State for an offence for which he has already been finally acquitted or convicted in accordance with the law and penal procedure of that State.
2. The provisions of the preceding paragraph shall not prevent the reopening of the case in accordance with the law and penal procedure of the State concerned, if there is evidence of new or newly discovered facts, or if there has been a fundamental defect in the previous proceedings, which could affect the outcome of the case.
3. No derogation from this Article shall be made under Article 15 of the Convention.

Article 5

Spouses shall enjoy equality of rights and responsibilities of a private law character between them, and in their relations with their children, as to marriage, during marriage and in the event of its dissolution. This Article shall not prevent States from taking such measures as are necessary in the interests of the children.

Appendix V

THE INTERNATIONAL COVENANT ON CIVIL AND POLITICAL RIGHTS, 1966

PREAMBLE

The States Parties to the present Covenant,

Considering that, in accordance with the principles proclaimed in the Charter of the United Nations, recognition of the inherent dignity and of the equal and inalienable rights of all members of the human family is the foundation of freedom, justice and peace in the world,

Recognizing that these rights derive from the inherent dignity of the human person,

Recognizing that, in accordance with the Universal Declaration of Human Rights, the ideal of free human beings enjoying civil and political freedom and freedom from fear and want can only be achieved if conditions are created whereby everyone may enjoy his civil and political rights, as well as his economic, social and cultural rights,

Considering the obligation of States under the Charter of the United Nations to promote universal respect for, and observance of, human rights and freedoms,

Realizing that the individual, having duties to other individuals and to the community to which he belongs, is under a responsibility to strive for the promotion and observance of the rights recognized in the present Covenant,

Agree upon the following articles:

PART I

Article 1

1. All peoples have the right of self-determination. By virtue of that right they freely determine their political status and freely pursue their economic, social and cultural development.

2. All peoples may, for their own ends, freely dispose of their natural wealth and resources without prejudice to any obligations arising out of international economic co-operation, based upon the principle of mutual benefit, and international law. In no case may a people be deprived of its own means of subsistence.

3. The States Parties to the present Covenant, including those having responsibility for the administration of Non-Self-Governing and Trust Territories, shall promote the realization of the right of self-determination, and shall respect that right, in conformity with the provisions of the Charter of the United Nations.

Part II

Article 2

1. Each State Party to the present Covenant undertakes to respect and to ensure to all individuals within its territory and subject to its jurisdiction the rights recognized in the present Covenant, without distinction of any kind, such as race, colour, sex, language, religion, political or other opinion, national or social origin, property, birth or other status.

2. Where not already provided for by existing legislative or other measures, each State Party to the present Covenant undertakes to take the necessary steps, in accordance with its constitutional processes and with the provisions of the present Covenant, to adopt such legislative or other measures as may be necessary to give effect to the rights recognized in the present Covenant.

3. Each State Party to the present Covenant undertakes:

   (a) To ensure that any person whose rights or freedoms as herein recognized are violated shall have an effective remedy, notwithstanding that the violation has been committed by persons acting in an official capacity;

   (b) To ensure that any person claiming such a remedy shall have his right thereto determined by competent judicial, administrative or legislative authorities, or by any other competent authority provided for by the legal system of the State, and to develop the possibilities of judicial remedy;

   (c) To ensure that the competent authorities shall enforce such remedies when granted.

Article 3

The States Parties to the present Covenant undertake to ensure the equal right of men and women to the enjoyment of all civil and political rights set forth in the present Covenant.

Article 4

1. In time of public emergency which threatens the life of the nation and the existence of which is officially proclaimed, the State Parties to the present Covenant may take measures derogating from their obligations under the present Covenant to the extent strictly required by the exigencies of the situation, provided that such measures are not inconsistent with their other obligations under international law and do not involve discrimination solely on the ground of race, colour, sex, language, religion or social origin.

2. No derogation from Articles 6, 7, 8 (paragraphs 1 and 2), 11, 15, 16 and 18 may be made under this provision.

3. Any State Party to the present Covenant availing itself of the right of derogation shall immediately inform the other States Parties to the present Covenant, through the

intermediary of the Secretary-General of the United Nations of the provisions from which it has derogated and of the reasons by which it was actuated. A further communication shall be made, through the same intermediary on the date on which it terminates such derogation.

Article 5

1. Nothing in the present Covenant may be interpreted as implying for any State, group or person any right to engage in any activity or perform any act aimed at the destruction of any of the rights and freedoms recognized herein or at their limitation to a greater extent than is provided for in the present Covenant.
2. There shall be no restriction upon or derogation from any of the fundamental human rights recognized or existing in any State Party to the present Covenant pursuant to law, conventions, regulations or custom on the pretext that the present Covenant does not recognize such rights or that it recognizes them to a lesser extent.

PART III

Article 6

1. Every human being has the inherent right to life. This right shall be protected by law. No one shall be arbitrarily deprived of his life.
2. In countries which have not abolished the death penalty, sentence of death may be imposed only for the most serious crimes in accordance with the law in force at the time of the commission of the crime and not contrary to the provisions of the present Covenant and to the Convention on the Prevention and Punishment of the Crime of Genocide. This penalty can only be carried out pursuant to a final judgment rendered by a competent court.
3. When deprivation of life constitutes the crime of genocide, it is understood that nothing in this Article shall authorize any State Party to the present Covenant to derogate in any way from any obligation assumed under the provisions of the Convention on the Prevention and Punishment of the Crime of Genocide.
4. Anyone sentenced to death shall have the right to seek pardon or commutation of the sentence. Amnesty, pardon or commutation of the sentence of death may be granted in all cases.
5. Sentence of death shall not be imposed for crimes committed by persons below eighteen years of age and shall not be carried out on pregnant women.
6. Nothing in this Article shall be invoked to delay or to prevent the abolition of capital punishment by any State Party to the present Covenant.

Article 7

No one shall be subjected to torture or cruel, inhuman or degrading treatment or punishment. In particular, no one shall be subjected without his free consent to medical or scientific experimentation.

Article 8

1. No one shall be held in slavery; slavery and the slave-trade in all their forms shall be prohibited.
2. No one shall be held in servitude.
3. (*a*) No one shall be required to perform forced or compulsory labour;
    (*b*) Paragraph 3 (*a*) shall not be held to preclude, in countries where imprisonment with hard labour may be imposed as a punishment for a crime, the performance of hard labour in pursuance of a sentence to such punishment by a competent court;
    (*c*) For the purpose of this paragraph the term 'forced or compulsory labour' shall not include:
        (i) Any work or service, not referred to in sub-paragraph (*b*), normally required of a person who is under detention in consequence of a lawful order of a court, or of a person during conditional release from such detention;
        (ii) Any service of a military character and, in countries where conscientious objection is recognized, any national service required by law of conscientious objectors;
        (iii) Any service exacted in cases of emergency or calamity threatening the life or well-being of the community;
        (iv) Any work or service which forms part of normal civil obligations.

Article 9

1. Everyone has the right to liberty and security of person. No one shall be subjected to arbitrary arrest or detention. No one shall be deprived of his liberty except on such grounds and in accordance with such procedures as are established by law.
2. Anyone who is arrested shall be informed, at the time of arrest, of the reasons for his arrest and shall be promptly informed of any charges against him.
3. Anyone arrested or detained on a criminal charge shall be brought promptly before a judge or other officer authorized by law to exercise judicial power and shall be entitled to trial within a reasonable time or to release. It shall not be the general rule that persons awaiting trial shall be detained in custody, but release may be subject to guarantees to appear for trial, at any other stage of the judicial proceedings, and, should occasion arise, for execution of the judgment.
4. Anyone who is deprived of his liberty by arrest or detention shall be entitled to take proceedings before a court, in order that that court may decide without delay on the lawfulness of his detention and order his release if the detention is not lawful.
5. Anyone who has been the victim of unlawful arrest or detention shall have an enforceable right to compensation.

Article 10

1. All persons deprived of their liberty shall be treated with humanity and with respect for the inherent dignity of the human person.

2. (*a*) Accused persons shall, save in exceptional circumstances, be segregated from convicted persons and shall be subject to separate treatment appropriate to their status as unconvicted persons;

(*b*) Accused juvenile persons shall be separated from adults and brought as speedily as possible for adjudication.

3. The penitentiary system shall comprise treatment of prisoners the essential aim of which shall be their reformation and social rehabilitation. Juvenile offenders shall be segregated from adults and be accorded treatment appropriate to their age and legal status.

Article 11

No one shall be imprisoned merely on the ground of inability to fulfil a contractual obligation.

Article 12

1. Everyone lawfully within the territory of a State shall, within that territory, have the right to liberty of movement and freedom to choose his residence.

2. Everyone shall be free to leave any country, including his own.

3. The above-mentioned rights shall not be subject to any restrictions except those which are provided by law, are necessary to protect national security, public order (*ordre public*), public health or morals or the rights and freedoms of others, and are consistent with the other rights recognized in the present Covenant.

4. No one shall be arbitrarily deprived of the right to enter his own country.

Article 13

An alien lawfully in the territory of a State Party to the present Covenant may be expelled therefrom only in pursuance of a decision reached in accordance with law and shall, except where compelling reasons of national security otherwise require, be allowed to submit the reasons against his expulsion and to have his case reviewed by, and be represented for the purpose before, the competent authority or a person or persons especially designated by the competent authority.

Article 14

1. All persons shall be equal before the courts and tribunals. In the determination of any criminal charge against him, or of his rights and obligations in a suit at law, everyone shall be entitled to a fair and public hearing by a competent, independent and impartial tribunal established by law. The Press and the public may be excluded from all or part of a trial for reasons of morals, public order (*ordre public*) or national security in a democratic society, or when the interest of the private lives of the parties so requires, or to the extent strictly necessary in the opinion of the court in special

circumstances where publicity would prejudice the interests of justice; but any judgement rendered in a criminal case or in a suit at law shall be made public except where the interest of juvenile persons otherwise requires or the proceedings concern matrimonial disputes or the guardianship of children.

2. Everyone charged with a criminal offence shall have the right to be presumed innocent until proved guilty according to law.

3. In the determination of any criminal charge against him, everyone shall be entitled to the following minimum guarantees, in full equality:

  (*a*) To be informed promptly and in detail in a language which he understands of the nature and cause of the charge against him;

  (*b*) To have adequate time and facilities for the preparation of his defence and to communicate with counsel of his own choosing;

  (*c*) To be tried without undue delay;

  (*d*) To be tried in his presence, and to defend himself in person or through legal assistance of his own choosing; to be informed, if he does not have legal assistance, of this right; and to have legal assistance assigned to him, in any case where the interests of justice so require, and without payment by him in any such case if he does not have sufficient means to pay for it;

  (*e*) To examine, or have examined, the witnesses against him and to obtain the attendance and examination of witnesses on his behalf under the same conditions as witnesses against him;

  (*f*) To have the free assistance of an interpreter if he cannot understand or speak the language used in court;

  (*g*) Not to be compelled to testify against himself or to confess guilt.

4. In the case of juvenile persons, the procedure shall be such as will take account of their age and the desirability of promoting their rehabilitation.

5. Everyone convicted of a crime shall have the right to his conviction and sentence being reviewed by a higher tribunal according to law.

6. When a person has by a final decision been convicted of a criminal offence and when subsequently his conviction has been reversed or he has been pardoned on the ground that a new or newly discovered fact shows conclusively that there has been a miscarriage of justice, the person who has suffered punishment as a result of such conviction shall be compensated according to law, unless it is proved that the non-disclosure of the unknown fact in time is wholly or partly attributable to him.

7. No one shall be liable to be tried or punished again for an offence for which he has already been finally convicted or acquitted in accordance with the law and penal procedure of each country.

Article 15

1. No one shall be held guilty of any criminal offence on account of any act or omission which did not constitute a criminal offence, under national or international law, at the time when it was committed. Nor shall a heavier penalty be imposed than the one that was applicable at the time when the criminal offence was committed. If, subsequent to the commission of the offence, provision is made by law for the imposition of a lighter penalty, the offender shall benefit thereby.

2. Nothing in this article shall prejudice the trial and punishment of any person for any act or omission which, at the time when it was committed, was criminal according to the general principles of law recognized by the community of nations.

Article 16

Everyone shall have the right to recognition everywhere as a person before the law.

Article 17

1. No one shall be subjected to arbitrary or unlawful interference with his privacy, family, home or correspondence, nor to unlawful attacks on his honour and reputation.
2. Everyone has the right to the protection of the law against such interference or attacks.

Article 18

1. Everyone shall have the right to freedom of thought, conscience and religion. This right shall include freedom to have or to adopt a religion or belief of his choice, and freedom, either individually or in community with others and in public or private, to manifest his religion or belief in worship, observance, practice and teaching.
2. No one shall be subject to coercion which would impair his freedom to have or to adopt a religion or belief of his choice.
3. Freedom to manifest one's religion or beliefs may be subject only to such limitations as are prescribed by law and are necessary to protect public safety, order, health, or morals or the fundamental rights and freedoms of others.
4. The States Parties to the present Covenant undertake to have respect for the liberty of parents and, when applicable, legal guardians to ensure the religious and moral education of their children in conformity with their own convictions.

Article 19

1. Everyone shall have the right to hold opinions without interference.
2. Everyone shall have the right to freedom of expression; this right shall include freedom to seek, receive and impart information and ideas of all kinds, regardless of frontiers, either orally, in writing or in print, in the form of art, or through any other media of his choice.
3. The exercise of the rights provided for in paragraph 2 of this article carries with it special duties and responsibilities. It may therefore be subject to certain restrictions, but these shall only be such as are provided by law and are necessary:

(*a*) For respect of the rights or reputations of others;

(*b*) For the protection of national security or of public order (*ordre public*), or of public health or morals.

Article 20

1. Any propaganda for war shall be prohibited by law.

2. Any advocacy of national, racial or religious hatred that constitutes incitement to discrimination, hostility or violence shall be prohibited by law.

Article 21

The right of peaceful assembly shall be recognized. No restrictions may be placed on the exercise of this right other than those imposed in conformity with the law and which are necessary in a democratic society in the interests of national security or public safety, public order (*ordre public*), the protection of public health or morals or the protection of the rights and freedoms of others.

Article 22

1. Everyone shall have the right to freedom of association with others, including the right to form and join trade unions for the protection of his interests.

2. No restrictions may be placed on the exercise of this right other than those which are prescribed by law and which are necessary in a democratic society in the interests of national security or public safety, public order (*ordre public*), the protection of public health or morals or the protection of the rights and freedoms of others. This Article shall not prevent the imposition of lawful restrictions on members of the armed forces and of the police in their exercise of this right.

3. Nothing in this article shall authorize States Parties to the International Labour Organization Convention of 1948 concerning Freedom of Association and Protection of the Right to Organize to take legislative measures which would prejudice, or to apply the law in such a manner as to prejudice, the guarantees provided for in that Convention.

Article 23

1. The family is the natural and fundamental group unit of society and is entitled to protection by society and the State.

2. The right of men and women of marriageable age to marry and to found a family shall be recognized.

3. No marriage shall be entered into without the free and full consent of the intending spouses.

4. States Parties to the present Covenant shall take appropriate steps to ensure equality of rights and responsibilities of spouses as to marriage, during marriage and at its dissolution. In the case of dissolution, provision shall be made for the necessary protection of any children.

Article 24

1. Every child shall have, without any discrimination as to race, colour, sex, language, religion, national or social origin, property or birth, the right to such measures of protection as are required by his status as a minor, on the part of his family, society and the State.
2. Every child shall be registered immediately after birth and shall have a name.
3. Every child has the right to acquire a nationality.

Article 25

Every citizen shall have the right and the opportunity, without any of the distinctions mentioned in Article 2 and without unreasonable restrictions:

- (*a*) To take part in the conduct of public affairs, directly or through freely chosen representatives;
- (*b*) To vote and to be elected at genuine periodic elections which shall be universal and equal suffrage and shall be held by secret ballot, guaranteeing the free expression of the will of the electors;
- (*c*) To have access, on general terms of equality, to public service in his country.

Article 26

All persons are equal before the law and are entitled without any discrimination to the equal protection of the law. In this respect, the law shall prohibit any discrimination and guarantee to all persons equal and effective protection against discrimination on any ground such as race, colour, sex, language, religion, political or other opinion, national or social origin, property, birth or other status.

Article 27

In those States in which ethnic, religious or linguistic minorities exist, persons belonging to such minorities shall not be denied the right, in community with the other members of their group, to enjoy their own culture, to profess and practise their own religion, or to use their own language.

Appendix VI

HOME OFFICE POLICY DP/2/93

MARRIAGE AND CHILDREN

Introduction

1. The attached instruction provides guidance on cases involving marriage and children, and takes into account the effect of the European Convention on Human Rights. Article 8 of the Convention guarantees the right to respect for family life and recent European Court cases have demonstrated that, <u>however unmeritorious the applicant's immigration history</u>, the Court is strongly disposed to find a breach of Article 8 where the effect of an immigration decision is to separate an applicant from his/her spouse or child.

2. The instruction is divided into two sections:

Section A: Marriage Policy

Section B: Children

3. The guidance on marriage policy in DP 4/88 and 5/90 is now superseded.

4. Any enquiries about this instruction should be addressed to the Enforcement Policy Group, Room 809 (Extensions 2600/2602).

Enforcement Policy Group
January 1993

IMG/89 47/558/5

Section A: Marriage Policy

1. All deportation and illegal entry cases must be considered on their individual merits. Where enforcement action is under consideration or has been initiated and the offender is married a judgment will need to be reached on the weight to be attached to the marriage as a compassionate factor.

2. As a general rule deportation action under section 3(5)(a) or section 3(5)(b) (in non-criminal cases), or illegal entry action should not be initiated or pursued where the subject has a genuine and subsisting marriage to a person settled in the United Kingdom if:

    (a) the marriage pre-dates enforcement action; and

    (b) the marriage has lasted 2 years or more or, in the case of a common-law relationship (see paragraph 7 below), the couple have cohabited for 2 years or more. It does not automatically follow, however, that deportation/removal is the right course where this test is not met. Full account should be taken of any evidence that a strong relationship has existed for more than 2 years (this will include any reasons why the couple did not marry earlier, eg waiting for a divorce to be finalised, saving to buy their own home); or

    (c) the settled spouse has lived here from an early age or it is otherwise unreasonable to expect him/her to accompany on removal; or

    (d) one or more children of the marriage has the right of abode in the United Kingdom, most commonly as a result of having been born in the United Kingdom to a parent settled here. It should be noted that an illegitimate child born in the United Kingdom only obtains British citizenship under the British Nationality Act 1981 if the mother is a British citizen or is settled in the United Kingdom. Under the 1981 Act the status of the father of an illegitimate child has no bearing on the nationality of the child unless he subsequently marries the mother and legitimises the child.

    Note: (i) The subject's immigration history is of little relevance once it has been concluded that the marriage is genuine and subsisting.

    (ii) Enforcement action may be inappropriate where the spouse or the foreign national is pregnant with a child who would have the right of abode here even if born outside the United Kingdom.

    (iii) The presence of the settled spouse's children by a former relationship will also be an availing factor provided that the children have the right of abode in the United Kingdom, are still dependent and that we can be satisfied that they either live with or have frequent contact with the settled spouse.

3. In considering whether it is reasonable for a spouse to accompany on removal under paragraph 2(c) above, whilst the onus is on the United Kingdom settled spouse to make out a case for why it is unreasonable for him/her to join the family outside the United Kingdom, in general terms cases should be conceded if the United Kingdom settled spouse

    (a) has strong family ties in the United Kingdom; or

    (b) has lengthy residence in the United Kingdom; or

    (c) suffers from ill health such that his/her quality of life would be significantly impaired if he/she were to accompany his/her spouse on removal.

4. There will be a presumption to proceed with section 3(5)(a), 3(5)(b) (in non-criminal cases) or illegal entry action (subject to consideration of other relevant factors) in marriage cases where there are no children with the right of abode in the United Kingdom if:

   (a) neither partner is settled in the United Kingdom; or
   (b) the marriage is one of convenience: that is, the couple do not intend to live together permanently as husband and wife; or
   (c) the couple are separated.

Divorced or separated parents

5. The fact that the European Court is strongly disposed to find a breach of Article 8 of the European Convention where the effect of an immigration decision is to separate a parent from his/her child is also relevant in cases involving divorced or separated parents. Where one parent is settled in the United Kingdom and the removal of the other would result in deprivation of frequent and regular access currently enjoyed by either parent, section 3(5)(a), 3(5)(b) (in non-criminal cases) or illegal entry action should be abandoned. Reliance cannot be placed on the argument that the United Kingdom settled parent can travel abroad to continue access.

6. Cases will arise where a person to be deported/removed has custody of a child with the right of abode in the United Kingdom by a previous partner who is no longer in contact with the child. Here, the crucial question is whether it is reasonable for the child to accompany the parent to live abroad. The factors to be considered are:

   (a) the age of the child (in most cases a pre-school age child could reasonably be expected to adapt to life abroad);
   (b) the strength of the child's ties with the United Kingdom, including other United Kingdom resident family members;
   (c) any medical conditions which would be better treated here;
   (d) the standard of living (including educational facilities) in the country to which the parent is being removed.

Common-law relationships

7. Where there is conclusive evidence that a genuine and subsisting common-law relationship akin to marriage exists, it should be considered under this instruction as if it were a marriage. The onus rests firmly on the individual who seeks to benefit to provide conclusive evidence of the nature of the relationship.

Criminal convictions

8. The test in cases where someone liable to immigration control has family ties here which would normally benefit him/her under paragraphs 1–6 above yet has criminal convictions is whether removal can be justified as "necessary in the interests of a democratic society". This is usually interpreted by the European Court as serious crime punished with imprisonment (for example, crimes of violence, drug offences

(other than possession), murder, terrorism) but minor offences (even where the individual has a long criminal record) or a poor immigration history do not carry much weight. What is reasonable in any particular case will depend not only on the nature of the offence but also on the settled spouse's strength of ties with the United Kingdom. Where action is deemed to be in the interests of a democratic society it would normally be capable of being taken under section 3(5)(b) or 3(6) deportation powers.

Marriages of convenience to EC nationals

9. Foreign nationals who contract a valid marriage to an EC national exercising Treaty rights in the United Kingdom (for example by working) have hitherto been accepted as benefiting from the provisions of Community law in line with his/her spouse, effectively preventing enforcement action (barring serious criminal convictions) at least while the spouse continues to exercise Treaty rights. It has become clear, however, that immigration offenders can exploit this approach by entering into marriages of convenience with EC nationals.

10. Current legal advice is that the removal of a person who has married an EC national exercising Treaty rights may be justified where there are *exceptionally strong grounds for suspicion* that the marriage is one of convenience, ie that the couple do not intend to live together permanently as man and wife and the marriage was contracted for immigration purposes.

Section B: Children

Part 1: Adoption, wardship, custodianship and residence orders

11. This part of the instruction provides guidance on handling cases where there is reason to believe that the purpose of adoption, custodianship, wardship or residence order proceedings is to frustrate enforcement action.

Definitions

12. Adoption: A child adopted by order of a court in the United Kingdom is a British citizen (and thus not liable to immigration control) from the date of the order if an adoptive parent is a British citizen at that date. An adoption by order of a foreign court may not be recognised in United Kingdom law: in such cases advice should be sought from B2 Division.

Custodianship: This represents a less final relationship than adoption and vests 'legal custody of the child in the adult(s) caring for him/her. Where a custodianship order is made the child's immigration status is unchanged but he/she should not be removed from the jurisdiction of the court while the order remains in force.

Wardship: Children who are wards of court should not be removed from the United Kingdom without the court's leave.

Residence Orders: Residence orders are very similar in effect to wardship and children subject to residence orders should not be removed from the United Kingdom without the leave of the court.

Intervention

13. The Family Court will generally attach much more weight to the child's welfare than to irregularities surrounding the immigration status of the child or a parent. Where however it is clear that the court proceedings are designed purely to enable the child or the parent to evade immigration control consideration may be given to instructing the Treasury Solicitor with a view to intervention in the proceedings. <u>There must be evidence, not just a suspicion, that there has been a serious attempt to circumvent the immigration control</u> and decisions to intervene must be taken at not less than SEO level.
14. Where intervention has been agreed the papers should be copied to the Treasury Solicitor's office as soon as possible. Their normal practice is then to apply for the Secretary of State to be joined as a respondent, and to file an affidavit setting out the child's and/or parents' immigration history and the Secretary of State's objections.

Part 2: Abandoned children

15. Enforcement action against children and young persons under the age of 16 who are on their own in the United Kingdom should only be contemplated when the child's voluntary departure cannot be arranged. In all cases removal must not be enforced unless we are satisfied that the child will be met on arrival in his/her home country and that care arrangements are in place thereafter. To this end, caseworkers should contact the Welfare Section of the appropriate Embassy or High Commission as well as the local Social Services Department. If there is evidence, not just a suspicion, that the care arrangements are seriously below the standard normally provided in the country concerned or that they are so inadequate that the child would face a serious risk of harm if returned, consideration should be given to abandoning enforcement action.
16. Where deportation or removal remains the right course, consideration will need to be given to whether an escort is necessary on the journey.

Enforcement Policy Group
January 1993

IMG 89 47/558/5

Index